For Tom, Andrew, and Mike Watters

*For Tom Moser; Fredrika, Rick, and Lucy; Tom, Jr.,
Cathy, and Polly*

Contents

PART II
Argument in the American Tradition

Chapter 5: Identities 101

American Identities through History 102

Franklin's eighteenth-century woodcut, reportedly the first American cartoon.

An introductory chapter to the renowned work, *Democracy in America.*

A detailed cartoon from the popular weekly magazine, *Puck.*

An early twentieth-century poster designed to garner financial support for World War I.

An American Indian's view of the conflict of Anglo and Indian cultures.

A fictional representation of an African American's experience in the dominant culture.

Chapter 6: American Dreams   153

Chapter 9: Justice and Civil Liberties   359

Preface

∞

We developed the third edition of *Creating America* to provide a book that focuses on argumentation and persuasion in the context of American history and tradition: a book that brings together materials revolving around issues that have always concerned Americans. This edition maintains the focus of the previous two on argumentation in context, but with some major additions. The chapter formerly called "War and the Enemy" is now "War and Violence," to allow for a consideration of a wider range of materials and experience. Part I, Contexts for Reading and Writing Arguments, is now four separate chapters. Chapter One, "Arguments in American Cultures," is an overview of the historical scope, design, and intent of the book. Chapter Two, "The Art and Craft of Persuasion," is a three-part assessment and analysis of distinct persuasive components. The first part of the chapter, "Persuasion and Audience," provides the rhetorical underpinning for argumentation, with explanations and examples of the relationship between rhetor and audience, the purpose and effect of Aristotelian appeals, and common uses and abuses of logic. The second section in this chapter, "Persuasion in Diverse Genres," discusses specific genres included in the text—essays, legal cases, fiction, poetry, film, advertisements, speeches, and so on—and illustrates the persuasive elements they share as well as those advantages that are unique to each of them. The final part of the chapter, "Elements of Persuasion," concentrates on those components that all writers use to some degree, such as assertions, examples, assumptions, definitions, and refutations, and that constitute the practical continuum of those underlying rhetorical assumptions discussed in the first part of the chapter. Chapter Two also contains two new student essays as illustrations: an analysis of visual persuasion in a famous Vietnam War photograph, and an analysis of refutation in the Supreme Court case, *Brown v. Board of Education.*

Chapters Three and Four are devoted to different but related aspects of essay writing. Chapter Three, "Writing Essays," moves students through the whole writing process, from strategies for pre-writing to developing a thesis, organizing an essay, and shaping an argument. In order to concretize these suggestions, we have also included, under the sections which discuss expository, analytical, and argumentative writing, examples of each kind of essay, followed by discussion of their rhetorical and developmental strategies. The expository essay, from the 1920s, is a paean to New York energy by a Korean immigrant—"A Korean Discovers New York." The analytical essay is a student's deconstruction of a well-known Vietnam anti-war poster which plays off the very famous James Montgomery Flagg World War I poster of Uncle Sam. And in the argumentative essay, a philosopher makes the case for "Affirmative Action in Context."

Chapter Four, "Research," is about integrating research into writing. Building on Chapter Three, it guides the student through all the steps of the research process: approaching a topic and gathering information (including on-line information); strategies for internet research, search engines, ways of evaluating web-based information, and sample web sites; detailed discussions and samples of library sources; and sections on drafting, revision, and documentation.

Teachers integrating the rhetorical material with readings, as well as teachers wishing to use the readings alone and teach with a different model of argument, such as the Toulmin model, will find a rich range of materials in Part II, "Argument in the American Tradition." Part II offers textual and visual arguments for analysis and discussion. Chapter 5, "Identities," includes a range of materials from early discussions of what is uniquely American to contemporary struggles of building community yet maintaining cultural identity. Chapter 6, "American Dreams," includes selections on both political and material dreams and success. Chapter 7, "Images of Gender and Family," offers different perspectives on what makes a family and what constitutes the particular roles and rights of men, women, and children; Chapter 8, "Work and Play," looks at the business of America—business; and at the business of play, or contemporary American sports. Chapter 9, "Justice and Civil Liberties," brings together core readings and images of American freedoms and the struggles that precede and accompany them. Chapter 10, "War and Violence," offers visual and textual arguments about how we idealize our friends and demonize our enemies. Chapter 11, "Frontiers," analyzes both the idea and the reality of the frontier and the West.

Each chapter includes an introduction to the core theme or issue. Selections follow, with headnotes for context and background information; journal prompts to guide reflective writing; and questions for discussion and writing, with a focus on analysis and argumentation. In each chapter we include a recommended film that should be available as a video rental in most colleges or communities. Most chapters also include at least one student essay, generally written in response to a chapter writing suggestion; inclusion of these essays is based on the premise that student writing is an appropriate focus for analysis and discussion.

Creating America, third edition, is designed for use in a first-year course in composition, particularly one emphasizing argumentative writing. The underlying pedagogy is based on an Aristotelian model, but it is informed by the theories of Kenneth Burke, Carl Rogers, and feminist critics. Our premise is that people use, to quote Aristotle, "all of the available means of persuasion" to argue a point; therefore, we do not treat argument and persuasion separately. Rather, we focus on the appeals to ethos, pathos, and logos, introducing induction and deduction under logos as the basic principles by which to evaluate and through which to develop arguments. The selections represent a range of arguments, from rather combative debate to more dialogic, narrative explorations of difficult questions and complex issues.

Acknowledgments

We gratefully acknowledge our colleagues at Stanford University, Stanford University Library, and the Hoover Institution Archives: Dr. Elena Danielson, Director of the Hoover Institution Archives; Cissie Hill and Remy Squires; Maggie Kimball, Archivist, Stanford University Libraries; Susan Wyle, instructor in the Program in Writing and Rhetoric; and Hector Cuevas of Undergraduate Advising.

We also offer our profound thanks to the colleagues, mentors, family, and friends who have in so many ways supported or contributed to this process. Tom Moser and Tom, Andy, and Mike Watters, Barbara Charlesworth Gelpi, Albert Gelpi, Joan L'Heureux, John L'Heureux, Andrea Lunsford, Linda Jo Bartholemew, George Dekker, Maryvonne LeMoal Menget, and the staff of Freshman and Sophomore Programs: Shari Palmer, Marina Bonnano, Dena Slothower, Carlos Seligo, Gari Gene, Mona Kitasoe, and Irene Cervantes; Drs. Ginny Bassi, Patrick Miles, Jean Sarris, and Allen Valcov; SMC Access Team; and the San Mateo coffee group: Susan Cohn, Rosa Lee, Drs. Elizabeth Lee and Laurie Spencer, Jennifer Raiser, and Carolyne Cohn. We owe a special debt to our editor at Prentice-Hall, Corey Good, whose work on our behalf has been above and beyond the call of duty, and to Jennifer Collins and Karen Berry. We have been extremely fortunate in our reviewers, whose feedback and advice deserve much credit for any improvements in this edition: William R. Brown, Philadelphia University; Ryan Chandlee, University of Minnesota; William E. Sheidley, University of Southern Colorado; Susan Hoffman, Indiana State University; Troy Nordman, Butler County Community College; and James Allen, College of DuPage.

Above all we thank our students, who continue to challenge and inspire us, and we offer a special thanks to our families.

Joyce Moser, Stanford University
Ann Watters, Stanford University

1

∞

Arguments in
American Cultures

W hen the founding fathers were about to publish the Declaration
of Independence and set themselves on a course that would put
them in direct conflict with the British government, Benjamin Franklin
is reported to have said, "Gentlemen, we must all hang together, or assuredly we shall all hang separately."

In a sense, this book takes Franklin's observation and applies it
more generally to thinking and writing about the nation Franklin and
his co-revolutionists were in the process of establishing. The pieces of
American life—people who come from many countries, cultures, and
religions; states that differ from one another in topography, industry,
and demographics; huge variations in urban and suburban lifestyles,
in income and interests—are so heterogeneous that they could have
hardly been expected to coexist as they have for more than two hundred years, but they have. *Creating America* offers a way of examining
and writing about what it is that has caused them to hang together.

Reading American Cultures

The selections assembled in this book are not limited to any one
time period; there are eighteenth-century cartoons, nineteenth- and
twentieth-century advertisements, and contemporary films; great political speeches from the 1770s to the present; essays on relations between men and women and between parents and children; paintings
of Yosemite in the 1870s; propaganda posters from World War I,
and Henry David Thoreau on civil disobedience; Frederick Douglass
on the horrors of slavery, Jacqueline Navarra Rhoads on the horrors
of war, and Studs Terkel on the pleasure and pain of a good day's
work.

Our central premise is that certain ideas run back to the earliest
days of America as a political and social entity and continue to do so
today, and those threads can be read across centuries and across gen-

res. Every generation of Americans reinterprets and reargues these ideas in the light of its own experience. This book provides a wide array of materials that vary in kind and across time—fiction, essays, cartoons, posters, journals, paintings, poetry, legal proceedings, advertisements, movies—and thus form a core sample of American culture.

The ability to analyze these materials can work both ways. An eighteenth-century etching about what constitutes appropriate behavior for a young woman instructs us about earlier norms and helps us to understand more recent conflicts about feminism, freedom, and self-expression. And a contemporary advertisement that sells sex in order to sell clothing also helps us understand the limits against which earlier generations of women defined themselves.

In the same way, F. Scott Fitzgerald's article "Early Success," from *The Crack-Up,* is highly informative about the American association of romance and money, which Fitzgerald understood so well; but so is advertising music on MTV. Reading Susan B. Anthony on the First Amendment and freedom of speech may give you insight into the argument about whether the Internet should be censored, and reading Martin Luther King Jr. on nonviolent resistance may help you understand why his intellectual ancestor, Thoreau, refused to pay taxes and insisted, with some relish, on going to jail to protest a war he could not support.

Persuasion

As you study the selections in this book, you will find that most of the authors are engaged in arguments of one kind or another about a particular political stance, a contemporary ethical problem, or the status quo. Frequently the fight is not so much about an individual opponent as about an idea or a belief. However varied the subject matter or the historical events surrounding it, this kind of argument is characteristically a manifestation of disagreement in a democracy. It is argument that encourages rather than stifles disagreement and allows the expression of different, even completely opposing points of view, and it protects the right of individual Americans to say and express ideas that other Americans find highly offensive. It is argument designed not to bludgeon opposition into submission but rather to persuade.

The target of such persuasive argument is often the American public at large or a particular group of citizens within a larger political unit. Americans take for granted their right to argue publicly and privately and to criticize their government, their elected officials, their school boards, their neighbors. This chapter provides suggestions for analyzing and using persuasion as a basis for your own experiments in reading and writing critically about American materials.

Persuasion is a process in which a *rhetor*—a speaker, writer, or artist—tries to elicit a desired response from an *audience* by identifying commonalities in the interests of both parties. It is a process that deals not in certainties but in probabilities—in arguing from evidence or reasons and assumptions to a conclusion. This textbook is designed to enable you to develop your ability to understand and analyze the strategies of persuasion in what you read and to develop your own ability to write persuasively. Studying persuasive texts can help you to become a more critical reader and listener and to communicate more clearly and effectively. By focusing on diverse kinds of arguments in American culture, by looking at context and purpose, by looking beneath the surface at strategies and appeals, you will see persuasion all around you in daily life—not only in books you read, but also in advertising, flyers, posters, news magazines, newspapers, and so forth. A persuasive text is one that asserts a point of view and seeks a desired response; it attempts to induce the readers to agree with whatever is being expounded on. A description of orderly governance in an American Indian tribe, for example, implicitly argues for respect for that culture. Sometimes the desired response is self-sacrifice; a poster advertising war bonds appeals to the interests of the audience—whether self-interest or desire to belong—to garner financial support for the war effort. Ultimately, persuasion can change beliefs, behavior, or even government policy; in *Brown* v. *Board of Education,* a legal argument citing inequities in segregated education changed the law of the land and the future of millions of Americans.

Persuasion and American Cultures

American cultures have common threads that are woven in tremendous diversity. Persuasive appeals in public discourse must take this into account in order to succeed, tapping into the assumptions and common values and beliefs while acknowledging divergent views. More so than the speakers and writers in more homogeneous cultures, Americans wishing to persuade their fellow Americans must understand something about their audience: who they are, what they believe and assume, how they communicate, and what they value. Some assumptions and values remain constant over time, but each age brings with it a different view anchored in that particular time and culture. Examining persuasive texts from different time periods in American history and from different cultural perspectives may help us to understand our own age and culture better while considering them in a larger historical context.

As the preceding discussion suggests, the themes in this text represent some of the core debates in American history. Who are Americans? What are their dreams? What makes an American family? What are Americans' values about work and success? What are their concepts of justice and liberty? Why do they construct an "other" or enemy, and how do they take action against the other? What is their image of the frontier, and how, having reached the geographic limits of the continent, do they search for new frontiers? Each type of question or problem lends itself to a particular aspect of argumentation.

In the second chapter, we begin to explore those aspects, including the relationship between the rhetor and the audience—a fluid and often exasperating connection that changes with time, history, and experience. The connection is especially complicated if, as is often the case with selections in this book, a document written for one audience in one generation has proved to be so important that it continues to be read by future generations who were not part of the original equation. What you need to recognize is that you, as a contemporary reader, have a relationship with the text which is as valid and as important as that of any member of the original audience. And the way you read that text will depend, in part, on the experience, beliefs, and assumptions you bring to it.

It will also depend on other issues raised in Chapter 2—the differences between past and present audiences; the appeals that others make to you and that you can use to persuade others; the logical errors that can throw an argument off or intentionally mislead you as the reader, and the ways you can recognize them in your work or anyone else's; and persuasion in action—for example, the way all or some of these techniques work even in a supposedly objective piece of writing such as a news story.

Besides persuasive techniques there are all the ways in which we shape them. Essays are probably the form you're most familiar with as a writer, but even essays come in different permutations—expository, argumentative, reflective, or, in much of the best work, a combination of any or all three of them. Legal cases, of which there are several in this book, would seem to lend themselves entirely to logical arguments, but in fact no legal argument that isn't also persuasive is going to convince a jury or a reader. And a great legal narrative has a lot in common with the ability to tell a good story.

Fiction and poetry are often posited as forms that rely on emotion or aesthetics, but in fact a really persuasive poem or story has a logic and inevitability that many essays don't; fiction and poetry can deal indirectly with such abstract issues as justice or love or political freedom, and end by making them more concrete and specific than a direct statement written in expository form. (See the story "In the Land of the Free" in the American Dreams chapter.)

Finally, this next chapter deals with the enormous persuasive power of visual texts and the many forms they can take—illustrations, comics, posters, advertisements, photographs, music videos, movies.

Keep in mind that an advertisement has a writer, designers, a producer, and other people who make creative decisions about how to present the product and what audience to gear the ad toward. Similarly, a movie involves hundreds of people, from the director and the writers to the cinematographers and film editors; every line of dialogue and every camera angle is the result of someone's choices. Once you realize how much choice is involved, you also become more aware of alternatives. The film or the ad or the poster could have been done differently, and its success in reaching you, the audience, will depend partly on your awareness that art is no more haphazard than the most closely reasoned legal argument.

Whatever the form, it always depends on a set of assumptions, conscious or unconscious; there are always particular appeals to you, and there is an underlying structure which may be completely convincing or so full of logical errors that all persuasive content is lost. As you look at the next chapter, remember that reading, writing, and viewing are all interactive; in exploring the text, you are also developing your own argumentative and persuasive capabilities.

2

The Art and Craft
of Persuasion

There are three interrelated parts to this chapter. The first part, Persuasion and Audience, focuses on how closely the rhetor's, or speaker's, effectiveness is tied to his or her ability to identify correctly the audience and appeal to it appropriately. A rhetor who fails to do so will not connect, and therefore will not persuade. Many factors, cultural, personal, and intellectual, go into being a successful rhetor. This section identifies and explains the most significant ones, including the eternally useful Aristotelian appeals, as well as the logical errors that can derail your argument and make it very difficult for you to get your point across.

The second part of the chapter, Persuasion and Diverse Genres, is a practical overview of how many venues there are in which to use persuasive strategies: not only texts, such as essays and legal cases, but also visual representations, such as advertisements, films, cartoons, and photographs. To show you how analysis of an image can be done, we have included a student essay on the famous Vietnam War photograph "Saigon Execution" in which a man is killed at the instant the picture is being taken (you will find that photograph in the chapter on War and Violence). This essay is an example of one way in which a visual representation can be analyzed for its rhetorical appeals in much the same way as a more traditionally written text.

Finally, Elements of Persuasion breaks out the constituent parts on which both textual and visual persuasion rely: assumptions, assertions, examples, and refutations. Another student essay, this time on the most famous Supreme Court case of the last hundred years, *Brown v. Board of Education,* shows how rhetorical strategies—appeals to ethos and logos—can combine with a persuasive element, refutation, to overthrow a legal precedent, and, by the way, change American history.

Persuasion and Audience

Rhetor and Audience

Understanding the arts of persuasion entails understanding how others persuade you and how you can persuade others through your own arguments. Although some scholars have stated that argument relies on logic and persuasion on emotion, Aristotelian rhetoric makes no such clear-cut distinction. Aristotle's *Rhetoric* suggests that reason, beliefs and values, and emotion—*logos, ethos,* and *pathos*—work together to engage the whole person and guide him or her toward appropriate judgment of the issue at hand. A traditional view suggests that argument entails an adversarial relationship between two sides— generally writer or speaker and audience. In debate, for example, the two opposing sides each offer arguments that the other side then refutes; in propaganda, the audience is inundated with generally one-sided, unsupported assertions. Such persuasion is rhetoric "to gain advantage, of one sort or another," as critic Kenneth Burke notes, and to some degree, it reflects Aristotle's primary definition of rhetoric as "understanding all of the available means of persuasion."

More recently some scholars have argued for different approaches to argumentation. Drawing on the work of psychologists such as Carl Rogers, they outline a model that suggests that both rhetor, or communicator, and audience are participants in the argument and should work together, much like a client and therapist, to pursue knowledge and truth. Some feminist critics suggest that our traditional views of argumentation are male-centered, adversarial, and combative; they emphasize a more collaborative approach to argumentation, with negotiation rather than debate as the dominant mode. In such an approach, both sides identify their common interests and attempt to close the distance between their respective positions.

Another view suggests rereading Aristotle to understand the connection between rhetor and audience. (The term *rhetor* will in this textbook refer to an individual attempting to persuade orally or in written text or image.) In this view, the rhetor and audience work together to pursue and develop a solution to a problem, a difference of opinion, or an issue. Audience and rhetor are dynamically involved in argument, and no argument can begin from scratch; the rhetor relies on and presumes a certain background on the part of the audience, including certain assumptions, beliefs, values, and reservoir of knowledge.

Audiences and Cultures

Scholars of rhetoric have shown that persuasion in homogeneous cultures tends to leave many reasons and assumptions unexpressed; a shared heritage tends to include a fair number of shared assumptions and values. In a heterogeneous society such as the United States, arguments rely on some common ground, but they tend to be more forcefully and clearly articulated, with premises and steps in the logic more often stated than assumed. The argumentative style and organization tend to be more indirect in countries where a direct approach could be considered offensive and where the rhetor might instead broach a subject, move away from it, then return to supporting points later. The point, again, is to analyze audiences carefully, to visualize them and consider their beliefs, values, attitudes, and style of interaction, rather than concentrating only on one's own point of view. Understanding audience assumptions and expectations is crucial in developing persuasive argumentative strategies.

Audiences from Other Times

Analyzing arguments written for readers from other time periods brings with it its own complexity. Although the basic strategies of argument remain much the same through the ages, the role of public debate and the particular concerns and issues vary with each age and culture. The early America of European colonial culture was largely agricultural, with people living on farms and in towns isolated from each other; it took days for information to reach New York City from Philadelphia. Today Americans and the rest of the world are connected by global media. Colonial culture was more homogeneous, but space and time separated its communications; American society today is more diverse, but most Americans are exposed to the same news and popular culture. Superficially, then, we have more in common, but the increased variety in cultures means that we come to the discussion with different cultural perspectives. People who seek to persuade others in American cultures and media cannot count on the kinds of shared assumptions held by the audiences of Benjamin Franklin or Thomas Jefferson. Understanding persuasive texts from other times, then, will require not only analyzing the texts themselves but also considering the assumptions, values, beliefs, and needs of the audiences for whom they were intended.

Audience and Appeals: Ethos, Pathos, and Logos

In order to induce others to identify with them or their point of view, rhetors use a number of strategies. Aristotle outlined three modes of persuasion that relate to the connection between writer and audience: appeals to ethos, pathos, and logos.

Appeals to Ethos　Appeals to ethos are appeals to the underlying values and beliefs of the audience. There are two benefits to this kind of appeal. First, it helps rhetors establish their own credibility and authority—or, as Aristotle puts it, "the personal character" of the speaker. A politician who presents himself as the product of an economically poor environment is appealing to the American belief in success as a product of hard work. Academic writers who present themselves as well informed and capable of using the language and convention of their disciplines, as well as relying on credible scholarly resources, are appealing to the American belief in expertise, research, and inquiry.

The appeal to ethos has a second function as well, one that is more subtle, but very important. Rhetors draw on the values and beliefs they share with the audience, not only to establish their own authority, but also to suggest the underlying premises which will support whatever arguments and conclusions they are trying to make. And two different rhetors can appeal to the same underlying value or belief for entirely different purposes. For example, when Franklin Delano Roosevelt vilified the Japanese during World War II, he was appealing to the deep-seated American belief in fair play which had been violated by the Japanese sneak attack on Pearl Harbor. When Martin Luther King Jr. appealed to that ingrained sense of fairness, he was arguing, not for the purposes of identifying an enemy, but for the civil rights of all Americans.

Let's look at an example of persuasion that uses appeals to ethos as unspoken premises to support a conclusion. Consider, for example, the statement as illustrated in the photo.

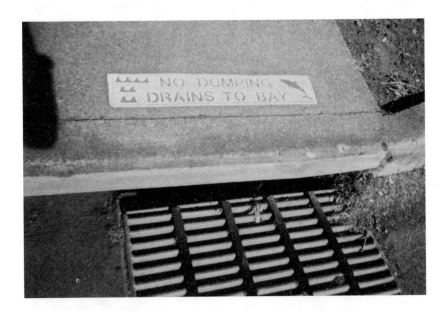

This stenciled statement-plus-images can be found painted near drains in many cities and towns. Such appeals target local concerns; in some areas, *bay* would be replaced with *river* or *ocean*, and sometimes the images would be different—birds rather than fish, for example. The argument includes an assertion (do not dump waste here), a reason (because it will drain to the bay), and implied consequences (and damage the waterways and wildlife).

Although the argument seems to rest primarily on reason, appeals to values and beliefs pervade this argument. The rhetor assumes that the audience values the environment, represented in the water symbol and the small animal outline, and that viewers will accept some responsibility for protecting natural resources.

Consider alternative messages for this argument: for example, instead of "drains to bay," the rhetor could have stated, "$500 fine." Why might the rhetor appeal to ethos rather than threaten violators with a fine? What are the advantages, and disadvantages, of appealing to values and beliefs in this rhetorical situation?

Appeals to Pathos   The good rhetorician, said Aristotle, seeks to understand the emotions and then to put the audience in the right frame of mind to hear an argument. Appeals to pathos, like appeals to ethos, relate to identification. If one can empathize, one can identify with another, put oneself in the other's position, and understand the other's feelings and point of view. Critics have argued that emotional appeals are less appropriate than logos or ethos appeals, perhaps over concern about manipulating audience emotions or relying on emotional appeals to cover up a lack of logic and evidence. Yet persuasion engages the whole individual, and pathos appeals can create a more balanced argument or a more ethical decision. Cost-benefit analyses may argue against any intervention in postcommunist Eastern Europe, but showing the human costs and suffering, in text or images, may provide a kind of evidence that eludes the rigorous economical and political analyses. By the same token, logically staking out the political benefits of uninterrupted oil shipments to the United States may not present the whole picture unless one includes the human costs, on both sides, of a war in the Middle East.

In the "no dumping" argument cited earlier, the rhetor didn't select images of snakes and rats, for example, but rather more appealing animals that evoke a desire to protect, such as a dolphin. Further, most of these arguments are painted in blue and white, which mirror colors found in nature and suggest pristine natural surroundings, rather than mudslides or other unappealing natural phenomena. Are there any disadvantages to using emotional appeals in this rhetorical situation? Do these appeals go far enough in persuading the reader? How might physical location, culture and local customs, economic status, or other elements of the rhetorical situation affect the selection of appeals?

The rhetor cannot generally invoke emotions directly by asking the readers to feel a certain way or to empathize with someone. He or she must use language, examples, and details that clearly convey situations with which the audience can identify. Appeals to pathos are frequently made through specific detail or connotative language—language that evokes feelings or emotional responses. In the Prologue to *Invisible Man*, for example, Ralph Ellison invites the reader to identify with a man who is invisible in his society; Ellison persuades readers to see another point of view by invoking their empathy for the narrator's situation.

Appeals to Logos   Appeals to logos refer to the logic and shape of the argument. Nearly every argument at least pretends to possess some logic in the form of reasons why the audience should change their views. Aristotle cites two basic methods of developing logos appeals: induction, arguing from evidence; and deduction, arguing from general principles.

In *induction*, the rhetor generalizes from a number of observations, specific cases, or examples and draws inferences or conclusions based on data. Induction deals not with certainties but with probabilities; the rhetor cannot test every single case or provide an infinite number of examples, so he or she uses examples and evidence to draw conclusions about another case or a larger population.

When the rhetor reasons from examples to a conclusion, she asks the audience to make an inductive leap—a leap of faith from the known and verifiable specific cases presented in the argument, across an unknown and unknowable stretch, to a probable conclusion. The relevance, breadth, and number of examples reduce the leap audiences must make and therefore strengthen the credibility of the argument. Because rhetors have a limited amount of time and space to devote to their examples, they must select those most persuasive and most suited to the audience and purpose. When Martin Luther King Jr. describes driving all night because he can't find a motel that will accept his business, or having to explain to his child why she can't play in a playground that is for whites only, or seeing that his people's wives, mothers, and sisters are denied the respected title of "Mrs." and that grown men are called "boy," his vivid, specific examples make a strong case for the conclusion that Americans of African descent endure relentless and pervasive racism. In academic writing as well, each author must include relevant, sufficient, and representative examples to build a persuasive case for the conclusion. Scientists carefully record data about sampling, methods, and observations to substantiate credibly the conclusions they draw from their data.

Inductive arguments can go wrong in one of two ways: either the evidence is inadequate for the conclusion drawn, or the reasoning from evidence to conclusion is faulty. Readers of academic prose as well as other kinds of arguments must be critical of the kinds of examples offered and mindful of biased or inadequate sampling. They should also examine critically the "leap" they are asked to make from evidence to conclusion.

Say, for example, a friend of yours works in a hospital transcribing medical notes written by physicians. On his first day of work, he sees six patient charts, and all six contain doctors' notes in handwriting that is almost illegible. He might conclude that doctors have terrible handwriting. If he tells you, "All doctors have terrible handwriting," he would be guilty of overgeneralizing. In fact, he hasn't seen all doctors' handwriting. If he said, "All of the doctors whose handwriting I have seen write illegibly," he would be making a statment that is accurate (assuming others share his standards) but is limited to the sample he describes. Induction, like other forms of argumentation, is open to question; if it weren't, there would be no reason for debate. But reasonable people will be likely to accept the conclusions one draws if they are based on sufficient evidence and if the conclusion logically follows from the evidence. What we most want induction to do is to enable us to generalize from a sample to larger populations and other cases; we want to be able to say, with some degree of certainty, that the conclusion is true based on our evidence.

Deduction, the other primary method of organizing arguments, takes a general principle (also called a premise or an assumption) and draws a conclusion or makes an assertion based on it. The *syllogism* is a classic outline of deduction used to test the logic of the argument. It entails a statement of a general premise, a specific case, and a conclusion derived from the general premise and specific case. For example, consider the following statements:

> All physicians have terrible handwriting.
> Dr. Weller is a physician.
> Therefore, Dr. Weller has terrible handwriting.

Clearly the generalization forming the conclusion of the argument is highly questionable. Sketching out an argument in this form frequently enables readers to examine both the premises being made and the conclusions being drawn. Generally, though, arguments don't occur in this explicit form. More often, writers persuade through collapsed arguments, with generalizations and assumptions left out or buried within the argument.

Such a compact deductive argument, known as an *enthymeme,* unites the author's statement and conclusion with a part of the argument that is understood or assumed by the audience. The syllogism generally spells out the general principle, the specific case, and the conclusion. The enthymeme leaves out one of the premises, often the generalization or underlying assumption. Drawing from the example, the argument would appear something like this:

> Dr. Weller, being a physician, has terrible handwriting.

or

> Of course Dr. Weller has terrible handwriting—she's a physician.

Both statements have buried within them the outlined argument in the syllogism, but rather than sketching out all the steps, the rhetor relies on assumptions shared with the audience. The rhetor's task is to analyze the audience and to know how much background information to supply, what definitions to include or exclude, what the audience already accepts or believes, what points must be argued and supported with evidence. In the compact argument of the enthymeme, the rhetor assumes that the audience will supply certain links in the chain of argument.

A number of selections in this book provide examples of deductive arguments. The Declaration of Independence (Chapter 9) argues extensively from principle, explicitly stating premises and assumptions, testing those premises against a specific case (the British government of the colonies), and then drawing the conclusion that the break with Britain is justified. If one accepts the premises—governments derive their authority from the consent of the governed; governments exist to protect the rights of life, liberty, and the pursuit of happiness—then one must accept the validity of the conclusion—that governments that do not protect these rights no longer deserve their authority and should be abolished.

Errors in Logic

Arguments can go wrong in a number of ways. Critical readers and careful writers need to question the arguments in what they read and take care with the evidence, assumptions, and reasons they offer and the conclusions they draw. In a deductive argument, a critical reader can argue with the reasons and assumptions, sometimes called premises, on which the conclusion is based, or question the reasoning process from premises to conclusions. In inductive reasoning, one can question the evidence offered or the conclusion drawn about that evidence. Both methods can lead to a number of errors in logical argumentation, or fallacies. Below are some of the most common fallacies.

1. *Hasty generalization.* Leaping in logic from a very few cases to a broad conclusion can be considered hasty generalization. If, for example, we find that two senators have financial assets worth millions of dollars and we conclude that all public officials are wealthy, we

have made a leap that is unsupported by the evidence. We have leaped too hastily from examples to a conclusion.

2. *Inadequate or biased sampling.* This fallacy is related to hasty generalization. If a writer's conclusions are based on too few samples or a skewed or biased collection of samples, the conclusions are not necessarily generalizable to the larger issue or population. If we sampled only the senators included in a list of the fifty wealthiest Americans to draw conclusions about all senators, we would be using a biased sample. We need to cast our net wider and draw from a more representative sampling. Drawing at random a sample of ten or twenty from the list of one hundred senators and examining their financial statements would give us more representative and complete data and enable us to make generalizations about the larger population of senators.

3. *Straw man.* A straw man in argumentation is a false target: the writer sets up a misstatement of the opponent's view and then attacks that misstatement instead of the real argument. An argument attacking someone who does not support specific prochoice legislation might suggest that the opponent wants "all women barefoot and pregnant" instead of discussing the specific legislation in question.

4. *Ad hominem.* In the ad hominem argument, literally meaning "against the man," the writer attacks an individual holding the position rather than the position. If a writer says, "Governor Jones is in favor of nationalized health insurance, so it must be a bad idea," that writer is attacking the governor but not addressing the merits of his specific arguments.

5. *False analogy.* Argument by analogy is one of the weakest strategies and highly vulnerable to attack. A false analogy entails erroneously suggesting that two people, situations, or issues are analogous or comparable in certain ways. In recent years, any number of potential military conflicts have been argued against because they might represent "another Vietnam," whether or not there are, in fact, any similarities between the two situations.

6. *Post hoc ergo propter hoc.* Literally, this expression translates into "after this, therefore because of this." The mistake in logic lies in suggesting that because A happened before B, A caused B. The watchword in statistics and many social sciences, however, is that correlation does not equal causation. Because the divorce rate increased after the advent of widespread television viewing, there is no reason to conclude that television viewing causes divorce.

7. *False dilemma.* A false dilemma is an either-or situation in which the writer implies that we have only two choices: "Either we get rid of television once and for all, or we resign ourselves to being a nation with the leading divorce rate in the civilized world."

8. *Slippery slope.* In this lapse in logic, the writer argues that one first step will inevitably lead to disastrous consequences. For example, someone opposed to genetic engineering might argue, "Once we allow scientists to map human chromosomes, we will see people murdering their children because they don't have blond hair and blue eyes."

9. *Begging the question.* Begging the question is essentially assuming something as a given that has not been proved. A related strategy, circular reasoning, restates the proposition as a conclusion. "Students who have bad grades and don't study should not be allowed to watch television because viewing might be detrimental to their schoolwork."

10. *Non sequitur.* Literally, this term means, "It does not follow." Advertisements are full of fallacious reasoning but make something of a specialty of non sequiturs: "Crock Cola tastes great: America's fastest-growing cola company!" Taste and relative corporate growth are juxtaposed as if one leads to the other; such, regrettably for consumers, is not necessarily the case. Sometimes the term *non sequitur* is used more generally to indicate any lapse in logic.

Understanding Persuasion in Practice

In addition to evaluating the appeals to ethos, pathos, and logos in an argument, taking arguments apart on a structural, sentence-by-sentence level to see how they work can be instructive. Understanding both general principles of persuasion and specific, sentence-level strategies enables us to evaluate the arguments that confront us daily, in college studies and in our communities.

Examples of persuasion surround us in academic texts, mass media, personal conversations—even as we walk down the street. Let's examine a specific piece of persuasion encountered on a college campus recently. A flyer posted on the wall of a campus building has the following message spray-painted on it, in red letters on a white background, as if through a stencil:

> Oil in Kuwait
> Oil in Panama
> No Oil in Bosnia
> Get it?

Unpacking the argument takes a bit of thought and involves reader response and input to make the argument work. First, we observe that this is not an impromptu message, because it was created through a stencil, which presumes multiple applications of the message in various locations. The somewhat diffuse red spray–paint draws attention to the message and suggests blood; the rhetor, through the parallel structure of the phrases, argues that the situations are analogous: that the United States intervened militarily in other countries when doing so was in its own best interests; that it has not intervened in Bosnia because there is no economic motive to do so. In a rather taunting manner, the rhetorical question of the last line invites audience engagement in the discussion.

As it happens, some audience members—people of the academic community who passed by the notice—did engage in the argument. Written in ballpoint pen ink between lines two and three are, "No oil in Vietnam" and "No oil in Grenada," a reference to other U.S. military involvement without apparent economic benefit.

Except for the rhetorical question, each of the other elements in the argument is a phrase, which the audience has to fill in to complete a statement. Those statements might look something like this:

> The United States intervenes militarily in other countries only to protect its interests, such as access to suppliers of oil.
> Bosnia is not a supplier of oil.
> Therefore the United States will not intervene militarily to protect its interests in Bosnia.

For the conclusion to be true, the premises leading to the conclusion must be true. If they are not, the argument breaks down. When critiquing an argument, the audience can question the premises or the reasoning process that leads to the conclusion or claim. The scrawled messages in ballpoint pen refute the argument by attacking the premise that the Untied States intervenes militarily only when oil is at stake.

Examining the style of the message, we see that the rhetor made use of an excellent stylistic tactic, parallelism. The grammatical structures of the first three lines are equivalent: noun, preposition, noun, with a negative added to the last line. Parallel structures can help to clarify and emphasize connections and equivalence between ideas, as the rhetor was trying to suggest.

Let's examine another use of helpful grammatical structure, a balanced sentence:

> When guns are outlawed, only outlaws will have guns.

What is your immediate reaction to this slogan? Imagine you saw it on a bumper sticker of a car. Does it seem sensible or logical? Now read it aloud and take it apart.

> When guns are outlawed.
> Only outlaws will have guns.

First, examine the rhythm. Which words are stressed? How do the stresses contribute to the rhythm? What words are then distressed and deemphasized? How does the sense of balance, of equivalence, contribute to the sense of logic or make it seem that the slogan "makes sense"?

Now look critically at the diction, or word choice. First look at the ambiguous term, *guns*. Does it refer to handguns? Shotguns? Rifles? Semiautomatics? Uzis? What does *outlawed* mean? Does it mean people must register for a gun? That they must wait ten days before purchasing one so that the seller can check for a criminal record? Does it mean children can't buy guns? Then examine that unstressed word, *only*. Is it true that only outlaws or criminals will have guns? What about police officers? Forest rangers? Brinks guards? The assumptions and assertions of the slogan do not bear up under close examination. In a fleeting statement as on a bumper sticker or in a cartoon, such arguments can sometimes make an impression or erode the position of the opposition just a bit.

Though you need to avoid falling into fallacious arguments, or those in which the logic breaks down, as in the example of the bumper sticker, you can use structures such as parallelism and balance to show viable relationships between things and ideas. You can choose whether to use *denotative* language, which is explicit language that attempts to convey objectivity, or *connotative* language, which is emotion-laden language that attempts to evoke an image or idea. By the same token, you can understand when you are being hornswoggled or fooled by eloquent language disguising a weak argument.

Let's look at the way another rhetorical strategy, antithesis, which is a balanced structure with opposing elements, can reinforce the effects of language:

> We observe today
> not a victory of party
> but a celebration of freedom.

These opening lines to John F. Kennedy's "Inaugural Address" stress the orderly changing of administrations, emphasizing not the rancorous 1960 presidential race against and defeat of Richard Nixon, not the onset of Democratic rule, but the sense that the inauguration itself is a link of history, part of the ritual of democratic government. A few lines later, Kennedy makes use of highly connotative language to evoke a sense of tradition, grandeur, and solemnity:

> For I have sworn before you and Almighty God the same, solemn oath our forebears prescribed nearly a century and three quarters ago.

Why would a modern president—one who used the relatively new medium of television to his advantage, one who represented youth and change, one who frightened some citizens simply by virtue of being Catholic—speak in archaic, formal diction? How do you think you would have reacted to such a speech? What tone, approach, and mood does this rhetor evoke? And how do these strategies support his goals?

Sometimes simple repetition of a key phrase can drive a point home forcefully and eloquently. You may have been told in the past to avoid being repetitious; now is a good time to examine the difference between needless, annoying repetition that occurs when you have not taken care with your essay or paragraph organization, and repetition that reinforces points and ideas, suggests connections between ideas, clarifies meaning, and delivers pleasing balance and rhythm to the audience. As we saw with the bumper sticker, rhythm and balance are no substitute for logic and evidence; nevertheless, well-crafted prose is itself more persuasive than plodding, hard-to-follow prose. And unless you are deliberately trying to obfuscate or muddy up the issues, clarity too is a virtue. Let's look at an eloquent example of *anaphora*, or a repeated sentence opener, from Martin Luther King Jr.'s "I Have a Dream" speech.

> So let freedom ring from the prodigious hilltops of New Hampshire.
> Let freedom ring from the mighty mountains of New York.
> Let freedom ring from the heightening Alleghenies of Pennsylvania!
> Let freedom ring from the snowcapped Rockies of Colorado!
> Let freedom ring from the curvaceous peaks of California!
> But not only that;
> Let freedom ring from Stone Mountain of Georgia!
> Let freedom ring from Lookout Mountain of Tennessee!
> Let freedom ring from every hill and molehill of Mississippi.
> From every mountainside, let freedom ring!

This section follows King's recitation of the lyrics to "America" and picks up the thread of the last line of that song in the repeated "let freedom ring," and the image of "from every mountainside" in the second to last line of the song. Examine the progression of King's lines. What geographical regions are included? Then examine the break, midway, and the change in direction. In what ways does this repetition, attached to the diverse regions, reinforce a theme?

You can read the full text of this speech in Chapter 6. As you review this and other selections, remember to analyze not only themes and overall structure but also patterns of sentences, words, and images; all contribute to and underscore the persuasive message of the rhetor.

Persuasion works on many levels: to engage the audience, to get them to identify with the point of view of the rhetor, and, if possible, to move them in belief or in action to the position suggested by the rhetor. Because argument relies on moving beyond the supporting materials to draw conclusions, whether that support is based on examples or derived from a general proposition, the strength and effectiveness of appeals to ethos, pathos, and logos are crucial in persuading audiences. Such appeals operate at the level of the main points, the supporting points, and down to individual words and sentences.

Persuasion in Diverse Genres

There are any number of genres in which a writer or artist can be persuasive; some of them are clearly argumentative, like a pro-and-con debate or a legal case; some of them less obviously so, like fiction, poetry, or film. But all of them can be successful at conveying a point of view or swaying an audience. In this book we include a variety of genres with strong persuasive elements. The brief explanations that follow are designed to help you read these materials, regardless of medium, for ideas, themes, and argumentative and persuasive content, as well as for the pleasure of encountering American writers and artists on their home ground.

Essays

Essays may be reflective, analytical, expository, or argumentative. The essay was invented by the Renaissance writer Michel de Montaigne. He used it as a way of getting to know himself better. Informal, ironic, funny, full of anecdotes and charm, Montaigne's essays started as quotations on which he made comments and ended as an exploration of his psychological makeup and view of the world. He tested out his thoughts, pains, prejudices, and pleasures against the measure of his own intelligence. Great essays demand a high level of honesty from the writer, but they also provide a kind of immediacy and intimacy, a one-on-one exchange between reader and writer that is very satisfying. The essay persuades through a form of verbal seduction— by enabling the reader to look with the writer's eyes and the writer's own viewpoint. Reflective essays also present the personality of the writer distinctively; when you get to know a great essayist, invariably you will recognize his or her voice.

In an expository essay, the writer gives information in order to explain a point of view on a topic. This kind of essay presents you, as the writer, with an opportunity to work out your ideas in a broad context—on the environment, for example, or privacy, or relations between men and women. Your research, reflections, and analyses all contribute to the assertions you make and how you make them, but the goal of an expository essay is to express or explain your ideas clearly and to persuade the reader to accept the merit of your thesis or main point, rather than to change the reader's opinion or behavior.

An argumentative essay argues a point of view or presupposes an opposing point of view, and it is geared directly to anticipating and refuting that point of view. Like the expository essay, it clearly puts ideas in the public arena, but with the goal of stimulating debate, eliciting criticism, or convincing readers to change the way they think or what they do or to persuade them to take action in a particular direction. The best argumentative essays, however, are not divorced from the writer; they engage readers most thoroughly when the author is passionate about the subject matter.

Occasionally an author is able to write an essay that is simultaneously analytical and expository or argumentative, for example, the excerpt from Thoreau's *Civil Disobedience* in Chapter 9. Thoreau tells us about himself—his potential beliefs, how he expresses them, why he believes civil disobedience to unjust laws is the most accurate expression of his individuality and personality. He is so eloquent on the importance of the lone conscience in a democracy, the trouble with Congress, and the moral obligation to stand up and be counted at any cost that his personal creed also becomes a persuasive argument for nonviolent resistance as a general political tool. Few essayists can manage to combine all forms of the essay in one, but Thoreau will give you some idea of how many forms of self-expression and powerful persuasion a good essay can present.

Fiction and Poetry

We don't often think of fiction or poetry as persuasive writing because the arguments they make are more subtly stated, enveloped in character and language and plot. They are *about* someone or something. In fact, a great story or poem can move people profoundly and change their ideas, or enlighten them, in ways that more direct forms of address cannot. For example, Ralph Ellison's *Invisible Man* is a novel about an African American man who finds himself both literally and figuratively invisible in white America. Nowhere in the text does Ellison deliver a lecture on prejudice, or the corrupting influence of racism, or the tragic denial of ordinary freedoms. (See Chapter 5 for the Prologue of this novel.) But his characters, the voice of the narrator, and the story are so lucid and so affecting that the theme argues more profoundly than any explicit statement could.

Poetry is characterized by a kind of compression that makes its point through concentrated images and language. In her poem "Dear John Wayne," Louise Erdrich makes a forceful argument against the treatment Native Americans have received in the media, in popular culture, and in the way other Americans perceive them (see Chapter 11). Rather than assemble statistics about life on the reservation, she sets out an illustration whose point is vividly clear: the experience of Indian teenagers at a drive-in movie, watching John Wayne, the all-American hero, shoot apparently endless numbers of their ancestors in a movie battle. The oversimplification of the movie's portrait of good guys and bad guys, combined with the ordinariness of watching a movie at a drive-in, urge us to rethink our perspective and reevaluate our ideas—the goal of every well-written argument.

Legal Cases

Legal cases are a good way to clarify the elements of persuasive argument because that's exactly what they are about: two opponents in a court of law, arguing against each other in order to persuade a judge or jury to decide in their favor, knowing that only one side can win, and using every psychological and intellectual strategy they can think of to get the decision to go their way.

Trials are adversarial by definition; there have to be two sides and a neutral third party—a judge or a jury guided by a judge. Once the verdict has been reached, based on the evidence—once the third party has been persuaded by one side or the other—the trial is over. If the losing side is dissatisfied with the verdict, it can write an appeal, a piece of purely persuasive writing that goes to a panel of judges who then decide if they want to overrule the trial court decision or have the case tried again.

The U.S. Supreme Court is the court of last resort for appeals, but certain threshold conditions must be met for an appeal to be submitted to it; for example, the Court can decide to rule on a case involving the interpretation or application of the Constitution of the United States to a particular situation. Two of the cases in this book are Supreme Court cases. As you read the decisions the Court made in *Plessy* v. *Ferguson* and *Brown* v. *Board of Education,* keep four points in mind.

First, the Court often relies on the accumulated body of law already decided in related cases—called *precedent*—to explain why it is not overturning the verdict in the case before it. Occasionally—and *Brown* is the most famous example in American law—the Court rejects all precedent and makes a new law or takes the law, and the country, in a new direction.

Second, every year the Court receives many requests to hear cases on appeal and accepts only a fraction—usually those involving issues of substantial national importance. When it refuses a case, whatever the previous state or federal court decided remains unchanged.

Third, once the Supreme Court makes a decision, it is the law, until or unless Congress passes a different one. There is no higher court of appeal. It is a remarkable feature of our political life that Americans accept the Court's authority, though many of them may disagree with individual decisions.

Finally, Supreme Court decisions are rarely unanimous. With nine justices, the vote on a given case can be anything from 9-to-0 to 5-to-4. When you turn to *Plessy*, you will first read the majority decision, which prevailed. Then you will see Justice John Harlan's minority dissent—an opinion written by a justice who disagrees with the majority or is not persuaded by its reasoning and wants to set the reasons down clearly. *Brown,* in contrast, was decided unanimously.

Sometimes a dissenting opinion in one case forms the basis for a majority decision in another case years later. That is what happened between the *Plessy* decision and the *Brown* case almost fifty years afterward; Justice Harlan's argument against racial segregation was rejected in his lifetime, but in 1954 the Supreme Court found his language persuasive and used it in reversing the *Plessy* decision.

Images

This text includes a range of images, from historical to contemporary. We are persuaded daily by images—advertisements, editorial cartoons, Web sites, television programs, and the like. Advertisements convince us to buy certain food, drink, or clothing or to cultivate a certain appearance; films and television programs attract us by creating certain heroes, reinforcing our ideas, or invoking our fantasies and our need to escape. Posters and editorial cartoons communicate social expectations or political ideas to vast audiences. Visual images can persuade where words might fail.

Increasingly, scholars are attending to other elements of visual persuasion. Discussions of visual rhetoric may include not only photographs, paintings, cartoons, advertisements, and posters, but also Web sites and business documents which persuade visually not only through conventional images, but also through the appearance, format, and placement of text. Graphics, visual display of data, and other elements of a document are more and more commonly used to increase the clarity and the persuasiveness of textual documents as well.

Your experience as a viewer will serve you well in analyzing how the persuasiveness of images works, even when the images are previously unfamiliar to you. For example, you've seen automobile advertisements all your life; you don't have to have lived in the 1950s to get the point of an advertisement for a 1958 car complete with enormous fins and a huge front grill. And when you see an eighteenth-century etching showing a woman confined within the outlines of a compass, you will probably have little difficulty in figuring out that it illustrates the limits of what women were allowed to do. Although pictures from different times are directed to different audiences and your own reaction to those from the past may be different from those of the original viewers, keep in mind that the skill involved in "reading" images is one you practice every time you look at the advertisements in a magazine, a television show, or a movie.

Following is a brief overview of the varieties of visual images in this book, as well as some strategies for analyzing and enjoying them.

Photographs, Paintings, and Cartoons   Photographs punctuate news coverage. Whether still photos in a newspaper or "live-action video" on a television news program, photographs bring the story to life and capture the event in ways that complement the textual material and sometimes supplant it entirely. They appear to be objective records, yet the photographer "edits" by choosing to leave certain things out of the picture. Photographs are taken from a certain perspective, from a specific point of view; they record, but they also select; they capture the event, but at the same time they leave out part of the picture, often the larger context. Photos taken to report the news can move viewers to change their point of view and, in some cases, to change policy; the Pulitzer Prize–winning photographs in Chapter 10 are examples of the persuasive power of photography.

As with other expressive media, perhaps it is less common to think of paintings as persuasive, even when they capture specific events or appear to be recording a simple moment in time. Alfred Bierstadt's *Giant Redwood Trees of California* in Chapter 11 may seem to be simply an impressive landscape. But the interpolation of tiny figures—and Native American figures at that—is what articulates the scale of the trees. And at the same time, because the viewers of the painting would typically be white, those Native American figures help to explain what the wilderness used to be like and how it is changing.

Editorial cartoons make no pretense of objectivity. Often visual images with brief text, they must capture attention and make a point in only a second or two. Benjamin Franklin's woodcut and the *U.S. Hotel* cartoon, both in Chapter 5, and most of the editorial cartoons in contemporary newspapers tap into cultural references common to rhetor and audience as a kind of shorthand for longer arguments. In a sense, they are visual enthymemes, because the audience supplies the missing links in the argument in order to get the point.

Posters   Posters developed out of nineteenth-century technology and the need to communicate with a larger audience. They advertised performances and goods, appealed for labor and military recruits, and in time of war and national distress sought to maintain morale and denounce the enemy. Posters were a dominant communication device from the late nineteenth century until the rise of newsreel, radio, and later television. They were still useful, as a quickly and cheaply produced mass medium, but their impact declined as the other media appeared. For posters to persuade (and that was generally their purpose), they had to be able to attract attention and to inform. The audience generally would have been passersby, so, rather like political cartoons, they had to make their point quickly. Effective posters generally convey a strong impression in a matter of seconds, and a single strong element and strategic use of color, such as a bold color accent on a muted background, can draw the eye to the core issue or theme immediately. Other elements can be more subtle; in one poster in the Hoover Archives collection, for example, a German poster stressing soldiers' efforts to save women and children of the fatherland includes a small cross hanging around a woman's neck, tapping into the "Christian" identity of the woman and, presumably, her soldier-savior.

In evaluating posters as persuasive discourse, we look to some of the same criteria we use in judging other works of art. Although we can't always know the artist's personal beliefs or the extent to which the poster represents mass opinion, we can examine the rhetorical strategies employed by the artist and the themes implicit in the poster. We can assume that the posters were meant to inform or persuade and that the appeals employed by the artist were designed to evoke audience response. We can then make inferences about the intended audience, remembering that we are generalizing from the data the posters provide. We can look to color, placement of objects in the poster, designs, motifs, and themes to analyze their effectiveness.

Advertisements Like posters, advertisements reveal much about the cultures in which they appear, or at least the dominant culture of the society. Often shortchanging logic in favor of associations and emotional appeals, ads can appear in print or on video, radio, or film; they can be made up of text or image or both; and their arguments can be expected and explicit or unexpected and implicit. Purveyors of products go to great effort to have their products featured in films. Ads have also moved to a more explicit form in home videos. And an enormous battle has been waged as schools and school boards have debated whether to accept offers of free television equipment in exchange for including a certain amount of advertising in the television "curriculum." Even a historically advertising-free medium, public television, is offering longer and longer "thanks" to corporate sponsors of its programs.

As in writing about art, posters, and texts, writing about advertisements entails evaluating purpose, appeals, and aesthetics. The purpose is generally evident: the purchase of a product. Much fruitful analysis of advertising focuses on the assumptions, the flaws in logic, and the ethos, pathos, and logos appeals in the ads. Many of the points made earlier about these appeals pertain to advertising. Logical fallacies are rampant. Emotional appeals are often evident but are also often hidden beneath ostensibly logical claims. For example, an advertisement for soup might claim that soups will warm a child up before the child runs outside on a cold day; such an ad relies on emotional appeals (warmth, nurturing, home and health) more than physiological fact.

Critically assessing the layout, color, and image of advertisements can yield rich information about its persuasive tactics. Often products are strategically placed on the page, or near certain parts of the anatomy of a model; other times, a product (lipstick, beverage) is deliberately presented in a sexually suggestive position. Sometimes the advertiser wants part of the ad to recede into the background. For example, look at some magazine advertisements for cigarettes and try to find the surgeon general's warning. A good way to see where the eye falls in magazine ads is to flip through a magazine and notice which part of the page you see first; then assess what key feature of the product is made prominent and which is pushed to the side.

The language of advertising is highly connotative, associative, and image-laden; writers have to convey maximum impact in the fewest words possible. Student writers could indeed learn a lot about conciseness by examining well-written advertisements. The structure of textual arguments in advertising, though, is something to avoid in academic arguments; it is commonly designed to shortchange logic and to get consumers to draw a particular inference (they should buy a certain product) from the limited "data" presented.

There is no getting away from advertising in mainstream American culture. There are different ways of approaching the issue—from economic, sociological, psychological, political, and aesthetic perspectives, to name a few. You may wish to investigate some of these perspectives as you develop longer, documented essays for college courses. Professor Jean Kilbourne, for example, examines damaging attitudes toward and treatment of women in advertisements in the lecture/film *Still Killing Us Softly* that may be available through your college library. For the purposes of this text, we focus on the rhetorical strategies used to persuade audiences.

Films

We have included a film selection in each chapter. Film critic Robin Wood says that movies express not only the dreams of the people who make them but the dreams of the audience watching them. No other art form is more wholly or characteristically American. Hollywood became known long ago as the "Dream Factory," and there is no aspect of American life that is not refracted sooner or later through the lens of a camera. Sometimes the result is realistic; sometimes it is more an expression of wish fulfillment or escapism. Sometimes it is insulting; minorities watched movies for generations, looking for images of themselves and seeing nothing or seeing themselves portrayed in stereotypical or debased characterizations. But it would be impossible to imagine modern American culture without movies. And every theme in this book has provided and continues to provide material for the vast film audience. Movies are so embedded in our lives that many of the most profound notions Americans have about themselves are as much a result of what they see on the screen as of what they read or learn from experience.

We can look for common themes shared by the posters, political cartoons, films, fiction, essays, and arguments to find the common denominators in the way different media treat particular themes. You can pursue research by looking up particular themes or issues (women in the workforce, support on the home front, vilification of the enemy) that interest you and then analyzing treatment of them in the different media. Maybe your library has access to back issues of *Life* magazine, for example. One student researched issues of *Time* magazine from the 1940s, found an article entitled "How to Tell Your Friends from the Japs," and was able to trace racial stereotypes from posters and cartoons as well as the popular general interest magazines of the times. Other sources for this kind of research include Sam Keen's book *Faces of the Enemy* and the film of the same name, a thoughtful look at the ways in which we create an enemy through various media, including posters and cartoons. Another excellent source for propaganda and war-era posters is *Persuasive Images,* by Peter Paret et al.

Numerous Web sites are devoted to visual persuasion. You may find some useful examples on some of the following Web sites.

http://cartooning.about.com/arts/cartooning/mbody.htm   (cartooning)

http://www.nara.gov/exhall/powers/powers.html   (powers of persuasion)

http://www.nara.gov/   (national archives and record administration)

Analyzing an Image

The essay that follows, written by student Ray Tsao, is an example of how a photograph, one of the most famous photographs from the Vietnam War, can be analyzed for its use of visual rhetoric, particularly the Aristotelian appeals to ethos and pathos. This is a visceral image, and still a shocking one; Tsao's essay captures the complicated political and emotional charge this photograph carried in a highly partisan time, as well as those elements which make it a timeless picture of war. (The photo may be found in the chapter on war and violence.)

∞ *Persuasiveness in "Saigon Execution"*

RAY TSAO

The Vietnam War divided the United States as never before; civilian sentiment diverged sharply from government action. Undoubtedly, Edward T. Adams presented a stark contrast to wartime propaganda in his photograph, "Saigon Execution." Whereas the U.S.

government had focused on appealing to logic, in arguing that the fall of a democratic Vietnam would result in the proliferation of communism, Adams's photograph relies more on appeals to ethos and pathos, offering a powerful antiwar message precisely because of its ability to refute logical arguments.

Taken in the broadest sense, Adam's photograph was the almost reasonable portrayal of the execution of a Vietcong suspect. The context of war overrode what was essentially the murder of the human being. The execution was a path in which the audience followed quite readily; in order for the war to be won, enemies had to be killed. Therefore, the Vietcong suspect's death was but one of thousands in Vietnam; clearly, more would follow as the war was waged. However, Adams was able to present the suspect's death in another light.

The details in the photograph gave a dose of realism to the audience back home. Indeed, the gritty details of war apparent in "Saigon Execution," the broken windows, half-destroyed buildings, ravaged streets and patrolling soldiers, were substantially different from the picturesque "clean" war depicted in government propaganda. This was no conflict staged in an unnamed jungle or battleground; it was set amidst the friendly confines of "home." Furthermore, the audience could empathize with the Vietnamese, imagining their houses in the middle of a battlefield. More compelling, however, were the two individuals in the photograph, Police Chief Colonel Nguyen Loan and the Vietcong suspect.

The suspect easily attracts the attention and sympathy of the audience. He looks like little more than a teenager, his arms clasped behind his back and hunched over, his expression nothing but fear and horror. In addition, his casual plaid shirt is markedly different from Loan's combat fatigues. This is neither a heavily armed commando nor a vicious criminal, but a frightened boy. The idea that people similar to the suspect were being executed was one both alien and disturbing to the audience back home, not only for the loss of life but also the loss of innocence.

By the same token, Loan came across as a forbidding figure—as the symbol of South Vietnamese and U.S. power, but hardly justice. With both his face and body averted, it is difficult to relate to him. Much like the grim reaper, the police chief is a faceless agent of death. Obviously, Loan's emotions remain unclear to the audience, and whether he felt sympathy or took pleasure in executing the suspect became irrelevant. However, with his right hand gripping the gun, there was no question which man has the power.

"Saigon Execution" succeeded in disputing propaganda on the home front and giving the audience a taste of the realism that came with the Vietnam conflict. More than ever, it became unclear which side was "right." Was it necessary to occupy someone's homeland and impose a government which the civilians disavowed? The photograph—which won a Pulitzer Prize—did little to help the U.S. government's position. Adam's photograph achieved what antiwar activists had hoped: by confusing the line between "friend" and "enemy," it forced American viewers to reevaluate the necessity of the Vietnam conflict.

The purpose of this short essay is to demonstrate that a photograph can make an argument, and a persuasive one at that. Because it was not staged—the photographer was shooting a roll of film when the execution took place—the killing was on the evening news all over America, and it shocked the viewers. Ray Tsao's point is that this picture appeals to ethos and pathos, and thereby undercuts the official government argument for the war, which was based on logic. But what you should keep in mind when you look at the photo and read the essay is the way Tsao goes about proving his point—by looking closely at all the details of the photograph, including the street and buildings in the background, the shirt of the Viet Cong, the look on his face, and the body language and posture of the colonel. It is those details that give him the basis for analyzing the underlying appeals in the picture, and that kind of close reading is crucial to analyzing the persuasiveness of any image, in or out of this book—an advertisement in a magazine, a painting, a cartoon.

Tsao's reading of the photo is not exhaustive—Is the look on the Viet Cong's face one of terror, or is it the physiological result of being shot? Is the colonel's face averted, or is he just aiming his gun? What difference does it make that the photo is shot from up close and not a hundred feet away?

Tsao's methodology is invaluable for helping you to analyze visuals yourself. The next time you see an advertisement that gets to you, that you think is either wonderful or terrible, take the time to stop and look at it, really look at it. Look closely, and ask yourself why you think it worked, or didn't. What clues do you find? How did you come to the conclusion you did? See how many details you can list: where figures and objects are, where shadows and light are, what the perspective is, what the language says, where the words are placed on the page. This close reading will also begin to formulate ideas about who the audience is, why you react the way you do, and what underlying assumptions, values, and beliefs you bring with you that affect the way you see the world you live in.

Elements of Persuasion

As you examine the visual and textual arguments in this book, you may find it helpful to be able to recognize the rhetorical building blocks on which they rely: assumptions, assertions, examples, and refutations. You will never read an essay or novel or poem, or see an advertisement or a film, that does not make use of some or all of these elements. You use them yourself in ordinary conversation every time you talk to a friend. The difference is that in conversation they are generally spur of the moment, extemporaneous. In your own writing, you have the choice and control over which elements you use, how, and in what combinations. They are the DNA of persuasion, both essential and capable of infinite versatility.

Once you have thought about material presented earlier in this chapter—who is your audience, how do you want to appeal to it and why, what genre you want to use—you can use the elements that follow to structure and guide your writing. It's not a question of choosing one over the other; if you make any assertions, or if there are assumptions you start out with, you will always need examples to back them up. If you are arguing against someone else's ideas, then you need ammunition—assertions, examples—to show that your idea is better. As you become more conscious of these elements, which you use intuitively in your everyday life, you will also find it more natural and effective to use them in your writing.

Assumptions and Assertions

In everyday life we make countless assumptions: that the water will flow out of the tap when we turn it on, that the bus will come more or less on time to take us to school or work. That sometimes the water main breaks or the bus is quite late does not change the fact that we take these things for granted. When we arrive at school, we assume that a paper we turn in will be read and evaluated; we assume that the data we obtain from reliable sources—books, reputable journals, people we trust—are reported accurately. Sometimes we explicitly state the assumptions on which we are operating; for example, we might say, "With inflation holding steady for the rest of the quarter, we predict stable interest rates."

Assumptions are the unseen glue in an argument, providing the connection between the evidence or proof and the conclusions drawn from that proof. They are underlying principles on which we base our claims and part of the shared values or wisdom of a community, whether a society, culture, workplace, or academic discipline. We might conclude, for example, that a family might be dysfunctional based on our own criteria for functional families. Or we might assume that nuclear families have always been the norm, until we reflect on other community structures such as clans, tribes, and the like, or research alternative families in American history.

There is nothing inherently bad about assumptions; life would be extremely difficult if we had to start from scratch every day. But critical readers and careful writers do need to recognize assumptions in arguments, particularly those that are unstated. Careful readers question assumptions in the arguments they read, interrogating the text (or image) and writing notes in the margins or a notebook: "Who says? Why do you say that? Do you have any proof? Why did you draw that conclusion?" They will check for missing links between evidence and claim, or a jump from reason to conclusion that does not seem warranted by the reason itself. In addition to asking questions, one can diagram a selection by blocking out on paper the conclusion and the specific reasons that support it, and then examine them for underlying assumptions.

Assertions are the conclusions one draws based on some combination of reasons and assumptions. The main assertion in an essay is often referred to as a *thesis statement.* Reasons are the support the writer offers—the evidence on which she or he has based those assertions. Assumptions are the often unstated beliefs, values, and principles we hold that interplay with other assumptions and reasons. Some writers refer to assumptions and reasons as premises; the term *premise* is prominent in discussions of formal logic and the syllogism, or deductive argument in outline form. For the sake of clarity, we will use *assertions* consistently throughout this text but will note synonyms that other writers sometimes use.

Assertions vary in tone and in language because of differences in the assumptions that underlie them and because of differences in temperament, background, and purpose. Some assertions are factual; some are statements of values; some are drawn from research; and some are meant as calls to action, to suggest changes in policy or procedure.

The whole middle section of the Declaration of Independence is a list of assertions about all the terrible things King George III did to the colonies which finally forced the colonists to declare their independence. Chapter 9, Justice and Civil Liberties, includes the first draft of the Declaration along with the final version, so you can see how different in tone and effect the two versions are.

In the same chapter, Susan B. Anthony's speech after she got arrested for trying to vote in 1872 makes assertions that were unacceptable to most Americans at the time—that the Constitution meant to include women in the phrase, "We the People," that the Declaration meant to include women in the phrase, "All men are created equal," and that being denied the right to vote was a denial of the Fourteenth and Fifteenth Amendments. By using the language of our most revered documents to phrase her assertions, Anthony was laying claim to a political legitimacy which could not be expressed in any other terms.

Examples

Technically, an example is a single part chosen to show the nature or character of a whole, or a sample of a larger unit, or a typical sample of something; George Washington is an example of an American president, and Chris Rock is an example of a comedian.

Practically, though, examples fulfill two crucial functions in writing. First, they enable an audience to identify emotionally and/or intellectually with the writer or the writer's subject. This identification is especially important if the writer wants to move the audience to action, or knows that the audience is hostile or indifferent or just unfamiliar with the material. For instance, in the speech "I Have a Dream," Martin Luther King Jr. included examples of how prejudice affected the lives of African Americans doing ordinary things—like trying to book a hotel room or get a seat on a bus—to explain the effects of racial segregation to an audience, many of whose members had no personal experience of segregation. These common and easily understandable examples help persuade through *identification*—identification between King and his audience, between the people he is talking about and the people he is talking to.

The second role that example fills is to support persuasion through *evidence*; examples can act as proof for general statements or assertions. Just as abstractions without examples are emotionally uninvolving, assertions without examples are unconvincing. Examples are as essential to a persuasive argument as results are to an experiment.

The following two paragraphs show the difference between a paragraph without clear examples and the same paragraph rewritten by the author to include examples. The argument concerns whether dropping the atomic bomb on Japan hastened the end of World War II. The writer, Paul Fussell, is criticizing John Kenneth Galbraith, the economist, who thought that the atomic bomb made no difference.

Without Examples

On the other hand, John Kenneth Galbraith is persuaded that the Japanese would have surrendered by November without an invasion. He thinks the atomic bombs were not decisive in bringing about the surrender and he implies that their use was unjustified. What did he do in the war? He was in the Office of Price Administration in Washington, and then he was director of the United States Strategic Bombing Survey. He was thirty-seven in 1945, and I don't demand that he experience having his ass shot off. I just note that he didn't. In saying this I'm aware of its offensive implications ad hominem. But here I think that approach justified. What's at stake in an infantry assault is so entirely unthinkable to those without any experience of one, even if they possess very wide-ranging imaginations and sympathies, that experience is crucial in this case.

With Examples

On the other hand, John Kenneth Galbraith is persuaded that the Japanese would have surrendered surely by November without an invasion. He thinks the A-bombs were unnecessary and unjustified because the war was ending anyway. The A-bombs meant, he says, "a difference, at most, of two or three weeks." But at the time, with no indication that surrender was on the way, the kamikazes were sinking American vessels, the *Indianapolis* was sunk (880 men killed), and Allied casualties were running to over 7,000 per week. "Two or three weeks," says Galbraith. Two weeks more means 14,000 more killed and wounded, three weeks more, 21,000. Those weeks mean the world if you're one of those thousands or related to one of them. During the time between the dropping of the Nagasaki bomb on August 9 and the actual surrender on the 15th, the war pursued its accustomed course: on the 12th of August eight captured American fliers were executed (heads chopped off); the fifty-first United State submarine, *Bonefish,* was sunk (all aboard drowned); the destroyer *Callaghan* went down, the seventieth to be sunk, and the Destroyer Escort *Underhill* was lost. That's a bit of what happened in six days of the two or three weeks posited by Galbraith. What did he do in the war? He worked in the Office of Price Administration in Washington. I don't demand that he experience having his ass shot off. I merely note that he didn't.

The first paragraph gives no evidence to support or refute Galbraith's contention that the use of the bombs was unnecessary. The second, with its example upon example of the numbers and types of casualties that occurred in the last days of the war, certainly puts the writer in a stronger position to persuade the reader that Galbraith was wrong.

Refutation

Refutation is proof that an argument or statement is wrong. It comes into existence only when there is an opponent or another side. Refutation means that someone else has gone first; it is the answer to an assumption, or a point of view, or a statement with which one disagrees.

In one sense, then, refutation is not a completely independent rhetorical strategy; it needs to bounce off and argue against something else. The emphasis in refutation is less on stating one's own principles than on taking the material presented by an opponent and dismantling it.

In another sense, refutation is based on instinct, on the impulse to react negatively when we hear an idea that infuriates us or strikes us as stupid or unethical or unjust. But refutation is more disciplined than that. An artful, well-prepared writer or speaker uses refutation to overturn an opponent's argument or to take his or her ideas and reverse them to advantage.

It is possible to refute an argument logically without necessarily having a deep intellectual belief in the view expressed by the refutation. For example, an excellent logician could refute the argument of someone he or she agrees with by pointing up inconsistencies; a member of a debating team could be randomly assigned either side of an argument and would be expected to find ways to damage the other side's approach. And criminal attorneys are routinely expected to fulfill their duty of defending people whom they dislike, distrust, or even believe to be guilty, mostly by refuting the prosecution's evidence and raising doubt in the mind of a jury or judge.

The higher forms of refutation, however, are neither mechanical nor uncommitted. They come from one's involvement with an issue or a principle, and they do more than decimate the opposing viewpoint; they can change the way people think and move them to action.

In extraordinary cases—like those expressed in Chapter 9 by Henry David Thoreau, Frederick Douglass, and Martin Luther King Jr.—refutation can acquire a significant symbolic authority, which resonates over time to larger and more distant audiences. It can even move and inspire otherwise ordinary people to risk their own security and freedom in the name of an idea. Thoreau, for example, argued so powerfully for the effectiveness of nonviolent resistance over the use of force that both Mahatma Gandhi and Martin Luther King Jr. were able to apply his approach to two of the most powerful civil rights movements of the twentieth century.

In the following essay, student writer William West analyzes Chief Justice Earl Warren's successful use of refutation in *Brown* v. *Board of Education* to overthrow a legal precedent that had stood for fifty years. You will notice that refutation is not the only element from this chapter that Warren employs; he also relies heavily on Aristotelian appeals, and he gives many examples. But refutation of an older legal decision is his main purpose, and all the other tools at his disposal are chosen and organized with that purpose in mind.

∞ *Refutation in* Brown v. Board of Education

WILLIAM WEST

A court of law does not have open to it the same avenues for supporting its opinions that an ordinary rhetor has. Legal argumentation and writing are governed by conventions, one of the most important of which is precedent. Because the Supreme Court case of *Brown* v.

Board of Education overturned *Plessy* v. *Furguson,* which had stood for over half a century, the court had to be careful to fully justify its rejection of precedent. In his opinion for the court, Chief Justice Earl Warren carefully creates an argument which uses logical appeals to justify overturning *Plessy,* and appeals to ethos to give the ruling more validity.

The contested issue in the case is whether so-called "separate but equal" educational facilities are truly equal and afford black students the equal protection under the law required by the Fourteenth Amendment.

The first part of the Court's opinion outlines the general facts of the case and the arguments presented by both sides. This approach both appeals to the belief in impartial and balanced justice and forms the groundwork for later argument. Only after he has laid this groundwork does Justice Warren begin to criticize the *Plessy* ruling.

In calling *Plessy* into question, Justice Warren repudiates the idea that it should stand simply because it is based on tradition. He begins with a logical reminder of how much times have changed since *Plessy* was decided. That leads to his point that the test *Plessy* used, that of counting only tangible factors in judging whether separate public facilities can also be equal facilities, is also out of date. He argues that "We cannot turn the clock back . . . to 1896 when *Plessy* v. *Ferguson* was written. We must consider public education in light of . . . its present place in American life and throughout the nation."

Having introduced the idea that times have changed, and thereby implied that precedents can be changed too, Warren proposes that the test for separate but equal schools deserves a more modern test than the one in *Plessy.* In this way, he compensates for getting rid of the old logical appeal to precedent by substituting a newer logical appeal to the realities of the modern world.

However, Justice Warren then goes on to make an additional appeal, this time to widely held American values. He writes that education is "required in the performance of our most basic public responsibilities" and is "the very foundation of good citizenship." Phrases such as these evoke commonly held beliefs about the importance of education and participation in democracy. No one can easily argue, at least in the abstract, against the ideal of preparing young girls and boys to be good citizens. Warren implicitly asks whites who support these notions in the abstract to extend them to the particular case of segregated black students.

Finally, after having laid the necessary groundwork, Warren makes his assertion: certain intangible differences between segregated schools "deprive the children of the minority group of equal educational opportunities." This is the conclusion of the logical inquiry that he proposed earlier. He then supports this conclusion by presenting other court rulings, which, although they did not overturn *Plessy* outright, nonetheless identified inequality in specific cases. In addition he supplies psychological evidence, "amply supported by modern authority," that segregation gives black students a feeling of inferiority. The cases presented as evidence serve as concrete examples of how facilities can be truly unequal and serve as new precedents.

Throughout this opinion Warren uses appeals to ethos and logos together to justify the controversial act of overturning a long-standing precedent. On the one hand, he appeals to logic. On the other hand, he invokes the American belief in good citizenship and democratic participation. This ethical appeal provides the implied support for Warren's conclusion that separate cannot be equal, and that *Plessy* is unconstitutional. The significance of combining the appeals to logos and ethos in a legal context is clearly what underlies the structure of Warren's argument.

The chapter on Justice and Civil Liberties from which this student essay is drawn contains some of the most effective examples of persuasive argument this country has produced, including the Declaration of Independence and Martin Luther King Jr.'s "Letter from Birmingham Jail." West's topic is particularly interesting, not only because of the significance of the Supreme Court's decision in *Brown* v. *Board of Education,* but because it unpacks the most significant rhetorical element in that decision. We can see its constituent parts—the appeals, the examples, the assertions. But the focus is on the ultimate goal of justifying the refutation of an older Court decision and replacing it with a new decision which reads the Constitution in a completely different way. By analyzing the rhetorical parts that together combine to form a good refutation, West gives us an insight into how any refutation can be constructed.

We hope that these suggestions for analyzing persuasive strategies, audiences, cultures, and genres will help you to learn to read diverse arguments critically and to become more aware of your own abilities as readers, viewers, and writers. Chapter 3 offers suggestions for developing your essays, from prewriting to thesis to organizing your ideas, and Chapter 4 is a guide to incorporating research materials into your writing.

In order to integrate critical reading and persuasive writing, the chapters in Part II, "Argument in the American Tradition," combine critical readings with suggestions for analytical and persuasive writing. Each chapter develops a core thematic issue and links that issue to important aspects of argumentation through an introduction, diverse persuasive materials, an end-of-chapter discussion, and assignments that develop your ability to construct your own effective arguments. We hope that the arguments you find included in this book, as well as the suggestions for good writing, will stimulate your imagination, your critical thinking, and your understanding of persuasion in what you read and what you write. Debate in American culture rages on, and we hope you will jump in and become part of our ongoing discussion and debate—part of the American tradition.

3

Writing Essays

Developing Essays

In writing an essay, you start with an idea or something you've wondered about, or you get an idea, maybe from reading or discussion. You read, review, discuss, perhaps take notes—and in the process integrate what you are learning with what you already know. Writing is a way of learning; we write to elicit what we already know and to develop and clarify thoughts and ideas. Writing essays and other prose forces us to develop, organize, and transmit clearly our ideas, evidence, and interpretations. Writing is also a way to record information and demonstrate knowledge. It remains the primary means of disseminating knowledge and information in the academic world, and despite the pervasiveness of visual and audio media, it remains a crucial means of communication in the rest of society as well.

There are several different kinds of persuasive writing: reports, exposition, and argumentation. The writing situation—the audience, purpose, and subject—dictates the form that is needed. This book focuses on argumentation, but we suggest considering persuasion in communication not as a discrete, separate genre but as a continuum with varying degrees of argumentative edge.

Along the continuum of persuasion in written discourse, *reports* tend to be the least overtly persuasive. A report writer presents information accurately in a relatively unbiased manner; indeed, the writer's thoroughness and accuracy may in themselves be persuasive of a certain conclusion, but the report itself does not necessarily suggest that conclusion. A lab report is an example of the kind of report writing commonly used in college. In business, people other than the report writer often make decisions based on the report, although some reports also include recommendations.

An *expository essay* is more persuasive; it asserts a point of view and is persuasive insofar as the writer wants to convince readers of the merits of his or her case. The expository or analytical essays most college students write often work in conjunction with other texts and materials; that is, the writer is responding to a text, an idea, a concept, or a situation. Such essays often entail developing a point of view or an assertion about a subject and then supporting that point of view with evidence from personal observation, a literary text, or a prominent theory in the field. Essays analyzing a literary work or a historical event are good examples of the kinds of expository writing commonly practiced in college courses.

An *argumentative essay* clearly attempts to persuade its readers to identify with the writer, to change their minds, to change their behavior, and to adopt or abandon a policy or course of action. The argument rests on assumptions, assertions, and evidence.

All three kinds of essays can integrate research. We suggest that you consider research a process you undertake whenever the response to a question or the testing of a hypothesis requires that you look beyond your own knowledge and experience for supporting evidence which might have persuaded the reader of the truth of your experience but wouldn't necessarily suggest that it is pervasive in American society. Instead, outside experts and evidence present a far more convincing case. In the sections that follow, we first discuss developing essays that may not require outside research and then outline suggestions for integrating research.

Techniques for Developing Essays

All forms of writing involve a process of prewriting, writing, and revising. During this process, it may be helpful to use some of the following prompts and questions to help you think about, focus, structure, and develop your paper.

Strategies for Prewriting

1. Freewrite. Start with a focused freewrite, that is, writing without attention to grammar, style, or spelling. Keep pen to page, or fingers to keyboard, and write for five or ten minutes to get started. Do you have some general topic area to think about? Jot down everything you can think of about your topic. Then review your notes and try again with a more focused view of some aspect of the topic that came up in the freewrite. If you don't have an assignment or a specific topic in mind, freewriting can help you figure out what you might find interesting to write about.

2. Brainstorm. Write down ideas, images, possible directions—anything that comes to mind about your potential topic—in a list down the page, rather than in the continuous flow of the freewrite. Review your list and try again, focusing on something interesting that came up in the brainstorming.

3. *Do invisible writing.* If you have access to a computer, this exercise may be useful. Turn off the monitor or screen brightness and write continuously without viewing what you are writing. This technique is useful for people who tend to get writer's block or censor their writing and ideas even before they can get the words out.

4. *Review what you have written.* Do you see possibilities to focus on? Do you see connections or angles you didn't think of before? If so, select one of the exercises above—freewriting, brainstorming, or invisible writing—that seemed the most productive for you, and do another session of writing on the focused area you discovered in the exercises. Review the topic and see if it looks promising for further development. Devise a tentative core point or hypothesis.

5. *Consider your own biases.* After you have developed a tentative focus, the next couple of exercises may be useful. First, write out all of your biases or preconceived notions about the topic. This is particularly important if you are developing an argumentative researched essay. It is crucial that you conduct your research in an open-minded manner, one that enables you to seek out material and data on both sides of the question. An argument implies an opposition, so take care to look at both sides in your research as well as in your structuring of your argument.

6. *Construct a dialogue between the two sides.* Personify each side of the argument and have the two sides debate the issue. That is, assign a position or a personality to each side, and let them argue for a while, with you writing the script.

7. *Refine your topic and focus.* In a sentence, try to write what the focus and approach of your paper will be. If you can't write it now, at least narrow your topic to something that seems manageable for the length and depth of the paper assigned.

8. *Try the journalistic method.* After generating some material about your topic, it might be useful to adopt a systematic approach based on the journalistic method, which asks and responds to the following questions: what, who, when, where, why, and how.

- *What* is happening, or what has happened, in terms of your topic?
- *Who* (or perhaps *what*) was or is involved in your topic? Who or what does something, or to whom or to what does something happen?
- *When* did it happen?
- *Where* did it happen? What is the background of the situation?
- *Why* did it happen? Why did the agent (*who*) cause it to happen? What are the implications of this purpose?
- *How* was the action or event brought about? What were the means, methods, resources involved?

While working with whichever prewriting and planning methods you find most helpful, you will find that one or more areas of focus emerge. As you review your prewriting and planning material, you are in a good position to develop a tentative thesis statement. You will likely go back and forth between prewriting and drafting, adjusting the thesis and content as you go, but explicit attention to your thesis now will pay off when you strive to organize and develop your essay further.

Developing a Core Assertion: The Thesis Statement

Critical readers learn to detect and analyze the main idea in a text. Persuasive writers develop a thesis statement to focus and guide the development of their essays. By *thesis statement,* we mean the core assertion, the main point being argued for and supported. In an expository or informative essay, the thesis statement indicates your limited topic and your approach to that topic; it still asserts a point of view or perspective, but it tends not to have an argumentative edge to it. A thesis statement in a persuasive piece of discourse seeks to argue for a certain position or point of view, not merely informing but pushing for some change in viewpoint or attitude on the part of the audience. An expository thesis statement does not necessarily provoke a response or an argument; a persuasive thesis statement generally does. Whereas readers of informative or explanatory information will want to see the evidence or support that led to the thesis statement, the persuasive essay will also need to respond to counterarguments; the thesis itself will generally be a stronger assertion of a position than the expository thesis statement. Clearly there is overlap between expository and argumentative thesis statements, but the edge of an opinion, statement of belief, or more forceful assertion generally signals to the reader that an argument follows. For example, an essay might include one of the following core assertions.

- "Martin Luther King Jr.'s 'I Have a Dream' speech was the turning point of the March on Washington."
- "Martin Luther King Jr.'s 'I Have a Dream' speech confronted white America with its own sorry record on civil rights for black Americans."
- "If America is to support the ideals for which Martin Luther King Jr. fought, it must do more than pay lip service to civil rights rulings—it must enforce them."

The first statement could serve as the thesis for an expository essay; it selects and limits a topic and conveys an approach and an attitude toward that topic. The writer may try to convince the reader as to the merits of his case but does not invite counterarguments or try to change attitudes. The second statement also focuses the topic and indicates an approach; in addition, it addresses beliefs and values and engages the reader through value-laden terms (*confronted, sorry*), though it could soften them (i.e., *poor record*) and still argue a point. This sentence invites debate, if not dialogue. The third sentence doesn't argue a point of view or value judgment, like the second sentence, but it proposes a course of action: enforcing civil rights legislation. Buried within the third statement is the assumption or principle that all Americans should support the values for which King fought.

Many expository thesis statements look something like the first sentence; some arguments about values, beliefs, and principles look like the second; proposals or attempts to move the reader to a specific course of action often look like the third. There are many different variations and types of sentences, and we will examine them throughout this book. Essentially, though, a thesis is an assertion that focuses the topic; it indicates an approach to be followed in the essay or other discourse, and in the case of persuasive and argumentative works, it argues for a position, a belief or value, or a course of action.

A thesis is not a statement of acknowledged fact; if it were, there would be little point in discussion. It is not an effusion of emotion or a matter of taste; those too defy reasoned debate. It is an element that reflects and guides the essay. An essay exists to amplify or prove the thesis; the thesis is an encapsulation of the essay. The two must echo and reinforce each other if the essay is to be coherent, to be linked throughout.

Not all pieces of writing explicitly state a thesis. Some use implication, meaning the audience has to infer, or figure out, from the essay what the point or assertion is. Generally, argumentative essays clearly state a position, but pieces that are less explicitly persuasive often do not. The etching *Keep Within Compass* in Chapter 7 states its point, though the values and beliefs supporting that point are implied through other text and the artwork.

As you practice writing, you will generally need to develop a clear statement of purpose, focus, approach, or proposal. Not every piece of writing you will ever do will need a clear, explicit thesis statement, but generally college writing (and much out-of-college writing) will require you to state your position or point clearly and then support it with appropriate evidence. When do you devise a thesis statement? That depends. If you have an idea of what you want to assert, even if it is not fully formed or is tentative, write it down, perhaps trying several variations. Often freewriting a bit after you have jotted down several possibilities will help you to discern what it is you are trying to say. If you are exploring a topic—say, an analysis of an argumentative piece—read, discuss, and take notes until you feel ready to develop a working thesis statement. Some students find that a simple outline for a thesis statement can help them focus it. While writing down a topic or a phrase is a good start, it is more difficult to get off the fence and state an assertion or proposal. Two outlines that students have found useful are the following:

1. I shall argue that _____.

This format reminds you that you need to assert something, not just throw out a topic, even a narrowed topic, although that is a useful stage in the process before you develop a thesis.

2. Although _____, I believe/I shall argue that _____
   because _____.

This outline can guide you by making sure you are looking at potential objections to your argument, that you assert something, and that you have lined up some evidence to support your view.

These are working outlines and need not appear in your essay. In fact, the second outline could produce an exceedingly cumbersome thesis, or at least an inelegant one. But you will be able to decide how explicit to make your thesis statement as you revise, and you will be able to refine the language in revision as well. The Hofstadter selection in Chapter 11 is a superb example of an explicitly stated thesis.

As noted earlier, writing is generally not a linear process that takes you from point A to point B in orderly succession; rather it is a recursive process—writers return to earlier parts of the process as needed—perhaps reviewing and refining the focus or brainstorming examples to support a key point. But after some productive effort at prewriting and crafting a thesis statement, you will be in a good position to consider how you want to structure your material. Some writers have found the following techniques helpful.

Organizing and Drafting the Essay

Break your topic into parts. After generating yet more information, through prewriting and as appropriate through research and note taking, think about how you might break down or analyze the parts of your topic. Draft out the major divisions or aspects of your topic on paper or on screen. Don't worry about the form of the outline; just get the major divisions on paper so you can see where your project is going and so that you have a sense of the magnitude and direction of the topic at this state.

Go back to the question of focus. Does your tentative thesis statement still capture the gist of your ideas? If not, review your notes, your preliminary thoughts and ideas, and the materials you have developed. Try to understand where they are taking you. What connections can you make? What inferences can you make from your findings? Draft several thesis statements; one or two probably will come close to representing the direction in which your research is taking you.

Consider coherence. Having listed the major divisions of your subject area, consider whether all of the parts you have set forth still belong in your paper. Are all parts closely related to the key question of your preliminary focus? If not, will you adapt your thesis or throw out the irrelevant material?

Review your main topic divisions. Does an order suggest itself? Does there seem to be a best way to present your points to the reader?

Pay attention to contradictions and opposing views. At what point do they suggest themselves? If you are writing a persuasive essay, opposing views may come up at any time in the process; if they don't come to mind, you'll need to seek them out. Ask yourself questions. Why isn't what I propose already in place? Why wouldn't people want what I am advocating? If you don't consider and deal with opposing views, the reader will certainly be thinking of them, and you will undercut your credibility if you don't concede to or refute opposing arguments.

Refocus your thesis statement. Try to write a more focused thesis statement to state the argument or point you want to make (review notes on thesis statements in the introduction).

Write out a plan. If at this point you see the overall pattern of your paper emerging, take the time now to write a prospectus—a plan that summarizes the purpose, organization, and main points of your paper. If you are not yet ready to do so, answer some of the following questions:

- Why is the subject important to you or to potential readers? Why have you chosen to write about it, and what do you plan to transmit to others?

- How much additional reading will you need to do, and where will you go to find the information you need?

- How much background information do your readers need to understand the significance of your topic or the issues involved?

- What points will you be making about your topic, and what kinds of evidence will you include?

Consider methods and sources of research. For researched essays, review the rest of the chapter for advice about taking notes, integrating sources, and documenting sources.

Revising the Draft

After you get the basic structure of the rough draft down, review the logic of your assertions. Determine whether they still support the thesis and whether the thesis still allows you to engage the parts of your topic that you want to cover. Thesis and support must remain connected and mutually reinforcing. Review your draft and determine if you need more evidence or if you should cut out parts that don't seem relevant. Peer feedback at this stage can be useful. Exchange drafts with a classmate and try to give each other "big picture" feedback on the thesis, basic structure, and supporting evidence. Then revise your essay as needed to attend to criticism from your peer. Remember, though, that as the author, you have the final decision over changes you make. Accept feedback, but use your own judgment in deciding how much and what kind of advice to take.

You should certainly spell-check your paper if you are using a computer to write it, but such tools do not find all the errors and lapses in good style that your draft may have. Peer feedback is also helpful for detecting errors that you may not find, since at this point in the draft your eyes may see what they expect to see (or want to see) rather than what is on the page. You and a peer should both go over your paper in fine detail, attending to issues of style, appropriateness of language, level of diction, proper syntax, and correct documentation style.

Organizing Tools

Writers use different approaches for organizing their essays. The following are some of the most common. There is no hard and fast rule here about which approach to take; the point is that some organizing principle will work for you, and any one you use is better than none. The alternative is writing an essay at two o'clock in the morning, and finally getting sleepy enough to convince yourself that those loosely related ideas you've been looking at on your computer screen really form a unified presentation. That approach is about as effective as it sounds. Here are a couple of techniques to help you lay more effective groundwork for your writing.

Outlines

An outline indicates the framework of your essay. It summarizes the core assertion and key supporting points. When you make an outline you can put in the points you're sure of, and doing that may help you to see what's missing. Constructing an outline can help you sort out the relationships between various ideas as well as determine whether your thesis is narrow enough and where you need to provide additional specific support (i.e., more examples). An outline can also help you to reorder and reorganize points, keeping related ideas together and enabling you to check the overall order and flow of ideas.

Some students prefer a very rough kind of outline of the major sections that indicates the purpose of each section. It's possible to limit yourself very successfully to a working thesis statement and several topic sentences—essentially listing what could be the main sentence in each paragraph. That kind of outline gives you a road map to follow as you build the essay.

A more formal outline indicates the subordinate elements under each major heading; a detailed outline might include Roman numerals for section headings, numbers for subsections, and letters of the alphabet for individual ideas. If you can organize this kind of outline, you will have a lot of the work for your essay in front of you before you even start writing out the text in paragraphs.

A topic sentence outline, in which you actually write out your points in complete sentences instead of listing topics or ideas in fragments, has a real advantage. It forces you to make your assertion or state your assumption, and that means you have to set forth your claims and examine them and the evidence you have to support them. This is a highly objective way of seeing what you really have, because it's the closest you can come to reading your work as though it had been written by someone else.

Index Cards and Notebooks

Index cards are an informal approach that many writers use. If you feel that you can't put down every idea because you don't really know yet what you think or because you really don't like outlines and don't do them thoroughly, try writing on a bunch of index cards. Put one idea on each card in big letters. Number the cards. That way you can always add supporting evidence or secondary ideas without losing track of your materials. For your own sake, however, keep a rubber band around the cards or stash them in one place; there are few occurrences more discouraging to the use of this or any other system than losing all the work that went into it.

The alternative—and the more writing you do the better this is—is to have one notebook dedicated to your writing. Carry it with you, and put everything, including library information, brainstorming ideas, and possible thesis sentences, in it. Scribble sentence fragments, try out opening paragraphs. A notebook is private, and inexpensive, and all the information is together in one place. Professional writers almost always have a notebook with them so they can put down ideas whenever they occur. That habit—writing down ideas as you have them, rather than hoping you'll remember them until you have time later—can help preserve your thoughts when they are freshest and most likely to suggest other connections.

Laptops and Computers

Computers are clearly helpful for storing large quantities of information in multiple formats. Many students have access to computers either at home or at school, and use them for writing drafts. They are a good repository for your preliminary work, as well as for any potential reference you come across, and for any idea that you got from free writing, brainstorming, or any of the other exercises earlier in this chapter. If you are fortunate enough to have a laptop, take it to the library with you and put everything on it, just as if you were using index cards. You can use the computer to see what kind of outline, if any, would work for you. You can try a rough or detailed outline, or make files for each of them.

Sample Essays

Generating and organizing material for your essay depends to some degree on the type of essay you are writing. Earlier we discussed reports, expository essays, and argumentative essays. Often essays will be both argumentative and expository (see Susan B. Anthony and Wallace Stegner selections), but there is usually a dominant mode. Expository essays can be reflective; they can tell about a place or an incident. The dreaded "What I Did on my Summer Vacation" topic from elementary school calls for an expository response—you're not mounting an argument over whether you did or didn't go to Disneyland with your grandparents. "Nurses in Vietnam," Jacqueline Navarro Rhoads's narrative about her experiences during the Vietnam War, is also expository. It's a story about what happened to her and to people she knew, and how she felt. Analytical essays are a type of expository essay that involve taking something apart— a poem, a picture, a set of assertions, a group of assumptions, even an argument—and explaining how it works, what it aims to do, and how well it succeeds. Argumentative essays are aimed at proving a point or points, and sometimes at doing so by dismantling someone else's argument, or taking on someone else's ideas. In the next section, we provide samples of each of these modes, so that you can see them side by side and get a better sense of their strategies.

Expository Essays   The following example of an expository essay is by Korean American Younghill Kang, who emigrated to the United States in 1921 and whose writing is an attempt to mediate between

Asian and American experience from an immigrant's perspective. This essay describes his arrival in New York.

∞ A Korean Discovers New York

YOUNGHILL KANG

From an old walled Koran city some thousand years old—Seoul—famous for poets and scholars, to New York. I did not come directly. But almost. A large steamer from the Orient landed me in Vancouver, Canada, and I travelled over three thousand miles across the American continent, a journey more than half as far as from Yokohama to Vancouver. At Halifax, straightway I took another liner. And this time for New York. It was in New York I felt I was destined really "to come off from the boat." The beginning of my new existence must be founded here. In Korea *to come out from the boat* is an idiom meaning to be born, as the word "pai" for "womb" is the same as "pai" for "boat"; and there is the story of a Korean humorist who had no money, but who needed to get across a river. On landing him on the other side, the ferryman asked for his money. But the Korean humorist said to the ferryman who too had just stepped out, "You wouldn't charge your brother, would you? We both came from the same boat." And so he travelled free. My only plea for a planet-ride among the white-skinned majority of this New World is the same facetious argument. I brought little money, and no prestige, as I entered a practical country with small respect for the dark side of the moon. I got in just in time before the law against Oriental immigration was passed.

But New York, that magic city on rock yet ungrounded, nervous, flowing, million-hued as a dream, became, throughout the years I am recording, the vast mechanical incubator of me.

It was always of New York I dreamed—not Paris nor London nor Berlin nor Munich nor Vienna nor age-buried Rome. I was eighteen, green with youth, and there was some of the mystery of nature in my simple immediate response to what was for me just a name . . . like the dogged moth that directs its flight by some unfathomable law. But I said to myself, "I want neither dreams nor poetry, least of all tradition, never the full moon." Korea even in her shattered state had these. And beyond them stood waiting—death. I craved swiftness, unimpeded action, fluidity, and amorphous New. Out of action rises the dream, rises the poetry. Dream without motion is the only wasteland that can sustain nothing. So I came adoring the crescent, not the full harvest moon, with winter over the horizon and its waning to a husk.

"New York at last!" I heard from the passengers around me. And the information was not needed. In unearthly white and mauve, shadow of white, the city rose, like a dream dreamed overnight, new, remorselessly new, impossibly new . . . and yet there in all the arrogant pride of rejoiced materialism. These young, slim, stately things a thousand houses high (or so it seemed to me, coming from an architecture that had never defied the earth), a tower of Babel each one, not one tower of Babel but many, a city of Babel towers, casually, easily strewn end up against the skies—they stood at the brink, close-crowded, the brink of America, these Giantesses, these Fates, which were not built for a king nor a ghost nor any man's religion, but were materialized by those hard, cold, magic words—opportunity, enterprise, prosperity, success—just business words out of world-wide commerce from a land rich in natural resource. Buildings that sprang white from the rock. No earth clung to their skirts. They leaped like Athene from the mind synthetically; they spurned the earth. And there was no monument to the machine-age like America.

I could not have come farther from home than this New York. Our dwellings, low, weathered, mossed, abhorring the lifeless line—the definite, the finite, the aloof—loving rondures and an upward stroke, the tilt of a roof like a boat always aware of the elements in which it is swinging—most fittingly my home was set a hemisphere apart, so far over the globe that to have gone on would have meant to go nearer not farther. How far my little grass-roofed, hill-wrapped village from this gigantic rebellion which was New York! And New York's rebellion called to me excitedly, this savagery which piled great concrete block on concrete block, topping at the last moment as in an afterthought, with crowns as delicate as pinnacled ice; this lavishness which, without a prayer, pillaged coal mines and waterfalls for light, festooning the great nature-severed city with diamonds of frozen electrical phenomena—it fascinated me, the Asian man, and in it I saw not Milton's Satan, but the one of Blake.

It's clear as one reads this essay that for Kang, who came from an ancient culture, the newness and enormous energy of New York were immensely attractive to him before he ever came to America. Let's look at a couple of his assertions:

> It was in New York I felt I was destined really "to come off the boat."
> The beginning of my new existence must be founded here.

These assertions are supported by a couple of explanations—that off the boat in Korean is the same as being born, that coming to New York means starting a new life in a new country. Kang's focus is not just on his immigrant status, however, but on what New York seemed to offer that no other place could. Kang uses elaborate metaphorical language to express this view: ". . . that magic city on rock yet ungrounded, nervous, flowing, million hued as a dream, became, throughout the years I am recording, the vast mechanical incubator of me."

If we examine this image briefly, we can see how Kang's exposition of the central idea—the nature of New York and it's significance to his own development—is packed into one sentence. His language is poetic and deliberately contradictory; New York is both a city on rock and a place that is as yet ungrounded; it's nervous and multicolored, a great organism, but it's also a machine, an incubator. And since an incubator keeps newborn babies alive until they're well enough to manage on their own, this metaphor also reinforces Kang's previous image of coming to New York to be reborn.

In the latter part of the essay, the exposition turns more toward what New York has to offer. Kang names the economic possibilities—"opportunity, enterprise, prosperity, success" and the fact that New York is America's best monument to the machine age (a reference that goes back to the incubator metaphor and forward to the final paragraph).

But having drawn contrasts throughout this essay between Korea and New York, Kang returns to that idea by contrasting the "little grass-roofed, hill-wrapped village" he was born in with New York's architecture. Like the earlier metaphor, which describes New York as simultaneously an organism and a machine, the metaphor here describes skyscrapers as concrete blocks "with crowns as delicate as pinnacled ice."

This kind of exposition is deliberately poetic, piled with language and metaphor, imagery and simile. What makes it work is that these expository techniques are an expression of the main idea in the essay—that New York is attractive to Kang because it is so full of energy, variety, and possibility. Kang's idea of New York and the words he uses to describe it are full of the same nervous energy, and through them he communicates both the unruliness of the city and the sense of liberation it gives him. This is an expository essay in which the writer's language is profoundly in tune with his thesis.

Analytical Essays Most students are familiar with essays analyzing texts. They have written essays responding to literature and focusing on characters, images, or historical and philosophical contexts for the text. In analyzing argumentative or persuasive texts, students focus more on the ways in which the elements of a text work together to create an argument. They may focus on the contribution of imagery to evoke appeals to emotions, or they might evaluate the ways in which persuasive language sway a reader to adopt a certain point of view. They also examine the underlying assumptions and premises in a text and evaluate the logic of the conclusion drawn from those premises.

An example of an essay analyzing a persuasive text that is also a literary work is student writer Chris Countryman's essay on the Langston Hughes poem "Let America be America Again," in Chapter 6. Let's take a look at his thesis statement:

> In his poem "Let America be America Again" Langston Hughes uses evocative language and structural techniques to help emphasize the separation he feels underclass Americans experience in a country they helped create.

In this thesis statement, we see the topic, the focus, and the direction of his analysis: he will focus on the ways in which language and poetic structure convey the theme and argument—that certain groups of people whose contributions helped create America have been kept from full participation in their society. We recommend turning to Chapter 6 to this poem and the full essay for an excellent example of textual analysis.

Note that Countryman's essay is not simply a catalog of words and poetic structures in the poem; it is, rather, an examination of the ways in which these strategies contribute to Hughes's argument. An analysis of a text must be in service of a thesis—an assertion you make about the text or its argument. Such an essay, like other essays, needs an introduction to help orient the reader, as well as a logical organization to help the reader stay with the argument. Some organizational strategies range from following the order of the text to adopting a global-to-local focus (overall impression to specifics).

Less commonly, you may have been asked to analyze an image, in the form of an advertisement or painting. As noted in Chapter 2, a number of predominantly visual images can be persuasive. Much of the information we now receive incorporates visual images with text—from war propaganda to political cartoons to the nightly news to the majority of Web pages. Increasingly, scholars and writers are grappling with the notion of "visual rhetoric," or the ways in which the visual elements of a text convey information or stance. As with textual rhetoric, visual rhetoric incorporates the rhetorical situation of audience and purpose. As with textual analysis, you will need to tease apart and analyze (1) any text accompanying the image; (2) the elements of the image; and (3) the ways in which these elements and the accompanying text put forth assertions, rely on assumptions, and draw conclusions.

In keeping with our practice of encouraging you to "read" visuals for their rhetoric, audience, purpose, and techniques, we present an essay by student Erica Heiman. Here she analyzes a poster which turned a famous American patriotic image—that of Uncle Sam saying "I Want You!"—into a statement of protest.

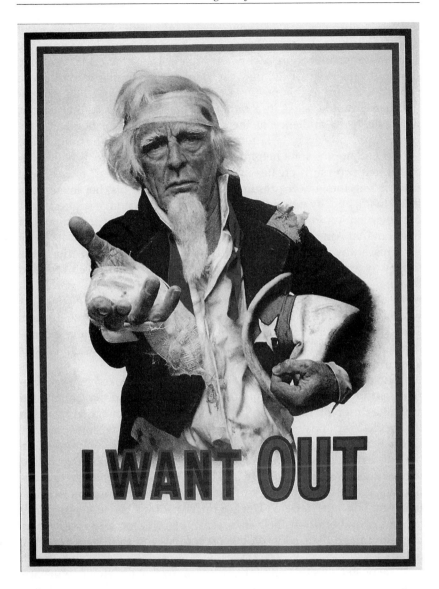

∞ *I Want Out*

ERICA HEIMAN

Propaganda posters do not always encourage patriotic action; in times of protest, propaganda posters may carry messages of antipatriotism and ask for an end to action. The Vietnam War was one such event in America's history, when many questioned the validity of U.S.

involvement in the conflict, especially in light of the huge numbers of casualties the war was creating and had been for more than five years. This image, produced in 1971 by an organization that called itself the Committee to Help Unsell the War, depicts the familiar icon of Uncle Sam. Uncle Sam in this poster is represented similarly to the way in which he was depicted in a famous World War I recruiting poster, with which the audience of the poster was no doubt familiar. This Uncle Sam, however, is tattered and pathetic, reaching out to the viewer and hoping for a helping hand. The poster acts on two levels to encourage protest: it creates sympathy for the tortured, tattered old man, letting the viewer presume the same fate for his/her loved ones in Vietnam; and, by perverting a classic American icon, it suggests that our intervention in Vietnam corrupts the classic ideals of dignity and freedom that America holds sacred.

This antiwar image catches the viewer's attention in much the same way as the original prowar poster did earlier in the century. The image is confrontational and personalized, addressing the viewer directly with an appeal. To avoid responding to an appeal of this sort would seem an affront to the old man who is asking a personal favor. The staring eyes of the figure seem to follow the viewer, and disconcert him enough to prevent him from walking by the poster without glancing at it.

Though this poster and its predecessor both evoke emotional responses in the viewer, the emotions that each one hopes to conjure up are quite different. Instead of the dignified, fatherly image with which the World War I poster presented potential enlistees, this one portrays Uncle Sam as a torn and tattered pathetic individual who needs a helping hand. The old Uncle Sam, in his stern glory, invokes in the viewer a sense of responsibility and pride. He calls on them to take action and mobilize themselves in the name of American integrity and freedom. This new, tattered Uncle Sam asks for his viewers' pity. Their action depends not on their own sense of pride or responsibility in themselves and their country, but on compassion for this bedraggled old man.

The poster stirs this pity for Uncle Sam so that the viewer will suppose the same fate for the entire American army, which had been fighting in Vietnam for over five years. In addition to representing the army as a whole, Uncle Sam can also quickly become any soldier, any son or husband, in the mind of an American viewer. This poster, then, targets those with family and friends in Vietnam, fighting until their bodies give out and they reach out their hands to beg for help. And in addition to representing the soldiers beloved by the viewers of this poster, the poster gives a face to those whom they have never met. By representing an army with one face, this image personalizes the suffering of an entire army, and makes it easier to sympathize with its plight.

In addition to asking viewers to reexamine what is happening to America's army halfway across the world, this poster asks them to re-examine the values that they endorse by supporting the war effort. Uncle Sam, a symbol inspiring American patriotism and pride, has deteriorated drastically, and the strong, spirited slogan "I Want You" has become a wailing "I Want Out." This perversion of such a classic American icon indicates that present U.S. policy is a corruption of the classic American ideals that Uncle Sam represents. The Vietnam War was an extremely controversial conflict: Many called into question the validity of U.S. involvement in a country on the other side of the world because of a clash in ideology. War protestors saw U.S. involvement in the war as putting limits on people's freedoms, an act very much at odds with presumed American ideals. The "I Want Out" poster is taking this antiwar standpoint. It presents the contrast between classic American ideals and the ideals represented by the Vietnam War as the contrast between the old representation of Uncle Sam and the new, pathetic one. The poster asks the viewer to protest the war in order to uphold American dignity and idealism.

Uncle Sam represents both a person and a concept in this Vietnam War protest poster. As a person, he is a soldier, injured and tired, stirring the viewer's sympathy. As a concept, he is American idealism, and his deterioration appeals to the viewer's system of values. In this way, this 1971 propaganda poster stirs the audience's sympathies and convictions in encouraging an end to the war.

Heiman organized her essay as follows: She began by challenging the conventional role of propaganda posters in encouraging patriotism. This approach provides a context for both the role of the poster in general and the specific role of this poster in protest. She provides additional context for this particular poster and the context for protest in her reference to the Vietnam War. She includes the provenance of the poster to provide context regarding the poster's author and alludes to its roots in the 1917 version of the poster. She ends this background information with her thesis statement to orient the reader to the aspects of the poster that she will discuss in her essay.

The next paragraph discusses the overall impression the poster conveys to its audience. She then contrasts the two posters in terms of the emotional impact on the audience. The next paragraph analyzes the way in which the poster extends its emotional impact from the "bedraggled old man" of the poster to American fighting men in general and family members and friends in particular. Heiman then steps back to reflect on the poster's assertions: that viewers should reevaluate their support for the war; that the patriotic fervor of the traditional

Uncle Sam has been perverted in U.S. policy in Vietnam; and that, in fact, protesting the war will in fact uphold the earlier, idealistic and dignified image of Uncle Sam. Heiman concludes her essay by placing this American icon in its context as representing both individuals damaged by the war and the concept of American idealism.

Other analytical essays in this text include "Building Beliefs" by Daniel McKenzie (Chapter 7) and "Propaganda in FDR's 'Pearl Harbor Address'" by Neil A. Van Os (Chapter 10). Examining these essays can help you to develop your own range of strategies to construct analytical essays on textual and visual arguments.

Argumentative Essays   Although the prewriting and organizing suggestions described earlier should prove helpful in developing an argumentative essay, some writers prefer to conceptualize their more persuasive essays a bit differently, envisioning the argument as a more engaged and interactive process than writing exposition. Further, you will at times be engaged in arguments that are not assigned exercises or responses to texts or discussion questions, but rather evolve out of circumstances within and outside of your academic studies.

For most argument assignments, you will need to argue a point of view or propose a course of action. You may be assigned a topic, or you may be able to select one based on your interests or observations. There are argument assignments in this text; check the end of selection and end of chapter assignments. You could consider writing an argument about something practical and close to home. Such topics might include campus residence regulations, gender studies/distribution requirements, theme residence halls, need-blind admission, scholarships for athletes/musicians/others, alcohol policy, or early admissions. You could write a letter to the campus newspaper or another newspaper or write a guest editorial, whether you choose a subject close to home or one with broad implications. Alternatively, you could write a letter directly to an administrator on campus, such as an academic or student affairs dean.

You could also consider a literary topic—*Huckleberry Finn* is/is not a great work or should/should not be required reading in high school courses, for example. Or, you could write about something philosophical or political—U.S. troops should/should not go to Central Europe/Africa/Central America; the United States should trade with Cuba, pay reparations to Guatemala, send aid to Kosovo, and the like. In any event, make sure your topic is substantial enough to merit your effort and the reader's time. Beware of entirely idiosyncratic arguments that matter to you and no one else. (For example, most instructors would probably rather not read arguments about why you and your friend should become "more involved.") Limit your topic appropriately for the length of the assignment: you're better off focusing on the topic and dealing with it in depth than staying general and floundering around in superficialities. Finally, consider avoiding the usual litany (abortion, capital punishment) unless you feel you truly have something unique to add to the discussion.

If you select a current event, make sure that your argument is your own and not an editorial writer's, although certainly you would be wise to consider the key arguments offered in various periodicals. In summary, you might draw from literature, from science or social science, from public policy, from experience and personal interests, from philosophy, and from the assignments in this text. Aim for a topic that challenges you but that is feasible in the time and space allowed.

Many students' arguments have one fatal flaw: They do not discuss the opposing or alternative views. Remember that traditional argument assumes an opposition; if there were no opposition or alternative view, there would be no need to argue. You should bring up the most compelling arguments on the other side, because assuredly your audience will be thinking of them anyway. When you bring them up yourself, you are, first of all, appealing to ethos and demonstrating that you have faith in your own position—enough to face the other side. This action gives you more credibility. Further, you are often able to refute those opposing arguments by demonstrating why they are faulty (in premises, in logic) or by bringing up even more convincing arguments and evidence to the contrary. But even if you cannot refute opposing views and must concede them, you have established yourself as a rhetor who is reasonable, fair-minded, and able to consider other views.

Use the appeals and evidence that seem appropriate to the topic and audience at hand (and you might consider indicating your audience, perhaps in a footnote if it is not apparent from the context and content). You may decide that appeals to ethos and logos are the most powerful, but do not underestimate appeals to pathos if they suit your rhetorical situation.

In any case, you should follow the guidelines for a good essay:

- Get in step with the reader (intro)
- Focus the core topic of the essay (thesis)
- Develop and support that thesis (body of essay) with focused paragraphs (clear topic idea for each) that address and develop the subtopics of the essay
- Leave your readers with a memorable conclusion that puts the issue in a larger context or leaves the reader with a thought-provoking image or statement that provides a sense of closure

Writers have different approaches to organizing their essays. Some prefer a very rough outline of the major sections or large chunks of the essay, indicating the purpose of each section. Such an approach might have a rough organization as follows for an inductive essay:

Context

Prevailing view/beliefs/interpretations

Problems with current view

Your alternative view, supported by evidence

The larger conclusion/context, adjusted to take into account re-
    vised view of context, text, or problem

Other writers prefer to envision the argument's structure as a thesis statement with an argumentative edge that captures the central claim or core assertion, with major subclaims or premises then supporting the thesis by serving as topic sentences. These subclaims are, in turn, supported by evidence, either reasons or examples or both. A basic outline, then, would consist of thesis statement and topic sentences supporting the thesis. Some of those topic sentences will be introduc-ing or stating alternative or opposing views—counterclaims to your core assertion/thesis. The body of those paragraphs would then con-cede or refute the counterclaim.

You may outline your essay in a number of ways, and there is no perfect formula, but consider adapting one of the following structures:

*Deductive/Direct Organization: Intro, State Your Point/Thesis
and Then Provide*

A	B
key supporting arguments	key supporting points
key opposing arguments	opposing point/rebuttal
rebuttal	opposing point/rebuttal (etc.)
conclusion	conclusion

Or, with an Inductive/Indirect Organization

A	B
intro	intro
opposing view	opposing view/rebuttal
opposing view	opposing view/rebuttal
opposing view	opposing view/rebuttal
rebuttal	

Thesis and Additional Support Not Covered in the Rebuttals

| conclusion | conclusion |

Although the sample outline indicates that you will be dealing with "opposing views," often the views are not diametrically opposed, but rather are simply different ways to approach the problem or topic—alternative views rather than opposites. Again, the crucial element here is anticipating and dealing with alternatives or objections to your point of view and your key assertions.

There are, as noted, variations on these approaches, but the point is to be mindful of organization and to select the best organization for your topic. For example, if your topic is controversial or your thesis is likely to meet with opposition, you may get a fairer hearing if you can dispatch a few opposing arguments or concerns before stating your position.

The conclusion is your last chance to make your points with the reader: Don't raise any new issues except, perhaps, to forecast a potential effect or result if you plan is/is not followed. Leave your reader with a thought-provoking point, a reinforcement of your theme or core issue (but don't be repetitious!), or a striking image or memorable statement. You could look at a few editorials in the newspapers to see what you find effective yourself as a critical reader.

Pay special attention to language and maintain a reasonable tone throughout the argument. If you engage in the written equivalent of ranting and raving, your reader will react the way you do when you experience someone verbally ranting and raving at you. Watch out for patronizing or irritating language ("well obviously," etc.).

Know your readers! Unless you have designated a specific audience, think of your reader as an educated generalist who may not know the particular arguments or jargon of your topic. You'll need to communicate clearly without patronizing or offending your audience. Remember that you are writing an essay, not giving a speech, and you will need to adjust your style accordingly. For example, directly addressing the reader—"Look, if everyone contributed just $1 a day"—might be workable in a speech, but the rhetorical situation of the written argument calls for a less colloquial style. Further, to persuade effectively, you will need to understand your reader if you want your reader to identify with you or if you want to appeal to common values or concerns. You will also need to consider your reader to figure out the best organization for your argument.

A clear argumentative essay can be very powerful. Professor Cornell West, a philosopher who was formerly the head of African American Studies at Princeton and is currently at Harvard, writes in the following essay about a controversial topic—affirmative action—and lays out a series of argumentative points as part of a larger philosophical question.

∞ *Affirmative Action in Context*

CORNEL WEST

Today's affirmative action policy is not the appropriate starting point for a substantive debate on affirmative action. Instead, we must begin with the larger historical and moral context of the recent controversy. Why was the policy established in the first place? What were the alternatives? Who questioned its operation, and when? How did it come about that a civil rights initiative in the 1960s is viewed by many as a civil rights violation in the 1990s? Whose civil rights are we talking about? Is there a difference between a right and an expectation? What are the limits of affirmative action? What would the consequences be if affirmative action disappeared in America?

The Aim of Affirmative Action

The vicious legacy of white supremacy—institutionalized in housing, education, health care, employment, and social life—served as the historical context for the civil rights movement in the late 1950s and 1960s. Affirmative action was a *weak* response to this legacy. It constituted an imperfect policy conceded by a powerful political, business, and educational establishment in light of the pressures of organized citizens and the disturbances of angry unorganized ones.

The fundamental aim of affirmative action was to put a significant dent in the tightly controlled networks of privileged white male citizens who monopolized the good jobs and influential positions in American society. Just as Catholics and Jews had earlier challenged the white Anglo-Saxon Protestant monopoly of such jobs and positions, in the 1960s blacks and women did also. Yet since the historical gravity of race and gender outweighs that of religion and ethnicity in American society, the federal government had to step in to facilitate black and female entry into the U.S. mainstream and malestream. This national spectacle could not but prove costly under later, more hostile circumstances.

The initial debate focused on the relative lack of fairness, merit, and public interest displayed by the prevailing systems of employment and education, principally owing to arbitrary racist and sexist exclusion. In the 1960s, class-based affirmative action was not seriously considered, primarily because it could easily have been implemented in such a way as to perpetuate exclusion, especially given a labor movement replete with racism and sexism. Both Democratic and Republican administrations supported affirmative action as the painful way of trying to create a multiracial democracy in which women and people of color were not second-class citizens. Initially, affirmative action was opposed by hard-line conservatives, usually the same ones who opposed the civil rights movement led by Dr. Martin Luther King, Jr. Yet the pragmatic liberals and conservatives prevailed.

The Neoconservative Opposition

The rise of the neoconservatives unsettled this fragile consensus. By affirming the principle of equality of opportunity yet trashing any mechanism that claimed to go beyond merit, neoconservatives drove a wedge between civil rights and affirmative action. By claiming that meritocratic judgments trump egalitarian efforts to produce tangible results, neoconservatives cast affirmative action policies as multiracial reverse racism and the major cause of racial divisiveness and low black self-esteem in the workplace and colleges.

Yet even this major intellectual and ideological assault did not produce a wholesale abandonment of affirmative action on behalf of business, political, and educational elites. The major factor that escalated the drive against affirmative action was the shrinking job possibilities—along with stagnating and declining wages—that were squeezing the white middle class. Unfortunately, conservative leaders seized this moment to begin to more vociferously scapegoat affirmative action, and to seek its weakening or elimination.

Their first move was to define affirmative action as a program for "unqualified" women and, especially, black people. Their second move was to cast affirmative action as "un-American," a quota system for groups rather than a merit system for individuals. The third move was to claim that anti-discrimination laws are enough, given the decline or end of racism among employers. The latest move has been to soothe the agonized consciences of liberals and conservatives by trying to show that black people are genetically behind whites in intelligence; hence, nothing can be done.

The popularity—distinct from the rationality—of these moves has created a climate in which proponents of affirmative action are on the defensive. Even those of us who admit the excesses of some affirmative action programs—and therefore call for correcting, not eliminating, them—give aid and comfort to our adversaries. This reality reveals just how far the debate has moved in the direction of the neoconservative and conservative perceptions in the country. It also discloses that it is far beyond weak policies like affirmative action to confront the legacies of white supremacy and corporate power in the United States—legacies visible in unemployment and underemployment, unaffordable health care and inadequate child care, dilapidated housing and decrepit schools for millions of Americans, disproportionately people of color, women, and children.

The idea that affirmative action violates the rights of fellow citizens confuses a right with an expectation. We all have a right to be seriously and fairly considered for a job or position. But calculations of merit, institutional benefit, and social utility produce the results. In the past, those who were never even considered had their rights violated; in the present, those who are seriously and fairly considered yet still not selected do not have their rights violated but rather had their expectations frustrated.

For example, if Harvard College receives more than ten thousand applications for fourteen hundred slots in the freshman class and roughly four thousand meet the basic qualifications, how does one select the "worthy" ones? Six thousand applicants are already fairly eliminated. Yet twenty-six hundred still will not make it. When considerations of factors other than merit are involved, such as whether candidates are the sons or daughters of alumni, come from diverse regions of the country, or are athletes, no one objects. But when racial diversity is involved, the opponents of affirmative action yell foul play. Yet each class at Harvard remains about 5 to 7% black—far from a black takeover. And affirmative action bears the blame for racial anxiety and division on campus in such an atmosphere. In short, neoconservatives and conservatives fail to see the subtle (and not-so-subtle) white supremacist sensibilities behind their "color-blind" perspectives on affirmative action.

The Limits of Affirmative Action

Yet it would be myopic of progressives to make a fetish of affirmative action. As desirable as those policies are—an insight held fast by much of corporate America except at the almost lily-white senior management levels—they will never ameliorate the plight and predicament of poor people of color. More drastic and redistributive measures are needed in order to address their situations, measures that challenge the maldistribution of wealth and power and that will trigger cultural renewal and personal hope.

If affirmative action disappears from the American scene, many blacks will still excel and succeed. But the larger signal that sends will be lethal for the country. It is a signal that white supremacy now has one less constraint and black people have one more reason to lose trust in the promise of American democracy.

In examining West's argument, it's a good idea to start with the title, because "Affirmative Action in Context" suggests a historical and/or social perspective which is crucial to his organizational sense. This perspective is born out by the first two sentences:

> Today's affirmative action policy is not the appropriate starting point for a substantive debate on affirmative action. Instead, we must begin with the larger historical and moral context of the recent controversy.

What West then proceeds to do is divide his argument into three distinct sections: The Aim of Affirmative Action, The Neoconservative Opposition, and The Limits of Affirmative Action. In the first part, he explains the birth of affirmative action as a weak response to the legacy of white supremacy, an effort supported by pragmatic liberals and conservatives as a way of facilitating "black and female entry into the U.S. mainstream and malestream." In the second and longest part of the essay, West describes how neoconservative opponents of affirmative action transformed the argument from one about social justice to a referendum on reverse racism and the hiring of unqualified women and blacks. In the final section, he asserts that affirmative action is not the answer to everything; it is too mild to affect the lives of poor people of color, but it's better than nothing and destroying it would give black people "one more reason to lose trust in the promise of American democracy."

This summary indicates the progression of West's contextual argument, from the distant to the more recent past to the present and the future. That chronological approach is helpful in developing momentum for the whole essay, and it is one that you may find useful in your own work. But West does something else as well. Within each section he makes specific assertions that form the backbone of his argument. For example, in the main second section he numbers three separate attacks on affirmative action. Then he moves to the moral question of redressing past wrongs through current social action, and explains the distinction between having one's rights violated and one's expectations disappointed. He follows that with a good example of induction; many worthy students do not get into Harvard; no one objects to special consideration for athletes, children of alumni, and so on; neoconservatives do object, however, to special consideration for blacks. Conclusion: neoconservatives who insist they are "color-blind" in fact fail to recognize their own racially based sensibilities.

The culmination of West's argumentation is as much a moral as a logical construction, but it also helps bring us as readers back to the opening page of the essay. He says that the end of affirmative action will eliminate one more constraint on white supremacy. White supremacy is also the subject of his first section, The Aim of Affirmative Action. By repeating the phrase at the end, West suggests that though a lot of time may have passed since the heyday of white supremacy, the actual situation may be more static than one would have thought.

In effect, he refutes the arguments in favor of ending affirmative action, appeals to his readers' logic, applies inductive reasoning, and finishes with a moral warning. His essay is a compendium of well-wrought rhetorical strategies. You don't have to use all of them, but you might want to refer back to this essay when you are thinking about and preparing your own argument, implicitly or explicitly refuting someone else's point of view, or searching for a structure to hold your argument in hand.

We close this chapter with one more sample essay, this one by student writer Kris Andeen, whose assignment was to analyze a visual image, a painting by the famous American illustrator Norman Rockwell (see Chapter 9, Justice and Civil Liberties, for another Rockwell picture). We chose this essay not only because it gives you one more example of how to analyze visual rhetoric and read a picture like a text, but also because we wanted you to see how a student starting from scratch goes through the entire process of completing such a project. This selection includes Kris Andeen's prewriting, his planning, draft, final revision, and reflection. We hope that this complete record of one student's efforts will give you both encouragement and additional tools to help with your own work.

Kris's assignment for his writing class was to find a visual argument and analyze it. He browsed through some books containing World War I and II era posters at the school library and selected "Hasten the Homecoming—Buy Victory Bonds" by Norman Rockwell. He made a color photocopy of the poster to attach to the submitted essay. Then he brainstormed a list of his first impressions of the poster, jotting them all down as they came to him. He could also have searched the Web and downloaded an appropriate image, taking care to cite his source appropriately.

Next, he reviewed what he had learned about Aristotle's appeals—to ethos, pathos, and logos—and examined the poster with those elements in mind, generating more material on the poster. The outline that follows organized these impressions:

"Hasten the Homecoming—Buy Victory Bonds," USA, 1939–1945. Norman Rockwell painting, originally for *Saturday Evening Post*

1. First Impressions
   A. First thing which draws the eye is red line: "Buy Victory Bonds."
      1. This makes sense since it is most important part of the poster.
   B. After one's eyes have seen red "Buy Victory Bonds," the eyes are next taken to the red sweater of the mother who is reaching out to her son.
      1. Her eyes point toward her son, which is next place viewer's eyes look.

C. After viewer has seen son, he/she begins to see the rest of the picture, but by this point, a central association has been made in the viewer's mind: "Buy victory bonds, and the men will come home."

    1. Rest of picture reveals 16 faces witnessing the soldier's return—17, if you count the dog!!

    2. All faces are smiling (with exception of one), which associates happiness with the return of the soldier.

Norman Rockwell, "Hasten the Homecomng. Buy victory bonds." Poster.(c)1943. Norman Rockwell Family Trust. Photo courtesy of the Franklin D. Roosevelt Library.

2. All faces are smiling (with exception of one), which associates happiness with the return of the soldier.

3. Obviously, this is not a mansion, but a lower-class, more common American home. Therefore, the ad will appeal to a large percentage of the American population.

4. It appears as though some previous problems with the roof are being repaired.

5. There also appear to be light shining down on the scene from the upper right-hand corner of the picture as if it is just coming out of the clouds.

II. Appeals

A. Appeals to Ethos

1. The family portrayed in the poster represents the common American family of the time.
   a. excited, motherly figure
   b. Pops is smoking a pipe
   c. lots of kids (neighborhood too)
   d. Sparky, the dog

2. The scene represents the common American neighborhood.
   a. After depression ('30s), people still living in lower-class homes.
   b. Clothes dried on clothesline.
   c. The classic American sweetheart is waiting for soldier-boy just around the corner.

3. The headlines for the poster, "Hasten the Homecoming—Buy Victory Bonds," are printed in red and blue against a white background→red, white, and blue→patriotism, nationalism.

B. Appeals to Pathos

1. If you did not have any children/family members in the war, this poster still might make you feel sorry for those with loved ones at war, so you might be convinced to buy victory bonds to bring your neighbor's son home. Neighbors *are* shown in the picture, with smiles on their faces.

2. If you were a wealthy American, you might feel sorry for lower-class citizens upon seeing this poster, and thus be convinced to buy victory bonds.

C. Appeals to Logos

1. As earlier stated, this poster seems to suggest that if one were to buy victory bonds, then the men of the war could come home faster, thus bringing happy smiles, repairs, and bright sunshine.

III. Audience

I believe this poster can be aimed at three types of people: families with relatives fighting in the war, neighbors of people fighting in the war and their families, and wealthy citizens who feel sorry for lower-class families with relatives in the war.

After putting the project aside for a day or two, Kris tried to compose a draft based on his working outline. He considered and reconsidered his dominant impression or thesis—the main assertion or inference he would make based on his material—so that he would be able to focus the essay and make sure it stayed on track. Kris identified this as his dominant point: "the poster's strength lay in its ability to identify with the common American."

After reviewing the biographical notes on Rockwell in the book of posters and in a reference book on American biographies, Kris drafted some background information for the introduction to provide context and help prepare the reader to listen to his analysis. The introduction led smoothly into the thesis for this draft. For the draft, Kris didn't use all the material he had generated; the assignment was to write a two- to three-page analysis of a visual argument, and he had generated enough material for a longer paper. Once he developed his thesis around the notion of identifying with the common person, he was able to determine what to keep and what to let go. The first body paragraph focuses on Rockwell's use of the family in the poster; he then expands his point to involve the neighborhood; he then shifts to broader American attitudes, values, and desire for an end to the war. All paragraphs stay focused on the theme of appeals to the common American. The draft below includes some comments from both an instructor and a peer.

Kris Andeen
English 1D5
10/1/97
Draft

The Common American

Norman Rockwell's work represents a hallmark of the American

great
background

You ordinarily need a noun after "this" to avoid reference errors.

dream. His paintings during the early half of this century are known for portraying the common American. The U.S. government recognized this and used one of his cover paintings for *The Saturday Evening Post* in a poster encouraging financial support for World War II. Although

Yes, the thesis can be placed at end of intro to lead into essay.

Rockwell probably wasn't commissioned by the U.S. government to paint this picture, it served the government's purposes quite well. The

the poster's? Or the other way works because Americans can identify w/ the scene

poster's strength lies in its ability to identify with the common Ameri- *portrayed?*

can. Indeed, Rockwell was so skilled at depicting the people of the

time, that his painting could have been used for any of a number of

move to end of essay?

causes and still have been successful.
    check w.c.

    The first way which this poster appeals to the common American
                        dominant?   *rephrase?*
is through the family, the most dominating figure of which (in this

painting) is the mother. Thanks to her bright red sweater, Mom stands

out as the first figure that catches the viewer's eye. Traditionally, she

represents the passionate, caring head of the family, just as she is por-

trayed here with her arms outstretched. She is also shown as a white

person (as is the whole neighborhood) as white people represented the

largest racial percentage of the nation's population. Also seen on the

front porch is Dad, who appears to have just gotten out of his recliner,

pipe still in hand. Again, this fits the classic image we have of the fa-

therly figure who rests after a day at work in his recliner with his pipe

and slippers. And of course, the American family is not a small one—
                                                      whom
indeed, there are plenty of children about, some of which may be

assumed are siblings. But Rockwell doesn't stop at human

figures—Sparky, the dog, plays a crucial role in the classic American

family, and he too can be seen running anxiously towards) the

returning soldier

        Another way in which Rockwell is able to identify with the people

vague   of the time is to associate with the neighborhood. In this painting, the neighborhood plays an even larger role than the family. So what did

the common American neighborhood look like from 1939 to 1945?

One must remember that during this time, not only was the U.S. at war,

Usually capitalized

but it was still recovering from the great depression. A very large per-

unclear sentence

centage of the population lived in the city and inner-city housing

wasn't any more beautiful then than it is now. The brick house, the

clotheslines, the garbage-ridden street, the sweetheart around the cor-

ner, the hordes of frolicking children (they weren't inside playing Nin-

(He's also dealing with class issues.)

tendo or surfing the Web back then), the repairman on the roof, and

Victory Bonds are not just for the wealthy, etc.

even the faded paint on the porch all contribute in providing an arche-

Needed?

typal image of the urban American neighborhood. *(Once again,)* Rock-

well has identified with the American population by meticulously

allegorizing the American home.

One last key theme in identifying with America is happiness and

Check w.c.—needed? most precise?

an odium for war. The American people don't like to be active in wars.

There are many reasons for this; increased stress on the household,

Could use, such as . . . or a colon. But the semicolon won't work here.

possible increase on the price of imports, and the threat of attack. But

most of all, Americans are troubled by the absence of loved ones who

may or may not return after the war. With the return of the soldier in

Rockwell's painting we see a number of happy connotations. For one,

Write out numbers up to 99 (a convention).

Avoid shifts to 2nd person point of view

there are 16 smiling faces in the picture, and that's if you don't count

Sparky. We also see (consciously or unconsciously) green leaves

emerging from the tree which otherwise appears not to have any fo- *great*
details
liage. This suggests Springtime and a new happiness. Another sugges-

tion of such happiness is that while most of the scene appears to be

very dark, with the exception of Mom's clothesline, there appears to be

a bright light shining down from the upper right-hand corner of the pic-

ture. This implies the sun breaking through the clouds of wartime, an-
                          Transition? Needed?
other concept which America most certainly welcomes. So once again,
                                 Ref?
Rockwell has identified with the American through its desire for an end

to the war and the return of happy times.

Happy times are just what the American public wanted. Norman

Rockwell was aware of this and by incorporating such values into his

painting he was able to identify with the nation. His abilities in relating
                                        Resource? (See if you want the connotation
to the nation's people made him a valuable tool for the U.S. govern- *that "tool"*
                                                                       provides.)
ment. The power of such identification in art could just as well have

been used to rouse the country in a cultural diversity campaign. If Mom
                                                    for example,
were stretching her arms out to a newly arrived Japanese family, then

the same concepts of identification would work in promoting the ac-

ceptance of the Japanese culture. Indeed, Rockwell's work, with its na-

tionalistic morals and commonplace subjects, provides an excellent *Good*
                                                                    analysis
example of the power of ethos appeals.

To revise this essay, Kris chose to keep the focus that he developed
in this draft, so his work was primarily geared toward crafting

smoother transitions and effective prose. He had already incorporated evidence from the "text," or image, to support his assertions; indeed, in an inductive process he had generated his evidence and then used inferences from that evidence to make a point. In the essay, the inferences are structured as topic sentences, which are then, in turn, supported by the evidence, examples, and images from the poster.

Kris's draft went through two reviews before final submission, including one peer review. Because this essay was written early in the term, peers were not yet well skilled in providing substantial feedback, so much of the peers' suggestions focused on word choice or mechanics. The instructor's suggestions targeted focus and placement of the thesis (end of introduction or end of essay), selection of evidence to support topic ideas, and some matters of style that needed attention (inappropriate transitions, word choice). Kris also chose to change his title from "The Common American" to "End of the Tunnel," because the artist's strategy of identification with the common man or woman was, in fact, a means to a larger end—expressing the persuasive message that the end of the war is near and that the troops will be home even sooner if we all do our part and buy Victory Bonds. The title ties in well with the conclusion, where Kris amplifies this point.

Kris's final essay, while not perfect, is an excellent example of how a writer analyzes, selects, focuses, and organizes material to develop a coherent expository essay on a visual argument. Kris made particular choices and used a particular approach in doing the analysis and writing the essay. You could take the same image and come up with a very different essay, because your own ideas, creativity, ability to analyze, interests, and skill would determine the outcome.

Kris Andeen
English 1D5
Revision

End of the Tunnel

Norman Rockwell's art represents a hallmark of the American dream. His paintings in the early half of this century are known for portraying the common American and his/her struggles and joys in this society. The U.S. government recognized Rockwell's talent, and in 1939 they used one of his cover paintings for *The Saturday Evening Post* in a

poster encouraging financial support for World War II. Although Rockwell wasn't commissioned by the U.S. government to paint this picture,
it served the government's purposes quite well. The poster's persuasive
strength lay in the ease with which the common American could identify with the scene portrayed.

The first way in which this poster appealed to the common American was through the family. The most dominant figure of the family, in
this painting, is the mother. Thanks to her brilliant red sweater, Mom
stands out as the first figure who catches the viewer's eye. Traditionally, she represents the passionate, caring head of the family, just as she
is portrayed here with her arms outstretched. She is also shown as a
white person (as is the whole neighborhood) since white people represented the largest racial percentage of the nation's population. Also
seen on the front porch is Dad, who appears to have just gotten out of
his recliner, pipe still in hand. Rockwell's painting fits the classic image
we have of the fatherly figure who rests after a day at work in his recliner with his pipe and slippers. And of course, the American family is
not a small one—indeed, there are plenty of children about, some of
whom may be assumed are siblings. But Rockwell doesn't stop at
human figures—Sparky, the dog, plays a crucial role in the classic
American family, and he too can be seen running anxiously toward the
returning soldier.

Another way in which Rockwell was able to identify with the people of the time was to associate his painting with the American neighborhood. In this painting, the neighborhood plays an even larger role than the family. So what did the common American neighborhood look like from 1939 to 1945? One must remember that during this time the U.S. was not only at war, but it was still recovering from the Great Depression. A large percentage of the population lived in the city, and inner-city housing wasn't any more beautiful then than it is now. The brick apartment building, the clotheslines, the garbage-ridden street, the sweetheart around the corner, the hordes of frolicking children (they weren't inside playing Nintendo or surfing the Web), the repairman on the roof, and even the faded paint on the porch all contribute in providing an archetypal image of the urban American neighborhood. In a sense, Rockwell has painted his audience's neighborhood, providing a mirror in which they may see themselves.

One last key theme in identifying with America is happiness and a repugnance for war. The American people don't like to be active in wars. There are many reasons for this isolationist mindset, such as increased stress on the household, possible increase on the price of imports, and the threat of attack. But most of all, Americans are troubled by the absence of loved ones who may or may not return after the war. With the return of the soldier in Rockwell's painting we see a number of happy connotations. For one, there are *sixteen* smiling faces in the picture, and that's if you don't count Sparky. We also see (consciously or subconsciously) green leaves emerging from the tree which otherwise appears barren. This emerging foliage suggests Springtime and a new happiness. Another suggestion of such happiness is that while the lighting in most of the scene is very dark (with the exception of Mom's clothesline), there appears to be a bright light shining down from the upper right-hand corner of the picture. Such illumination implies the sun breaking through the clouds of wartime, another concept which America most certainly welcomes. Subconsciously, these hints of joy suggest a light at the end of the tunnel, a tunnel of war and depression which all Americans were anxious to exit.

An end to the tunnel is just what the American public wanted. Norman Rockwell was aware of this desire and by incorporating such values into his painting he was able to identify with the nation. The power of such identification in Rockwell's art is so strong that it could have been used successfully to support any number of causes. For example, if Mom were stretching her arms out to a newly arrived Japanese family, then the same concepts of identification would work in promoting the acceptance of the Japanese culture. Indeed, Rockwell's work, with its nationalistic morals and commonplace subjects, provides an excellent example of the power of ethos appeals.

Kris wrote the following reflection on how he went about completing his essay assignment:

> Our assignment was to choose an advertisement and write about the different ways in which it appealed to its audience. We weren't restricted to war ads, but I was familiar with war ads since we had been analyzing them in class. So I went to the library and looked up books about war advertising. There were quire a few books, each filled with full-color war ads. I checked out a few of the books and chose three possible posters to write about. Then I wrote possible hypotheses for each and reasoned that the Rockwell poster had the strongest, most supportable thesis.
>
> Since my thesis focused on Rockwell's remarkable appeals to ethos, I wrote down every aspect of the scene that was common to the American family. My list was long, and with such a list of supporting images, writing the essay itself wasn't very difficult. My outline was basic. The first paragraph would be my lead-in, with some background on Rockwell and the thesis. Each paragraph of the body would cite different aspects of the poster and their relation to the common American. The closing paragraph would wrap up my argument, restating the thesis.
>
> As far as revision went, I read back through my essay to check for fluency in tone and clear progression of thought. Transitions were important and I was careful to use varied transitions where necessary. My professor also read through the rough draft and made some suggestions. For example, she cited my continual use (near the end of each paragraph) of the phrase "once again," or "again we see . . ." I had been using these types of phrases to wrap up each paragraph and tie the paragraphs back to the thesis. However, the use of "again" was repetitive and unoriginal, and I was overrelying on these words to make connections between my points. We were able to rephrase each of these instances, creating a more diverse paragraph structure.
>
> Finally, after making all of my own revisions and those that my professor suggested in our conference, I subjected my prose to my class peers. My peers and their reactions were valuable since they provided me with different, fresh feedback. Then I revised my paper for style and mechanics one more time and submitted the essay.

4

Research

Integrating Research into Writing

College is a community of scholars. The academic community develops and transmits scholarly opinion, research findings, and reports in papers, books, lectures, and, in some cases, computer programs. Being part of that community entails pursuing the ongoing and exciting enterprise known as research. As you begin to conduct research, you take part in worldwide conversations and construction of knowledge. As you see how to integrate research into your writing and writing into your research, you learn to set other ideas and evidence next to your own and to draw connections between them.

A writer who invites other voices into the text must strive to represent their views fairly, to credit them appropriately, and to manage these multiple voices in such a way that she remains the author of this particular paper and the dominant voice in it. The experts can support her, but she must make the core proposal and maintain control of the flow of conversation. She must also take responsibility for everything in the paper and must stand behind her core assertion, her key supporting points, and the evidence she includes.

Researched essays sometimes get a poor reputation for being long, dry exercises in library treasure hunts or fussy documentation styles. To maintain this view is to miss one of the most exciting aspects of the academic community: learning to think, read, write, and contribute as a scholar. As you learn to conduct and carry out research, to use the library, to communicate with other scholars, you claim membership in the community and also equip yourself to become a thoughtful, contributing member of society.

Research activities are complex and recursive processes. As in writing an essay, you start with an idea—maybe from reading or through class discussion. You discuss, read, review, perhaps take notes, and in the process integrate what you are learning with what you already know. You determine what you know enough about and what you need to learn more about—and that "learning more about" is one of the main reasons you do research. During the process of research, it may be useful to employ some of the prompts and questions included in the earlier section on techniques for developing essays to help you think about, focus, structure, and develop your paper. Generally your process of writing researched essays will entail the steps of prewriting, close reading, note taking, organizing ideas, drafting, and revising.

Before proceeding, it may be useful to look at the role of research in expository and argumentative essays. Remember that they are different parts of a continuum, with exposition developing an assertion that is not highly controversial and argument developing an assertion with an argumentative edge.

Expository essays can be based on your own experience, observations, reflections, interpretations of readings, and the like. They are used to explain, and although they convey a point of view and develop an assertion, their goal is not necessarily to change beliefs or behavior. Sometimes you will research a subject to add credibility to the assertions you make in your expository essay; you will analyze a development, a historical process, the causes of a situation, the potential effects of some event. You might research the history of jazz or different drafts of a novel, or convey the history or the background of some event or issue. Expository essays in the humanities might include materials from the text to support an interpretation; essays in the sciences and social sciences generally incorporate evidence acceptable in their disciplines to support their assertions, whether that evidence is statistics or observations. The point of the evidence is generally to suggest how the assertion or conclusion was obtained and to support the writer's interpretations.

In an *argumentative essay,* you need to be concerned with the skeptical reader who asks, "Who says so?" and "Why should I believe it?" To answer the first question, you bring in reinforcements in the form of expert opinion and testimony to back up any claims. While your voice needs to remain dominant in the essay, the authority of the experts you quote adds support to your argument. To answer the second question, you turn to evidence—examples, observations, statistics, or whatever other data are respected in the discipline.

An argumentative essay that integrates outside research is still similar to one that does not in that its goal is to persuade people to change their minds—about the ramifications of European settlement of the American continent, or the behavior of an ethnic group toward other Americans, or support of educational or public policy. For example, Susan Faludi's essay in Chapter 7 offers substantial evidence to support her argumentative thesis that there is a backlash against the modest gains American women have made. In deciding the landmark case *Brown* v. *Board of Education* (Chapter 9), the Supreme Court used a sociologist's report to help decide the case.

Research has an important place in both expository and argumentative essays, but special caution must be exercised in argumentative essay research. As you browse through potential sources, it may be tempting to fall prey to "selective attention," a situation in which you look for evidence that supports your view and avoid materials that contradict it. Remember that you must consider opposing views; similarly, in researching controversial or argumentative topics, you need to consider material that contradicts your hypothesis or your belief. Such open-mindedness will help you develop sound scholarly research methods and ultimately will strengthen your paper by demonstrating that you have researched alternatives to your belief or proposal. Dealing with contradictory evidence in your essay will appeal to ethos by ensuring readers that you have a broad background in the topic, that you are not trying to slant the evidence in your favor, and that your argument is strong and well supported enough to withstand contrary evidence. In any case, your readers will already be considering opposing views; your willingness to acknowledge them will only strengthen your case.

Beginning the Process

Begin by selecting the general topic area and developing a research question. If you have been assigned a topic, determine some aspect of it that interests you and that you can develop fully in the time and space allowed. If you choose your own topic, be guided by your interests but also by the limits of time and paper length; having the freedom to choose a topic often entails a more careful assessment of what you can manage. Additional concerns about topic selection for a documented essay include selecting a subject about which you can find enough materials with the resources available to you; also, since you will likely spend considerable time with your topic, you should find a subject that genuinely engages your interest. Finally, remember your role as a contributing member of the academic community; don't bother researching something that is obvious or a foregone conclusion. And consider researching subjects about which you can truly contribute: legislative research that serves the public interest, for example, or environmental research that can help your community or school make informed decisions about policy.

An underappreciated aspect of research papers, especially in first-year courses, is developing a research question. When you identify a question to which you truly want to find some answers, you are more likely to be interested in your topic and to keep an open mind as you research. For example, "Was the Civil War truly about economic issues?" or "What stereotypes have remained constant through different stages in American history?" are both much more likely to help you focus and develop a topic than if you say to yourself, "Maybe I can write about the Civil War or about prejudice." A research question can guide your research, help you to develop a working thesis, and prevent you from floundering around in a sea of readings, papers, notes, and miscellaneous unfocused ideas.

You will also need to establish a schedule. Determine the due dates for your paper and any intermediate due dates for parts of the paper during the research process. Often instructors establish checkpoints by which time you will have established a research question, tentative thesis, preliminary research, a working bibliography, an annotated bibliography, a working outline and revised thesis statement, a draft, peer reviews, a revision. If you have not received such guidelines, make your own, and stick to the schedule. It is too easy to let big projects slide in the face of daily competing demands for your time and interest. The results of waiting too long to start include finding that most of the best sources have been checked out, that you don't have time to do careful research, and that you are fresh out of ideas late in the night before the draft is due.

As with any writing project, consider the audience. Understanding the audience is crucial in making decisions about the subject and focus of the researched essay. If you are writing about literature in a composition class, you are in the position of being a generalist writing to an expert in the field. Your audience knows more about the topic than you do, but you bring with you new insights on the topic and unique responses to the texts you are interpreting. You may also uncover unique connections between sources and new insights in recent critical interpretations. In that same composition class, when you research particular topics of interest that are not literary topics, you will probably become the expert on the topic at hand. You will then have to be particularly aware of your readers' backgrounds and assumptions about your topic.

When you write as an expert to other experts, as you do when you are advancing in your chosen major or discipline, you have the advantage of a common language and a common understanding of the core concepts of the discipline. If you are writing papers for your courses, you will still be writing to specialists who know more than you do in the discipline, but you will have less explaining of terminology to do and can draw on shared assumptions and background knowledge.

Let us say that you are interested in physics or astronomy—in string theory or dark matter in the universe or nanotechnology. Your interest in the topic may carry you through the extensive technical research that will be needed, but if you are writing the essay in response to an open assignment in your writing class, the additional task remains of translating concepts and technical jargon for an audience of writing class peers and instructor. Such a writing situation is not restricted to writing courses; scientists and scholars frequently must translate the concepts of their work either to publish in general periodicals or to write grant proposals to outside funding sources who may be highly educated but unfamiliar with the particulars of the scientist's work.

Gathering Information

In addition to thinking about the functions of research and researched essays in college, you should consider expanding your sense of sources. Probably in high school, you used books, articles, and Web sites as sources for papers, and these remain excellent choices, but in the academic community other sources now become necessary and helpful. For example, your college faculty includes experts in various fields and disciplines; plan to visit these faculty to obtain their expert opinions on issues related to your research. Faculty are away from time to time, so plan ahead; call the department and find out who in the field is knowledgeable about the issue in question. Then ask for that professor's office hours and call to schedule an appointment. Try to read this person's articles or books before your visit, so that you can ask informed questions and can use the time to best advantage. Experts in business, schools, and industry are other people you can interview for information about topics you might be researching. Other members of the community can help as well. If you are doing oral histories, for example, as Studs Terkel does (Chapter 8), you will be interviewing people to find out their stories or their attitudes about some part of their lives.

To assemble background information about your topic, ask yourself some questions about what you know. Where did you first learn about the topic? Do you have class materials or notes? Do you know people who can serve as resources? And finally, how will you start your library search strategy?

The first part of your search for information should help you to develop a brief overview of the topic: important names, dates, and terminology associated with the topic; related subjects and terms to use for searching for articles; and a list of potential sources for information. After collecting a basic list of core terms and key words, you are ready to search in more depth.

Using On-line Resources in Research

You have probably already used the World Wide Web in a preliminary search of your general topic area, or perhaps just to look around for some promising topic ideas. Even though the library has been the traditional starting point in research for generations past, libraries are not just about books—they are about information. Because historically we have been accustomed to using books and periodicals as the primary means of transmitting knowledge, we sometimes think that on-line resources represent different categories of information and require entirely different research strategies. Although there are some special approaches to utilizing Internet-based resources, they, like the library, essentially represent the storage, indexing, retrieval, and dissemination of information. It is therefore not surprising that libraries have invested heavily in ways to access on-line resources beyond the physical boundaries of the traditional library system. A key difference between on-line and more traditional "hard copy" resources, however, is the speed of transmission of information.

When you search the World Wide Web, for example, you can start a search, refine it, click on a topic area, click on the title of a linked page, and generally zip around all kinds of resources in a matter of minutes. Links between related topics are often already in place, and you can explore several closely related areas, explore your own topic in depth, save your places with "bookmarks," print out materials, get bibliographies—accomplish what would have been a painstaking, time-intensive process in a matter of moments.

A second key feature of Web-based research, mentioned above, is the linking of information. Find the Purdue Writing Center site, for example, and in moments you have access to all kinds of related sites, including the Library of Congress and the different rooms and the displays currently featured. Any number of sites related to writing and research are accessible from the initial page, and often different sites will lead you to other interesting, related ones. And many sites have information not easily available in most libraries. If you wanted to investigate traditional music of an American Indian tribe, for example, you could likely find a site with a sample recording and background information.

Access to a wide range of information, however, does not guarantee accuracy or even a truly representative sampling of knowledge on a given topic. Although a selection of library books may be limited—librarians can't buy every book printed—researching on-line creates the opposite problem. Your desktop can be overloaded with all kinds of on-line information, some of which may be authoritative and the rest questionable. The time you save in physically going from place to place in the library, the reference room, the bookshelves, back to the catalog for another search, and the like, should be devoted to evaluating on-line sources. Nearly anyone can create a Web page and post information. You have to use your scholarly skills, as well as common sense, in determining the credibility of such sources. The Library of Congress Web site, for example, has tremendous authority behind it, whereas Joe Zook's Cool Disco Revival may not (then again, it may have recordings of popular disco tunes or a top-ten list of disco hits, and if you are researching popular culture, you went to the right place after all). But if you are just starting to inform yourself about a topic, you can start browsing and learn what the principal divisions or elements of your topic are and follow your interest and the available links.

Linking on the Web is not an exact science, however, and it's important not to overrely on the links; they are someone else's idea of how topics should be connected. Use links to interesting Web pages to inform yourself in a general area of knowledge, but only as part of a larger, thoughtful research strategy. And when you have ten thousand "hits" for your search, it's time to reconsider your focus.

Strategies for Internet Research

Internet-based sources include indexes similar to those that have existed in print for some time. Reference sources include Web-based dictionaries, encyclopedias, almanacs, quotations, resources for questions, people locators, and medical/legal reference sites. A number of sites are devoted to news and have counterparts in print and other media: the *New York Times, Times of London, Chicago Tribune, Irish Times,* and *San Jose Mercury News* are examples. Most of the Internet-accessed indexes students are likely to use now have a Web interface for access on-line.

Search Engines   You are likely to begin your search by using a search engine, or a mechanism for retrieving and sorting information from the Web. As of this writing, a list of search engines for the Web includes Alta Vista, Ask Jeeves, Dogpile, Excite, Go.com, GoTo, HotBot, Infoseek, Lycos, MetaCrawler, Yahoo, and Web Crawler. You would access them from your home page, and in fact your computer may open to one of these pages as a default. Some sample addresses include *http://www.altavista.com/, http://www.excite.com/,* and *http://www.yahoo.com/.*

Different search engines have different options that may be helpful—some permit you to limit the language of the search (e.g., English), others let you specify other parameters such as specific dates or let you ask questions. One way to start a search is to review the search engine's index. This process would be most helpful when you have a general category of interest (environment or health, for example) but have not yet defined or identified a specific area of interest (geothermal energy in the Philippines, or stem cell research, for example). In browsing the list of categories, you may find a more focused area of interest to pursue.

Many searches, though, begin by indicating a key word or words, hitting the search or "go" button, and waiting to see how many and what kind of "hits" you got. Often a frustration is that you get either a vast array of Web sites too numerous to evaluate effectively or a collection of sites just off topic enough to be of little value. A way to focus your search is to use Boolean searching. In Boolean searching, named for mathematician George Boole, you add related terms to limit the type and number of Web sites returned in your search. Boolean searches use the words "and," "or," and "not," as well as quotes and parentheses, to indicate terms to be considered together while searching. These terms may be adapted by various search engines, so experiment with a few basic searches trying out different terms to see how they work.

Evaluating Web-Based Information   Because Web-based materials have not been through the winnowing process of peer-reviewed journals, librarian selection, or publisher review, you will need to be particularly critical in your evaluation of Web sources. Several guidelines are listed:

- Author: One criterion to consider is authorship and authority. Who is the author? What are his or her credentials? Affiliations? Is the publisher also the author? Is an organization the author? Are any organizational affiliations acknowledged? Are any affiliations likely to bias the information in unacknowledged ways? Who pays for the site? If there is advertising, can it be readily distinguished from the ostensible content of the site? Has there been a review process?

- Purpose: What is the purpose of the site? Information? Instruction? Advocacy? Entertainment? Sales? Creating or maintaining a community of users? An entry point to other sites?

- Quality of content: Can the information be verified as accurate? Is it credible? Is it current, with date of site's creation, date the information was placed, and date site was last updated visible? Are there links to other sites? Is there a Web creator to access for comments and questions? How does the information on this site compare with other sites and other media on this topic?

Below are some examples of Web sites that might be useful in researching themes related to American Cultures.

http://nativeamculture.about.com/culture/nativeamculture/mbody.htm
   (Native American culture)

http://afroamculture.about.com/culture/afroamculture/mbody.htm
   (African American culture)

http://www.newton.mec.edu/Angier/DimSum/
   chinadimsumaconnection.html   (Chinese American culture)

http://www.dla.utexas.edu/depts/ams/Jazz/Jazz.html   (an on-line
   journal on jazz scholarship published by the University of
   Texas)

http://www.library.yale.edu/pubstation/databases/chicano.html
   (Chicano database)

http://www.library.yale.edu/pubstation/databases/hlas.html
   (handbook of Latin American studies)

http://www.soci.swt.edu/areas/europeanbib.htm   (multicultural
   relations: bibliographies: European Americans)

http://www.soci.swt.edu/areas/multicltrlinks.htm   (multicultural
   relations links)

Finally, a caution: ownership of text can get especially murky on
the Web. Text is easily uploaded, downloaded, modified, integrated,
and otherwise manipulated and shaped. You still bear the responsibility of ethical scholarship: When you quote, quote exactly and give
credit. When you summarize or integrate information, particularly if it
is unique in content or phrasing, credit the source. If you are ever
tempted to do the unthinkable and to lift a paper or part of a paper off
the Web, or to overrely on a source for an assignment, remember:
Your instructor and classmates have access to the Web just like you
do. A sobering lesson at our institution occurred when two students
both plagiarized the same paper off the Web. But these reminders
should be beside the point: As a scholar and a thinker, you need to do
your own original thinking and writing. Sources will help you think
through and then build your own arguments—not argue in your place
while you tag along for the ride.

Keep in mind, then, good sense, critical thinking skills, and traditional research techniques and let them guide you through the maze of
networked information.

Using Library Sources

Library sources, both print and other media, will probably serve
as your core materials for research, so it is important to get to know
your library system. You have probably already used reference materials and library books to find information you needed; you may be
less familiar with alternatives—electronic media, for example, including on-line, or networked, researching capabilities and CD-ROMs,
which store large amounts of information and are updated frequently.
Familiarize yourself with such data-gathering resources as soon as
possible, because they will become more and more prominent in the
future. Ask your instructor or a librarian for class or individual instruction on using them. Some public libraries now have such sources

to search for magazine articles; generally, they are "user friendly" and entail only punching a few clearly marked buttons.

Materials in the library fall into three categories. *Primary sources* are original materials, such as interviews, survey data, oral histories, photographs, posters, advertisements, paintings, and literary works. What constitutes a primary resource depends on the field and context, but generally they are the raw data about which others may write or which they may interpret. Examples of primary sources in this book are *Keep within Compass* and the writings of Frederick Douglass. Student writer John Wu used statistical evidence as a primary source in his research paper (Chapter 7).

Secondary sources are materials written *about* the primary sources: Authors describe, interpret, or otherwise integrate primary sources into their writings. Langston Hughes's poem "Let America Be America Again" (Chapter 6) is an example of a primary source. Chris Countryman's essay analyzing the poem is a secondary source. A student analyzing propaganda materials could use both primary materials, such as posters, and secondary materials to develop an analytical or argumentative essay about techniques of propaganda.

Tertiary sources are third-level materials, such as bibliographies, which list collections of both primary and secondary sources. *The Mexican American: A Selected and Annotated Bibliography* is a tertiary source.

The sources you need will vary depending on the research stage. Initially, general sources, such as general or specialized encyclopedias, can provide an overview of the topic and identify the core concepts and issues. Encyclopedias range from the general, such as *Encyclopaedia Britannica,* to the specialized, such as encyclopedias of music, religion, social science, and the like. Encyclopedias and specialized dictionaries are shelved in the reference sections of the library, and they generally are listed in on-line catalogs as well. While you are doing basic general information gathering, look up your topic's key words in the Library of Congress Subject Headings reference guide, which should be available in the reference room as well. As on-line searches for materials become more and more important in conducting research, it is essential that you have a good working list of key words with which to conduct your searches. For example, people researching Latino studies may need to use key words such as *ethnic identity, Cuban Americans,* or *Puerto Rico—U.S.*

Once you have general background information, you can start digging for additional, more focused materials. Compile a list of selections in books, academic journals, and general interest magazines to help you find more detailed information.

To find books on your topic, consult either the card catalog or whatever on-line computer catalog your institution or local library uses. Start with the list of key words and browse for titles that look interesting. Consider both general and more specific levels of your topic, and pay special attention to any bibliographies or books that indicate that they include bibliographies.

To find articles, search periodical indexes in both print and media forms. You are probably familiar with the *Reader's Guide to Periodical Literature*, but you may not yet have used specialized indexes. Some important ones are the *Humanities Index, Social Science Index, General Science Index, Alternative Press Index, Index to Black Periodicals, Women's Studies Abstracts, Historical Abstracts, MLA Bibliography, PAIS International, Psych Abstracts*, and, for general information, a newspaper index such as *The New York Times Index*.

The electronic media include both general and specific magazine and journal indexes as well as reference sources. Lexis-Nexis, as one example, provides full texts of articles in business, general news, and law. Specialized sources you may have access to include *Bibliography of Native North Americans, EconLit, PsychLit, Art Index*, and the on-line *Oxford English Dictionary*, as well as duplication of print versions of *MLA Bibliography* and *Historical Abstracts*.

In addition to the general reference and research sources already outlined, your library may have some specialized sources for research on American themes. Following are some of the possible categories of specialized references and some examples of the kinds of material you may be able to find to help you investigate your subject.

General Sources for American Themes

American Writers before 1800

American Writers

American Drama Criticism: Interpretations, 1890–1977

MLA International Bibliography

American Humanities Index

The Democracy Reader: Classic and Modern Speeches, Essays, Poems, Declarations, and Documents on Freedom and Human Rights

The Bill of Rights: A Documentary History

Encyclopedia of the American Constitution

Documentary History of the Modern Civil Rights Movement

Slavery in the Courtroom: Annotated Bibliography of Cases

Black Slavery in the Americas

The American Civil Liberties Union: An Annotated Bibliography

Social Reform and Reaction in America: An Annotated Bibliography

Women's Rights Movement in the United States

Encyclopedia of the American Constitution

Index on Censorship

The Anthropology of War: A Bibliography

Encyclopedia of Military History

Peace Research Abstracts Journal

American Public Opinion Index

American Public Opinion Data

Public Opinion, 1935–1946

The Gallup Poll: Public Opinion (annual)

An American Profile: Opinions and Behavior, 1972–1989

Public Opinion Polls and Survey Research: Selective Annotated Bibliography of U.S. Guides and Studies from the 1980s

Statistical Abstracts of the United States (from the U.S. Census Bureau)

Historical Statistics of the United States: Colonial Times to 1970

Social Indicators III: Selected Data and Social Conditions and Trends in the United States

American Statistics Index

The Official Washington Post *Index*

Immigration and Ethnicity: A Guide to Information Sources

Statistical Abstracts of the United States

We the People: An Atlas of America's Ethnic Diversity

America: History and Life

Film Studies

The American Film Industry: A Historical Dictionary

The Film Encyclopedia

Blacks in American Films and Television

The Hispanic Image on the Silver Screen: An Interpretive Filmography from Silents

Contemporary Theatre, Film and Television

Who's Who in American Film

Film Study: An Analytical Bibliography

The New Film Index: A Bibliography of Magazine Articles in English, 1930–1970

Ethnic and Racial Images in American Film and Television: Historical Essays and Bibliography

Blacks in Film and Television: A Pan-African Bibliography of Films, Filmmakers, and Performers

Film Literature Index

New York Times *Film Reviews*

Film Review Index

Index to Critical Reviews

African American Studies

Some key words for searching: Afro-Americans—Race-Identity; Afro-American Press; Afro-Americans—History; Black Power—United States; Civil Rights—United States; School Integration—United States.

The African American Encyclopedia

Dictionary of Afro-American Slavery

Encyclopedia of Black America

Encyclopedia of Southern Culture

Notable Black American Women

Black Women in America

The Harlem Renaissance: A Historical Dictionary

The Negro Almanac: A Reference Work on the Afro-American into Sound, 1898–1935

Women of Color and Southern Women: A Bibliography of Social Science Research

Afro-American Folk Culture

Afro-American History

Afro-American Reference: An Annotated Bibliography of Selected Resources

Black Adolescence: Current Issues and Annotated Bibliography

Black American Writers: Bibliographical Essays

The Black Family in the United States

Black Rhetoric: A Guide to Afro-American Communication

Index to Black Periodicals

Latino Studies

Some key words for searching: Mexican Americans—Ethnic Identity; Hispanic Americans—Ethnic Identity; Cuban Americans; Mexican American Women; Migrant Agricultural Laborers; Puerto Ricans—U.S.

Chicano Literature: A Reference Guide

Dictionary of Mexican American History

Bibliografia Chicana: A Guide to Information Sources

A Bibliography of Criticism of Contemporary Chicano Literature

Bibliography of Mexican American History

Chicano Anthology Index: A Comprehensive Author, Title, and Subject Index to Chicano Anthologies, 1965–1987

The Chicana Studies Index: Twenty Years of Gender Research, 1972–1991

Latinos in the United States: A Historical Bibliography

The Mexican American: A Selected and Annotated Bibliography

Mexican American Biographies: A Historical Dictionary

Statistical Handbook on U.S. Hispanics

The Chicano Index

Latin American Studies

Native American Studies

The Library of Congress term for the aboriginal peoples of the Western Hemisphere, including the Inuit, is *Indians*. The Western Hemisphere is divided into regions: North America, Mexico, Central America, West Indies, and South America. Works on Indians of a particular region are listed as, for example, *Indians of North America*. Individual tribal names are used as appropriate, such as *Navaho Indians* or *Choctaw Indians*. Other key words include Western Algonquin Indians; Athapascan Indians; Caddoan Indians; Eskimos; Mound-builders; Ojibwa Indians; Piegan Indians; Shoshoni Indians; Tinne Indians; United States—Civilization—Indian influences.

Atlas of Ancient America

Atlas of the North American Indian

A Concise Dictionary of Indian Tribes of North America

Dictionary of Daily Life of Indians of the Americas

Encyclopedia of Native American Religions: An Introduction

Encyclopedia of Native American Tribes

Handbook of the American Frontier: Four Centuries of Indian-White Relationships

Handbook of North American Indians

Native American Almanac: A Portrait of Native America Today

American Indian Women: A Guide to Research

Native American Folklore, 1879–1979: An Annotated Bibliography

Native North Americans: Crime, Conflict, and Criminal Justice: A Research Bibliography

Southwest Native American Arts and Material Culture: A Guide to Research

Bibliography of Native North Americans on Disc (on CD-ROM)

Who Was Who in Native American History: Indians and Non-Indians from Early Contacts Through 1900

Native Women: A Statistical Overview

Reports of the American Indian Family History Project

Statistical Record of Native North Americans

Nations Within a Nation: Historical Statistics of American Indians

Asian American Studies

The Library of Congress uses *Asian American,* but other headings include the following: American Literature—Asian American Authors; Chinese Americans; East Indians; Filipino Americans; Filipinos in the United States; Hawaiians; Japanese Americans; Korean Americans; Oceanian Americans; Pacific Islander Americans; Vietnamese Americans.

Asian-Americans Information Directory

The Chinese in America, 1920–1973

The Filipinos in America, 1898–1974

The Koreans in America, 1882–1974

Dictionary of Asian American History

Japanese American History: An A to Z Reference from 1868 to the Present

Harvard Encyclopedia of American Ethnic Groups

Refugees in the United States

Asian American Literature: An Annotated Bibliography

The Asian American Media Reference Guide, 2d ed.

Asian American Studies: An Annotated Bibliography and Research Guide

A Comprehensive Bibliography for the Study of American Minorities

Images of Color: A Guide to Media from and for Asian, Black, Latino and Native American Communities

Immigrant Women in the United States: A Selectively Annotated Multidisciplinary Bibliography

Pacific/Asian American Research

A Selected Bibliography on the Asians in America

South Asians in North America: An Annotated and Selected Bibliography (covers 1900–1986)

Biographical Sources

Chinese American Portraits: Personal Histories, 1828–1988

Who's Who Among Asian Americans

Statistical Record of Asian Americans

A number of sources already listed can also be good sources for information on Asian Americans.

Focusing the Search

Once you have found a general overview of your subject and a list of potential sources, deepen your search for materials. Many of the general and bibliographical sources are in the reference area of your library or can be accessed on-line; your next step will probably be to collect some important books and periodical articles in the field.

In some fields, books will be your most important sources; a scholarly book has the advantage of being an in-depth examination of some issue or element in the field. A periodical, on the other hand, by virtue of the recurrent issuing of the material, offers less in-depth but more current information.

Books are generally spread out through the library storage system in what are commonly called *stacks*. Sometimes the stacks are closed, and you need to request books you want from the circulation desk. If stacks at your library are open, you can browse the shelves in your subject area. If the book you tracked down in a bibliography isn't available, perhaps another interesting book is. Or perhaps other nearby books on the shelves look helpful. You should plan on taking some time in the stacks and perusing tables of contents, introductory chapters, and bibliographies of books in the area of your topic.

Working with Sources

As you assemble general, preliminary, and increasingly specialized sources, you will need to keep track of your materials, both the original sources and your notes on them. Few experiences in academia are more frustrating than finding an excellent piece of information or an idea and then losing track of where you located it. Different writers approach notes and note taking in different ways.

First, you have to determine what you are looking for when you read sources. In addition to keeping in mind the general advice offered in Chapter 1 for reading critically, pay special attention to the following questions when critiquing sources:

1. What is the theme? What is the author's purpose in writing? Who are the intended audiences? What are the author's assumptions? Do you share those assumptions? Do the author's assumptions or emphasis indicate bias?

2. What is the overall idea the author develops? What is the primary organizing plan (cause-effect, problem-solution, definition, process)?

3. Is the evidence presented clearly? Is it persuasive? Do the author's conclusions logically follow from the evidence?

4. How does the selection connect with other readings? Does it provide information on other sources? Does it provide an example of a point made in another source? Does it contradict another source? Are there points of comparison or contrast with another source? What common threads run through the sources?

Taking Notes   As a fellow scholar in the academic community, you are expected not to take your sources at face value but to challenge and question them, to assess the merit of their arguments and the logic of their conclusions critically.

Be an active, assertive reader. Question information as you read it; argue with the text. If you own the book or you are using photocopies, make extensive marginal notes. Otherwise, use note cards, computer "note cards," or notepaper to keep track of your information. Try to use a medium for taking notes that allows you to sort the notes by topic as you collect more information.

As you take notes, write down not only the information itself but key words, phrases, reactions to points the author makes, critical arguments and comments, and reactions you may have. *But take great care to keep track of exactly what information comes from the sources and which comments are your own reflections on the source.* When information or ideas appear in a number of sources (usually three or more), most writers will consider it common knowledge in the field and will not document the source. Until you have researched enough to know what will need citing, however, you should keep track of the sources in your notes.

There are three different types of notes we generally use to record our research of sources: summaries, paraphrase, and direct quotation. *Summaries* of information from the source help you to make sure you have digested the material and help you to translate the information into your own words. They pull out the key ideas of a source. *Paraphrases* are a kind of running commentary or translation of the original source; they capture essentially all of the material in the original. Paraphrase is a frequent suspect in plagiarism, the unacknowledged use of the ideas or phrases of others. The difference between summary and paraphrase can be seen in the following example, based on an excerpt from "The Gettysburg Address."

Original

Four score and seven years ago our fathers brought forth on this continent, a new nation, conceived in Liberty, and dedicated to the proposition that all men are created equal.

Now we are engaged in a great civil war, testing whether that nation, or any nation so conceived and so dedicated, can long endure. We are met on a great battlefield of that war. We have come to dedicate a portion of that field as a final resting-place for those who here gave their lives that that nation might live. It is altogether fitting and proper that we should do this.

Summary

Eighty-seven years ago a country was founded on the principles of freedom and equality. We are now involved in a war that will test whether the nation and those principles will survive. Appropriately, we gather on a battlefield of that war to dedicate a cemetery for those who died here fighting for the nation's survival.

Paraphrase

Eighty-seven years ago the founding fathers created on the American continent a new country, born in freedom and committed to the ideal that everyone is created equal.

We are now involved in a large-scale civil war that will determine if a nation with such ideals and such a purpose can last. We meet at the site of one of the great battles of that war and we are here to dedicate part of the battlefield as a cemetery for those who died here to save the nation. It is appropriate that we do so.

Direct quotations *must* be taken down exactly as written and put inside quotation marks. They should be saved for those occasions when the quotation so perfectly captures a concept, idea, or image that it would require a great deal more time and space to say the same thing that would have much less impact. They, too, need to be carefully documented. Sometimes you can summarize an author's point and then put key or specialized words into quotations. If you use only parts of a quotation by an author, be sure to use ellipses—three spaced dots—to indicate that you have left material out; be careful not to change the author's intended meaning. For a quotation within a quotation, use single quotation marks; if the author quotes someone else you want to quote directly, your citation would say, for example, "(Pritchard, qtd. in Garcia 32)." Keep careful track of who says what in your sources so that you can quote accurately.

Avoiding Plagiarism   Plagiarism is the unacknowledged use of the ideas or words of others. Whether accidental or intentional, plagiarism is a serious offense. To avoid plagiarism, you should follow these general guidelines.

Cite your sources in the following cases: an original idea from a source, whether you summarize it, paraphrase it, or quote it directly; factual information that is not common knowledge; any exact wording or unique phrasing taken from a source.

There is no need to cite when material is considered common knowledge; that is, it appears in a number of sources or can be verified by agreed-on measurement or criteria. How many sources must it appear in? Some scholars suggest a minimum of three sources; others say five. We have found that if the material is general background information and occurs in three sources or more, it can safely be considered common knowledge. But if you are writing about some scientific findings and it is relevant that a number of scientists duplicated certain results, then you would be better off citing even a large number of studies, as the confirmation of some findings by others is crucial to the information's credibility. Again, you need to develop judgment about audience, purpose, and subject as you make such decisions. Too many citations can interrupt the flow of your paper or give the impression that the sources' voices are taking over your paper, but when in doubt, it is better to cite rather than not.

Plagiarism is essentially the passing off of the ideas or words of others as your own. Keep in mind the spirit of the law and you will be guided by it as you make specific decisions about particular pieces of information in your essay.

Writing Drafts

As you collect information, review notes, and sift through ideas and evidence, connections should begin to form in your mind, and responses to your initial research question begin to suggest themselves. You can foster this process by reviewing notes as you collect new information, determining where the new sources fit with the material you already know. Take time at regular intervals to freewrite about your topic, either in a journal or in scheduled bursts of freewriting at the computer after a research session.

Some writers find it helpful to take notes from different sources and then begin to sort them by subtopic; or go back to their research question and divide the question into smaller questions; or review the working hypothesis, refine it, and divide it into categories. For example, a paper on the myth of the model minority could focus on the family ethos of work, the glass ceiling in corporations, the different patterns of immigration from Asia, the relative economic and educational status of each group, and so on. Sometimes a diagram or flowchart helps, with lines and circles connecting various parts of the material. Whatever your method, try to begin lining up the general elements of the material.

Consider the kinds of supporting assertions you can make based on your evidence; review your tentative thesis or hypothesis and refine it, if needed, based on your findings. Review your supporting assertions in light of your refined thesis. Those supporting assertions can become your topic ideas. Line up those supporting assertions in the order in which your reader needs to hear them and in an order that links up one point to the next. Then draft a working outline based on the assertions you have identified, work through the material to find the support for your assertions, and write a rough draft. At this stage, you are primarily interested in getting the basic structure down. Although you should keep track of where your information is coming from, don't worry too much about the specifics of documentation or style: "(Smith 21)" or "(Smith teaching article p. 21)" in some form is sufficient at this stage, but try to keep track of article and page number. Checking spelling and worrying about specifics of grammar are tasks for a later stage of writing. Just get your core argument down. Save your file often if you are working on the computer! If you are writing out or typing your draft, photocopy it as you write large parts of it to guard against losing your work.

Documentation

When you converse in the academic community, you generally need to use the conventions of the various disciplines to communicate ideas and research findings. As you begin to think of yourself as a part of the scholarly community, you will see how citation forms work as a kind of shorthand that permits scholars to share their findings with others in the national and international academic communities and helps those scholars follow up on each other's work. The cooperative nature of research may help explain the very specific formats used in different disciplines. In the social sciences, for example, the date of a research study is crucial, so the American Psychological Association (APA) format puts the date right after the author's name. In humanities fields, on the other hand, where the date of the findings is less important, the Modern Language Association (MLA) format for in-text citations contains a name or book title and page number. In the "Works Cited" list as well, the date comes last.

You may have been instructed to use a particular documentation style. An excellent resource is the MLA's Web site or an alternative such as *www.wisc.edu/writing/Handbook/DocMLA*. Your instructor may provide guidance, or you can use a style book. Both MLA and APA have style books. Some examples of style manuals in other disciplines include *Council of Biology Editors Style Manual: A Guide for Authors, Editors, and Publishers; A Manual for Authors of Mathematical Papers;* and *Style Manual for Guidance in the Preparation of Papers.*

Most composition courses suggest following either the MLA or APA style. If you have a choice and you know you are interested in humanities or social science, you may want to start using the format you are likely to use in future classes and to buy the appropriate manual. Following are the general guidelines for documenting your essays and citing your sources.

How to Document Sources   Most disciplines are moving toward parenthetical within-text citation, and that is the style we will use here. In APA style, supply the last name of the author(s) and the year of publication: (Garcia & Collins, 1988). In MLA style, if you are referring to a work by an author, cite the author's name and a page number: (Garcia 38). Note that in MLA style you don't need a comma or "p." to indicate page number. If Garcia's name or book or article title is implied in the context, you can simply use the page number (38) as the reference. If you are citing two works by Garcia, you can use a brief title of the work (Messages 28) to indicate to the reader which work this particular quotation comes from. Look at the documented student essays in this book for samples; John Wu (Chapter 7) documented his essay in correct MLA style. If you have substantive notes or "asides" to the reader, you can include those as footnotes or endnotes. If you use endnotes, place them at the end of the paper, but before your list of references.

References/Works Cited   within the general guidelines for documentation, there are specific forms that should be followed for different types of sources. A "Works Cited" list is now commonly used with MLA style; it contains only the references actually cited in the paper. The APA style uses a "References" list with all relevant readings that may have influenced the paper.

Sample Documentation   the following lists provide samples of common works that you will use. Note that underlining may be substituted for italics if you are writing by hand or on a typewriter.

A book by one author

> *MLA:*   Sowell, Thomas. *Ethnic America.* New York: Basic Books, 1981.
> *APA:*   Sowell, T. (1981). *Ethnic America.* New York: Basic Books.

A book by two authors

> *MLA:*   Neesom, Lisa, and George Madera. *Early American Art.* Englewood Cliffs: Prentice-Hall, 1955.

APA: Neesom, M., & Madera, G. (1955). *Early American art.* Englewood Cliffs, NJ: Prentice-Hall.

A book by three authors

MLA: Lewis, Peter, A. J. McGee, and Martin Washington. *American Folk Art.* 3rd ed. New York: McGraw-Hill, 1993.

APA: Lewis, P., McGee, A. J., & Washington, M. (1993). *American folk art* (3rd ed.). New York: McGraw-Hill.

A book with more than three authors

MLA: Isselbacher, Kurt J., et al. *Harrison's Principles of Internal Medicine.* 9th ed. New York: McGraw-Hill, 1980.

APA: Isselbacher, K. J., Adams, D. A., Braunwald, E., Petersdorf, R. G., Wilson, J. D. (1980). *Harrison's principles of internal medicine* (9th ed.). New York: McGraw-Hill.

The edited work of an author

MLA: Hawthorne, Nathaniel. *The Portable Hawthorne.* Ed. Malcolm Cowley. New York: Viking, 1969.

APA: Hawthorne, N. (1969). *The portable Hawthorne.* (M. Cowley, Ed.). New York: Viking Press.

A work in an anthology

MLA: Hawthorne, Nathaniel. "Young Goodman Brown." *Heritage of American Literature.* Ed. James E. Miller, Jr., with Kathleen Farley. Vol. 1. New York: Harcourt Brace, 1991. 1413–21.

APA: Hawthorne, N. (1991). Young Goodman Brown. In J. E. Miller, Jr. (Ed.), *Heritage of American literature: Vol. 1* (pp. 1413–1421). New York: Harcourt Brace.

A work in translation

MLA: Pushkin, Aleksander. *Eugene Onegin.* Trans. Vladimir Nabokov. 4 vols. New York: Bollingen Foundation, 1964.

APA: Pushkin, A. (1964). *Eugene Onegin* (Vols. 1–4). (V. Nabokov, Trans.). New York: Bollingen Foundation.

An article in a journal with separate pagination for each issue

MLA: Budd, Matthew A. "Human Suffering: Road to Illness or Gateway to Learning?" *Advances: The Journal of Mind-Body Health* 3 (Summer 1993): 28–35.

APA: Budd, M. A. (1993, Summer). Human suffering: Road to illness or gateway to learning? *Advances: The Journal of Mind-Body Health, 3,* 28–35.

An article in a journal with continuous pagination

MLA: Frey, Olivia. "Beyond Literary Darwinism: Women's Voices and Critical Discourse." *College English* 52 (1990): 507–26.

APA: Frey, O. (1990). Beyond literary Darwinism: Women's voices and critical discourse. *College English, 52,* 507–526.

An unsigned newspaper article or editorial

MLA: "Small Companies Earn Big Honors." *San Francisco Examiner* 20 May 1994: B1.

APA: Small companies earn big honors. (1994, May 20). *San Francisco Examiner,* p. B1.

A signed newspaper article or editorial

MLA: Ulrich, Allan. "Variations on a Gould-en Theme." *San Francisco Examiner* 20 May 1994: C1.

APA: Ulrich, A. (1994, May 20). Variations on a Gould-en theme. *San Francisco Examiner,* p. C1.

A public document

MLA: United States Department of Health and Human Services, Administration for Children, Youth and Families, Children's Bureau. *Child Welfare Strategies in the Coming Years.* Washington: Office of Human Development Services, 1978.

APA: U.S. Department of Health and Human Services, Administration for Children, Youth and Families, Children's Bureau. (1978). *Child welfare strategies in the coming years.* Washington: Office of Human Development Services.

A film

MLA: *Judgment at Nuremberg.* Stanley Kramer, dir. United Artists, 1961.

APA: Kramer, S. (Director). (1961). *Judgment at Nuremberg* [Film]. United Artists.

A lecture

MLA: Rebholz, Ronald. "Shakespeare and the Power of an Idea." Centennial Lecture Series. Stanford U. 23 Sept. 1991.

> *APA:* Rebholz, Ronald. (1991, September 23). *Shakespeare and the power of an idea*. Lecture presented at the Centennial Lecture Series, Stanford University.

An interview

> *MLA:* Garcia, Juana. Personal interview. 3 Dec. 1993.
> *APA:* Garcia, J. (1993, December 3). [Interview].

A computer program

> *MLA:* Watters, Ann. *The Art of Persuasion.* Vers. 1.0. Computer software, CD-ROM. Focus Interactive, 1995.
> *APA:* Watters, A. (1995). The art of persuasion [Computer software]. Menlo Park, CA: Focus Interactive.

Legal cases

> Plessy v. Ferguson, 163 U.S. 537 (1896).

Internet and World Wide Web sources

> Standards are gradually emerging for Internet and World Wide Web resources. The functional rule remains: Provide for the reader sufficient information to document your results and to guide your reader to the same source. Insofar as possible, include author, title, date of publication of source, date you accessed it, and URL or means of access.

(Note: Both the MLA and APA follow the style set forth in *A Uniform System of Citation*, 15th edition, published by the Harvard Law Review Association in 1991.)

5

Identities

Whom do you visualize when you hear the term *American?* Do you identify a specific gender, race, occupation, or age that you consider typical? Do you see a white male banker? A Native American high school student? A family of migrant farmers? A Chinese American factory worker? All of these people can be American citizens, of course, but is there one that seems *more* American to you than the others?

America is a confluence of cultures: American Indians who have lived here for millennia; European and Asian immigrants who came here in search of a better life; people of African descent brought by force. Over time, these cultures have mingled and evolved into something new and recognizably American. How do all of these disparate identities come together to form an American identity?

In understanding American identities, we need to come to terms with unity and division, with separateness and common ground. The question, What do we mean by American? encompasses a host of related questions: Is there a distinctly American identity? Is there one overriding, generalized American culture? Or are there only disparate subcultures that form strategic alliances for survival? Should we retain the old metaphor of the melting pot, into which various cultures are tossed, melted down, and pulled out as generic Americans? If so, what are the characteristics of that generic American? If we reject the metaphor of the melting pot, what should we use as a more fitting metaphor: A mosaic? A puzzle?

Identity has always been a difficult question nagging the collective American mind. We wonder how much we have in common besides living in the same country. We argue about a common culture, a shared set of values—whether there is one, whether we should try to cobble one together, whether we should try to revise one that has been thrust upon us or simply evolved. We debate whether it is more important for Americans of a particular ethnic, racial, or cultural heritage to celebrate that history or to feel part of mainstream America—or whether both can coexist.

The question of who or what is an American is clearly important on a personal level as each of us comes to terms with who we are. But it is also a pressing political issue because citizenship, government entitlements, voting rights, job protection, civil liberties, and every other advantage or opportunity that America offers depend ultimately on whether a person is considered a true American.

American Identities through History

As long as there has been an America, Americans have wondered and argued about who they were. The dominant issues and topics have shifted over time, but the same concerns have surfaced time and time again. All of the authors in this chapter have taken part in the debate about Americans and American identities, about individuality and cohesion, on both personal and political levels.

One of the first issues was whether there was—or could be—a unified American identity at all. Before the American Revolution, European settlers typically thought of themselves as residents of their own colonies and subjects of European monarchs, not as part of a unified new nation. In the 1750s, however, with the French and Indian War looming, Benjamin Franklin and others began calling for a union of the colonies for mutual protection. Franklin's lithograph *Join, or Die* is a graphic representation of the advantages of such unity: self-preservation rather than destruction.

After the Revolution, when political unity had been established, observers began offering assessments of the American character and culture, based almost exclusively on the Anglo Americans of the northeast and eastern seaboard. Alexis de Tocqueville attempts to define the American character by describing the political and social history of its most dominant group, and he identifies that group as English settlers, especially in New England. The approach that he takes—seeing the English character as the origin of true American culture—is one that almost all succeeding writers have had to address.

Although Tocqueville and other historians at the time focused on the British ancestry of mainstream America, many other cultures were contributing to the American identity. Over the course of the nineteenth century, the American population became more and more diverse: Irish fleeing famine; Jews and Catholics fleeing religious persecution; Italians, Swedes, Chinese, Russians, and others seeking jobs and opportunities. How were all these people—whose looks, languages, and actions were generally quite different from the dominant Anglo culture—to be incorporated into the American identity?

These immigrants generally favored assimilation. After arriving in America, each group found itself faced with further hardship and discrimination because they were so easily identified as "foreign." Their desire to succeed became a desire to escape the unwanted attention of other groups, to merge with mainstream American culture. The dominant ideal became that of the melting pot, with foreign differences melted away and identical Americans rolling off the assembly line.

At one time or another, every foreign element or influence associated with new immigrants was considered suspect. The artist who created *The U.S. Hotel* cartoon clearly wanted to preserve America for Americans—that is, for the people who were already here and the few newcomers who would completely accept those established cultural values. At other times, especially when America was faced with an outside enemy, all Americans were considered acceptable, regardless of their heritage. The divisiveness of *The U.S. Hotel* is completely absent from the propagandistic posters from World War I like *Victory Liberty Loan*, which proudly presented a diverse but united America.

One name often missing even from a picture of multicultural America is a recognizable Native American. European immigrant groups were not, of course, writing their history on a blank page. For countless generations, Native Americans had identified themselves with the American land. Luther Standing Bear articulates the argument that the true American is the Indian, identified with the essence of the American continent. Another group struggling in the early twentieth century to be recognized as full-fledged Americans were African Americans. Because the American identity had always been defined in terms of whites, African Americans were, as Ralph Ellison pointed out, invisible. In the Prologue to *Invisible Man*, Ellison uses the metaphor of invisibility to explore how the prevailing definition of *American* has kept some groups dominant and others excluded.

By the mid–twentieth century, the melting pot ideal was falling into disfavor. Clearly, not all Americans had been accounted for, and those who had been were beginning to challenge the value of assimilation. Critic Kenneth Burke suggests, "If men were not apart from one another, there would be no need for the rhetorician to proclaim their unity." John F. Kennedy, elected president in 1960, sought to unite the divided nation by proclaiming its unity. In his inaugural address, he defines a new American identity based on the nation's role in the international scene and its presumed unity of purpose.

Nearly two decades later Poet Robert Pinsky addresses political and public dimensions of America in "Local Politics," an exerpt from his long poem "An Explanation of America."

In recent decades, many writers have focused on forging a coherent personal identity as Americans living within a cultural mosaic. Some commentators, such as historian and educator Arthur Schlesinger Jr., suggest that recognition of America's ethnic subcultures have gone too far. In his essay "The Cult of Ethnicity," he argues that the traditional American values of integration and assimilation have been rejected to the detriment of society. Another historian, Ronald Takaki, professor and multicultural education proponent, brings his research and his perspective to a more multicultural and integrative understanding of America's roots. In "Prospero Unbound: The Market Revolution," he succinctly raises issues of America's political and cultural identity and the role of economics in forging those identities. Jean Wakatsuki Houston takes a more personal perspective in her speech, "A Tapestry of Hope," making a strong case, without insult or accusation, for the strength to be found in America's diversity. In "Chicana," the chapter's student essay, student writer Martha Serrano argues for her right to define her own identity, choosing a label that accurately reflects her heritage. The film for this chapter, *The Joy Luck Club*, highlights the forging of several young Chinese American women's identities within and across cultures.

As you read and reflect on the selections that follow, consider not only your own personal identity and cultural origins but also the social and political implications of your identity and that of others as you begin to take part in the obligations and privileges of citizenship: open debate, difference of opinion, and the need to take a stand on important issues. Ask yourself the questions that the readings pose: Who is an American? Who is entitled to what America has to offer? What are our common bonds, our goals, our ethics and beliefs as a society?

∞ *Join, or Die* (1754)

BENJAMIN FRANKLIN

Benjamin Franklin (1706–1790), American statesman, author, printer, inventor, was apprenticed at age twelve to his brother, a printer, and in 1723 went to Philadelphia, where he eventually set up his own paper and published Poor Richard's Almanac. *Franklin was active throughout the American Revolution and was a signer of the Declaration of Independence. "Join, or Die," considered the first American cartoon, was Franklin's contribution to the debate about unity among the colonies as the French and Indian War approached. Franklin was the delegate from Pennsylvania as seven colonies sent representatives to negotiate with the Iroquois Nation, but his argument for a union of colonies with "one general government" for common defense would serve in other crises as well. To make his point, Franklin draws upon a myth that is familiar to his audience: a cut-up snake that is reassembled before sundown will come back to life.*

For Journals

Some created images, such as the American flag or the Statue of Liberty, evoke a sense of America for many people. What images from nature, whether plant or animal, embody your sense of America?

For Discussion

1. What is the primary argument of the cartoon? What does Franklin want the audience to do? Why?

2. Woodcuts with a moral or lesson in text below a visual image date back centuries. What are some advantages of making an argument in both text and image? What audiences can an author hope to reach in this way?

3. What are some of the advantages of visual argument over text, especially a simple design, as in this cartoon? Consider your own responses to other visual images, such as cartoons and advertisements, as well as the response you would expect of Franklin's contemporaries.

4. Mid-twentieth-century audiences may find the image of a snake threatening or disturbing, but what of the largely agrarian American population of the mid–eighteenth century? Do you suspect they had a similar response? Why might Franklin have wanted to identify the united colonies as a dangerous creature? Consider the use of other, similar slogans in early U.S. history, such as "don't tread on me," frequently accompanying an image of a coiled snake.

5. If a separated snake can unite its parts before sundown and survive, to what symbolic, political sundown is Franklin drawing an analogy?

6. What identity does Franklin foresee for the colonies? In what ways is this identity a precursor to other identities for America?

For Writing

1. Look through some newspapers, especially in the editorial pages, and select a political cartoon dealing with some aspect of American identity (foreign policy or immigration, for example). Analyze the allusions or references in the cartoon that readers need to know in order to understand the point of it. Will audiences fifty, one hundred, or two hundred years from now understand the cartoon you have selected? Explain your answer.

2. Research some aspect of American history or politics at the beginning of the twentieth century by looking at cartoons from the era—during an election, for example. You could review old newspapers or look at a cartoon collection at the library. Alternatively, browse through old newspapers or magazines and see what you can infer about the social or political debates of the times. To what extent do you understand the allusions or jokes? Why do you think this is so? Write up your findings in an analytical essay; if possible, include photocopies of the cartoons you analyze.

◈ *Origin of the Anglo-Americans* (1839)

ALEXIS DE TOCQUEVILLE

Count Alexis [Charles Henri Maurice Clerel] de Tocqueville (1805–1859), magistrate and political observer, held a number of positions in the French government. His observations of and writings on the workings of democracy in the United States, based on an extended visit to America, comprise the well-known work Democracy in America (De la démocratie en Amérique), *from which the following selection is excerpted. Written between 1835 and 1839, this work is considered a landmark study of American institutions and is often quoted to this day. It is valuable in studying both historical and contemporary aspects of American cultures.*

After the birth of a human being, his early years are obscurely spent in the toils or pleasures of childhood. As he grows up, the world receives him, when his manhood begins, and he enters into contact

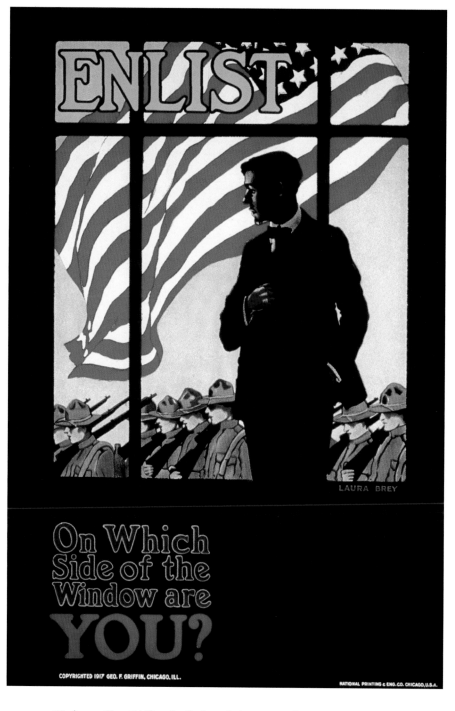

∞ *Enlist: On Which Side of the Window Are YOU?* (1917)

See the headnote and discussion questions for this poster on pages 221–223.

∾ Destroy this Mad Brute (1917)

H.R. HOPPS

The images and theme of this World War I poster, developed and circulated in the United States, were resurrected by German propagandists early in the second world war.

Questions for Discussion

1. What are the appeals to logos? Analyze them by articulating the premises and conclusion of the textual argument this poster presents.

2. Examine the poster's appeals to pathos and logos. Which do you find more persuasive? Which do you think were more effective for the intended audience?

Questions for Writing

1. Do some searching to find the 1939 German poster based on this American poster. You may find it on the Web, but it is in the book, *Persuasive Images* (Paret et al.), which catalogues some posters of the Hoover Archives at Stanford University. Analyze the effectiveness of the more recent German poster.

2. Examine a number of posters from World War I and then from World War II. Write an essay in which you analyze the themes common to one era; alternatively, compare and contrast images and strategies of persuasion from World War I and World War II.

3. Using an appropriate secondary text such as Paul Fussell's *Wartime* (an excerpt appears in this text in the War and Violence chapter) or Jacques Ellul's *Propaganda,* write an essay in which you apply the principles discussed in the secondary reading to a number of posters, your primary sources; or, looking at it another way, discuss the ways in which your primary sources illustrate the arguments discussed in the secondary readings.

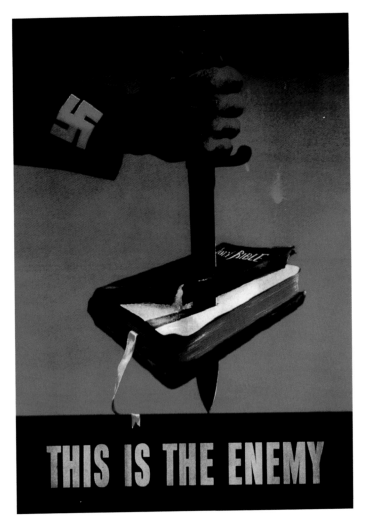

∞ This Is the Enemy (1943)

This unsigned poster is part of a series designed to inform Americans about Nazism.

Questions for Discussion

1.   Analyze the composition of the poster—the objects, the positions, the color scheme. How do they contribute to the persuasive message?

2.   Which persuasive appeals predominate? How are these appeals effective?

Questions for Writing

1.   Research propaganda posters that appear to have a religious theme and write an essay in which you analyze the effectiveness of these appeals.

2.   Write an essay in which you compare and contrast posters that appear to use religious appeals with those that rely on other types of appeals (protecting home and family, appealing to self-interest, and the like).

∞ Brownie Brand Crate Label (1927)

1. Keeping in mind that the unknown artist who did this advertisement was trying to sell Washington State pears, what feeling besides the freshness of the fruit does this picture convey to you? Look at the landscape, the mountains, the colors, their relation to each other in assigning emotional values to this picture.

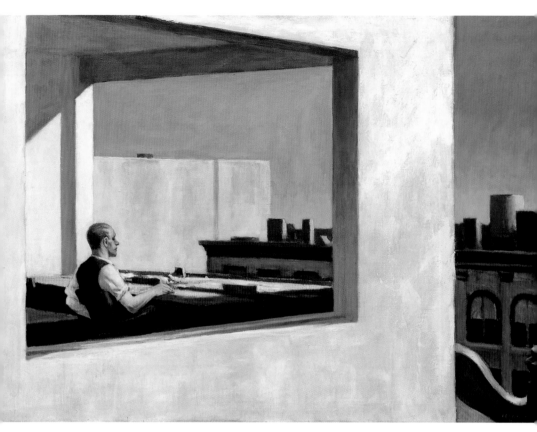

Edward Hopper (1882–1967), "Office in a Small City," 1953. Oil on canvas, H. 28 in. W. 40 in. Signed (lower left) Edward Hopper. The Metropolitan Museum of Art, George A. Hearn Fund, 1953. (53.183)

∞ *Office in a Small City* (1953)

EDWARD HOPPER

1. Edward Hopper painted many scenes of individuals in the city; what kind of daily office life do you imagine for the man in this painting? What adjectives would you use to describe him? Self-contained? Lonely? Exposed? Relaxed? Look closely at the picture, and, however you choose to describe him, use details from the painting to explain your choice.

2. With your classmates each contributing a sentence, make up a story about the life, work, and/or thoughts of the person in this picture.

with his fellows. He is then studied for the first time, and it is imagined that the germ of the vices and the virtues of his maturer years is then formed. This, if I am not mistaken, is a great error. We must begin higher up; we must watch the infant in his mother's arms; we must see the first images which the external world casts upon the dark mirror of his mind, the first occurrences which he witnesses; we must hear the first words which awaken the sleeping powers of thought, and stand by his earliest efforts,—if we would understand the prejudices, the habits, and the passions which will rule his life. The entire man is, so to speak, to be seen in the cradle of the child.

The growth of nations presents something analogous to this; they all bear some marks of their origin. The circumstances which accompanied their birth and contributed to their development affect the whole term of their being. If we were able to go back to the elements of states, and to examine the oldest monuments of their history, I doubt not that we should discover in them the primal cause of the prejudices, the habits, the ruling passions, and, in short, of all that constitutes what is called the national character. We should there find the explanation of certain customs which now seem at variance with the prevailing manners; of such laws as conflict with established principles; and of such incoherent opinions as are here and there to be met with in society, like those fragments of broken chains which we sometimes see hanging from the vaults of an old edifice, and supporting nothing. This might explain the destinies of certain nations which seem borne on by an unknown force to ends of which they themselves are ignorant. But hitherto facts have been wanting to researches of this kind: the spirit of inquiry has only come upon communities in their latter days; and when they at length contemplated their origin, time had already obscured it, or ignorance and pride adorned it with truth-concealing fables.

America is the only country in which it has been possible to witness the natural and tranquil growth of society, and where the influence exercised on the future condition of states by their origin is clearly distinguishable. . . . America, consequently, exhibits in the broad light of day the phenomena which the ignorance or rudeness of earlier ages conceals from our researches. Near enough to the time when the states of America were founded, to be accurately acquainted with their elements, and sufficiently removed from that period to judge of some of their results, the men of our own day seem destined to see further than their predecessors into the series of human events. Providence has given us a torch which our forefathers did not possess, and has allowed us to discern fundamental causes in the history of the world which the obscurity of the past concealed from them. If we carefully examine the social and political state of America, after having studied its history, we shall remain perfectly convinced that not an opinion, not a custom, not a law, I may even say not an event, is upon record which the origin of that people will not explain. The readers of this book will find in the present chapter the germ of all that is to follow, and the key to almost the whole work.

The emigrants who came at different periods to occupy the territory now covered by the American Union differed from each other in many respects; their aim was not the same, and they governed themselves on different principles. These men had, however, certain features in common, and they were all placed in an analogous situation. The tie of language is, perhaps, the strongest and the most durable that can unite mankind. All the emigrants spoke the same tongue; they were all offsets from the same people. Born in a country which had been agitated for centuries by the struggles of faction, and in which all parties had been obliged in their turn to place themselves under the protection of the laws, their political education had been perfected in this rude school; and they were more conversant with the notions of right, and the principles of true freedom, than the greater part of their European contemporaries. At the period of the first emigrations, the township system, that fruitful germ of free institutions, was deeply rooted in the habits of the English; and with it the doctrine of the sovereignty of the people had been introduced into the bosom of the monarchy of the house of Tudor. . . .

Another remark, to which we shall hereafter have occasion to 5 recur, is applicable not only to the English, but to . . . all the Europeans who successively established themselves in the New World. All these European colonies contained the elements, if not the development, of a complete democracy. Two causes led to this result. It may be said generally, that on leaving the mother country the emigrants had, in general, no notion of superiority one over another. The happy and the powerful do not go into exile, and there are no surer guaranties of equality among men than poverty and misfortune. It happened, however, on several occasions, that persons of rank were driven to America by political and religious quarrels. Laws were made to establish a gradation of ranks; but it was soon found that the soil of America was opposed to a territorial aristocracy. To bring that refractory land into cultivation, the constant and interested exertions of the owner himself were necessary; and when the ground was prepared, its produce was found to be insufficient to enrich a proprietor and a farmer at the same time. This land was then naturally broken up into small portions, which the proprietor cultivated for himself. Land is the basis of an aristocracy, which clings to the soil that supports it; for it is not by privileges alone, nor by birth, but by landed property handed down from generation to generation, that an aristocracy is constituted. A nation may present immense fortunes and extreme wretchedness; but unless those fortunes are territorial, there is no true aristocracy, but simply the class of the rich and that of the poor.

All the British colonies had then a great degree of family likeness at the epoch of their settlement. All of them, from their beginning, seemed destined to witness the growth, not of the aristocratic liberty of their mother country, but of that freedom of the middle and lower orders of which the history of the world had as yet furnished no complete example. In this general uniformity, however, several striking differences were discernible, which it is necessary to point out. Two branches may be distinguished in the great Anglo-American family, which have hitherto grown up without entirely commingling; the one in the South, the other in the North.

Virginia received the first English colony; the emigrants took possession of it in 1607. The idea that mines of gold and silver are the sources of national wealth was at that time singularly prevalent in Europe; a fatal delusion, which has done more to impoverish the European nations who adopted it, and has cost more lives in America, than the united influence of war and bad laws. The men sent to Virginia were seekers of gold, adventurers without resources and without character, whose turbulent and restless spirit endangered the infant colony, and rendered its progress uncertain. Artisans and agriculturists arrived afterwards; and, although they were a more moral and orderly race of men, they were hardly in any respect above the level of the inferior classes in England. No lofty views, no spiritual conception, presided over the foundation of these new settlements. The colony was scarcely established when slavery was introduced; this was the capital fact which was to exercise an immense influence on the character, the laws and the whole future of the South. Slavery . . . dishonors labor; it introduces idleness into society, and with idleness, ignorance and pride, luxury and distress. It enervates the powers of the mind, and benumbs the activity of man. The influence of slavery, united to the English character, explains the manners and the social condition of the Southern States.

In the North, the same English character . . . received totally different colors. Here . . . the two or three main ideas which now constitute the basis of the social theory of the United States were first combined. . . . They now extend their influence . . . over the whole American world. The civilization of New England has been like a beacon lit upon a hill, which, after it has diffused its warmth immediately around it, also tinges the distant horizon with its glow. . . .

The settlers who established themselves on the shores of New England all belonged to the more independent classes of their native country. Their union on the soil of America at once presented the singular phenomenon of a society containing neither lords nor common people, and we may almost say, neither rich nor poor. These men possessed, in proportion to their number, a greater mass of intelligence than is to be found in any European nation of our own time. All, perhaps without a single exception, had received a good education, and many of them were known in Europe for their talents and their acquirements. The other colonies had been founded by adventurers without families; the emigrants of New England brought with them the best elements of order and morality; they landed on the desert coast accompanied by their wives and children. But what especially distinguished them from all others was the aim of their undertaking. They had not been obliged by necessity to leave their country; the social position they abandoned was one to be regretted, and their means of subsistence were certain. . . . In facing the inevitable sufferings of exile, their object was the triumph of an idea.

The emigrants, or, as they deservedly styled themselves, the Pil- 10 grims, belonged to that English sect the austerity of whose principles had acquired for them the name of Puritans. Puritanism was not merely a religious doctrine, but it corresponded in many points with the most absolute democratic and republican theories. It was this tendency which had aroused its most dangerous adversaries. Persecuted by the government of the mother country, and disgusted by the habits of a society which the rigor of their own principles condemned, the Puritans went forth to seek some rude and unfrequented part of the world, where they could live according to their own opinions, and worship God in freedom. . . . Puritanism . . . was scarcely less a political than a religious doctrine. No sooner had the emigrants landed on the barren coast . . . than it was their first care to constitute a society, by subscribing the [Mayflower Compact]:

"In the name of God. Amen. We, whose names are underwritten, the loyal subjects of our dread Sovereign Lord King James, &s, &c., Having undertaken for the glory of God, and advancement of the Christian Faith, and the honour of our King and country, a voyage to plant the first colony in the northern parts of Virginia; Do by these presents solemnly and mutually, in the presence of God and one another, covenant and combine ourselves together into a civil body politick, for our better ordering and preservation, and furtherance of the ends aforesaid: and by virtue hereof do enact, constitute, and frame such just and equal laws, ordinances, acts, constitutions, and offices, from time to time, as shall be thought most meet and convenient for the general good of the Colony: unto which we promise all due submission and obedience. . . ."

This happened in 1620, and from that time forwards the emigration went on. The religious and political passions which ravaged the British empire during the whole reign of Charles I drove fresh crowds of sectarians every year to the shores of America. In England, the stronghold of Puritanism continued to be in the middle classes; and it was from the middle classes that most of the emigrants came. The population of New England increased rapidly; and whilst the hierarchy of rank despotically classed the inhabitants of the mother country, the colony approximated more and more the novel spectacle of a community homogeneous in all its parts. A democracy, more perfect than antiquity had dared to dream of, started in full size and panoply from the midst of an ancient feudal society.

For Journals

Whom do you think of as the first Americans?

For Discussion

1.   Why do you think Tocqueville frames his study of America and Americans using the analogy of studying the child to know the man? How does this image illuminate and clarify his purpose?

2.   To what in the Anglo Americans' history does Tocqueville attribute their knowledge of the principles of freedom? Are you persuaded by his conclusion? Do you think his contemporaries would have been?

3.   How does Tocqueville characterize New England and the Puritans? Pay special attention to the passages he cites to illuminate "the spirit of these pious adventurers." What conclusions does he draw from his evidence? Do you think his contemporary audience would have been convinced? Are you convinced of the Puritans' character based on the passage he cites?

4.   According to Tocqueville, what effects does slavery have on a society in general? What do you infer from his remark, "The influence of slavery, united to the English character, explains the manners and the social condition of the Southern states"?

5.   Tocqueville writes in paragraph 4, "The tie of language is, perhaps, the strongest and the most durable that can unite mankind." What assumption is he making about language and culture? How does this approach to culture define "American"? Do you agree with his assumption and with this definition? How do you think his contemporaries would have reacted to his assertion?

For Writing

1.   Drawing from your discussions in response to discussion items 3 and 4 above, write an essay in which you compare and contrast Tocqueville's treatment of North and South and the American identities that developed in each region. Which identity do you find more clearly articulated? Which assertions are more persuasive? Do you find his generalizations merited, based on the evidence he offers? How is your assessment of his argument biased by your own cultural or geographical identity?

2.   Tocqueville's discussion of a common language has had strong reverberations in recent debates over "English only" in schools and over policies establishing English as the official language of the United States. Research one of these issues, checking recent journal, newspaper, and magazine indexes for both educational journals and popular magazines, as well as books, so that you have up-to-date information. Develop a thesis about the topic and support it with well-reasoned arguments based on evidence from your research.

∞ *The U.S. Hotel Badly Needs a Bouncer* (ca. 1890)

JOSEPH KEPPLER

The following cartoon was published in Puck, *the first successful American weekly humor magazine.* Puck *was started in 1876 by Joseph Keppler, one of the well-known color cartoonist of the great age of political cartooning, which flourished from approximately 1870 to 1900. While other American magazines printed perhaps one cartoon per issue, Keppler published three a week in* Puck, *perhaps accounting in part for the magazine's popularity. Color cartoons at that time were larger than those we are used to today.* Puck, *for example, included full-page cartoons on the front and back covers and a two-page spread. This golden age of cartooning and the production of* Puck, *which was published until 1918, coincided with a huge influx of European immigrants in America—some 14 million between 1869 and 1900. It is not surprising that issues of immigration, and American identity, appeared as the subject matter for such cartoons.*

For Journals

Do you think there are certain people who should be encouraged to come to America or discouraged from coming?

For Discussion

1.   Study the cartoon, noting the figures and their appearance, their arrangement, the relationships between them, and their identities. What sorts of people are represented by which types of figures? Which are the "good" identities of qualities? Which are the undesirable traits?

2.   Discuss the overall point of the cartoon. From what evidence, or examples, did you infer that point? What assumptions about America, Americans, and immigrants are implied? State the cartoon's argument in your own words.

3.   Why do you believe the artist chose the metaphor of the hotel? What effect does this metaphor have on the argument? Do you believe America should be a hotel rather than a home? Should bouncers be able to evict people?

4.   How might the artist's contemporaries have reacted to the cartoon? Judging from the artist's persuasive strategies, what can you infer from the cartoon about immigration issues of the times? About the cartoon's audiences and their beliefs and values? Does the message seem more directed at getting people to behave well or encouraging them to regulate the behavior of others?

For Writing

1.   Compare the argument and assumptions in *The U.S. Hotel* with other selections in this chapter, such as Ralph Ellison's Prologue to *Invisible Man*. Alternatively, compare the persuasiveness of this cartoon with the posters in Chapter 10, "War and Violence." What common strategies or themes do you find?

2.   Select a recent social or political cartoon—from the editorial pages of a newspaper, for example—on an issue related to American identities, such as immigration. Compare and contrast the cartoon you choose with *The U.S. Hotel*, focusing on strategies of persuasion and the artists' implicit assumptions about their audiences.

3.   How do you think audiences have changed since this cartoon was published? In what ways have they remained the same? How have strategies or techniques of persuasion changed or remained the same?

∽ *Victory Liberty Loan*   (1919)

HOWARD CHANDLER CHRISTY

World War I began in Europe in 1914, and the United States entered the war in 1917. In the year and a half following the U.S. declaration of war, civilian efforts to support the war included some $18 billion in war-bond purchases. War bonds, or funds through which consumers lent money to the government at a modest interest rate, helped finance war matériel without harsh increases in federal income taxes; to some extent, bonds were said to help deal with currency inflation that can ensue when there are few consumer goods to buy. More important, though, Americans were also persuaded to "buy into" the war through purchasing bonds. William Gibbs McAdoo, who, was then secretary of the Treasury, wrote: "We went directly to the people, and that means to everybody—to business men, workmen, farmers, bankers, millionaires, school-teachers, laborers. We capitalized on the profound impulse called patriotism. It is the quality of coherence that holds a nation together; it is one of the deepest and most

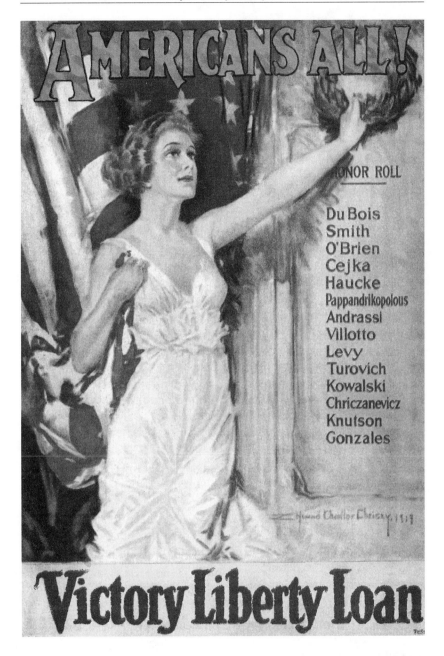

powerful of human motives." Artists such as Christy were commissioned to create posters to advertise the bonds, while film stars and others appeared at rallies to urge people to buy bonds—and to support the war. This particular design was quite successful both during and for some time after the war.

For Journals

What visual symbols remind you of America? What kinds of symbols appeal to your sense of patriotism?

For Discussion

1. What draws your eye when you first look at the poster? What are the poster's most prominent features? What did the artist want the viewer to see and feel first? Why?

2. Is the clothing of the female figure in the poster what you expect for its era? How would you account for her style of dress?

3. What do the wreath, the gold star, and the honor roll symbolize? (In what other contexts have you seen these symbols?) The woman is literally draping herself in the American flag. What do her posture and gestures suggest?

4. Read the list of names under the heading "Honor Roll" carefully. What do you notice? What point is the artist trying to make?

5. Who do you think was the intended audience for this poster? Explain your answer.

For Writing

1. Compare and contrast the assumptions about the American identity evident in this poster and in the cartoon *The U.S. Hotel.* Are the assumptions similar or different? Explain your assessment.

2. Select a modern advertisement that tries to appeal to Americans with a variety of ethnic heritages. Write an essay analyzing the choice of persuasive strategies in the ad and their effectiveness.

3. If you were asked to provide a poster or flyer to appeal to patriotism, what design choices would you make? Try to design such a poster or flyer (you may want to take an existing one and give it a patriotic edge), writing out the text and sketching the images you would use. Write an essay explaining your choices.

✑ *What the Indian Means to America* (1933)

LUTHER STANDING BEAR

Luther Standing Bear (1868–1947), a member of a Teton Sioux tribe, attended the government Indian school at Carlyle, Pennsylvania, and later worked in jobs ranging from storekeeper to minister to performer in Buffalo Bill's Wild West Show. Having lived during and observed firsthand the forcible removal of Native Americans to reser-

vations during the rapid expansion of the West, Standing Bear found the government practices untenable. His views are set out in My People the Sioux *(1928),* My Indian Boyhood *(1931),* Stories of the Sioux *(1934), and* Land of the Spotted Eagle *(1933), from which the following selection is excerpted. In this essay, Standing Bear identifies the American Indian as the one who truly understands the American lands.*

The feathered and blanketed figure of the American Indian has come to symbolize the American continent. He is the man who through centuries has been moulded and sculpted by the same hand that shaped its mountains, forests, and plains, and marked the course of its rivers.

The American Indian is of the soil, whether it be the region of forests, plains, pueblos, or mesas. He fits into the landscape, for the hand that fashioned the continent also fashioned the man for his surroundings. He once grew as naturally as the wild sunflowers; he belongs just as the buffalo belonged.

With a physique that fitted, the man developed fitting skills—crafts which today are called American. And the body had a soul, also formed and moulded by the same master hand of harmony. Out of the Indian approach to existence there came a great freedom—an intense and absorbing love for nature; a respect for life; enriching faith in a Supreme Power; and principles of truth, honesty, generosity, equity, and brotherhood as a guide to mundane relations. . . .

The white man does not understand the Indian for the reason that he does not understand America. He is too far removed from its formative processes. The roots of the tree of his life have not yet grasped the rock and soil. The white man is still troubled with primitive fears; he still has in his consciousness the perils of this frontier continent, some of its fastnesses not yet having yielded to his questing footsteps and inquiring eyes. He shudders still with the memory of the loss of his forefathers upon its scorching deserts and forbidding mountaintops. The man from Europe is still a foreigner and an alien. And he still hates the man who questioned his path across the continent.

But in the Indian the spirit of the land is still vested; it will be until 5 other men are able to divine and meet its rhythm. Men must be born and reborn to belong. Their bodies must be formed of the dust of their forefathers' bones.

The attempted transformation of the Indian by the white man and the chaos that has resulted are but the fruits of the white man's disobedience of a fundamental and spiritual law. The pressure that has been brought to bear upon the native people, since the cessation of armed conflict, in the attempt to force conformity of custom and habit has caused a reaction more destructive than war, and the injury has not only affected the Indian, but has extended to the white population as well. Tyranny, stupidity, and lack of vision have brought about the situation now alluded to as the "Indian Problem."

There is, I insist, no Indian problem as created by the Indian himself. Every problem that exists today in regard to the native population is due to the white man's cast of mind, which is unable, at least reluctant, to seek understanding and achieve adjustment in a new and a significant environment into which it has so recently come.

The white man excused his presence here by saying that he has been guided by the will of his God; and in so saying absolved himself of all responsibility for his appearance in a land occupied by other men.

Then, too, his law was a written law; his divine decalogue reposed in a book. And what better proof that his advent into this country and his subsequent acts were the result of divine will! He brought the Word! There ensued a blind worship of written history, of books, of the written word, that has denuded the spoken word of its power and sacredness. The written word became established as a criterion of the superior man—a symbol of emotional fineness. The man who could write his name on a piece of paper, whether or not he possessed the spiritual fineness to honor those words in speech, was by some miraculous formula a more highly developed and sensitized person than the one who had never had a pen in hand, but whose spoken word was inviolable and whose sense of honor and truth was paramount. With false reasoning was the quality of human character measured by man's ability to make with an implement a mark upon paper. But granting this mode of reasoning be correct and just, then where are to be placed the thousands of illiterate whites who are unable to read and write? Are they, too, "savages"? Is not humanness a matter of heart and mind, and is it not evident in the form of relationship with men? Is not kindness more powerful than arrogance; and truth more powerful than the sword?

True, the white man brought great change. But the varied fruits of 10 his civilization, though highly colored and inviting, are sickening and deadening. And if it be the part of civilization to maim, rob, and thwart, then what is progress? . . .

After subjugation, after dispossession, there was cast the last abuse upon the people who so entirely resented their wrongs and punishments, and that was the stamping and labeling of them as savages. To make this label stick has been the task of the white race and the greatest salve that it has been able to apply to its sore and troubled conscience now hardened through the habitual practice of injustice.

But all the years of calling the Indian a savage has never made him one; all the denial of his virtues has never taken them from him; and the very resistance he has made to save the things inalienably his has been his saving strength—that which will stand him in need when justice does make its belated appearance and he undertakes rehabilitation.

All sorts of feeble excuses are heard for the continued subjection of the Indian. One of the most common is that he is not yet ready to accept the society of the white man—that he is not yet ready to mingle as a social entity.

This, I maintain, is beside the question. The matter is not one of making over the external Indian into the likeness of the white race—a process detrimental to both races. Who can say that the white man's way is better for the Indian? Where resides the human judgment with the competence to weigh and value Indian ideals and spiritual concepts; or substitute for them other values?

Then, has the white man's social order been so harmonious and 15 ideal as to merit the respect of the Indian, and for that matter the thinking class of the white race? Is it wise to urge upon the Indian a foreign social form? Let none but the Indian answer!

Rather, let the white brother face about and cast his mental eye upon a new angle of vision. Let him look upon the Indian world as a human world; then let him see to it that human rights be accorded to the Indians. And this for the purpose of retaining for his own order of society a measure of humanity. . . .

The spiritual health and existence of the Indian was maintained by song, magic, ritual, dance, symbolism, oratory (or council), design, handicraft, and folk-story.

Manifestly, to check or thwart this expression is to bring about spiritual decline. And it is in this condition of decline that the Indian people are today. There is but a feeble effort among the Sioux to keep alive their traditional songs and dances, while among other tribes there is but a half-hearted attempt to offset the influence of the Government school and at the same time recover from the crushing and stifling regime of the Indian Bureau.

One has but to speak of Indian verse to receive uncomprehending and unbelieving glances. Yet the Indian loved verse and into this mode of expression went his deepest feelings. Only a few ardent and advanced students seem interested; nevertheless, they have given in book form enough Indian translations to set forth the character and quality of Indian verse.

Oratory receives a little better understanding on the part of the 20 white public, owing to the fact that oratorical complications include those of Indian orators.

Hard as it seemingly is for the white man's ear to sense the differences, Indian songs are as varied as the many emotions which inspire them, for no two of them are alike. For instance, the Song of Victory is spirited and the notes high and remindful of an unrestrained hunter or warrior riding exultantly over the prairies. On the other hand, the song of the *Cano unye* is solemn and full of urge, for it is meant to inspire the young men to deeds of valor. Then there are the songs of death and the spiritual songs which are connected with the ceremony of initiation. These are full of the spirit of praise and worship, and so strong are some of these invocations that the very air seems as if surcharged with the presence of the Big Holy.

The Indian loved to worship. From birth to death he revered his surroundings. He considered himself born in the luxurious lap of Mother Earth and no place was to him humble. There was nothing between him and the Big Holy. The contact was immediate and personal, and the blessings of Wakan Tanka flowed over the Indian like rain showered from the sky. Wakan Tanka was not aloof, apart, and ever seeking to quell evil forces. He did not punish the animals and the birds, and likewise He did not punish man. He was not a punishing God. For there was never a question as to the supremacy of an evil power over and above the power of Good. There was but one ruling power, and that was *Good.*

Of course, none but an adoring one could dance for days with his face to the sacred sun, and that time is all but done. We cannot have back the days of the buffalo and the beaver; we cannot win back our clean blood-stream and superb health, and we can never again expect the beautiful *rapport* we once had with Nature. The springs and lakes have dried and the mountains are bare of forests. The plow has changed the face of the world. Wi-wila is dead! No more may we heal our sick and comfort our dying with a strength founded on faith, for even the animals now fear us, and fear supplants faith.

And the Indian wants to dance! It is his way of expressing devotion, of communing with unseen power, and in keeping his tribal identity. When the Lakota heart was filled with high emotion, he danced. When he felt the benediction of the warming rays of the sun, he danced. When his blood ran hot with success of the hunt or chase, he danced. When his heart was filled with pity for the orphan, the lonely father, or bereaved mother, he danced. All the joys and exaltations of life, all his gratefulness and thankfulness, all his acknowledgments of the mysterious power that guided life, and all his aspirations for a better life, culminated in one great dance—the Sun Dance.

When the Indian has forgotten the music of his forefathers, when 25 the sound of the tomtom is no more, when noisy jazz has drowned the melody of the flute, he will be a dead Indian. When the memory of his heroes are no longer told in story, and he forsakes the beautiful white buckskin for factory shoddy, he will be dead. When from him has been taken all that is his, all that he has visioned in nature, all that has come to him from infinite sources, he then, truly, will be a dead Indian. His spirit will be gone, and though he walk crowded streets, he will, in truth, be—*dead!*

But all this must not perish; it must live, to the end that America shall be educated no longer to regard native production of whatever tribe—folk-story, basketry, pottery, dance, song, poetry—as curios, and native artists as curiosities. For who but the man indigenous to the soil could produce its song, story, and folk-tale; who but the man who loved the dust beneath his feet could shape it and put it into undying, ceramic form; who but he who loved the reeds that grew beside still waters, and the damp roots of shrub and tree, could save it from seasonal death, and with almost superhuman patience weave it into enduring objects of beauty—into timeless art!

Regarding the "civilization" that has been thrust upon me since the days of reservation, it has not added one whit to my sense of justice; to my reverence for the rights of life; to my love for truth, honesty, and generosity; nor to my faith in Wakan Tanka—God of the Lakotas. For after all the great religions have been preached and expounded, or have been revealed by brilliant scholars, or have been written in books and embellished in fine language with finer covers, man—all man—is still confronted with the Great Mystery.

So if today I had a young mind to direct, to start on the journey of life, and I was faced with the duty of choosing between the natural way of my forefathers and that of the white man's present way of civilization, I would, for its welfare, unhesitatingly set that child's feet in the path of my forefathers. I would raise him to be an Indian!

For Journals

What do you know about the relationship between American Indians and the land?

For Discussion

1. How does Standing Bear establish the argument that the American Indian is not only the true symbol but also the essence of the American continent? In what ways do the American Indian and the land share an identity?

2. Standing Bear contrasts the American Indians and the whites in terms of their relationship with the land. What does he mean when he asserts that "in the Indian the spirit of the land is still vested"? How can others inherit that spirit?

3. According to Standing Bear, in what ways are whites foreigners in America? What kind of assimilation do white people need to undergo so as not to be aliens? How is this process similar to and different from other kinds of assimilation you have heard of?

4. How have the pressure and "conformity of custom" injured both American Indians and whites?

5. How do whites justify their presence in America and their subjugation of Indians? How does the author refute these arguments? Standing Bear published this selection in 1933 as part of a larger work. How do you think his audiences responded to the initial arguments of whites and to Standing Bear's refutation? How do you respond?

For Writing

1.   Write an essay summarizing Standing Bear's definition of a true American and then either offer support for or refute his position.

2.   Research the Trail of Tears, the establishing of the reservation system, or some other specific issue in the history of Indian-white relations in America, and write a documented essay explaining the issue or event. Alternatively, investigate the current status of the relationship between one or more of the Native American nations and the U.S. government, focusing on the degree to which Indian-white relations have, or have not, changed since the publication of Standing Bear's books in the late 1920s and early 1930s.

∞ *Prologue to* Invisible Man   (1947)

RALPH ELLISON

Born in Oklahoma in 1914 and educated at the Tuskegee Institute in Alabama, Ralph Ellison established his considerable reputation with his first and only novel, Invisible Man, *first published in 1947 and reprinted numerous times since, most recently in 1990. This selection from the Prologue is typical of Ellison's lyrical and unflinching portrayal of black identity in American society, an identity the novelist has fleshed out more fully in collections of essays such as* Shadow and Act *(1964) and* Going to the Territory *(1986). Ellison lectured at Yale, Columbia, and New York Universities, and remains a dominant figure on the American literary landscape even after his death in 1994.*

I am an invisible man. No, I am not a spook like those who haunted Edgar Allan Poe; nor am I one of your Hollywood-movie ectoplasms. I am a man of substance, of flesh and bone, fiber and liquids—and I might even be said to possess a mind. I am invisible, understand, simply because people refuse to see me. Like the bodiless heads you see sometimes in circus sideshows, it is as though I have been surrounded by mirrors of hard, distorting glass. When they approach me they see only my surroundings, themselves, or figments of their imagination—indeed, everything and anything except me.

Nor is my invisibility exactly a matter of a biochemical accident to my epidermis. That invisibility to which I refer occurs because of a peculiar disposition of the eyes of those with whom I come in contact. A matter of the construction of their *inner* eyes, those eyes with which they look through their physical eyes upon reality. I am not complaining, nor am I protesting either. It is sometimes advantageous to be unseen, although it is most often rather wearing on the nerves. Then too, you're constantly being bumped against by those of poor vision. Or again, you often doubt if you really exist. You wonder whether you aren't simply a phantom in other people's minds. Say, a figure in a nightmare which the sleeper tries with all his strength to destroy. It's when you feel like this that, out of resentment, you begin to bump people back. And, let me confess, you feel that way most of the time. You ache with the need to convince yourself that you do exist in the real world, that you're a part of all the sound and anguish, and you strike out with your fists, you curse and you swear to make them recognize you. And, alas, it's seldom successful.

One night I accidentally bumped into a man, and perhaps because of the near darkness he saw me and called me an insulting name. I sprang at him, seized his coat lapels and demanded that he apologize. He was a tall blond man, and as my face came close to his he looked insolently out of his blue eyes and cursed me, his breath hot in my face as he struggled. I pulled his chin down sharp upon the crown of my head, butting him as I had seen the West Indians do, and I felt his flesh tear and the blood gush out, and I yelled, "Apologize! Apologize!" But he continued to curse and struggle, and I butted him again and again until he went down heavily, on his knees, profusely bleeding. I kicked him repeatedly, in a frenzy because he still uttered insults though his lips were frothy with blood. Oh yes, I kicked him! And in my outrage I got out my knife and prepared to slit his throat, right there beneath the lamplight in the deserted street, holding him in the collar with one hand, and opening the knife with my teeth—when it occurred to me that the man had not *seen* me, actually; that he, as far as he knew, was in the midst of a walking nightmare! And I stopped the blade, slicing the air as I pushed him away, letting him fall back to the street. I stared at him hard as the lights of a car stabbed through the darkness. He lay there, moaning on the asphalt; a man almost killed by a phantom. It unnerved me. I was both disgusted and ashamed. I was like a drunken man myself, wavering about on weakened legs. Then I was amused: Something in this man's thick head had sprung out and beaten him within an inch of his life. I began to laugh at this crazy discovery. Would he have awakened at the point of death? Would Death himself have freed him for wakeful living? But I didn't linger. I ran away into the dark, laughing so hard I feared I might rupture myself. The next day I saw his picture in the *Daily News*, beneath a caption stating that he had been "mugged." Poor fool, poor blind fool, I thought with sincere compassion, mugged by an invisible man!

Most of the time (although I do not choose as I once did to deny the violence of my days by ignoring it) I am not so overtly violent. I remember that I am invisible and walk softly so as not to awaken the sleeping ones. Sometimes it is best not to awaken them; there are few things in the world as dangerous as sleepwalkers. I learned in time though that it is possible to carry on a fight against them without their realizing it. For instance, I have been carrying on a fight with Monopolated Light & Power for some time now. I use their service and pay them nothing at all, and they don't know it. Oh, they suspect that power is being drained off, but they don't know where. All they know is that according to the master meter back there in their power station a hell of a lot of free current is disappearing somewhere into the jungle of Harlem. The joke, of course, is that I don't live in Harlem but in a border area. Several years ago (before I discovered the advantages of being invisible) I went through the routine process of buying service and paying their outrageous rates. But no more. I gave up all that, along with my apartment, and my old way of life: That way based upon the fallacious assumption that I, like other men, was visible. Now, aware of my invisibility, I live rent-free in a building rented strictly to whites, in a section of the basement that was shut off and forgotten during the nineteenth century, which I discovered when I was trying to escape in the night from Ras the Destroyer. But that's getting too far ahead of the story, almost to the end, although the end is in the beginning and lies far ahead.

The point now is that I found a home—or a hole in the ground, as 5 you will. Now don't jump to any conclusion that because I call my home a "hole" it is damp and cold like a grave; there are cold holes and warm holes. Mine is a warm hole. And remember, a bear retires to his hole for the winter and lives until spring; then he comes strolling out like the Easter chick breaking from its shell. I say all this to assure you that it is incorrect to assume that, because I'm invisible and live in a hole, I am dead. I am neither dead nor in a state of suspended animation. Call me Jack-the-Bear, for I am in a state of hibernation.

My hole is warm and full of light. Yes, *full* of light. I doubt if there is a brighter spot in all New York than this hole of mine, and I do not exclude Broadway. Or the Empire State Building on a photographer's dream night. But that is taking advantage of you. Those two spots are among the darkest of our whole civilization—pardon me, our whole *culture* (an important distinction, I've heard)—which might sound like a hoax, or a contradiction, but that (by contradiction, I mean) is how the world moves: Not like an arrow, but a boomerang. (Beware of those who speak of the *spiral* of history; they are preparing a boomerang. Keep a steel helmet handy.) I know; I have been boomeranged across my head so much that I now can see the darkness of lightness. And I love light. Perhaps you'll think it strange that an invisible man should need light, desire light, love light. But maybe it is exactly because I *am* invisible. Light confirms my reality, gives birth to my form. A beautiful girl once told me of a recurring nightmare in which she lay in the center of a large dark room and felt her face expand until it filled the whole room, becoming a formless mass while her eyes ran in bilious jelly up the chimney. And so it is with me. Without light I am not only invisible, but formless as well; and to be unaware of one's form is to live a death. I myself, after existing some twenty years, did not become alive until I discovered my invisibility.

For Journals

Are there groups of people in your community—ethnic minorities, older people, disabled people—whom you rarely notice?

For Discussion

1. How is the notion of invisibility developed in this selection? Why do you think Ellison uses the idea of invisibility? What associations does it have? What could a person do—or not do—if invisible?

2. The speaker notes that he found a home, a "hole in the ground," literally in a basement of a building restricted to whites. What is significant about his living in such a place? What is special, literally and metaphorically, about the light and the power company?

3. In what sense is the invisible man's identity related to and developed by how others see him? Consider his growing awareness of being invisible, the incident with the blond stranger, and his relationship with the power company.

4. In an introduction to *Invisible Man* that accompanied an edition printed in 1981, Ellison writes, "My task was one of revealing the human universals hidden within the plight of one who was both black and an American." What do you infer from this selection about the plight of those who live with this double identity?

For Writing

1. Write an essay discussing the effects of others' perceptions on developing one's own identity, whether in terms of ethnicity, race, culture, nationality, or age. You could develop this assignment as a personal essay; alternatively, you could investigate and incorporate recent research on the subject, found in psychology or sociology books and journals.

2. Ellison wrote that his task in *Invisible Man* was to deal with "the sheer rhetorical challenge involved in communicating across our barriers of race and religion, class, color, and region—barriers which consist of the many strategies of division that were designed, and still function, to prevent what would otherwise have been a more or less natural recognition of the reality of blackness." How does he cope with the rhetorical challenges—obstacles to persuasion—he mentions here? In what ways do his metaphor of invisibility and the voice and tone of the speaker serve to meet those challenges?

∞ *Inaugural Address* (1961)

JOHN F. KENNEDY

*John Fitzgerald Kennedy (1917–1963) was born in Brookline, Massachusetts,
and graduated from Harvard University. He served as a torpedo boat commander in
the Pacific during World War II and received both the Navy Medal and the Purple
Heart for his service. For his book* Profiles in Courage *(1956) Kennedy won the
Pulitzer Prize, and after a career in Congress he became the youngest elected and first
Roman Catholic president. His administration was cut tragically short when rifle fire
from an assassin in Dallas, Texas, ended his life in 1963. Kennedy's famous inaugural
address exemplifies the youth, vitality, and vision of a generation and remains a classic of American rhetoric.*

We observe today not a victory of party but a celebration of freedom—symbolizing an end as well as a beginning, signifying renewal
as well as change. For I have sworn before you and Almighty God the
same solemn oath our forebears prescribed nearly a century and three-
quarters ago.

The world is very different now. For man holds in his mortal
hands the power to abolish all forms of human poverty and all forms
of human life. And yet the same revolutionary beliefs for which our
forebears fought are still at issue around the globe: the belief that the
rights of man come not from the generosity of the state but from the
hand of God.

We dare not forget today that we are the heirs of that first revolution. Let the word go forth from this time and place, to friend and foe
alike, that the torch has been passed to a new generation of Americans—born in this century, tempered by war, disciplined by a hard
and bitter peace, proud of our ancient heritage—and unwilling to witness or permit the slow undoing of those human rights to which this
nation has always been committed, and to which we are committed
today at home and around the world.

Let every nation know, whether it wishes us well or ill, that we
shall pay any price, bear any burden, meet any hardship, support any
friend, oppose any foe to assure the survival and the success of liberty.

This much we pledge—and more.   5

To those old allies whose cultural and spiritual origins we share,
we pledge the loyalty of faithful friends. United, there is little we cannot do in a host of cooperative ventures. Divided, there is little we
can do—for we dare not meet a powerful challenge at odds and split
asunder.

To those new states whom we welcome to the ranks of the free, we
pledge our word that one form of colonial control shall not have
passed away merely to be replaced by a far more iron tyranny. We

shall not always expect to find them supporting our view. But we shall always hope to find them strongly supporting their own freedom—and to remember that, in the past, those who foolishly sought power by riding the back of the tiger ended up inside.

To those people in the huts and villages of half the globe struggling to break the bonds of mass misery, we pledge our best efforts to help them help themselves, for whatever period is required—not because the Communists may be doing it, not because we seek their votes, but because it is right. If a free society cannot help the many who are poor, it cannot save the few who are rich.

To our sister republics south of the border, we offer a special pledge: to convert our good words into good deeds—in a new alliance for progress—to assist free men and free governments in casting off the chains of poverty. But this peaceful revolution of hope cannot become the prey of hostile powers. Let all our neighbors know that we shall join with them to oppose aggression or subversion anywhere in the Americas. And let every other power know that this hemisphere intends to remain the master of its own house.

To that world assembly of sovereign states, the United Nations, 10 our last best hope in an age where the instruments of war have far outpaced the instruments of peace, we renew our pledge of support—to prevent it from becoming merely a forum for invective, to strengthen its shield of the new and the weak, and to enlarge the area in which its writ may run.

Finally, to those nations who would make themselves our adversary, we offer not a pledge but a request: that both sides begin anew the quest for peace, before the dark powers of destruction unleashed by science engulf all humanity in planned or accidental self-destruction.

We dare not tempt them with weakness. For only when our arms are sufficient beyond doubt can we be certain beyond doubt that they will never be employed.

But neither can two great and powerful groups of nations take comfort from our present course—both sides overburdened by the cost of modern weapons, both rightly alarmed by the steady spread of the deadly atom, yet both racing to alter that uncertain balance of terror that stays the hand of mankind's final war.

So let us begin anew, remembering on both sides that civility is not a sign of weakness, and sincerity is always subject to proof. Let us never negotiate out of fear. But let us never fear to negotiate.

Let both sides explore what problems unite us instead of belabor- 15 ing those problems which divide us.

Let both sides, for the first time, formulate serious and precise proposals for the inspection and control of arms—and bring the absolute power to destroy other nations under the absolute control of all nations.

Let both sides seek to invoke the wonders of science instead of its terrors. Together let us explore the stars, conquer the deserts, eradicate disease, tap the ocean depths, and encourage the arts and commerce.

Let both sides unite to heed in all corners of the earth the command of Isaiah—to "undo the heavy burdens . . . [and] let the oppressed go free."

And if a beachhead of cooperation may push back the jungle of suspicion, let both sides join in creating a new endeavor, not a new balance of power, but a new world of law, where the strong are just and the weak secure and the peace preserved.

All this will not be finished in the first one hundred days. Nor will 20
it be finished in the first one thousand days, nor in the life of this administration, nor even perhaps in our lifetime on this planet. But let us begin.

In your hands, my fellow citizens, more than mine, will rest the final success or failure of our course. Since this country was founded, each generation of Americans has been summoned to give testimony to its national loyalty. The graves of young Americans who answered the call to service surround the globe.

Now the trumpet summons us again—not as a call to bear arms, though arms we need; not as a call to battle, though embattled we are—but a call to bear the burden of a long twilight struggle, year in and year out, "rejoicing in hope, patient in tribulation," a struggle against the common enemies of man: tyranny, poverty, disease, and war itself.

Can we forge against these enemies a grand and global alliance, north and south, east and west, that can assure a more fruitful life for all mankind? Will you join in that historic effort?

In the long history of the world, only a few generations have been granted the role of defending freedom in its hour of maximum danger. I do not shrink from this responsibility—I welcome it. I do not believe that any of us would exchange places with any other people or any other generation. The energy, the faith, the devotion which we bring to this endeavor will light our country and all who serve it—and the glow from that fire can truly light the world.

And so, my fellow Americans: Ask not what your country can do 25
for you—ask what you can do for your country.

My fellow citizens of the world: Ask not what America will do for you, but what together we can do for the freedom of man.

Finally, whether you are citizens of America or citizens of the world, ask of us here the same high standards of strength and sacrifice which we ask of you. With a good conscience our only sure reward, with history the final judge of our deeds, let us go forth to lead the land we love, asking His blessing and His help, but knowing that here on earth God's work must truly be our own.

For Journals

What have you learned, from people older than you or in the media, about the Kennedy administration? What images, expressions, and values come to mind?

For Discussion

1. Identify the audience for and purpose of an inaugural address. What special demands do they place on the speaker? Kennedy was not only the youngest and first-ever Catholic president elected; he also won by an exceedingly narrow margin. What additional demands did he need to meet? What strategies did he use to meet these demands? Was he successful?

2. How does Kennedy define his generation? How does he link these definitions to the goals of his administration?

3. What rhetorical strategies does Kennedy use to unite his audience and evoke a sense of shared purpose? Focus specifically on word choice and on literary or biblical allusions in the speech. How do you think most people in Kennedy's audience reacted, either consciously or unconsciously, to his words? Do you think such a speech would be suitable for an audience of your contemporaries? Why or why not?

4. Study the themes of the address. What do you infer about how Americans at that time defined their role in international affairs? In what ways does their identity rest on a contrast with the Soviet Union?

5. Kennedy draws a particular portrait of America and Americans. Write out or discuss in your own words the visions, goals, and ideas either suggested by or articulated in the speech.

For Writing

1. Choose a topic from one of the burning issues of the early 1960s—civil rights, space exploration, communism, youth culture, rock music, free speech, or something else—to explore. Develop a research question; then collect information by reading books and essays on the topic and also by finding and evaluating magazines, newspapers, television shows, radio broadcasts, and music lyrics or albums of the time that were written on the topic. Try to interview people who were young adults at the time. Develop your findings into a presentation to share with your peers.

2. Communicating clearly through a speech is different from communicating through writing. Good public speakers must take advantage of word choice, strong organization, parallelism, rhythm, and other elements of style to make their points. In other words, they take many features of good prose and accentuate them. Write an essay analyzing the use of one or more of these stylistic features in Kennedy's address. Try to show how the president used stylistic devices to emphasize his themes.

∞ *"Local Politics,"* FROM An Explanation of America (1979)

ROBERT PINSKY

Robert Pinsky (1940–) Poet Laureate of the United States and professor at Boston University, grew up in Long Branch, New Jersey. In addition to a best-selling translation of Dante's Inferno, *he has published four volumes of original poems, most recently collected in* The Figured Wheel: 1966–1996; The Sounds of Poetry: A Brief Guide, *and an anthology of poems,* Handbook of Heartbreak, *are forthcoming. As other poets laureate had done, notably Robert Hass and Rita Dove, Pinsky has worked to bring a larger audience to poetry, developing, for example, the Favorite Poem Archive through which one thousand citizens from all professions and backgrounds have been invited to record their favorite poems in what has been termed a "cultural database." Pinsky, who is also poetry editor for the on-line magazine* SLATE, *has received numerous awards for his poems, translations, and prose works. The selection that follows, "Local Politics," is from a section of the long poem subtitled, "Its Many Fragments."*

III. Local Politics

And so the things the country wants to see
Are like a nest made out of circumstance;
And when, as in the great old sermon "The Eagle
Stirreth Her Nest," God like a nesting eagle
Pulls out a little of the plush around us   5
And lets the thorns of trial, and the bramble,
Stick through and scrape and threaten the fledgling soul,
We see that that construction of thorn and bramble
Is like a cage: the tight and sheltering cage
Of Law and circumstance, scraping through the plush   10
Like death—whenever the eagle stirreth her nest,
The body with its bony cage of law
And politics, the thorn of death and taxes.

You, rich in rhetoric and indignation,
The jailbird-lawyer of the Hunnewell School,   15
Come home from some small, wicked parliament
To elaborate a new theme: forceful topics
Touching the sheeplike, piggish ways of that tyrant

And sycophantic lout, the Majority.
The two lame cheers for democracy that I   20
Borrow and try to pass to you ("It is
The worst of all the forms of government,
Except for all the others"—Winston Churchill)
You brush aside: Political Science bores you,
You prefer the truth, and with a Jesuit firmness   25
Return to your slogan: "Voting *is not* fair."
I have another saw that I can scrape
For you, out of the hoard of antique hardy
Cliches and Great Ideas, quaintly-toothed
Black ironwork that we heap about our youth   30
Voting is one of the *"necessary evils."*
Avoid all groups and institutions, they
Are necessary evils: necessary
Unto the general Happiness and Safety,
And evil because they are deficient in being.   35
Such is the hardware; and somewhere in between
The avoidance and the evil necessity
We each conclude a contract with the Beast.

America is, as Malcolm X once said,
A prison. And that the world and all its parts   40
Are also prisons (Chile, the Hunnewell School,
One's own deficient being, each prison after
It's own degree and kind), does not diminish
Anything that he meant about his country:
When the Dan Ryan Expressway in Chicago   45
Was flooded, "Black youths" who the paper said
Pillaged the stranded motorists like beached whales
Were rioting prisoners . . . a weight of lead
Sealed in their hearts was lighter for some minutes
Amid the riot.   50
                    Living inside a prison,
Within its many other prisons, what
Should one aspire to be? a kind of chaplain?
But chaplains, I have heard, are often powers,
Political, within their prisons, patrons   55
And mediators between the frightened groups:
Blue People, Gray People, and their constricting fears,
The mutual circumstance of ward and warder.

No kind of chaplain ever will mediate
Among the conquering, crazed immigrants   60
Of El Camino and the Bergen Mall,

The Jews who dream up the cowboy films, the Blacks
Who dream the music, the people who dream the cars
And ways of voting, the Japanese and Basques
Each claiming a special sense of humor, as do   65
Armenian photo-engravers, and the people
Who dream the saws: *"You cannot let men live*
Like pigs, and make them freemen, it is not safe,"
The people who dream up the new diseases
For use in warfare, the people who design   70
New shapes of pants, and sandwiches sumptuous
Beyond the dreams of innocent Europe: crazed
As carpet-bombing or the Berlin Airlift—
Crazed immigrants and prisoners, rioting
Or else, alone as in the secrecy   75
Of a narrow bunk or cell, whittling or painting
Some desperate weapon or crude work of art:
A spoon honed to a dagger or a bauble,
A pistol molded from a cake of soap,
A fumbling poem or a lurid picture   80
Urgent and sentimental as a tattoo. . . .
The Dorians, too, were conquering immigrants,
And hemmed in by their own anarchic spirits
And new peninsula, they too resorted
To invented institutions, and the vote,   85
With a spirit nearly comic, and in fear.

The plural-headed Empire, manifold
Beyond my outrage or my admiration,
Is like a prison which I leave to you
(And like a shelter)—where the people vote,   90
And where the threats of riot and oppression
Inspire the inmates as they whittle, scribble,
Jockey for places in the choir, or smile
Passing out books on weekdays.
                                   On the radio,   95
The FM station that plays "All Country and Western"
Startled me, when I hit its button one day,
With a voice—inexplicable and earnest—
In Vietnamese or Chinese, lecturing
Or selling, or something someone wanted broadcast,   100
A paid political announcement, perhaps. . . .
"All politics is local politics"
Said Mayor Daley (in pentameter):
And this then is the locus where we vote,

Prisonyard fulcrum of knowledge, fear and work—   105
Nest where an Eagle balances and screams,
The wild bird with its hardware in its claws.

For Journals

What is your impression of "local politics" in America? Did the 2000 elections affect your views of local or national politics in America? Explain.

For Discussion

1.   Read the poem outloud, and read it at least twice before discussion. Does the language seem to be "elevated diction" or does it sound like everyday English? Give examples from the text.

2.   Examine the metaphors and allusions in the text. In what way do they contribute to your understanding of the poem? Select one of the references, and, based on your knowledge or your research, explain what you think the reference contributes to the poem's meaning. For example, why might the image of the eagle open and close this selection?

3.   The narrator refers to several cliches or old "saws" or slogans about democracy and specifically about voting. How do you interpret his assertions? What do you believe to be the narrator's point of view? Whom might he be addressing? Focus on specific assertions, such as that "Voting is one of the *'necessary evils'*" and the explanation of that term that follows.

4.   How do you interpret the point that America is a prison? For whom? And how so? What would it mean to be the chaplain in a prison?

5.   Near the end of the selection, the narrator is startled when the FM station that plays "All Country and Western" suddenly features a Chinese or Vietnamese speaker. What does this image say about America? How might it "explain" America?

For Writing

1.   Using discussion question 2 as a starting point, write an essay analyzing the imagery of this poem.

2.   Assuming a reader who would argue that the majority is indeed a "tyrant and sycophantic lout," write a paper arguing for the rule of the majority and the importance of the vote.

3. Considering the events of the 2000 elections, would you agree that voting is "one of the 'necessary evils' . . . necessary / Unto the general Happiness and Safety, / And evil because they are deficient in being"? Discuss.

4. Research one or several of the references in this poem, perhaps working with fellow students to write brief explanations of each and putting your findings together in an annotation of this poem that you contribute to your classroom or school library.

∽ The Cult of Ethnicity (1991)

ARTHUR M. SCHLESINGER JR.

Arthur M. Schlesinger, Jr. (1917–), educator and historian, is well known for his service during the Kennedy and Johnson administrations. His books, which have earned him awards such as the Pulitzer Prize and National Book Award, include The Age of Jackson *(1945),* The Age of Roosevelt *(1957, 1959, 1960),* A Thousand Days: John F. Kennedy in the White House *(1965),* Robert Kennedy and His Times *(1978), and, more recently,* The Disuniting of America *(1992). The following essay appeared in* Time *magazine.*

The history of the world has been in great part the history of the mixing of peoples. Modern communication and transport accelerate mass migrations from one continent to another. Ethnic and racial diversity is more than ever a salient fact of the age.

But what happens when people of different origins, speaking different languages and professing different religions, inhabit the same locality and live under the same political sovereignty? Ethnic and racial conflict—far more than ideological conflict—is the explosive problem of our times.

On every side today ethnicity is breaking up nations. The Soviet Union, India, Yugoslavia, Ethiopia, are all in crisis. Ethnic tensions disturb and divide Sri Lanka, Burma, Indonesia, Iraq, Cyprus, Nigeria, Angola, Lebanon, Guyana, Trinidad—you name it. Even nations as stable and civilized as Britain and France, Belgium and Spain, face growing ethnic troubles. Is there any large multiethnic state that can be made to work?

The answer to that question has been, until recently, the United States. "No other nation," Margaret Thatcher has said, "has so successfully combined people of different races and nations within a single culture." How have Americans succeeded in pulling off this almost unprecedented trick?

We have always been a multiethnic country. Hector St. John de 5 Crèvecoeur, who came from France in the 18th century, marveled at the astonishing diversity of the settlers—"a mixture of English, Scotch, Irish, French, Dutch, Germans and Swedes ... this promiscuous breed." He propounded a famous question: "What then is the American, this new man?" And he gave a famous answer: "Here individuals of all nations are melted into a new race of men." *E pluribus unum.*

The U.S. escaped the divisiveness of a multiethnic society by a brilliant solution: the creation of a brand-new national identity. The point of America was not to preserve old cultures but to forge a new, American culture. "By an intermixture with our people," President George Washington told Vice President John Adams, immigrants will "get assimilated to our customs, measures and laws: in a word, soon become one people." This was the ideal that a century later Israel Zangwill crystallized in the title of his popular 1908 play *The Melting Pot.* And no institution was more potent in molding Crèvecoeur's "promiscuous breed" into Washington's "one people" than the American public school.

The new American nationality was inescapably English in language, ideas and institutions. The pot did not melt everybody, not even all the white immigrants; deeply bred racism put black Americans, yellow Americans, red Americans and brown Americans well outside the pale. Still, the infusion of other stocks, even of nonwhite stocks, and the experience of the New World reconfigured the British legacy and made the U.S., as we all know, a very different country from Britain.

In the 20th century, new immigration laws altered the composition of the American people, and a cult of ethnicity erupted both among non-Anglo whites and among nonwhite minorities. This had many healthy consequences. The American culture at last began to give shamefully overdue recognition to the achievements of groups subordinated and spurned during the high noon of Anglo dominance, and it began to acknowledge the great swirling world beyond Europe. Americans acquired a more complex and invigorating sense of their world—and of themselves.

But, pressed too far, the cult of ethnicity has unhealthy consequences. It gives rise, for example, to the conception of the U.S. as a nation composed not of individuals making their own choices but of inviolable ethnic and racial groups. It rejects the historic American goals of assimilation and integration.

And, in an excess of zeal, well-intentioned people seek to trans- 10 form our system of education from a means of creating "one people" into a means of promoting, celebrating and perpetuating separate ethnic origins and identities. The balance is shifting from *unum* to *pluribus.*

That is the issue that lies behind the hullabaloo over "multiculturalism" and "political correctness," the attack on the "Eurocentric" curriculum and the rise of the notion that history and literature should be taught not as disciplines but as therapies whose function is to raise minority self-esteem. Group separatism crystallizes the differences, magnifies tensions, intensifies hostilities. Europe—the unique source of the liberating ideas of democracy, civil liberties and human rights—is portrayed as the root of all evil, and non-European cultures, their own many crimes deleted, are presented as the means of redemption.

I don't want to sound apocalyptic about these developments. Education is always in ferment, and a good thing too. The situation in our universities, I am confident, will soon right itself. But the impact of separatist pressures on our public schools is more troubling. If a Kleagle of the Ku Klux Klan wanted to use the schools to disable and handicap black Americans, he could hardly come up with anything more effective than the "Afrocentric" curriculum. And if separatist tendencies go unchecked, the result can only be the fragmentation, resegregation and tribalization of American life.

I remain optimistic. My impression is that the historic forces driving toward "one people" have not lost their power. The eruption of ethnicity is, I believe, a rather superficial enthusiasm stirred by romantic ideologues on the one hand and by unscrupulous con men on the other: self-appointed spokesmen whose claim to represent their minority groups is carelessly accepted by the media. Most American-born members of minority groups, white or nonwhite, see themselves primarily as Americans rather than primarily as members of one or another ethnic group. A notable indicator today is the rate of intermarriage across ethnic lines, across religious lines, even (increasingly) across racial lines. "We Americans," said Theodore Roosevelt, "are children of the crucible."

The growing diversity of the American population makes the quest for unifying ideals and a common culture all the more urgent. In a world savagely rent by ethnic and racial antagonisms, the U.S. must continue as an example of how a highly differentiated society holds itself together.

For Journals

What are your beliefs about what makes someone "American"?

For Discussion

1.   What does Schlesinger mean by "the cult of ethnicity"? Do you agree with his definition? What is his assertion about it? What evidence does he offer for support? What counterpoints does he neglect?

2.   The author suggests that a focus on ethnicity, if "pressed too far," results in rejecting assimiliation and integration. Do you agree that re-

jecting these historic goals is unhealthy? How do you think the author defines "too far"? How should a society determine when the focus on ethnicity, at the expense of assimilation, has gone too far?

3.   Set up a debate in your whole class, with half the class taking the "assimilation" perspective and half the class arguing for recognizing ethnic diversity. Have someone keep track of the main points made by each side, on the board or overhead projector. Then, evaluate the merit and persuasiveness of arguments made on each side. (This activity could also be carried out in small groups.)

4.   Do you agree with the author's assertion that "most American-born members of minority groups, white or nonwhite, see themselves primarily as American rather than primarily as members of one or another ethnic group"? Discuss, providing evidence to support your view.

For Writing

1.   Using material developed in discussion item 3, write a response to Schlesinger arguing in favor of maintaining unique ethnic cultural traditions and groups in American society. Be sure to respond to his main points as you shape your own argument.

2.   If you agree with Schlesinger, write an argument that takes the same stand and responds to Schlesinger's likely critics, again using material generated in discussion item 3 as a starting point.

3.   How would one of the other authors in this chapter respond to Schlesinger? Create an imaginary dialogue between Schlesinger and Ellison, Standing Bear, or Serrano, debating one or more of the key points raised in this essay.

∞ Prospero Unbound: The Market Revolution (1993)

RONALD TAKAKI

Ronald Takaki (1939–), who is the grandson of Japanese plantation laborers in Hawaii, is a professor in Asian American studies and ethnic studies at the University of California at Berkeley, as well as a proponent of multicultural education. He holds a Ph.D. in American history. In 1988 Takaki was awarded the Goldwin Smith University Lectureship at Cornell University and became the Distinguished Messenger Lecturer, Cornell's most prestigious lecturer appointment, in 1993. His publications include Iron Cages: Race and Culture in 19th Century America *(1979),* Pau Hana: Plantation Life and Labor in Hawaii *(1983),* Strangers from a Different

Shore: A History of Asian Americans *(1989), and the work in which this selection was published,* A Different Mirror: A History of Multicultural America *(1993). Forthcoming is the book* Hiroshima: Why America Dropped the Atomic Bomb.

Like John Winthrop, Jefferson believed Americans had a special destiny and responsibility: "The eyes of the virtuous all over the earth are turned with anxiety upon us, as the only depositories of the sacred fire of liberty, and . . . our falling into anarchy would decide forever the destinies of mankind, and seal the political heresy that man is incapable of self-government." Here was a republican vision of "the city upon a hill." To be self-governing meant that men in America no longer needed a parent country, especially a king. Like Prospero, they would re-create themselves in the New World.[1]

If Americans were to be a virtuous people, would all of the people in the new nation be allowed to become Americans? Shortly before the beginning of the American Revolution, Benjamin Franklin noted that the number of "purely white People" in the world was proportionately very small. All Africa was black or tawny, Asian chiefly tawny, and "America (exclusive of the new comers) wholly so." The English were the "principle Body of white People," and Franklin wanted more of this type in America. "And while we are . . . *Scouring* our Planet, by clearing America of Woods, and so making this Side of our globe reflect a brighter Light to the Eyes of Inhabitants in Mars or Venus," he declared, "why should we in the Sight of Superior Beings, darken its People? Why increase the Sons of Africa, by Planting them in America, where we have so fair an opportunity, by excluding all Blacks and Tawnys, of increasing the lovely White. . . ?"[2]

Independence had given new importance to this question. The Founding Fathers needed to define political membership for the new republic. In Congress, they enacted the Naturalization Act of 1790. In supporting this law, they affirmed their commitment to the "pure principles of Republicanism" and their determination to develop a citizenry of good and "useful" men. Only the "worthy part of mankind" would be encouraged to settle in the new republic and be eligible for citizenship. Prospective citizens would be required to go through a probationary period so they would have time to understand republican principles and demonstrate "proper and decent behavior." Through this careful screening, the government would exclude "vagrants," "paupers," and "bad men." But the policymakers went further in their efforts to create a homogeneous society. Applicants for naturalized citizenship were required to reside in the United States for two years as well as provide "proof" of good character in court and document their republican fitness. They also had to be "white." This law reflected what Thomas Jefferson envisioned as a society composed of "a people speaking the same language, governed in similar forms, and by similar laws." The Naturalization Act excluded from citizenship not only nonwhite immigrants but also a group of people already here—Indians. Though they were born in the United States, they were regarded as members of tribes, or as domestic subjects; their status was considered analogous to children of foreign diplomats born here. As domestic "foreigners," Native Americans could not seek naturalized citizenship, for they were not "white."[3]

Republicanism provided a psychology that would fuel economic acquisition and expansion in America. In the act of independence, Americans had seized not only power from the king but also the freedom to create a vibrant economy. The Protestant ethic had defined work as virtuous, requiring the habits of self-control and the accumulation of wealth as a sign of salvation; republicanism was now proclaiming worldly goods as markers of virtue. The war for political independence had secured economic freedom for America: freedom to convert Indian lands west of the Appalachians into private property, to trade whenever and with whomever they wished, to import products like tea and molasses without paying taxes to an external authority, to issue their own currency, to develop their own manufacturing, and in general, to expand the market.[4]

This republican "errand into the wilderness" generated a frenetic 5 pursuit for individual materialistic success. Visiting the United States in the 1830s, Alexis de Tocqueville noticed "an inordinate love of material gratification" among Americans. Democracy itself seemed to be its source. "When the reverence that belonged to what is old has vanished," he explained, "birth, condition, and profession no longer distinguished men . . . hardly anything but money remains to create strongly marked differences between them and to raise some of them above the common level." Money had become the nexus of social relations. "When all the members of the community are independent of or indifferent to each other, the co-operation of each of them can be obtained only by paying for it: This infinitely multiplies the purposes to which wealth may be applied and increases its value." Unbound, like Prospero, white men were no longer restrained by laws made in the old country as they ushered America into the era of the Market Revolution—the "take-off" years that transformed America into a highly complex industrial economy.[5]

In 1800, the United States had a population of six million, of which only 320,000 were listed as urban. A large percentage of the rural population was engaged in subsistence farming, growing food crops mainly for their own needs. Living in the interior regions, many of these farmers found that the transportation of surplus crops to the market was too expensive. The cost of carrying a ton of goods only thirty miles overland was as much as shipping it three thousand miles from America to Europe. Thus commercial activity was limited to the areas near the seaboard and navigable waterways.

By 1860, this static economy had been transformed. Advances in transportation such as the steamboat an the railroad now linked the three major regions—the East, West, and South. Each region represented a division of production. New England and the Middle Atlantic states concentrated on manufacturing and commerce and relied on the West for foodstuffs for its growing urban population and the South for raw cotton to supply its textile factories. In 1860, the total value of manufactured goods in the East was $1,270,937,679, compared to only $540,137,811 for the other two regions combined. The western states of Ohio, Indiana, and Illinois exported grain and livestock to the East and South while depending on the East for manufactured goods. In 1860, the West shipped a million barrels of flour and 31 million barrels of grain through Buffalo to the East, and $185,211,254 worth of produce through New Orleans to the South. The South, mainly Georgia, South Carolina, Alabama, Mississippi, and Louisiana, became the cotton kingdom, producing fiber for the textile mills of the East and purchasing foodstuffs from the West and manufactured goods from the East. Meanwhile, cotton had become the country's most important export product. Cotton constituted 39 percent of the total value of exports from 1816 to 1820 63 percent from 1836 to 1840, and over 50 percent from 1840 to 1860.

The causes of this tremendous economic transformation were multiple. The shipping boom of the early 1800s had enabled merchants like Francis Lowell to accumulate capital to invest in manufacturing ventures. The proliferation of banks and the expansion of the credit system made it possible for farmers to borrow money and buy land for commercial agriculture. Technological progress introduced new machinery and paved the way for factory production. Government intervention in the form of protective tariffs and the development of transportation also contributed to the advance of the market. The transportation revolution laid vast networks of turnpikes, canals, and railroads across the country: between 1815 and 1860, freight charges for shipments overland had been reduced by 95 percent.[6]

But the most "decisive" impetus of the Market Revolution was cotton. "Cotton was strategic," observed economist Douglas C. North, "because it was the major independent variable in the interdependent structure of internal and international trade. The demands for western foodstuffs and northeastern services and manufactures were basically dependent upon the income received from the cotton trade." Dominant in the export trade, cotton was crucial in the development of interregional specialization. The income derived from the export of cotton helped to finance enterprises throughout the American economy.[7]

The development of the cotton export sector depended on the appropriation of Indian lands and the expansion of slavery. The major cotton-producing states—Alabama, Mississippi, and Louisiana—were carved out of Indian territory. Tribe after tribe in the South was forced to cede their lands to the federal government and move west of the Mississippi River. Eleven treaties of cession were negotiated with these tribes between 1814 and 1824; from these agreements the United States acquired millions of acres of lands, including one-fifth of Mississippi and three-quarters of Alabama. Sales of Indian lands were followed by increases in the slave population: between 1820 and 1850, the number of slaves jumped from 42,000 to 343,000 in Alabama, 33,000 to 310,000 in Mississippi, and 69,000 to 245,000 in Louisiana. Cotton production in Alabama, Arkansas, Florida, Louisiana, and Mississippi nearly doubled, from 559,000 bales in 1833 to 1,160,000 ten years later.

The Market Revolution opened the way to the making of an even more multicultural America, for it led to the massive influx of laborers from Ireland, the war against Mexico with its annexation of the Southwest territories, and eventually to American expansion into Asia and Chinese immigration to America. The inclusion of these new groups of Calibans created a greater "pluribus," a racially and culturally diverse "giddy multitude" that challenged the vision of Jefferson's "homogeneous" America and Franklin's society of "the lovely White." The economy fastened these different peoples to each other, their histories woven into the tapestry of a greater "unum" called America. Working in the textile mills of New England, Irish immigrant women manufactured fabric made from cotton grown on former Indian land and picked by enslaved blacks; meanwhile, Irish immigrant men labored in New England shoe factories, making shoes from hides shipped by Mexican workers in California. Chinese and Irish railroad workers laid the transcontinental tracks that closed the frontier and changed forever the lives of Indians in the West. America was becoming a nation of peoples from many different shores.

But as the Market Revolution buttressed the institution of slavery and the westward expansion into Indian territory, the very boundlessness of this racial and ethnic diversity generated a need to reinforce interior borders. This dilemma of preserving racial homogeneity while becoming a multicultural society perplexed the policymakers of the new nation. They were especially concerned about two of the groups. "Next to the case of the black race within our bosom," worried James Madison, "that of the red on our borders is the problem most baffling to the policy of our country."[8]

Notes

1. Jefferson to John Hollins, May 5, 1811, in Andrew A. Lipscomb and Albert E. Bergh (eds.), *Writings of Thomas Jefferson*, 20 vols. (Washington, D.C., 1904), vol. 13, p. 58. For the definitive study of the economy and society of the first half of the nineteenth

century, see Charles Sellers, *The Market Revolution: Jacksonian America, 1815–1846* (New York, 1991). My appreciation to Professor Sellers for his inspiration and teaching.

   2. Benjamin Franklin, *Observations Concerning the Increase of Mankind,* in Leonard W. Labaree (ed.), *The Papers of Benjamin Franklin* (New Haven, Conn., 1959–), vol. 4, p. 234.

   3. *Debates and Proceedings in the Congress of the United States, 1789–1791,* 2 vols. (Washington, D.C.), vol. 1, pp. 998, 1284; vol. 2, pp. 1148–1156, 1162, 2264; Thomas Jefferson to James Monroe, November 24, 1801, in Paul L. Ford (ed.), *The Works of Thomas Jefferson,* 20 vols. (New York, 1892–1899), vol. 9, p. 317; Felix S. Cohen, *Handbook of Federal Indian Law* (Albuquerque, N. Mex., 1958), pp. 153–159.

   4. Max Weber, *The Protestant Ethic and the Spirit of Capitalism* (New York, 1958; originally published in 1930).

   5. Alexis de Tocqueville, *Democracy in America,* 2 vols. (New York, 1945; originally published in 1935), vol. 2, pp. 23, 239, 137. See also Douglass C. North, *The Economic Growth of the United States, 1790–1860* (New York, 1966).

   6. See George R. Taylor, *The Transportation Revolution, 1815–1860* (New York, 1962).

   7. North, *Economic Growth,* p. 129.

   8. James Madison, quoted in Michael Paul Rogin, *Fathers and Children: Andrew Jackson and the Subjugation of the American Indian* (New York, 1975), p. 319.

For Journals

Write your impressions about the ways in which economic needs fostered America's development as a multicultural society. Consider writing about Westward expansion or immigration of labor from Africa and Europe.

For Discussion

1. In the first paragraph, the author alludes to Prospero, who, in Shakespeare's *The Tempest,* is exiled to an island inhabited by the "savage" Caliban, a place his daughter Miranda describes as a "brave new world." Why do you think Takaki utilizes this analogy? Who would fulfill the role of Prospero in the New World? Who would have the role of Caliban?

2. Takai refers to Thomas Jefferson's belief that America has a special duty and responsibility to demonstrate the merit of self-government. In what ways might this belief have shaped the society America has become? Do you get a sense, from Tocqueville's description (earlier in this chapter), that most Americans held this view? Do you believe they hold it today?

3. Are you surprised by Benjamin Franklin's assertions about race? Why or why not?

4. The author raises the question of who would be allowed to become Americans and how the founder would "define political membership for the new republic." To what degree do you think that race played a part in this definition? To what degree did the need for labor and other market forces shape a response to this question? To what degree do you believe this same market displaced American Indians and reinforced the institution of slavery?

For Writing

1. Individually or in groups, research the role of various historical figures referred to in this selection: John Winthrop, Thomas Jefferson, Benjamin Franklin, as well as the literary references from *The Tempest*. Compare notes and devise an annotated version of this reading for your class.

2. Research some element of America's economic history, such as the role of transportation systems such as the railroad; technology; urban versus rural economies; employment categories of various ethnic groups; and the like. For example, Irish, Italian, and Chinese immigrants had diverse occupational trends.

3. Check out Takaki's book, *A Different Mirror: A History of Multicultural America*, and read in an area that interests you; you could follow up, for example, on the racial worries Madison raises. You could then research further a specific topic, such as the Trail of Tears and the forced Indian removal.

∞ *A Tapestry of Hope*
America's Strength Was, Is, and Will Be Its Diversity (1994)

JEANNE WAKATSUKI HOUSTON

Jeanne Wakatsuki Houston (1934–) was born in Los Angeles and lived in Santa Monica with her family until the Japanese attack on Pearl Harbor on December 7, 1941; her father was a fisherman. After the attack, President Roosevelt signed an order (see Chapter 10, "War and Violence") that led to the internment of many thousands of Japanese Americans in camps on the grounds that they might prove disloyal. They did not, but they lost their homes and livelihoods; the Wakatsukis were forced to spend three and a half years in a camp called Manzanar, in the Owens Valley in California. In 1973, Wakatsuki Houston and her husband, writer James Houston, wrote what became the most famous Japanese American memoir of the internment camps, Farewell to Manzanar. The following speech was delivered by Wakatsuki Houston at the graduation ceremonies at De Anza College in California in June 1994.

Many years ago—43 to be exact—when I stood on the ground where De Anza College now stands, I looked out onto lush orchards, fragrant with blossoms in springtime and ladened with plump fruit in summer. I viewed acres of foliage carpeting the earth with green— patches of beans, tomatoes, and squash, and long furrows of strawberries, glistening red under their leafy canopies. In those days I knew this area well, for I had spent several summers picking those berries at a large strawberry ranch called Esperanza, located not far from here.

Esperanza, the Spanish word for "hope," was farmed by Japanese families in partnership with the Driscoll brothers. They were sharecroppers. My father sharecropped with the Driscolls at another ranch in South County from 1951 to 1955.

In 1945 when our family re-entered society after three and a half years of incarceration at Manzanar, a concentration camp for Japanese-Americans during World War II, my father's fishing license was revoked. It forced him to seek a livelihood outside a successful pre-war fishing occupation.

Starting at economic zero, at age 59 he seized the opportunity to begin again and brought his family to San Jose from Southern California to farm strawberries. Although my father had been in this country for more than 35 years, and his family, including my mother, had been born here, we arrived at this luscious valley like new immigrants, refugees from another world.

Why do I tell you this? I tell you this because when I picked those berries I never dreamed I would be speaking at a college that someday would rise up within view of where I knelt in the dirt. It was beyond my imagination. But here I am sharing with you some thoughts and insights I have accrued since those days in the strawberry fields more than 40 years ago.

As Santa Clara Valley's landscape has changed, so has its con- 5 sciousness. I'm not going to lecture about how tough it was then to be Asian, to be poor, and to be a woman. But I would like to say a few words to remind us how we have changed, how things are different— especially in attitudes toward ethnic diversity.

When I was growing up in the '50s, being "American" and acceptable into mainstream society meant one had to assimilate, melt into one great pot where the broth was predominantly Anglo-European flavored.

No one talked about the concept of cultural diversity as a mosaic or as a tapestry of multi-colored threads that when woven together created a vibrantly rich and textured fabric. "Real Americans" were white. People of color had to think and act "white" to prove their "Americanness." And while I was growing up after the war, muted by the internment experience, it never occurred to me to question this attitude.

Not even when I was told I should not continue with a journalism major at San Jose State because I was "Oriental" and a female. There were no jobs in the field. So I changed my major to social welfare. And when I was told again by the head of Juvenile Probation Services that they could not hire me as a probation officer because the community was not "ready" for "Orientals," I did not protest—although I had been educated enough by then to know it was wrong. But that was the '50s.

Equal opportunity laws were non-existent. I remained silent, returning to the safety zone of invisibility and "don't make waves" mentality.

Rediscovering Our Histories

Then in the '60s, the Black Power movement changed forever the 10 way racial and ethnic minorities thought of themselves. Black leaders led us to rediscover our cultural backgrounds and our histories. We rediscovered our participation in and our contributions to the development of this country, and with this recognition came a sense of pride and identity.

For the first time in U.S. history, an awareness of values inherent in America's sub-cultures rose into public consciousness. We began to see that when individuals have a strong sense of identity, of pride in one's heritage, this sense of self-worth strengthens the larger society. Not only were attitudes changing in the dominant culture, but also subgroups themselves began to recognize that America is a land of immigrants, and that all immigrants had a hand in developing it.

Thirty years ago, the word "immigrant" seemed reserved for people of color, individuals from the Third World. Today, this still seems to be the prevailing myth. I hear so often the comment, "America is becoming—so multi-cultural with all this immigration from Asia and south of the border." Some people are surprised or mystified or threatened by this idea that the country is becoming so diverse, when in fact, it always has been.

From the moment Portuguese and Italian sailors landed in the New World to mingle with indigenous peoples in what we now call the West Indies, America began its cross-cultural heritage. And up North, more than 500 indigenous tribes, speaking as many different languages, for centuries had lived on this vast and fertile continent.

Ethnicity is not the exclusive property of people of color. We all have ethnicity. We are descendants of individuals from China, Ireland, Ethiopia, Vietnam, El Salvador, Canada—to name a few. Ideally, Americans should not have a problem with identity; we must realize there is no need to "wanna-be ethnic"—because, in fact, we all are.

"The World Is Watching"

I would like to share an experience I had two years ago when I 15 was in Japan. I met a Japanese man, a visionary who founded a grassroots movement called "the Sweet Potato Movement." It was a calling back to the land from the cities, the dense urban areas he referred to as the "fourth world."

He surprised me with this comment, "The world is watching America deal with its diversity. For the Japanese, America is the role model for democracy. We may be strong economically, but we need your country to lead us in human rights and values. You must succeed if democracy is to succeed around the world."

He was one of many Japanese I met who saw multi-culturalism as a pivotal test for America's democratic ideals.

I like to view our diversity as a metaphor, a microcosm of the macrocosm of a world of nations. I like to see America as a great experiment, a laboratory for testing ideals—the big test today being tolerance and cooperation. If we can't get along in our own communities because of our cultural differences, how can we expect nations around the world to co-exist peacefully?

One of our greatest challenges is to embrace our differences while seeking out the common bonds that hold us together. What are those bonds? What are those threads, the warp in the loom that sets the pattern for who we are as Americans? For me, those threads are the ideals of freedom, equality, opportunity, justice. I also include the human qualities of gratitude, generosity, curiosity and love. Those threads together provide the strength and foundation around which our individual cultural differences weave, making each and every one of us unique and interesting Americans.

As I noted earlier, there was a major shift in perception to reach 20 the point of agreement that we are, indeed, a multi-cultural society, that we began with diversity. But there is a difference between cultural diversity and cross-cultural understanding. They are not synonymous. The great opportunity now is to seek out ways to enhance cross-cultural understanding and not fall back on separatism and attitudes of "our tribe against theirs."

The Search for Scapegoats

Today, in a time of economic crisis, there are those in our political leadership who are all too ready to find scapegoats.

More and more, it seems, those scapegoats are immigrants. The voices of fear echo daily on the front pages of newspapers, in our television broadcasts: "They are different from us. They have no idea of democracy and freedom. They won't speak our language and they keep to themselves."

Those are the words used today to describe the newest Americans. How many of us who lived through the racism and internment of Japanese-Americans during World War II remember what it was like to have those words directed against one innocent group?

In 1942, we had no one to speak up for us. But after the war, empowered by the Civil Rights movement of the '60s, Japanese-

Americans began a 10-year drive for redress from our government. It culminated with the passage of the Civil Liberties Act of 1988, which officially apologized for the internment.

Japanese-Americans were vindicated in the eyes of history. But 25 this victory was not for Japanese-Americans alone. It was a great victory for all Americans, for it proved our Constitution is not just a piece of parchment under glass in the National Archives. It is a living, vital contract that binds us all together as Americans.

And if that contract is broken—as it was in 1942—it is not just the rights of individuals that are threatened, but the very fabric of this nation. And we know that the fabric is woven from threads representing many different groups. If one of those threads is cut, stretched out of proportion, or bleached of color, the design becomes listless and in danger of unraveling.

I began this talk with a memory, a powerful memory, which should underline one of the ironic possibilities of living in America. Who knows what the future holds for any of us? But whatever measure of success we have achieved is because we own a certain capacity. That capacity is hope.

When I was a teenager picking strawberries on that ranch, so appropriately named "Esperanza," I did not have vision. I could not envision the future I have today. Yet, I did have an unexplainable pull to fulfill some possibility, some unknown challenge. I now know that urge to fulfill was hope, a submerged belief in my own power, in the possibility I could accomplish "something."

Today I salute the accomplishments of all people and their faith—their faith in themselves and thus, in a future for this country.

For Journals

Do you believe there is strength in cultural diversity? Why or why not?

For Discussion

1.   Graduation speeches tend to exhort the graduates to action, but they have a reputation for being rather long and dry. Imagine yourself in the audience listening to this speech. How do you think you would have reacted, and why? What strategies does Houston use in this speech to keep her audience's attention and to enable them to follow her points? Consider language, paragraphing, and other rhetorical strategies you have studied.

2.   Houston begins her speech with a memory, an anecdote, to lead into her argument. How effective do you find this strategy? What other introductions might Houston have used? Do you think they would be more, or less, effective than the speech as given?

3. What strategies does the author use to identify with her audience? To what beliefs and values does she appeal? To what emotions?

For Writing

1. Using material developed in response to the discussion questions as a starting point, write an essay analyzing the persuasive strategies in this speech.

2. Houston writes, "Ethnicity is not the exclusive property of people of color. We all have ethnicity." Write an essay exploring your own ethnicity identity. Draw upon memories, stories, family history, oral histories, or outside research to develop and support your dominant theme.

∞ *Chicana* (1994)

MARTHA SERRANO

Martha Serrano grew up in Los Angeles. In her adolescent years she was a member of a gang, but she dropped out of it to concentrate on high school studies. A recent college graduate, she plans to attend law school and work on behalf of her people. As part of a first-year writing course, Serrano wrote the essay that follows in response to writing assignment 1 at the end of this chapter.

Don't call me Hispanic. Don't call me Latina. Don't call me Mexican. Don't call me Mexican American. I want to be called Chicana. I am *mestiza*—indigenous and Spanish. My heritage is struggle and strength. I join my strength and struggle to that of my *hermanas*, my sisters. I am a woman of *Aztlan*, the southwestern United States. I don't want to be called Hispanic because I don't want people to tell me who I am and where I come from.

Most, if not all, of the people who call me Hispanic do not know that "Hispanic" is a term imposed on Americans of Latin descent by federal regulators, unprepared educators, and merchants who want our money but not us. In the mid 1970s, the U.S. Census Bureau first admitted that its 1970 census had seriously undercounted persons of Latin American descent in the United States. Under pressure from Latino activists to avoid a repetition of that mistake in the 1980 head count, the bureau searched for an all-encompassing word to describe the diverse assortment of Latin Americans living in this country: Mexican Americans and Mexican citizens, Puerto Ricans and Cuban Americans, and "other Hispanics" was the Census Bureau's solution.

The term "Hispanic" denies my cultural heritage. However, a Chicana is both Hispanic and Indian. For the Chicana, her world has been shaped by historical forces beyond the barrio and this country. My ancestors are the *conquistadores* and the conquered indigenous people of 1492. Our vanquished heritage has always haunted us and has been ignored by American historians.

The term "Chicana" is linked to my indigenous past. The roots of the word date back to the conquest of *El Valle de México.* Back then, Mexico was pronounced "meshico." The Spaniards had no letter or sound in their alphabet for the Nahuatl "sh" or hard "j" so they put an "x" in its place. In Meshico, "Mejico" became "Mexico" and "Tejas," "Texas." Mexico's Catholicism (which came from the encounter between Spaniards and Native Americans), and its food, art, and customs manifest Indian presence. Moreover, the Mexican dialect of Spanish, used to create world-famous prose and poetry, is influenced by Aztec words.

The first *mestizos* were born of Spanish soldiers and indigenous 5 maidens. This scorned underclass was called Meshicanos and evolved to shicanos, Chicanos. Culturally, in the past, the word "Chicano" was a pejorative, class-bound adjective. Latinos used to associate the word "Chicano" with violent gangsters who had nothing better to do but hang out in the street and cause trouble. Now, however, it is the root idea of a new cultural identity for my people. It reveals a growing solidarity and the development of a common social praxis. Today, the widespread use of the word signals a rebirth of pride and confidence. It embodies an ancient truth: "Man is never closer to his true self as when he is close to his community."

All Chicanos agree that being Chicano/a is more than being an American of Mexican descent; it is a way of thinking. It means being politically and culturally aware. It means knowing who you are and where you came from. It means being proud of your ethnic background and history. Most important of all, it means resisting assimilation into American mainstream society. Chicanos fight for self-determination and tackle issues facing the Chicano community. Chicanos struggle for the betterment of *La Raza,* the people.

Chicanos are *mestizos,* or the blending of two races and cultures. No matter what our differences may be, all Chicanos believe that education, especially higher education, leads to progress and the development of our community. We believe that once our people get educated, we can go to our own lawyers, doctors, architects, engineers, and others to help build a stronger and united Chicano community. However, we believe that education must contribute to the formation of a complete man or woman who truly values life and freedom. I am Chicana!

For Journals

Are there particular ways in which people categorize you that you dislike? What do you know about the origins of these labels?

For Discussion

1. Do your intellect and emotion respond in the same way to Serrano's argument? If not, how do your reactions conflict? Do you find her introduction effective? Explain your answer.

2. What connections is Serrano making between the term "Chicana" and cultural identity? What is the connection between the individual, and community, and culture in forming identity?

3. Serrano describes the history of the terms "Chicana" and "Hispanic" to support her view that the former is the better term for her identity and her people. Are you persuaded by the information she provides? Could she offer other arguments to support her view?

4. Serrano rejects the term "Hispanic" as one imposed by others. Should people be able to name and define their own ethnicity and culture as they wish?

5. Serrano writes of resisting assimilation; some of the other readings in this chapter, however, assume that assimilation is good. Working in groups or pairs in class, argue that being American does or does not entail assimilation into mainstream American society. In the process, try to come up with a working definition of assimilation for contemporary Americans.

For Writing

1. Compare and contrast Serrano's idea of cultural identity with Ellison's. Alternatively, construct a dialogue between Serrano and Jeanne Wakatsuki Houston on claiming a cultural identity.

2. Analyze the ways in which exposure to others of your ethnic group or national origin has, or has not, helped you form an identity.

∞ Film: *The Joy Luck Club* (1994)

This film follows the story of four lifelong friends, including both their joys and tragedies, and shows how their experiences have not only shaped their own lives, but have also affected their hopes and dreams for their children. It is based on the novel, of the same name, by Amy Tan. (139 minutes)

For Journals

This film contains both tragic and comic elements. Write a journal entry reflecting on your emotional response to the film and to its central characters.

For Discussion

1.   Comment on the technique of narrative, or storytelling, in the film, exploring, for example, the ways in which it weaves together past and present. How does such a technique contribute to your understanding of the characters and their cultures?

2.   Which story line was most compelling to you? Why? Cite material from the film to support your view.

3.   In what ways does the interplay of ethnic heritage and American identity become apparent? Cite specific examples or incidents from the film to support your view.

For Writing

1.   Take a specific example or scene from the film, such as the scene in which the young white man, Rick, comes to dinner, and analyze the film's handling of cross-cultural differences. How does the scene implicitly convey a point about cultures and customs? What does the scene later in the film, with the same characters, suggest to you about cultural differences?

2.   Write a review of the film for your school paper, your class, or a friend. Would you recommend it? Why or why not? In your review, remember to introduce the topic, develop a dominant impression or core assertion, and then briefly summarize the plot before analyzing the film's strengths and weaknesses.

Writing Assignments

1.   Write a memoir, narrative, or autobiography that conveys a sense of your personal identity as an American and what the term "American" means to you. Review the readings by Ellison, Standing Bear, and Serrano to find ways in which these authors developed their self-definition or search for identity. Make sure to determine a specific focus or claim about your identity rather than string together examples or anecdotes without a persuasive intent.

2.   Investigate past or contemporary issues in immigration policy. Examine how people are defined as American citizens, who is a citizen automatically and who must apply, what kinds of restrictions are in place, whether different categories of immigrants are able to enter in higher numbers, and why. Some research questions you might consider include the following: What kinds of immigrants does American policy favor? How can definitions be used to favor particular groups? In what ways have policies changed over the years? Present your thesis and findings in an essay that documents this research.

3. Imagine that you are an advertising copywriter who has been asked to create a public relations campaign for a political candidate that defines the best that America and Americans have to offer. The audience is a group of U.S. citizens. Sketch out your strategy, propose it to your client, and argue that your strategy will be effective.

Alternatively, design a campaign for a U.S. tourism organization that will target an overseas audience from a country or region you designate. It might be interesting, for example, to devise a campaign encouraging citizens of countries of the former Soviet Union to visit the United States.

4. Currently, scholars, activists, and students are discussing the notion of "identity politics"—or the belief that people from nondominant cultures should define themselves rather than have identities imposed on them by others. Martha Serrano's essay is an example of the kinds of debate revolving around conflicts between how people identify themselves and how others define them. Research this concept in recent periodicals, and write an essay explaining the concept to your classmates or other peer group. Alternatively, argue for a redefinition of an ethnic group or culture with which you identify.

6

⚭

American Dreams

The selections in this chapter revolve around the most familiar but elusive expression of the American national character, the American dream. It is an expression that turns up everywhere in our culture; open any newspaper or watch any news program, and you will probably find more samples like these:

- An African American banker helps provide mortgages to minority applicants. The headline of the newspaper story is "The American Dream"; the subtitle is "Doing Well by Doing Good."
- Three promising navy officers, a woman and two men, are killed in a double murder and suicide. The news story focuses on the poignancy of the loss by pointing out that all three officers were on the way to achieving the American dream.
- A teenage television actor becomes wealthy and famous; a television magazine program reporting on his newfound stardom calls it an example of the American dream.

As these examples show, the American dream is so well established—both as an expression and as an idea—that no one feels the need to define it; however, no one seems to agree on exactly what it means. Perhaps the closest we can come is to say that the American dream represents both what Americans believe themselves entitled to and what they believe themselves capable of. In other words, it is the promise inherent in the idea of America itself.

The idea of America actually began with a mistake; Renaissance Europeans in search of a route to the East Indies stumbled on it. As the famous naval historian Samuel Eliot Morrison remarked, they spent the next fifty years trying to get around or through it. Actually finding such a continent, even by accident, had exciting and unsettling impact on the European imagination. As a result, early European dreams about America reflected a curious combination of fantasy and science fiction. Writers who had never been to America described Native Americans with feathers sprouting from their feet, precious stones growing out of their chests, heads that grew from below their shoulders, no government, no private property, a taste for cannibalism, and a life span of 150 years.

Of course the reality was very different, and dreams changed, from the discovery of golden cities to the acquisition of land for farming. But two early elements were fixed—that America represented the possibility of prosperity and that whoever came here could make a new start.

From the beginning, then, the American dream has existed as a series of evolving promises and discrepancies, of continuous conflicts and renewed possibilities for achievement, of the tension between faith in a glorious promise and the more difficult task of making that promise come true under less-than-ideal conditions. These contradictions are elements in a three-hundred-year debate that continues to this day, because, while most Americans believe in the American dream, there is much disagreement on its particulars. We argue that what the dream consists of—money, social equality, power, success, democratic ideals; we argue about the means to achieve it—hard work, luck, aggressiveness, drive or the will to succeed at any cost; we argue about who is entitled to it—long-term residents, new immigrants, everyone, or just the lucky few. And finally, we argue over how much each person is entitled to—the complete fulfillment of his or her dream, or just the right to compete?

American Dreams through History

The selections in this chapter reflect reality and myth, coexisting contradictions, disappointing experience, and renewed optimism in pursuing the American dream. The first selection, an excerpt from Sir Walter Raleigh's 1595 report on Guiana, emphasizes America as a source of untold riches, untouched land, and unfettered sexuality, all waiting to be improved, saved, and used by Europeans. Raleigh's story also promises access to El Dorado, the golden city whose multiple mythical locations, often in the west, would find their ultimate home in legends about golden California. But in 1595, Raleigh makes what may be the first English argument for acquisition of territory in the Americas based on how rich that acquisition would make the country that conquered it. That argument would continue to be made for the next 250 years, by English, French, and Spanish explorers, all intent on conveying to the folks back home that America was worth any price, and eventually by Americans justifying the westward movement of the United States.

The Europeans' fascination with America, or their dream of it, encouraged the production of images and writings that were less factual than fictional, not to mention exotic. Although an early tradition of accurate and beautiful drawings of animals, plants, and birds, culminating in John J. Audubon's great folios in the nineteenth century, faithfully portrayed the continent, Europeans who had never been to America would have had difficulty separating relatively scientific drawings from the purely fanciful, even bizarre versions that competed for their attention.

The most popular allegorical representations depicted America as a woman, sometimes beautiful and sexual, sometimes armed and dangerous, sometimes both simultaneously. Often she carried a bow and arrow, like an Amazon warrior or Diana, goddess of the hunt.

There were, of course, Americans to whom this dream of unbelieveable wealth became a reality. In the latter part of the nineteenth century, those Americans tended to be men of talent, enormous energy and often considerable ruthlessness who made their fortunes from promoting, expanding, and developing the country's industrial power. One of the most interesting and complex of these men was Andrew Carnegie, who came to the United States as a poverty-stricken Scottish immigrant of twelve and made a huge fortune in coal and railroads. What was different about Carnegie was an apparent conflict between his drive to succeed on an unparalleled scale, and an inheritance of social activism from his immediate family, who had experienced discrimination and displacement in Scotland. The result was that on the one hand Carnegie was extremely rich, and on the other hand he felt the need to address wealth as a burden and a responsibility as well as a privilege. In his famous essay in this chapter, he proposes the rather unusual idea that the best thing rich men can do for themselves and their children is to give away all their money so that it does the most good.

The actual experience of coming to America, however, was far more complicated and traumatic than the visual iconography which resulted from the European longing for what F. Scott Fitzgerald would eventually describe in *The Great Gatsby* as "the fresh green breast of the New World." As emigration to America increased in the nineteenth century, Asians, southern Europeans, and eastern Europeans entered the mix. For most of them, the untold wealth of America remained as remote and insubstantial as a picture (see *California, the Cornucopia of the World*). Instead, life in America involved a continual, often painful effort to learn English, find a community, and make what living they could. Chinese Americans, for example, had the extra burden of struggling not only against the usual traumas of immigration, but also against the especially harsh anti-Chinese laws to which they were subject. Sui Sin Far, in "In the Land of the Free," examines the results of miscommunication and differing cultural values in an encounter between a young Chinese immigrant mother and the well-meaning but uncomprehending American woman who disrupts her life, and that of her child, with tragic consequences.

The dream remained equally elusive for some of the people who had lived in America the longest. Langston Hughes, the African American poet, writer, and leader in the great cultural explosion of the Harlem Renaissance in the 1920s, repeatedly questioned why the dream of success and equality that was so clear in theory remained so inaccessible in practice to so many. Both angry and hopeful, he wrote a series of poems, including "Let America Be America Again," in which he underlined the contradictions between the dream of opportunity and fulfillment and a much grimmer reality, between what America held out as a promise and what it delivered.

A decade later, America was in the midst of the Great Depression, an economic disaster so enormous that it made an indelible impression on those who lived through it. Fifteen million people were out of work. The poor got poorer, and, more than at any other time in our history, the middle class, the primary carriers of belief in the rewards of work and the inevitability of success, found themselves unemployed. The savings of a lifetime disappeared when banks failed; frugality and honesty were not rewarded; and confidence in one's ability to mold the future was destroyed.

Margaret Bourke-White, a famous photographer for *Life* and *Time* magazines, took many pictures of Americans coping with the terrors of the Depression; one of her best photos, the ironically titled "There's No Way like the American Way," captures an image of poor people juxtaposed with an image of a rich, secure America that seems utterly distant from their experience. For F. Scott Fitzgerald, the Depression had psychological as well as financial aspects. Probably no writer had understood better the enormous energy behind the American love of success, and he experienced it himself when he became a best-selling author at the age of twenty-three with his college novel, *This Side of Paradise.* His later novel, *The Great Gatsby,* had a hero who could never have been anything but American in his ambition, his drive, and his naive if ruthless faith in the connections between love and money. But by 1937, Fitzgerald was forgotten, drinking too much and writing about disintegration—his own and the country's—in a series of essays called *The Crack-Up.* The selection here, "Early Success," is his own remarkably objective look at what it means to succeed when you're too young to understand either success or failure.

America didn't fully recover from the Great Depression until the beginning of World War II, when the need for war matériel put factories on overtime and created an immense need for laborers. Another side effect of the war was that millions of women who had never expected to work outside the home suddenly found themselves recruited for well-paying jobs vacated by the men who had joined the armed forces. For the first time, many found themselves in business, earning money and feeling successful in ways that had traditionally been reserved for men.

As soon as the war ended and the men returned, though, women were rerouted back into domestic life with a vengeance. Magazines like *Woman's Day* emphasized not their lost earning power but their ability to make a good tuna casserole. Men, on the other hand, were expected to provide more and more material proof of their own success at the office: the split-level ranch house in the suburbs, the healthy 2.3 children, and an ever-changing model of American-made car.

While millions of Americans enthusiastically pursued the vision of suburban fulfillment, their belief in it was not always supported by the results. In fact the continuing effort to keep up with the Joneses, to have a nicer yard and a newer car, fresh-faced children and a happy marriage, could be exhausting. Like earlier versions of the American dream, the model for post-war happiness was a demand for a particular kind of success, which seemed to equate money and possessions with personal achievement. For Americans who believed it, the failure to garner that success was devastating. In 1949, playwright Arthur Miller gave immortal expression to the unease and desperation that underlie the darker side of the American dream in his play, *Death of a Salesman*. In this chapter we excerpt the epilogue, or Requiem, of *Salesman*. Through the tragedy of the title character, Willie Loman, Miller gives us an extraordinary insight into the price ordinary Americans can pay in their pursuit of an unreliable dream.

African Americans, as usual, were still largely excluded from the new prosperity. African American soldiers who fought for their country in World War II returned to find that jobs, houses, and good education were as difficult to come by as ever. There were some changes. President Truman had desegregated the armed forces in 1948 by executive order, and a Supreme Court case the same year overturned a real estate transaction in which a clause called a restrictive covenant could forbid selling to someone of a particular color or religion. But in 1951, Jim Crow was still the only way of life in the South, and African American migration to the big northern and midwestern cities had shifted rather than eliminated a struggle to survive. Langston Hughes, ever sensitive and responsive to the situation, made his discontent explicit in a short, powerful, and angry poem, "Harlem," which forms a kind of psychological companion piece to "Let America Be America Again." By now the dream of diverse populations finding common cause in their mutual political and economic disenfranchisement has been replaced by a grim impatience.

But the more idealistic sense of fulfillment that Langston Hughes had articulated in his poetry was still a factor in the American agenda. In 1963, thirty years after Hughes made his plea for a renewed commitment to the American dream, Martin Luther King Jr., the leader of the modern civil rights movement, made the most famous American speech of the twentieth century: the largely extemporaneous address at the Lincoln Memorial, "I Have a Dream." At the time, most southern blacks could not share a water fountain, a beach, a bus seat, a school room, or a voting booth with southern whites. King, a believer in the power of nonviolent resistance, had already led a successful bus boycott in Montgomery, Alabama, and a long series of marches, demonstrations, and sit-ins at ordinary places like lunch counters; he had been arrested by southern sheriffs and was the frequent recipient of death threats. But a huge civil rights march in Washington, D.C., gave him the opportunity to address a larger American audience and to locate civil rights at the political center of the American dream, to make one the expression of the other.

These two strains of the American dream—the ideals of opportunity and achievement based on character, perseverance, and fairness, versus the charms of getting rich quick, winning or borrowing money, and keeping ahead of, rather than even with, the Joneses—continue to dominate contemporary American life. Jacob Weisberg, the editor of an on-line magazine, explores in "United Shareholders of America" the debilitating effects of stock market madness on middle-class Americans. He sees the passion for betting one's future on rising stock prices as yet another instance of how short Americans' memories are; not only have they forgotten the causes of the Great Depression, but they still think they can circumvent the less glamorous paths to the dream, like saving money, by engaging in what is effectively a different kind of sweepstakes.

On a somewhat more hopeful note, urban studies expert Witold Rybczynski, visits a new community, Celebration, which attempts to reinvigorate the American sense of community while accommodating it to the computer age, in effect seeking the best of the past and the present. The fact that "Tomorrowland," as he calls it, was built by the Disney Corporation raises interesting issues about how much the American dream owes both to nostalgia and self-perpetuated mythology.

Student Chris Countryman returns to the themes that Martin Luther King Jr. spoke of and that Langston Hughes wrote so hopefully. In his essay on "Let America Be America Again," Countryman proves how eloquent the voice of a poet, shaping lines and stanzas, can be in arguing that the best way for the American dream to be realized is for America to return to its first, best promise.

Finally, in the film *Avalon*, we see a classic example of the dream at work in three generations of one family, beginning with brothers who immigrate to America early in the twentieth century and encompassing their children and grandchildren, with unexpected results.

All selections in this chapter, separated as they are by time and distance, speak to us in distinct and recognizable American voices. In Chapter 5, you read about Americans trying to establish their identities by defining, for themselves as much as for anyone else, who an American is. This chapter's selections continue that process by trying to express what Americans want and what they feel are their unique opportunities; the selections appeal to a common sense of possibility that both shapes our ambitions and survives our experience.

∞ FROM *The Discovery of the Large, Rich, and Beautiful Empire of Guiana,*
with a relation of the great and golden city of Manoa[1] *(which the Spaniards call El Dorado). Performed in the year 1595 by Sir Walter Raleigh Knight*

SIR WALTER RALEIGH

Sir Walter Raleigh (1562–1618) was one of the most remarkable and versatile members of the court of Queen Elizabeth I. A soldier, poet, explorer, and a great favorite of the queen, he traveled to the Americas in the hope of convincing England that the new continent was worth fighting for, and that contesting with Spain for colonial domination would bring incalculable riches. He failed to find gold—what he reports here are at best secondhand stories and legends—and after Elizabeth's death, Raleigh was imprisoned in the Tower of London by the new ruler, James I. Aside from one more abortive trip to the Americas, he spent the rest of his life in the Tower, and was executed in 1618.

The empire of Guiana is directly east from Peru towards the sea, and lieth under the equinoctial line, and it hath more abundance of gold than any part of Peru, and as many or more great cities than ever Peru had when it flourished most: I have been assured by such of the Spaniards[2] as have seen Manoa the imperial city of Guiana, which the Spaniards call El Dorado, that for the greatness, for the riches, and for the excellent seat, it far exceedeth any of the world.

---

[1]Raleigh had reports from several Spaniards of an unexplored Indian kingdom between the Oronoco and Amazon rivers and of the city the Spaniards called "El Dorado" in testimony to its gold. Called "Manoa" by the native inhabitants, that city was reportedly founded by the Inca emperor of Peru as a new capital after the Spanish invasion.

[2]This is probably disingenuous; Raleigh could hardly have met personally Spaniards claiming to have seen Manoa, but he would have heard or read some plausible-sounding secondhand accounts.

                                    *   *   *

I will promise these things that follow, which I know to be true. Those that are desirous to discover may be satisfied with this river,[3] above 2000 miles east and west, and 800 miles south and north, and of these, the most either rich in gold, or in other merchandises. The common soldier shall here fight for gold, and pay himself instead of pence, with plates of half a foot broad, whereas he breaketh his bones in other wars for provender and penury. Those commanders and chieftains that shoot at honor and abundance, shall find there more rich and beautiful cities, more temples adorned with golden images, more sepulchres filled with treasure, than either Cortez found in Mexico, or Pizarro in Peru: and the shining glory of this conquest will eclipse all those so far extended beams of the Spanish nation. There is no country which yieldeth more pleasure to the inhabitants, either for the common delights of hunting, hawking, fishing, fowling, or the rest, than Guiana doth.

Both for health, good air, pleasure, and riches I am resolved it cannot be equalled by an region either in the east or the west. Moreover the country is so healthful, as of an hundred persons and more (which lay without shift most sluttishly, and were every day almost melted with heat in rowing and marching, and suddenly wet again with great showers, and did eat of all sorts of corrupt fruits, and made meals of fresh fish without seasoning, of tortugas,[4] of crocodiles, and besides lodged in the open air every night) we lost not any one, nor had one ill disposed to my knowledge, nor found any calentura, or other of those pestilent diseases which dwell in all hot regions.

Where there is store of gold, it is in effect needless to remember other commodities for trade: but it hath towards the south part of the river, great quantities of brazil-wood, and diverse berries that dye a most perfect crimson and carnation. All places yield abundance of cotton, of silk, of balsam, and of those kinds most excellent and never known in Europe, of all sorts of gums, of Indian pepper: and what else the countries may afford within the land we know not, neither had we time to abide the trial, and search. The soil besides is so excellent and so full of rivers, as it will carry sugar, ginger, and all those other commodities, which the West Indies have.

The Navigation is short, for it may be sailed with an ordinary 5 wind in six weeks, and in the like time back again.

Guiana is a country that hath yet her maidenhead, never sacked, turned, nor wrought, the face of the earth hath not been torn, nor the virtue and salt of the soil spent by manurance, the graves have not

---

[3]The Oronoco.
[4]Tortoises.

been opened for gold, the mines not broken with sledges, nor their images pulled down out of their temples. It hath never been entered by any army of strength, and never conquered by any Christian prince. It is besides so defensible, that if two forts be built in one of the provinces which I have seen, the flood setteth in so near the bank, where the channel also lieth, that no ship can pass up but within a pike's length of the artillery, first of the one, and afterwards of the other.

Guiana hath but one entrance by the sea (if it hath that) for any vessels of burden: so as whosoever shall first possess it, he shall be found unaccessible for any enemy, except he come in wherries, barges, or canoes, or else in flat bottomed boats, and if he do offer to enter it in that manner, the woods are so thick two hundred miles together upon the rivers of such entrance, as a mouse cannot sit in a boat unhit from the bank. By land it is more impossible to approach, for it hath the strongest situation of any region under the sun, and it so environed with impassable mountains on every side, as it is impossible to victual any company in the passage: which hath been well proved by the Spanish nation, who since the conquest of Peru have never left five years free from attempting this empire, or discovering some way into it, and yet of three and twenty several gentlemen, knights, and noblemen, there was never any that knew which way to lead an army by land, or to conduct ships by sea, anything near the said country. Don Antonio de Berreo[5] (whom we displanted) the last: and I doubt much, whether he himself or any of his yet know the best way into the said empire.

The West Indies were first offered Her Majesty's grandfather[6] by Columbus a stranger, in whom there might be doubt of deceit, and besides it was then thought incredible that there were such and so many lands and regions never written of before. This empire is made known to Her Majesty by her own vassal, and by him that oweth to her more duty than an ordinary subject, so that it shall ill sort with the many graces and benefits which I have received to abuse Her Highness, either with fables or imaginations. The country is already discovered, many nations won to Her Majesty's love and obedience, and those Spaniards which have latest and longest laboured about the conquest, beaten out, discouraged and disgraced, which among these nations were thought invincible. Her Majesty may in this enterprise employ all those soldiers and gentlemen that are younger brethren, and all captains and chieftains that want employment, and the charge will be only the first setting out in victualling and arming them: for after the

---

[5]One of Raleigh's informants, a captured Spanish officer at Trinidad.
[6]Henry VII.

first or second year I doubt not but to see in London a Contractation House[7] of more receipt for Guiana, than there is now in Seville for the West Indies.

I am resolved that if there were but a small army a foot in Guiana, marching towards Manoa the chief city of Inca, he would yield to Her Majesty by composition so many hundred thousand pounds yearly, as should both defend all enemies abroad, and defray all expenses at home, and that he would besides pay a garrison of three or four thousand soldiers very royally to defend him against other nations.

For whatsoever prince shall possess it, shall be greatest, and if the 10 King of Spain shall enjoy it, he will become unresistible. Her Majesty hereby shall confirm and strengthen the opinions of all nations, as touching her great and princely actions.

I trust in God, this being true, will suffice, and that he which is King of all Kings and Lord of Lords, will put it into her heart which is Lady of Ladies to possess it.

For Journals

Have you ever heard of El Dorado? Atlantis? Utopia? What do you associate with any of those terms?

For Discussion

1. Which audience or audiences would you guess Raleigh intended this writing for? Look for evidence for your choice in the text.

2. Aside from its reported gold and treasure, what other benefits does Raleigh attribute to Guiana that would be attractive to the English?

3. Raleigh refers to Guiana, in effect, as virgin. That phraseology is common among writers describing America—virgin land, virgin wilderness. Why would they apply that term to a country, and what does use of that term suggest about their attitude toward America?

For Writing

1. Look at the illustration later in this chapter, California Cornucopeia. Write an essay in which you compare Raleigh's picture of a rich and waiting Guiana with a rich and fruitful California. Consider: What are the main attractions of each place as portrayed in these selec-

---

[7]Place for receiving the goods contracted to be sent back to the projectors who would finance the Guiana expedition.

tions? How different are they? Use details from the text and the picture as evidence.

Alternatively, if you were going to compose an ad which illustrates the mythic wonders of Guiana the way the nineteenth century advertisement pushes the advantages of California, what would your advertisement for Guiana look like? Using the California ad as a model, what would be included? What writing would you put on it? What details would you emphasize?

2. There were may histories/reports/legends written about the Americas, sometimes by people who had never been there, sometimes by naturalists interested in flora and fauna, sometimes by explorers trying to describe what they had seen while glorifying their own exploits. Research and write a paper on one of them, such as Captain John Smith on Jamestown, Hakluyt's Voyages, or Thomas Hariot's account of the Indians in Virginia. (These are available both in libraries and in most anthologies of English literature.) Choose one or two chapters to discuss. You can either compare them with Raleigh, or treat them on their own terms. In either case, examine them with the following in mind: What are their expectations? Are they disappointed? Frightened? How attractive or dangerous do they make the new world seem? And what educated guesses can you make as to their audience and purpose? As always, use the text as evidence.

∽ *Wealth* (1889)

ANDREW CARNEGIE

Andrew Carnegie (1835–1919) emigrated from Scotland to the United States. He began his career as a weaver like his father, but then he became a telegraph messenger boy and eventually a telegraph operator and superintendent. He made his fortune in railroads, communications, and steel; he sold his interest to J. P. Morgan in 1901 for $250 million. When he retired from public life, he dedicated much of his fortune to establishing institutions for the public good, including Carnegie Tech (later Carnegie-Mellon University), Carnegie Hall, the Carnegie Foundation, the Carnegie Endowment for Peace, and libraries in many towns and cities in the United States and Britain. Most of his writings concern the importance of preserving and maintaining world peace, but he also wrote about business and money.

The problem of our age is the proper administration of wealth, so that the ties of brotherhood may still bind together the rich and poor in harmonious relationship. The conditions of human life have not only been changed, but revolutionized, within the past few hundred years. In former days there was little difference between the dwelling, dress, food, and environment of the chief and those of his retainers. The Indians are to-day where civilized man then was. When visiting the Sioux, I was led to the wigwam of the chief. It was just like the others in external appearance, and even within the difference was trifling between it and those of the poorest of his braves. The contrast between the palace of the millionaire and the cottage of the laborer with us to-day measures the change which has come with civilization. . . .

The price which society pays for the law of competition, like the price it pays for cheap comforts and luxuries, is also great; but the advantages of this law are also greater still, for it is to this law that we owe our wonderful material development, which brings improved conditions in its train. . . .

We start, then, with a condition of affairs under which the best interests of the race are promoted, but which inevitably gives wealth to the few. Thus far, accepting conditions as they exist, the situation can be surveyed and pronounced good. The question then arises. . . .

What is the proper mode of administering wealth after the laws upon which civilization is founded have thrown it into the hands of the few? And it is of this great question that I believe I offer the true solution. It will be understood that *fortunes* are here spoken of, not moderate sums saved by many years of effort. . . .

There are but three modes in which surplus wealth can be disposed of. It can be left to the families of the decedents; or it can be bequeathed for public purposes; or, finally, it can be administered during their lives by its possessors. . . . [T]he question which forces itself upon thoughtful men in all lands is: Why should men leave great fortunes to their children? If this is done from affection, is it not misguided affection? Observation teaches that, generally speaking, it is not well for the children that they should be so burdened. Neither is it well for the state. Beyond providing for the wife and daughters moderate sources of income, and very moderate allowances indeed, if any, for the sons, men may well hesitate, for it is no longer questionable that great sums bequeathed oftener work more for the injury than for the good of the recipients. Wise men will soon conclude that, for the best interests of the members of their families and of the state, such bequests are an improper use of their means. . . .

As to the second mode, that of leaving wealth at death for public uses, it may be said that this is only a means for the disposal of wealth, provided a man is content to wait until he is dead before it becomes of much good in the world. . . .

There remains, then, only one mode of using great fortunes; but in this we have the true antidote for the temporary unequal distribution of wealth. . . .

Poor and restricted are our opportunities in this life; narrow our horizon; our best work most imperfect; but rich men should be thankful for one inestimable boon. They have it in their power during their lives to busy themselves in organizing benefactions from which the masses of their fellows will derive lasting advantage, and thus dignify their own lives. . . .

This, then, is held to be the duty of the man of Wealth: First, to set an example of modest, unostentatious living, shunning display or extravagance; to provide moderately for the legitimate wants of those dependent upon him; and after doing so to consider all surplus revenues which come to him simply as trust funds. . . . [T]he man of wealth thus becoming the mere agent and trustee for his poorer brethren, bringing to their service his superior wisdom, experience, and ability to administer, doing for them better than they would or could do for themselves. . . .

. . . Or every thousand dollars spent in so called charity to-day, it is probable that $950 is unwisely spent; so spent, indeed, as to produce the very evils which it proposes to mitigate or cure. . . .

In bestowing charity, the main consideration should be to help those who will help themselves; to provide part of the means by which those who desire to improve may do so; to give those who desire to rise the aids by which they may rise; to assist, but rarely or never to do all. Neither the individual nor the race is improved by alms-giving. Those worthy of assistance, except in rare cases, seldom require assistance. The really valuable men of the race never do, except in cases of accident or sudden change. . . .

The rich man is thus almost restricted to following the examples of Peter Cooper, Enoch Pratt of Baltimore, Mr. Pratt of Brooklyn, Senator Stanford, and others, who know that the best means of benefiting the community is to place within its reach the ladders upon which the aspiring can rise—parks, and means of recreation, by which men are helped in body and mind; works of art, certain to give pleasure and improve the public taste, and public institutions of various kinds, which will improve the general condition of the people;—in this manner returning their surplus wealth to the mass of their fellows in the forms best calculated to do them lasting good.

Thus is the problem of Rich and Poor to be solved. The laws of accumulation will be left free; the laws of distribution free. Individualism will continue, but the millionaire will be but a trustee for the poor; intrusted for a season with a great part of the increased wealth of the community, but administering it for the community far better than it could or would have done for itself. The best minds will thus have reached a stage in the development of the race in which it is clearly seen that there is no mode of disposing of surplus wealth creditable to thoughtful and earnest men into whose hands it flows save by using it year by year for the general good. . . . "The man who dies thus rich dies disgraced."

Such, in my opinion, is the true Gospel concerning Wealth, obedience to which is destined some day to solve the problem of the Rich and the Poor, and to bring "Peace on earth, among men Good-Will."

For Journals

Describe what you think your standard of living is.

For Discussion

1. To what factors do you think Carnegie attributes his assertion that the standard of living is higher than ever before in history? How would you compare the American standard of living now to what Carnegie describes?

2. How do you think Carnegie would define civilization? In what ways, if any, is his definition a particularly American one?

3. According to Carnegie, what social price do we pay for the advantages of modern life? What price do you think we pay today for the modern advantages we enjoy?

4. How do you respond to Carnegie's argument that a great fortune in the hands of a few people can do society more good than a little money spread around among many people? How can a man who started with nothing argue that it's better for a few people to have a lot of money?

For Writing

1. Carnegie gives three possible models for how great American wealth should be distributed: rich people could leave it to their children; they could leave money in their wills for public purposes; or they could spend their money philanthropically during their lifetimes. Assume that you have found yourself in control of a great deal of money—and that you have already gratified your personal whims and those of your family. Write an essay arguing in favor of one of Carnegie's suggestions.

2. Assume that you have a great fortune; write a creative proposal explaining how you plan to spend that fortune for the public good. Make some specific suggestions for projects you would support, and be explicit about the American values or virtues you think your plan would encourage.

3. Carnegie said that, as a rule, individuals worthy of assistance don't need assistance, and that philanthropists should build parks, donate art, and create public institutions to improve the general condition of the people. On your own, or with other students, make plans to visit a homeless shelter to interview a counselor or social worker there. Then ask that worker to set up an interview between you and an individual or family receiving assistance from that institution. Write a summary of the interviews. Alternately, arrange a visit to your local parks department or to a museum that has a children's program; interview the administrator, and, if possible, some of the children who come to the program. In either case, conclude with your own evaluation of whether the service is an effective use of money for the public good.

∞ *California, the Cornucopia of the World* (1889)

The following poster was designed at a time when the population of California was smaller than that of Mississippi. What is now Los Angeles was a relatively small city consisting mostly of orange groves and palm trees. This poster is displayed in the Ellis Island Museum, located in the building where millions of immigrants first set foot on American soil.

For Journals

When you think of California, what images come to your mind? How many of them are represented in this poster?

For Discussion

1. Who do you think was the intended audience for this poster? What guesses can you make about their educational level? Their occupations? Their goals and dreams?

2. What does the artist want the audience to learn about California? What kinds of positive facts are incorporated into the picture? What does the artist want the audience to overlook or remain ignorant of?

3. The central image in the poster is the cornucopia overflowing with fruits, vegetables, and flowers. Why do you think this image was chosen? What associations does it bring to mind?

4. There are gaps in the information provided by this poster. For example, what does "untaken" land mean if Native Americans and Mexicans are living there? How can California be the cornucopia of the world if so many millions of its acres are still unfarmed? What other

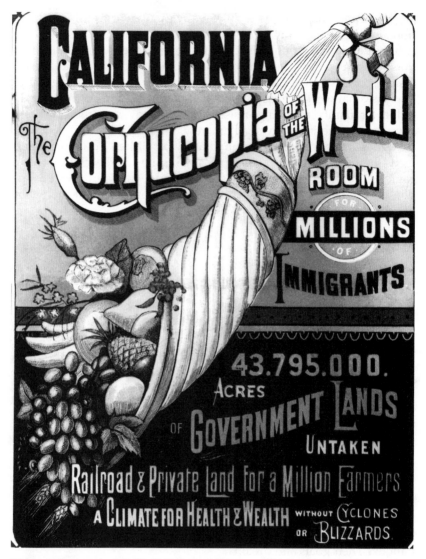

"California, Cornucopia of the World." Lithographic poster, c. 1880, Rand–McNally. From the Bella C. Landauer Collection, Neg. #41800. © Collection of the New -York Historical Society.

gaps can you find? What other kinds of information do you think the audience would want? Is this kind of advertising fair or unfair to the audience, and why?

For Writing

1. Look through some travel magazines for advertisements about a particular American place to visit. Be sure there are both pictures and text. Then write an essay answering discussion questions 1–4. You could begin with a visual exercise: look at the picture, close your eyes, and try to visualize it again; then look at it again, put it away, and try to write down everything you remember about it. What you remember—even incorrectly—will be a good guide to what made the biggest impression on you and will help you organize your ideas. Use examples from the text and images in the advertisement to support whatever conclusions you draw.

2. In his cultural history of California, *Inventing the Dream*, historian Kevin Starr says that developments and transformations in California set the standard for the rest of the nation and that California, particularly southern California and Hollywood, has a fixed place in the "daydream of America." Write an essay analyzing this idea. Here are some questions to consider: What are your mental images of California? What examples (such as movies, television, and music) portray the California dream Starr speaks of? How much do you identify the idea of California with the idea of the American dream?

∞ *In the Land of the Free* (ca. 1900)

SUI SIN FAR

Sui Sin Far (1865–1914) was the Chinese name of the daughter of an English father and a Chinese mother; her English name was Edith Eaton. She is the first Asian American whose fiction was published in the United States. This story is from a collection, Mrs. Spring Fragrance, *published in 1912.*

1

"See, Little One—the hills in the morning sun. There is thy home for years to come. It is very beautiful and thou wilt be very happy there."

The Little One looked up into his mother's face in perfect faith. He was engaged in the pleasant occupation of sucking a sweetmeat; but that did not prevent him from gurgling responsively.

"Yes, my olive bud; there is where thy father is making a fortune for thee. Thy father! O, wilt thou not be glad to behold his dear face. 'Twas for thee I left him."

The Little One ducked his chin sympathetically against his mother's knee. She lifted him on to her lap. He was two years old, a round, dimple-cheeked boy with bright brown eyes and a sturdy little frame.

"Ah! Ah! Ah! Ooh! Ooh! Ooh!" puffed he, mocking a tugboat 5 steaming by.

San Francisco's waterfront was lined with ships and steamers, while other craft, large and small, including a couple of white transports from the Philippines, lay at anchor here and there off shore. It was some time before the *Eastern Queen* could get docked, and even after that was accomplished, a lone Chinaman who had been waiting on the wharf for an hour was detained that much longer by men with the initials U.S.C. on their caps, before he could board the steamer and welcome his wife and child.

"This is thy son," announced the happy Lae Choo.

Hom Hing lifted the child, felt of his little body and limbs, gazed into his face with proud and joyous eyes; then turned inquiringly to a customs officer at his elbow.

"That's a fine boy you have there," said the man. "Where was he born?"

"In China," answered Hom Hing, swinging the Little One on his   10
right shoulder, preparatory to leading his wife off the steamer.

"Ever been to America before?"

"No, not he," answered the father with a happy laugh.

The customs officer beckoned to another.

"This little fellow," said he, "is visiting America for the first time."

The other customs officer stroked his chin reflectively.   15

"Good day," said Hom Hing.

"Wait!" commanded one of the officers. "You cannot go just yet."

"What more now?" asked Hom Hing.

"I'm afraid," said the customs officer, "that we cannot allow the boy to go ashore. There is nothing in the papers that you have shown us— your wife's papers and your own—having any bearing upon the child."

"There was no child when the papers were made out," returned   20
Hom Hing. He spoke calmly; but there was apprehension in his eyes and in his tightening grip on his son.

"What is it? What is it?" quavered Lae Choo, who understood a little English.

The second customs officer regarded her pityingly.

"I don't like this part of the business," he muttered.

The first officer turned to Hom Hing and in an official tone of voice, said:

"Seeing that the boy has no certificate entitling him to admission   25
to this country you will have to leave him with us."

"Leave my boy!" exclaimed Hom Hing.

"Yes; he will be well taken care of, and just as soon as we can hear from Washington he will be handed over to you."

"But," protested Hom Hing, "he is my son."

"We have no proof," answered the man with a shrug of his shoulders; "and even if so we cannot let him pass without orders from the Government."

"He is my son," reiterated Hom Hing, slowly and solemnly. "I am 30 a Chinese merchant and have been in business in San Francisco for many years. When my wife told to me one morning that she dreamed of a green tree with spreading branches and one beautiful red flower growing thereon, I answered her that I wished my son to be born in our country, and for her to prepare to go to China. My wife complied with my wish. After my son was born my mother fell sick and my wife nursed and cared for her; then my father, too, fell sick, and my wife also nursed and cared for him. For twenty moons my wife care for and nurse the old people, and when they die they bless her and my son, and I sent for her to return to me. I had no fear of trouble. I was a Chinese merchant and my son was my son."

"Very good, Hom Hing," replied the first officer. "Nevertheless, we take your son."

"No, you not take him; he my son too."

It was Lae Choo. Snatching the child from his father's arms she held and covered him with her own.

The officers conferred for a few moments; then one drew Hom Hing aside and spoke in his ear.

Resignedly Hom Hing bowed his head, then approached his wife. 35 " 'Tis the law," said he, speaking in Chinese, "and 'twill be but for a little while—until tomorrow's sun arises."

"You, too," reproached Lae Choo in a voice eloquent with pain. But accustomed to obedience she yielded the boy to her husband, who in turn delivered him to the first officer. The Little One protested lustily against the transfer; but his mother covered her face with her sleeve and his father silently led her away. Thus was the law of the land complied with.

2

Day was breaking. Lae Choo, who had been awake all night, dressed herself, then awoke her husband.

" 'Tis the morn," she cried. "Go, bring our son."

The man rubbed his eyes and arose upon his elbow so that he could see out of the window. A pale star was visible in the sky. The petals of a lily in a bowl on the windowsill were unfurled.

" 'Tis not yet time," said he, laying his head down again.   40

"Not yet time. Ah, all the time that I lived before yesterday is not so much as the time that has been since my Little One was taken from me."

The mother threw herself down beside the bed and covered her face.

Hom Hing turned on the light, and touching his wife's bowed head with a sympathetic hand inquired if she had slept.

"Slept!" she echoed, weepingly. "Ah, how could I close my eyes with my arms empty of the little body that has filled them every night for more than twenty moons! You do not know—man—what it is to miss the feel of the little fingers and the little toes and the soft round limbs of your little one. Even in the darkness his darling eyes used to shine up to mine, and often have I fallen into slumber with his pretty babble at my ear. And now, I see him not; I touch him not; I hear him not. My baby, my little fat one!"

"Now! Now! Now!" consoled Hom Hing, patting his wife's shoul- 45 der reassuringly; "there is no need to grieve so; he will soon gladden you again. There cannot be any law that would keep a child from its mother!"

Lae Choo dried her tears.

"You are right, my husband," she meekly murmured. She arose and stepped about the apartment, setting things to rights. The box of presents she had brought for her California friends had been opened the evening before; and silks, embroideries, carved ivories, ornamental lacquer-ware, brasses, camphorwood boxes, fans, and chinaware were scattered around in confused heaps. In the midst of unpacking the thought of her child in the hands of strangers had overpowered her, and she had left everything to crawl into bed and weep.

Having arranged her gifts in order she stepped out on to the deep balcony.

The star had faded from view and there were bright streaks in the western sky. Lae Choo looked down the street and around. Beneath the flat occupied by her and her husband were quarters for a number of bachelor Chinamen, and she could hear them from where she stood, taking their early morning breakfast. Below their dining-room was her husband's grocery store. Across the way was a large restaurant. Last night it had been resplendent with gay colored lanterns and the sound of music. The rejoicings over "the completion of the moon," by Quong Sum's firstborn, had been long and loud, and had caused her to tie a handkerchief over her ears. She, a bereaved mother, had it not in her heart to rejoice with other parents. This morning the place was more in accord with her mood. It was still and quiet. The revellers had dispersed or were asleep.

A roly-poly woman in black sateen, with long pendant earrings in 50 her ears, looked up from the street below and waved her a smiling greeting. It was her old neighbor, Kuie Hoe, the wife of the gold embosser, Mark Sing. With her was a little boy in a yellow jacket and lavender pantaloons. Lae Choo remembered him as a baby. She used to like to play with him in those days when she had no child of her own. What a long time ago that seemed! She caught her breath in a sigh, and laughed instead.

"Why are you so merry?" called her husband from within.

"Because my Little One is coming home," answered Lae Choo. "I am a happy mother—a happy mother."

She pattered into the room with a smile on her face.

The noon hour had arrived. The rice was steaming in the bowls and a fragrant dish of chicken and bamboo shoots was awaiting Hom Hing. Not for one moment had Lae Choo paused to rest during the morning hours; her activity had been ceaseless. Every now and again, however, she had raised her eyes to the gilded clock on the curiously carved mantelpiece. Once, she had exclaimed:

"Why so long, oh! why so long?" Then, apostrophizing herself: 55 "Lae Choo, be happy. The Little One is coming! The Little One is coming!" Several times she burst into tears, and several times she laughed aloud.

Hom Hing entered the room; his arms hung down by his side.

"The Little One!" shrieked Lae Choo.

"They bid me call tomorrow."

With a moan the mother sank to the floor.

The noon hour passed. The dinner remained on the table.   60

3

The winter rains were over: the spring had come to California, flushing the hills with green and causing an ever-changing pageant of flowers to pass over them. But there was no spring in Lae Choo's heart, for the Little One remained away from her arms. He was being kept in a mission. White women were caring for him, and though for one full moon he had pined for his mother and refused to be comforted he was now apparently happy and contended. Five moons or five months had gone by since the day he had passed with Lae Choo through the Golden Gate; but the great Government at Washington still delayed sending the answer which would return him to his parents.

Hom Hing was disconsolately rolling up and down the balls in his abacus box when a keen-faced young man stepped into his store.

"What news?" asked the Chinese merchant.

"This!" The young man brought forth a typewritten letter. Hom Hing read the words:

"Re Chinese child, alleged to be the son of Hom Hing, Chinese 65 merchant, doing business at 425 Clay Street, San Francisco.

"Same will have attention as soon as possible."

Hom Hing returned the letter, and without a word continued his manipulation of the counting machine.

"Have you anything to say?" asked the young man.

"Nothing. They have sent the same letter fifteen times before. Have you not yourself showed it to me?"

"True!" The young man eyed the Chinese merchant furtively. He 70 had a proposition to make and was pondering whether or not the time was opportune.

"How is your wife?" he inquired solicitously—and diplomatically.

Hom Hing shook his head mournfully.

"She seems less every day," he replied. "Her food she takes only when I bid her and her tears fall continually. She finds no pleasure in dress or flowers and cares not to see her friends. Her eyes stare all night. I think before another moon she will pass into the land of the spirits."

"No!" exclaimed the young man, genuinely startled.

"If the boy not come home I lose my wife sure," continued Hom 75 Hing with bitter sadness.

"It's not right," cried the young man indignantly. Then he made his proposition.

The Chinese father's eyes brightened exceedingly.

"Will I like you to go to Washington and make them give you the paper to restore my son?" cried he. "How can you ask when you know my heart's desire?"

"Then," said the young fellow, "I will start next week. I am anxious to see this thing through if only for the sake of your wife's peace of mind."

"I will call her. To hear what you think to do will make her glad," 80 said Hom Hing.

He called a message to Lae Choo upstairs through a tube in the wall.

In a few moments she appeared, listless, wan, and hollow-eyed; but when her husband told her the young lawyer's suggestion she became electrified; her form straightened, her eyes glistened; the color flushed to her cheeks.

"Oh," she cried, turning to James Clancy. "You are a hundred man good!"

The young man felt somewhat embarrassed; his eyes shifted a little under the intense gaze of the Chinese mother.

"Well, we must get your boy for you," he responded. "Of 85 course"—turning to Hom Hing—"it will cost a little money. You can't get fellows to hurry the Government for you without gold in your pocket."

Hom Hing stared blankly for a moment. Then: "How much do you want, Mr. Clancy?" he asked quietly.

"Well, I will need at least five hundred to start with."

Hom Hing cleared his throat.

"I think I told to you the time I last paid you for writing letters for me and seeing the Custom boss here that nearly all I had was gone!"

"Oh well then we won't talk about it, old fellow. It won't harm the boy to stay where he is, and your wife may get over it all right."

"What that you say?" quavered Lae Choo.

James Clancy looked out of the window.

"He says," explained Hom Hing in English, "that to get our boy we have to have much money."

"Money! Oh, yes."

Lae Choo nodded her head.

"I have not got the money to give him."

For a moment Lae Choo gazed wonderingly from one face to the other; then, comprehension dawning upon her, with swift anger, pointing to the lawyer, she cried: "You not one hundred man good; you just common white man."

"Yes, ma'am," returned James Clancy, bowing and smiling ironically.

Hom Hing pushed his wife behind him and addressed the lawyer again: "I might try," said he, "to raise something; but five hundred—it is not possible."

"What about four?"

"I tell you I have next to nothing left and my friends are not rich."

"Very well!"

The lawyer moved leisurely toward the door, pausing on its threshold to light a cigarette.

"Stop, white man; white man, stop!"

Lae Choo, panting and terrified, had started forward and now stood beside him, clutching his sleeve excitedly.

"You say you can go to get paper to bring my Little One to me if Hom Hing give you five hundred dollars?"

The lawyer nodded carelessly; his eyes were intent upon the cigarette which would not take the fire from the match.

"Then you go get paper. If Hom Hing not can give you five hundred dollars—I give you perhaps what more that much."

She slipped a heavy gold bracelet from her wrist and held it out to the man. Mechanically he took it.

"I go get more!"

She scurried away, disappearing behind the door through which she had come.

"Oh, look here, I can't accept this," said James Clancy, walking back to Hom Hing and laying down the bracelet before him.

"It's all right," said Hom Hing, seriously, "pure China gold. My wife's parent give it to her when we married."

"But I can't take it anyway," protested the young man.

"It is all same as money. And you want money to go to Washing- 115
ton," replied Hom Hing in a matter-of-fact manner.

"See, my jade earrings—my gold buttons—my hairpins—my
comb of pearl and my rings—one, two, three, four, five rings; very
good—very good—all same much money. I give them all to you. You
take and bring me paper for my Little One."

Lae Choo piled up her jewels before the lawyer.

Hom Hing laid a restraining hand upon her shoulder. "Not all, my
wife," he said in Chinese. He selected a ring—his gift to Lae Choo
when she dreamed of the tree with the red flower. The rest of the jewels he pushed toward the white man.

"Take them and sell them," said he. "They will pay your fare to
Washington and bring you back with the paper."

For one moment James Clancy hesitated. He was not a sentimental 120
man; but something within him arose against accepting such payment
for his services.

"They are good, good," pleadingly asserted Lae Choo, seeing his
hesitation.

Whereupon he seized the jewels, thrust them into his coat pocket,
and walked rapidly away from the store.

4

Lae Choo followed after the missionary woman through the mission nursery school. Her heart was beating so high with happiness that
she could scarcely breathe. The paper had come at last—the precious
paper which gave Hom Hing and his wife the right to the possession of
their own child. It was ten months now since he had been taken from
them—ten months since the sun had ceased to shine for Lae Choo.

The room was filled with children—most of them wee tots, but
none so wee as her own. The mission woman talked as she walked.
She told Lae Choo that little Kim, as he had been named by the school,
was the pet of the place, and that his little tricks and ways amused and
delighted every one. He had been rather difficult to manage at first
and had cried much for his mother; "but children so soon forget, and
after a month he seemed quite at home and played around as bright
and happy as a bird."

"Yes," responded Lae Choo. "Oh, yes, yes!" 125

But she did not hear what was said to her. She was walking in a
maze of anticipatory joy.

"Wait here, please," said the mission woman, placing Lae Choo in
a chair. "The very youngest ones are having their breakfast."

She withdrew for a moment—it seemed like an hour to the
mother—then she reappeared leading by the hand a little boy dressed

in blue cotton overalls and white-soled shoes. The little boy's face was round and dimpled and his eyes were very bright.

"Little One, ah, my Little One!" cried Lae Choo.

She fell on her knees and stretched her hungry arms toward her 130 son.

But the Little One shrunk from her and tried to hide himself in the folds of the white woman's skirt.

"Go 'way, go 'way!" he bade his mother.

For Journals

There's an idea of America as a melting pot and another of America as a tossed salad; which one do you think better describes the mix of cultures in this country?

For Discussion

1. In the first sentence of this story, Lae Choo, arriving in San Francisco with her infant son, expresses her dream for his happy future in America: "See, Little One—the hills in the morning sun. There is thy home for years to come. It is very beautiful and thou wilt be very happy there." But things don't work out exactly as planned; in fact, in each of the four parts of this story, dreams are derailed, if not destroyed. What are these dreams, whose are they, and how are they changed by circumstances?

2. How does the involvement of white Americans in the lives of Hom Hing, Lae Choo, and their child highlight cultural differences between the Chinese and the white American characters? Do these involvements have positive or negative consequences? What are the intentions of the Americans?

3. Earlier in this chapter you saw a poster advertising California, printed roughly at the time this story was written. What elements of life in California are left out of the poster, yet would affect the dreams of people like Hom Hing and Lae Choo?

4. The classic image of the immigrant experience in America is the melting pot, in which everyone becomes part of the larger American community. Does Sui Sin Far's representation of the Chinese immigrant experience support this idea? What examples can you find in the text that best convey her sense of what the Chinese immigrants' attitude is toward assimilation and the larger American culture?

5. What do you think of the story's title? What does it tell you about expectation and reality in the lives of the Chinese characters?

For Writing

1. Write an essay in which you look at this story from the point of view of the missionary lady. How do you think she would have depicted the last scene in the story, when Lae Choo finally gets her son back? Do you think her dreams for him will be fulfilled? What dreams might the son himself have? To find evidence for your essay, reread the last scene and look at the various exchanges: between Lae Choo and the missionary lady, Lae Choo and her son, and the son and the missionary lady.

2. Compare Amy Tan's *The Joy Luck Club*, from the previous chapter, with this story. Be sure to include the following points: the attitudes of the native-born Chinese American women to their immigrant mothers; the attitude of the mothers toward raising children in America; Tan's descriptions of contemporary life in San Francisco's Chinatown.

3. Research and write a report on one of the following topics: the cultural life in San Francisco's Chinatown at the turn of the century; the anti-Chinese immigration laws, including the prohibition of marriage; the role of Chinese laborers in building the transcontinental railroad; the prevalence of Chinese medicine and the unavailability of American health care in Chinatown; the way the Chinese in America were portrayed around 1900 in American newspapers, such as the *New York Times* and the *San Francisco Chronicle*, and in tabloids, such as the *Police Gazette* (see Chapter 11).

∞ *Let America Be America Again* (1938)

LANGSTON HUGHES

Langston Hughes (1902–1967) was one of the premier figures of the Harlem Renaissance—that jubilant outpouring of black art and culture in New York City in the 1920s. Hughes uses the rhythms of jazz, blues, and gospel music to celebrate and probe the role of black people in American society. His collections of verse include The Dream Keeper *(1932),* The Way of White Folks *(1934),* Shakespeare in Harlem *(1941), and* Montage of a Dream Deferred *(1951).*

Let America be America again.
Let it be the dream it used to be.
Let it be the pioneer on the plain
Seeking a home where he himself is free.

(America never was America to me.)   5

Let America be the dream the dreamers dreamed—
Let it be that great strong land of love

Where never kings connive nor tyrants scheme
That any man be crushed by one above.

(It never was America to me.) 10

O, let my land be a land where Liberty
Is crowned with no false patriotic wreath,
But opportunity is real, and life is free,
Equality is in the air we breathe.

(There's never been equality for me, 15
Nor freedom in this "homeland of the free.")

Say who are you that mumbles in the dark?
And who are you that draws your veil across the stars?

I am the poor white, fooled and pushed apart,
I am the red man driven from the land. 20
I am the refugee clutching the hope I seek—
But finding only the same old stupid plan

Of dog eat dog, of mighty crush the weak.
I am the Negro, "problem" to you all.
I am the people, humble, hungry, mean— 25
Hungry yet today despite the dream.
Beaten yet today—O, Pioneers!
I am the man who never got ahead,
The poorest worker bartered through the years.
Yet I'm the one who dreamt our basic dream 30
In that Old World while still a serf of kings,
Who dreamt a dream so strong, so brave, so true,
That even yet its mighty daring sings
In every brick and stone, in every furrow turned
That's made America the land it has become. 35
O, I'm the man who sailed those early seas
In search of what I meant to be my home—
For I'm the one who left dark Ireland's shore,
And Poland's plain, and England's grassy lea,
And torn from Black Africa's strand I came 40
To build a "homeland of the free."

The free?
Who said the free? Not me?
Surely not me? The millions on relief today?
The millions who have nothing for our pay 45

For all the dreams we've dreamed
And all the songs we've sung
And all the hopes we've held
And all the flags we've hung,
The millions who have nothing for our pay—　　　　　　50
Except the dream we keep alive today.

O, let America be America again—
The land that never has been yet—
And yet must be—the land where every man is free.
The land that's mine—the poor man's, Indian's, Negro's, ME—　　55
Who made America,
Whose sweat and blood, whose faith and pain,
Whose hand at the foundry, whose plow in the rain,
Must bring back our mighty dream again.

　　O, yes,　　　　　　　　　　　　　　　　　60
　　I say it plain,
　　America never was America to me,
And yet I swear this oath—
America will be!

For Journals

What do you know about the America of the 1930s and the Great Depression? What do you think they have to do with the subject of the poem?

For Discussion

1. With whom, or with what, does Hughes identify the America that is "the dream it used to be" (line 2)? In the first three stanzas, which examples of the dream does he celebrate?

2. Beginning with line 52, Hughes gives examples of the people he thinks of as the real source of the American dream, a dream that must be "the poor man's, Indian's, Negro's, ME" (line 55) in order to be valid. How can this viewpoint coexist with the idea of an America exemplified by the founding fathers, including Benjamin Franklin (see Chapter 8)?

3. Analyze the poem as an argument. What are the two sides? What are they fighting over? What points does each side make? Where does the poem "turn"? How would you describe the tone of the speaker? Optimistic? Cheerful? Bitter? What do you consider the most persuasive part of the poem?

4.   What does it mean for America to be America again, as the title says, if it never was in the first place? Since the population of America is almost all descended from people who came from somewhere else, including all the nationalities Hughes mentions, is there any evidence in the poem to support the possibility of change? Where would it come from?

5.   Considering how much of the American dream revolves around success, how do you respond to the fact that Hughes identifies the dream with examples of people who are not successful—"I am the man who never got ahead, / The poorest worker bartered through the years" (lines 28–29)? Do you think he is distorting the definition of the dream, or redefining it? Why?

For Writing

1.   Write an essay that provides a persuasive answer to the following questions: If the people who originated the American dream are left out of it, what about the dream is still worthwhile to them? Why do they still want it? Read several newspaper or magazine articles about the problems and attitudes that prospective immigrants to America currently encounter. Support your essay with examples and, if possible, with actual quotations from immigrants about their desires to come to this country.

2.   Hughes was active as a writer both during and after the Harlem Renaissance. Research and write an essay on one of the following: the historical and social background for the Harlem Renaissance; the work of any of the artists, musicians, and writers involved in the Renaissance, for example, Jean Toomer, Zora Neale Hurston, Duke Ellington, Richard Wright, Countee Cullen, or Lou Jones; the history of the Cotton Club and the entertainers who worked there; the story of the Apollo Theater; or other work by Langston Hughes, including his great collection of short stories, *The Best of Simple*.

∞ *There's No Way like the American Way* (1937)

MARGARET BOURKE-WHITE

Margaret Bourke-White (1904–1971) was a photojournalist who covered major news stories for Life *magazine when that publication was home to the world's best photographers. As well as the work she did on the Great Depression, she is famous for her photographs of the invasion of Russia in World War II and the liberation of concentration camps.*

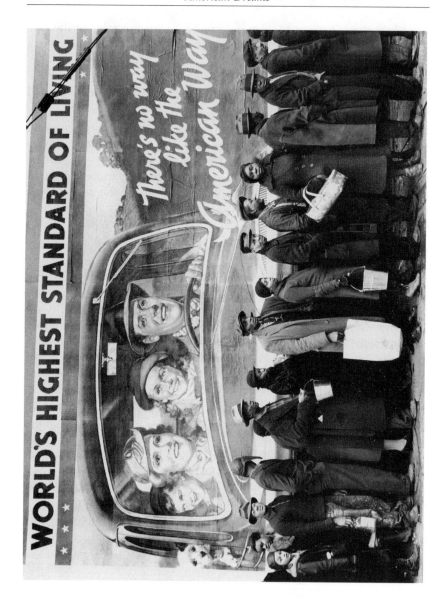

One of Bourke-White's most famous photographs is this picture of Americans in 1937, during the Great Depression, standing in line at an emergency relief station in the aftermath of an Ohio flood that killed hundreds of people and left thousands of others homeless.

For Journals

What do you know about the Great Depression of the 1930s? Was anyone in your family affected by it?

For Discussion

1.   From looking at this photo, what would you say was the image of the ideal American family in 1937? How is that image affected by the fact that in 1937 the Depression was in full force, with roughly 15 million Americans out of work?

2.   There are two verbal assertions in this photograph, both of them slogans on the billboard. How does the rest of the photograph, including the line of people, support or refute those statements?

3.   How do you suppose the people in the line would respond to the billboard behind them? What is your response to it?

4.   The composition of a great photograph is never accidental. Since the line of people was longer than the billboard, what do you think were Bourke-White's reasons for taking a photograph of those particular people under that particular billboard? Would it have a different impact if the flood victims were white? Is their color or their economic situation more important?

5.   If you had to translate this photo into a verbal assertion about life in America in 1937, what would it be? What details of the photograph would you choose to support your statement?

For Writing

1.   Today America still has problems of homelessness and unemployment. Look in recent newspapers or magazines for a picture or pictures of homeless or unemployed Americans. Write a reflective essay in which you consider the following: whether you could imagine yourself or your family in a similar situation and whether your choice of your major in school is affected by your concerns for the future.

2.   Bourke-White took this photograph from a particular point of view. Using back copies of magazines, contemporary magazines, or books of photographs, find an American photograph from a historic event—for example, the Civil War, the Great Depression, one of the world wars, a political assassination, the civil rights struggle in the South, a presidential campaign—in which the photographer makes a judgment about the event through the image. Research the background of the event to be sure you understand the historical context. Then write an essay in which you respond to the following questions: What is the photo's impact on you? Has the meaning of the photo changed over time? What biases or values or assumptions do you think the photographer is expressing? What details in the photograph support your assertions?

∞ *Early Success* (1937)

F. SCOTT FITZGERALD

While still in his twenties, F. Scott Fitzgerald (1897–1940) was already famous for his stories and novels. An extremely careful prose stylist, he was never prolific, but he had to produce a lot of short stories for magazines to pay for the expensive lifestyle that he and his wife had become accustomed to. By the time he died in 1940 of a heart attack, he had survived years of alcoholism and the decline of his reputation. But he had produced three remarkable novels: The Great Gatsby, Tender Is the Night, *and the unfinished* The Last Tycoon. *Since his death, he has become one of the most widely read and written-about American authors. This selection is an article from* The Crack-Up, *a collection of Fitzgerald's articles, letters, and notes in which he writes, with devastating honesty, about his early success, his later disintegration, and how he put himself back together.*

October, 1937

Seventeen years ago this month I quit work or, if you prefer, I retired from business. I was through—let the Street Railway Advertising Company carry along under its own power. I retired, not on my profits, but on my liabilities, which included debts, despair, and a broken engagement and crept home to St. Paul to "finish a novel."

That novel, begun in a training camp late in the war, was my ace in the hole. I had put it aside when I got a job in New York, but I was as constantly aware of it as of the shoe with cardboard in the sole, during all one desolate spring. It was like the fox and goose and the bag of beans. If I stopped working to finish the novel, I lost the girl.

So I struggled on in a business I detested and all the confidence I had garnered at Princeton and in a haughty career as the army's worst aide-de-camp melted gradually away. Lost and forgotten, I walked quickly from certain places—from the pawn shop where one left the field glasses, from prosperous friends whom one met when wearing the suit from before the war—from restaurants after tipping with the last nickel, from busy cheerful offices that were saving the jobs for their own boys from the war.

Even having a first story accepted had not proved very exciting. Dutch Mount and I sat across from each other in a car-card slogan advertising office, and the same mail brought each of us an acceptance from the same magazine—the old *Smart Set*.

"My check was thirty—how much was yours?"

5

"Thirty-five."

The real blight, however, was that my story had been written in college two years before, and a dozen new ones hadn't even drawn a personal letter. The implication was that I was on the down-grade at twenty-two. I spent the thirty dollars on a magenta feather fan for a girl in Alabama.

My friends who were not in love or who had waiting arrangements with "sensible" girls, braced themselves patiently for a long pull. Not I—I was in love with a whirlwind and I must spin a net big enough to catch it out of my head, a head full of trickling nickels and sliding dimes, the incessant music box of the poor. It couldn't be done like that, so when the girl threw me over I went home and finished my novel. And then, suddenly, everything changed, and this article is about that first wild wind of success and the delicious mist it brings with it. It is a short and precious time—for when the mist rises in a few weeks, or a few months, one finds that the very best is over.

It began to happen in the autumn of 1919 when I was an empty bucket, so mentally blunted with the summer's writing that I'd taken a job repairing car roofs at the Northern Pacific shops. Then the postman rang, and that day I quit work and ran along the streets, stopping automobiles to tell friends and acquaintances about it—my novel *This Side of Paradise* was accepted for publication. That week the postman rang and rang, and I paid off my terrible small debts, bought a suit, and woke up every morning with a world of ineffable toploftiness and promise.

While I waited for the novel to appear, the metamorphosis of ama- 10 teur into professional began to take place—a sort of stitching together of your whole life into a pattern of work, so that the end of one job is automatically the beginning of another. I had been an amateur before; in October, when I strolled with a girl among the stones of a southern graveyard, I was a professional and my enchantment with certain things that she felt and said was already paced by an anxiety to set them down in a story—it was called *The Ice Palace* and it was published later. Similarly, during Christmas week in St. Paul, there was a night when I had stayed home from two dances to work on a story. Three friends called up during the evening to tell me I had missed some rare doings: a well-known man-about-town had disguised himself as a camel and, with a taxi-driver as the rear half, managed to attend the wrong party. Aghast with myself for not being there, I spent the next day trying to collect the fragments of the story.

"Well, all I can say is it was funny when it happened." "No, I don't know where he got the taxi-man." "You'd have to know him well to understand how funny it was."

In despair I said:

"Well, I can't seem to find out exactly what happened but I'm going to write about it as if it was ten times funnier than anything you've said." So I wrote it, in twenty-two consecutive hours, and wrote it "funny," simply because I was so emphatically told it was funny. *The Camel's Back* was published and still crops up in the humourous anthologies.

With the end of the winter set in another pleasant pumped-dry period, and, while I took a little time off, a fresh picture of life in America began to form before my eyes. The uncertainties of 1919 were over—there seemed little doubt about what was going to happen—America was going on the greatest, gaudiest spree in history and there was going to be plenty to tell about it. The whole golden boom was in the air—its splendid generosities, its outrageous corruptions and the tortuous death struggle of the old America in prohibition. All the stories that came into my head had a touch of disaster in them—the lovely young creatures in my novels went to ruin, the diamond mountains of my short stories blew up, my millionaires were as beautiful and damned as Thomas Hardy's peasants. In life these things hadn't happened yet, but I was pretty sure living wasn't the reckless, careless business these people thought—this generation just younger than me.

For my point of vantage was the dividing line between the two generations, and there I sat—somewhat self-consciously. When my first big mail came in—hundreds and hundreds of letters on a story about a girl who bobbed her hair—it seemed rather absurd that they should come to me about it. On the other hand, for a shy man it was nice to be somebody except oneself again: to be "the Author" as one had been "the Lieutenant." Of course one wasn't really an author any more than one had been an army officer, but nobody seemed to guess behind the false face.

All in three days I got married and the presses were pounding out *This Side of Paradise* like they pound out extras in the movies.

With its publication I had reached a stage of manic depressive insanity. Rage and bliss alternated hour by hour. A lot of people thought it was a fake, and perhaps it was, and a lot of others thought it was a lie, which it was not. In a daze I gave out an interview—I told what a great writer I was and how I'd achieved the heights. Heywood Broun,[1] who was on my trail, simply quoted it with the comment that I seemed to be a very self-satisfied young man, and for some days I was notably poor company. I invited him to lunch and in a kindly way told him that it was too bad he had let his life slide away without accomplishing anything. He had just turned thirty and it was about then that I wrote a line which certain people will not let me forget: "She was a faded but still lovely woman of twenty-seven."

---

[1]Broun (1888–1939) was a journalist and critic.

In a daze I told the Scribner Company that I didn't expect my novel to sell more than twenty thousand copies and when the laughter died away I was told that a sale of five thousand was excellent for a first novel. I think it was a week after publication that it passed the twenty thousand mark, but I took myself so seriously that I didn't even think it was funny.

These weeks in the clouds ended abruptly a week later when Princeton turned on the book—not undergraduate Princeton but the black mass of faculty and alumni. There was a kind but reproachful letter from President Hibben, and a room full of classmates who suddenly turned on me with condemnation. We had been part of a rather gay party staged conspicuously in Harvey Firestone's car of robin's-egg blue, and in the course of it I got an accidental black eye trying to stop a fight. This was magnified into an orgy and in spite of a delegation of undergraduates who went to the board of Governors, I was suspended from my club for a couple of months. The *Alumni Weekly* got after my book and only Dean Gauss had a good word to say for me. The unctuousness and hypocrisy of the proceedings was exasperating and for seven years I didn't go to Princeton. Then a magazine asked me for an article about it and when I started to write it, I found I really loved the place and that the experience of one week was a small item in the total budget. But on that day in 1920 most of the joy went out of my success.

But one was now a professional—and the new world couldn't possibly be presented without bumping the old out of the way. One gradually developed a protective hardness against both praise and blame. Too often people liked your things for the wrong reasons or people liked them whose dislike would be a compliment. No decent career was ever founded on a public and one learned to go ahead without precedents and without fear. Counting the bag, I found that in 1919 I had made $800 by writing, that in 1920 I had made $18,000, stories, picture rights and book. My story price had gone from $30 to $1,000. That's a small price to what was paid later in the Boom, but what it sounded like to me couldn't be exaggerated. 20

The dream had been early realized and the realization carried with it a certain bonus and a certain burden. Premature success gives one an almost mystical conception of destiny as opposed to will power—at its worst the Napoleonic delusion. The man who arrives young believes that he exercises his will because his star is shining. The man who only asserts himself at thirty has a balanced idea of what will power and fate have each contributed, the one who gets there at forty is liable to put the emphasis on will alone. This comes out when the storms strike your craft.

The compensation of a very early success is a conviction that life is a romantic matter. In the best sense one stays young. When the primary objects of love and money could be taken for granted and a shaky eminence had lost its fascination, I had fair years to waste, years that I can't honestly regret, in seeking the eternal Carnival by the Sea. Once in the middle twenties I was driving along the High Corniche Road through the twilight with the whole French Riviera twinkling on the sea below. As far ahead as I could see was Monte Carlo, and though it was out of season and there were no Grand Dukes left to gamble and E. Phillips Oppenheim[2] was a fat industrious man in my hotel, who lived in a bathrobe—the very name was so incorrigibly enchanting that I could only stop the car and like the Chinese whisper: "Ah me! Ah me!" It was not Monte Carlo I was looking at. It was back into the mind of the young man with cardboard soles who had walked the streets of New York. I was him again—for an instant I had the good fortune to share his dreams, I who had no more dreams of my own. And there are still times when I creep up on him, surprise him on an autumn morning in New York or a spring night in Carolina when it is so quiet that you can hear a dog barking in the next county. But never again as during that all too short period when he and I were one person, when the fulfilled future and the wistful past were mingled in a single gorgeous moment—when life was literally a dream.

For Journals

If, like Fitzgerald, you could become famous for something while you are still very young, what would it be?

For Discussion

1. What dream does Fitzgerald start with? Based on this essay, how would you describe his version of the American dream he found himself living?

2. Fitzgerald couldn't marry his girlfriend until he wrote a book that made money, and he wrote about money often: not having any, suddenly having a lot, losing it. How significant a role do you think money does or doesn't play in achieving success in this country, either in work or in love or in both?

3. Fitzgerald was able to speak ironically about himself even in his worst moments. Looking closely at the text, what examples can you find of irony and self-mockery? How persuasive are these examples in suggesting the changes Fitzgerald underwent in the process of going from an unknown to a famous writer?

---

[2]Oppenheim (1866–1946) was an English author who wrote over 100 novels.

4. What argument does Fitzgerald make in favor of later achievement rather than the kind of early fame that he enjoyed? How convincing are his assertions about the effects of fame on character? What examples can you think of concerning contemporary writers, actors, musicians, and so on who became very successful early and later had difficulties handling the results? What in Fitzgerald's experience could be extrapolated to help in such circumstances?

For Writing

1. Read the other essays in *The Crack-Up,* which Fitzgerald wrote about his own breakdown and subsequent recovery. Write an essay in which you examine the following questions: How does "Early Success" fit in this group? In what ways, if any, does Fitzgerald achieve success after his professional and personal failures?

2. Fitzgerald's most famous remark about success and money was an opening line to one of his stories, written in 1926: "Let me tell you about the very rich. They are different from you and me." Answering Fitzgerald, in a story as well, Ernest Hemingway responded, "Yes, they have more money." Write an essay in which you argue either that Fitzgerald was correct—that possession of a lot of money creates deep differences psychologically as well as culturally—or that Hemingway was right. Give your own interpretation of both remarks. You can use other selections in this book—by Andrew Carnegie, Benjamin Franklin, Charlotte Perkins Gilman, and others—as well as your own observations and experience to support your assertions.

∞ *Requiem* FROM Death of a Salesman (1949)

ARTHUR MILLER

Arthur Miller (1915–) grew up in Brooklyn, in a Jewish immigrant family; because of financial problems his parents experienced in the Depression, he didn't attend college—at the University of Michigan—until 1934. While there he discovered playwriting and won his first two awards. He has always written plays that were both socially conscious and which drew heavily on his own life experience; his play After the Fall, *for example, evokes the complexity and ultimate impossibility of his marriage to his second wife, Marilyn Monroe. The overwhelming preponderance of Miller's work, however, portrays the experiences of ordinary middle-class Americans, and the absolute importance of taking responsibility for the consequences of one's actions. The play which made him famous,* Death of a Salesman, *is still his most performed and admired work, not only in the United States but also in China, where Miller helped mount a hugely famous production in the 1980's, and in Europe.*

The following excerpt is the Requiem—really the epilogue—from *Death of a Salesman*. The play is about the last day in the life of the main character, Willy Loman, a salesman who has spent his time reaching for some version of the American dream in which he would come out as the number one man. Instead, Willy, over sixty and over the hill professionally, loses his job, which he hasn't been good at in years; his relations with his two sons come to a crisis; and as the ghosts of his past wander into his mind and across the stage, we watch him disintegrate. He is, as Miller describes him, a man with a mercurial nature, a temper, little cruelties, and massive dreams. The dreams end with Willy's suicide; the Requiem takes place after his funeral, and the characters are his wife Linda, his friend Charlie, and his two sons, Happy and Biff.

Requiem

CHARLEY: It's getting dark, Linda.
Linda doesn't react. She stares at the grave.
BIFF: How about it, Mom? Better get some rest, heh? They'll be closing the gate soon.
Linda makes no move. Pause.
HAPPY, *deeply angered:* He had no right to do that. There was no necessity for it. We would've helped him.
CHARLEY, *grunting:* Hmmm.
BIFF: Come along, Mom.
LINDA: Why didn't anybody come?
CHARLEY: It was a very nice funeral.
LINDA: But where are all the people he knew? Maybe they blame him.
CHARLEY: Naa. It's a rough world, Linda. They wouldn't blame him.
LINDA: I can't understand it. At this time especially. First time in thirty-five years we were just about free and clear. He only needed a little salary. He was even finished with the dentist.
CHARLEY: No man only needs a little salary.
LINDA: I can't understand it.
BIFF: There were a lot of nice days. When he'd come home from a trip; or on Sundays, making the stoop; finishing the cellar; putting on the new porch; when he built the extra bathroom; and put up the garage. You know something, Charley, there's more of him in that front stoop than in all the sales he ever made.
CHARLEY: Yeah. He was a happy man with a batch of cement.
LINDA: He was so wonderful with his hands.
BIFF: He had the wrong dreams. All, all, wrong.
HAPPY, *almost ready to fight Biff:* Don't say that!
BIFF: He never knew who he was.
CHARLEY, *stopping Happy's movement and reply. To Biff:* Nobody dast blame this man. You don't understand: Willy was a salesman. And for

a salesman, there is no rock bottom to the life. He don't put a bolt to a nut, he don't tell you the law or give you medicine. He's a man way out there in the blue, riding on a smile and a shoeshine. And when they start not smiling back—that's an earthquake. And then you get yourself a couple of spots on your hat, and you're finished. Nobody dast blame this man. A salesman is got to dream, boy. It comes with the territory.

BIFF: Charley, the man didn't know who he was.

HAPPY, *infuriated:* Don't say that!

BIFF: Why don't you come with me, Happy?

HAPPY: I'm not licked that easily. I'm staying right in this city, and I'm gonna beat this racket! *He looks at Biff, his chin set.* The Loman Brothers!

BIFF: I know who I am, kid.

HAPPY: All right, boy. I'm gonna show you and everybody else that Willy Loman did not die in vain. He had a good dream. It's the only dream you can have—to come out number-one man. He fought it out here, and this is where I'm gonna win it for him.

BIFF, *with a hopeless glance at Happy, bends toward his mother:* Let's go, Mom.

LINDA: I'll be with you in a minute. Go on, Charley. *He hesitates.* I want to, just for a minute. I never had a chance to say good-by.

Charley moves away, followed by Happy. Biff remains a slight distance up and left of Linda. She sits there, summoning herself. The flute begins, not far away, playing behind her speech.

LINDA: Forgive me, dear. I can't cry. I don't know what it is, but I can't cry. I don't understand it. Why did you ever do that? Help me, Willy, I can't cry. It seems to me that you're just on another trip. I keep expecting you. Willy, dear, I can't cry. Why did you do it? I search and search and I search, and I can't understand it, Willy. I made the last payment on the house today. Today, dear. And there'll be nobody home. *A sob rises in her throat.* We're free and clear. *Sobbing more fully, released:* We're free. *Biff comes slowly toward her.* We're free . . . We're free . . .

Biff lifts her to her feet and moves out up right with her in his arms. Linda sobs quietly. Bernard and Charley come together and follow them, followed by Happy. Only the music of the flute is left on the darkening stage as over the house the hard towers of the apartment buildings rise into sharp focus.

CURTAIN

For Journals

If a parent of yours lost his or her job, what effect would it have on you and your family?

For Discussion

1. The excerpt you have here is the last page of the play, so you can only judge the play by what you find in these two pages. From this short selection, what troubles in Willy's life do you get a sense of? What is the most significant aspect of Willy to each of the characters, Charley, Biff, Happy, and Willy's widow Linda?

2. Requiem is a musical term; look it up in a dictionary so you have the exact definition, and then come up with your own reasons for why that is or isn't an effective term for what you've read.

3. There are versions of this play on film, including one starring Dustin Hoffman as Willy, which are available from video stores. Watch the film with your class and discuss the following: What are Willy's dreams? What are his relationships with his sons? Why are those relationships so troubled? Also discuss whether you think Willy's failure is personal to him or built into the dreams he follows, and what Linda means in the play's most famous line, "Attention must be paid."

4. The classical definition of a tragic play assumes the fall of a great man destroyed by a crucial flaw, usually hubris, or overweening pride, like Oedipus. One of the crucial questions that was asked in light of *Salesman's* success, and its powerful effect on audiences, is whether it's possible for a middle-class, ordinary American to be a tragic hero even though he is neither famous nor powerful. If you have seen a video of the play, discuss this question in relation to *Salesman*. If you have only read this excerpt, then draw on the experiences of people you know, on other readings or films you are aware of, and on your own ideas about what tragedy is in the context of the American dream.

For Writing

1. Write an essay based on question 3 or question 4 above. If you choose 3, write about only one or two of the issues raised in the question. If you choose 4, make up your own definition of an American tragic hero, and see whether you think Willy qualifies. Alternatively, once you come up with a definition, you can apply it to a character from another play or movie. In either case, you must refer to specific scenes and dialogue to keep your writing grounded in the play itself.

2. Watch the video of *All My Sons*, Miller's play about unacknowledged guilt and the family conflict that results because one of the central characters sold bad airplane parts to the Air Force during World War II and never admitted that American pilots died as a result. Write an essay in which you focus entirely on an aspect of *All My Sons*, such as the aftereffects of that decision on two or three of the main characters. Or you could write a paper in which you compare one relationship in this film such as that of the father and his surviving son to Willy and his relationship with Biff.

3. If you are a fan of F. Scott Fitzgerald's novel, *The Great Gatsby*, write a paper in which you compare the scene following Gatsby's funeral, especially his father's and the narrator's reactions, with the Requiem here and the family's reactions.

∞ *Harlem* (1951)

LANGSTON HUGHES

This poem, written more than a decade after "Let America Be America Again," poses a very different set of questions and answers.

What happens to a dream deferred?

Does it dry up
like a raisin in the sun?
Or fester like a sore—
And then run?   5
Does it stink like rotten meat?
Or crust and sugar over—
like a syrupy sweet?

Maybe it just sags
like a heavy load.   10

Or does it explode?

For Journals

To what social or political issues might this poem be applicable today?

For Discussion

1. Let America be America Again is distinguished, among other reasons, by Hughes's ability to incorporate a large number of voices in a kind of symphonic poetry. Whose voice or voices do you think are speaking in this poem?

2. This poem has only eleven short lines, but they include five different questions. Paraphrase each of those questions. What mood or moods do you think are suggested by such verbal phrases as dries up, festers, stinks, crusts over, or sags?

3. Why do you think Hughes separates the last line from the rest of the questions in the poem?

For Writing

1. Write an essay answering question 2 in the Discussion section. Besides paraphrasing the questions Hughes asks, assess how each verb he chooses suggests a slightly different mood, what the turning points in the poem are, and who the voice or voices belong to. Alternatively, look at another of Hughes's poems as a subject for analysis, particularly for his use of language and diction—for example, "Theme for English B" or "Brass Spitoons."

∞ *I Have a Dream* (1963)

MARTIN LUTHER KING JR.

Martin Luther King Jr. (1929–1968) was the leader of the nonviolent civil rights struggle. A minister from a family of ministers, he became a public figure while still in his twenties when he led a bus boycott in Montgomery, Alabama. Frequently threatened or arrested, he was the main organizer of sit-ins and marches in segregated southern towns and cities, particularly Birmingham, Alabama, in 1963. That summer he addressed a huge audience of civil rights workers who had marched in protest in Washington, D.C. His speech, delivered from the steps of the Lincoln Memorial, is one of the most famous of the century. King received the Nobel Peace Prize in 1964, the youngest person ever to do so. He was assassinated in Memphis, Tennessee, in 1968.

Five score years ago, a great American, in whose symbolic shadow we stand, signed the Emancipation Proclamation. This momentous decree came as a great beacon light of hope to millions of Negro slaves who had been seared in the flames of withering injustice. It came as a joyous daybreak to end the long night of captivity.

But one hundred years later, we must face the tragic fact that the Negro is still not free. One hundred years later, the life of the Negro is still sadly crippled by the manacles of segregation and the chains of discrimination. One hundred years later, the Negro lives on a lonely island of poverty in the midst of a vast ocean of material prosperity. One hundred years later, the Negro is still languishing in the corners of American society and finds himself an exile in his own land. So we have come here today to dramatize an appalling condition.

In a sense we have come to our nation's Capitol to cash a check. When the architects of our republic wrote the magnificent words of the Constitution and the Declaration of Independence, they were signing a promissory note to which every American was to fall heir. This note was a promise that all men would be guaranteed the unalienable rights of life, liberty, and the pursuit of happiness.

It is obvious today that America has defaulted on this promissory note insofar as her citizens of color are concerned. Instead of honoring this sacred obligation, America has given the Negro people a bad check; a check which has come back marked "insufficient funds." But we refuse to believe that the bank of justice is bankrupt. We refuse to believe that there are insufficient funds in the great vaults of opportunity of this nation. So we have come to cash this check—a check that will give us upon demand the riches of freedom and the security of justice. We have also come to this hallowed spot to remind America of the fierce urgency of *now*. This is no time to engage in the luxury of cooling off or to take the tranquilizing drug of gradualism. *Now* is the time to make real the promises of Democracy. *Now* is the time to rise from the dark and desolate valley of segregation to the sunlit path of racial justice. *Now* is the time to open the doors of opportunity to all of God's children. *Now* is the time to lift our nation from the quicksands of racial injustice to the solid rock of brotherhood.

It would be fatal for the nation to overlook the urgency of the mo-   5
ment and to underestimate the determination of the Negro. This sweltering summer of the Negro's legitimate discontent will not pass until there is an invigorating autumn of freedom and equality. 1963 is not an end, but a beginning. Those who hope that the Negro needed to blow off steam and will now be content will have a rude awakening if the nation returns to business as usual. There will be neither rest nor tranquility in America until the Negro is granted his citizenship rights. The whirlwinds of revolt will continue to shake the foundations of our nation until the bright day of justice emerges.

But there is something I must say to my people who stand on the warm threshold which leads into the palace of justice. In the process of gaining our rightful place we must not be guilty of wrongful deeds. Let us not seek to satisfy our thirst for freedom by drinking from the cup of bitterness and hatred. We must forever conduct our struggle on the high plane of dignity and discipline. We must not allow our creative protest to degenerate into physical violence. Again and again we must rise to the majestic heights of meeting physical force with soul force. The marvelous new militancy which has engulfed the Negro community must not lead us to a distrust of all white people, for many of our white brothers, as evidenced by their presence here today, have come to realize that their destiny is tied up with our destiny and their freedom is inextricably bound to our freedom. We cannot walk alone.

And as we walk, we must make the pledge that we shall march ahead. We cannot turn back. There are those who are asking the devotees of civil rights, "When will you be satisfied?" We can never be satisfied as long as the Negro is the victim of the unspeakable horrors of police brutality. We can never be satisfied as long as our bodies, heavy with the fatigue of travel, cannot gain lodging in the motels of the highways and the hotels of the cities. We cannot be satisfied as long as the Negro's basic mobility is from a smaller ghetto to a larger one. We can never be satisfied as long as a Negro in Mississippi cannot vote and a Negro in New York believes he has nothing for which to vote. No, no, we are not satisfied, and we will not be satisfied until justice rolls down like waters and righteousness like a mighty stream.

I am not unmindful that some of you have come here out of great trials and tribulations. Some of you have come fresh from narrow jail cells. Some of you have come from areas where your quest for freedom left you battered by the storms of persecution and staggered by the winds of police brutality. You have been the veterans of creative suffering. Continue to work with the faith that unearned suffering is redemptive.

Go back to Mississippi, go back to Alabama, go back to South Carolina, go back to Georgia, go back to Louisiana, go back to the slums and ghettoes of our northern cities, knowing that somehow this situation can and will be changed. Let us not wallow in the valley of despair.

I say to you today, my friends, that in spite of the difficulties and   10 frustrations of the moment I still have a dream. It is a dream deeply rooted in the American dream.

I have a dream that one day this nation will rise up and live out the true meaning of its creed: "We hold these truths to be self-evident; that all men are created equal."

I have a dream that one day on the red hills of Georgia the sons of former slaves and the sons of former slaveowners will be able to sit down together at the table of brotherhood.

I have a dream that the state of Mississippi, a desert state sweltering with the heat of injustice and oppression, will be transformed into an oasis of freedom and justice.

I have a dream that my four little children will one day live in a nation where they will not be judged by the color of their skin but by the content of their character.

I have a dream today.   15

I have a dream that the state of Alabama, whose governor's lips are presently dripping with the words of interposition and nullification, will be transformed into a situation where little black boys and black girls will be able to join hands with little white boys and white girls and walk together as sisters and brothers.

I have a dream today.

I have a dream that one day every valley shall be exalted, every hill and mountain shall be made low, the rough places will be made plain, and the crooked places will be made straight, and the glory of the Lord shall be revealed, and all flesh shall see it together.

This is our hope. This is the faith with which I return to the South. With this faith we will be able to hew out of the mountain of despair a stone of hope. With this faith we will be able to transform the jangling discords of our nation into a beautiful symphony of brotherhood. With this faith we will be able to work together, to pray together, to struggle together, to go to jail together, to stand up for freedom together, knowing that we will be free one day.

This will be the day when all of God's children will be able to sing   20 with new meaning.

> My country, 'tis of thee
> Sweet land of liberty,
>   Of thee I sing:
> Land where my fathers died,
> Land of the pilgrims' pride,
> From every mountainside
>   Let freedom ring.

And if America is to be a great nation this must become true. So let freedom ring from the prodigious hilltops of New Hampshire. Let freedom ring from the mighty mountains of New York. Let freedom ring from the heightening Alleghenies of Pennsylvania!

Let freedom ring from the snowcapped Rockies of Colorado!

Let freedom ring from the curvaceous peaks of California!

But not only that; let freedom ring from Stone Mountain of Georgia!

Let freedom ring from Lookout Mountain of Tennessee!

Let freedom ring from every hill and molehill of Mississippi. From every mountainside, let freedom ring.

When we let freedom ring, when we let it ring from every village and every hamlet, from every state and every city, we will be able to speed up that day when all of God's children, black men and white men, Jews and Gentiles, Protestants and Catholics, will be able to join hands and sing in the words of the old Negro spiritual, "Free at last! free at last! thank God almighty, we are free at last!"

For Journals

What have you heard or read about the civil rights movement? About Martin Luther King Jr.? If you have seen film or newsreels of the struggle between civil rights advocates and segregationists, how did you react to them?

For Discussion

1. What is King trying to convince African Americans they should do about segregation? What is he trying to convince white Americans to do?

2. King gave this speech at the Lincoln Memorial. Aside from the obvious location, why does he begin with a line reminiscent of the beginning of Lincoln's Gettysburg Address, "Four score and seven years ago"? What associations might he be trying to raise in the minds of his audience?

3. In order to identify the consequences of racial injustice in American life, King uses both unusual figures of speech, like the promissory note of equality (paragraph 3), and examples of the effects of prejudice in ordinary life, like not being able to get into a hotel (paragraph 7). Look for some more examples of both unusual language and ordinary experience. What do you think he gains from using both kinds of examples? How do the two together help make his argument more persuasive?

4. King says his dream is deeply rooted in the American dream. But he also uses Judeo-Christian references that are part of his background as a minister. Divide the speech into sections based on these two themes; with two of your peers, look through the speech for examples of religious and biblical language and references to the American dream. What values or ideas are expressed in those examples, as you see it?

5. King addresses the frustrated dreams of African Americans in the civil rights movement who thought progress was too slow and the irritation of northerners who thought it was too fast. Look at the section of the speech starting with, "We have also come to this hallowed spot to remind America of the fierce urgency of *now*" (the middle of paragraph 4). What examples does he use to address each group? Which examples advocate patience, and which ones express determination? Do you recognize the sources of any of his metaphorical examples?

6. The video of King's speech is available in many college libraries. If it is in yours, watch it in class. If not, read the speech out loud in class. In the last and most famous part of the speech, King begins paragraphs with the words, "I have a dream," and then "Let freedom ring." What kinds of fulfillment does he dream about in these passages? You might want to paraphrase his language to see how many kinds of dreams he evokes here.

For Writing

1. King gave this speech in the summer of 1963. Using contemporary newspaper and magazine reports and at least one biography of King or a history of the civil rights movement (Taylor Branch's *Parting the*

Waters is a good example), write a researched paper on the circumstances that preceded the march. Some points to include: Who was against it? Why were there fears about what would happen at the march? What was the response of the audience? The press? What was the aftermath? Did people who heard King's speech talk about their own dreams for America in response?

2. This speech is remarkable for the number of other texts it borrows from, rephrases, or uses for its own purposes—the Bible, the Declaration of Independence, the Gettysburg Address, Shakespeare, spirituals, and others. Write an essay in which you identify at least three examples of these borrowed texts, and explain why you think King picked them, what point they were used to make, and how persuasive you think they are. Then try to come up with examples of contemporary texts or songs that you would borrow from if you were delivering this speech today.

∞ *Tomorrowland* (1997)

WITOLD RYBCZYNSKI

Witold Rybczynski (1943–), the Martin and Margy Myerson Professor of Urbanism at the University of Pennsylvania, has written in-depth, thoughtful works on urban architecture, housing, and the uses of technology. His books include Taming the Tiger *(1983),* Looking Around: A Journey Through Architecture *(1993), and* City Life *(1995). This selection is an article he wrote in 1997 for the* New Yorker.

Famous firsts are recorded by sports statisticians, academic journals, and the Guinness Book. Everyday firsts are not. I've never heard of a statue to the suburbanite who sprinted through the first mall, or to the person who punched into the first ATM. I have these thoughts while I'm standing in front of 931 Jasmine Street. It is unlikely that there will ever be a commemorative plaque here, but perhaps there should be. The building itself, while attractive, is unremarkable. It is a one-story house of a type that is not uncommon in the South. The hipped roof extends over a deep front veranda. The walls are clapboard; the double-hung windows are shuttered. There is a U-Haul van in the driveway. I'm standing on the sidewalk watching Larry Haber move into his new home. He is a good sport and pauses so that I can take a photograph. Larry and his wife, Terri, and their two young children are the first residents of an unusual town: a town that is being built by an organization whose chief business is storytelling and make-believe—the Walt Disney Company.

It was Walt himself who had the idea of building a town. Exactly thirty years ago, he announced that he was going to create a showcase for advanced technology—a kind of urban laboratory. It would be called EPCOT, for Experimental Prototype Community of Tomorrow, and it would be an actual community. But Disney died before he could realize his vision of a city of the future, and his successors were unable to reconcile his coercive brand of social engineering with the demands of American home buyers. When EPCOT finally opened, in 1982, it did feature futuristic technology, but there were no residents. It was a theme park.

EPCOT is situated in Walt Disney World, on the enormous tract of land—twenty-eight thousand acres—that Disney owns outside Orlando, in central Florida. There are two other theme parks there—the Magic Kingdom and the Disney-MGM Studios—and a fourth, Disney's Animal Kingdom, is slated to open in 1998. Even so, about a third of the land remained unused. The idea of building a residential community had lingered on in the Disney Company's corporate memory, and when a master plan was being prepared under the aegis of the current C.E.O., Michael Eisner, it was determined that it was finally time to implement Walt's vision. There were also practical considerations: highway access to the theme parks and various wetlands restrictions made residential use attractive. "At that point, we could have gone in any direction," says Disney's Tom Lewis, who oversaw planning during the first five years of the project. "It could have been a second-home community or a resort or a retirement village. Instead, we decided that it would be a place where families would have their primary residences. We wanted it to be a real town."

The notion that Disney World could be a setting for real life will strike most people as improbable. Yet the town promises not only to be real but to be a model for others to follow. Celebration, as it is called, is not a theme park. It is an unincorporated town under the rule of Osceola County. There will be a school, a health campus, and an office park. Planned recreational facilities include a golf course, a lake, and miles of walking trails and bike paths. The town center will have restaurants, shops, offices, a supermarket, a bank, a small inn, and a cinema. When Celebration is completed, in ten or fifteen years, it could have as many as twenty thousand inhabitants. It is the most comprehensively planned new town since Columbia, Maryland, and Reston, Virginia, were built, in the mid-sixties. . . .

You would look in vain for manifestations of any of the current 5 vogues in high-fashion architecture. There is no free-form deconstructivism here, no corrugated-metal high tech. Instead, there are gable roofs with dormers, bay windows and porches, balustrades and columns. Like all houses built commercially in the United States today, these houses favor distinctly traditional styles. The Habers' house, on

Jasmine Street, is an example of Coastal, which is a loose interpretation of the type of house that was built in the South Carolina low country. It is a style characterized by deep one- or two-story porches, high ceilings, full-length windows, and first floors raised off the ground. Coastal is one of six—and only six—architectural styles permissible in Celebration; the others are Classical, Victorian, Colonial Revival, Mediterranean, and French. The six styles are defined in a pattern book, which insures that the builders achieve a degree of architectural clarity that is missing in most builder homes. Unusual, too, is Celebration's approach to parking. Alleys running behind the houses give access to garages in the rear, and many of these garages have rooms above them. Larry Haber has built a suite for his mother-in-law above his garage. . . .

The downtown buildings are owned by Disney and are leased to retail tenants. But there is no Banana Republic here. Instead of major national chains, Disney has chosen only local and regional shops and restaurants. The intention is to attract the public by creating an experience different from that found in a typical shopping mall, Don Killoren told me. Though a downtown like Celebration's, with but a single landlord, does resemble a shopping mall, there is one crucial difference here: this is a commercial area where people will also live. . . .

A lively downtown, apartments above shops, front porches, houses close to the street, and out-of-sight garages all add up to an old-fashioned sort of place. But there is more to Celebration than nostalgia and tradition. What families like the Habers really want—what most Americans really want—has less to do with architecture and urban design than with good schools, health care, safe neighborhoods, and a sense of community. "We understand that community is not something that we can engineer," I was assured by Todd Mansfield, who is an executive vice-president of Disney Imagineeering, the division that oversees the design and construction of all the company's enterprises. "But we think that it's something we can foster." Despite Disney's reputation for obsessively leaving nothing to chance, fostering has not meant controlling. The Celebration school (kindergarten through twelfth grade) will be owned and operated not by Disney but by the Osceola County School District. The school will open next year and will eventually serve about fourteen hundred students—from the surrounding county as well as from the town. What is unusual about the school, apart from pedagogical innovations, is that it's in the center of the town. Children will be able to walk and bike to class. This fall will see the opening of the Teaching Academy, a teacher-training facility that is owned by Disney, run by Disney and Stetson University, and housed in a handsome building designed by William Rawn, who is also the architect of the school.

The health campus, now under construction on the outskirts of town, is a large facility belonging to Florida Hospital and including outpatient surgery, advanced diagnostics, primary-care physicians, and a fitness center. A fibre-optic network will eventually link both the school and the health facility to individual homes. This is just the sort of technological innovation that Walt Disney imagined would be the cornerstone of life in the future. But Michael Eisner's Celebration is actually the opposite of Walt Disney's urban vision. Walt Disney imagined a world in which problems would be solved by science and technology. Celebration puts technology in the background and concentrates on putting in place the less tangible civic infrastructure that is a prerequisite for community. Home buyers agree to be governed by their own homeowners' association and by a set of restrictive deed covenants whose purpose is to strike a balance between individual freedom and communal responsibility. You can park your cars in front of your house, for example, but no more than two cars. You can sublet your house—or your garage apartment—but you can't lease individual rooms. You can hold a garage sale, but only once a year. Writers and artists can work out of their homes, but not dentists—unless they live in the "home business district," where professional offices are allowed. A real sense of community can't develop in a vacuum, however, and Disney seems to have gone out of its way to insure that Celebration will not become a hermetic place. It is neither walled nor gated, unlike many recent master-planned communities. None of the streets are private. Policing is by the county sheriff's office, not by hired security guards (although the homeowners' association may hire additional security if it chooses to). The golf course, designed by the Robert Trent Joneses—father and son—is a public daily-fee facility, not a private club.

Yet, in spite of these efforts to make Celebration open to the outside world, much of the public assumes—or, at least, hopes—that a Disney town will be a perfect town. "It's one of my fears," says Todd Mansfield, who is himself going to build a house in Celebration. "We have people who have purchased houses who think they're moving to Utopia. We keep having to remind them that we can't provide safeguards for all the ills of society. We will have everything that happens in any community." He's right. I'm confident that despite the advanced Honeywell security systems there will be break-ins. Despite the fibreoptic networks, there will be children with learning problems. Despite the state-of-the-art medical technology, there will be sickness. And, despite the sociable appearance of the front porches, there will be neighborly disputes. If there weren't, Celebration would not be the real place that Disney says it will become. . . .

For Journals

When you see the name Disney, what immediate associations come to your mind? How many of them come from your childhood?

For Discussion

1.   Since Celebration looks like a traditional community, why does Rybczynski call the article "Tomorrowland"? Why not "Yesterdayland"?

2.   Look up the meaning of the word *nostalgia* in the dictionary. In what ways does Celebration play upon that concept? Why?

3.   What assumptions about the idea of a Disney town did Rybczynski have when he came to see Celebration? Find examples of them in the text. What assumptions did you start with?

4.   When you finished reading this article, were you convinced that Celebration was in fact as close as possible to an ideal community? Why would or wouldn't you want to live there?

5.   Since early in this century, most Americans have lived in cities. What, if any, features of Celebration could be adapted to improve city living?

For Writing

1.   Write an essay in which you set forth your idea of dream community—its appearance, its size, its neighborhoods, its values, and the kinds of people who would live there.

2.   Listen to the Disney song "Tomorrowland," and write an essay in which you compare the world described in the lyrics with the community described in Rybczynski's article.

3.   There's a long history of both writing about ideal communities and attempting to establish them: Plato's *Republic*, Thomas More's *Utopia*, and various real-life experiments. Research and write a paper on one of the following American attempts to set up the perfect place to live: Brook Farm, the Oneida Community, the Shakers, or the effort in Colorado to form a self-sustaining community within a bubble.

∞ United Shareholders of America (1998)

JACOB WEISBERG

Jacob Weisberg is the chief political correspondent for the on-line magazine Slate. *This article is from an issue of the* Sunday New York Times *devoted entirely to Americans and their relationship to money.*

. . . With half the country in the market, the gap is no longer just between those with incomes going up and those with stagnant incomes. It's between those with a steadily escalating net worth multiplying in the market and those who have little prospect of building any net worth. It makes the separation between haves and have-nots seem more like a division between will-always-haves and won't-ever-haves.

The market creates a powerful argument for ignoring inequality. It does so not just by highlighting the self-interest of the investing majority but also by fostering political values based on the market. At a basic level, Wall Street is drawing the majority of Americans into a very different idea of citizenship and a very different experience of democracy than the one the country had long been familiar with.

There are superficial similarities between political democracy and shareholder democracy. Shareholders elect management to run a company in their interest. If management fails, the majority of owners can vote them out. But a publicly held company is a democracy without any care for equality. Shareholders have voting rights, but they do not all have the same rights. Voting power is proportionate to one's ownership stake. In a corporation, the majority owners owe no special obligation to the minority. To expend resources on the interests of nonshareholders—by analogy the nation or society as a whole—would be a breach of fiduciary responsibility.

As Alexander Hamilton noted, economic institutions do teach civic lessons, and the experience of voting one's shares as opposed to voting one's conscience has affected the mind-set and the rhetoric of American politics. Ronald Reagan was the first to pose a challenge to an incumbent President in terms of narrow, personal self-interest. "Are you better off now than you were four years ago?" he asked in 1980, implying that voters should assess management's performance in quantitative terms. The citizen's position in relation to the country is increasingly referred to as an ownership stake—the view taken by the C.E.O. candidate Ross Perot in 1992. Results overwhelm questions of democratic legitimacy. . . .

The shareholder-citizen in whose image politics is being remade is 5 not a new player on the American stage. In fact, he is the reincarnation of an old character. The new ideal of the financially autonomous individual, who manages his own investments so as not to be dependent on government, the community or institutions, embodies the eternal American aspiration to individualism and self-sufficiency. Investing man is a successor to the Jeffersonian ideal of the yeoman farmer, whose ability to satisfy his own modest needs was taken as an underpinning of democratic health.

But the contemporary shareholder-citizen is at the same time an impoverished embodiment of that ideal, concentrating on material aspects of independence while largely excluding the experience of community and cultivation of civic virtue. An idea of material sufficiency that might have seemed appropriate just a few years ago has been supplanted by an ever-rising standard of how much is necessary for true happiness. Rather than fostering the kind of democratic citizen who can be trusted to govern, as Jefferson's ideal did, the market ideal of citizenship is about developing the means to withdraw from unsatisfactory common institutions—public schools, the Social Security system, even the need to work. The explicit version of this ideology, libertarianism, has been gaining adherents and credibility in recent years. It is the political philosophy fostered by the stock market.

The citizen-investor serves his fellow citizens badly by his inclination to withdraw from the community. He tends to serve himself badly as well. He does so by focusing his pursuit of happiness on something that very seldom makes people happy in the way they expect it to.

A hundred years ago, during another popular spasm of enthusiasm for investment, a President was more likely to remind the country of this human truth than to indulge its fascination with the market. In his 1893 Fourth of July proclamation, President Grover Cleveland warned the nation to "guard against the sordid struggle for unearned wealth" and to "hold fast to the American idea that work is honorable and economy a virtue." He viewed getting rich in the stock market as a dismal aspiration, not just for America but for Americans.

For Journals

How do you expect to provide for yourself financially when you leave school?

For Discussion

1. How does using language reminiscent of the Declaration of Independence or phrases with political overtones—like "citizen-investor"—strengthen Weisberg's argument against the get-rich quick mentality?

2. Weisberg's definition of the American dream is a middle-class standard of living for all. How would your personal definition of the American dream compare with his? With the definition of your parents? Your friends?

For Writing

1. Go the library or a magazine stand and find one or two articles that have advice about money—making it, saving it, losing it, managing with very little of it—as their subject. Write an essay in which you consider the following questions: What assumptions, explicit or implicit, does the writer make about Americans and their attitude toward money? What are the strongest and weakest points the writer makes, and why? Does the author make any connections between money and the achievement or destruction of the American dream? If so, what are they?

2. Write an essay on an incident from your own life that you think best illustrates your attitude toward money and toward the issues of responsibility, selfishness, and involvement that Weisberg raises. As objectively as possible, analyze your own relationship to money and what you think it can and cannot do for you.

∞ Structured Appeal: Let America Be America Again (1997)

CHRIS COUNTRYMAN

Chris Countryman is a college student from California who wrote this essay as part of his second-quarter writing class. His assignment was to analyze a persuasive text, and he chose this Langston Hughes poem from his course text.

Not all arguments come in the form of emotional speeches or legalistic essays: cartoons, newspaper articles, and even photographs can persuade as well, and sometimes much more efficiently. Poetry exemplifies this type of argumentation. Because many forms of verse follow a less restrictive format than the typical essay, poets have much more freedom to arrange elements of structure to enhance the argumentative nature of a work. In his poem "Let America Be America Again" Langston Hughes uses evocative language and structural techniques to help emphasize the separation he feels underclass Americans experience in a country they helped create.

From the beginning Hughes crafts the structure of his poem to match the nature of his thesis. The first section of his poem alternates between four-line stanzas and short sentences in parentheses. The use of these two stylistically different forms creates individual voices which present the division Hughes sees in American society. Hughes's word choice enhances this contrast. In the opening lines Hughes chooses slow, balanced sentences: "Let America be America again. / Let it be the dream it used to be. / Let it be the pioneer on the plain / Seeking a home where he himself is free" (lines 1–4). These lines resound with confidence and grandeur, and evoke a powerful patriotic image of the rugged frontiersman representing America in search of a land to claim in the name of freedom. Hughes contrasts this formal stanza with a short, much more personal line set off in parentheses:

"(America never was America to me)" (line 5). Several techniques come into play here. The line's physical separation from the narrative highlights to the separation in viewpoint, and the enclosure in parentheses suggests an unequal relationship and differing viewpoints, the dominant majority's American dream and the submissive minority's American reality. Hughes's parenthetical interjection mimics the structure of the first line, but in replacing "again" in line 1 with "to me" he shifts the focus from past glory to present, and very personal, isolation.

The second and third verse paragraphs, up through line 10, follow the same pattern. Again, the first stanza employs highly connotative words in balanced structures, including the repetition of "dream" in the first line and the images of conniving kings and scheming tyrants (lines 6, 8). By repeating the formula of four-line stanza followed by interjection, Hughes creates a dialogue emphasizing the fact that all of these paragraphs address the same subject, America's deviation from the ideal. Hughes's formatting changes and word choice, however, give each speaker an entirely different message. One voice calls for a return to past greatness, the other claims that greatness never existed.

As the poem progresses Hughes alters his word choice and structure in order to bring about a reversal in this dialogue. After the short couplet in italics Hughes's speakers switch roles: the previously parenthetical voice gains new strength and the old narrator fades away. Hughes now indicates forcefulness by printing the second voice in normal text. In the stanza starting at line 19 Hughes has his second voice imitate the first, employing the same type of balanced sentence structure but with a twist. Instead of "America" he substitutes "I," emphasizing the isolation of the underprivileged from their own country.

In the next section Hughes concentrates on the collective identity, 5 history, and struggle of the various groups that compose the American underclass, and his choice of imagery and structure reflects this move toward unity. Having established the stereotypical vision of the American foundation experience in his earlier stanzas, Hughes falls back on these emotionally charged images to retell American history in terms of the role of currently underprivileged minorities. Now the Negroes, poor whites, and red men are the "Pioneers"; it is they who are the "serf[s] of kings" (lines 19–31). Hughes also returns to images and phrases from earlier in the poem. The modern-day victims of America "dreamt our basic dream" and built a "homeland of the free" (lines 30, 41). Hughes inserts more parallel constructions near the end of the paragraph to emphasize the shared trials of the true American pioneers: ". . . all the dreams we've dreamed / And all the songs we've sung / And all the hopes we've held / And all the flags we've hung" (lines 46–49). In addition the structure of the poem as a whole changes to reflect Hughes's argumentative tactic. Instead of individual stanzas,

Hughes casts this section of the poem in a single unified paragraph, mirroring the unified cause of Hughes's unsung American patriots.

In many ways poetry as an argumentative form bears a closer resemblance to photography or other artwork than to essays. While structural concerns certainly occupy an essay's author, the incredible flexibility of poetry allows the poet to balance phrases and order stanzas much like a photographer might arrange objects in a scene to create a certain effect. Poetry also relies heavily on visual language. Although poetic arguments may tend toward emotional appeals, they are no less valid than pathos appeals in essays, and can be much more effective. Certainly in Hughes's "Let America Be America Again" these images, combined with a carefully planned structure, create a powerful, and ultimately convincing, argument.

For Journals

Do you read poetry on your own? Do you think of it as a vehicle for intellectual expression?

For Discussion

1. What is Countryman's thesis about the use of poetry or other forms of art to make an argument or appeal?

2. Countryman does a very close reading of this poem to explain how the argument is constructed. What are the crucial voices and dialogues in the poem? What points of view do they express?

3. Given the different voices, how do the historical references to pioneers help structure the unity achieved at the end of the poem between various excluded groups like poor white, black, and red Americans?

4. How persuasive is Countryman's point that poetry resembles photography? What other arts do you think can pose an argument the way poetry can?

For Writing

"Let America Be America Again" was one of a series of poems Hughes wrote about his disappointment and hope for the realization of his country's potential. Pick another poem from the series, and apply Countryman's analytical structure to it: What appeal is Hughes making in the poem? How many different voices can you find, and what points of view can you identify? Pay attention to individual words, especially pronouns, to help establish the various voices. Finally, be sure to look for the argument that the language of the poem conveys, and rephrase it in your own words.

∞ *Film: Avalon* (1990)

The subject of this film is the story of a Jewish American family, taking place mostly in the late 1940s and 1950s in Baltimore. It begins and ends with the memory of Sam's arrival as an immigrant from Russia in 1914, and focuses on his wife, son, daughter-in-law, and grandson Michael. (126 minutes)

For Journals

Do any of the traditions in this family—large Thanksgiving dinners, a family circle, time spent with cousins during childhood, tension between a mother-in-law and her daughter-in-law, a relationship with a beloved grandparent—remind you of your own family? How?

For Discussion

1. Who do you think is the hero of this film? What does this character do or represent that qualifies him for that status? In what ways is he central to the film's meaning?

2. Why does the film begin and end with Sam's arrival in the United States on the Fourth of July, 1914? Why is the Fourth of July also the day of the fire? Why do you think holidays like the Fourth of July and Thanksgiving play such a prominent role in this film?

3. What kinds of changes in the meaning of the Fourth of July have taken place in the film between Sam's first impressions of the holiday and the day his son makes a commercial for his discount store by advertising an Independence Day sale that promises independence from high prices?

4. When the family earns enough money to move from a city neighborhood to the suburbs, Michael asks, "Is this a good thing?" Is it? What do they gain and what do they give up in the move?

5. Look at the following scenes: the robbery and stabbing of Jules; the fight between Sam and his brother, Gabriel, first at Thanksgiving and then at the family circle; the time the family spends at the country club. What role does money play in the way the family begins to split up? Where else in the movie do you see the effects of money, both positive and negative.

For Writing

1. Write an essay in which you trace the development of the three main male characters in the film—Sam, the grandfather; Jules, the son; and Michael, the grandson. Pick one or two scenes to examine closely, which you think best illustrate their relationships (for example, Michael confessing that he thinks he burned the store down; Sam taking Michael and his cousins to sleep out on the Fourth of July; Michael coming to visit Sam in the nursing home and bringing his son with him).

2.   Referring back to discussion item 2, write an essay about all the times in this film that the Fourth of July is the focus for some significant event in the family members' lives. Comment on closeness, disintegration, assimilation, growing up, or any other major themes you observe.

3.   The writer and director of the film, Barry Levinson, is from Baltimore and has set much of his work there. Look at one of his other films, such as *Diner* or *Tin Men,* or an episode of his television series, *Homicide,* and write an essay in which you compare the different ways he portrays life in Baltimore. What constitutes a family or a family substitute? What do family members fight about? What do they consider their most valuable relationships and traditions?

4.   Look up the original meaning of the place name Avalon. What kind of place was it supposed to be? Write a paper in which you describe Avalon and explain why that title is meaningful for this movie, its themes, and one or two of the main characters.

Writing Assignments

1.   Find an advertisement in a magazine or newspaper that uses examples of American symbols directly (for example, advertising U.S. savings bonds by showing the emblem of the American bald eagle) or indirectly (e.g., savings bank using Benjamin Franklin's portrait as a logo, or a jeans company that embroiders an American flag on the pocket). There are many such examples; you also might want to look at CD covers and movie advertisements. Write an analysis of the ad in which you consider the following questions: Who is the audience? Why do you think that advertiser included an example of American symbolism in the ad? Why was the particular example chosen? How effective is that example in conveying American values? How successful or unsuccessful do you think this approach is?

2.   The selections in this chapter each express some element of the American dream. Write an essay in which you argue for your own idea of what the American dream means—both what you think it means to most Americans and what it means to you. How do you see the American dream in members of your family? In yourself? What el-

ements are crucial to it? Because you are dealing with a broad idea, it is especially important to include specific examples of what you believe the dream to be and how it manifests itself in you and your family. Do not confine yourself to generalizations like "My parents want me to have a better life than they have." Use your examples to explain their lives, including disappointments or worries, and to show what you really dream of for yourself.

3. Langston Hughes was vitally interested in the promise of the American dream and in the importance of making it accessible to all Americans. With his work in mind, listen to and read the lyrics of contemporary songs, including rap lyrics, that talk about American dreams and nightmares. Write an analytical essay in which you discuss the vision of American life, especially urban life, set forth in these songs, including what they say about dreams for the future. Cite examples from the lyrics to support your assertions. You can use Hughes as a point of comparison if you want to.

4. Imagine that you have to explain the American dream to an English-speaking visitor from another country and that you have to compose a popular culture curriculum featuring contemporary materials that would make the dream clearer to a stranger. Prepare a list of examples for this visitor drawn from each of the following categories: four movies to see; two to four musicians to listen to; two works of fiction and two works of nonfiction to read; and two magazines to read. After each selection, write a paragraph explaining why this particular example says something about the American dream, and what that is.

5. Go to the newsstand or your library and pick up the following: one issue of what is usually known as a women's magazine (*Family Circle, Ladies' Home Journal,* and so on), one issue of a magazine addressed to different women's interests (*Cosmopolitan, Mademoiselle,* and so on), and one issue of a magazine addressed largely to men (*GQ, Esquire,* and so on). Be sure that the magazines you choose have *at least one article apiece* on the home (entertaining at home, decorating the home, cooking for friends or family, spending time with children at home, and so on). Write an essay comparing the images of house and home you find in these publications. What dreams of American home life do you think they advertise? Do the dreams of home revealed in articles in a men's magazine differ from those in the articles for women? If so, in what ways? Are any of the articles more informative than others? If they include photographs, how do the illustrations support the articles' points of view and persuade readers to accept them?

7

∾

Images of Gender
and Family

A t the core of American identities and American dreams lies the
family. Whether a colonial-era farm household, an immigrant extended family, a native clan or tribe, an urban domestic partnership, or
a suburban nuclear family, families serve as a connection between the
individual and the outside world. The individual's identity, his or her
dreams, in large part depend on the family of origin or a family of
choice. The individual is shaped through beliefs, values, and assumptions that the family holds about the world and that are based on the
family members' experiences and collective memory. The family itself,
in turn, derives its value from the social, cultural, political, and philosophical assumptions and beliefs and the economic needs of the larger
culture.

Questions about the family are pervasive in contemporary American society: What is the "definition" of a family? Who can belong to a
family? What are appropriate gender roles within families? What restraints does the concept of family place on women? On men? On children? What happens to a society in which the nuclear family is no
longer the dominant configuration? What are "family values"? Are
they positive beliefs and aspirations that optimize growth and diversity for all, or narrow-minded strictures and intolerances that seek to
shut out differences of approach or opinion? The debates over these issues are becoming increasingly rancorous.

And yet this kind of conflict is not new. The history of our country
is one of uneasy inequality between men and women. Revolutionary-
era rhetoric depended heavily on a philosophy that was based on
equality and on political rights, but those concepts applied to men
only. Industrialization brought with it not only manufacturing jobs
and manufactured goods but also exploitation of children for labor.
World War I saw tremendous support for the war effort and for social
services from women, but although women finally gained the vote in
1920, they received few additional rights thereafter. World War II

brought new and demanding jobs for women to support the war effort but as soon as the men returned from war, society's needs for employment for men and for social stability issued a new message to women: go home, stay home, and raise children. The civil rights and women's movements of the sixties and seventies brought attention to gross civil injustices, but the Equal Rights Amendment failed to pass. Women have made some strides in business and government, but cries from the media, to politicians, to the religious right have declared that feminism and women's liberation have brought women in particular and society in general nothing but grief.

Despite this inequality of the sexes, the idea of the stable American family—and, concomitantly, a stable American society—has been with us for a long time. Recent debates decry the "decline" of the family and blame societal ills on a perceived lack of family stability. But to some degree we have idealized the family of the past. The current divorce rate is 50 percent of first marriages within forty years, but in the colonial era, marriages averaged only twelve years or less because of the death of one spouse. We deplore the numbers of absentee parents, but up to half of all colonial-era children lost at least one parent before the age of twenty-one, and before the 1920s, divorced fathers had no legal obligation to pay child support. We are rightfully concerned about problems in educating youth, but in the 1940s fewer than half of the students entering high school were able to finish. We mourn the death of the extended family, yet children are now more likely than at any earlier time in our history to have living grandparents and to be in contact with them. Many factories in the nineteenth century employed children under the age of eleven, and during the early industrial period, from 1850 to 1885, children worked at home, in tenement sweatshops, in mines and mills. Domestic workers supported middle-class nurturing and mothering, but their own children frequently served as maids or garment workers. During the years of the Great Depression, in the 1930s, families united for their own collective survival, but incompatible people who were stuck together in this manner, with few resources and little hope, would sometimes produce phenomena all too familiar in other eras: withdrawn or violent men; exhausted, overextended women; children with no resources with which to face the future.

Gender and Family in American History

Early recorded history of the colonies and the Revolution suggests that while the United States was founded on principles of equality, women were either invisible or were assumed to absorb the political views of their husbands or male relatives, just as their husbands were able to absorb their property upon marriage. They were expected to support economic embargoes against Britain and to supply provisions and support for the war, and they could be tried for treason during the Revolution. Men were expected to carry out the public duties of government and commerce. Some early Republicans and philosophers may have noticed the contradictions in promoting arguments about equal rights while restricting those rights to male landowners, but few questioned assumptions that women's work should be restricted to the home (though in the largely rural society, work at home was substantial).Women's sphere was the domestic arena; men participated in and ruled the public domain and debated affairs of state. One way to cope with this dichotomy was to state that the two realms were different but equal. As we examine this discussion, we will question just how equal those realms truly were, both in actuality and in perception.

The first selection in the chapter, the etching *Keep within Compass*, comes from the early post–Revolutionary period and taps into the notion of dual spheres for men and women. As such, it is part of a long-standing tradition of defining women's roles by circumscribing them and fostering a desire for stability. One change that did result from the Revolution, however, was that divorce was slightly easier for women to obtain, which may help explain why the etching contrasts the contented "virtuous woman" with images of what can happen to her if she steps outside her role. For a far more graphic example of the consequences that befell one young woman who was victimized for failing to stay within traditional lines of demarcation, read the dissent of Judge Wilner in *Rusk* v. *State*. This late-twentieth-century case makes a somewhat frightening companion piece to *Keep within Compass*.

In the nineteenth century, little challenged the assumptions of the twin spheres of domesticity and public realm, though domestic life, particularly in rural areas, certainly entailed labor, since families generally produced their own food and household goods and sometimes bartered for other needed commodities. Industrialization brought with it goods produced outside the home or farm, and along with increasing industry came the need for cheap labor. Immigrants, women, and children became part of that massive workforce. In the mid–nineteenth century, as household production decreased, wage labor and professional occupations developed, giving rise to an increasing middle class. Upper- and middle-class women could maintain a role focused on domesticity while men earned the family income, but the cost was borne by the laborers, often slaves and other men, women, and children, in mills, fields, and factories.

The second decade of the twentieth century saw worldwide turmoil brought about by World War I and social turmoil as U.S. women agitated for the vote, which they finally obtained in 1920. In a society in which women were assumed to carry on the emotional, sentimental, and moral needs of society as men pursued individualistic and public pursuits, women were to give love and nurturing freely, uncontaminated by the market forces of the newly industrialized society.

In addition to their role as breadwinners, men were assumed to be strong heroes and the protectors of women and children. War-era rhetoric and propaganda in particular appealed to manly attributes such as physical strength and a muscular build.

The World War I recruiting poster included in this chapter, *Enlist: On Which Side of the Window Are YOU?* makes a graphic statement about proper spheres for men and women, goading the male viewer into taking his rightful place in the public domain by using shame as a persuasive technique. The Charles Atlas body-building advertisement, published in 1944 during the height of America's involvement in World War II, uses classic appeals focusing on the shame of weakness and on men's desire to be real "red-blooded" Americans—with fame, and the admiration of women, as the ultimate prize.

While invoking beliefs about what a "real man" should be, particularly in time of war, propaganda artists also utilized expectations about a man's role in protecting home and family from danger. The selection "Powers of Persuasion," from the National Archives and Records Administration Web site, demonstrates how propaganda posters of World War II elicited protective feelings about home and family to "bring the war home" to Americans and rally support for the war.

Student writer Daniel McKenzie analyzed one of these posters titled "Keep These Hands Off!" and the ways in which it evoked emotion and traditional family values to achieve its persuasive purpose. Although of Canadian origin, this poster served as a model for a series of U.S. persuasive strategies attempting to base their emotional appeals on traditional American values.

Some advertisers took the next logical step and showcased both the woman/prize and the resulting offspring in a manner that clearly defined every role within the nuclear family. In the Edsel advertisement "They'll Know You've Arrived," gender and family roles are clearly delineated: the father and son are "action" figures in the foreground, next to the car, while the mother and daughter are relegated to watching from the sidelines. No competent wartime factory workers or Rosie Riveters here—women are back to the domestic sphere.

In the years that followed the civil rights and free speech movements of the 1960s, the women's movement increasingly argued for equality for women in society, especially in the home and workplace. Progress was slow, an even within liberal or left-wing social and political movements, such as the Student Nonviolent Coordinating Committee, male leaders typically assigned women to clerical or support duties rather than leadership roles. Increasing numbers of women in the workplace, relative to the postwar era of the 1950s and early 1960s, brought changes in the stable (to some, but stultifying to others) nuclear family. Long-standing assumptions that the nuclear family is the core of American communities underlie much of mainstream culture and affect how some Americans perceive cultures that differ from mainstream family values.

Assumptions also run deep about what is and is not appropriate behavior, particularly in women. We began this chapter with a look at an eighteenth-century etching exhorting women to stay in their place. Almost two hundred years later, in a famous "date rape" legal case, *Rusk* v. *State,* we see that if a woman doesn't "keep to her place" she is in essence putting herself in harm's way. Judge Wilner, the author of the minority opinion included in this chapter, articulates some of these assumptions as he argues against overturning the conviction of the rapist in this case. Ultimately the conviction was reinstated, but the case represents a sobering look at the assumptions and values that we take with us into policy and legal arenas.

In the late 1980s and early 1990s, on the heels of the social changes of the previous two decades, gay and lesbian rights movements further challenged the concept and value of the heterosexual nuclear family; moreover, they brought the debate over homosexual marriages into the open. Thomas Stoddard, attorney and gay rights leader, argues that "Marriage Is a Fundamental Right" and that same-gender marriages are a civil rights issue. Attorney Bruce Fein's essay, "Reserve Marriage for Heterosexuals," cites legal precedent, as does Stoddard's, but also draws on our fears for children and our beliefs about two-parent families to make Fein's case.

As the century has progressed, women have appeared to make gains in politics, economics, the workplace, and society generally. But despite these gains—or, according to author Susan Faludi, because of them—women don't "have it all." In fact, women have never been worse off, in her view. Faludi reports on her extensive study of the negative reaction to women's modest gains of the 1970s and 1980s in her book *Backlash: The Undeclared War against American Women.* In the introduction to the book, entitled "Blame It on Feminism," Faludi articulates the assumptions made by those who castigate the ill effects of feminism and then challenges them with reasoning as well as evidence and statistics.

The post–civil rights movement era also shows increasing concern over the needs of children. Some 20 percent of children still grow up in poverty, abuse, and neglect; some are born addicted to drugs and alcohol. In one battle for children's rights being fought through the courts, child advocates are arguing for increased legal rights for young people. An adult who has worked on behalf of children's rights for years, child advocate and Children's Defense Fund founder Marian Wright Edelman, explains the values, assumptions, and beliefs that led her to her life's work on behalf of children. Edelman's essay, "A Family Legacy," describes the family and extended family of community from which she learned the values of hard work, discipline, doing for others, and repaying the privileges of intellectual and material gifts by serving the community. Both Faludi, as a feminist author, and Edelman, as the leader of the Children's Defense Fund, address concerns related to those of Dr. Mary Pipher, author of *Reviving Ophelia: Saving the Selves of Adolescent Girls.* Pipher asks us to consider why young girls in our culture feel the need to stifle their voices, their energy, their creativity, and to ponder a corollary to this process—the incidence of depression, eating disorders, addictions, and suicide attempts. These young girls existing in a difficult culture are, she suggests, "Saplings in the Storm," and our society needs to look long and hard at what we are doing to them.

Not only girls, but also young boys are being acculturated in ways that do not promote either their growth or a healthy society, suggest authors Daniel J. Kinglon and Michael Thompson. In fact, we rear our young men in "The Culture of Cruelty," a culture without security either for the bullied or for the bully, a culture that, in the schoolyards and the hallways and the locker room, is not all that far removed from the fictional world of William Golding's *Lord of the Flies.*

While some ethnic cultures within American society sometimes appear to have resolved problems that others find perplexing, image is not necessarily reality, and easy generalizations can flatten out layers of complexity. The final reading in the chapter looks at an image of Asian American families. In a researched essay, "Making and Unmaking the 'Model Minority,'" student writer John Wu studies a label once applied to Jewish immigrants and now applied to Asian Americans. He analyzes assumptions and beliefs about the values transmitted through families about family, work, and success, and about the values assumed by society to be held by American families of Asian descent. This chapter's film selection, *Mi familia (My Family),* reflects in a visual medium the assumptions, values, and conflicts of a multigenerational Mexican American family coping with the differing assumptions, values, and conflicts of the dominant culture.

As you read the following selections, reflect on your own image of family and what the role of each member within it should be. Try also to identify and articulate the deeper assumptions on which these ideas are based. Do you think your images and assumptions are typical for an American? Are you comfortable with the fact that other Americans may have different family values?

∞ *Keep within Compass* (ca. 1790)

A metaphor that surfaces decade after decade in conveying social worlds is that of the circle, or in some cases, the three-dimensional sphere. Sometimes referring to a social class, other times to occupations, the image is frequently used, from the late eighteenth century through the twentieth century, to describe the designated and circumscribed roles for men and women: men's world of greater economic, industrial, and political society, and women's world of the home.

"Keep Within Compass," England, 1785–1805. Graphic on laid paper, H. 9.310 cm. Courtesy, Winterthur Museum. 1954.0093.001A

This etching draws upon a centuries-old tradition of emblems, which combine visual elements and a moral lesson. Combining a didactic picture with a textual moral statement, the etching depicts four unpleasant scenes with which the "virtuous" woman is threatened if she does not remain within her own sphere or circle: raising a child in poverty and misery, working as a domestic or tavern worker, selling in the street, and prostituting herself to soldiers. Such scenes contrast with the well-dressed, happy-looking gentlewoman depicted next to flowers and a large home.

For Journals

Write about what you imagine to be the daily life of eighteenth-century American women: women of means, with landed or wealthy families, and women without family or financial support.

For Discussion

1. What is your overall impression of the etching? What draws your eye? What is emphasized? Why do you think the etching was drawn to create this impression and this emphasis? Relative to the entire circle, how much space is allotted to the virtuous woman?

2. Who are the intended audiences? Do different elements of the etching appeal to different audiences? To different audience concerns?

3. Why do you think the artist used a compass to make his point? In the late eighteenth century, who would have been likely to wield a compass? Who, then, would be setting the limits on women?

4. Analyze the etching as a moral lesson or argument with supporting subtopics and evidence, including the smaller pictures and the additional printed messages. Write out a text outline of the argument. What is inside the compass? What are "good" women supposed to do? What is outside the compass? What are women not supposed to do? Is this what you would expect?

5. Why is it important that a woman be "a crown to her husband"? Do you think the authors of this etching would expect a man to be a crown to his wife? What associations does the crown bring to mind?

6. In what ways might the assumptions apparent in this etching be relevant today? Do you see any connections between this two-hundred-year-old image and arguments about date rape today? (See the legal augments regarding the noted "date rape" case later in this chapter.)

For Writing

1. In what ways are gender roles still restricted today? Draw a contemporary version of this etching for men or for women. Then write an essay explaining your diagram.

2.   Argue that women are no longer restricted by gender roles—or that men are more restricted in their choices and behavior than women are.

3.   Do research in art or literature of the American colonial period to examine the role of women or home life. Examine art books from your library, primary materials such as diaries if they are available, or secondary sources about the period. What do you conclude about women's or men's role in the home or in society during this period? Write a documented essay reporting your conclusions.

∞ Enlist: On Which Side of the Window Are YOU? (1917)

This American poster (see page 222), based on an earlier British poster, uses an approach that differs from the positive appeals to ethos and pathos that characterize many other war recruitment posters. You may want to review Chapter 1 for additional information on posters as a medium of persuasion.

For Journals

Do you believe men and women have an equal responsibility to participate in military service?

For Discussion

1.   Examine the elements of the poster. What first catches your eye? What next? Is the man inside the window confined in any way? Where does he seem to belong? What is the argument of the poster? What are the appeals used to persuade the audience? How do light and shading affect the message?

2.   Look closely at the man, his appearance, and his posture; then, look at the soldiers. What differences do you notice? What is implied by those differences?

3.   Compare and contrast this image to that of *Keep within Compass.* What do you infer about a woman's proper role? What is, conversely, a man's proper sphere? In what ways did women's and men's roles change, or remain constant, between 1790 and 1917? In what ways have they changed, and in what ways remained constant, since 1917?

For Writing

1.   Review all the war era images in this book. What are the common themes and appeals? How do their strategies differ? Select two posters

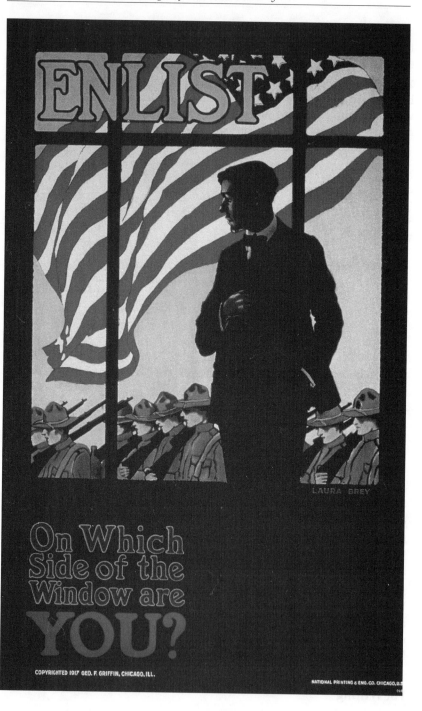

and write an essay comparing and contrasting them. Alternatively, select some other focus—appeals to ethos, for example—and develop an essay drawing evidence from the posters.

2. Using books of posters, a library collection, or a museum brochure, research other war era posters. You might look for particular ways in which the posters portray "the enemy" or particular kinds of appeals in posters from different countries.

∞ *Powers of Persuasion* (2000)

NATIONAL ARCHIVES AND RECORD ADMINISTRATION WEB SITE

This Web site is an excellent resource for examining primary materials from the National Archives. (URL is http://www.nara.gov/exhall/powers/homes.html.) This specific site presents several propaganda posters that utilize values, beliefs, and emotions about home and family.

The Archives provides several posters on this theme, included here (see p. 224), as well as a list of related posters you may want to review and write about.

For Journals

What comes to mind when you imagine the holdings of the National Archives? What kinds of materials do you expect it to contain?

For Discussion

1. Take each poster in turn, and analyze the appeals to pathos, ethos, and logos. Be sure to consider logical fallacies evident in the posters.

2. Compare notes in class as to which poster you find most persuasive and why. Do you notice any patterns in terms of gender or culture with regard to persuasiveness of the posters?

For Writing

Select one of these posters, or one of the other posters listed, and write an essay analyzing the poster's appeals.

∞ *Building Beliefs* (2000)

DANIEL MCKENZIE

Daniel McKenzie is a college student from Richmond, CA. Dan wrote this essay for his expository writing class; his assignment was to select and analyze a persuasive

image. Despite a number of potential approaches, he focuses his essay on the ways in which the poster evokes emotion and traditional family values to persuade its audience.

Persuasive imagery is often a complex and intricately woven collection of emotional and psychological appeals. Almost without fail such images target their audience by invoking the most fundamental and commonly shared values of the period, and the propaganda posters of World War II were no exception. In a period where both national security and national interest were constantly in danger, propaganda posters were used to persuade civilians to invest both emotionally and financially in the war effort. G. K. Odell's poster entitled "Keep These Hands Off" is a quintessential example of World War II propaganda. Although Odell employs a wide variety of persuasive elements including appeals to authority and logic, he most effectively utilizes emotion and traditional family values to cajole the audience into unified support of the war effort.

Odell's poster immediately attracts the viewer's attention with a powerful emotional appeal. Positioned at the center of the painting is a young, beautiful, and seemingly angelic mother holding a small child, presumably her own. What is most striking about this portrait is the way in which the woman appears to make eye contact with the viewer. The woman's peaceful yet pleading expression involves the viewer at a very personal and intimate level; one is drawn in immediately and it is this initial draw that makes the poster so effective. Once caught by the mother's unavoidable gaze the viewer cannot help but notice the infant held in her arms. The child seems to be looking off into the distance, unaware of the imminent danger posed by the encroaching claws positioned both above and below. It is this innocence, the innocence and potential of youth, that draws in the viewer closer still and causes him or her to feel a sense of emotional attachment to both mother and child.

Attached to this immediate invocation of emotion is Odell's strategic reliance on traditional and widespread beliefs—a critical aspect of any persuasive piece. Odell exploits two of the most deeply entrenched traditions of society—family values and gender roles. The sacred human relationship between mother and child is clearly threatened by the two dark hands representing the Axis powers. In addition, the poster implicitly communicates the value placed upon a peaceful and unthreatened childhood. It becomes the duty of the viewer to "keep these hands off" and ensure that such values are not jeopardized. Furthermore, Odell chooses not to depict any men in danger, only a woman and her child. The poster appeals to what are now outdated gender roles, namely, that women are vulnerable and incapable of defending themselves; it becomes the responsibility of the viewer to rescue the mother and child from their perilous situation. In this way the image draws viewers into the situation at hand, holds them responsible for the rescue and protection of both the mother and child, and requires their intervention through the only way possible—the purchase of victory bonds.

In addition, Odell employs a clever and more subtle use of color, shape, and shading to communicate his message. Both the mother and child are dressed in white clothing, symbolic of purity, innocence, and cleanliness. The dark hands descending upon the mother and child are further demonized by their apparent willingness to endanger and violate such a striking image of beauty and purity. Moreover, it is no coincidence that the two hands representing the Axis powers are colored so darkly. Darkness has long been associated with danger, fear, and destruction; associating the Axis powers with such concepts vividly portrays them as inherently evil. The use of color and shading to prompt certain emotional responses is an indispensable component of artwork. In addition, the hands themselves seem to be monsterlike, and in fact, inhuman. In this way the Axis powers are not only depicted as evil, but monsterlike, savage, incapable and undeserving of sympathy.

This characterization of the enemy as inhuman is an important psychological aspect of warfare; it is one that disguises immense human suffering and exonerates those forced to kill in battle. Enemy creation is also a quite effective tool in uniting a nation against a single identifiable threat. Only when taking this aspect into consideration can the poster's persuasive genius be fully appreciated. By identifying the Axis powers as a threat to traditional and widespread values, Odell inflames powerful emotions and in doing so provides the audience with a reason to unite, to fight for the common interest, and, ultimately, to invest in the war effort through the purchase of victory bonds.

The most essential components of a successful war effort are solidarity of purpose, high national morale, demonization of the enemy, and financial resources; Odell relied on, and intelligently invoked, the traditional values and emotions of his audience in order to provoke a response that would mobilize the most successful war effort possible. Thus, Odell not only appealed to certain preestablished values to attract the attention and interest of his audience; he also used these values to provoke and motivate his audience into action. Powerful persuasion often builds upon established beliefs. Odell not only understood this principle, he implemented his understanding successfully.

For Journals

Freewrite about your emotional responses to this poster.

For Discussion

1. First, review the poster being discussed. Analyze your own reactions to it. Does McKenzie's essay seem close to the mark? Why or why not?

2. McKenzie discusses the ways in which color, shading, juxtaposition, and the central image all contribute to the persuasive message. Is his assessment persuasive? Why or why not?

For Writing

1. Analyze this poster using a different focus or thesis.

2. Taking a similar focus as a starting point, write an essay analyzing the use of gender and family values to persuade through an image—either a propaganda poster in this text or elsewhere, or in an advertisement.

∽ *Fame Instead of Shame* (1944)

Charles Atlas (1893–1972) was a bodybuilder who made a fortune in the mail-order business promoting his techniques for developing a muscular male body. Appealing to men's desire to be "real red-blooded men" and using shame among other tactics, Atlas's beach anecdote of the muscle man kicking sand in a skinny man's face became the classic example of male-to-male bullying and competition—and of a cultural stereotype of manliness.

For Journals

What kinds of appeals dominate advertisements for men in the magazines you read?

For Discussion

1. List several assumptions that the author of this advertisement makes about the readers. Do such assumptions seem realistic? What is assumed about what men want? About what women want in a man? About attractiveness, maturity, competition? What expectations of men are conveyed?

2. How does Atlas define "a real man"? Examine the language, the physique of the cartoon figures, the appeals to emotion, the appeals to authority. How persuasive do you think this advertisement was in 1944? To what degree is it significant that the ad appeared during World War II? Do you think the ad would be effective today? Why or why not? How would an advertisement for a similar product be marketed today?

3. The advertisement contains a number of enthymemes (concise deductive arguments with conclusions that depend on the assumptions of the audience in order to make sense). Identify one or two; state them and supply the missing assumption.

4. Do you detect any appeals to logos, or logic, in the text? What are they? What is the evidence supplied to support the appeals? (See discussion of appeals to logos in Chapter 2.)

5. Considering both images and text, compare and contrast the stereotypical roles conveyed in *Keep within Compass* and in this advertisement. Which gender seems to have a more narrowly defined role in society? Have times changed for either gender?

For Writing

1.   Write an essay arguing that expectations for men and their role in American society have, or have not, changed since this advertisement was published. You can focus on this advertisement, or you can find a related contemporary advertisement and compare and contrast the two.

2.   Review a variety of magazines from the 1920s through the 1960s, looking for advertisements that convey gender roles or expectations. What is suggested in them about men's and women's roles? Abut children or children's gender roles? Write an essay developing your position. If possible, include photocopies of the advertisements you use.

∞ *They'll Know You've Arrived* (1958)

FORD MOTOR CO.

The Edsel car was one of the most embarrassing debacles in the automotive industry generally, and for the Ford Motor Company specifically, in the 1950s. Decades later, middle-aged and older Americans still allude to the Edsel in describing a colossal mistake, particularly in product development. But as the advertisement here suggests, the Edsel was marketed as a part of post–World War II prosperity, and ads such as this appeared in mainstream, middle-class magazines.

For Journals

What kinds of advertisements do you find most appealing? Do some types draw your eyes more than others? Do some appeal to your desire for status and success?

For Discussion

1.   Who are the active people in the advertisement? Who are the passive onlookers? Where are the people in the photograph relative to the product being displayed? What do these positions in the photograph convey to you about gender roles, power, and targeted audiences for the advertisement?

2.   The headline plays on the word *arrived* to indicate not only transportation but also status and success. Examine the smaller text at the bottom of the ad. In what ways does it reinforce the connection made in the headline between success, money, and consumption?

3.   What assertions does the advertisement make about success? What appeals to ethos, or credibility and shared values; to pathos, or

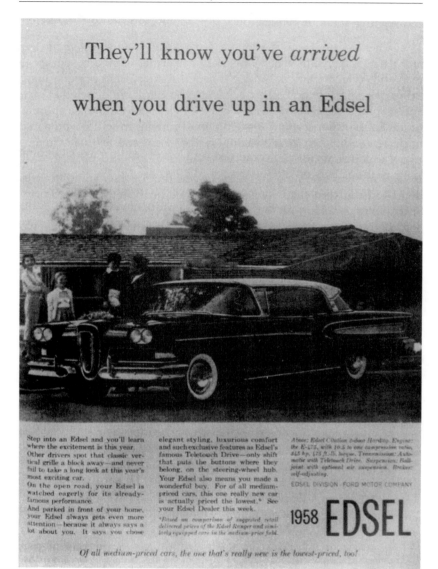

emotions; to logos, or logic, do the text and photograph make? Do both parts of the ad rely on the same types of appeals?

4.   The Edsel became a notoriously unpopular car and the butt of many jokes. Is there a car or other type of product today that you think may become the "Edsel" of tomorrow despite currently being considered a status symbol?

For Writing

1. In her article "You've Come a Long Way, Madison Avenue" in *Lear's* magazine, author Betsy Sharkey has argued that ads sell sex to men and style to women. Browse through some current popular magazines, and find several advertisements you think are directed at men and several directed at women. Does the evidence you find support or refute Sharkey's assertion? Develop an argument in which you agree or disagree with Sharkey, drawing on the visual and textual evidence of the advertisements to support your view.

2. For many years, cigarettes were advertised for their ability to help depress the appetite and even for their good health side effects. Lucky Strike, for example, used to run an ad that said, "Reach for a Lucky—instead of a sweet" and "It's toasted—No Throat Irritation—No Cough." Find an advertisement that you think is particularly misleading or unrealistic, and write an essay in which you analyze the elements of the ad.

3. In *Satisfaction Guaranteed*, her book on American consumerism, Susan Strasser says that Americans had to be trained to want products and to believe that they needed them so that they would go out and buy things and spend money. Based on your own observations and experience, do you agree or disagree with Strasser? Develop your argument into an essay supported by examples and details you have observed or experienced.

∞ *Rusk v. State*
Court of Special Appeals of Maryland, 406 A. 2d 624 (1979)

JUDGE WILNER

This legal opinion comes from the second of three parts in a court proceeding. In the first part, Mr. Rusk was convicted of rape and sentenced to ten years in prison. In the second part, he appealed for his conviction to be overturned, and he won. Judge Wilner served on the appeals court panel that heard Mr. Rusk's request, but unlike the majority of the court, he felt that Mr. Rusk's original sentence was correct. In the minority opinion presented here, he explains why he thinks Mr. Rusk was in fact guilty of rape. (In the third phase, Mr. Rusk's victim appealed for his conviction to be reinstated and the court agreed, relying for its decision on Wilner's reasoning in this earlier appeal.)

Wilner, Judge, dissenting.

With the deepest respect for the generally superior wisdom of my colleagues who authored or endorsed the majority Opinion, but with the equally profound conviction that, in this case, they have made a serious mistake, I record this dissent. . . .

Md. Annot. Code art. 27, § 463(a) considers three types of conduct as constituting second degree rape. We are concerned only with the first: a person is guilty of rape in the second degree if he (1) engages in vaginal intercourse with another person, (2) by force or threat of force, (3) against the will, and (4) without the consent of the other person. There is no real question here as to the first, third, or fourth elements of the crime. The evidence was certainly sufficient to show that appellant had vaginal intercourse with the victim, and that such act was against her will and without her consent. The point at issue is whether it was accomplished by force or threat of force; and I think that in viewing the evidence, that point should remain ever clear. *Consent is not the issue here, only whether there was sufficient evidence of force or the threat of force.*

Unfortunately, courts, including in the present case a majority of this one, often tend to confuse these two elements—force and lack of consent—and to think of them as one. They are not. They mean, and require, different things. See *State v. Studham,* 572 P.2d 700 (Utah, 1977). What seems to cause the confusion—what, indeed, has become a common denominator of both elements—is the notion that the victim must actively resist the attack upon her. If she fails to offer sufficient resistance (sufficient to the satisfaction of the judge), a court is entitled, or at least presumes the entitlement, to find that there was no force or threat of force, or that the act was not against her will, or that she actually consented to it, or some unarticulated combination or synthesis of these elements that leads to the ultimate conclusion that the victim was not raped. Thus it is that the focus is almost entirely on the extent of resistance—*the victim's acts, rather than those of her assailant.* Attention is directed not to the wrongful stimulus, but to the victim's reactions to it. Right or wrong, that seems to be the current state of the Maryland law; and, notwithstanding its uniqueness in the criminal law, and its illogic, until changed by statute or the Court of Appeals, I accept it as binding.

But what is required of a woman being attacked or in danger of attack? How much resistance must she offer? Where is that line to be drawn between requiring that she either risk serious physical harm, perhaps death, on the one hand, or be termed a willing partner on the other? Some answers are given in *Hazel v. State,* 221 Md. 464, 157 A.2d 922 (1960), although, as in so many cases, they were stated in the context of both the requirement of force and the lack of consent. The Court said, at pp. 469, 470, 157 A.2d at p. 925:

"Force is an essential element of the crime and to justify a conviction, the evidence must warrant a conclusion either that the victim resisted and her resistance was overcome by force or that she was prevented from resisting by threats to her safety. But no particular amount of force, either actual or constructive, is required to constitute rape. Necessarily that fact must depend upon the prevailing circumstances. As in this case force may exist without violence. *If the acts and threats of the defendant were reasonably calculated to create in the mind of the victim—having regard to the circumstances in which she was placed—a real apprehension, due to fear, of imminent bodily harm, serious enough to impair or overcome her will to resist, then such acts and threats are the equivalent of force.* . . .

"With respect to the presence or absence of the element of consent, it is true, of course, that however reluctantly given, consent to the act at any time prior to penetration deprives the subsequent intercourse of its criminal character. *There is, however, a wide difference between consent and a submission to the act. Consent may involve submission, but submission does not necessarily imply consent. Furthermore, submission to a compelling force, or as a result of being put in fear, is not consent.* . . .

"The authorities are by no means in accord as to what degree of resistance is necessary to establish the absence of consent. However, the generally accepted doctrine seems to be that a female—who was conscious and possessed of her natural, mental and physical powers when the attack took place—must have resisted to the extent of her ability at the time, unless it appears that she was overcome by numbers or was so terrified by threats as to overpower her will to resist. . . . Since resistance is necessarily relative, the presence or absence of it must depend on the facts and circumstances in each case. . . . *But the real test, which must be recognized in all cases, is whether the assault was committed without the consent and against the will of the prosecuting witness.*

"The kind of fear which would render resistance by a woman unnecessary to support a conviction of rape includes, but is not necessarily limited to, a fear of death or serious bodily harm, or a fear so extreme as to preclude resistance, or a fear which would well nigh render her mind incapable of continuing to resist, or a fear that so overpowers her that she does not dare resist." (Citations omitted.) (Emphasis supplied.)

From these pronouncements in *Hazel*, this Court has articulated 10 what the majority refers to as a "rule of reason"—*i.e.*, that "where the victim's story could not be corroborated by wounds, bruises or disordered clothing, the lack of consent could be shown by fear based upon reasonable apprehension." *Winegan* v. *State*, 10 Md.App. 196, 200, 268 A.2d 585, 588 (1970); *Goldberg* v. *State*, 41 Md.App. 58, 395 A.2d 1213 (1979). *As so phrased*, I do not consider this to be a rule of reason at all; it is highly unreasonable, and again mixes the element of consent with that of force. But what I do accept is what the Court of Appeals said in *Hazel*: (1) if the acts and threats of the defendant were reasonably calculated to create in the mind of the victim—having regard to the circumstances in which she was placed—a real apprehension, due to fear, of imminent bodily harm, serious enough to impair or overcome her will to resist, then such acts and threats are the equivalent of force; (2) submission is not the equivalent of consent; and (3) the real test is whether the assault was committed without the consent and against the will of the prosecuting witness.[1]

Upon this basis, the evidence against appellant must be considered. Judge Thompson recounts most, but not quite all, of the victim's story. The victim—I'll call her Pat—attended a high school reunion. She had arranged to meet her girlfriend Terry there. The reunion was over at 9:00, and Terry asked Pat to accompany her to Fell's Point.[2] Pat had gone to Fell's Point with Terry on a few prior occasions, explaining in court: "I've never met anybody [there] I've gone out with. I met people in general, talking in conversation, most of the time people that Terry knew, not that I have gone down there, and met people as dates." She agreed to go, but first called her mother, who was babysitting with Pat's two-year-old son, to tell her that she was going with Terry to Fell's Point, and that she would not be home late. It was just after 9:00 when Pat and Terry, in their separate cars, left for Fell's Point, alone.[3]

They went to a place called Helen's and had one drink. They stayed an hour or so and then walked down to another place (where they had another drink), stayed about a half hour there, and went to a third place. Up to that point, Pat conversed only with Terry, and did not strike up any other acquaintanceships. Pat and Terry were standing against a wall when appellant came over and said hello to Terry, who was conversing with someone else at the time. Appellant then began to talk with Pat. They were both separated, they both had young children; and they spoke about those things. Pat said that she had been ready to leave when appellant came on the scene, and that she only talked with him for five or ten minutes. It was then about midnight. Pat had to get up with her baby in the morning and did not want to stay out late.

---

[1]Other courts have stated the rule this way: A rape victim is not required to do more than her age, strength, surrounding facts and all attending circumstances make it reasonable for her to do to manifest her opposition. See *Dinkens* v. *State,* 92 Nev. 74, 546 P.2d 228 (1976); *State* v. *Studham,* 572 P.2d 700 (Utah 1977). See also *Schrum* v. *Com.,* 219 Va. 168, 246, S.E.2d 893 (1978). [Author's note]

[2]Fell's Point is an old section of Baltimore City adjacent to the harbor. It has been extensively renovated as part of urban renewal and, among refurbished homes and shops, hosts a number of cafes and discotheques. It is part of the City's night scene. [Author's note]

[3]Pat said that Terry and she lived at opposite ends of town and that Fell's Point was sort of midway between their respective homes. [Author's note]

Terry wasn't ready to leave. As Pat was preparing to go, appellant asked if she would drop him off on her way home.[4] She agreed because she thought he was a friend of Terry's. She told him, however, as they walked to her car, "I'm just giving a ride home, you know, as a friend, not anything to be, you know, thought of other than a ride." He agreed to that condition.

Pat was completely unfamiliar with appellant's neighborhood. She had no idea where she was. When she pulled up to where appellant said he lived, she put the car in park, but left the engine running. She said to appellant, "Well, here, you know, you are home." Appellant then asked Pat to come up with him and she refused. He persisted in his request, as did she in her refusal. She told him that even if she wanted to come up, she dared not do so. She was separated and it might cause marital problems for her. Finally, he reached over, turned off the ignition, took her keys, got out of the car, came around to her side, opened the door, and said to her, "Now, will you come up?"

It was at this point that Pat followed appellant to his apartment, 15
and it is at this point that the majority of this Court begins to substitute its judgment for that of the trial court and jury. We know nothing about Pat and appellant. We don't know how big they are, what they look like, what their life experiences have been. We don't know if appellant is larger or smaller than she, stronger or weaker. We don't know what the inflection was in his voice as he dangled her car keys in front of her. We can't tell whether this was in a jocular vein or a truly threatening one. We have no idea what his mannerisms were. The trial judge and the jury could discern some of these things, of course, because they could observe the two people in court and could listen to what they said and how they said it. But all we know is that, between midnight and 1:00 A.M., in a neighborhood that was strange to Pat, appellant took her car keys, demanded that she accompany him, and most assuredly implied that unless she did so, at the very least, she might be stranded.

Now, let us interrupt the tale for a minute and consider the situation. Pat did not honk the horn; she did not scream; she did not try to run away. Why, she was asked. "I was scared. I didn't think at the time what to do." Later, on cross-examination: "At that point, because I was scared, because he had my car keys. I didn't know what to do. I was someplace I didn't even know where I was. It was in the city. I didn't know whether to run. I really didn't think, at that point, what to do. Now, I know that I should have blown the horn. I should have run.

---

[4]Her testimony about this, on cross-examination, was: "I said I was leaving. I said, excuse me. It's nice meeting you; but I'm getting ready to leave; and he said, 'which way are you going,' and I told him; at that time, he said, 'Would you mind giving me a lift?'" [Author's note]

There were a million things I could have done. I was scared, at that point, and I didn't do any of them." What, counsel asked, was she afraid of? "Him," she replied. What was she scared that he was going to do? "Rape me, but I didn't say that. It was the way he looked at me, and said, 'Come on up, come on up;' and when he took the keys, I knew that was wrong. I just didn't say, are you going to rape me."

So Pat accompanied appellant to his apartment. As Judge Thompson points out, appellant left her in his apartment for a few minutes.[5] Although there was evidence of a telephone in the room, Pat said that, at the time, she didn't notice one. When appellant returned, he turned off the light and sat on the bed. Pat was in a chair. She testified: "I asked him if I could leave, that I wanted to go home, and I didn't want to come up. I said, 'Now, I came up. Can I go?'" Appellant, who, of course, still had her keys, said that he wanted her to stay. He told her to get on the bed with him, and, in fact, took her arms and pulled her on to the bed. He then started to undress her; he removed her blouse and bra and unzipped her pants. *At his direction,* she removed his clothes. She then said:

> "I was still begging him to please let, you know, let me leave. I said, 'you can get a lot of other girls down there, for what you want,' and he just kept saying, 'no;' and then I was really scared, because I can't describe, you know, what was said. It was more the look in his eyes; and I said, at that point—I didn't know what to say; and I said, 'If I do what you want, will you let me go without killing me?' Because I didn't know, at that point, what he was going to do; and I started to cry; and when I did, he put his hands on my throat, and started lightly to choke me; and I said, 'If I do what you want, will you let me go?' And he said, yes, and at that time, I proceeded to do what he wanted me to."

He "made me perform oral sex, and then sexual intercourse." Following that:

> "I asked him if I could leave now, and he said, 'Yes;' and I got up and got dressed; and he got up and got dressed; and he walked me to my car, and asked if he could see me again; and I said, 'Yes;' and he asked me for my telephone number; and I said, 'No, I'll see you down Fell's Point sometime,' just so I could leave."[6]

At this point, appellant returned her car keys and escorted her to her car. She then drove off:

---

[5]On direct examination, she twice said that he left the room "for a minute" after telling her to sit down. On cross-examination, she said she couldn't remember how long he was gone, but, at counsel's suggestion, said that it was not longer than five minutes. [Author's note]

[6]Pat explained this last comment further: "I didn't know what else to say. I had no intention of meeting him again." [Author's note]

"I stopped at a gas station, that I believe was Amoco or Exon (sic), and went to the ladies' room. From there I drove home. I don't know—I don't know if I rode around for a while or not; but I know I went home, pretty much straight home and pulled up and parked the car.

"I was just going to go home, and not say anything."

Q. "Why?"

A. *"Because I didn't want to go through what I'm going through now."*   25

Q. "What, in fact, did you do then?"

A. "I sat in the car, thinking about it a while, and I thought I wondered what would happen if I hadn't of done what he wanted me to do. So I thought the right thing to do was to go report it, and I went from there to Hillendale to find a police car." (Emphasis supplied.)

How does the majority Opinion view these events? It starts by noting that Pat was a 21-year-old mother who was separated from her husband but not yet divorced, as though that had some significance. To me, it has none, except perhaps (when coupled with the further characterization that Pat and Terry had gone "bar hopping") to indicate an underlying suspicion, for which there is absolutely no support in the record, that Pat was somehow "on the make." Even more alarming, and unwarranted, however, is the majority's analysis of Pat's initial reflections on whether to report what had happened. Ignoring completely her statement that she "didn't want to go through what I'm going through now," the majority, in footnote 1, cavalierly and without any foundation whatever, says:

> "If, in quiet contemplation after the act, she had to wonder what would have happened, her submission on the side of prudence seems hardly justified. Indeed, if *she* had to wonder afterward, how can a fact finder reasonably conclude that she was justifiably in fear sufficient to overcome her will to resist, at the time." (Emphasis in the original.)

It is this type of reasoning—if indeed "reasoning" is the right   30 word for it—that is particularly distressing. The concern expressed by Pat, made even more real by the majority Opinion of this Court, is one that is common among rape victims, and largely accounts for the fact that most incidents of forcible rape go unreported by the victim. See *F.B.I. Uniform Crime Reports* (1978), p. 14; *Report of Task Force on Rape Control,* Baltimore County (1975); *The Treatment of Rape Victims in the Metropolitan Washington Area,* Metropolitan Washington Council of Governments (1976), p. 4. See also *Rape and Its Victims: A Report for Citizens, Health Facilities, and Criminal Justice Agencies,* LEAA (1975). If appellant had desired, and Pat had given, her wallet instead of her body, there would be no question about appellant's guilt of robbery. Taking the car keys under those circumstances would certainly have supplied the requisite threat of force or violence and negated the element of consent. No one would seriously contend that because she failed to raise a hue and cry she had consented to the theft of her money. Why then is such life-threatening action necessary when it is her personal dignity that is being stolen?

For Journals

What is your understanding of the crime of rape? What are your biases or attitudes toward survivors of rape?

For Discussion

1.   Much of Judge Wilner's argument rests on a clear definition. What is the subject of his definition? What kinds of evidence does he use to substantiate his definition? Which kind is most effective?

2.   Judge Wilner recounts, from the majority opinion, the story of "Pat," the woman who was raped by a man she had met in a bar. Why do you think he did so? What attitude toward her story did he have? What do you infer was the attitude toward Pat's story of the majority justices (who overturned the rape conviction)?

3.   Examine the etching *Keep within Compass* presented earlier in this chapter. Do you sense any connection between the values and attitudes conveyed in the etching and in this court case? Explain. You could look, for example, at Judge Wilner's comment about the selection of details in the majority opinion, such as that "Pat" was a 21-year-old mother who was separated but not divorced and had gone "bar-hopping" with a friend.

For Writing

1.   Judge Wilner's argument refutes the majority opinion in *Rusk* v. *State.* Using discussion item 3 as a starting point, examine the assumptions held by the majority and opposing views, perhaps comparing and contrasting them with the message of the etching.

2.   Research the other arguments in this case: the majority opinion in *Rusk* v. *State,* and the arguments in the *State* v. *Rusk* (the original conviction). You could select one argument to analyze in depth, examining types of appeals, use of evidence, or arguments. Or select one particular type of appeal (such as appeal to ethos) and examine the ways in which it is used in the series of arguments.

∞ *Marriage Is a Fundamental Right* (1989)

THOMAS STODDARD

Thomas Stoddard (1948–) is an attorney and serves as executive director of the Lambda Defense and Education Fund, a gay rights organization. He is the author of The Rights of Gay People *(1983) and frequently speaks out on gay civil rights is-*

sues. *In the essay that follows, which first appeared in the* New York Times, *Stoddard argues on behalf of a controversial but fundamental issue: the rights of same-gender couples to marry.*

"In sickness and in health; 'til death do us part." With those words, millions of people each year are married, a public affirmation of a private bond that both society and the newlyweds hope will endure. Yet for nearly four years, Karen Thompson was denied the company of the one person to whom she had pledged life-long devotion.

Her partner is a woman, Sharon Kowalski, and their home state of Minnesota, like every other in the United States, refuses to permit same-sex marriages.

Karen Thompson and Sharon Kowalski are spouses in every respect except the legal. They exchanged vows and rings. The lived together until November 13, 1983—when Kowalski, as the result of an automobile accident, was rendered unable to walk and barely able to speak.

Thompson sought a ruling granting her guardianship over her partner, but Kowalski's parents opposed the petition and obtained sole guardianship. They then moved Kowalski to a nursing home 300 miles away from Thompson and forbade all visits between the two women.

In February 1989, in the wake of a reevaluation of Kowalski's 5 mental competence, Thompson was permitted to visit her partner again. But that prolonged injustice and anguish inflicted on both women hold a moral for everyone.

Marriage, the Supreme Court declared in 1967 in *Loving* v. *Virginia,* is "one of the basic civil rights of man" (and, presumably, of woman as well). The freedom to marry, said the Court, is "essential to the orderly pursuit of happiness."

Marriage is far more than a symbolic state. It can be the key to survival—emotional and financial. Marriage triggers a universe of rights, privileges and presumptions. In every jurisdiction in this country, a married person can share in a spouse's estate even when there is no will. She typically has access to the group insurance and pension programs offered by the spouse's employer, and she enjoys tax advantages.

The decision whether or not to marry belongs properly to individuals, not to the government. While marriage historically has required a male and a female partner, history alone cannot sanctify injustice.

If tradition were the only measure, most states still would limit matrimony to partners of the same race. As recently as 1967, before the Supreme Court declared in *Loving* that miscegenation statutes are unconstitutional, sixteen states still prohibited marriages between a white person and a black person. When all the excuses were stripped away, it was clear that the only purpose of those laws was to maintain white supremacy.

Those who argue against reforming the marriage statutes because 10 they believe that same-sex marriage would be "anti-family" overlook the obvious: Marriage creates families and promotes social stability. In an increasingly loveless world, those who wish to commit themselves to a relationship founded upon devotion should be encouraged, not scorned. Government has no legitimate interest in how that love is expressed.

And it can no longer be argued—if it ever could—that marriage is fundamentally a procreative unit. Otherwise, states would forbid marriage between those who, by reason of age or infertility, cannot have children, as well as those who elect not to.

The case of Sharon Kowalski and Karen Thompson demonstrates that sanctimonious illusions can lead directly to the suffering of others. Denied the right to marry, these women were left to the whims and prejudices of others, and of the law.

It is time for the marriage statutes to incorporate fully the concept of equal protection of the law by extending to the many millions of gay Americans the right to marry.

For Journals

Freewrite for five or ten minutes on your assumptions about or biases toward same-gender marriages or domestic partnerships.

For Discussion

1. Why do you think Stoddard begins with an anecdote? Why do you think he focuses on women? On the issue of caring for sick loved ones? How does this strategy shift the focus of the debate?

2. How does Stoddard's introductory strategy counter his readers' assumptions about the issue of gay marriage?

3. Stoddard's assertion is that same-gender marriage is not antifamily, as some have charged, but rather profamily. Does he adequately counter the antifamily arguments? Does he adequately support his assertions that same-gender marriage "creates families and promotes social stability" (paragraph 10)? In what ways is he transforming traditional definitions of family to do so?

4. What appeals to values and beliefs does Stoddard make? What appeals to emotion? To logic? Which do you find most persuasive?

5. Although this essay was first published in the *New York Times*, a newspaper with a general rather than legal audience, Stoddard (who is an attorney) is comfortable citing legal precedent to support his argument. Do you think his evidence is convincing to a diverse audience? Stoddard's article was later reprinted in the *Journal of the American Bar Association*. Do you think that audience is more, or less, likely to accept the arguments he makes?

For Writing

1.   Write a rebuttal to Stoddard, arguing with the specific points he makes, challenging his assumptions or premises, and making any additional points to support the opposing view. You may develop your argument using appeals to ethos, pathos, or logos, or appeals to values and beliefs, to emotion and empathy, to logic and evidence. (See Chapter 2, on ethos, pathos, and logos.) Or you may wish to integrate evidence from outside sources into your arguments. If you do, be sure to read about both sides of the issue and to use your evidence to represent the opposing views fairly and ethically and in accord with the author's intended meaning. (See Chapter 4, "Research," for additional information on research.)

3.   With a peer or in groups, write a dialogue between two people debating this topic or another controversial social issue. Then exchange dialogues with another peer or group. Evaluate the assumptions, premises, and appeals used in the dialogues. Summarize your findings, and share them with your class.

∞ *Reserve Marriage for Heterosexuals* (1990)

BRUCE FEIN

Bruce Fein, an attorney living in Washington, D.C., is the author of Significant Decisions of the Supreme Court *(1979–1980). He has contributed articles to the* National Review *and* American Legion Magazine. *Fein's article first appeared in the* Journal of the American Bar Association, *which also reprinted the preceding selection by Thomas Stoddard.*

Authorizing the marriage of homosexuals, like sanctioning polygamy, would be unenlightened social policy. The law should reserve the celebration of marriage vows for monogamous male-female attachments to further the goal of psychologically, emotionally and educationally balanced offspring.

As Justice Oliver Wendell Holmes noted, the life of the law has not been logic, it has been experience. Experience confirms that child development is skewed, scarred or retarded when either a father or mother is absent in the household.

In the area of adoption, married couples are favored over singles. The recent preferences for joint child-custody decrees in divorce proceedings tacitly acknowledge the desirability of child intimacies with both a mother and father.

As Supreme Court Justice Byron White recognized in *Taylor* v. *Louisiana* (1975): "[T]he two sexes are not fungible; a community made up exclusively of one is different from a community of both; the subtle interplay of influence one on the other is among the imponderables" (quoting from *Ballard* v. *United States*).

A child receives incalculable benefits in the maturing process by 5 the joint instruction, consolation, oversight and love of a father and mother—benefits that are unavailable in homosexuals households. The child enjoys the opportunity to understand and respect both sexes in a uniquely intimate climate. The likelihood of gender prejudice is thus reduced, an exceptionally worthy social objective.

The law should encourage male-female marriage vows over homosexual attachments in the interests of physically, mentally, and psychologically healthy children, the nation's most valuable asset.

Crowning homosexual relationships with the solemnity of legal marriage would wrongly send social cues that male-female marriages are not preferable. And there is no constitutional right to homosexual marriage since homosexual sodomy can be criminalized. See *Bowers* v. *Hardwick* (1986).

The fact that some traditional marriages end in fractious divorce, yield no offspring, or result in families with mistreated children does not discredit limiting marriage to monogamous female-male relationships. Anti-polygamy laws are instructive. They seek to discourage female docility, male autocracy, and intra-family rancor and jealousies that are promoted by polygamous marriages. That some might not exhibit such deplorable characteristics is no reason for their repeal or a finding of constitutional infirmity.

To deny the right of homosexual marriage is not an argument for limiting other rights to gays, because of community animosity or vengeance. These are unacceptable policy motivations if law is to be civilized.

Several states and localities protect homosexuals against discrimi- 10 nation is employment or housing. In New York, a state law confers on a homosexual the rent-control benefits of a deceased partner. Other jurisdictions have eschewed special legal rights for homosexuals, and the military excludes them. Experience will adjudge which of the varied legal approaches to homosexual rights has been the most enlightened.

Sober debate over homosexual rights is in short supply. The subject challenges deep-rooted and passionately held images of manhood, womanhood and parenthood, and evokes sublimated fears of community ostracism or degradation.

Each legal issue regarding homosexuality should be examined discretely with the recognition that time has upset many fighting faiths and with the goal of balancing indiviudal liberty against community interests. With regard to homosexual marriage, that balance is negative.

For Journals

Freewrite for five to ten minutes on the assumptions about marriage you had as a child and now have as an adult. How do children fit into the image you have in mind?

For Discussion

1. What kinds of appeals does Fein make? Consider particularly his core assertion: that children will suffer from same-gender marriages. What assumptions about the purpose of marriage does his argument rest on? Is the argument that children are the key consideration in marriage laws one that would be as persuasive to general audiences as Fein believes it will be to lawyers?

2. In addition to citing legal cases, Fein cites authorities such as Oliver Wendell Holmes. But he then states that "experience confirms that child development is skewed, scarred or retarded when either a father or mother is absent in the household" (paragraph 2). Are you persuaded by his citing of "experience"? If not, what additional evidence could he offer that might be more convincing?

3. Fein's overall organizational pattern is direct: he asserts and then supports. How might writing for an audience of lawyers have dictated this pattern? Would it have been equally effective writing for a general audience?

4. Fein also argues by making an analogy to polygamous marriages. How convincing is the analogy? How appropriate is it to the argument?

5. Fein differentiates and separates this issue from other civil rights issues. Do you accept his premise that marriage rights differ fundamentally from other civil rights?

6. Examine the logic of Fein's arguments, such as the one in paragraph 7. It may be helpful to outline the premises and conclusion for each argument he makes. Which of his arguments stand up to the analysis? Which ones are weak? Which ones could be strengthened with evidence?

For Writing

1. Write a letter of rebuttal to Fein. Use a different approach and different arguments than Thomas Stoddard (this chapter) uses in "Marriage Is a Fundamental Right." Keep in mind the biases and assumptions you wrote about in your journal assignment for the Stoddard article.

2.   Compare and contrast Fein's and Stoddard's arguments, focusing on the effectiveness of their appeals, their use of evidence, and their patterns of development. Which argument makes more appeals to emotion? To logic? To traditions, values, beliefs? Keeping in mind your own biases and attitudes toward the topic, which argument seems more sound?

∞ *Blame It on Feminism* (1991)

SUSAN FALUDI

Susan Faludi (1959–) graduated summa cum laude from Harvard University in 1981. Ten years later she won the Pulitzer Prize for an article about the leveraged buyout of Safeway supermarkets and the National Book Critics Circle Award for Backlash: The Undeclared War Against American Women *(1991), an extensive study of the social and political reaction against feminism and women's modest progress toward equal rights. Faludi has been a regular contributor to the magazines* Ms. *and* Mother Jones, *and her writing sometimes skeptically examines the status of women in contemporary society. She describes* Backlash *as a book that "arms women with information and a good dose of cynicism," adding, "It's also very large, so it can be thrown at misogynists."*

To be a woman in America at the close of the 20th century—what good fortune. That's what we keep hearing, anyway. The barricades have fallen, politicians assure us. Women have "made it," Madison Avenue cheers. Women's fight for equality has "largely been won," *Time* magazine announces. Enroll at any university, join any law firm, apply for credit at any bank. Women have so many opportunities now, corporate leaders say, that we don't really need equal opportunity policies. Women are so equal now, lawmakers say, that we no longer need an Equal Rights Amendment. Women have "so much," former President Ronald Reagan says, that the White House no longer needs to appoint them to higher office. Even American Express ads are saluting a woman's freedom to charge it. At last, women have received their full citizenship papers.

And yet . . .

Behind this celebration of the American woman's victory, behind the news, cheerfully and endlessly repeated, that the struggle for women's rights is won, another message flashes. You may be free and equal now, it says to women, but you have never been more miserable.

This bulletin of despair is posted everywhere—at the newsstand, on the TV set, at the movies, in advertisements and doctors' offices and academic journals. Professional women are suffering "burnout" and succumbing to an "infertility epidemic." Single women are grieving from a "man shortage." The *New York Times* reports: Childless women are "depressed and confused" and their ranks are swelling. *Newsweek* says: Unwed women are "hysterical" and crumbling under a "profound crisis of confidence." The health advice manuals inform: High-powered career women are stricken with unprecedented outbreaks of "stress-induced disorders," hair loss, bad nerves, alcoholism, and even heart attacks. The psychology books advise: Independent women's loneliness represents "a major mental health problem today." Even founding feminist Betty Friedan has been spreading the word: she warns that women now suffer from a new identity crisis and "new 'problems that have no name.'"

How can American women be in so much trouble at the same time 5 that they are supposed to be so blessed? If the status of women has never been higher, why is their emotional state so low? If women got what they asked for, what could possibly be the matter now?

The prevailing wisdom of the past decade has supported one, and only one, answer to this riddle: it must be all that equality that's causing all that pain. Women are unhappy precisely *because* they are free. Women are enslaved by their own liberation. They have grabbed at the gold ring of independence, only to miss the one ring that really matters. They have gained control of their fertility, only to destroy it. They have pursued their own professional dreams—and lost out on the greatest female adventure. The women's movement, as we are told time and again, has proved women's own worst enemy.

"In dispensing its spoils, women's liberation has given my generation high incomes, our own cigarette, the option of single parenthood, rape crisis centers, personal lines of credit, free love, and female gynecologists," Mona Charen, a young law student, writes in the *National Review*, in an article titled "The Feminist Mistake." "In return it has effectively robbed us of one thing upon which the happiness of most women rests—men." The *National Review* is a conservative publication, but such charges against the women's movement are not confined to its pages. "Our generation was the human sacrifice" to the women's movement, *Los Angeles Times* feature writer Elizabeth Mehren contends in a *Time* cover story. Baby-boom women like her, she says, have been duped by feminism: "We believed the rhetoric." In *Newsweek*, writer Kay Ebeling dubs feminism "the Great Experiment That Failed" and asserts "women in my generation, its perpetrators, are the casualties." Even the beauty magazines are saying it: *Harper's Bazaar* accuses the women's movement of having "lost us [women] ground instead of gaining it."

In the last decade, publications from the *New York Times* to *Vanity Fair* to the *Nation* have issued a steady stream of indictments against the women's movement, with such headlines as WHEN FEMINISM FAILED, OR THE AWFUL TRUTH ABOUT WOMEN'S LIB. They hold the campaign for women's equality responsible for nearly every woe besetting women, from mental depression to meager savings accounts, from teenage suicides to eating disorders to bad complexions. The "Today" show says women's liberation is to blame for bag ladies. A guest columnist in the *Baltimore Sun* even proposes that feminists produced the rise in slasher movies. By making the "violence" of abortion more acceptable, the author reasons, women's rights activists made it all right to show graphic murders on screen.

At the same time, other outlets of popular culture have been forging the same connection: in Hollywood films, of which *Fatal Attraction* is only the most famous, emancipated women with condominiums of their own slink wild-eyed between bare walls, paying for their liberty with an empty bed, a barren womb. "My biological clock is ticking so loud it keeps me awake at night," Sally Field cries in the film *Surrender*, as, in an all too common transformation in the cinema of the '80s, an actress who once played scrappy working heroines is now showcased groveling for a groom. In prime-time television shows, from *thirtysomething* to *Family Man*, single, professional, and feminist women are humiliated, turned into harpies, or hit by nervous breakdowns; the wise ones recant their independent ways by the closing sequence. In popular novels, from Gail Parent's *A Sign of the Eighties* to Stephen King's *Misery*, unwed women shrink to sniveling spinsters or inflate to fire-breathing she-devils; renouncing all aspirations but marriage, they beg for wedding bands from strangers or swing axes at reluctant bachelors. We "blew it by waiting," a typically remorseful careerist sobs in Freda Bright's *Singular Women;* she and her sister professionals are "condemned to be childless forever." Even Erica Jong's high-flying independent heroine literally crashes by the end of the decade, as the author supplants *Fear of Flying*'s saucy Isadora Wing, a symbol of female sexual emancipation in the '70s, with an embittered careerist-turned-recovering-"co-dependent" in *Any Woman's Blues*—a book that is intended, as the narrator bluntly states, "to demonstrate what a deadend the so-called sexual revolution had become, and how desperate so-called free women were in the last few years of our decadent epoch."

Popular psychology manuals peddle the same diagnosis for contemporary female distress. "Feminism, having promised her a stronger sense of her own identity, has given her little more than an identity *crisis*," the best-selling advice manual *Being a Woman* asserts. The authors of the era's self-help classic *Smart Women/Foolish Choices* proclaim that women's distress was "an unfortunate consequence of feminism," because "it created a myth among women that the apex of self-realization could be achieved only through autonomy, independence, and career." 10

In the Reagan and Bush years, government officials have needed no prompting to endorse this thesis. Reagan spokeswoman Faith Whittlesey declared feminism a "straitjacket" for women, in the White House's only policy speech on the status of the American female population—entitled "Radical Feminism in Retreat." Law enforcement officers and judges, too, have pointed a damning finger at feminism, claiming that they can chart a path from rising female independence to rising female pathology. As a California sheriff explained it to the press, "Women are enjoying a lot more freedom now, and as a result, they are committing more crimes." The U.S. Attorney General's Commission on Pornography even proposed that women's professional advancement might be responsible for rising rape rates. With more women in college and at work now, the commission members reasoned in their report, women just have more opportunities to be raped.

Some academics have signed on to the consensus, too—and they are the "experts" who have enjoyed the highest profiles on the media circuit. On network news and talk shows, they have advised millions of women that feminism has condemned them to "a lesser life." Legal scholars have railed against "the equality trap." Sociologists have claimed that "feminist-inspired" legislative reforms have stripped women of special "protections." Economists have argued that well-paid working women have created "a less stable American family." And demographers, with greatest fanfare, have legitimated the prevailing wisdom with so-called neutral data on sex ratios and fertility trends; they say they actually have the numbers to prove that equality doesn't mix with marriage and motherhood.

Finally, some "liberated" women themselves have joined the lamentations. In confessional accounts, works that invariably receive a hearty greeting from the publishing industry, "recovering Superwomen" tell all. In *The Cost of Loving: Women and the New Fear of Intimacy*, Megan Marshall, a Harvard-pedigreed writer, asserts that the feminist "Myth of Independence" has turned her generation into unloved and unhappy fast-trackers, "dehumanized" by careers and "uncertain of their gender identity." Other diaries of mad Superwomen charge that "the hard-core feminist viewpoint," as one of them puts it, has relegated educated executive achievers to solitary nights of frozen dinners and closet drinking. The triumph of equality, they report, has merely given women hives, stomach cramps, eye-twitching disorders, even comas.

But what "equality" are all these authorities talking about?

If American women are so equal, why do they represent two- 15 thirds of all poor adults? Why are more than 80 percent of full-time working women making less than $20,000 a year, nearly double the male rate? Why are they still far more likely than men to live in poor housing and receive no health insurance, and twice as likely to draw no pension? Why does the average working woman's salary still lag as far behind the average man's as it did twenty years ago? Why does the average female college graduate today earn less than a man with no more than a high school diploma (just as she did in the '50s)—and why does the average female high school graduate today earn less than a male high school dropout? Why do American women, in fact, face the worst gender-based pay gap in the developed world?

If women have "made it," then why are nearly 80 percent of working women still stuck in traditional "female" jobs—as secretaries, administrative "support" workers and salesclerks? And, conversely, why are they less than 8 percent of all federal and state judges, less than 6 percent of all law partners, and less than one half of 1 percent of top corporate managers? Why are there only three female state governors, two female U.S. senators, and two Fortune 500 chief executives? Why are only nineteen of the four thousand corporate officers and directors women—and why do more than half the boards of Fortune 500 companies still lack even one female member?

If women "have it all," then why don't they have the most basic requirements to achieve equality in the work force? Unlike virtually all other industrialized nations, the U.S. government still has no family-leave and child care programs—and more than 99 percent of American private employers don't offer child care either. Though business leaders say they are aware of and deplore sex discrimination, corporate America has yet to make an honest effort toward eradicating it. In a 1990 national poll of chief executives at Fortune 1000 companies, more than 80 percent acknowledged that discrimination impedes female employees' progress—yet, less than 1 percent of these same companies regarded *remedying* sex discrimination as a goal that their personnel departments should pursue. In fact, when the companies' human resource officers were asked to rate their department's priorities, women's advancement ranked last.

If women are so "free," why are their reproductive freedoms in greater jeopardy today than a decade earlier? Why do women who want to postpone childbearing now have fewer options than ten years ago? The availability of different forms of contraception has declined, research for new birth control has virtually halted, new laws restricting abortion—or even *information* about abortion—for young and poor women have been passed, and the U.S. Supreme Court has shown little ardor in defending the right it granted in 1973.

Nor is women's struggle for equal education over; as a 1989 study found, three-fourths of all high schools still violate the federal law banning sex discrimination in education. In colleges, undergraduate women receive only 70 percent of the aid undergraduate men get in grants and work-study jobs—and women's sports programs receive a pittance compared with men's. A review of state equal-education laws in the late '80s found that only thirteen states had adopted the minimum provisions required by the federal Title IX law—and only seven states had anti-discrimination regulations that covered all education levels.

Nor do women enjoy equality in their own homes, where they still 20 shoulder 70 percent of the household duties—and the only major change in the last fifteen years is that now middle-class men *think* they do more around the house. (In fact, a national poll finds the ranks of women saying their husbands share equally in child care shrunk to 31 percent in 1987 from 40 percent three years earlier.) Furthermore, in thirty states, it is still generally legal for husbands to rape their wives; and only ten states have laws mandating arrest for domestic violence—even though battering was the leading cause of injury of women in the late '80s. Women who have no other option but to flee find that isn't much of an alternative either. Federal funding for battered women's shelters has been withheld and one third of the 1 million battered women who seek emergency shelter each year can find none. Blows from men contributed far more to the rising numbers of "bag ladies" than the ill effects of feminism. In the '80s, almost half of all homeless women (the fastest growing segment of the homeless) were refugees of domestic violence.

The word may be that women have been "liberated," but women themselves seem to feel otherwise. Repeatedly in national surveys, majorities of women say they are still far from equality. Nearly 70 percent of women polled by the *New York Times* in 1989 said the movement for women's rights had only just begun. Most women in the 1990 Virginia Slims opinion poll agreed with the statement that conditions for their sex in American society had improved "a little, not a lot." In poll after poll in the decade, overwhelming majorities of women said they needed equal pay and equal job opportunities, they needed an Equal Rights Amendment, they needed the right to an abortion without government interference, they needed a federal law guaranteeing maternity leave, they needed decent child care services. They have none of these. So how exactly have we "won" the war for women's rights?

Seen against this background, the much ballyhooed claim that feminism is responsible for making women miserable becomes absurd—and irrelevant. . . . The afflictions ascribed to feminism are all myths. From "the man shortage" to "the infertility epidemic" to "female burnout" to "toxic day care," these so-called female crises have had their origins not in the actual conditions of women's lives but rather in a closed system that starts and ends in the media, popular culture, and advertising—an endless feedback loop that perpetuates and exaggerates its own false images of womanhood.

Women themselves don't single out the women's movement as the source of their misery. To the contrary, in national surveys 75 to 95 percent of women credit the feminist campaign with *improving* their lives, and a similar proportion say that the women's movement should keep pushing for change. Less than 8 percent think the women's movement might have actually made their lot worse.

What actually is troubling the American female population, then? If the many ponderers of the Woman Question really wanted to know, they might have asked their subjects. In public opinion surveys, women consistently rank their own *inequality*, at work and at home, among their most urgent concerns. Over and over, women complain to pollsters about a lack of economic, not marital, opportunities; they protest that working men, not working women, fail to spend time in the nursery and the kitchen. The Roper Organization's survey analysts find that men's opposition to equality is "a major cause of resentment and stress" and "a major irritant for most women today." It is justice for their gender, not wedding rings and bassinets, that women believe to be in desperately short supply. When the *New York Times* polled women in 1989 about "the most important problem facing women today," job discrimination was the overwhelming winner; none of the crises the media and popular culture had so assiduously promoted even made the charts. In the 1990 Virginia Slims poll, women were most upset by their lack of money, followed by the refusal of their men to shoulder child care and domestic duties. By contrast, when the women were asked where the quest for a husband or the desire to hold a "less pressured" job or to stay at home ranked on their list of concerns, they placed them at the bottom.

As the last decade ran its course, women's unhappiness with in- 25 equality only mounted. In national polls, the ranks of women protesting discriminatory treatment in business, political, and personal life climbed sharply. The proportion of women complaining of unequal employment opportunities jumped more than ten points from the '70s, and the number of women complaining of unequal barriers to job advancement climbed even higher. By the end of the decade, 80 percent to 95 percent of women said they suffered from job discrimination and unequal pay. Sex discrimination charges filed with the Equal Employment Opportunity Commission rose nearly 25 percent in the Reagan years, and charges of general harassment directed at working women climbed 208 percent. In the decade, complaints of sexual harassment jumped 70 percent. At home, a much increased proportion of women complained to pollsters of male mistreatment, unequal relationships, and male efforts to, in the words of the Virginia Slims poll, "keep women down." The share of women in the Roper surveys who agreed that men were "basically kind, gentle, and thoughtful" fell from almost 70 percent in 1970 to 50 percent by 1990. And outside their homes, women felt more threatened, too: in the 1990 Virginia Slims poll, 72 percent of women said they felt "more afraid and uneasy on the streets today" than they did a few years ago. Lest this be attributed only to a general rise in criminal activity, by contrast only 49 percent of men felt this way.

While the women's movement has certainly made women more cognizant of their own inequality, the rising chorus of female protest shouldn't be written off as feminist-induced "oversensitivity." The monitors that serve to track slippage in women's status have been working overtime since the early '80s. Government and private surveys are showing that women's already vast representation in the lowliest occupations is rising, their tiny presence in higher-paying trade and craft jobs stalled or backsliding, their minuscule representation in upper management posts stagnant or falling, and their pay dropping in the very occupations where they have made the most "progress." The status of women lowest on the income ladder has plunged most perilously; government budget cuts in the first four years of the Reagan administration alone pushed nearly 2 million female-headed families and nearly 5 million women below the poverty line. And the prime target of government rollbacks has been one sex only: one-third of the Reagan budget cuts, for example, came out of programs that predominantly serve women—even more extraordinary when one considers that all these programs combined represent only 10 percent of the federal budget.

The alarms aren't just going off in the work force. In national politics, the already small numbers of women in both elective posts and political appointments fell during the '80s. In private life, the average amount that a divorced man paid in child support fell by about 25 percent from the late '70s to the mid '80s (to a mere $140 a month). Domestic-violence shelters recorded a more than 100 percent increase in the numbers of women taking refuge in their quarters between 1983 and 1987. And government records chronicled a spectacular rise in sexual violence against women. Reported rapes more than doubled from the early '70s—at nearly twice the rate of all other violent crimes and four times the overall crime rate in the United States. While the homicide rate declined, sex-related murders rose 160 percent between 1976 and 1984. And these murders weren't simply the random, impersonal by-product of a violent society; at least one-third of the women were killed by their husbands or boyfriends, and the majority of that group were murdered just after declaring their independence in the most intimate manner—by filing for divorce and leaving home.

By the end of the decade, women were starting to tell pollsters that they feared their sex's social status was once again beginning to slip. They believed they were facing an "erosion of respect," as the 1990

Virginia Slims poll summed up the sentiment. After years in which an increasing percentage of women had said their status had improved from a decade earlier, the proportion suddenly shrunk by 5 percent in the last half of the '80s, the Roper Organization reported. And it fell most sharply among women in their thirties—the age group most targeted by the media and advertisers—dropping about ten percentage points between 1985 and 1990.

Some women began to piece the picture together. In the 1989 *New York Times* poll, more than half of black women and one-fourth of white women put it into words. They told pollsters they believed men were now trying to retract the gains women had made in the last twenty years. "I wanted more autonomy," was how one woman, a thirty-seven-year-old nurse, put it. And her estranged husband "wanted to take it away."

The truth is that the last decade has seen a powerful counter- 30 assault on women's rights, a backlash, an attempt to retract the handful of small and hard-won victories that the feminist movement did manage to win for women. This counterassault is largely insidious: in a kind of pop-culture version of the Big Lie, it stands the truth boldly on its head and proclaims that the very steps that have elevated women's position have actually led to their downfall.

The backlash is at once sophisticated and banal, deceptively "progressive" and proudly backward. It deploys both the "new" findings of "scientific research" and the dime-store moralism of yesteryear; it turns into media sound bites both the glib pronouncements of pop-psych trend-watchers and the frenzied rhetoric of New Right preachers. The backlash has succeeded in framing virtually the whole issue of women's rights in its own language. Just as Reaganism shifted political discourse far to the right and demonized liberalism, so the backlash convinced the public that women's "liberation" was the true contemporary American scourge—the source of an endless laundry list of personal, social, and economic problems.

But what has made women unhappy in the last decade is not their "equality"—which they don't yet have—but the rising pressure to halt, and even reverse, women's quest for that equality. The "man shortage" and the "infertility epidemic" are not the price of liberation; in fact, they do not even exist. But these chimeras are the chisels of a society-wide backlash. They are part of a relentless whittling-down process—much of it amounting to outright propaganda—that has served to stir women's private anxieties and break their political wills. Identifying feminism as women's enemy only furthers the ends of a backlash against women's equality, simultaneously deflecting attention from the backlash's central role and recruiting women to attack their own cause.

Some social observers may well ask whether the current pressures on women actually constitute a backlash—or just a continuation of

American society's long-standing resistance to women's rights. Certainly hostility to female independence has always been with us. But if fear and loathing of feminism is a sort of perpetual viral condition in our culture, it is not always in an acute stage; its symptoms subside and resurface periodically. And it is these episodes of resurgence, such as the one we face now, that can accurately be termed "backlashes" to women's advancement. If we trace these occurrences in American history . . . , we find such flare-ups are hardly random; they have always been triggered by the perception—accurate or not—that women are making great strides. These outbreaks are backlashes because they have always arisen in reaction to women's "progress," caused not simply by a bedrock of misogyny but by the specific efforts of contemporary women to improve their status, efforts that have been interpreted time and again by men—especially men grappling with real threats to their economic and social well-being on other fronts—as spelling their own masculine doom.

The most recent round of backlash first surfaced in the late '70s on the fringes, among the evangelical right. By the early '80s, the fundamentalist ideology had shouldered its way into the White House. By the mid '80s, as resistance to women's rights acquired political and social acceptability, it passed into the popular culture. And in every case, the timing coincided with signs that women were believed to be on the verge of breakthrough.

Just when women's quest for equal rights seemed closest to achieving its objectives, the backlash struck it down. Just when a "gender gap" at the voting booth surfaced in 1980, and women in politics began to talk of capitalizing on it, the Republican party elevated Ronald Reagan and both political parties began to shunt women's rights off their platforms. Just when support for feminism and the Equal Rights Amendment reached a record high in 1981, the amendment was defeated the following year. Just when women were starting to mobilize against battering and sexual assaults, the federal government stalled funding for battered-women's programs, defeated bills to fund shelters, and shut down its Office of Domestic Violence—only two years after opening it in 1979. Just when record numbers of younger women were supporting feminist goals in the mid '80s (more of them, in fact, than older women) and a majority of all women were calling themselves feminists, the media declared the advent of a younger "postfeminist generation" that supposedly reviled the women's movement. Just when women racked up their largest percentage ever supporting the right to abortion, the U.S. Supreme Court moved toward reconsidering it.

In other words, the antifeminist backlash has been set off not by women's achievement of full equality but by the increased possibility that they might win it. It is a preemptive strike that stops women long before they reach the finish line. "A backlash may be an indication that women really have had an effect," feminist psychiatrist Dr. Jean Baker Miller has written, "but backlashes occur when advances have been small, before changes are sufficient to help many people. . . . It is almost as if the leaders of backlashes use the fear of change as a threat before major change has occurred." In the last decade, some women did make substantial advances before the backlash hit, but millions of others were left behind, stranded. Some women now enjoy the right to legal abortion—but not the 44 million women, from the indigent to the military work force, who depend on the federal government for their medical care. Some women can now walk into high-paying professional careers—but not the more than 19 million still in the typing pools or behind the department store sales counters. (Contrary to popular myth about the "have-it-all" baby-boom women, the largest percentage of women in this generation remain typists and clerks.)

As the backlash has gathered force, it has cut off the few from the many—and the few women who have advanced seek to prove, as a social survival tactic, that they aren't so interested in advancement after all. Some of them parade their defection from the women's movement, while their working-class peers founder and cling to the splintered remains of the feminist cause. While a very few affluent and celebrity women who are showcased in news articles boast about having "found my niche as Mrs. Andy Mill" and going home to "bake bread," the many working-class women appeal for their economic rights— flocking to unions in record numbers, striking on their own for pay equity and establishing their own fledgling groups for working women's rights. In 1986, while 41 percent of upper-income women were claiming in the Gallup poll that they were not feminists, only 26 percent of low-income women were making the same claim.

Women's advances and retreats are generally described in military terms; battles won, battles lost, points and territory gained and surrendered. The metaphor of combat is not without its merits in this context and, clearly, the same sort of martial accounting and vocabulary is already surfacing here. But by imagining the conflict as two battalions neatly arrayed on either side of the line, we miss the entangled nature, the locked embrace, of a "war" between women and the male culture they inhabit. We miss the reactive nature of a backlash, which, by definition, can exist only in response to another force.

In times when feminism is at a low ebb, women assume the reactive role—privately and most often covertly struggling to assert themselves against the dominant cultural tide. But when feminism itself becomes the tide, the opposition doesn't simply go along with the reversal: it digs in its heels, brandishes its fists, builds walls and dams. And its resistance creates countercurrents and treacherous undertows.

The force and furor of the backlash churn beneath the surface, 40 largely invisible to the public eye. On occasion in the last decade, they have burst into view. We have seen New Right politicians condemn women's independence, antiabortion protesters fire-bomb women's clinics, fundamentalist preachers damn feminists as "whores" and "witches." Other signs of the backlash's wrath, by their sheer brutality, can push their way into public consciousness for a time—the sharp increase in rape, for example, or the rise in pornography that depicts extreme violence against women.

More subtle indicators in popular culture may receive momentary, and often bemused, media notice, then quickly slip from social awareness: A report, for instance, that the image of women on prime-time TV shows has suddenly degenerated. A survey of mystery fiction finding the numbers of female characters tortured and mutilated mysteriously multiplying. The puzzling news that, as one commentator put it, "So many hit songs have the B-word [bitch] to refer to women that some rap music seems to be veering toward rape music." The ascendancy of virulently misogynist comics like Andrew Dice Clay—who called women "pigs" and "sluts" and strutted in films in which women were beaten, tortured, and blown up—or radio hosts like Rush Limbaugh, whose broadsides against "femi-Nazi" feminists made his syndicated program the most popular radio talk show in the nation. Or word that in 1987, the American Women in Radio & Television couldn't award its annual prize for ads that feature women positively: it could find no ad that qualified.

These phenomena are all related, but that doesn't mean they are somehow coordinated. The backlash is not a conspiracy, with a council dispatching agents from some central control room, nor are the people who serve its ends often aware of their role: some even consider themselves feminists. For the most part, its workings are encoded and internalized, diffuse and chameleonic. Not all of the manifestations of the backlash are of equal weight or significance either; some are mere ephemera, generated by a culture machine that is always scrounging for a "fresh" angle. Taken as a whole, however, these codes and cajolings, these whispers and threats and myths, move overwhelmingly in one direction: they try to push women back into their "acceptable" roles—whether as Daddy's girl or fluttery romantic, active nester or passive love object.

Although the backlash is not an organized movement, that doesn't make it any less destructive. In fact, the lack of orchestration, the absence of a single string-puller, only makes it harder to see—and perhaps more effective. A backlash against women's rights succeeds to the degree that it appears *not* to be political, that it appears not to be a struggle at all. It is most powerful when it goes private, when it lodges inside a woman's mind and turns her vision inward, until she images the pressure is all in her head, until she begins to enforce the backlash, too—on herself.

In the last decade, the backlash has moved through the culture's secret chambers, traveling through passageways of flattery and fear. Along the way, it has adopted disguises: a mask of mild derision or the painted face of deep "concern." Its lips profess pity for any woman who won't fit the mold, while it tries to clamp the mold around her ears. It pursues a divide-and-conquer strategy: single versus married women, working women versus homemakers, middle- versus working-class. It manipulates a system of rewards and punishments, elevating women who follow its rules, isolating those who don't. The backlash remarkets old myths about women as new facts and ignores all appeals to reason. Cornered, it denies its own existence, points an accusatory finger at feminism, and burrows deeper underground.

Backlash happens to be the title of a 1947 Hollywood movie in which a man frames his wife for a murder he's committed. The backlash against women's rights works in much the same way: its rhetoric charges feminists with all the crimes it perpetrates. The backlash line blames the women's movement for the "feminization of poverty"— while the backlash's own instigators in Washington pushed through the budget cuts that helped impoverish millions of women, fought pay equity proposals, and undermined equal opportunity laws. The backlash line claims the women's movement cares nothing for children's rights—while its own representatives in the capital and state legislatures have blocked one bill after another to improve child care, slashed billions of dollars in federal aid for children, and relaxed state licensing standards for day care centers. The backlash line accuses the women's movement of creating a generation of unhappy single and childless women—but its purveyors in the media are the ones guilty of making single and childless women feel like circus freaks.

To blame feminism for women's "lesser life" is to miss entirely the point of feminism, which is to win women a wider range of experience. Feminism remains a pretty simple concept, despite repeated— and enormously effective—efforts to dress it up in greasepaint and turn its proponents into gargoyles. As Rebecca West wrote sardonically in 1913, "I myself have never been able to find out precisely what feminism is: I only know that people call me a feminist whenever I express sentiments that differentiate me from a doormat."

The meaning of the word "feminist" has not really changed since it first appeared in a book review in the *Athenaeum* of April 27, 1895, describing a woman who "has in her the capacity of fighting her way back to independence." It is the basic proposition that, as Nora put it in Ibsen's *A Doll's House* a century ago, "Before everything else I'm a human being." It is the simply worded sign hoisted by a little girl in the 1970 Women's Strike for Equality: I AM NOT A BARBIE DOLL. Feminism asks the world to recognize at long last that women aren't decorative ornaments, worthy vessels, members of a "special-interest group." They are half (in fact, now more than half) of the national population, and just as deserving of rights and opportunities, just as capable of participating in the world's events, as the other half. Feminism's agenda is basic: It asks that women not be forced to "choose" between public justice and private happiness. It asks that women be free to define themselves—instead of having their identity defined for them, time and again, by their culture and their men.

The fact that these are still such incendiary notions should tell us that American women have a way to go before they enter the promised land of equality.

For Journals

How do you define the term *feminism?*

For Discussion

1. According to Faludi, what is the real reason for women's unhappiness in contemporary American society? What role do men play in this reason?

2. Reread the first two paragraphs of the selection. In what ways does the introduction set the approach, direction, and tone for the rest of the argument?

3. Faludi's basic assertion is that there has been a backlash, or resistance, against gains in women's rights. Examine her key points and supporting evidence. Are you persuaded by her assertions and her supporting evidence that there is, indeed, a backlash? Explain the reasons for your answer.

4. What are the implications for the American family of what Faludi is discussing? For example, she cites recent reports in the popular press about a "man shortage," an "infertility epidemic," and "hysterical" unwed women (paragraph 4). To what degree are concerns about the future and stability of families feeding the backlash? Do you think those fears are unfounded or appropriate?

5. Faludi cites a range of sources, first to summarize the backlash argument that it is "all that equality that's causing all the pain" (paragraph 6) and then to question what "equality" is under discussion. Analyze Faludi's use of statistics and sources, in both her representation of the opposing view and in support of her own assertions.

6. Faludi cites Mona Charen, writing in the conservative *National Review*, who says that feminism has effectively "robbed us of one thing upon which the happiness of most women rests—men" (paragraph 7).

Do you think a male writer would be likely to make such an assertion about feminism?

For Writing

1.   Write a dialogue between Faludi and either the originator of *Keep within Compass* or Charles Atlas, asserting arguments consistent with each person's position and refuting the opposing view in the way you think each one might. Considering the various viewpoints represented in the chapter, to what degree have the arguments over women's and men's roles changed over the years?

2.   The author cites Rebecca West, who wrote in 1913 that "people call me a feminist whenever I express sentiments that differentiate me from a doormat" (paragraph 46). Drawing from your journal writings, this article, other readings you have done, or conversations and experiences you have had, define what you mean by "feminist" and argue that feminism is, or is not, ultimately beneficial to women, men, and families.

∞ A Family Legacy (1992)

MARIAN WRIGHT EDELMAN

Marian Wright Edelman (1939–), attorney and founding president of the Children's Defense Fund, is one of five children of a Baptist minister. She graduated from Spelman College, a historically black institution, and Yale Law School; she was the first woman to pass the state bar exam in Mississippi. Edelman has spent her professional life as an activist for disadvantaged Americans, especially children. She has received many honors and awards, and her writings include Children out of School in America *(1974),* Black and White Children in America *(1980), and* Families in Peril: An Agenda for Social Change *(1987). The essay that follows is the first chapter of her book* The Measure of Our Success: A Letter to My Children and Yours.

South Carolina is my home state and I am the aunt, granddaughter, daughter, and sister of Baptist ministers. Service was as essential a part of my upbringing as eating and sleeping and going to school. The church was a hub of Black children's social existence, and caring Black adults were buffers against the segregated and hostile outside world that told us we weren't important. But our parents said it wasn't so, our teachers said it wasn't so, and our preachers said it wasn't so. The message of my racially segregated childhood was clear: let no man or woman look down on you, and look down on no man or woman.

We couldn't play in public playgrounds or sit at drugstore lunch counters and order a Coke, so Daddy built a playground and canteen behind the church. In fact, whenever he saw a need, he tried to respond. There were no Black homes for the aged in Bennettsville, so he began one across the street for which he and Mama and we children cooked and served and cleaned. And we children learned that it was our responsibility to take care of elderly family members and neighbors, and that everyone was our neighbor. My mother carried on the home after Daddy died, and my brother Julian has carried it on to this day behind our church since our mother's death in 1984.

Finding another child in my room or a pair of my shoes gone was far from unusual, and twelve foster children followed my sister and me and three brothers as we left home.

Child-rearing and parental work were inseparable. I went everywhere with my parents and was under the watchful eye of members of the congregation and community who were my extended parents. They kept me when my parents went out of town, they reported on and chided me when I strayed from the straight and narrow of community expectations, and they basked in and supported my achievements when I did well. Doing well, they made clear, meant high academic achievement, playing piano in Sunday school or singing or participating in other church activities, being helpful to somebody, displaying good manners (which is nothing more than consideration toward others), and reading. My sister Olive reminded me recently that the only time our father would not give us a chore ("Can't you find something constructive to do?" was his most common refrain) was when we were reading. So we all read a lot! We learned early what our parents and extended community "parents" valued. Children were taught—not by sermonizing, but by personal example—that nothing was too lowly to do. I remember a debate my parents had when I was eight or nine as to whether I was too young to go with my older brother, Harry, to help clean the bed and bedsores of a very sick, poor woman. I went and learned just how much the smallest helping hands and kindness can mean to a person in need.

The ugly external voices of my small-town, segregated childhood 5 (as a very young child I remember standing and hearing former South Carolina Senator James Byrnes railing on the local courthouse lawn about how Black children would never go to school with whites) were tempered by the internal voices of parental and community expectation and pride. My father and I waited anxiously for the *Brown* v. *Board of Education* decision in 1954. We talked about it and what it would mean for my future and for the future of millions of other Black children. He died the week before *Brown* was decided. But I and other children lucky enough to have caring and courageous parents and other adult role models were able, in later years, to walk through the new and heavy doors that *Brown* slowly and painfully opened—doors that some are trying to close again today.

The adults in our churches and community made children feel valued and important. They took time and paid attention to us. They struggled to find ways to keep us busy. And while life was often hard and resources scarce, we always knew who we were and that the measure of our worth was inside our heads and hearts and not outside in our possessions or on our backs. We were told that the world had a lot of problems; that Black people had an extra lot of problems, but that we were able and obligated to struggle and change them; that being poor was no excuse for not achieving; and that extra intellectual and material gifts brought with them the privilege and responsibility of sharing with others less fortunate. In sum, we learned that service is the rent we pay for living. It is the very purpose of life and not something you do in your spare time.

When my mother died, an old white man in my hometown of Bennettsville asked me what I do. In a flash I realized that in my work at the Children's Defense Fund I do exactly what my parents did—just on a different scale. My brother preached a wonderful sermon at Mama's funeral, but the best tribute was the presence in the back pew of the town drunk, whom an observer said he could not remember coming to church in many years.

The legacies that parents and church and teachers left to my generation of Black children were priceless but not material: a living faith reflected in daily service, the discipline of hard work and stick-to-itness, and a capacity to struggle in the face of adversity. Giving up and "burnout" were not part of the language of my elders—you got up every morning and you did what you had to do and you got up every time you fell down and tried as many times as you had to get it done right. They had grit. They valued family life, family rituals, and tried to be and to expose us to good role models. Role models were of two kinds: those who achieved in the outside world (like Marian Anderson, my namesake) and those who didn't have a whole lot of education or fancy clothes but who taught us by the special grace of their lives the message of Christ and Tolstoy and Gandhi and Heschel and Dorothy Day and Romero and King that the Kingdom of God was within—in what you are, not what you have. I still hope I can be half as good as Black church and community elders like Miz Lucy McQueen, Miz Tee Kelly, and Miz Kate Winston, extraordinary women who were kind and patient and loving with children and others and who, when I went to Spelman College, sent me shoeboxes with chicken and biscuits and greasy dollar bills.

It never occurred to any Wright child that we were not going to college or were not expected to share what we learned and earned with the less fortunate. I was forty years old before I figured out, thanks to my brother Harry's superior insight, that my Daddy often responded to our requests for money by saying he didn't have any change because he *really* didn't have any rather than because he had nothing smaller than a twenty dollar bill.

I was fourteen years old the night my Daddy died. He had holes in his shoes but two children out of college, one in college, another in divinity school, and a vision he was able to convey to me as he lay dying in an ambulance that I, a young Black girl, could be and do anything; that race and gender are shadows; and that character, self-discipline, determination, attitude, and service are the substance of life.

I have always believed that I could help change the world because I have been lucky to have adults around me who did—in small and large ways. Most were people of simple grace who understood what Walker Percy wrote: You can get all As and still flunk life.

Life was not easy back in the 1940s and 1950s in rural South Carolina for many parents and grandparents. We buried children who died from poverty (and I can't stand it that we still do). Little Johnny Harrington, three houses down from my church parsonage, stepped on and died from a nail because his grandmother had no doctor to advise her, nor the money to pay for health care. (Half of all low-income urban children under two are still not fully immunized against preventable childhood diseases like tetanus and polio and measles.) My classmate, Henry Munnerlyn, broke his neck when he jumped off the bridge into the town creek because only white children were allowed in the public swimming pool. I later heard that the creek where Blacks swam and fished was the hospital sewage outlet. (Today thousands of Black children in our cities and rural areas are losing their lives to cocaine and heroin and alcohol and gang violence because they don't have enough constructive outlets.) The migrant family who collided with a truck on the highway near my home and the ambulance driver who refused to take them to the hospital because they were Black still live in my mind every time I hear about babies who die or are handicapped from birth when they are turned away from hospitals in emergencies or their mothers are turned away in labor because they have no health insurance and cannot pay pre-admission deposits to enter a hospital. I and my brothers and sister might have lost hope—as so many young people today have lost hope—except for the stable, caring, attentive adults in our family, school, congregation, civic and political life who struggled with and for us against the obstacles we faced and provided us positive alternatives and the sense of possibility we needed.

At Spelman College in Atlanta, I found my Daddy and Mama's values about taking responsibility for your own learning and growth reinforced in the daily (except Saturday) chapel service. Daily chapel attendance was compulsory and enforced by the threat of points taken off one's earned grade average as a result of truancy. For all my rebellion then, I remember now far more from the chapel speakers who came to talk to us about life and the purpose of education than from any class. And during my tenure as chairwoman of Spelman's board, I advocated reinstitution of some compulsory assemblies (monthly, not daily!) so our young women would have to hear what we adults think is important.

Many of my mentors and role models, such as Dr. Benjamin Mays, then president of Morehouse College, Whitney Young, dean of the School of Social Work at Atlanta University and later National Urban League head, M. Carl Holman, a professor at Clark College, later head of the National Urban Coalition, Dr. Howard Thurman, dean of the Chapel at Boston University, and Dr. King, all conveyed the same message as they spoke in Sisters Chapel at Spelman: education is for improving the lives of others and for leaving your community and world better than you found it. Other important influences during my Spelman years—Ella Baker, Septima Clark, Howard Zinn, Charles E. Merrill, Jr., and Samuel Dubois Cook—stretched my vision of the future and of one person's ability to help shape it. I'm still trying to live up to their teachings and to the examples of the extraordinary ordinary people whom I had the privilege to serve and learn from after law school during my civil rights sojourn in Mississippi between 1963 and 1968.

Fannie Lou Hamer, Amzie Moore, Winson and Dovie Hudson, 15 Mae Bertha Carter, school desegregation and voting rights pioneers in Mississippi, and Unita Blackwell, who rose from sharecropper to mayor of rural Mayersville, Mississippi—and countless courageous men and women who gave their voices and homes and lives to get the right to vote and to secure for their children a better life than they had—guide and inspire me still. Those largely unknown and usually unlettered people of courage and commitment, along with my parents, remind me each day to keep trying and to let my little light shine, as Mrs. Hamer sang and did through her inspiring life. In a D.C. neighborhood church, I recently saw a banner that reminded me "there is not enough darkness in the world to snuff out the light of even one small candle."

I have always felt extraordinarily blessed to live in the times I have. As a child and as an adult—as a Black woman—I have had to struggle to understand the world around me. Most Americans remember Dr. King as a great leader. I do too. But I also remember him as someone able to admit how often he was afraid and unsure about his next step. But faith prevailed over fear and uncertainty and fatigue and depression. It was his human vulnerability and his ability to rise above it that I most remember. In this, he was not different from many Black adults whose credo has been to make "a way out of no way."

The Children's Defense Fund was conceived in the cauldron of Mississippi's summer project of 1964 and in the Head Start battles of

1965, where both the great need for and limits of local action were apparent. As a private civil rights lawyer, I learned that I could have only limited, albeit important, impact on meeting epidemic family and child needs in that poor state without coherent national policy and investment strategies to complement community empowerment strategies. I also learned that critical civil and political rights would not mean much to a hungry, homeless, illiterate child and family if they lacked the social and economic means to exercise them. And so children—my own and other people's—became the passion of my personal and professional life. For it is they who are God's presence, promise, and hope for humankind.

For Journals

How do you think American families measure their success? What kinds of achievements or possessions are often used to measure success?

For Discussion

1. The subtitle of Edelman's book, of which this selection is the first chapter, is "A Letter to My Children and Yours." Why do you believe Edelman is addressing her remarks to these audiences? How do the audiences shape her message?

2. Edelman and the children of her community grew up knowing that they were valued and important. How did the adults of the community transmit these beliefs? What were the adults' expectations of the children? What did the children assume about their role in the community?

3. Edelman writes of the legacies from her family and community—of service, of doing for others, of making the most of intellectual and material gifts. How have such legacies changed her life? How have they influenced her work?

4. Edelman concludes, "Service is the rent we pay for living" (paragraph 6). What are the assumptions on which she bases this statement?

5. Edelman's community served as an extended family in supporting her and other children. In what ways was her upbringing like, and unlike, that of children growing up in the 1980s and 1990s? What has changed for the better? For the worse? What has not changed?

6. Edelman writes that her father died with "holes in his shoes but two children out of college, one in college, another in divinity school, and a vision" (paragraph 10). How does Edelman's measure of her father's success compare to, and contrast with, statements of family values and beliefs evident in other readings in this book? (Look, for example, at Martin Luther King Jr.'s "I Have a Dream," in Chapter 6, and at "Bricklayer's Boy," in Chapter 8 and "Making and Unmaking the 'Model Minority,'" in Chapter 7.)

For Writing

1. Write an essay examining, and explaining, the values and beliefs with which you were raised. What did you learn about your role in the family? In the community? What were the expectations of your parents and any extended family you have? You could focus on education, community involvement, music, or some other aspect of your youth.

2. Research a current issue in children's rights—for example, health care, legal protection, or issues of abuse. In addition to drawing on books, periodicals, and government documents, try to interview people in your community who work on behalf of children in the area you are researching. What are the controversies? Write up your research in a documented essay.

3. Write a letter to the children you have or expect to have, or to nieces or nephews or other relatives. Explain to them the legacies that you grew up with and that you hope you will pass on to them.

∞ *Saplings in the Storm* (1994)

MARY PIPHER

Mary Pipher, Ph.D., is a clinical psychologist in private practice in Lincoln, Nebraska. She teaches part-time at the University of Nebraska Wesleyan University. Dr. Pipher is also a commentator for Nebraska Public Radio. This selection is from her book Reviving Ophelia: Saving the Selves of Adolescent Girls.

When my cousin Polly was a girl, she was energy in motion. She danced, did cartwheels and splits, played football, basketball and baseball with the neighborhood boys, wrestled with my brothers, biked, climbed trees and rode horses. She was as lithe and as resilient as a willow branch and as unrestrained as a lion cub. Polly talked as much as she moved. She yelled out orders and advice, shrieked for joy when she won a bet or heard a good joke, laughed with her mouth wide open, argued with kids and grown-ups and insulted her foes in the language of a construction worker.

We formed the Marauders, a secret club that met over her garage. Polly was the Tom Sawyer of the club. She planned the initiations, led the spying expeditions and hikes to haunted houses. She showed us the rituals to become blood "brothers" and taught us card tricks and how to smoke.

Then Polly had her first period and started junior high. She tried to keep up her old ways, but she was called a tomboy and chided for not acting more ladylike. She was excluded by her boy pals and by the girls, who were moving into makeup and romances.

This left Polly confused and shaky. She had temper tantrums and withdrew from both the boys' and girls' groups. Later she quieted down and reentered as Becky Thatcher. She wore stylish clothes and watched from the sidelines as the boys acted and spoke. Once again she was accepted and popular. She glided smoothly through our small society. No one spoke of the changes or mourned the loss of our town's most dynamic citizen. I was the only one who felt that a tragedy had transpired.

Girls in what Freud called the latency period, roughly age six or 5 seven through puberty, are anything but latent. I think of my daughter Sara during those years—performing chemistry experiments and magic tricks, playing her violin, starring in her own plays, rescuing wild animals and biking all over town. I think of her friend Tamara, who wrote a 300-page novel the summer of her sixth-grade year. I remember myself, reading every children's book in the library of my town. One week I planned to be a great doctor like Albert Schweitzer. The next week I wanted to write like Louisa May Alcott or dance in Paris like Isadora Duncan. I have never since had as much confidence or ambition.

Most preadolescent girls are marvelous company because they are interested in everything—sports, nature, people, music and books. Almost all the heroines of girls' literature come from this age group—Anne of Green Gables, Heidi, Pippi Longstocking and Caddie Woodlawn. Girls this age bake pies, solve mysteries and go on quests. They can take care of themselves and are not yet burdened with caring for others. They have a brief respite from the female role and can be tomboys, a word that conveys courage, competency and irreverence.

They can be androgynous, having the ability to act adaptively in any situation regardless of gender role constraints. An androgynous person can comfort a baby or change a tire, cook a meal or chair a meeting. Research has shown that, since they are free to act without worrying if their behavior is feminine or masculine, androgynous adults are the most well adjusted.

Girls between seven and eleven rarely come to therapy. They don't need it. I can count on my fingers the girls this age whom I have seen: Coreen, who was physically abused; Anna, whose parents were divorcing; and Brenda, whose father killed himself. These girls were courageous and resilient. Brenda said, "If my father didn't want to stick around, that's his loss." Coreen and Anna were angry, not at themselves, but rather at the grown-ups, who they felt were making mistakes. It's amazing how little help these girls needed from me to heal and move on.

A horticulturist told me a revealing story. She led a tour of junior-high girls who were attending a math and science fair on her campus. She showed them side oats grama, bluestem, Indian grass and trees— redbud, maple, walnut and willow. The younger girls interrupted each other with their questions and tumbled forward to see, touch and smell everything. The older girls, the ninth-graders, were different. They hung back. They didn't touch plants or shout out questions. They stood primly to the side, looking bored and even a little disgusted by the enthusiasm of their younger classmates. My friend asked herself, What's happened to these girls? What's gone wrong? She told me, "I wanted to shake them, to say, 'Wake up, come back. Is anybody home at your house?'"

Recently I sat sunning on a bench outside my favorite ice-cream 10 store. A mother and her teenage daughter stopped in front of me and waited for the light to change. I heard the mother say, "You have got to stop blackmailing your father and me. Every time you don't get what you want, you tell us that you want to run away from home or kill yourself. What's happened to you? You used to be able to handle not getting your way."

The daughter stared straight ahead, barely acknowledging her mother's words. The light changed. I licked my ice-cream cone. Another mother approached the same light with her preadolescent daughter in tow. They were holding hands. The daughter said to her mother, "This is fun. Let's do this all afternoon."

Something dramatic happens to girls in early adolescence. Just as planes and ships disappear mysteriously into the Bermuda Triangle, so do the selves of girls go down in drives. They crash and burn in a social and developmental Bermuda Triangle. In early adolescence, studies show that girls' IQ scores drop and their math and science scores plummet. They lose their resiliency and optimism and become less curious and inclined to take risks. They lose their assertive, energetic and "tomboyish" personalities and become more deferential, self-critical and depressed. They report great unhappiness with their own bodies.

Psychology documents but does not explain the crashes. Girls who rushed to drink in experiences in enormous gulps sit quietly in the corner. Writers such as Sylvia Plath, Margaret Atwood and Olive Schreiner have described the wreckage. Diderot, in writing to his young friend Sophie Volland, described his observations harshly: "You all die at 15."

Fairy tales capture the essence of this phenomenon. Young women eat poisoned apples or prick their fingers with poisoned needles and fall asleep for a hundred years. They wander away from home, encounter great dangers, are rescued by princes and are transformed into passive and docile creatures.

The story of Ophelia, from Shakespeare's *Hamlet*, shows the de- 15 structive forces that affect young women. As a girl, Ophelia is happy and free, but with adolescence she loses herself. When she falls in love with Hamlet, she lives only for his approval. She has no inner direction; rather she struggles to meet the demands of Hamlet and her father. Her value is determined utterly by their approval. Ophelia is torn apart by her efforts to please. When Hamlet spurns her because she is an obedient daughter, she goes mad with grief. Dressed in elegant clothes that weigh her down, she drowns in a stream filled with flowers.

Girls know they are losing themselves. One girl said, "Everything good in me died in junior high." Wholeness is shattered by the chaos of adolescence. Girls become fragmented, their selves split into mysterious contradictions. They are sensitive and tenderhearted, mean and competitive, superficial and idealistic. They are confident in the morning and overwhelmed with anxiety by nightfall. They rush through their days with wild energy and then collapse into lethargy. They try on new roles every week—this week the good student, next week the delinquent and the next, the artist. And they expect their families to keep up with these changes.

My clients in early adolescence are elusive and slow to trust adults. They are easily offended by a glance, a clearing of the throat, a silence, a lack of sufficient enthusiasm or a sentence that doesn't meet their immediate needs. Their voices have gone underground—their speech is more tentative and less articulate. Their moods swing widely. One week they love their world and their families, the next they are critical of everyone. Much of their behavior is unreadable. Their problems are complicated and metaphorical—eating disorders, school phobias and self-inflicted injuries. I need to ask again and again in a dozen different ways, "What are you trying to tell me?"

Michelle, for example, was a beautiful, intelligent seventeen-year-old. Her mother brought her in after she became pregnant for the third time in three years. I tried to talk about why this was happening. She smiled a Mona Lisa smile to all my questions. "No, I don't care all that much for sex." "No, I didn't plan this. It just happened." When Michelle left a session, I felt like I'd been talking in the wrong language to someone far away.

Holly was another mystery. She was shy, soft-spoken and slow-moving, pretty under all her makeup and teased red hair. She was a Prince fan and wore only purple. Her father brought her in after a suicide attempt. She wouldn't study, do chores, join any school activities or find a job. Holly answered questions in patient, polite monosyllables. She really talked only when the topic was Prince. For several weeks we talked about him. She played me his tapes. Prince somehow spoke for her and to her.

Gail burned and cut herself when she was unhappy. Dressed in 20 black, thin as a straw, she sat silently before me, her hair a mess, her ears, lips and nose all pierced with rings. She spoke about Bosnia and the hole in the ozone layer and asked me if I liked rave music. When I asked about her life, she fingered her earrings and sat silently.

My clients are not different from girls who are not seen in therapy. I teach at a small liberal arts college and the young women in my classes have essentially the same experiences as my therapy clients. One student worried about her best friend who'd been sexually assaulted. Another student missed class after being beaten by her boyfriend. Another asked what she should do about crank calls from a man threatening to rape her. When stressed, another student stabbed her hand with paper clips until she drew blood. Many students have wanted advice on eating disorders.

After I speak at high schools, girls approach me to say that they have been raped, or they want to run away from home, or that they have a friend who is anorexic or alcoholic. At first all this trauma surprised me. Now I expect it.

Psychology has a long history of ignoring girls this age. Until recently adolescent girls haven't been studied by academics, and they have long baffled therapists. Because they are secretive with adults and full of contradictions, they are difficult to study. So much is happening internally that's not communicated on the surface.

Simone de Beauvoir believed adolescence is when girls realize that men have the power and that their only power comes from consenting to become submissive adored objects. They do not suffer from the penis envy Freud postulated, but from power envy.

She described the Bermuda Triangle this way: Girls who were the 25 subjects of their own lives became the objects of others' lives. "Young girls slowly bury their childhood, put away their independent and imperious selves and submissively enter adult existence." Adolescent girls experience a conflict between their autonomous selves and their need to be feminine, between their status as human beings and their vocation as females. De Beauvoir says, "Girls stop being and start seeming."

Girls become "female impersonators" who fit their whole selves into small, crowded spaces. Vibrant, confident girls become shy, doubting young women. Girls stop thinking, "Who am I? What do I want?" and start thinking, "What must I do to please others?"

This gap between girls' true selves and cultural prescriptions for what is properly female creates enormous problems. To paraphrase a

Stevie Smith poem about swimming in the sea, "they are not waving, they are drowning." And just when they most need help, they are unable to take their parents' hands.

Olive Schreiner wrote of her experiences as a young girl in *The Story of an African Farm*. "The world tells us what we are to be and shapes us by the ends it sets before us. To men it says, work. To us, it says, seem. The less a woman has in her head the lighter she is for carrying." She described the finishing school that she attended in this way: "It was a machine for condensing the soul into the smallest possible area. I have seen some souls so compressed that they would have filled a small thimble."

Margaret Mead believed that the ideal culture is one in which there is a place for every human gift. By her standards, our Western culture is far from ideal for women. So many gifts are unused and unappreciated. So many voices are stilled. Stendhal wrote: "All geniuses born women are lost to the public good."

Alice Miller wrote of the pressures on some young children to 30 deny their true selves and assume false selves to please their parents. *Reviving Ophelia* suggests that adolescent girls experience a similar pressure to split into true and false selves, but this time the pressure comes not from parents but from the culture. Adolescence is when girls experience social pressure to put aside their authentic selves and to display only a small portion of their gifts.

This pressure disorients and depresses most girls. They sense the pressure to be someone they are not. They fight back, but they are fighting a "problem with no name." One girl put it this way: "I'm a perfectly good carrot that everyone is trying to turn into a rose. As a carrot, I have good color and a nice leafy top. When I'm carved into a rose, I turn brown and wither."

Adolescent girls are saplings in a hurricane. They are young and vulnerable trees that the winds blow with gale strength. Three factors make young women vulnerable to the hurricane. One is their development level. Everything is changing—body shape, hormones, skin and hair. Calmness is replaced by anxiety. Their way of thinking is changing. Far below the surface they are struggling with the most basic of human questions: What is my place in the universe, what is my meaning?

Second, American culture has always smacked girls on the head in early adolescence. This is when they move into a broader culture that is rife with girl-hurting "isms," such as sexism, capitalism and lookism, which is the evaluation of a person solely on the basis of appearance.

Third, American girls are expected to distance from parents just at the time when they most need their support. As they struggle with countless new pressures, they must relinquish the protection and closeness they've felt with their families in childhood. They turn to their none-too-constant peers for support.

Parents know only too well that something is happening to their 35 daughters. Calm, considerate daughters grow moody, demanding and distant. Girls who loved to talk are sullen and secretive. Girls who liked to hug now bristle when touched. Mothers complain that they can do nothing right in the eyes of their daughters. Involved fathers bemoan their sudden banishment from their daughters' lives. But few parents realize how universal their experiences are. Their daughters are entering a new land, a dangerous place that parents can scarcely comprehend. Just when they most need a home base, they cut themselves loose without radio communications.

Most parents of adolescent girls have the goal of keeping their daughters safe while they grow up and explore the world. The parents' job is to protect. The daughters' job is to explore. Always these different tasks have created tension in parent-daughter relationships, but now it's even harder. Generally parents are more protective of their daughters than is corporate America. Parents aren't trying to make money off their daughters by selling them designer jeans or cigarettes, they just want them to be well adjusted. They don't see their daughters as sex objects or consumers but as real people with talents and interests. But daughters turn away from their parents as they enter the new land. They befriend their peers, who are their fellow inhabitants of the strange country and who share a common language and set of customs. They often embrace the junk values of mass culture.

This turning away from parents is partly for developmental reasons. Early adolescence is a time of physical and psychological change, self-absorption, preoccupation with peer approval and identity formation. It's a time when girls focus inward on their own fascinating changes.

It's partly for cultural reasons. In America we define adulthood as a moving away from families into broader culture. Adolescence is the time for cutting bonds and breaking free. Adolescents may claim great independence from parents, but they are aware and ashamed of their parents' smallest deviation from the norm. They don't like to be seen with them and find their imperfections upsetting. A mother's haircut or a father's joke can ruin their day. Teenagers are furious at parents who say the wrong things or do not respond with perfect answers. Adolescents claim not to hear their parents, but with their friends they discuss endlessly all parental attitudes. With amazing acuity, they sense nuances, doubt, shades of ambiguity, discrepancy and hypocrisy.

Adolescents still have some of the magical thinking of childhood and believe that parents have the power to keep them safe and happy.

They blame their parents for their misery, yet they make a point of not telling their parents how they think and feel; they have secrets, so things can get crazy. For example, girls who are raped may not tell their parents. Instead, they become hostile and rebellious. Parents bring girls in because of their anger and out-of-control behavior. When I hear about this unexplainable anger, I ask about rape. Ironically, their parents should have known about the danger and been more protective; afterward, they should have sensed the pain and helped.

Most parents feel like failures during this time. They feel shut out, 40 impotent and misunderstood. They often attribute the difficulties of this time to their daughters and their own failings. They don't understand that these problems go with the developmental stage, the culture and the times.

Parents experience an enormous sense of loss when their girls enter this new land. They miss the daughters who sang in the kitchen, who read them school papers, who accompanied them on fishing trips and to ball games. They miss the daughters who liked to bake cookies, play Pictionary and be kissed goodnight. In place of their lively, affectionate daughters they have changelings—new girls who are sadder, angrier and more complicated. Everyone is grieving.

Fortunately adolescence is time-limited. By late high school most girls are stronger and the winds are dying down. Some of the worst problems—cliques, a total focus on looks and struggles with parents—are on the wane. But the way girls handle the problems of adolescence can have implications for their adult lives. Without some help, the loss of wholeness, self-confidence and self-direction can last well into adulthood. Many adult clients struggle with the same issues that overwhelmed them as adolescent girls. Thirty-year-old accountants and realtors, forty-year-old homemakers and doctors, and thirty-five-year-old nurses and schoolteachers ask the same questions and struggle with the same problems as their teenage daughters.

Even sadder are the women who are not struggling, who have forgotten that they have selves worth defending. They have repressed the pain of their adolescence, the betrayals of self in order to be pleasing. These women come to therapy with the goal of becoming even more pleasing to others. They come to lose weight, to save their marriages or to rescue their children. When I ask them about their own needs, they are confused by the question.

Most women struggled alone with the trauma of adolescence and have led decades of adult life with their adolescent experiences unexamined. The lessons learned in adolescence are forgotten and their memories of pain are minimized. They come into therapy because their marriage is in trouble, or they hate their job, or their own daughter is giving them fits. Maybe their daughter's pain awakens their own pain. Some are depressed or chemically addicted or have stress-related illnesses—ulcers, colitis, migraines or psoriasis. Many have tried to be perfect women and failed. Even though they followed the rules and did as they were told, the world has not rewarded them. They feel angry and betrayed. They feel miserable and taken for granted, used rather than loved.

Women often know how everyone in their family thinks and feels except themselves. They are great at balancing the needs of their coworkers, husbands, children and friends, but they forget to put themselves into the equation. They struggle with adolescent questions still unresolved: How important are looks and popularity? How do I care for myself and not be selfish? How can I be honest and still be loved? How can I achieve and not threaten others? How can I be sexual and not a sex object? How can I be responsive but not responsible for everyone?

As we talk, the years fall away. We are back in junior high with the cliques, the shame, the embarrassment about bodies, the desire to be accepted and the doubts about ability. So many adult women think they are stupid and ugly. Many feel guilty if they take time for themselves. They do not express anger or ask for help.

We talk about childhood—what the woman was like at ten and at fifteen. We piece together a picture of childhood lost. We review her own particular story, her own time in the hurricane. Memories flood in. Often there are tears, angry outbursts, sadness for what has been lost. So much time has been wasted pretending to be who others wanted. But also, there's a new energy that comes from making connections, from choosing awareness over denial and from the telling of secrets.

We work now, twenty years behind schedule. We reestablish each woman as the subject of her life, not as the object of others' lives. We answer Freud's patronizing question "What do women want?" Each woman wants something different and particular and yet each woman wants the same thing—to be who she truly is, to become who she can become.

Many women regain their preadolescent authenticity with menopause. Because they are no longer beautiful objects occupied primarily with caring for others, they are free once again to become the subjects of their own lives. They become more confident, self-directed and energetic. Margaret Mead noticed this phenomenon in cultures all over the world and called it "pmz," postmenopausal zest. She noted that some cultures revere these older women. Others burn them at the stake.

Before I studied psychology, I studied cultural anthropology. I have always been interested in that place where culture and individual psychology intersect, in why cultures create certain personalities and not others, in how they pull for certain strengths in their members, in how certain talents are utilized while others atrophy from lack of attention. I'm interested in the role cultures play in the development of individual pathology.

For a student of culture and personality, adolescence is fascinating. It's an extraordinary time when individual, developmental and cultural factors combine in ways that shape adulthood. It's a time of marked internal development and massive cultural indoctrination.

I want to try in this book to connect each girl's story with larger cultural issues—to examine the intersection of the personal and the political. It's a murky place; the personal and political are intertwined in all of our lives. Our minds, which are shaped by the society in which we live, can oppress us. And yet our minds can also analyze and work to change the culture.

An analysis of the culture cannot ignore individual differences in women. Some women blossom and grow under the most hostile conditions while others wither after the smallest storms. And yet we are more alike than different in the issues that face us. The important question is, Under what conditions do most young women flower and grow?

Adolescent clients intrigue me as they struggle to sort themselves out. But I wouldn't have written this book had it not been for these last few years when my office has been filled with girls—girls with eating disorders, alcohol problems, posttraumatic stress reactions to sexual or physical assaults, sexually transmitted diseases (STDs), self-inflicted injuries and strange phobias, and girls who have tried to kill themselves or run away. A health department survey showed that 40 percent of all girls in my midwestern city considered suicide last year. The Centers for Disease Control in Atlanta reports that the suicide rate among children age ten to fourteen rose 75 percent between 1979 and 1988. Something dramatic is happening to adolescent girls in America, something unnoticed by those not on the front lines.

At first I was surprised that girls were having more trouble now. 55 After all, we have had a consciousness-raising women's movement since the sixties. Women are working in traditionally male professions and going out for sports. Some fathers help with the housework and child care. It seems that these changes would count for something. And of course they do, but in some ways the progress is confusing. The Equal Rights Amendment was not ratified, feminism is a pejorative term to many people and, while some women have high-powered jobs, most women work hard for low wages and do most of the "second shift" work. The lip service paid to equality makes the reality of discrimination even more confusing.

Many of the pressures girls have always faced are intensified in the 1990s. Many things contribute to this intensification: more divorced families, chemical addictions, casual sex and violence against women. Because of the media, which Clarence Page calls "electronic wallpaper," girls all live in one big town—a sleazy, dangerous tinsel town with lots of liquor stores and few protected spaces. Increasingly women have been sexualized and objectified, their bodies marketed to sell tractors and toothpaste. Soft- and hard-core pornography are everywhere. Sexual and physical assaults on girls are at an all-time high. Now girls are more vulnerable and fearful, more likely to have been traumatized and less free to roam about alone. This combination of old stresses and new is poison for our young women.

Parents have unprecedented stress as well. For the last half-century, parents worried about their sixteen-year-old daughters driving, but now, in a time of drive-by shootings and car-jackings, parents can be panicked. Parents have always worried about their daughters' sexual behavior, but now, in a time of date rapes, herpes and AIDS, they can be sex-phobic. Traditionally parents have wondered what their teens were doing, but now teens are much more likely to be doing things that can get them killed.

This book will tell stories from the front lines. It's about girls because I know about girls. I was one, I see them in therapy, I have a teenage daughter and I teach primarily young women. I am not writing about boys because I have had limited experience with them. I'm not saying that girls and boys are radically different, only that they have different experiences.

I am saying that girls are having more trouble now than they had thirty years ago, when I was a girl, and more trouble than even ten years ago. Something new is happening. Adolescence has always been hard, but it's harder now because of cultural changes in the last decade. The protected place in space and time that we once called childhood has grown shorter. There is an African saying, "It takes a village to raise a child." Most girls no longer have a village.

Parents, teachers, counselors and nurses see that girls are in trouble, 60 but they do not realize how universal and extreme the suffering is. This book is an attempt to share what I have seen and heard. It's a hurricane warning, a message to the culture that something important is happening. This is a National Weather Service bulletin from the storm center.

For Journals

Think back to what your life was like when you were ten years old, then at age fifteen. In what ways did you change the way you thought of yourself? Of your role as a young woman or young man?

For Discussion

1. What is the "storm" that the author writes about? Who are the "saplings"?

2. Pipher quotes the writer Diderot as saying to a young woman, "You all die at 15." What do you think Diderot means? Do you agree or disagree? Cite examples from the text, or from your own observation or experience, to support your view.

3. The author integrates several different types of evidence—specific cases, literary examples, assertions, and authority—to support her key assertions. Which do you find most persuasive, and why?

For Writing

1. Using your journal writing as a starting point, write a reflective essay on your own passage into adolescence. Use a specific anecdote or examples to illustrate your essay.

2. Research rites of passage for adolescence in American cultures or in other countries and cultures. Be sure to focus your topic so that you can develop the paper well in the space available.

3. Write a response to Pipher. If you agree with her, provide a case example that supports her view. If you disagree, offer convincing evidence that refutes her assertion.

∞ Making and Unmaking the "Model Minority" (1994)

JOHN WU

John Wu is a college student who was born in Taipei, Taiwan, and lived there until 1983. His family then moved to Arcadia, California, where they still live. Wu hopes to pursue a career in film and television; his parents still hope that he will go into law. Wu wrote this researched essay in response to a writing assignment asking him to examine assumptions about his identity and his family values.

Asians in America used to be the "yellow peril" and were considered unassimilable. Today, Asian Americans are the "model minority" and are seemingly assimilating into the white, middle-class mainstream. This change in public perception affirms the improving fortune of Asian Americans as a group in recent years. Rosy pictures, however, do not capture the full realities facing this diverse and aggregate population under the rubric of "Asian American." Labeling an entire group overlooks the individuality of its members. Labels lead to generalizations and stereotypes. Generalizations and stereotypes lead to prejudice. And prejudice is the seed of racism. For this reason, many Asian Americans reject the model minority label despite its complimentary nature.

Whether celebrated or renounced, the model minority label carries with it expectations that are uncomfortably familiar to second-generation Asian Americans whose immigrant parents want nothing less for their children than for them to be the "model minority." This familiarity is the source of unease and ambivalence about the outright rejection of the model minority image. Because the sense of familial duty and filial piety is deeply embedded in most Asian cultures, second-generation Asian Americans often feel obligated to live up to the visions of the immigrant parents and to fulfill the American dream.

There are many explanations for why the model minority story emerged. Bob Suzuki, in what is considered the first major rebuttal to the model minority thesis, titled "Education and the Socialization of Asian Americans: A Revisionist Analysis of the 'Model Minority' Thesis," suggests that the timing, which coincided with the racial crisis of the sixties, was not accidental. He writes: "The activists charged that the actual status of Asian Americans was being deliberately distorted to fit the 'model minority' image in an attempt to discredit the protests and demands for social justice of other minority groups by admonishing them to follow the 'shining example' set by Asian Americans" (Suzuki 24). The concept of model minority absolves the guilt of the white majority for the bleak condition which other minority groups face. It permits white Americans to feel better about America and its history of flagrant racial discrimination and botched race relations.

More important, the model minority story keeps the American dream alive. Americans hold dear the idea that an individual, regardless of any disadvantaged background, can succeed in this society as long as he or she works hard. Commenting on the need of the model minority myth, Ronald Takaki, professor of ethnic studies at the University of California at Berkeley, explains: "Here is a society that is very nervous about the black underclass and gloomy about the economy. These are tough economic times . . . you need a model minority to reassure people, they need to be told the American dream still works . . . 'look at these immigrants, they can still do it'" (qtd. in Kamen). Thus the success of Asian Americans reassures the dominant culture that the American dream is still realizable.

Within the Asian American community, the current debate is no 5 longer whether Asian Americans are the model minority; rather, it is over whether we should completely discard the label or take pride in its positive aspects. What almost all commentators agree on is that the expectations brought about by the model minority stereotype present problems for Asian Americans. Consider the following description in the *Washington Post:* "Armed with little more than a will to succeed, they open stores where no other entrepreneur will venture. They streak to the top in the technical worlds of computers and mathematics. Their workers are the most dedicated and tireless, their children are the smartest. They are wealthy and self-sufficient" (Kamen). This near-mythical description is an example of the overall depiction of Asian Americans by the media "as industrious and intelligent, enterprising and polite, with good values and strong families, equally successful as children in school and as adults in business and medicine and science and engineering" (Shaw).

These popular media stereotypes create expectations of how Asian Americans are supposed to be. Ironically, these expectations are the same ones that immigrant parents often have of their children. In school, Asian American students are expected to excel. Placing much hope on education as the key to success, parents want and expect their children to work extra hard in school. They accept nothing but the best marks and the highest scores as evidence of hard work and success. Educators also expect Asian American students to be brilliant in the classroom, particularly in math and science. These two sources of high expectations create an enormous pressure for Asian American students. Those who cannot deliver perfect scores and top marks often suffer from low self-esteem and low confidence. Some community activists believe that the expectations of the society and the parents are a contributing factor to an increase in suicides among Asian American youth (Kamen).

As adults, Asian Americans have limited career choices because of the model minority label and of parental expectations. Stereotypes of Asian Americans as good in technical fields are not bad in and of themselves. The implication, though, is that Asian Americans are not good in anything else. Hence we see few successful Asian Americans in areas like politics, sports, and entertainment. In fact, many doors to nontechnical fields are virtually dead-bolted to Asian Americans. This limited career track is also enforced by many Asian parents who push their children in certain directions. Having self-sacrificed by leaving a familiar home, immigrant parents place all of their hopes on their children to succeed, to be better than they. They tend to encourage their children to stick to safe fields where success is rewarded by hard work and not by luck.

Asian Americans are also seen as people who "do not rock the boat." This expectation is usually entangled with the stereotype of being quiet and unassertive. Many non-Asians regard Asian Americans as people who are easy to work with but are not leaders, which may explain why few Asian Americans are in the top management level despite the high percentage of professionals in the corporate world. The emphasis on stoicism in many Asian cultures is the other source for the "do not rock the boat" expectation. Immigrant parents usually teach their children not to fight back against harassment or not to complain about academic pressures (Lee). In the same way, the society expects Asian Americans to overcome any obstacles of racism and discrimination. As Leonard

Downie, managing editor of the *Washington Post,* observes, "These are just quiet people who come here, go to work and go to school and do a good job and don't ask for coverage and don't make themselves very visible in the community" (qtd. in Shaw).

Beyond these expectations, the dominant culture and new immigrants share one more thing in common—the American dream. The dominant culture, still embracing the American dream, wishes to believe that American society is colorblind and that individualism is a practicable principle (Chan 171). The model minority tale grants them that wish: Asian Americans are living the American dream because they have the initiative and they work hard. Children of immigrant parents are well aware of the American dream. It is the reason, at least partially, many Asian immigrants have come to the United States. They come in search of better opportunities. With expectations of success conjured by the American dream, immigrant parents self-sacrifice so their children can have a better education, a better career, and a better life. Knowing the sacrifices of the immigrant parents, second-generation Asian Americans feel obligated to work hard to meet the expectations and, in a way, repay the first generation. These are the same expectations as those of the society on Asian Americans in general as a model minority.

These expectations exact a psychological toll on Asian Americans. 10
Suzuki explains that "over-anxious attempts by Asian Americans to gain acceptance have stripped them of their dignity and have caused many of them to suffer from severe psychological disorders characterized by lack of confidence, low self-esteem, expressive conformity and alienation" (25). This situation is especially acute among Asian American students. Feeling obligated to succeed, they work extremely hard in school. Their diligence, though praised by teachers, is frowned upon by non-Asian peers. As a result, Asian American students often feel isolated and alienated. This situation is compounded when Asian American students cannot meet the expectations demanded of them. In essence, they are "doubly burdened" (Shaw). On the one hand, they are attempting to meet the standards of their parents and end up feeling isolated from the peer community. On the other, their inability to meet those standards distances them from their parents.

Because of the pluralist nature of American society, every minority group member feels as if he or she is serving as a model for the group as a whole. As Asian Americans, we constantly feel as if we have to prove ourselves to white Americans that we are just as "good." Perhaps we have achieved our goal because we are now a model minority. But because we do not have our individuality, we are not as "good" as they.

Labels and stereotypes hinder individuality. The model minority myth precludes the possibility that some Asian Americans may not be upwardly mobile and successful. Yet our parents expect us to become upwardly mobile and successful. Our parents' expectations personalize the society's model minority expectations for us. For second-generation Asian Americans, the Asian sense of duty to the family and filial piety still run strong. We feel obligated to live up to the goals of our parents. At the same time, we want to be our own person; we want to be successful on our own terms. We want to reject the labels and the stereotypes but we cannot deny the positive achievements of Asian Americans. We are in a schizophrenic state of trying to become the "model minority" for our parents while trying to unmake the "model minority" of white America.

Works Cited

Chan, Sucheng. *Asian Americans: An Interpretive History.* Boston: Twayne, 1991.

Kamen, Al. "Myth of 'Model Minority' Haunts Asian Americans." *Washington Post,* 22 June 1992: A1.

Lee, Felicia. "'Model Minority' Label Taxes Asian Youths." *New York Times,* 20 Mar. 1990: B1.

Shaw, David. "Asian-Americans Chafe Against Stereotype of 'Model Citizen.'" *Los Angeles Times,* 11 Dec. 1990: A31.

Suzuki, Bob. "Education and the Socialization of Asian Americans: A Revisionist Analysis of the 'Model Minority' Thesis." *Amerasia* 4.2 (1977): 23–51.

For Journals

Do people make assumptions about you, based on your ethnicity or gender?

For Discussion

1. Identify the main idea and key supporting points in Wu's essay. To what extent do his own assumptions link and support the evidence to his main idea?

2. What assumptions of society is Wu questioning? Of white American society? Of Asian Americans and their families?

3. To what extent are the values Wu writes about transmitted through families? Through society?

4. If you were to exchange drafts with Wu in peer review, what suggestions would you make for a revision?

For Writing

1. Select a social issue of concern and interest to you and, as Wu does, challenge the assumptions with reasoning and evidence.

2. Do others make assumptions about your family values and beliefs? Write an essay explaining your value system to others with the goal of clarifying misperceptions and communicating what you consider to be a true picture of your value system.

∞ "The Culture of Cruelty," FROM Raising Cain: Protecting the Emotional Life of Boys (2000)

DANIEL J. KINDLON AND MICHAEL THOMPSON

Daniel J. Kindlon is a researcher and a psychology professor at Harvard as well as a psychologist specializing in adolescent boys. Michael Thompson is a child psychologist and staff psychologist at an all-boys school. They have more than thirty-five years of combined experience working with boys and their families. The following selection is a chapter from their larger work on male adolescence in America. You may wish to consider it a companion reading to "Reviving Ophelia," a selection about girls' adolescence that appeared earlier in this chapter.

> Cruelty and fear shake hands together.
> —Honoré de Balzac

Almost every man has boyhood memories of camaraderie and a coming-of-age story to tell. Maybe it's about a friend, or his gang of friends, and the memorable times they spent together—riding bikes, shooting hoops, going to movies, or just "hanging out." Or maybe his story isn't about friends but about an event, a moment as vivid in memory as on the day it happened years ago. These are the stories men like to tell.

There are other coming-of-age stories that men don't tell so eagerly or won't tell at all, even years later, because the emotional pain of the experience remains as deeply disturbing as on the day it happened when they were ten or twelve or fourteen. These are stories of boy cruelty—of domination, humiliation, fear, and betrayal—that most women never hear and most men and boys are reluctant or unable to share even with one another.

Beginning around age ten, as a boy approaches puberty, normal cognitive development makes him more aware of himself and his place in the group and raises the stakes in the many diverse competitions that consume boys: who is stronger, who is more attractive to girls, who gets better grades, who is a better basketball player, who is richer and has better things, and who can get the upper hand in teasing verbal combat. A boy's eagerness for autonomy, the fact that he now receives less teacher supervision, and his desire to cut loose from his parents' influence make him a willing recruit into the peer culture. At the same time, the group demands conformity and holds him up to ridicule for any failure to conform. Whether it is the TV shows he watches, the books he reads, the shoes he wears, the color of his socks, the length of his shorts, the cut of his hair, the sound of his laugh, or the length of his stride, *anything* a boy says or does that's different can and will be used against him. The physical changes of this age, in height, musculature, voice, and facial hair, for insistence, only add to a boy's self-consciousness. Almost all boys hide their hurt because to admit it appears weak. And they all look to make preemptive strikes when possible—to divert attention from themselves and onto others. In this psychological war no boys are truly protected, and there are no real "winners."

Boys are desperate for role models as they head into this uncertain age, and in most cases the dominant image of masculinity is one that requires strength and stoicism. Among themselves boys engage in continuous psychological warfare. Older boys pick on younger boys—dominating them by virtue of their greater size—and younger boys mimic them, creating an environment that pits the strong against the weak, the popular against the unpopular, the power brokers against the powerless, and the conformity-driven "boy pack" against the boy who fails in any way to conform with pack expectations.

The headmistress of an East Coast boarding school wrote to us to share her concerns about cruel teasing that had become especially virulent among the boys at the school, going beyond the garden-variety insults and name-calling to more subtle psychological "pranks" that showed a disturbing undercurrent of emotional cruelty.

One incident had occurred one afternoon in the common room of the dormitory, when an eleventh-grade boy, flanked by somber-faced friends, pretended to be distraught and in emotional shock about the death of his father. Another boy approached him to console him, sincerely believing the boy was in the saddest of circumstances. After stringing the caring boy along for several minutes, the boy confessed the ruse—his parents were alive and well—and with the joke splendidly revealed, he and his friends had a good laugh. The compassionate boy was made a laughing-stock and felt foolish and angry at the trick. And he learned his lesson: he wouldn't be so quick with compassion the next time around.

Other troubling incidents she described could have come from any school or neighborhood in America where young adolescent boys gather:

On one unpopular boy's birthday, a number of boys sang "Happy Birthday" to him but pretended to forget his name. When it was clear that he was embarrassed, they apologized, then brought out his cake—a block of ice covered with frosting.

In the school gym locker room, some boys urinated on other boys' belongings or into their shampoo bottles. There were incidents of "nipple twisting," painful and humiliating to the victim. Boys mooned one another or mooned and rubbed themselves against boys targeted for harassment. Boys left used condoms or trash on other boys' clothes or in their lockers.

Neither the victim nor his friends generally report these incidents   10 to teachers, for the most part because they know the acts are so intimate and so obviously hurtful that any teacher or parent would disapprove and there would be penalties to pay; the repercussions could be worse than the original incident. Showing the hurt also would be an admission of defeat and would only heighten a boy's vulnerability to new waves of scorn and attack. Every boy knows this. Why would a boy sit uncomfortably through an entire afternoon of classes rather than set foot in the boys' rest room to relieve himself, as one of our students confided he often did? Because an open row of urinals is an invitation to humiliation. All it takes is a quick push on the back, and a boy knocked off balance is left with wet pants and endless ridicule. Not only the aggressor will tease; any other boys who see or hear of the incident will, too. They will taunt him with it and whisper and snicker about it until someone more humiliated is pushed to the forefront.

We consulted at a school where the members of the lacrosse team periodically would take two small ninth-grade boys out to a field and force them to fight each other. If they resisted, said the bigger boys, the rest of the team would beat them up anyway. And so these smaller boys would fight, and the older boys would videotape it and show it around school.

Despite collegial appearances, all boys live with fear in this culture of cruelty. They also adhere to its code, and are loyal to its tenets even though they may not feel as if they fit in, because they view it as an inevitable test of their manliness.

With every lesson in dominance, fear, and betrayal, a boy is tutored away from trust, empathy, and relationship.[1] This is what boys lose to the culture of cruelty. What they learn instead is emotional guardedness, the wariness with which so many men approach relationships for the rest of their lives.

This is a culture that offers no security. Some boys are more frequently targeted than others, some more often lead the assaults, but all boys know they are vulnerable. As a self-possessed and popular boy confided: "Everybody thinks you've got it so easy when you're on top, but being on top just means that you have to worry all the time about slipping or somebody gaining on you. All it takes is one mistake or a bad day, and all sorts of people are waiting to take you down." For a boy not so high in the pecking order, life can be brutal—physically and psychologically—when the whim of the pack turns against him or, worse, turns a humiliated boy against himself, resulting in serious emotional problems, suicide, or violence. Boys who are under constant pressure to assert power or be labeled a weakling are more likely to level cruelty at others with little recognition of, or regard for, its emotional impact. Boys are cruel, in part because they are afraid, and their need to defend against that fear is ironclad.

Colin, an insightful eleventh grader, reflects on his experiences in the seventh grade: "You get into a habit of saying stuff to people, and it gets to a point where you don't even think about what you're saying anymore—like 'You're a dork'—and then it happens so much, it gets worse and worse, and then it's just like another word, like 'and' or 'I,' and you don't think of it as a word that can hurt somebody. I don't think you see the consequences of it. When you punch somebody in the eye, you see that they get a black eye, but when you and thirty other people call somebody a loser ten times day, you don't see the kid having low self-esteem or being hurt by it. You might see it if he cried or something, but then that's only like pouring fuel on the fire: everybody goes after him for crying."

We are realistic. We know that powerful influences shape the culture of cruelty and perpetuate it. To the extent that the period of puberty and early adolescence is for all kids a time of radical change, self-definition, and emotional insecurity, it is to some degree inevitable that boys will become rivals, friends, enemies.[2] But just as one boy's careless taunt can inflict a lasting wound on another boy, so can even a few boys change the climate dramatically with their decision to resist joining in the teasing or to stand up for a boy under attack. If the culture of cruelty thrives on boys' fears of vulnerability, then the challenge is to replace their fears with a greater understanding of their own emotional struggle and in so doing diminish their need for cruelty and their tolerance of it.

Michael with Seventh-Grade Boys: Learning to Talk . . . but Not Too Much

The principal of a suburban middle school asks me to meet with two sections of seventh-grade boys for an hour. She says there is a lot of teasing among the boys, and she's hoping that conversation will be more effective without girls present.

The meeting takes place in a dark classroom in the late afternoon. All the boys—about forty of them—are sitting at desks with their huge book bags on the floor beside them. It is quite a sight, these boys with their fresh, open faces. They look so handsome, so adultlike, and yet they are not.

The boys arrange themselves in groups immediately upon entering the room, while some boys keep to themselves, and some hug the wall. There is always a center group, very close together, that conveys a sense of power and popularity. "You are going to hear from *us*," their position tells me. I cannot exactly explain the underlying theory of power seating in a school, but I know it when I see it. Within seconds it's clear which boys want to be the center of attention, which boys are going to compete for my time, which boys want to dominate the conversation, and which boys are going to be on the margins.

I begin by asking them why boys tease one another. To them it's a 20 dumb question. Because it's funny, says one, everyone knows that. The joke is right there, the stupid behavior is obvious; someone *has* to point it out. Then I ask them what the most painful moment—emotionally speaking—has been for them in school. There is an uncomfortable silence as the boys glance around the room at one another and shift in their chairs. A boy starts to describe an athletic injury, and I remind him that we are talking about hurt feelings. Someone describes having dropped a test tube filled with a smelly mixture in science lab, and how everyone started to tease him about being a klutz. Another boy says he used to get made fun of because he wore braces.

Then Steven, one of the boys sitting alone and against the wall, begins to talk about being regularly tormented on the bus, having his books grabbed out of his backpack, his papers scattered, and how all the kids laugh when he goes to pick them up. The tone of his voice signals us all that his pain is recent and deep. The discomfort in the room is palpable. His tormentors are here, and he is telling their "secret" to a "stranger."

What is most unnerving to the boys, however, is the emotion in Steven's voice. He has taken the wraps off; this is real. Boys start to squirm or giggle; a few nudge one another. Little noises arise from around the room. I can tell that Steven knows he is breaking the code of silence but doesn't care; he has my attention, and he is going to tell his story.

I am torn, because as a psychologist, I want to encourage this self-disclosure, but Steven has opened himself up for a whole new round of teasing. He is not reading the cues. If he goes on this way, exposing his vulnerabilities, the group will gang up on him. I want to help Steven speak his truth without having him become the victim, the "Piggy" of the group, like the classic vulnerable boy in William Golding's *Lord of the Flies.*

"Piggy" is the classic scapegoat in the literature of boy cruelty, the overweight boy in *Lord of the Flies.* In the novel, shipwrecked schoolboys, ranging in age from six to thirteen, struggle to maintain civilization and democracy but ultimately fail, succumbing to crueler impulses to shame and punish each other. Even the most fair-minded leader among the boys is, at some point, drawn into the pack's frenzied taunting of Piggy, the pudgy, bespectacled picture of vulnerability and the voice of reason. Finally, as the mob of boys grows restless in a violent swell of discord about duty assignments, Piggy cries out for calm deliberation, and he is killed.

In many schools the book is a standard part of the curriculum in 25 seventh- and eighth-grade English classes. For the girls it is a powerful piece of fiction about the human potential for cruelty. For the boys the story is real: it's as close as the crowded hall between classes or the locker room before gym period. It accurately captures their own, only slightly more civilized world. It is a place every man has been. A boy lives that story, too, aware every day that the group could turn on him in a flash, that every moment holds the "Piggy" potential, and that, if he is targeted, it will be almost impossible for anyone—even a friend—to stand up with him against the crowd. Except in the most violent communities, most boys don't face the potential of physical annihilation so much as they experience a marginalization—being made to feel worthless or virtually nonexistent—that can be emotionally debilitating.

I stop Steven and thank him for his contribution. He starts to speak on two later occasions in the meeting, and when I see the other boys becoming scornful, I close him down. I will seek him out, either directly or through the middle school principal, and find some time to speak with him privately.

Striving for Masculinity: In Search of the Big Impossible

It is normal for a child to seek the respect or appreciation of peers. Friendship provides affection, intimacy, and reliable alliance. From either a friend or the group, you can get practical assistance, nurturance, companionship, and enhancement of worth. What only a group can provide is a sense of inclusion, which all children crave.

For boys on the cusp of adolescence, this desire to fit in is supercharged by their developing gender identity need to establish themselves as successful males. In the Eastern Highlands of Papua, New Guinea, the Fox Indians call manhood the "Big Impossible."[3] What an appropriate name for manhood, which in so many cultures is recognized only after a rite of passage that tests the mettle of a boy against the fire of cultural expectations. Inherent in this thinking is the idea that to be a real man requires something more than simple anatomical maleness, that a boy must rise to a performance challenge that will earn him his manly status. When masculinity is defined as an achievement, then manhood becomes "a prize to be won or wrested through struggle" and a "precarious or artificial state," as David Gilmore notes in *Manhood in the Making*.

Yet performance-based masculine identity is virtually impossible to achieve in any lasting way. "You're only as good as your last game," they say in baseball. Boys understand this message on a personal level. In the boys' world, you can never, ever be satisfied with your performance. You have to prove yourself anew, continuously. This unending quest to fit in, to be cool, inevitably pits boys against one another—and against the men in their lives as well. In this psychologically competitive male environment, part of proving yourself is to belittle others.

A boy lives in a narrowly defined world of developing masculin- 30 ity in which everything he does or thinks is judged on the basis of the strength or weakness it represents: you are either strong and worthwhile, or weak and worthless. He must also be willing to fight. Even if you have never fought, and never intend to fight, you have to pretend to yourself that you can and will. A respected boy is someone who can "handle himself," as one nonviolent fifteen-year-old put it, which he said meant mentally taking the measure of another boy and assessing whether you could beat him up if you had to.

A common debate in many households is how to counsel a boy who is being harassed by bullies. Mothers take the position that "violence doesn't solve anything"; fathers have no qualms about telling a ten-year-old son to "punch out" the jerk, acknowledging that the punch might not get rid of the bully—but that that isn't the point. Walking away from tormentors is a sign of weakness, and the lasting feeling of cowardice is greater punishment than any blow.

Boys not only feel the pressure to appear masculine, but they feel that, in doing so, they must be clearly *not* feminine—perhaps even antifeminine—and so they consciously and deliberately attack in others and in themselves traits that might possibly be defined as feminine. This includes tenderness, empathy, compassion, and any show of emotional vulnerability. Whether these pressures produce a street fighter or not, they impose a standard for masculinity that all boys accept and use to judge themselves.

Howard, a teacher from a family of teachers, confided a story from his own youth, when his parents sent him to a camp in Vermont famous for its manly traditions. Every Friday night there was an "American Indian" ceremony by the campfire. All of the older boys, who had "passed the test," dressed up as "braves" and marched down to the campfire in single file. All of the younger boys were "squaws," who marched down at the end of the line with blankets over their heads. A boy remained a squaw until he had passed the "test," which involved singing a complicated "Indian" song filled with unfamiliar words.

Because of his nervousness, Howard could not learn the words to the song. Even so, each Friday night he stood up and tried to sing it, in front of the group, in front of all the "braves," and each time he tried, he failed. For that entire first summer, every Friday night he had to wear the blanket again and be a "squaw."

To be labeled a girl—a "squaw"—is the most humiliating thing 35 that can happen to a boy. To have the "honor" of manhood withheld from him because he could not memorize the words to a camp song added further insult to Howard's injury. In a life distinguished by a wealth of experience and accomplishments, Howard still carries this memory with him as one of the most unremittingly cruel and humiliating experiences of his life.

Notes

1. Alferi, T., D. N. Ruble, and E. T. Higgins. "Gender Stereotypes during Adolescence: Developmental Changes and the Transition to Junior High School." *Developmental Psychology* 32 (1996): 1129–37.

2. Anthony, E. *American Manhood: Transformation in Masculinity from the Revolution to the Modern Era*. New York: Basic Books, 1993.

3. Faludi, Susan. "The Naked Citadel." *The New Yorker*, September 5, 1994, 62–81.

For Journals

Write about a time around puberty when you became acutely aware of social expectations about your gender role.

For Discussion

1. From your experience or observation, does this selection accurately represent struggles of late childhood and early adolescence for boys and young men? Why or why not? How does the knowledge that the authors are psychologists affect your view of their authority on this topic?

2. Do you agree with the authors that "the dominant image of masculinity is one that requires strength and stoicism"? Do the authors suggest positive as well as negative outcomes from this culture? Do you believe there are positive as well as negative aspects to this image? Discuss.

3. The authors suggest that "a greater understanding of their own emotional struggle" will diminish boys' need for and tolerance of cruelty. Would you agree? Why or why not?

4. The authors note different approaches in dealing with bullies— with mothers frequently suggesting "violence doesn't solve anything" and fathers telling boys to "punch out the jerk." Do the authors appear to side with one or the other? Do you? Develop a class discussion on this topic with several class members observing and tracking the discussion. Then analyze the arguments made in terms of the gender of the discussants. What themes or patterns emerge, if any?

For Writing

1. Write a response to the authors, either agreeing with their point of view or refuting it. Support your response with personal experience or observation.

2. Analyze the premises, evidence, and conclusions of the authors. What points are strongest? Which evidence is most persuasive? Compare, for example, the authors' unsupported premises and those backed by case histories or anecdotal evidence.

3. Integrate this selection as a secondary source and revisit the William Golding novel, *Lord of the Flies*. How does this reading inform your reading of the novel?

4. Compare and contrast this selection with the Pipher selection on adolescent girls. What common themes emerge? What striking contrasts do you find?

∞ *Film:* Mi Familia (*My Family*) (1995)

This film's subject is the story and struggles of the three-generation Sanchez family, seen through the eyes of the eldest son, a writer. The narrative includes the father's journey on foot from Mexico to California in the 1920s, a brother's tragic death in the 1950s, and social and economic struggles in contemporary America. (121 minutes)

For Journals

What do you expect from a film about a Mexican American family? If you are Mexican American, what themes or issues do you think are likely to appear in this film?

For Discussion

1. In what ways is the Sanchez family similar to your own family? In what ways is it different?

2. The film begins, and ends, with images of the bridges connecting East Los Angeles with Los Angeles. What is the significance of those bridges? What do they mean to the members of the Sanchez family?

3. Jose Sanchez comes to California to find a relative who was born in California "when it was still Mexico." Discuss the political implications of this situation in terms of people who are, and are not, considered "American."

4.   Mrs. Sanchez suffers extreme difficulties in order to be reunited with her husband and children. Discuss the ways in which this element of the film, as well as other particular examples, conveys values and beliefs about family.

5.   Compare and contrast the values and beliefs that the parents and children have about work and money.

For Writing

1.   Write a review of this film for your campus newspaper, or write a letter to a friend urging him or her to see the film (or not). If you are unfamiliar with the genre of film reviews, read several from your local newspaper. The review captures reader interest, makes a claim about the film's merit or lack thereof, and usually briefly summarizes the film in a way that does not give away the plot or any surprises. The reader should be able to make an informed decision about viewing the film based on your review.

2.   Select one scene in the film and write about how it illuminates a larger theme or idea that the film as a whole suggests (for example, the father's journey, the mother's river crossing, the wedding scene, one of the scenes in which a new romantic partner is introduced to the family).

3.   Research and write a documented essay about one of the actual or historical events or situations referred to in the film, such as forced relocation of American citizens who "looked Mexican" during the Great Depression of the 1930s.

Writing Assignments

1.   Select a reading in this chapter, and diagram the assumptions on which it rests. Put the main point in a box at the top of the page and then draw boxes and connecting lines showing the supporting assumptions and reasons. How do you think the writer knew which assumptions to state explicitly and which ones would be understood or automatically accepted by the audience?

2.   Examine a piece of artwork or other visual image that appears in another chapter in this book. Articulate the implicit and explicit assumptions and values on which it is based, and write an essay analyzing what such assumptions tell us about the audiences for which the image was intended.

3.   Develop your own argument on the subject of women's or men's proper role in society, on same-gender domestic partnerships, on in-

terracial adoption, or on some other social issue of concern to you. Exchange essays with a peer, preferably one who has taken an opposing view or has written on a different subject. Write refutations of each other's essays, and turn in both originals and refutations. Did you find yourselves refuting primarily the assumptions, the reasons, the conclusions drawn, or some of each part of the argument in equal amounts?

4. Examine your own values and beliefs about family and gender. Do some private freewriting, reflecting on how you have come to hold those values. What are your assumptions about family life? The work ethic? Dating roles? Parental roles? Friendship between genders? Marriage or partnership roles? Write a reflective essay exploring the process through which you have come to hold these particular beliefs.

5. Interview your parents or grandparents or other people of their generations; ask them about the expectations they grew up with about dating, gender roles, or family and parental duties. Do they still hold those assumptions? What do they think of current customs? Write an essay summarizing your findings and share it with other class members. Alternatively, compare the assumptions held by the people you interviewed with those you hold, and analyze the similarities and differences.

6. In a group, and if everyone is willing to share, put up butcher paper around the classroom and have everyone write his or her name, ethnic background, parents' and grandparents' occupations, and any sayings, proverbs, legacies (ideas they've passed down to you or possessions that represent these ideas). After everyone has finished, silently review the material, looking for connections, themes, values, or assumptions that emerge. Discuss them as a class, or write up your reflections privately or to share.

7. Design a flyer to inform an audience about a social issue. Write an essay explaining your design, focusing on the assumptions you made about your audience and the premises on which your flyer is based.

8

∞

Work and Play

The relationship of Americans to work is one of the most complicated dynamics in our culture. The ethics of worth, beliefs about
wealth and the importance of money, and ways of measuring success
for ourselves and others all come into the discussion. Work, like religion, family, the American dream, and other deeply rooted beliefs, is
closely identified with who we are, how we value ourselves, and how
we in turn are valued, or not valued, by society.

Americans believe that everyone deserves at least the chance to be
successful; perhaps that's how most would interpret the Declaration of
Independence's guarantee of the pursuit of happiness. But they have
never agreed on how success is to be achieved or measured and are
torn between the Protestant work ethic—a belief in hard work and
diligence rewarded by middle-class prosperity—and the fantasy of
wealth gained without any work, through the blind luck of buying a
winning lottery ticket or marrying the boss's only child.

Between those two extremes, Americans have historically entertained a variety of beliefs about work, some of them mutually inconsistent. The Calvinist theology that prevailed in early New England
included the belief that God chooses to save some unworthy souls as a
sign of infinite mercy; these fortunate few are called the elect. Gradually that austere tenet of faith came to include an assumption that
someone living the comfortable life must be doing it with God's help;
thus, outward success was viewed as proof of good work habits and
God's favor. Calvinism has long since ceased to dominate our country's religious life, but the connection of high pay, status, and success
with personal self-worth has remained embedded in American culture
and consciousness.

Industrialization, especially after the Civil War, brought factory
jobs and long hours. The fortunate few—the elect of industrial America—were known as the robber barons. Many of these railroad, mine,
and factory owners came from poor or ordinary backgrounds and

293

made inconceivably vast amounts of money. Poorer Americans both resented and worshipped them; low pay and terrible working conditions were the reality for most Americans, and their highest goal was to become middle class. But secretly they dreamed that perhaps their children would do better—much better.

Part of the reward system for doing better and entering the middle class was the opportunity to enjoy a privilege that was once reserved for the rich—leisure time in which to engage in a pleasurable activity such as a sport or a craft, to be a spectator at professional sports events, to go to the theater or to a musical performance, or even to travel. Well-off Victorian America offered baseball, tennis, boating, parlor games and card games, and bicycling. For the very poor, of course, leisure was still a rare luxury, but some sports, such as baseball and boxing, were more generally available to everyone. Baseball was probably the most democratized sport of all, played before the Civil War, spread by prisoners on both sides during the Civil War, played in cities, by immigrants as well as native-born Americans, by blacks as well as whites. However, when baseball, like other American institutions, embraced segregation in the late nineteenth century, it established what would eventually become a truism about sports in America—they represented a microcosm of the country as a whole, and, in this case, a tragic reflection of inequalities in other areas of American life.

Baseball was significant in another way too. It became the first American sport to turn into a business, and big business at that. Eventually, other sports that were originally strictly amateur—football and basketball, for example—followed its lead. College stars went on to play on professional teams, with salaries, owners, fans, local pride, local economies, and a lot of money at stake. The area of athletics that remained amateur the longest (that is, with no real money involved) was women's college sports. Many of them—track and field, field hockey, softball—still draw women for the love of the sport alone. But others—women's tennis, golf, and particularly basketball—now imitate men's sports in the sense that the best college athletes can now join professional tours or leagues. At the same time, the Olympics highlight sports in which women are particularly well established, such as gymnastics and figure skating, and a gold medal means endorsements and high salaries, not to mention product advertisements, celebrity, and pictures of the champion emblazoned on Wheaties boxes.

These changes certainly signal a definite move toward equality and recognition that great women athletes are as interesting, if not more interesting, to watch than men. But these opportunities are not an unalloyed blessing: now some women athletes experience the problems of commercialization and overmarketing that were previously the preserve of men alone. Whether women's sports handle those problems any differently remains to be seen.

The most significant American writing about work and play is both a response to and a reflection of the values behind them and the national experience that shaped them. The selections in this chapter sample a spectrum of those values, examine various kinds of work and play, and offer possibilities for combining the two. They also raise related issues: the tenuousness of life in this country for those who lack paying work or whose work is unfulfilling and poorly paid; the corruption of the amateur ideal by the reality of sports finances; the questionable status of women in a culture in which husbands work outside and supply the paychecks and wives work at home but do not earn money; the significance of work and money as satisfying, non-gendered activities; the benefits of athletic competition and the dangers of completely commercialized sports. Finally, this chapter raises the question of balance—between work and play, between amateur and professional, between the lives of working men and women, between Americans' faith in the redeeming possibilities of work as well as their desire to escape it.

Work and Play through History

The selections in this chapter revolve around two areas: work and play. Work-related issues include needing a job, having a job and getting the most out of it, looking for job security, or dealing with the trauma of losing it. Play includes both sports and a less determinate but valuable category called leisure—the time and the freedom to choose a night out, a vacation, a stay at home, or nothing at all.

Benjamin Franklin worked at many jobs in his lifetime—some for money, some for science, some for public service—but his overall brilliance makes it difficult to know where his work ended and his leisure began. He seems to have enjoyed working as a printer—a vocation which made him wealthy, gratified his early ambitions, and enabled him to retire very early. But he also seems to have enjoyed swimming, teaching himself languages while playing chess, and finding ways to establish the first circulating library in the country, the fire department, the American Philosophical Society, and the University of Pennsylvania. And if he sometimes found diplomacy with France stressful, he so charmed the French that they followed him around as if he were a rock star. In the first selection, taken from the *Autobiography*, we see him as a child and a young man. Brilliant, rebellious, ambitious, he comes into conflict with an older brother, sets out on his own, and embarks on a process of self-education that would last his entire life and enrich his country immeasurably. Whatever he does, he does with an energy, intelligence, and humor that make him, still, the most remarkable of Americans.

In another part of the *Autobiography,* Franklin reports on a widow who proved infinitely more successful at running a business than her husband. Franklin's conclusion—that women should be educated about money, accounting, and business transactions—was far ahead of its time, and it fell on deaf ears. But it found an echo, more than a century later, in the groundbreaking work of Charlotte Perkins Gilman who knew from personal experience what it meant to have no control over one's finances, and therefore one's independence; what it meant to be a well-brought up Victorian woman suffocated by conventions and restrictions. She wrote a remarkable story, "The Yellow Wallpaper," about a young mother who has a breakdown that is exacerbated by the condescending and wrong-headed ministrations of her doctor and husband. Gilman's understanding of what it meant for married women to have no legal or financial independence led to her innovative study *Women and Economics,* which is excerpted here. It made her the first professional American woman economist.

Well-off Americans were spared the grinding poverty exposed in Jacob Riis's famous photograph of women sewing in a tenement around 1907 (although Gilman would have understood the economic extremities that brought it about). In the early part of this century, Riis documented the lives of immigrants in New York's Lower East Side, letting the images of sweatshops, illness, crowded living conditions, and desperate determination speak for themselves. At the same time, Americans who were poorer than Gilman but much better off than the women in Riis's photograph, namely blue- and white-collar workers, were beginning to enjoy a variety of relatively inexpensive pleasures such as amusement parks, vaudeville shows, early movie theaters (called picture palaces), and inner-city baseball parks. In his social history *Going Out,* David Nasaw explains how the beginnings of American mass entertainment came into being, who got to enjoy it and who didn't, and how the growth of the big cities and the development of electric lights made that entertainment possible.

For those more prosperous Americans whose income enabled them to travel, the favorite destination was Europe, particularly London and Paris. But as the 1914 Hawaiian postcard of famous swimmer and surfer Duke Kahanamoku shows, the idea of being an American tourist in America was beginning to take shape, especially if the destination could be shown as exotic and attractive. Hawaii was certainly far enough from the mainland and unknown enough to qualify as practically a foreign place to most Americans, and the postcard wisely plays up the different pleasures it has to offer.

Equally welcoming—and equally powerful in its representation of the body as an object of worship—is the 1927 cover of Bernarr Macfadden's highly successful magazine, *Physical Culture*. The young woman on the cover, like Duke Kahanamoku, is emblematic of American health and energy, consciously developed and energetically pursued. Just as Duke is an advertisement for Hawaii, the cover girl promotes Macfadden's somewhat eccentric ideology, in which a healthy body is a necessary precondition to moral excellence. And a blooming female body, scantily dressed by 1927 standards, isn't a bad idea for attracting readers.

The only short story in this chapter, John Steinbeck's famous "The Chrysanthemums," is paired with Woody Guthrie's song, "Union Maid." Steinbeck, the middle-class chronicler of fishermen, farmers, and union organizers, among others, and Guthrie, the itinerant song-smith, were committed to similar causes. Their sympathies were with the dispossessed, the underdogs, the honest poor. Steinbeck's story, written only a couple of years after *The Grapes of Wrath*, is about a woman on a Salinas Valley farm whose work with flowers is the only source of beauty and fulfillment she knows, and who is vulnerable because of it. Guthrie's song, "Union Maid," is one of the many he wrote to honor and empower ordinary people who suffered from substandard working conditions, low wages, and the sometimes violent efforts of companies to discourage the formation of unions. It is unusual, though, in that it is dedicated to women workers.

Studs Terkel, the journalist and interviewer who is, in his own way, as much of a historian of American culture as Steinbeck and Guthrie, devoted an entire book, *Working*, to what all kinds of Americans, from celebrities to unknown citizens, do for a living and how they feel about what they do. The interview with Mr. Bates, a stone-mason, depicts a man at the fortunate end of the work spectrum, who has spent his whole life at a job he loves and which gives him great pride and satisfaction. His delight in his craft, his sense of having made something which lasts, is almost as palpable as the stone with which he works. So is his understanding that he may be the last of his breed. No doubt Benjamin Franklin, who so enjoyed seeing anyone do a job well, especially a craftsman, would have enjoyed Mr. Bates enormously.

Reporter Alfred Lubrano, on the other hand, raises a further issue of work satisfaction and complicates it with a question: What happens when a blue-collar father, like Mr. Bates, raises a son who, thanks to education, rises into the middle class and the world of white-collar work and values? Like F. Scott Fitzgerald, Lubrano recognizes the darker side of the work ethic, but he is also an example of how contemporary writers continue to reevaluate that ethic in the light of their own experience. Lubrano can neither deny nor escape the cost to familial intimacy and comfort when a son succeeds at a kind of work his father cannot share.

The next three selections deal with issues arising from the one area of American life in which work and play presumably coincide: the world of amateur sports. The central issue in sports historian Leonard Koppett's article is the intrusion of the classic American reward for work—money—into the supposedly amateur life of college sports teams. The result, according to Koppett, is hypocrisy. Colleges insist that they observe the division between work and play in their athletic programs, but in truth student/athletes get paid under the table and amateurism becomes a byword for corruption.

Student Katie Norris, in another argumentative essay, explores some of the physical and psychological dangers confronting adolescent female athletes, and suggests some solutions. And another veteran sportswriter, C. W. Nevius, carries the arguments of Koppett and Davis to their logical if depressing conclusions by examining children's sports—Little League, Pop Warner, gymnastics, hockey, and other venues—in a series of articles for the *San Francisco Chronicle*. In this selection, he examines how the obsessive parents and ill-tempered coaches of children's teams contribute to an atmosphere of competition and violence that would be excessive at a professional football game and that completely violates the notion of child's play.

Finally the film *Jerry Maguire,* a comedy about a seeming contradiction in terms—the moral rebirth of a sports agent—provokes another look at the sports/work/ethics dilemma, as well as a witty reminder that all honest work has dignity, and that doing a job honestly and well may be the hardest work of all.

∽ FROM *Autobiography* (1771)

BENJAMIN FRANKLIN

Benjamin Franklin (1706–1790) had established himself as a printer, writer, and public servant in Philadelphia, the biggest city in the colonies, by the time he was twenty-four years old. He was able to retire at forty-two and spend the rest of his life in service to science, philanthropy, and the young country he helped to found. He also found time to teach himself several languages, start America's first lending library and fire department, invent the Franklin stove and bifocals, and lay the basis for the American Philosophical Society and the University of Pennsylvania. A hugely successful American representative in France, and an early supporter of the abolition of slavery, he wrote of himself with a characteristic mixture of objectivity and self-mockery. The following selection shows him in his rebellious youth, and gives one of his early experiments—personal rather than scientific—whose failure he managed to learn from.

My elder Brothers were all put Apprentices to different Trades. I was put to the Grammar School at Eight Years of Age, my Father intending to devote me as the Tithe of his Sons to the Service of the Church. My early Readiness in learning to read (which must have been very early, as I do not remember when I could not read) and the Opinion of all his Friends that I should certainly make a good Scholar, encourag'd him in this Purpose of his. . . . But my Father in the mean time, from a View of the Expence of a College Education which, having so large a Family, he could not well afford, and the mean Living many so educated were afterwards able to obtain, Reasons that he gave to his Friends in my Hearing, altered his first Intention, took me from the Grammar School, and sent me to a School for Writing & Arithmetic kept by a then famous Man, Mr Geo. Brownell, very successful in his Profession generally, and that by mild encouraging Methods. Under him I acquired fair Writing pretty soon, but I fail'd in the arithmetic, & made no Progress in it.—At Ten Years old, I was taken home to assist my Father in his Business, which was that of a Tallow Chandler and Sope-Boiler. A Business he was not bred to, but had assumed on his Arrival in New England & on finding his Dying Trade would not maintain his Family, being in little Request. Accordingly I was employed in cutting Wick for the Candles, filling the Dipping Mold, & the Molds for cast Candles, attending the Shop, going of Errands, &c.—I dislik'd the Trade and had a strong Inclination for the Sea; but my Father declar'd against it; however, living near the Water, I was much in and about it, learnt early to swim well, & to manage Boats, and when in a Boat or Canoe with other Boys I was commonly allow'd to govern, especially in any case of Difficulty; and upon other Occasions I was generally a Leader among the Boys, and sometimes led them into Scrapes. . . .

To return, I continu'd thus employ'd in my Father's Business for two Years, that is till I was 12 Years old; and my Brother John, who was bred to that Business having left my Father, married and set up for himself at Rhodeisland, there was all Appearance that I was destin'd to supply his Place and be a Tallow Chandler. But my Dislike to the Trade continuing, my Father was under Apprehensions that if he did not find one for me more agreable, I should break away and get to Sea, as his Son Josiah had done to his great Vexation. He therefore sometimes took me to walk with him, and see Joiners, Bricklayers, Turners, Braziers, &c. at their Work, that he might observe my Inclination, & endeavour to fix it on some Trade or other on Land.—It has ever since been a Pleasure to me to see good Workmen handle their Tools; and it has been useful to me, having learnt so much by it, as to be able to do little Jobs my self in my House, when a Workman could not readily be got; & to construct little Machines for my Experiments while the Intention of making the Experiment was fresh & warm in my Mind. . . .

From a Child I was fond of Reading, and all the little Money that came into my Hands was ever laid out in Books. . . .

This Bookish Inclination at length determin'd my Father to make me a Printer, tho' he had already one Son, (James) of that Profession. In 1717 my Brother James return'd from England with a Press & Letters to set up his Business in Boston. I lik'd it much better than that of my Father, but still had a Hankering for the Sea.—To prevent the apprehended Effect of such an Inclination, my Father was impatient to have me bound to my Brother. I stood out some time, but at last was persuaded and signed the Indentures, when I was yet but 12 Years old. . . .

My Brother had in 1720 or 21, begun to print a Newspaper. It was 5 the second that appear'd in America, & was called *The New England Courant.* The only one before it, was *The Boston News Letter.* I remember his being dissuaded by some of his Friends from the Undertaking, as not likely to succeed, one Newspaper being in their Judgment enough for America.—At this time 1771 there are not less than five & twenty.— . . . Tho' a Brother, he considered himself as my Master, & me as his Apprentice; and accordingly expected the same Services from me as he would from another; while I thought he demean'd me too much in some he requir'd of me, who from a Brother expected more Indulgence. Our Disputes were often brought before our Father, and I fancy I was either generally in the right, or else a better Pleader, because the Judgment was generally in my favour: But my Brother was passionate & had often beaten me, which I took extreamly amiss;* and thinking my Apprenticeship very tedious, I was continually wishing for some Opportunity of shortening it, which at length offered in a manner unexpected.

One of the Pieces in our News-Paper, on some political Point which I have now forgotten, gave Offence to the Assembly. He was taken up, censur'd and imprison'd for a Month by the Speaker's Warrant, I suppose because he would not discover his Author. I too was taken up & examin'd before the Council; but tho' I did not give them any Satisfaction, they contented themselves with admonishing me, and dismiss'd me; considering me perhaps as an Apprentice who was bound to keep his Master's Secrets. During my Brother's Confinement, which I resented a good deal, notwithstanding our private Differences, I had the Management of the Paper, and I made bold to give our Rulers some Rubs in it, which my Brother took very kindly, while others began to consider me in an unfavourable Light, as a young Genius that had a Turn for Libelling & Satyr. My Brother's Discharge was accompany'd with an Order of the House, (a very odd one) *that James*

---

*I fancy his harsh & tyrannical Treatment of me, might be a means of impressing me with that Aversion to arbitrary Power that has stuck to me thro' my whole Life.

Franklin should no longer print the Paper called The New England Courant. There was a Consultation held in our Printing House among his Friends what he should do in this Case. Some propos'd to evade the Order by changing the Name of the Paper; but my Brother seeing Inconveniences in that, it was finally concluded on as a better Way, to let it be printed for the future under the Name of *Benjamin Franklin.* . . .

. . . the Paper went on accordingly under my Name for several Months. At length a fresh Difference arising between my Brother and me, I took upon me to assert my Freedom, presuming that he would not venture to produce the new Indentures. It was not fair in me to take this Advantage, and this I therefore reckon one of the first Errata of my Life: But the Unfairness of it weigh'd little with me, when under the Impressions of Resentment, for the Blows his Passion too often urg'd him to bestow upon me. Tho' He was otherwise not an ill-natur'd Man: Perhaps I was too saucy & provoking.—

When he found I would leave him, he took care to prevent my getting Employment in any other Printing-House of the Town, by going round & speaking to every Master, who accordingly refus'd to give me Work. I then thought of going to New York as the nearest Place where there was a Printer: and I was then rather inclin'd to leave Boston. . . .

Walking in the Evening by the Side of the River a Boat came by, which I found was going towards Philadelphia, with several People in her. They took me in, and as there was no Wind, we row'd all the Way; and about Midnight not having yet seen the City, some of the Company were confident we must have pass'd it, and would row no farther, the others knew not where we were, so we put towards the Shore, got into a Creek, landed near an old Fence with the Rails of which we made a Fire, the Night being cold, in October, and there we remain'd till Daylight. Then one of the Company knew the Place to be Cooper's Creek a little above Philadelphia, which we saw as soon as we got out of the Creek, and arriv'd there about 8 or 9 a Clock, on the Sunday morning, and landed at the Market street Wharff.—

. . . I now open'd a little Stationer's Shop. I had in it Blanks of all   10
Sorts the correctest that ever appear'd among us, being assisted in that by my Friend Brientnal; I had also Paper, Parchment, Chapmen's Books, &c. One Whitemash a Compositor I had known in London, an excellent Workman now came to me & work'd with me constantly & diligently, and I took an Apprentice the Son of Aquila Rose. I began now gradually to pay off the Debt I was under. . . . In order to secure my Credit and Character as a Tradesman, I took care not only to be in *Reality* Industrious & frugal, but to avoid all *Appearances* of the Contrary. I drest plainly; I was seen at no Places of idle Diversion; I never went out a-fishing or shooting; a Book, indeed, sometimes debauch'd me from my Work; but that was seldom, snug, & gave no Scandal: and

to show that I was not above my Business, I sometimes brought home the Paper I purchas'd at the Stores, thro' the Streets on a Wheelbarrow. Thus being esteem'd an industrious thriving young Man, and paying duly for what I bought, the Merchants who imported Stationary solicited my Custom, others propos'd supplying me with Books, & I went on swimmingly. . . .

It was about this time that I conceiv'd the bold and arduous Project of arriving at moral Perfection. I wish'd to live without committing any Fault at any time; I would conquer all that either Natural Inclination, Custom, or Company might lead me into. As I knew, or thought I knew, what was right and wrong, I did not see why I might not *always* do the one and avoid the other. But I soon found I had undertaken a Task of more Difficulty than I had imagined: While my Care was employ'd in guarding against one Fault, I was often surpriz'd by another. . . .

The Precept of *Order* requiring that *every Part of my Business should have its allotted time*, one Page in my little Book contain'd the following Scheme of Employment for the Twenty-four Hours of a natural Day,

The Morning Question, What Good shall I do this Day?	5 6 7 8	Rise, wash, and address *Powerful Goodness;* contrive Day's Business and take the Resolution of the Day; prosecute the present Study: and breakfast. —
	9 10 11	Work.
	12 1	Read, or overlook my Accounts, and dine.
	2 3 4 5	Work.
	6 7 8	Put Things in their Places, Supper, Musick, or Diversion, or Conversation, Examination of the Day.
Evening Question, What Good have I done to-day?	9 10 11 12 1 2 3 4	Sleep. —

. . . My Scheme of Order, gave me the most Trouble, and I found, that tho' it might be practicable where a Man's Business was such as to leave him the Disposition of his Time, that of a Journey-man Printer for instance, it was not possible to be exactly observ'd by a Master, who must mix with the World, and often receive People of Business at their own Hours.—*Order* too, with regard to Places for Things, Papers, &c. I found extreamly difficult to acquire. I had not been early accustomed to it, & having an exceeding good Memory, I was not so sensible of the Inconvenience attending Want of Method. This Article therefore cost me so much painful Attention & my Faults in it vex'd me so much, and I made so little Progress in Amendment, & had such frequent Relapses, that I was almost ready to give up the Attempt, and content my self with a faulty Character in that respect. Like the Man who in buying an Ax of a Smith my Neighbour, desired to have the whole of its Surface as bright as the Edge; the Smith consented to grind it bright for him if he would turn the Wheel. He turn'd while the Smith press'd the broad Face of the Ax hard & heavily on the Stone, which made the Turning of it very fatiguing. The Man came every now & then from the Wheel to see how the Work went on; and at length would take his Ax as it was without farther Grinding. No, says the Smith, Turn on, turn on; we shall have it bright by and by; as yet 'tis only speckled. Yes, says the Man; but—*I think I like a speckled Ax best.*—And I believe this may have been the Case with many who having for want of some such Means as I employ'd found the Difficulty of obtaining good, & breaking bad Habits, in other Points of Vice & Virtue, have given up the Struggle, & concluded that *a speckled Ax was best.* . . . In Truth I found myself incorrigible with respect to *Order;* and now I am grown old, and my Memory bad, I feel very sensibly the want of it. But on the whole, tho' I never arrived at the Perfection I had been so ambitious of obtaining, but fell far short of it, yet I was by the Endeavour made a better and a happier Man that I otherwise should have been, if I had not attempted it.

For Journals

Do you think Franklin would succeed in a business today if he were starting one? Would his skills still be useful?

For Discussion

1. How would you describe Franklin's work ethic? Why does he work hard? What does he get out of his efforts? What are his own assertions about work? Look for supporting evidence in the text—either quotations or accounts of his work experience.

2. Franklin was very open about promoting his reputation as a hard-working and industrious young man. He says, "In order to secure my Credit and Character as a Tradesman, I took care not only to be in *Reality* Industrious & frugal, but to avoid all *Appearances* of the Contrary" (paragraph 4). What relationship do you think there is between his public advertisement of his hard work and his private success? Could he have one without the other? If he did, would that make his achievements less valuable to him? To you?

3. What do you think was Franklin's attitude toward success? How do you think he would have defined it? Would you define it differently? How much of Franklin's definition do you think has to do with money? Would you describe Franklin's idea of success as typically American? Atypically? Why?

4. How does the anecdote Franklin tells about the man who took his ax to a smith to be polished, but eventually took it back partly polished, support or not support the assertions he makes about self-improvement? Why would Franklin tell this story about himself?

5. Franklin believed, at least for a while, that he could get rid of all his bad habits and develop good ones instead. Look at his chart of how he wanted to spend his time every day. How much of this activity do you regard as work?

For Writing

1. Write an essay about your own work ethic. Whatever assertions you make about what you think of work and why it is or isn't important to you, try to be aware of the assumptions you are basing your ideas on. Consider the following questions: How important is making money to you? Is that why you work? Would you work if you didn't need the money? What would you do instead? It might be interesting to make up a chart like Franklin's, using your own assessment of how your time should be divided up daily for you to get the most out of it.

2. Starting with Franklin's *Autobiography*, research and write a paper on Philadelphia in the eighteenth century. Consider, for example, what people did for a living, what cultural institutions there were (aside from the ones that Franklin started himself), the role of the Quaker community, what food people ate, and what houses looked like and how they were furnished.

3. Franklin was the most prolifically talented American of his time, with the possible exception of Thomas Jefferson. Write a paper in which you research one of the following topics: his inventions and their uses; his role as ambassador to France during the American Revolution and his celebrity status there; his other publications, including *Poor Richard's Almanac*; his contributions to the Declaration of Independence and the Constitutional Convention; his troubled relationship with his own son, who supported the British during the Revolution; his political satires; or his antislavery writings.

4. Different audiences and people read the same text very differently. In his book *Studies in Classic American Literature* (1923), the twentieth-century English writer D. H. Lawrence detested Franklin and wrote of him:

> The perfectability of Man! The perfectability of the Ford car! The perfectability of which man? I am many men. Which of them are you going to perfect? I am not a mechanical contrivance. Education! Which of the various me's do you propose to educate, and which do you propose to suppress? . . . Old Daddy Franklin will tell you. He'll rig him up for you, the pattern American. . . . He knew what he was about, the sharp little man. He set up the first dummy American.

Write an essay comparing Lawrence's impression of Franklin with your own view of him, and use Franklin's text for examples. Consider these questions: What values, positive or negative, does Franklin represent to Lawrence? What does Lawrence seem to think the American dream is? Do you think one has to be an American to appreciate Franklin? Why or why not?

∽ FROM *Women and Economics* (1898)

CHARLOTTE PERKINS GILMAN

Born in Hartford, Connecticut, in 1860, Charlotte Perkins Gilman supported herself as an artist, teacher, and governess before discovering her gift for writing. In the 1890s she escaped destitution by publishing short stories like "Similar Cases" and "The Yellow Wallpaper," the latter a harrowing fictionalization of her own experience of nervous breakdown. Women and Economics *appeared in 1898 and was hailed as the most important work of its kind since John Stuart Mill's* Subjugation of Women. *Gilman committed suicide in 1934. She is recognized as one of the intellectual leaders of the women's movement in American history.*

What we do modifies us more than what is done to us. The freedom of expression has been more restricted in women than the freedom of impression, if that be possible. Something of the world she lived in she has seen from her barred windows. Some air has come through the purdah's[1] folds, some knowledge has filtered to her eager ears from the talk of men. Desdemona learned somewhat of Othello. Had she known more, she might have lived longer. But in the ever-

---

[1] Purdah is the Hindu word for hiding or concealing women from strangers by means of a veil or a curtain.

growing human impulse to create, the power and will to make, to do, to express one's new spirit in new forms,—here she has been utterly debarred. She might work as she had worked from the beginning,—at the primitive labors of the household; but in the inevitable expansion of even those industries to professional levels we have striven to hold her back. To work with her own hands, for nothing, in direct body-service to her own family,—this has been permitted,—yes, compelled. But to be and to do anything further from this she has been forbidden. Her labor has not been limited in kind, but in degree. Whatever she has been allowed to do must be done in private and alone, the first-hand industries of savage times. . . .

It is painfully interesting to trace the gradual cumulative effect of these conditions upon women: first, the action of large natural laws, acting on her as they would act on any other animal; then the evolution of social customs and laws (with her position as the active cause), following the direction of mere physical forces, and adding heavily to them; then, with increasing civilization, the unbroken accumulation of precedent, burnt into each generation by the growing force of education, made lovely by art, holy by religion, desirable by habit; and, steadily acting from beneath, the unswerving pressure of economic necessity upon which the whole structure rested. These are strong modifying conditions indeed.

The process would have been even more effective and far less painful but for one important circumstance. Heredity has no Salic law.[2] Each girl child inherits from her father a certain increasing percentage of human development, human power, human tendency; and each boy as well inherits from his mother the increasing percentage of sex-development, sex-power, sex-tendency. The action of heredity has been to equalize what every tendency of environment and education made to differ. This has saved us from such a female as the gypsy moth. It has held up the woman, and held down the man. It has set iron bounds to our absurd effort to make a race with one sex a million years behind the other. But it has added terribly to the pain and difficulty of human life,—a difficulty and a pain that should have taught us long since that we were living on wrong lines. Each woman born, re-humanized by the current of race activity carried on by her father and re-womanized by her traditional position, has had to live over again in her own person the same process of restriction, repression, denial; the smothering "no" which crushed down all her human desires to create, to discover, to learn, to express, to advance. . . .

To the young man confronting life the world lies wide. Such powers as he has he may use, must use. If he chooses wrong at first, he may choose again, and yet again. Not effective or successful in one

---

[2]Law prohibiting a woman from ascending a throne.

channel, he may do better in another. The growing, varied needs of all mankind call on him for the varied service in which he finds his growth. What he wants to be, he may strive to get. What he wants to get, he may strive to get. Wealth, power, social distinction, fame,—what he wants he can try for.

To the young woman confronting life there is the same world beyond, there are the same human energies and human desires and ambition within. But all that she may wish to have, all that she may wish to do, must come through a single channel and a single choice. Wealth, power, social distinction, fame,—not only these, but home and happiness, reputation, ease and pleasure, her bread and butter,—all must come to her through a small gold ring. This is a heavy pressure. It has accumulated behind her through heredity, and continued about her through environment. It has been subtly trained into her through education, till she herself has come to think it a right condition, and pours its influence upon her daughter with increasing impetus. Is it any wonder that women are oversexed? But for the constant inheritance from the more human male, we should have been queen bees, indeed, long before this. But the daughter of the soldier and the sailor, of the artist, the inventor, the great merchant, has inherited in body and brain her share of his development in each generation, and so stayed somewhat human for all her femininity.

For Journals

What is your response to Gilman's first assertion: "What we do modifies us more than what is done to us" (paragraph 1)?

For Discussion

1. According to Gilman, what different kinds of conditions have combined to make women dependent? Do you agree with her? If you do not, would you substitute other reasons to support her conclusion?

2. How do you respond to Gilman's views on heredity and its consequences for creativity in both men and women? Identify her central assertion about heredity, and rephrase it in your own terms. Do you accept her reasoning? What evidence do you have, personal or otherwise, to support or deny it?

3. What assertions does Gilman make about the effect of marriage on women's independence? Why is a gold wedding ring such a heavy burden to her? What do you think she would consider a successful woman's life?

4. Gilman is talking about the situation of middle- and upper-middle-class Victorian women. How valid or invalid do you find her assertions about women, independence, and the need for work today?

How do you think women who work entirely in the home today feel about their independence or the value of their work?

5. What is your evaluation of Gilman's belief that a young man confronting life can try for anything he wants, do any kind of work he wants, and keep getting new opportunities if the work he is doing doesn't suit him? Do you agree? Why or why not?

6. In her book on the history of American housework, *Never Done*, Susan Strasser writes, "When Charlotte Perkins Gilman described the food of her ideal future, she envisioned kitchenless houses; individuals and families would patronize establishments that served hot cooked food ready to eat, produced according to the industrial principles of the division of labor and economies of scale. Eighty years later her dream has come true at McDonald's." From what you have read of Gilman and what you know of McDonald's, how valid is Strasser's assertion?

For Writing

1. Write an essay in which you analyze a major compromise made by your mother, another female relative, a friend, or you for the sake of financial security. The choice can be personal or professional, and you can argue either for or against it, but, even if you disagree with the result, try to be objective. What reasons or assertions were given or assumed in making the trade-off? What values or beliefs supported it? What pressures, economic or otherwise, were brought to bear on the person who made the compromise?

2. Research and write a report to share with your peers about a Victorian American woman who found a way to combine work and marriage, or one who chose work over marriage (for example, political activists Susan B. Anthony and Carrie Chapman Catt, or writers such as Harriet Beecher Stowe, Louisa May Alcott, Kate Chopin, and Edith Wharton). Pay special attention to the economic and social obstacles these women had to struggle with in order to find fulfilling work.

∞ *Two Women Sewing* (ca. 1907)

JACOB RIIS

Jacob Riis (1849–1914) was born in Denmark and emigrated to the United States as a young man. He became famous as a reporter and social crusader whose books about immigrant life in New York at the turn of the century helped mobilize public opinion and educate his readers about the shocking working conditions and poverty in which many immigrants were forced to live. Riis was active in the movements to build

"Sewing and Starving in an Elizabeth Street Attic," c. 1890. Museum of the City of New York, Jacob A. Riis Collection, #146. © Museum of the City of New York.

small parks and playgrounds and to reform tenement houses and schools. His book include How the Other Half Lives *(1890),* The Children of the Poor *(1892),* Children of the Tenements *(1903), and* The Making of an American *(1901). This photograph is from* Children of the Tenements.

For Journals

What other documentary photographs, war photographs, or historical photographs have you seen? What made the greatest impression on you, and why?

For Discussion

1. With no other information except the picture itself, what can you deduce about the working conditions depicted in this photograph? Which details in this picture are the most persuasive in expressing the women's poverty or misery.

2. Describe the contents of this photograph in detail. How similar or different are the two women? How would you describe their body language? Why does including both of them create a more powerful image than just one figure would?

3.   If this picture were in color instead of black and white, what colors do you think would predominate? What are the advantages of using only black and white for documentary pictures? How might color change the overall effect?

For Writing

Jacob Riis was one of the most famous documentary photographers of his time. Look at a book on immigrant life (such as Irving Howe's *World of Our Fathers,* for example), and find another picture by Riis, by Alfred Stieglitz, or by any of the photographers who took pictures of immigrant workers in order to document the conditions under which they lived. Write an essay in which you compare and contrast the Riis picture here with another image of immigrant labor—sweatshop workers, immigrant neighborhoods in New York, street peddlers, and so on. Examine how the figures are arranged, how the background (other people, objects, or interiors) is composed, and how those details contribute to the overall impression. If you think the photographer is exposing an injustice, discuss what the injustice is, how you deduced its nature and seriousness from the photograph, and how persuasive the photograph is to you.

∞ FROM *Going Out* (1994)

DAVID NASAW

David Nasaw (1945–) is a professor of history at the College of Staten Island of the City University of New York. He is the author of Schooled to Order: A Social History of Public Schooling in the United States *(1972) and* Children of the City: At Work and at Play *(1985). This selection is from* Going Out *(1994), a social history of American popular entertainment—vaudeville, amusement parks, etc.—before World War II.*

. . . The rise of public amusements was a by-product of the enormous expansion of the cities. Commercial entertainments were, in this period at least, an urban phenomenon. Their rise and fall were inevitably and inextricably linked to the fortunes of the cities that sustained them.

Between 1870 and 1920, American cities flourished as never before. The urban population of the nation increased from under ten to over fifty-four million people. Per capita income and free time expanded as well. Between 1870 and 1900, real income for nonfarm employees increased by more than 50 percent, while the cost of living, as measured by the consumer price index, decreased by 50 percent. This increase in wages was accompanied by a steady decrease in work hours. The average manufacturing worker worked three and a half hours less in 1910 than in 1890; for many blue-collar workers, unionized employees, and white-collar workers, the decrease in the workweek was even more dramatic. It also was in this period that the Saturday half-holiday and the "vacation habit" arrived in the American city. Although . . . most workers still had to finance their own vacations, increasing numbers of white-collar employees were beginning to take days, even a week or more, off during the warm-weather months.

As Roy Rosenzweig and a generation of labor and social historians have argued, the quest for leisure time "reverberated through the labor struggles of the late nineteenth and early twentieth centuries. As a compositor told the U.S. Senate Committee on Relations Between Labor and Capital in 1883: 'A workingman wants something besides food and clothes in this country. . . . He wants recreation.'" "Going out" was more than an escape from the tedium of work, it was the gateway into a privileged sphere of everyday life. The ability to take time out from work for recreation and public sociability was the dividing line between old worlds and new. Peasants and beasts of burden spent their lives at work; American workers and citizens went out at night and took days off in the summer.

Recreation and play were not luxuries but necessities in the modern city. . . . Instead of the older "interfusion of free and work time," there was now "an increasing segregation of work and play into distinct categories." The fear of idle time as the devil's workshop gave way to a reverence for play, promoted alike by middle-class reformers and working-class organizers. As the Yiddish *Tageblatt* advised its Jewish readers in the spring of 1907, "He who can enjoy and does not enjoy commits a sin."

While all the city's workers, even its most recent immigrants, 5 joined the assembling public for commercial amusements, it was the workers in white collars who constituted the critical element in the construction of the new "nightlife." As the white-collar sector of the work force increased in size in the late nineteenth and early twentieth centuries, so did the potential audience for the new public amusements. In 1880, there had been 5,000 typists and stenographers in the nation. By 1910, the number had increased sixtyfold to 300,000, while the overall clerical work force had risen from 160,000 to more than 1.7 million. From a negligible 2.4 percent of the total work force in 1870, the number of clerical and sales workers grew to a substantial 11 percent by 1920. In the big cities, the percentage of white-collar workers was even greater: 24 percent of the Chicago work force in 1920 were white-collar workers, a large number of them women.

The city's white-collar workers were the most avid consumers of the commercial pleasures. Their work was increasingly regimented, concentrated, and tedious, creating a need for recreation. And, compared to that of blue-collar workers, it provided them with sufficient time, resources, and energy to go out at night. For factory, mill, and manual workers who had to get up at five in the morning to be at work by six, the consequences of a night "out" were considerable. Clerical and sales workers could, on the other hand, stay out late, get a good night's sleep, and still get to work on time.

The new amusements were "public" and "commercial" as well as urban. The terms, in this period at least, became almost interchangeable, as the city's showmen, learning the new calculus of public entertainments, lowered prices to welcome the largest possible audience to their establishments. . . . To succeed in the show business (as it was called throughout this period), the amusement entrepreneurs had to do more than build theaters; they had to provide commercial amusements and amusement sites that were public in the sense that they belonged to no particular social groups, exciting enough to appeal to the millions, and respectable enough to offend no one.

. . . Vaudeville had to be certified as a decent entertainment for mixed audiences, with no relation to the male-only variety show that had preceded it; the amusement parks had to be promoted as "clean" outdoor shows for the whole family; the moving-picture theaters had to be distinguished from the penny arcades and peep shows. The envelope in which it was delivered mattered as much as the content of the show. An otherwise "indecent" act became "decent" when presented in an amusement site certified as "respectable." It was permissible to stare at gyrating belly dancers on the world's fair midways, if the dancers in question were performing "authentic" foreign dances; women in tights or tight-fitting bathing suits could appear on the vaudeville stage, if they were billed as acrobats or championship swimmers; holding onto a member of the opposite sex was acceptable at the amusement park, if it happened "accidentally" on the cyclone.

                              *   *   *

No matter how hungry city folk might have been for cheap amusements or how eager the show businessmen were to provide them, the expansion in commercial amusements could not have occurred without accompanying advances in technology, in particular the electrification of the metropolis . . . the lighting of the city by electricity, the sine qua non for the expansion of urban "nightlife" in the late nineteenth and early twentieth centuries.

Incandescent lighting transformed the city from a dark and   10
treacherous netherworld into a glittering multicolored wonderland. Nineteenth-century authors had described city streets after dark as sinister and filled with danger. The gas lamps did not "light" up the night as much as cast into shadow the disreputable doings and per-

sonages of slum, tenderloin, and levee. In *New York by Gas-Light,* first published in 1850, George Foster, the *New-York Tribune* reporter and best-selling author, described in lurid detail "the fearful mysteries of darkness in the metropolis—the festivities of prostitution, the orgies of pauperism, the haunts of theft and murder, the scenes of drunkenness and beastly debauch, and all the sad realities that go to make up the lower stratum—the under-ground story—of life in New York!". . .

. . . Unlike gas lamps, which were highly flammable, electric lamps could be kept on all night. The street lamps illuminated not simply the lamppost beneath but both sides of the street with a clear, bright white light, not the sooty gray of the gas lamps. The commercial lights of restaurants, shops, and theaters added the merry twinkle that gave the "nocturnal round of business, pleasure and illumination . . . we think of as night life . . . its own special atmosphere."

The artificially illuminated streets provided city residents with an added incentive to leave their darkened or gas-lit flats to go out at night "when all the shop fronts are lighted, and the entrances to the theaters blaze out on the sidewalk like open fireplaces." As the journalist Richard Harding Davis wrote of Broadway in 1892, "It is at this hour that the clerk appears, dressed in his other suit, the one which he keeps for the evening, and the girl bachelor, who . . . has found her hall bedroom cold and lonely after the long working day behind a counter or at a loom and the loneliness tends to homesickness . . . puts on her hat and steps down a side-street and loses herself in the unending processions of Broadway, where, though she knows no one, and no one wants to know her, there is light and color, and she is at least not alone."

Earlier in the nineteenth century, young people who walked the streets after dark would have been admonished for placing themselves in mortal danger of moral contamination. But the electric street lights had gone a long way toward purging "nightlife" of its aura of licentiousness. Although there were no accurate statistics to prove the case, it was taken for granted that the electric street lamps were removing much of the danger that had lurked in the dark. A 1912 article in *The American City* listed first among "the advantages accruing from ornamental street lighting [a decrease in] lawlessness and crime. . . . 'A light is as good as a policeman.' . . . A criminologist of world-wide fame, and one who is considered an authority, says that he would rather have plenty of electric lights and clean streets than all the law and order societies in existence."

Electricity was not simply providing power to light the urban landscape but was reconfiguring it into a fairyland of illuminated shapes, signs, and brightly colored, sometimes animated, messages and images—forty-foot green pickles, gigantic pieces of chewing gum, Roman chariots racing on top of a hotel. The lights of the city created "a new kind of visual text," a new landscape of modernity. They foregrounded the city's illuminated messages, its theaters, tall buildings, hotels, restaurants, department stores, and "Great White Ways," while erasing its "unattractive areas and cast[ing] everything unsightly into an impenetrable darkness. If by day poor or unsightly sections called out for social reform, by night the city was a purified world of light, simplified into a spectacular pattern, interspersed with now-unimportant blanks."

The lights "marked" the city as a "sight" worthy of respect, even 15 admiration. But they also focused attention on the city as a source of amusement. The lighting of the lights signaled that the workday was over and the time for play at hand. . . .

Electrification made going out at night not only safer and more exciting but easier and cheaper than ever before. The dynamos and generators that lit the street lamps also powered the trolleys that tied together the city and its neighborhoods. Between 1890 and 1902, investment in electric and cable cars quadrupled, track mileage tripled, and fare passengers doubled. In 1890, only 15 percent of all American streetcars had been electrified, and the remainder were connected to horses. By 1902, 94 percent were electric. The flat nickel fare and free transfers between lines made streetcar travel accessible to more city residents and workers.

. . . The new "downtowns" were defined geographically by the convergence of the railroad and trolley lines and framed architecturally by the mammoth new terminals that welcomed out-of-towners into the heart of the city. The majority of those who resided temporarily in the nearby hotels had come for business purposes: to buy, sell, insure, inspect, or display their goods. Before, after, and sometimes even during business hours, however, they expected to be entertained. They were joined in this pursuit by white-collar workers who stayed "downtown" after work; by city residents who worked and lived in outlying residential neighborhoods but rode the streetcar to the theater district; and by suburbanites who were linked by electric "interurban" to the city and its nighttime pleasures. For all of them, the city was becoming as much a place of play as a place of work.

For Journals

Do you think of leisure as an entitlement? A privilege? A right? Why?

For Discussion

1. In your own words, state Nasaw's thesis about the development of leisure time in America. Which social and technological evidence does he present to describe this radical change in the lives of working people?

2. How does Nasaw explain the connection between work and leisure time for ordinary Americans? Is it more of a reward for working or a proof of success? Is it a status symbol or a physical necessity? Why shouldn't it continue to be reserved, as it previously had been, for wealthy people to enjoy?

3. What leisure activities that Americans pursue now are the modern parallels for the vaudeville shows and amusement parks that Nasaw describes? What needs to you think those activities fulfill for us now that distinguish us from the Americans whom Nasaw discusses?

4. What do you and your friends spend your leisure time on? Do you think of it as an opportunity to go out, or are you more likely to watch television? How active or passive is your use of free time, and why?

For Writing

1. Write an essay in which you respond to discussion question 4. Explain what your leisure time is for and how you spend it. Use Nasaw's thesis about leisure in America as a basis for comparison. In what ways do your ideas about leisure for Americans in general and for you in particular substantiate or contradict his argument?

2. If you have ever been to Disneyland, Disney World, Universal Studios, Las Vegas, Atlantic City, or any similar place that millions of Americans visit for leisure or vacation, write a description of your visit. Include your observations on who goes there and why, how they behave, whether you thought the entertainment and atmosphere were in good taste, and your own response to the experience. Support your conclusions with details from your own visit.

∞ *Duke Kahanamoku* (1914)

HAWAIIAN TOURIST BOARD

Duke Paoa Kahanamoku (1890–1968) was the greatest swimmer of his time. The winner of three Olympic gold medals, he set three world records in the 100-meter freestyle. After he retired from swimming he acted occasionally in movies, became the sheriff of Honolulu, and was a perpetually popular symbol of the Hawaiian islands.

For Journals

What would be your idea of a perfect place to spend a vacation? Describe in detail your idea of the ideal leisure environment.

For Discussion

1. What image does this postcard give you of Hawaii? Of Duke himself? On what details do you base your impressions?

2. This postcard has an inner picture and an outer border with scenery; how do these two strengthen the card's impact? What adjectives would you use to describe the mood or emotion that results from their interplay?

3. How would you describe Duke's pose—his tense body, clenched fists, and big smile? Is it welcoming? Challenging? Competitive? How does his pose contribute to the impression the tourist board wants to create?

4. Look at the text on the card; how does it tell a tourist that he or she would have a good time in Hawaii? Which American tourist audience do you think would be most attracted by this postcard? What other images of Hawaii might succeed in attracting visitors?

For Writing

This postcard is an early twentieth-century American manifestation of the leisure postcard, advertising various forms of play and vacations accessible to the middle class. Find a current poster (for example, in a travel agency), a postcard, or a magazine advertisement that promotes sports and leisure in Hawaii or anywhere else—Bermuda, the Rockies, New York City, and so on. Write an essay in which you describe the picture, compare it to Duke's postcard, and decide how much, if anything, has changed over seventy-five years in promoting leisure travel. What lifestyle is being advertised? What activity or kind of entertainment? Who is the presumed audience? Does the ad portray an idea of leisure that you find attractive?

∞ *Physical Culture* (1927)

Physical Culture magazine was edited by Bernarr Macfadden (1868–1955), who took it over in 1899. Macfadden was part showman, part entrepreneur, and he had a sensational career in marketing health products and promoting himself as a health guru. He raised the circulation of this monthly magazine from three thousand to one hundred thousand subscribers, partly by using somewhat revealing pictures of women. He also established "healthatoriums" and called himself a professor of psycultopathy and brain breathing.

For Journals

How important are exercise and leisure in your own life?

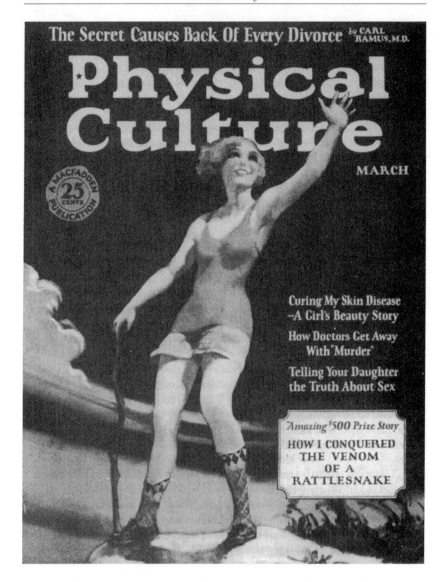

For Discussion

1. Judging from the appearance of the young woman on the cover and what she is wearing, what sport or sports is she supposed to be engaged in? Since she is a standard-bearer for health and exercise, why isn't she shown sweating or working hard?

2. Look at some contemporary exercise and self-improvement magazines, featuring young women on the cover. How is their image of a

healthy woman exercising similar to or different from the way this 1927 cover presents the same subject?

3.   How do you respond to this opinion of the editor of *Physical Culture:* "the individual was always solely responsible for his or her own condition—economic, social, or medical. If taken by some serious disease, people had only themselves to blame"? What attitude do you take toward the idea that you can control the state of your own well-being through your choices and behavior?

4.   Look at the articles listed on the front of the ad; how many of these would be of interest to you? Which ones address concerns relevant to your own experience?

For Writing

Referring back to discussion item 2, look at the covers of several contemporary magazines that advertise youth, health, and attractiveness: *Cosmopolitan, Self, Esquire,* a men's or women's fashion magazine, and so on. Pick one cover, and write an essay in which you compare it with the cover of *Physical Culture.* Look for the rhetorical strategies that underlie each. What is each ad trying to sell? What points do you think the magazine wants to convey to you about the connections between health and attractiveness? Health and youth? How are the topics of the articles listed on the cover of the contemporary magazine similar to or different from those on the *Physical Culture* cover?

∞ *The Chrysanthemums*[1] (1938)

JOHN STEINBECK

John Steinbeck (1902–1968) was born in Salinas, California, and grew up with a strong dislike for what he perceived as the middle-class morality of his hometown and a deep love for the surrounding Monterey Peninsula, its workers, farmers, and fishermen. He attended Stanford University on and off, studying marine biology and taking English classes. He worked as a caretaker in Lake Tahoe, an assistant in a laboratory, a reporter, and so on. His best-known work revolves around the Salinas Valley and Monterey, including Cannery Row, Tortilla Flats, Of Mice and Men, East of Eden, *and the novel with which he will always be associated,* The Grapes of Wrath *(1939). His ongoing interest was in the inherent heroism of ordinary people, especially under the pressure of social crisis. Steinbeck was awarded the Nobel Prize for Literature in 1962.*

---

[1]"The Chrysanthemums" was first collected in *The Long Valley* (1938).

The high grey-flannel fog of winter closed off the Salinas Valley from the sky and from all the rest of the world. On every side it sat like a lid on the mountains and made of the great valley a closed pot. On the broad, level land floor the gang plows bit deep and left the black earth shining like metal where the shares had cut. On the foothill ranches across the Salinas River, the yellow stubble fields seemed to be bathed in pale cold sunshine, but there was no sunshine in the valley now in December. The thick willow scrub along the river flamed with sharp and positive yellow leaves.

It was a time of quiet and of waiting. The air was cold and tender. A light wind blew up from the southwest so that the farmers were mildly hopeful of a good rain before long; but fog and rain do not go together.

Across the river, on Henry Allen's foothill ranch there was little work to be done, for the hay was cut and stored and the orchards were plowed up to receive the rain deeply when it should come. The cattle on the higher slopes were becoming shaggy and rough-coated.

Elisa Allen, working in her flower garden, looked down across the yard and saw Henry, her husband, talking to two men in business suits. The three of them stood by the tractor shed, each man with one foot on the side of the little Fordson. They smoked cigarettes and studied the machine as they talked.

Elisa watched them for a moment and then went back to her work. 5 She was thirty-five. Her face was lean and strong and her eyes were as clear as water. Her figure looked blocked and heavy in her gardening costume, a man's black hat pulled low down over her eyes, clodhopper shoes, a figured print dress almost completely covered by a big corduroy apron with four big pockets to hold the snips, the trowel and scratcher, the seeds and the knife she worked with. She wore heavy leather gloves to protect her hands while she worked.

She was cutting down the old year's chrysanthemum stalks with a pair of short and powerful scissors. She looked down toward the men by the tractor shed now and then. Her face was eager and mature and handsome; even her work with the scissors was over-eager, over-powerful. The chrysanthemum stems seemed too small and easy for her energy.

She brushed a cloud of hair out of her eyes with the back of her glove, and left a smudge of earth on her cheek in doing it. Behind her stood the neat white farm house with red geraniums close-banked around it as high as the windows. It was a hard-swept looking little house, with hard-polished windows, and a clean mud-mat on the front steps.

Elisa cast another glance toward the tractor shed. The strangers were getting into their Ford coupe. She took off a glove and put her strong fingers down into the forest of new green chrysanthemum sprouts that were growing around the old roots. She spread the leaves and looked down among the close-growing stems. No aphids were there, no sowbugs or snails or cutworms. Her terrier fingers destroyed such pests before they could get started.

Elisa started at the sound of her husband's voice. He had come near quietly, and he leaned over the wire fence that protected her flower garden from cattle and dogs and chickens.

"At it again," he said. "You've got a strong new crop coming."   10

Elisa straightened her back and pulled on the gardening glove again. "Yes. They'll be strong this coming year." In her tone and on her face there was a little smugness.

"You've got a gift with things," Henry observed. "Some of those yellow chrysanthemums you had this year were ten inches across. I wish you'd work out in the orchard and raise some apples that big."

Her eyes sharpened. "Maybe I could do it, too. I've a gift with things, all right. My mother had it. She could stick anything in the ground and make it grow. She said it was having planters' hands that knew how to do it."

"Well, it sure works with flowers," he said.

"Henry, who were those men you were talking to?"   15

"Why, sure, that's what I came to tell you. They were from the Western Meat company. I sold those thirty head of three-year-old steers. Got nearly my own price, too."

"Good," she said. "Good for you."

"And I thought," he continued, "I thought how it's Saturday afternoon, and we might go into Salinas for dinner at a restaurant, and then to a picture show—to celebrate, you see."

"Good," she repeated. "Oh, yes. That will be good."

Henry put on his joking tone. "There's fights tonight. How'd you   20
like to go to the fights?"

"Oh, no," she said breathlessly. "No, I wouldn't like fights."

"Just fooling, Elisa. We'll go to a movie. Let's see. It's two now. I'm going to take Scotty and bring down those steers from the hill. It'll take us maybe two hours. We'll go in town about five and have dinner at the Cominos Hotel. Like that?"

"Of course I'll like it. It's good to eat away from home."

"All right, then. I'll go get up a couple of horses."

She said, "I'll have plenty of time to transplant some of these sets, I   25
guess."

She heard her husband calling Scotty down by the barn. And a little later she saw the two men ride up the pale yellow hillside in search of the steers.

There was a little square sandy bed kept for rooting the chrysanthemums. With her trowel she turned the soil over and over, and smoothed it and patted it firm. Then she dug ten parallel trenches to

receive the sets. Back at the chrysanthemum bed she pulled out the little crisp shoots, trimmed off the leaves of each one with her scissors
and laid it on a small orderly pile.

A squeak of wheels and plod of hoofs came from the road. Elisa
looked up. The country road ran along the dense bank of willows and
cottonwoods that bordered the river, and up this road came a curious
vehicle, curiously drawn. It was an old spring-wagon, with a round
canvas top on it like the cover of a prairie schooner. It was drawn by
an old bay horse and a little grey-and-white burro. A big stubble-
bearded man sat between the cover flaps and drove the crawling team.
Underneath the wagon, between the hind wheels, a lean and rangy
mongrel dog walked sedately. Words were painted on the canvas, in
clumsy, crooked letters. "Pots, pans, knives, sisors, lawn mores,
Fixed." Two rows of articles, and the triumphantly definitive "Fixed"
below. The black paint had run down in little sharp points beneath
each letter.

Elisa, squatting on the ground, watched to see the crazy, loose-
jointed wagon pass by. But it didn't pass. It turned into the farm road
in front of her house, crooked old wheels skirling and squeaking. The
rangy dog darted from between the wheels and ran ahead. Instantly
the two ranch shepherds flew out at him. Then all three stopped, and
with stiff and quivering tails, with taut straight legs, with ambassador-
ial dignity, they slowly circled, sniffing daintily. The caravan pulled
up to Elisa's wire fence and stopped. Now the newcomer dog, feeling
out-numbered, lowered his tail and retired under the wagon with
raised hackles and bared teeth.

The man on the wagon seat called out, "That's a bad dog in a fight 30
when he gets started."

Elisa laughed. "I see he is. How soon does he generally get
started?"

The man caught up her laughter and echoed it heartily. "Sometimes not for weeks and weeks," he said. He climbed stiffly down,
over the wheel. The horse and the donkey drooped like unwatered
flowers.

Elisa saw that he was a very big man. Although his hair and beard
were greying, he did not look old. His worn black suit was wrinkled
and spotted with grease. The laughter had disappeared from his face
and eyes the moment his laughing voice ceased. His eyes were dark, and
they were full of the brooding that gets in the eyes of teamsters and of
sailors. The calloused hands he rested on the wire fence were cracked,
and every crack was a black line. He took off his battered hat.

"I'm off my general road, ma'am," he said. "Does this dirt road
cut over across the river to the Los Angeles highway?"

Elisa stood up and shoved the thick scissors in her apron pocket. 35
"Well, yes, it does, but it winds around and then fords the river. I
don't think your team could pull through the sand."

He replied with some asperity, "It might surprise you what them beasts can pull through."

"When they get started?" she asked.

He smiled for a second. "Yes. When they get started."

"Well," said Elisa, "I think you'll save time if you go back to the Salinas road and pick up the highway there."

He drew a big finger down the chicken wire and made it sing. "I 40 ain't in any hurry, ma'am. I go from Seattle to San Diego and back every year. Takes all my time. About six months each way. I aim to follow nice weather."

Elisa took off her gloves and stuffed them in the apron pocket with the scissors. She touched the under edge of her man's hat, searching for fugitive hairs. "That sounds like a nice kind of a way to live," she said.

He leaned confidentially over the fence. "Maybe you noticed the writing on my wagon. I mend pots and sharpen knives and scissors. You got any of them things to do?"

"Oh, no," she said quickly. "Nothing like that." Her eyes hardened with resistance.

"Scissors is the worst thing," he explained. "Most people just ruin scissors trying to sharpen 'em, but I know how. I got a special tool. It's a little bobbit kind of thing, and patented. But it sure does the trick."

"No. My scissors are all sharp." 45

"All right, then. Take a pot," he continued earnestly, "a bent pot, or a pot with a hole. I can make it like new so you don't have to buy no new ones. That's a saving for you."

"No," she said shortly. "I tell you I have nothing like that for you to do."

His face fell to an exaggerated sadness. His voice took on a whining undertone. "I ain't had a thing to do today. Maybe I won't have no supper tonight. You see I'm off my regular road. I know folks on the highway clear from Seattle to San Diego. They save their things for me to sharpen up because they know I do it so good and save them money."

"I'm sorry," Elisa said irritably. "I haven't anything for you to do."

His eyes left her face and fell to searching the ground. They 50 roamed about until they came to the chrysanthemum bed where she had been working. "What's them plants, ma'am?"

The irritation and resistance melted from Elisa's face. "Oh, those are chrysanthemums, giant whites and yellows. I raise them every year, bigger than anybody around here."

"Kind of a long-stemmed flower? Looks like a quick puff of colored smoke?" he asked.

"That's it. What a nice way to describe them."

"They smell kind of nasty till you get used to them," he said.

"It's a good bitter smell," she retorted, "not nasty at all." 55

He changed his tone quickly. "I like the smell myself."

"I had ten-inch blooms this year," she said.

The man leaned farther over the fence. "Look. I know a lady down the road a piece, has got the nicest garden you ever seen. Got nearly every kind of flower but no chrysanthemums. Last time I was mending a copper-bottom washtub for her (that's a hard job but I do it good), she said to me, 'If you ever run acrost some nice chrysanthemums I wish you'd try to get me a few seeds.' That's what she told me."

Elisa's eyes grew alert and eager. "She couldn't have known much about chrysanthemums. You can raise them from seed, but it's much easier to root the little sprouts you see there."

"Oh," he said., "I s'pose I can't take none to her, then." 60

"Why yes you can," Elisa cried. "I can put some in damp sand, and you can carry them right along with you. They'll take root in the pot if you keep them damp. And then she can transplant them."

"She'd sure like to have some, ma'am. You say they're nice ones?"

"Beautiful," she said. "Oh, beautiful." Her eyes shone. She tore off the battered hat and shook out her dark pretty hair. "I'll put them in a flower pot, and you can take them right with you. Come into the yard."

While the man came through the picket gate Elisa ran excitedly along the geranium-bordered path to the back of the house. And she returned carrying a big red flower pot. The gloves were forgotten now. She kneeled on the ground by the starting bed and dug up the sandy soil with her fingers and scooped it into the bright new flower pot. Then she picked up the little pile of shoots she had prepared. With her strong fingers she pressed them into the sand and tamped around them with her knuckles. The man stood over her. "I'll tell you what to do," she said. "You remember so you can tell the lady."

"Yes, I'll try to remember." 65

"Well, look. These will take root in about a month. Then she must set them out, about a foot apart in good rich earth like this, see?" She lifted a handful of dark soil for him to look at. "They'll grow fast and tall. Now remember this: In July tell her to cut them down, about eight inches from the ground."

"Before they bloom?" he asked.

"Yes, before they bloom." Her face was tight with eagerness. "They'll grow right up again. About the last of September the buds will start."

She stopped and seemed perplexed. "It's the budding that takes the most care," she said hesitantly. "I don't know how to tell you." She looked deep into his eyes, searchingly. Her mouth opened a little, and she seemed to be listening. "I'll try to tell you," she said. "Did you ever hear of planting hands?"

"Can't say I have, ma'am."   70

"Well, I can only tell you what it feels like. It's when you're pick-ing off the buds you don't want. Everything goes right down into your fingertips. You watch your fingers work. They do it themselves. You can feel how it is. They pick and pick the buds. They never make a mistake. They're with the plant. Do you see? Your fingers and the plant. You can feel that, right up your arm. They know. They never make a mistake. You can feel it. When you're like that you can't do anything wrong. Do you see that? Can you understand that?"

She was kneeling on the ground looking up at him. Her breast swelled passionately.

The man's eyes narrowed. He looked away self-consciously. "Maybe I know," he said. "Sometimes in the night in the wagon there—"

Elisa's voice grew husky. She broke in on him, "I've never lived as you do, but I know what you mean. When the night is dark—why, the stars are sharp-pointed, and there's quiet. Why, you rise up and up! Every pointed star gets driven into your body. It's like that. Hot and sharp and—lovely."

Kneeling there, her hand went out toward his legs in the greasy   75
black trousers. Her hesitant fingers almost touched the cloth. Then her hand dropped to the ground. She crouched low like a fawning dog.

He said, "It's nice, just like you say. Only when you don't have no dinner, it ain't."

She stood up then, very straight, and her face was ashamed. She held the flower pot out to him and placed it gently in his arms. "Here. Put it in your wagon, on the seat, where you can watch it. Maybe I can find something for you to do."

At the back of the house she dug in the can pile and found two old and battered aluminum saucepans. She carried them back and gave them to him. "Here, maybe you can fix these."

His manner changed. He became professional. "Good as new I can fix them." At the back of his wagon he set a little anvil, and out of an oily tool box dug a small machine hammer. Elisa came through the gate to watch him while he pounded out the dents in the kettles. His mouth grew sure and knowing. At a difficult part of the work he sucked his under-lip.

"You sleep right in the wagon?" Elisa asked.   80

"Right in the wagon, ma'am. Rain or shine I'm dry as a cow in there."

"It must be nice," she said. "It must be very nice. I wish women could do such things."

"It ain't the right kind of a life for a woman."

Her upper lip raised a little, showing her teeth. "How do you know? How can you tell?" she said.

"I don't know, ma'am," he protested. "Of course I don't know. 85
Now here's your kettles, done. You don't have to buy no new ones."

"How much?"

"Oh, fifty cents'll do. I keep my prices down and my work good.
That's why I have all them satisfied customers up and down the
highway."

Elisa brought him a fifty-cent piece from the house and dropped it
in his hand. "You might be surprised to have a rival some time. I can
sharpen scissors, too. And I can beat the dents out of little pots. I could
show you what a woman might do."

He put his hammer back in the oily box and shoved the little anvil
out of sight. "It would be a lonely life for a woman, ma'am, and a
scarey life, too, with animals creeping under the wagon all night." He
climbed over the singletree, steadying himself with a hand on the bur-
row's white rump. He settled himself in the seat, picked up the lines,
"Thank you kindly, ma'am," he said. "I'll do like you told me; I'll go
back and catch the Salinas road."

"Mind," she called, "if you're long in getting there, keep the sand 90
damp."

"Sand, ma'am? . . . Sand? Oh, sure. You mean around the chrysanthemums. Sure I will." He clucked his tongue. The beasts leaned luxuriously into their collars. The mongrel dog took his place between the
back wheels. The wagon turned and crawled out the entrance road
and back the way it had come, along the river.

Elisa stood in front of her wire fence watching the slow progress
of the caravan. Her shoulders were straight, her head thrown back, her
eyes half-closed, so that the scene came vaguely into them. Her lips
moved silently, forming the words "Good-bye—good-bye." Then she
whispered, "That's a bright direction. There's a glowing there." The
sound of her whisper startled her. She shook herself free and looked
about to see whether anyone had been listening. Only the dogs had
heard. They lifted their heads toward her from their sleeping in the
dust, and then stretched out their chins and settled asleep again. Elisa
turned and ran hurriedly into the house.

In the kitchen she reached behind the stove and felt the water
tank. It was full of hot water from the noonday cooking. In the bathroom she tore off her soiled clothes and flung them into the corner.
And then she scrubbed herself with a little block of pumice, legs and
thighs, loins and chest and arms, until her skin was scratched and
red. When she had dried herself she stood in front of a mirror in her
bedroom and looked at her body. She tightened her stomach and
threw out her chest. She turned and looked over her shoulder at her
back.

After a while she began to dress, slowly. She put on her newest
underclothing and her nicest stockings and the dress which was the

symbol of her prettiness. She worked carefully on her hair, penciled her eyebrows and rouged her lips.

Before she was finished she heard the little thunder of hoofs and 95 the shouts of Henry and his helper as they drove the red steers into the corral. She heard the gate bang shut and set herself for Henry's arrival.

His step sounded on the porch. He entered the house calling, "Elisa, where are you?"

"In my room, dressing. I'm not ready. There's hot water for your bath. Hurry up. It's getting late."

When she heard him splashing in the tub, Elisa laid his dark suit on the bed, and shirt and socks and tie beside it. She stood his polished shoes on the floor beside the bed. Then she went to the porch and sat primly and stiffly down. She looked toward the river road where the willow-line was still yellow with frosted leaves so that under the high grey fog they seemed a thin band of sunshine. This was the only color in the grey afternoon. She sat unmoving for a long time. Her eyes blinked rarely.

Henry came banging out of the door, shoving his tie inside his vest as he came. Elisa stiffened and her face grew tight. Henry stopped short and looked at her. "Why—why, Elisa. You look so nice!"

"Nice? You think I look nice? What do you mean by 'nice'?" 100

Henry blundered on. "I don't know. I mean you look different, strong and happy."

"I am strong? Yes, strong. What do you mean 'strong'?"

He looked bewildered. "You're playing some kind of a game," he said helplessly. "It's a kind of a play. You look strong enough to break a calf over your knee, happy enough to eat it like a watermelon."

For a second she lost her rigidity. "Henry! Don't talk like that. You didn't know what you said." She grew complete again. "I'm strong," she boasted. "I never knew before how strong."

Henry looked down toward the tractor shed, and when he 105 brought his eyes back to her, they were his own again. "I'll get out the car. You can put on your coat while I'm starting."

Elisa went into the house. She heard him drive to the gate and idle down his motor, and then she took a long time to put on her hat. She pulled it here and pressed it there. When Henry turned the motor off she slipped into her coat and went out.

The little roadster bounced along on the dirt road by the river, raising the birds and driving the rabbits into the brush. Two cranes flapped heavily over the willow-line and dropped into the river-bed.

Far ahead on the road Elisa saw a dark speck. She knew.

She tried not to look as they passed it, but her eyes would not obey. She whispered to herself sadly, "He might have thrown them off the road. That wouldn't have been much trouble, not very much. But he kept the pot," she explained. "He had to keep the pot. That's why he couldn't get them off the road."

The roadster turned a bend and she saw the caravan ahead. She 110
swung full around toward her husband so she could not see the little
covered wagon and the mismatched team as the car passed them.

In a moment it was over. The thing was done. She did not look
back.

She said loudly, to be heard above the motor, "It will be good,
tonight, a good dinner."

"Now you're changed again," Henry complained. He took one
hand from the wheel and patted her knee. "I ought to take you in to
dinner oftener. It would be good for both of us. We get so heavy out
on the ranch."

"Henry," she asked, "could we have wine at dinner?"

"Sure we could. Say! That will be fine."   115

She was silent for a while; then she said, "Henry, at those prize
fights, do the men hurt each other very much?"

"Sometimes a little, not often. Why?"

"Well, I've read how they break noses, and blood runs down their
chests. I've read how the fighting gloves get heavy and soggy with
blood."

He looked around at her. "What's the matter, Elisa? I didn't know
you read things like that." He brought the car to a stop, then turned to
the right over the Salinas River bridge.

"Do any women ever go to the fights?" she asked.   120

"Oh, sure, some. What's the matter, Elisa? Do you want to go? I
don't think you'd like it, but I'll take you if you really want to go."

She relaxed limply in the seat. "Oh, no. No. I don't want to go. I'm
sure I don't." Her face was turned away from him. "It will be enough
if we can have wine. It will be plenty." She turned up her coat collar so
he could not see that she was crying weakly—like an old woman.

For Journals

Do you believe that your own work would be just as valuable if you
did it for nothing, or do you think that being paid confers status on it?

For Discussion

1.   What reasons can you think of for choosing this particular title for
the story?

2.   Look closely at the scene in which she talks to the man on the
wagon. How does he manipulate her? Look for specific exchanges between them, and for turning points in Elisa's attitude toward him.

3.   Agree or disagree with the following two assertions: (a) Elisa is betrayed by both the stranger and by her husband, and (b) Elisa's love
for the flowers is her hobby.

4. Why is Elisa so hurt by the sight of the flowers on the road? How does Steinbeck prepare us for her reaction at the end the story?

For Writing

1. Write an essay in which you compare this story with Studs Terkel's interview with the stonemason, Mr. Bates, later in this chapter. Consider such questions as: What does their work mean to each of them? What kind of satisfaction does each draw from it? Which work situation would you prefer, Mr. Bates's or Elisa's? Why? Use the text as evidence so that your answers will be specific.

2. Write an essay based on discussion 2 above. Be sure to support your assertions about the nature of the exchange between Elisa and the man with quotes from the text, and include close readings of at least two passages, i.e., look at each sentence in the passage and try to locate the turning points, the changes in emotion, Elisa's frame of mind, and how the man uses her love of flowers to get what he wants.

∞ *Union Maid* (1940)

WOODY GUTHRIE

Woody Guthrie (1912–1967) was probably the greatest of all American folk-singers and composers. A native of Oklahoma, he spent most of his life on the road, hitching rides on freight trains or living in migrant worker camps. In hundreds of songs, he detailed the experiences of Americans caught in the throes of economic dislocation during the Great Depression: migrant workers, union organizers, wanderers and hobos, and particularly people forced to move from Oklahoma by the terrible dust storms of the 1930s. His most famous song, "This Land Is Your Land," has become a sort of informal national anthem.

> There once was a union maid
> Who never was afraid
> Of goons and ginks and company finks
> And the deputy sheriffs who made the raids;
> She went to the union hall   5
> When a meeting it was called,
> And when the company boys came 'round
> She always stood her ground.
>
> CHORUS:
> Oh, you can't scare me.   10
> I'm sticking to the union,

I'm sticking to the union,
I'm sticking to the union.
Oh, you can't scare me.
I'm sticking to the union,   15
I'm sticking to the union
Till the day I die.

This union maid was wise
To the tricks of company spies.
She never got fooled by a company stool,   20
She'd always organize the guys.
She always got her way
When she struck for higher pay,
She'd show her union card to the company guard
And this is what she'd say: 25

You gals who want to be free,
Just take a little tip from me:
Get you a man who's a union man
And join the Ladies' Auxiliary;
Married life ain't hard   30
When you've got a union card,
A union man has a happy life
When he's got a union wife.

For Journals

What songs do you associate with a specific event, cause, or place in
your life?

For Discussion

1. Describe the intended audience for this song. Is it aimed at people
similar to the characters in the song? Where can you imagine Guthrie
singing it, and why?

2. Given the subject matter, why do you think the song is written
from the point of view of a woman rather than a man? In what ways is
a woman's perspective presented in the song as similar to or different
from a man's? Would using a female narrator broaden or lessen its appeal to its intended audience?

3. Judging from the lyrics, what tactics were involved in discouraging the formation of unions? Guthrie made no secret of where his
sympathies lay. How does he convey them to you? How does he
characterize the other side? How persuasive is he?

For Writing

1. A lot of Guthrie's music was based on specific historical situations, such as the battle between pro- and antiunion forces or the effects of the Great Depression on farmers in the Midwest. But many of the songs have entered the larger culture. If you can get a tape or CD of Guthrie's music, listen to some of his other songs, such as "This Land Is Your Land." Pick two or three of the most popular songs, and write an essay in which you comment on their message, the effectiveness of the lyrics, and your description of the intended audience. What emotions is he expressing? In what sense is his evocation of America one that you recognize?

2. Songs are invariably associated with crucial developments in American history. Research the music related to one event—for example, the Civil War, World War I or II, the Great Depression, the Vietnam War. Write an essay in which you explain the circumstances in which it was written or became popular, the positive and negative reactions of audiences, the cause or event with which it was associated, and the ideas it represented.

∽ FROM *Working* (1972)

STUDS TERKEL

Studs Terkel (1912–) grew up and still lives in Chicago. Having worked as a disc jockey and a sports commentator, among other jobs, he has for many years hosted a daily interview program, which is broadcast all over the country; for a writer to be interviewed by Mr. Terkel is considered a great honor. Mr. Terkel is the author of several books, including Division Street: America *(1967),* The Good War *(1984), and* Hard Times *(1970). All of them use interviews with Americans from all walks of life to reveal the effect of historic events, like the Depression and World War II, on the lives of individuals. The following selection is from his book about Americans and what they do for a living, called* Working *(1974).*

The Mason

Carl Murray Bates

We're in a tavern no more than thirty yards from the banks of the Ohio. Toward the far side of the river, Alcoa smokestacks belch forth: an uneasy coupling of a bucolic past and an industrial present. The waters are polluted, yet the jobs out there offer the townspeople their daily bread.

He is fifty-seven years old. He's a stonemason who has pursued his craft since he was seventeen. None of his three sons is in his trade.

As far as I know, masonry is older than carpentry, which goes clear back to Bible times. Stone mason goes back way *before* Bible time: the pyramids of Egypt, things of that sort. Anybody that starts to build anything stone, rock, or brick, start on the northeast corner. Because when they built King Solomon's Temple, they started on the northeast corner. To this day, you look at your courthouses, your big public buildings, you look at the cornerstone, when it was created, what year, it will be on the northeast corner. If I was gonna build a septic tank, I would start on the northeast corner. (Laugh). Superstition, I suppose.

With stone we build just about anything. Stone is the oldest and best building material that ever was. Stone was being used even by the cavemen that put it together with mud. They built out of stone before they even used logs. He got him a cave, he built stone across the front. And he learned to use dirt, mud, to make the stones lay there without sliding around—which was the beginnings of mortar, which we still call mud. The Romans used mortar that's almost as good as we have today.

Everyone hears these things, they just don't remember 'em. But me being in the profession, when I hear something in that line, I remember it. Stone's my business. I, oh, sometimes talk to architects and engineers that have made a study and I pick up the stuff here and there.

Every piece of stone you pick up is different, the grain's a little different and this and that. It'll split one way and break the other. You pick up your stone and look at it and make an educated guess. It's a pretty good day layin' stone or brick. Not tiring. Anything you like to do isn't tiresome. It's hard work; stone is heavy. At the same time, you get interested in what you're doing and you usually fight the clock the other way. You're not lookin' for quittin'. You're wondering you haven't got enough done and it's almost quittin' time. (Laughs). I ask the hod carrier what time it is and he says two thirty. I say, "Oh, my Lord, I was gonna get a whole lot more than this."

I pretty well work by myself. On houses, usually just one works. 5 I've got the hod carrier there, but most of the time I talk to myself, "I'll get my hammer and I'll knock the chip off there." (Laughs.) A good hod carrier is half your day. He won't work as hard as a poor one. He knows what to do and make very move count makin' the mortar. It has to be so much water, so much sand. His skill is to see that you don't run out of anything. The hod carrier, he's above the laborer. He has a certain amount of prestige.

I think a laborer feels that he's the low man. Not so much that he works with his hands, it's that he's at the bottom of the scale. He always wants to get up to a skilled trade. Of course he'd make more money. The main thing is the common laborer—even the word *common* laborer—just sounds so common, he's at the bottom. Many that works with his hands takes pride in his work.

I get a lot of phone calls when I get home: how about showin' me how and I'll do it myself? I always wind up doin' it for 'em. (Laughs.) So I take a lot of pride in it and I do get, oh, I'd say, a lot of praise or whatever you want to call it. I don't suppose anybody, however much he's recognized, wouldn't like to be recognized a little more. I think I'm pretty well recognized.

One of my sons is an accountant and the other two are bankers. They're mathematicians, I suppose you'd call 'em that. Air-conditioned offices and all that. They always look at the house I build. They stop by and see me when I'm aworkin'. Always want me to come down and fix somethin' on their house, too. (Laughs.) They don't buy a house that I don't have to look at it first. Oh sure, I've got to crawl under it and look on the roof, you know. . . .

I can't seem to think of any young masons. So many of 'em before, the man lays stone and his son follows his footsteps. Right now the only one of these sons I can think of is about forty, fifty years old.

I started back in the Depression times when there wasn't any ap- 10 prenticeships. You just go out and if you could hold your job, that's it. I was just a kid then. Now I worked real hard and carried all the blocks I could. Then I'd get my trowel and I'd lay one or two. The second day the boss told me: I think you could lay enough blocks to earn you wages. So I guess I had only one day of apprenticeship. Usually it takes about three years of being a hod carrier to start. And it takes another ten or fifteen years to learn the skill.

I admired the men that we had at that time that were stonemasons. They knew their trade. So naturally I tried to pattern after them. There's been very little change in the work. Stone is still stone, mortar is still the same as it was fifty years ago. The style of stone has changed a little. We use a lot more, we call it golf. A stone as big as a baseball up to as big as a basketball. Just round balls and whatnot. We just fit 'em in the wall that way.

Automation has tried to get in the bricklayer. Set 'em with a crane. I've seen several put up that way. But you've always got in-between the windows and this and that. It just doesn't seem to pan out. We do have a power saw. We do have an electric power mix to mix the mortar, but the rest of it's done by hand as it always was.

In the old days they all seemed to want it cut out and smoothed. It's harder now because you have no way to use your tools. You have no way to use a string, you have no way to use a level or a plumb. You just have to look at it because it's so rough and many irregularities. You have to just back up and look at it.

All construction, there's always a certain amount of injuries. A scaffold will break and so on. But practically no real danger. All I ever did do was work on houses, so we don't get up very high—maybe two stories. Very seldom that any more. Most of 'em are one story. And so many of 'em use stone for a trim. They may go up four, five feet and then paneling or something. There's a lot of skinned fingers or you hit your finger with a hammer. Practically all stone is worked with hammers and chisels. I wouldn't call it dangerous at all.

Stone's my life. I daydream all the time, most times it's on stone. Oh, I'm gonna build me a stone cabin down on the Green River. I'm gonna build stone cabinets in the kitchen. That stone door's gonna be awful heavy and I don't know how to attach the hinges. I've got to figure out how to make a stone roof. That's the kind of thing. All my dreams, it seems like it's got to have a piece of rock mixed in it.

If I got some problem that's bothering me, I'll actually wake up in the night and think of it. I'll sit at the table and get a pencil and paper and go over it, makin' marks on paper or drawin' or however . . . this way or that way. Now I've got to work this and I've only got so much. Or they decided they want it that way when you already got it fixed this way. Anyone hates tearing his work down. It's all the same price but you still don't like to do it.

These fireplaces, you've got to figure how they'll throw out heat, the way you curve the fireboxes inside. You have to draw a line so they reflect heat. But if you throw out too much of a curve, you'll have them smoke. People in these fine houses don't want a puff of smoke coming out of the house.

The architect draws the picture and the plans, and the draftsman and the engineer, they help him. They figure the strength and so on. But when it comes to actually makin' the curves and doin' the work, you've got to do it with your hands. It comes right back to your hands.

When you get into stone, you're getting' away from the prefabs, you're getting' into the better homes. Usually at this day and age they'll start into sixty to seventy thousand and run up to about half a million. We've got one goin' now that's mighty close, three or four hundred thousand. That type of house is what we build.

The lumber is not near as good as it used to be. We have better fabricating material, such as plywood and sheet rock and things of that sort, but the lumber itself is definitely inferior. Thirty, forty years ago a house was almost entirely made of lumber, wood floors. . . . Now they have vinyl, they have carpet, everything, and so on. The framework wood is getting to be of very poor quality.

But stone is still stone and the bricks are actually more uniform than they used to be. Originally they took a clay bank . . . I know a church been built that way. Went right on location, dug a hole in the ground and formed bricks with their hands. They made the bricks that built the building on the spot.

Now we've got modern kilns, modern heat, the temperature don't vary. They got better bricks now than they used to have. We've got machines that make brick, so they're made true. Where they used to, they were pretty rough. I'm buildin' a big fireplace now out of old brick. They run wide, long, and it's a headache. I've been two weeks on that one fireplace.

The toughest job I ever done was this house, a hundred years old plus. The lady wanted one room left just that way. And this doorway had to be closed. It had deteriorated and weathered for over a hundred years. The bricks was made out of broken pieces, none of 'em were straight. If you lay 'em crooked, it gets awful hard right there. You spend a lifetime tryin' to learn to lay bricks straight. And it took a half-day to measure with a spoon, to try to get the mortar to match. I'd have so much dirt, so much soot, so much lime, so when I got the recipe right I could make it in bigger quantity. Then I made it with a coffee cup. Half a cup of this, half a cup of that . . . I even used soot out of a chimney and sweepin's off the floor. I was two days layin' up a little doorway, mixin' the mortar and all. The boss told the lady it couldn't be done. I said, "Give me the time, I believe I can do it." I defy you to find where that door is right now. That's the best job I ever done.

There's not a house in this country that I haven't built that I don't look at every time I go by. (Laughs.) I can set here now and actually in my mind see so many that you wouldn't believe. If there's one stone in there crooked, I know where it's at and I'll never forget it. Maybe thirty years, I'll know a place where I should have took that stone out and redone it but I didn't. I still notice it. The people who live there might not notice it, but I notice it. I never pass that house that I don't think of it. I've got one house in mind right now. (Laughs.) That's the work of my hands. 'Cause you see, stone, you don't prepaint it, you don't camouflage it. It's there, just like I left it forty years ago.

I can't imagine a job where you go home and maybe go by a year 25 later and you don't know what you've done. My work, I can see what I did the first day I started. All my work is set right out there in the open and I can look at it as I go by. It's something I can see the rest of my life. Forty years ago, the first blocks I ever laid in my life, when I was seventeen years old. I never go through Eureka—a little town down there on the river—that I don't look thataway. It's always there.

Immortality as far as we're concerned. Nothin' in this world lasts forever, but did you know that stone—Bedford limestone, they claim—deteriorates one-sixteenth of an inch every hundred years? And it's around four or five inches for a house. So that's gettin' awful close. (Laughs.)

For Journals

What skills or knowledge of a craft do you have or would you like to have?

For Discussion

1.   Usually the word *professional* is used to describe jobs that require a college education or advanced degrees. Judging from the text of this interview, explain Mr. Bates's sense of pride in his job. In what ways is he a professional?

2.   What do you think of the status hierarchy Mr. Bates sets up among levels of workers? Between him and his own sons who have white-collar jobs?

3.   How does Terkel's decision to call this interview "The Mason" instead of "Mr. Bates" establish his attitude toward Mr. Bates and his work? How does it affect your own attitude toward Mr. Bates?

4.   Looking at the text, identify the assertions Mr. Bates makes to connect the history of masonry and the possibilities for achieving immortality. Are those possibilities affected by the fact that no young masons are following in his footsteps? Is that irrelevant? Why or why not?

For Writing

1.   In the excerpt from his *Autobiography* at the beginning of this chapter, Franklin mentions how much he loved watching craftsmen do their work. Write an essay in which you compare Franklin's attitude toward work, pride in one's occupation, ambition, and excellence with Mr. Bates's ideas on the same subjects or on other work-related issues you find in the two texts. Use specific references and quotations from each to support your points.

2.   Do an interview with someone who you know who works hard at his or her job. Pick someone, in or outside the home, whose work you admire or are curious about. If you can, use a tape recorder for accuracy and show the person a copy of what you've written. Encourage this person to show you or tell you exactly what he or she does, how meaningful the work is or isn't, and what the most rewarding parts of it are. Be sure that whoever you interview understands that you are treating his or her work with respect.

∞ *Bricklayer's Boy* (1989)

ALFRED LUBRANO

Alfred Lubrano is a reporter for New York Newsday *and is a contributor to* Gentleman's Quarterly, *where this essay originally appeared. Lubrano frequently writes about personal relationships and family life. In the memoir that follows, he writes about the family and work values gained from his blue-collar upbringing and how they are, or are not, reconciled with his adult way of life.*

My father and I were college buddies back in the mid 1970s. While I was in class at Columbia, struggling with the esoterica du jour, he was on a bricklayer's scaffold not far up the street, working on a campus building.

Sometimes we'd hook up on the subway going home, he with his tools, I with my books. We didn't chat much about what went on during the day. My father wasn't interested in Dante, I wasn't up on arches. We'd share a *New York Post* and talk about the Mets.

My dad has built lots of places in New York City he can't get into: colleges, condos, office towers. He makes his living on the outside. Once the walls are up, a place takes on a different feel for him, as if he's not welcome anymore. It doesn't bother him, though. For my father, earning the dough that paid for my entrée into a fancy, bricked-in institution was satisfaction enough, a vicarious access.

We didn't know it then, but those days were the start of a branching off, a redefining of what it means to be a workingman in our family. Related by blood, we're separated by class, my father and I. Being the white-collar son of a blue-collar man means being the hinge on the door between two ways of life.

It's not so smooth jumping from Italian old-world style to U.S. yuppie in a single generation. Despite the myth of mobility in America, the true rule, experts say, is rags to rags, riches to riches. According to Bucknell University economist and author Charles Sackrey, maybe 10 percent climb from the working to the professional class. My father has had a tough time accepting my decision to become a mere newspaper reporter, a field that pays just a little more than construction does. He wonders why I haven't cashed in on that multi-brick education and taken on some lawyer-lucrative job. After bricklaying for thirty years, my father promised himself I'd never pile bricks and blocks into walls for a living. He figured an education—genielike and benevolent—would somehow rocket me into the consecrated trajectory of the upwardly mobile, and load some serious loot into my pockets. What he didn't count on was his eldest son breaking blue-collar rule No. 1: Make as much money as you can, to pay for as good a life as you can get.

He'd tell me about it when I was nineteen, my collar already fading to white. I was the college boy who handed him the wrong wrench on help-around-the-house Saturdays. "You better make a lot of money," my blue-collar handy dad wryly warned me as we huddled in front of a disassembled dishwasher I had neither the inclination nor the aptitude to fix. "You're gonna need to hire someone to hammer a nail into a wall for you."

In 1980, after college and graduate school, I was offered my first job, on a now-dead daily paper in Columbus, Ohio. I broke the news in the kitchen, where all the family business is discussed. My mother wept as if it were Vietnam. My father had a few questions: "Ohio? Where the hell is Ohio?"

I said it's somewhere west of New York City, that it was like Pennsylvania, only more so. I told him I wanted to write, and these were the only people who'd take me.

"Why can't you get a good job that pays something, like in advertising in the city, and write on the side?"

"Advertising is lying," I said, smug and sanctimonious, ever the 10
unctuous undergraduate. "I wanna tell the truth."

"The truth?" the old man exploded, his face reddening as it does when he's up twenty stories in high wind. "What's truth?" I said it's real life, and writing about it would make me happy. "You're happy with your family," my father said, spilling blue-collar rule No. 2. "That's what makes you happy. After that, it all comes down to dollars and cents. What gives you comfort besides your family? Money, only money."

During the two weeks before I moved, he reminded me that newspaper journalism is a dying field, and I could do better. Then he pressed advertising again, though neither of us knew anything about it, except that you could work in Manhattan, the borough with the water-beading high gloss, the island polished clean by money. I couldn't explain myself, so I packed, unpopular and confused. No longer was I the good son who studied hard and fumbled endearingly with tools. I was hacking people off.

One night, though, my father brought home some heavy tape and that clear, plastic bubble stuff you pack your mother's second-string dishes in. "You probably couldn't do this right," my father said to me before he sealed the boxes and helped me take them to UPS. "This is what he wants," my father told my mother the day I left for Columbus in my grandfather's eleven-year-old gray Cadillac. "What are you gonna do?" After I said my good-byes, my father took me aside and pressed five $100 bills into my hands. "It's okay," he said over my weak protests. "Don't tell your mother."

When I broke the news about what the paper was paying me, my father suggested I get a part-time job to augment the income. "Maybe you could drive a cab." Once, after I was chewed out by the city editor for something trivial, I made the mistake of telling my father during a visit home. "They pay you nothin', and they push you around too much in that business," he told me, the rage building. "Next time, you gotta grab the guy by the throat and tell him he's a big jerk."

"Dad, I can't talk to the boss like that."   15

"Tell him. You get results that way. Never take any shit." A few years before, a guy didn't like the retaining wall my father and his partner had built. They tore it down and did it again, but the guy still bitched. My father's partner shoved the guy into the freshly laid bricks. "Pay me off," my father said, and he and his partner took the money and walked. Blue-collar guys have no patience for office politics and corporate bile-swallowing. Just pay me off and I'm gone. Eventually, I moved on to a job in Cleveland, on a paper my father has heard of. I think he looks on it as a sign of progress, because he hasn't mentioned advertising for a while.

When he was my age, my father was already dug in with a trade, a wife, two sons and a house in a neighborhood in Brooklyn not far from where he was born. His workaday, family-centered life has been very much in step with his immigrant father's. I sublet what the real-estate people call a junior one-bedroom in a dormlike condo in a Cleveland suburb. Unmarried and unconnected in an insouciant, perpetual student kind of way, I rent movies during the week and feed single women in restaurants on Saturday nights. My dad asks me about my dates, but he goes crazy over the word "woman." "A girl," he corrects. "You went out with a girl. Don't say 'woman.' It sounds like you're takin' out your grandmother."

I've often believed blue-collaring is the more genuine of lives, in greater proximity to primordial manhood. My father is provider and protector, concerned only with the basics: food and home, love and progeny. He's also a generation closer to the heritage, a warmer spot nearer the fire that forged and defined us. Does heat dissipate and light fade further from the source? I live for my career, and frequently feel lost and codeless, devoid of the blue-collar rules my father grew up with. With no baby-boomer groomer to show me the way, I've been choreographing my own tentative shuffle across the wax-shined dance floor on the edge of the Great Middle Class, a different rhythm in a whole new ballroom.

I'm sure it's tough on my father, too, because I don't know much about bricklaying, either, except that it's hell on the body, a daily sacrifice. I idealized my dad as a kind of dawn-rising priest of labor, engaged in holy ritual. Up at five every day, my father has made a religion of responsibility. My younger brother, a Wall Street white-collar guy with the sense to make a decent salary, says he always felt safe when he heard Dad stir before him, as if Pop were taming the day for us. My father, fifty-five years old, but expected to put out as if he were three decades stronger, slips on machine-washable vestments of khaki cotton without waking my mother. He goes into the kitchen and turns on the radio to catch the temperature. Bricklayers have an occupational need to know the weather. And because I am my father's son, I can recite the five-day forecast at any given moment.

My father isn't crazy about this life. He wanted to be a singer and   20 actor when he was young, but that was frivolous doodling to his Italian family, who expected money to be coming in, stoking the stove that kept hearth fires ablaze. Dreams simply were not energy-efficient. My dad learned a trade, as he was supposed to, and settled into a life

of pre-scripted routing. He says he can't find the black-and-white publicity glossies he once had made.

Although I see my dad infrequently, my brother, who lives at
home, is with the old man every day. Chris has a lot more blue-collar
in him than I do, despite his management-level career; for a short time,
he wanted to be a construction worker, but my parents persuaded him
to go to Columbia. Once in a while he'll bag a lunch and, in a nice
wool suit, meet my father at a construction site and share sandwiches
of egg salad on semolina bread.

It was Chris who helped my dad most when my father tried to
change his life several months ago. My dad wanted a civil-service bricklayer foreman's job that wouldn't be so physically demanding. There
was a written test that included essay questions about construction
work. My father hadn't done anything like it in forty years. Why the hell
they needed bricklayers to write essays I have no idea, but my father
sweated it out. Every morning before sunrise, Chris would be ironing a
shirt, bleary-eyed, and my father would sit at the kitchen table and read
aloud his practice essays on how to wash down a wall, or how to build a
tricky corner. Chris would suggest words and approaches.

It was so hard for my dad. He had to take a Stanley Kaplan–like
prep course in a junior high school three nights a week after work for
six weeks. At class time, the outside men would come in, twenty-five
construction workers squeezing themselves into little desks. Tough
blue-collar guys armed with No. 2 pencils leaning over and scratching
out their practice essays, cement in their hair, tar on their pants, their
work boots too big and clumsy to fit under the desks.

"Is this what finals felt like?" my father would ask me on the phone
when I pitched in to help long-distance. "Were you always this nervous?" I told him yes. I told him writing's always difficult. He thanked
Chris and me for the coaching, for putting him through school this time.
My father thinks he did okay, but he's still awaiting the test results. In
the meantime, he takes life the blue-collar way, one brick at a time.

When we see each other these days, my father still asks how the 25
money is. Sometimes he reads my stories; usually he likes them, although he recently criticized one piece as being a bit sentimental: "Too
schmaltzy," he said. Some psychologists say that the blue-white-collar
gap between fathers and sons leads to alienation, but I tend to agree
with Dr. Al Baraff, a clinical psychologist and director of the Men-
Center in Washington, D.C. "The core of the relationship is based on
emotional and hereditary traits," Baraff says. "Class [distinctions] just
get added on. If it's a healthful relationship from when you're a kid,
there's a respect back and forth that'll continue."

Nice of the doctor to explain, but I suppose I already knew that.
Whatever is between my father and me, whatever keeps us talking
and keeps us close, has nothing to do with work and economic class.

During one of my visits to Brooklyn not long ago, he and I were in the car, on our way to buy toiletries, one of my father's weekly routines. "You know, you're not as successful as you could be," he began, blue-collar blunt as usual. "You paid your dues in school. You deserve better restaurants, better clothes." Here we go, I thought, the same old stuff. I'm sure every family has five or six similar big issues that are replayed like well-worn videotapes. I wanted to fast-forward this thing when we stopped at a red light.

Just then my father turned to me, solemn and intense. His knees were aching and his back muscles were throbbing in clockable intervals that registered in his eyes. It was the end of a week of lifting fifty-pound blocks. "I envy you," he said quietly. "For a man to do something he likes and get paid for it—that's fantastic." He smiled at me before the light changed, and we drove on. To thank him for the understanding, I sprang for the deodorant and shampoo. For once, my father let me pay.

For Journals

What did you learn from your family, implicitly or explicitly, about class and money?

For Discussion

1. What is your response to the voice and tone of the essay? Do the author and his family seem like people you would like to meet? Do any of his family members have values that you share?

2. Lubrano directly addresses issues of class, comparing blue-collar and white-collar lifestyles. What does he suggest is typical of each lifestyle?

3. The author mentions "blue-collar" rules. What do you think would be his "white-collar" rules? Do the "rules" lead to conflict in this family?

4. The essay is full of rich language and metaphor. Select some of the more vivid metaphors, and discuss ways in which they underscore and reinforce Lubrano's assertions about values.

5. What is the myth of mobility discussed in this essay? What is the connection of this myth to class values?

For Writing

1. Develop your journal writing into a reflective essay on the ways in which your family taught you values, attitudes, and beliefs. You could focus on a specific area, such as work or education.

2. Research and develop an expository essay on the myth of mobility and the notion of "rags to riches." Do you find evidence to support Lubrano's claim that the usual scenario is "rags to rags"?

∞ FROM *Sports Illusion, Sports Reality* (1994)

LEONARD KOPPETT

Leonard Koppett (1926–) has been a sports reporter for the New York Times *and the* New York Post. *The author of ten books about sports, he is one of this country's greatest experts on professional and amateur sports, as well as sports journalism. He is a member of the writers' division of both the Baseball Hall of Fame and the Basketball Hall of Fame.*

The Poison of Amateurism

One concept peculiar to sports deserves condemnation.

It is called *amateurism.* Amateurism has been pumping a poisonous hypocrisy through American society for more than a century, and continues to do so. Almost all the harmful effects of the sports establishment can be traced to this misnamed "ideal." And it's a virus that touches everyone everywhere, even those who have no apparent connection to sports.

Amateurism, as it has come to be defined and interpreted by the worldwide sports community, is evil *in principle.* That amateur "rules" are widely violated in practice is generally accepted, with a wink, or a sigh, or indignation, or indifference. And it is also well understood that tolerating these violations is hypocritical. What is rarely considered however, is that the amateur ideal—if perfectly observed and policed—is incompatible with any decent modern society, especially American society. In many twentieth-century cultures, it is simply an inapplicable term. In others, where its definition can be put into some sort of correspondence with reality, it reflects and promotes concepts those very societies renounce.

In short, amateurism doesn't work anywhere; if it did work, it would be a bad thing; and since it can't work and shouldn't, institutionalizing its respectability (through the American school system, primarily) corrupts the intellect as well as the ethical sense. . . . Why make such a designation as "amateur" in the first place? And why consider it a virtue?

In ordinary usage, *amateur,* as distinguished from *professional,* con- 5
notes less proficiency. As Tevye says about poverty in *Fiddler on the Roof,* it's no disgrace, but it's no great honor, either. When we speak of a musician (or any artist) as an amateur, we don't imply moral superi-

ority, or even praise. We are explaining the artist's status, either as a justification for lack of skill or as something to marvel at, if the skill is of professional quality. Do you know of anyone who prefers to be treated by an amateur doctor? Or defended by an amateur lawyer, before an amateur judge?

Note, incidentally, that this demarcation has nothing to do with talent. Professionalism is the cultivation of a talent through time, training, and dedication. An amateur may actually be more talented, in native aptitude, than a polished professional, but he or she hasn't developed that talent to the same degree.

In sports, unlike the arts, medicine, or law, the activity consists of pitting one competitor against another, for the express purpose of finding out which one will win. It would make admirable sense, therefore, to ensure fair competition by grading the participants, so that only those of reasonably equal abilities are brought together. And that's exactly what's done with weight classes in boxing or wrestling, age designations in Little League, major-league and minor-league affiliations among professional teams, and varsity and intramural distinctions in schools.

But what is the essential ingredient in developing athletic talent to the highest, world-class levels of proficiency? Time. Time to train, practice, concentrate, and gain competitive experience. So it would make perfect sense to separate amateurs from professionals on the basis of time and effort devoted to becoming proficient. The term *professional* itself signifies someone who has completed a rigorous, accepted program of preparation, and who makes the practiced activity his chief occupation.

But that is not how sports amateurism is defined. It is defined exclusively in terms of *remuneration.* . . .

The concept of sports organization, which didn't exist before the 10 1800s, and evolved in the England of Queen Victoria, wasn't pointless in the culture of that time. That was a time when "gentlemen" still didn't soil their hands with "commerce," if they could help it; when hereditary privilege was still the backbone of social status; when work performed for pay was considered vaguely degrading, if sometimes necessary; when affiliation to club or caste or family was still considered more important than personal worth or eccentricity.

It was also a time when the facilities and leisure time for sports activity were generally unavailable to ordinary or working-class people. The golf course, the running oval, the polo field, the cricket ground, the newly designed tennis court were the provinces of the upper class. (The working-class game was football—soccer—and it became openly professional without much fuss, throughout Europe and soon throughout the world.)

But athletic games are mastered by muscle, determination, reflexes, and alertness—commodities not restricted to "nice" people. In fact, since the lower classes were so much more numerous and gen-erally less inhibited, they could certainly overwhelm club members if they could compete under equal conditions for any extended period of time. So elevating the lack of remuneration to a symbol of moral purity was in tune with the social climate; and it was very, very convenient. In plain language, it kept the riff-raff out. For a while, that is.

At this point, someone is sure to ask about the ancient Greeks and their ideals. The ancient Olympics, which inspired the modern Games, had no cash prizes and were also our model for democracy and citizen participation, weren't they? No, they weren't. Ancient Greek "democracy," where it did exist briefly, was a slave-based soci-ety that supported a small upper layer of citizens. Professionalism was plentiful in the ancient Olympics, and prizes of great value were heaped upon winners by their communities. (Even at Olympia, the promoters knew how to avoid putting up expensive awards them-selves.)

In any case, the social forces of mid-Victorianism had nothing to do with American life, even then. But the practices and frames of refer-ence that became codified in the financial definition of amateurism were grafted onto American culture too.

The messages embedded in such concepts can be paraphrased 15 thus:

- Since athletic excellence can be achieved only through full-time application, and since tangible rewards for the fruits of this effort are forbidden, there must be something wrong with honest pay for honest work.

- Since superior achievement is honored but cannot be rewarded di-rectly (as it can for the artist or the surgeon), and since part-time effort can't achieve the goal, it must be all right to accept sponsor-ship, openly or covertly.

- Since everyone has to eat, and since only the "authorities" can de-termine whether you have complied with rules only the indepen-dently wealthy could live up to, it must be proper to lie (at worst) or pervert logic (at best) and stay eligible.

But what if every single individual in America were a paragon of integrity, and lies and subterfuge did not exist? Would we want a sys-tem that restricts competition to amateurs drawn only from a leisure class? That brands compensation for honest work as somehow dirty? That cheats a performer of a decent share of the tangible rewards his performances generate for those authorities who sell tickets and tele-vision rights, have salaried staffs, and share profits with ancillary businesses?

We would not want it, and we don't have it. In practice, everyone sees that value is given for value received in amateur sports. The high school athlete is rewarded with college admission he might not get otherwise—a ticket to upward mobility. The college athlete gets a free ride (worth thousands of dollars a year) and is in a position to obtain advantageous postgraduate opportunities through alumni and publicity. . . .

By subscribing to this definition, uncritically, American society has been infected with a debilitating disease. The entire school system, which forms the backbone of America's athletic programs, insists on an amateur posture. But the high school football or basketball star is perfectly aware of the tangible reward he is playing for: a free college education. And the college player knows he is getting it. His coaches know. And his teachers. And the school administrators. And his parents and family. And his nonplaying classmates. And his out-of-school friends. And all the neighbors and local businessmen who congratulate him on his athletic success. And he knows they know. And they know he knows.

A more pervasive institutionalization of hypocrisy is hard to imagine, and it is at work every single day, in millions of cases. The lesson is inescapable: It is all right to do one thing while professing its opposite. It's not only all right, it is warmly endorsed and fostered by the leaders of society and all the authority figures who fashion a child's values: parents, clergy, teachers, and government officials.

If you accept the idea that remuneration is O.K. when it is prop- 20 erly disguised, you cripple your moral sensibilities. If you accept the disguises at face value and say they are not really remuneration, you cripple your capacity to think straight. And for three generations, *everyone* who has been to school in America, not just the athletes, has been exposed to this moral flabbiness and intellectual dishonesty. The athlete, at least, earns his keep by actual effort, but everyone else sees—and enjoys and profits from, in many cases—the hypocrisy that is being accepted.

None of this, please note, involves *violations* of the serpentine rules. Those also abound, come to the attention of millions, and are usually accepted. When, in some particular instance, punishment is inflicted and self-righteous horror is expressed, the rarity and quixotic nature of the incident merely heightens everyone's perception of injustice. The violations, which can't be kept secret from those who participate in them, even if they are never uncovered officially, compound the problem but don't alter its basic nature.

The problem is that upholding amateurism as an ideal in an industrialized world guarantees daily indoctrination in false values. Work *should* be rewarded. World-class athletic performance, for the entertainment of millions of paying customers, is *work*. A privileged leisure class which could afford to play just for the love of it, is what Western civilization has been rejecting for the last two hundred years, in capitalistic countries no less than in socialistic ones.

In reality, there are millions of true amateurs playing sports everywhere—but not in front of ticket-buying audiences, for the purpose of mass entertainment. It's the deliberate confusion of two distinct functions—play and entertainment—that does the damage.

Why, then, does modern democratic society cling to the old definition? Cheap labor. The professional is controlled by whoever pays him: he must perform when and where and how the employer decides. But before he agrees, he can command a high price for his services (that is, a significant fraction of the income he generates for the promoter). The amateur, on the other hand, is controlled by *eligibility*. And that can't be negotiated. It's completely in the hands of the promoter—the school, club, IOC,[1] or whatever. To stay eligible, the amateur must accept what's offered: scholarship, books, room, training table, expense money, free equipment, lionization, promises, or even the products of cheating. These awards are substantial in themselves, but they add up to a smaller fraction of the promoter's budget than negotiated fees would.

Just as it suits the socialist world to have a no-money definition of amateurism imposed on market-exchange societies, it suits school and amateur-sports authorities to have the same definition imposed on the performers they "hire" so indirectly. You couldn't get away with that if you presented it openly. If nothing else, the antitrust laws would get in the way, but aside from that, the illusion of glamour, which draws spectators, would be tarnished by acknowledged cheapness.

So the package is wrapped in high-sounding morality. Amateurs are presented as "pure," "noble," "disinterested in profit," and "motivated by love of sport." Professionals are grubby, greedy, commerce-soiled mercenaries. And of course professionals must never, never, *never* be allowed to compete against amateurs, because they would show up the amateurs for what they really are—less proficient—and would destroy the amateurs' gate appeal.

There is only one appropriate word for such a system: *sick*.

For Journals

Do you participate or have you ever wanted to participate in any team or individual sports? Do you consider yourself a fan? Why or why not?

---

[1]International Olympic Committee.

For Discussion

1.   *Poison* is a very strong word to use. How does it fit Koppett's argument as he makes his case that amateurism, as it is practiced in America, is both hypocritical and unethical? Is use of such a strong word justified?

2.   In another part of his book, Koppett suggests that in a modern, affluent, high-technology society, watching sports provides a vicarious and pleasurable thrill without any personal danger. Do you agree? What are other reasons for watching athletes compete, either as amateurs or professionals?

3.   Koppett says that any sport pursued as the work of a lifetime is in fact work and should be rewarded as such. Does that explain the enormous salaries that professional athletes get paid? What other factors can you think of?

4.   If you had a chance to go to college on a full athletic scholarship, what arguments could you make to justify your position to a nonathlete who had to work twenty hours a week to qualify for an ordinary scholarship?

For Writing

1.   The old definition of *amateur* is "one who participates and always has participated in sport as an avocation without material gain of any kind." Based on Koppett's article, write an essay in which you either argue in support of this definition or make up one of your own. Incorporate your own experience as a spectator or as a participant.

2.   Elsewhere in his book, Koppett notices the tendency of many writers to use sports metaphors in writing about topics that have nothing to do with sports, such as business or politics. For example, X can't get to first base with that customer; Hertz is number one; the candidates are going for the knockout punch in their debate. Find a newspaper or magazine article which uses this kind of language and rewrite it in terms that do not refer to sports at all. Either omit those terms altogether or substitute typical terminology or slang from a different field, such as the military. Then write an assessment of how the change in language affects the tone and overall effect of the article.

3.   Research and write a paper on one of the following topics: the decision to allow professional athletes to compete in the Olympic Games; the salaries of professional athletes; charges of corruption or payoffs in the National Collegiate Athletic Association. For your sources, check newspaper and magazine articles, the work of sportswriters such as Koppett or Roger Angell, and, if you have access to it, the Internet.

∞ Sports, Body Image, and the American Girl (2000)

KATIE NORRIS

Katie Norris is a California college student.

In the 1980s, a generation after the passage of Title IX and several Olympics in which young female gymnasts and ice skaters became media stars, there was a noticeable increase in sports participation by women. The athletic ability of female athletes began to be recognized, and young girls were encouraged to become more active in the sports organizations in their communities and schools. Since then, women's athletic programs around the country have thrived and successfully proven themselves as a popular pastime of nearly one-half of all females in the United States. Many of them enrolled in dance classes or softball teams by the age of five.

Once a girl reaches high school, the intensity of her particular sport increases and demands more time, exertion, money, and ability. Trying to balance school, social life, adolescence, and a high level of athleticism is difficult for a teenage athlete, and as a result, many girls do not give their bodies appropriate attention. Because of the importance of staying healthy, all female athletes participating in high school sports should be given mandatory seminars to educate them about how to properly care for themselves, and to learn the connections between their emotional and physical well-being.

In high school, many female athletes resort to ways of enhancing their athletic performance that have nothing to do with hard work. Soccer players, softball players, volleyball players, and basketball players are among the athletes who often take steroids to increase the production of male hormones, which give women larger muscles that allow them to hit the ball harder, run faster, or kick farther. However, increasing testosterone in a teenage girl will dramatically effect her female hormones and damage her for the rest of her life. Educating young woman athletes about the effects of these drugs have could prevent their use in the future by other women athletes.

Eating disorders are also a common occurrence among female athletes in sports that require grace, flexibility, and agility. In the past decade, sports such as gymnastics, figure skating, and diving have been reporting an increase in the number of girls who have developed anorexia or bulimia. The less you weigh and the less body fat you have, the better, according to coaches and trainers. Young girls are often so pressured to conform to their coaches' expectations and social peer pressure that they feel they have no choice but to starve themselves or regurgitate their food. However, if they had a person to guide them and teach them the right way to stay in shape, the number of female athletes with eating disorders would decrease. Many girls are just not well informed of the dangers of eating disorders and the long-term health risks. Teaching female athletes from childhood on how to take care of their active bodies will prevent them from resorting to unhealthy habits.

Girls who learn about the dangers of eating disorders or unhealthy diet supplements will spread the word to other female athletes, as well as to younger girls, older girls, siblings, parents, and friends. The girls who are knowledgeable about healthy eating habits could act as informal peer counselors to other young women who are in danger. Seminars in high schools on health and body image, for example, are just one of the many steps that should be taken to inform young girls on how to value themselves and their health. 5

People who oppose this view believe that because female athletes are so consumed with their sports they fall into the body image issues that consume almost every teenage girl. These critics believe that an athlete does not need to be told how to maintain her body because her sport maintains it for her. However each sport requires a certain body type. Dancers are supposed to be slender and lightweight; gymnasts and figure skaters are supposed to be tiny and thin. Sports magazines often feature female athletes who both excel in their sport and have these body types. Teenage female athletes who read these magazines look to these women as role models, and quickly become the ones who are most at risk to develop eating disorders.

Another opposing view is that bringing in an expert on healthy body image to present a lecture to the female athletes would cost too much money and take up too much time. Proponents of this view feel that public high schools have too many other academic and athletic issues to deal with and that an extra seminar would not be worth the time and money. But if adding an extra seminar means reaching just one person and preventing her from making unhealthy choices in their life, don't you think it's worth it? That's much more important than a few extra dollars that would have been spent on some new soccer balls. In any case, schools would have control over hiring and paying a speaker, and deciding when and for how long the speaker should meet with the athletes. The meetings could be after school for a few days or during a couple of practices one afternoon. The time is minimal compared with what girls would learn. The information would help them make wise, healthy choices in their daily lives, and also help other girls around them who may see them as role models, in much the same way that the young female school athletes see athletes in magazines as role models.

Some people believe that the coaches are the ones qualified to inform girls about how to take care of their bodies and educate the girls on sport-related body issues. Softball, soccer, volleyball, basketball, and rugby coaches should give suggestions for body toning, strength enhancing, and mind and body coordination supplements, and dance, figure skating, and swim coaches should give suggestions for good weight loss techniques. This is a possibility. However coaches do not have PhDs in medicine or psychology; they are coaches and only know so much. More importantly, the coaches themselves may be the ones demanding and encouraging female athletes to attain a certain body type that's supposed to help them succeed in competition, regardless of what the girls have to go through and regardless of the negative long-term effects. Athletes need an outside influence to inform them of all their options and explain to them what products and techniques are beneficial or dangerous. An expert in the field of body-image issues can provide information in an unbiased way and can also be easier for an athlete to talk to than the coach who already judges and criticizes her. She'd be more comfortable talking to an objective outsider.

Adolescent teenage girls in high school sports deal with new pressures in their lives every day. Body image is just one more thing that they have to deal with. For an athlete, maintaining the right build, weight, strength, and flexibility are essential for excelling in sports. However, reaching that physical condition can be difficult, frustrating, and ultimately dangerous. When these girls grow older, they carry with them the side effects and aftermaths of what they did to their bodies. Many girls never recover from eating disorders, no matter how much counseling and medical help they've received, and the drugs and hormones that some girls take can alter their estrogen levels for life, preventing them from having children, and sometimes causing organ damage. No girls want these outcomes, and they would not decide to destroy their bodies if they really understood the consequences. But because many female athletes are unaware of the consequences, they treat their bodies badly and will continue to use harmful substances and techniques to enhance their athletic ability, or at least the body type they've been taught to admire. Teaching these young women how to deal with body issues and showing them the best ways to stay healthy will prevent an increase in substance abuse and eating disorders, thus keeping the future women of America healthier and happier.

For Journals

Have you or anyone in your family ever played in sports, like Little League, the elementary school soccer or hockey team, Pop Warner football, or any other organized children's sports? If not, what kind of less official play did you have as a child?

For Discussion

1. Restate Norris's main arguments in favor of educating young women athletes about staying healthy. Which do you find the most convincing, and why?

2. Davis also gives two opposing viewpoints. Do they seem more or less convincing than Norris's own argument? Why? What additional points could you make to strengthen them?

3. State your own version of Norris's thesis. Then come up with your own opening paragraph.

4. Look at a few contemporary magazines that focus on women's athletics. Pick several photographs of young women athletes in different sports who look to you like the ideal for that sport. For example, a woman basketball player, soccer player, gymnast, figure skater, rower, swimmer. How would you describe the differences between them? Which ones seem to you the most or least attractive and/or healthy?

For Writing

1. No image of the American young woman has been as powerful, as persistent, or as adaptable as the Barbie doll. Either go to a toy store, or check out the Barbie doll Web site, and examine the range of Barbie dolls available, including any professional sports Barbies. Write a paper in which you compare the differing images of young womanhood represented. Use the dolls themselves—their clothing, their accessories, their physical structure—as evidence for your comparisons.

2. Anorexia and bulimia are unusually common among first-year female college students, and there is a great deal of literature on the subject. Research and write a paper about the available information on those illnesses at your own or a different school. Possible sources include campus health professionals, journal articles, and health information handed out to entering students.

∞ The Cost of High Stakes
On Little League Games (2000)

C. W. NEVIUS

C. W. Nevius is a veteran sports columnist at the San Francisco Chronicle. *The following is one of a series of articles on the increased violence and the loss of control on America's playing fields; it was published on December 11, 2000.*

When he was 10 years old, Joseph Matteucci had a coach for his Castro Valley Little League team who was a "screamer." Joseph's mother, Alexandra, had concerns, but as a single parent she wanted to encourage her son to meet and play with other kids, so she didn't complain.

Another parent did not hold back however. In the parking lot after a game, he confronted the coach about the yelling at his son. The coach got out of the car and began throwing punches. The father went down in the barrage and when his wife rushed out to aid him, the coach slugged her too.

Joseph Matteucci, sitting in the car, saw it all and burst into tears. He quit Little League the next day. Alexandra Matteucci was relieved. Thank God she'd gotten her son out of that violent environment.

Six years later Joseph was dead.

An innocent bystander, he stopped by a spring Little League game 5 for 16-year-old players to pick up a friend. A brawl broke out after the game, the result of excessive taunting from spectators. A player swung a bat at one of his tormentors, he ducked, and Matteucci was hit in the back of the head. He died in less than 24 hours.

Some might call that 1993 incident a fluke, but the reality is the tragedy on that Castro Valley playground had all the elements of what has become an ugly trend in youth sports.

Violence has become commonplace on the fields of play in America, and the formula is simple, direct and brutal. Taunting from the sidelines escalates, coaches and spectators fail to quell the rising tensions, umpires or referees can not control the situation, and finally, rage boils over.

"Before it was coaches helping the kids who were having trouble controlling their emotions," says Jim Thompson, director of Stanford's Positive Coaching Alliance. "Now it is, 'Let's provide leadership to help the coaches control the parents.'"

The incidents of enraged parents are so out of proportion that they sound absurd. Orlando Lago, an assistant coach with the Hollywood, Fla., All-Stars, broke the jaw of umpire Tom Dziedzinski after a disputed call at third base in a Connie Mack game between high school teams.

Last January, police were called to a gym in Kirkland, Washing- 10 ton, when a heated confrontation at a wrestling match became so violent that a coach head-butted a parent and broke his nose. The wrestlers were 6 years old.

And the most shocking display took place in Reading, Mass., last July when Thomas Junta, a parent, beat to death Michael Costin, a hockey coach, at an ice rink. Junta, who was furious because he felt that Costin was allowing rough play, beat the coach to unconsciousness as his children begged him to stop. Junta, 42, has pleaded not guilty to charges of manslaughter.

But those are just the headlines. Anyone who has been to a youth sports game lately knows the truth. Parents are out of control. They scream at their kids, yell at the officials, and, in more cases than anyone would like to admit, something troubling happens.

Worse, every indicator shows it is becoming more common. Bob Still, spokesman for the National Association of Sports Officials, says his organization gets "between one and three" reports of physical assaults on an official each week.

"These are what we would call assaults as defined by law," says Still, whose organization has been tracking the numbers for 25 years. "The verbal attacks have always been there. But people acting out, coming on the field, there is a definite trend to more violence."

Kill the ump? It isn't so funny. Still says it has reached the point 15 that in 1998 his association began offering "assault insurance" to its 19,000 members. The policy pays medical bills, provides counseling, and offers legal advice as to how to prosecute attackers.

It doesn't take much imagination to project the short term result. Would you want to be a referee in this climate?

"Finding referees is the single most important thing we have to deal with right now," says Bob Maas, president of Pleasanton's highly competitive Balistic United Soccer League." You get out there, some parent yells at you, and you think, 'You know, I am missing the 49er game right now.'"

But the referee shortage is the symptom, not the problem. Fueled by unrealistic expectations and an unhealthy obsession with winning, parents have gone from cheerleaders to taskmasters. Having invested large sums in clinics and private instruction for their kids, anything but success is unacceptable.

Alexandra Matteucci, who now runs the Joseph Matteucci Foundation (*www.jmf4peace.org*), was speaking to a group in Los Angeles when she heard a recent example. A mother, watching her son in a baseball game for 12- to 15-year-olds, was furious when her son was taken out.

"She went out and sat on second base and refused to move until 20 they put her son back in," Matteucci said. "They didn't know what to do, so they put him back in the game."

That kind of acting out may have worked in that case, but how many kids want their parent to become a laughingstock? The yelling, the gestures, and the intense pressure can drive even avid athletes out of organized sports.

"I can't tell you how many times I have heard kids say, 'Shut up dad!'" says Danville's John Wondolowski, whose under-11 soccer team won the State Cup last spring.

When dad won't pipe down, the next step is off the field. Many kids drop sports—an estimated 70 percent quit before they reach the age of 12—but some also find another outlet. Skateboarders, mountain bikers, and surfers are just part of an emerging X Games generation. There are fewer rules, less structure, and—best of all—dad doesn't know the first thing about it.

"That's the protection," says Positive Coaching Alliance's Thompson. "No adults. It is not hyper competitive. Fifteen or 20 years ago adults didn't know anything about soccer. Now you've got guys who think they know all about it. My son is into surfing, skating, and snowboarding. His point was: Do I want to stand in line, wait to bat, and have the coach yell at me? Or do I want to sit out in the ocean?"

A kinder, gentler approach was the idea behind "Silent Sunday" 25 last October in a Cleveland suburb. Coaches and parents in the 217-team league were told not to yell at the players, not even to cheer good plays. Was it hard to break old habits? Well, some parents, afraid they couldn't resist the temptation, put duct tape over their mouths.

Another soccer coach turned the tables on his parents. He put them on the field for a practice and let the kids scream instructions at them as they scrambled to kick the ball. Reportedly, the parents were ready for the exercise to stop long before the kids.

Are those the only choices? Do kids either have to drop out of sports or duct tape their parents' mouths shut?

Well no, there are options, proposed by groups like Thompson's PSA and the Matteucci Foundation. It begins with what groups like Ballistic soccer calls "zero tolerance" for attacks on officials, but more than anything it involves changing perceptions for parents.

"After all," says Thompson, "when you go to a spelling bee, nobody screams at the officials. It isn't done."

"We turn our heads," says Still of the Association of Sports Offi- 30 cials. "We say, 'I'm going to let it go. It is no big deal. Bill is a good guy, he just lost it that one time.'"

That, says facilitators like Matteucci, has to stop. A clear ethics code must be established before the season begins and the parents must go over it. Expecting them to read a handout isn't enough. Matteucci advocates reading the code aloud before every game.

Second, parents who get out of control need to be told so, and in a way that makes it clear that they are out of step with the entire group. And, if the coach, or some of the other parents, cannot calm the transgressor down, enforce the rules and call a forfeit.

"Call the game," says Matteucci. "If we do, life goes on."

But most important, parents need to monitor their level of involvement with an eye toward scaling it down. Chances are, their son or daughter is not going to get a college scholarship, or appear on a Wheaties box. In 10 years, the best you can hope is that the kids still enjoy staying physically active and look back fondly on their sports career.

What's fun about sports if you don't win? Thompson recommends 35 changing the goal. He worked with a soccer team that was so outclassed that it lost every game. Instead of winning, or even scoring, the team decided to make its objective to get the ball over midfield five times in one game.

When they finally did it, cheers rang up and down their sideline, puzzling the opposing parents.

"They were asking, 'What are they so happy about?'" Thompson said. "Aren't we beating them by eight goals?"

Yes, but they were playing a different game.

For Journals

When you were a child, what famous people were you interested in and why did you admire them? Were any of them athletes?

For Discussion

1.   Nevius says that the two examples he gives of killings at ordinary kids' ball games are not as extreme as they might seem. What evidence does he use to support that claim?

2.   What do you think is at stake for the adults in these confrontations, and what kinds of effects could their behavior have on the children?

3.   Nevius relates the story of a mother who sat down on the baseball field when her son was taken out of the game, and refused to get up until he was put back in. What better ways would you suggest of dealing with this situation and for defusing the rage of other adult nonparticipants?

4.   Earlier in this chapter is the Duke Kahanamoku postcard showing the great Olympic swimmer joyfully surfboarding toward the viewer. What image or images come to your mind when reading this article?

For Writing

1.   Leonard Koppett writes about how the professionalization of bigtime college sports has made the idea of the pure amateur a bad joke, and Norris writes about the pressures on young girls to conform to particular body types, even at a risk to their health. Write an essay in which you compare what you believe to be the risks to young people posed by the first two articles to the risks to the children in Nevius's article. Which group do you see as being in the most danger? Why? Who is likely, in your opinion, to suffer the most long-term effects?

And finally, for whichever group—college athletes, adolescent women athletes, and children on sports teams—you see the most significant consequences, suggest your own remedies. Be as creative as you like; just try to find your own ethical solutions, even partial ones, to this growing problem.

∽ *Film: Jerry Maguire* (1997)

Jerry Maguire is a film about a sports agent who, in a tired moment, writes an unexpectedly honest memorandum about how hypocritical and greedy his profession has become. As a result he is fired by his employer and deserted by all but one of his clients—a mediocre football player who provides him with one last chance to truly help and inspire an athlete and redeem himself. (126 minutes)

For Journals

Does this film give you a higher or lower opinion of professional sports? What did you think before you saw this film, and on what were you basing your opinion?

For Discussion

1. What image of sports agents does the film communicate, particularly in the scenes at the office after Jerry sends around his mission statement? What do you think a sports agent is supposed to do?

2. Jerry Maguire can't express intimate feelings but is good at his job, and Rod Tidwell is good at personal intimacy but not so good at his job. What scenes in the film are crucial, in your opinion, to the gradual change in both men? How do they affect and help one another?

3. In what ways does this film portray sports as a business? What and who is marketed? What does success mean in this context? Look for specific scenes or exchanges of dialogue to prove your point.

4. The most famous line in this movie is "Show me the money!" But the end of the film is more sentimental than financial in impact. How well does the director lay the groundwork for this change? In what scenes does he prepare us to accept a kinder, gentler resolution of the problems the movie raises? Where, in particular, do you see Jerry Maguire changing his behavior?

For Writing

1. Watch the movie *Field of Dreams,* and write an essay in which you analyze at least two of the following issues: the pure pleasure of sport; baseball as the ultimate game of American mythology; nostalgia for an earlier America that we think was simpler than the America we live in; the powers of memory; impractical idealism versus cold business practices. Look for scenes in which these issues appear, and examine them for crucial dialogue or character development. Give specific examples from them as evidence for your conclusions.

2. The salaries of major league sports figures are much higher, even for average professional athletes, than they were ten years ago. In fact, Rod Tidwell's successful bid for a higher salary from his team would no longer be considered a great deal. Research and write a paper explaining the causes and effects of the enormous jump in major league salaries in either baseball or football. To find a range of facts and opinions, check the writings of Leonard Koppett, Roger Noll, Harry Edwards, or any other sports expert who has written extensively about the issue. Also, use the Internet to locate other articles on this subject.

Writing Assignments

1. Why do people work? Or more specifically, why do you or will you work? After brainstorming, reading, discussing, and recollecting some of the points made in class and in your readings, develop a core assertion as to the meaning, value, or purpose of work—to people in your family, to people of a certain class, to people of a certain ethnic culture or gender. Avoid vague generalizations. Focus on a specific assertion, and offer strong support for it.

2. Research advertisements or political cartoons from times gone by—from nineteenth-century publications to back issues of *Life* or other popular magazines from the 1940s. Analyze the values implied and the assertions made about work or play in the images. Alternatively, view one or two television comedies from the 1950s and 1960s, and analyze the values, assumptions, and assertions they convey, particularly those about work and gender, or play and gender.

3. Record oral histories of three different workers talking about what work means to them. Draft several questions to get your interview started and to suggest a focus. After the interviews, compare and contrast the view of your interviewees, looking for common and diverse threads among the histories. Develop a core claim or thesis, using the material from the interviews and, if you want, from the readings in this chapter and your own experience to support your view. Alternatively, do the same assignment, but by interviewing three people who are committed to a sport or sports on a regular basis.

4.   Examine the assertions made about blue-collar work or the importance of work in women's lives by this chapter's authors, especially Gilman and Steinem. Do particular types of factual assertions, evaluative assertions, or proposals dominate topic or selection? Which types are most persuasive? Write an analytical paper discussing your findings.

5.   Write a proposal for change in a program at your college or in your community: a change in the curriculum, such as revising the language or writing requirements; a change in scholarship or work-study funding; a change in alcohol policy in your residence; or a campus or community recycling program. Write the proposal in the form of a letter to the appropriate administrator, or for a more general audience, as a letter to the editor.

6.   Write an argumentative essay asserting your own view of the value of work, success, money, education, or some other belief that you hold. Pay special attention to the assumptions you are making and the evidence you are selecting to support your view, and be sure to back up any assumptions you make that your audience may not share or accept.

9

❦

Justice and Civil Liberties

E very morning, millions of American schoolchildren recite the pledge of allegiance to the flag, which ends, "With liberty and justice for all." That phrase refers to more people today than it has in the past; today it includes women, children, ethnic minorities, the aged, and the disabled. This is a country proudly self-conscious that its political system was established to be something new, that it offered a readjustment of rights and privileges more profound than anything that had ever been attempted before. So standards and expectations for justice and civil liberties have always been higher here, at least in theory, than anywhere else.

Given our ideals, however, the fact that for 250 years African Americans were bought and sold like furniture could not be easily explained, nor could the denial of their civil rights into modern times. So, more often than not, a consideration of social justice in America starts with racial justice.

Many of the high and low points associated with racial justice involve attempts of whites to deny or to correct past wrongs, and the attempts of African Americans to claim the promise of liberty and the American dream from which they had been excluded. At times, individual leaders—like Frederick Douglass—have taken upon themselves the role of spokespersons and protest leaders. Their job has been simultaneously to educate white Americans about the everyday injustices in African American life and to organize their constituencies to effect change.

The fact that laws did not change quickly, or that the laws did but attitudes did not, has led to a continuing and sometimes violent debate over what justice is, who is entitled to justice (and how much), and whether there is a way to compensate citizens for past wrongs. These issues raise profound questions for Americans about the depth of their commitment to ideals of freedom, opportunity, and political participation.

Race is not the only social struggle in America. As the definitions of justice and freedom became gradually more inclusive in the nineteenth century, one of the offshoots of the first struggle for civil rights was the increased consciousness in other segments of the population that they too were discriminated against. Foremost among these other groups were women—mostly white and middle class—who began organizing for the right to vote. Many of them had been abolitionists, and they turned the self-confidence and political skills they had honed during the fight against slavery to the fight for universal suffrage.

In Victorian America, however, constrained expectations of women as domestic goddesses who knew their place (at home with husband and children) meant that most men and many women were horrified by the open political participation of women and criticized them for being disobedient, unfeminine, and threatening to the status quo. Like African Americans who demanded to be treated equally, the suffragists were viewed as unnatural and ungrateful deviants from the norm who had forgotten their traditional virtues of deference and meekness.

In recent decades the gay rights movement has gained considerable momentum, though its members too have often been castigated as deviants from the norm who should stay in their place and not demand equal rights. Although gays have essentially secured civil liberties in arenas such as housing and employment, the ongoing debate about their presence in the armed forces indicates that the struggle is not fully resolved.

Indeed, complete civil liberties for ethnic and sexual minorities and women are still a long way from being assured as the twenty-first century begins. Unpopular causes and new ideas frequently make audiences angry, and while we all demand the right to say what we want, we are better at defending the speech of people who agree with us than that of people we think are wrong, misguided, extreme, disloyal, or simply very different. Fortunately, however, at all points in our history, this country has been graced by the presence of Americans who were willing to stand up—by themselves, if necessary—to defend the civil liberties in which they believed, particularly the freedoms of speech and press guaranteed by the First Amendment to the Constitution.

Justice and Civil Liberties through History

The writers and artists in this chapter all engaged in an ongoing argument in which the interpretations about the extent of civil liberties and the meaning of justice in America have varied wildly. The values in question were established first in the Declaration of Independence in 1776, then in the Constitution and the Bill of Rights in 1787, in the subsequent amendments to the Constitution, in two hundred years of legal decisions, in reform movements and political debates, in the trauma of a Civil War in which 618,000 Americans died at each other's hands, and in the words and lives of individuals who have made civil liberties and justice their personal business.

But the issues and rights that found their way into our government's defining documents did not spring full-blown from the founding fathers' heads. By the time the Revolution began, discussion of the question of individual rights already had a relatively long history in what was still a very young country. For example, in 1735, John Peter Zenger, a publisher, was put on trial for having printed articles critical of the British colonial government. His lawyer, Andrew Hamilton, based his ultimately successful defense of Zenger on the nature and importance of freedom of the press. That defense, which is the first selection in this chapter, is one of the crucial early cases in the establishment of basic American freedoms.

The men who dominated the American Revolution do not fit the usual image of revolutionaries. They were not poverty-stricken peasants revolting against an insensitive aristocracy but established, educated, and powerful men whose earliest loyalties were to England. Over time, however, they had come to feel capable of managing their own government; finally, they began to think of themselves differently—as Americans. But if they were not radical in the traditional sense, their great contribution to political history, a representative democracy headed by an elected leader, was a radical political development, and its first major expression, the Declaration of Independence, is a remarkable document. Like the Constitution that followed it eleven years later, it is written with such foresight and flexibility that it has stretched to accommodate the needs of later generations and previously excluded constituencies. Much of subsequent American political argument refers back to it or to its promise. Whenever the subject of justice, equality, and civil liberties comes up, either the phrases of the Declaration or the spirit—or both—hover over the discussion. For example, in the years before the Civil War, issues of equality and freedom were slowly if inexorably working their way to the forefront of American political consciousness, and some Americans were more sensitive than others to the impossibility of supporting slavery in a growing democracy with continental ambitions. Among those Americans were Henry David Thoreau and Frederick Douglass. Examples of their work in this chapter are, to differing degrees, early warning signals for the conflagration of the coming Civil War. Henry David Thoreau had a direct sense of the evils of slavery, and he interpreted the Declaration not only as an ideal for collective rebellion against injustice but as an injunction to every single American to heed his or her conscience, even if that meant disobeying the government. Thoreau's most famous piece on dissent, *Civil Disobedience,* which first appeared in 1849, has been a prod to American complacency and self-satisfaction ever since.

Thoreau spoke publicly against slavery because he was an abolitionist—a member of the movement that campaigned for the immediate end to slavery. The abolitionist movement was considered a collection of radicals by most northerners, but like all other campaigns it depended on good speakers to attract attention, audiences, and public support. Thoreau was not in the same class as Frederick Douglass as an orator—nobody was—although he was once called upon to substitute for Douglass at a meeting in Boston.

Douglass, a former slave and a brilliant activist and writer, also had a charismatic presence as a speaker. His powerful intellect and emotion come through intensely in his 1851 Independence Day speech in Rochester, New York, in which he forcefully reminded his white audience of the meaninglessness of the phrase "all men are created equal" for Americans who were enslaved.

Once the Civil War was over, racial division remained, but the political energy that had previously been concentrated on the abolition of slavery began to find its way into other protest movements, particularly the movement for women's right to vote. The intellectual leader and spokesperson of the suffrage movement, Susan B. Anthony, gave her famous speech, "Women's Right to Vote," after she was arrested for trying to register to vote in a presidential election. Like Douglass, also a supporter of women's rights, she was adept at turning the language of the Declaration of Independence and the Constitution back on her audience to prove her point.

By 1896, all the southern states had passed segregation laws against African Americans for the explicit purpose of undoing the civil rights they had won as a result of the Civil War, especially the Thirteenth, Fourteenth, and Fifteenth Amendments to the Constitution, which ended slavery and granted equal protection under the law and the right to vote. The Supreme Court undermined those amendments when, in 1896, it sided with the state of Louisiana in a case called *Plessy* v. *Ferguson,* and declared that black Americans who were forced to ride in separate train cars from whites were not being deprived of equal protection under the law. This is what became known as the "separate but equal" doctrine. Technically, the *Plessy* decision applied only to railroads, but its real effect was to institutionalize segregation in every area of southern public life: transportation, restaurants, beaches, churches, schools. The lone dissenter to the Court's ruling in *Plessy* was Justice John Harlan, a former slave owner who foresaw the tragic consequences of the decision very clearly.

The Supreme Court's interpretation of any case becomes the law of the land, until or unless the law changes or the interpretation changes. In the case of *Plessy*, the worst effects of segregation continued to make themselves felt everywhere in the ordinary experience, the psyches, and the economic suffering of African Americans in the South.

Perhaps the single most striking visual representation of that suffering is a series of photographs taken by the great southern writer Eudora Welty, in rural Mississippi during the worst days of segregation as well as the Depression. One of them is reproduced here: a photograph, called "Dolls," of two little African American girls, wearing their Sunday-best clothes and clutching two white dolls. In this picture Welty condenses the effects of the prejudice that the Supreme Court would eventually confront. In an entirely different mood, and with a very different purpose in mind—to remind Americans in World War II of what they were fighting for—Norman Rockwell's famous 1943 painting *Freedom of Speech*, which appeared on the cover of the *Saturday Evening Post*, offers a small-town New England, almost Jeffersonian image of our most cherished freedom being fully exercised by ordinary Americans.

Roughly half a century, two world wars, and a Depression after *Plessy*, Justice Harlan's lonely dissent was finally vindicated in what is probably the most famous Supreme Court decision of the twentieth century, *Brown* v. *Board of Education* (1954). In *Brown*, the Warren Court declared, in an unusual unanimous decision, that the "separate but equal" standard approved in *Plessy* is a contradiction in terms. Like *Plessy*, *Brown* was technically about only one kind of public segregation—in this instance, public schools. Like *Plessy*, however, it had a domino effect: the outlawing of segregation of children at school began, slowly, to dismantle segregation in the South.

But resistance to integration was fierce, and change was irregular and slow, opposed at every step by southern legislatures, governors, sheriffs, and private citizens who met peaceful efforts to integrate public facilities with hatred and often violence. The medium through which most Americans became acquainted with southern segregation and the civil rights movement was television. Pictures of police turning water cannons or attack dogs on unarmed marchers, including elderly men and women, or on college students asking for service at a lunch counter or a drink of water at a fountain marked "WHITES ONLY," made a powerful impression on Americans who had never been south of the Mason-Dixon line and whose only image of the South probably came from watching *Gone with the Wind*.

Martin Luther King Jr., the leader of the civil rights movement, was frequently arrested. During one incarceration in Birmingham, Alabama, King took the opportunity to respond to some of his critics, who had taken out an advertisement in the local paper criticizing him and his followers. Ironically, these particular opponents were not Ku

Klux Klan members or other white supremacists but southern clergy-men—and mostly black clergymen at that. King's answer, "Letter from Birmingham Jail," immediately became an unofficial primer for the ideology of nonviolent resistance.

In the 1970s and later, a whole new series of arguments about jus-tice and individual rights arose: for or against the Vietnam War, a new wave of the feminist movement, sex education in schools, gays in the military. In "What Is Hate Speech?," attorney and gadfly Alan Der-showitz defends the right to obnoxious freedom of speech. Probably one of the most incendiary civil liberties issues to emerge in recent years is the question of what can and should be allowed on the Inter-net. Student Vickie Chiang addresses this problem through a really in-teresting prism: adults who want the Internet access in libraries filtered to protect children from pornographic or obscene websites come into conflict with the free exchange of ideas and the First Amendment. How can all of these needs and rights be protected?

Finally, the film *The Long Walk Home* brings the issue of civil liber-ties back to where it started, in a story about the effects of the Mont-gomery bus boycott on two families, one black and one white.

As long as Americans continue to believe in the ideals of the Dec-laration of Independence and the Constitution, they will recognize, in-termittently and with considerable discomfort, that justice and civil liberty are easy to support but hard to practice. The tension between equality and conformity, individuality and difference, can lead to prej-udice. Americans do not always welcome the artists, writers, or politi-cal leaders who remind them of the American promise or of how much they have fallen short. The perpetually recurring question is how to make our potential actual, not once, but over and over again in the light of each generation's experience. Despite our frequent mis-takes, overt cynicism, philosophical laziness or failure of will, the un-derlying principles survive, independent of us yet depending on us to give them shape.

∞ *In Defense of Freedom of the Press* (1735)

ANDREW HAMILTON

Andrew Hamilton (1676–1741) was a native of Scotland who came to colonial America around 1700, remarkably enough not as a free man, but as an indentured servant. By 1735, he had been a teacher, studied law in London, served as a repre-sentative in the Maryland Assembly, and become one of the most famous lawyers in the country. In 1735, he defended John Peter Zenger, who had been arrested for crit-icizing the colonial British governor in his newspaper. This selection, the first major American defense of freedom of the press, is from Hamilton's argument before the jury.

May it please your honors, I agree with Mr. Attorney [Richard Bradley] that government is a sacred thing, but I differ very widely from him when he would insinuate that the just complaints of a number of men, who suffer under a bad administration, is libeling that administration. Had I believed that to be law, I should not have given the court the trouble of hearing anything that I could say in this cause. . . .

There is heresy in law as well as in religion, and both have changed very much; and we well know that it is not two centuries ago that a man would have burned as a heretic for owning such opinions in matters of religion as are publicly written and printed at this day. They were fallible men, it seems, and we take the liberty, not only to differ from them in religious opinion, but to condemn them and their opinions too; and I must presume that in taking these freedoms in thinking and speaking about matters of faith or religion, we are in the right; for, though it is said there are very great liberties of this kind taken in New York, yet I have heard of no information preferred by Mr. Attorney for any offenses of this sort. From which I think it is pretty clear that in New York a man may make very free with his God, but he must take special care what he says of his Governor. It is agreed upon by all men that this is a reign of liberty, and while men keep within the bounds of truth, I hope they may with safety both speak and write their sentiments of the conduct of men of power; I mean of that part of their conduct only which affects the liberty or property of the people under their administration; were this to be denied, then the next step may make them slaves. For what notions can be entertained of slavery beyond that of suffering the greatest injuries and oppressions without the liberty of complaining; or if they do, to be destroyed, body and estate, for so doing?

It is said, and insisted upon by Mr. Attorney, that government is a sacred thing; that it is to be supported and reverenced; it is government that protects our persons and estates; that prevents treasons, murders, robberies, riots, and all the train of evils that overturn kingdoms and states and ruin particular persons; and if those in the administration, especially the supreme magistrates, must have all their conduct censured by private men, government cannot subsist. This is called a licentiousness not to be tolerated. It is said that it brings the rulers of the people into contempt so that their authority is not regarded, and so that in the end the laws cannot be put in execution. These, I say, and such as these, are the general topics insisted upon by men in power and their advocates. But I wish it might be considered at the same time how often it has happened that the abuse of power has been the primary cause of these evils, and that it was the injustice and oppression of these great men which has commonly brought them into contempt with the people. The craft and art of such men are great, and who that is the least acquainted with history or with law can be ignorant of the specious pretenses which have often been made use of by men in power to introduce arbitrary rule and destroy the liberties of a free people. . . .

If a libel is understood in the large and unlimited sense urged by Mr. Attorney, there is scarce a writing I know that may not be called a libel, or scarce any person safe from being called to account as a libeler, for Moses, meek as he was, libeled Cain; and who is it that has not libeled the devil? For, according to Mr. Attorney, it is not justification to say one has a bad name. Eachard has libeled our good King William; Burnet has libeled, among many others, King Charles and King James; and Rapin has libeled them all. How must a man speak or write, or what must he hear, read, or sing? Or when must he laugh, so as to be secure from being taken up as a libeler? I sincerely believe that were some persons to go through the streets of New York nowadays and read a part of the Bible, if it were not known to be such, Mr. Attorney, with the help of his innuendoes, would easily turn it into a libel. As for instance: Isaiah 11:16: "The leaders of the people cause them to err, and they that are led by them are destroyed." But should Mr. Attorney go about to make this a libel, he would read it thus: "The leaders of the people" (*innuendo,* the Governor and council of New York) "cause them" (*innuendo,* the people of this province) "to err, and they" (the Governor and council meaning) "are destroyed" (*innuendo,* are deceived into the loss of their liberty), "which is the worst kind of destruction." Or if some person should publicly repeat, in a manner not pleasing to his betters, the tenth and the eleventh verses of the fifty-sixth chapter of the same book, there Mr. Attorney would have a large field to display his skill in the artful application of his innuendoes. The words are: "His watchmen are blind, they are ignorant," etc. "Yea, they are greedy dogs, they can never have enough." But to make them a libel, there is, according to Mr. Attorney's doctrine, no more wanting but the aid of his skill in the right adapting his innuendoes. . . .

The loss of liberty to a generous mind is worse than death; and yet 5 we know there have been those in all ages who, for the sakes of preferment or some imaginary honor, have freely lent a helping hand to oppress, nay, to destroy, their country. This brings to my mind that saying of the immortal Brutus, when he looked upon the creatures of Caesar, who were very great men, but by no means good men: "You Romans," said Brutus, "if yet I may call you so, consider what you are doing; remember that you are assisting Caesar to forge those very chains which one day he will make yourselves wear." This is what every man that values freedom ought to consider; he should act by judgment and not by affection or self-interest; for where those prevail, no ties of either country or kindred are regarded; as, upon the other hand, the man who loves his country prefers its liberty to all other considerations, well knowing that without liberty life is a misery. . . .

Power may justly be compared to a great river; while kept within its bounds, it is both beautiful and useful, but when it overflows its banks, it is then too impetuous to be stemmed; it bears down all before it, and brings destruction and desolation wherever it comes. If, then, this be the nature of power, let us at least do our duty, and, like wise men who value freedom, use our utmost care to support liberty, the only bulwark against lawless power, which, in all ages, has sacrificed to its wild lust and boundless ambition the blood of the best men that ever lived.

I hope to be pardoned, sir, for my zeal upon this occasion. It is an old and wise caution that "when our neighbor's house is on fire, we ought to take care of our own." For though, blessed be God, I live in a government where liberty is well understood and freely enjoyed, yet experience has shown us all (I am sure it has to me) that a bad precedent in one government is soon set up for an authority in another; and therefore I cannot but think it mine and every honest man's duty that, while we pay all due obedience to men in authority, we ought, at the same time, to be upon our guard against power wherever we apprehend that it may affect ourselves or our fellow subjects.

I am truly very unequal to such an undertaking, on many accounts. And you see I labor under the weight of many years and am borne down with great infirmities of body; yet old and weak as I am, I should think it my duty, if required, to go to the utmost part of the land, where my service could be of any use in assisting to quench the flame of prosecutions upon informations, set on foot by the government to deprive a people of the right of remonstrating, and complaining too, of the arbitrary attempts of men in power. Men who injure and oppress the people under their administration provoke them to cry out and complain, and then make that very complaint the foundation for new oppressions and prosecutions. I wish I could say there were no instances of this kind. But, to conclude, the question before the court, and you, gentlemen of the jury, is not of small nor private concern; it is not the cause of a poor printer, nor of New York alone, which you are now trying. No! It may, in its consequence, affect every free man that lives under a British government on the main continent of America. It is the best cause; it is the cause of liberty; and I make no doubt that your upright conduct, this day, will not only entitle you to the love and esteem of your fellow citizen, but every man who prefers freedom to a life of slavery will bless and honor you as men who have baffled the attempt of tyranny, and, by an impartial and uncorrupt verdict, have laid a noble foundation for securing to ourselves, our posterity, and our neighbors that to which nature and the laws of our country have given us a right—the liberty of both exposing and opposing arbitrary power (in these parts of the world at least) by speaking and writing truth. . . .

For Journals

If you were to write a letter to a newspaper on an issue that really mattered to you, what would it be about? How free would you feel to say what you wanted to?

For Discussion

1.   Libel is, very loosely defined, a printed statement that has the effect of damaging a person's standing in the community. The crucial legal principle Hamilton established here is that truth is always a defense to libel. Why does that make sense, and in what situations, if any, can you imagine this ruling being a protection for you?

2.   Hamilton is worried about what lawyers call the slippery slope—once a freedom is endangered, a process of further erosion begins, which is as hard to stop as sliding down a slippery slope. What specific harms will follow, and who will be hurt, if freedom of the press is not upheld in this case?

3.   John Peter Zenger, the defendant, was arrested for publishing articles critical of the British colonial government. What argument does the government make to justify the arrest? Do you think a government is ever justified in stopping someone from speaking or writing? If so, under what circumstances? If not, why not?

4.   What is the logic behind Hamilton's argument that if what Zenger did is libelous, then it's hard to find anyone who isn't? How does he strengthen his argument by including examples such as Moses and Isaiah of the Bible and Julius Caesar and Brutus of ancient Rome?

For Writing

1.   Go to the supermarket and buy or look at a tabloid newspaper. Pick out one or two articles directed at either the government or a famous person, and write an essay in which you explain why they might be considered libelous and why the writers of those articles should or should not be protected from prosecution. Remember that truth is a defense to libel, but an untrue statement is not. Two techniques of Hamilton's you could imitate in your paper are use of historical references to support an argument and stating the other side's argument before attacking it.

2.   The Constitutional question of preventing publication of documents damaging to the government has continued to come up in American history. Research and write a paper about the circumstances surrounding the publication of the Pentagon Papers in the *New York Times* during the Vietnam War. You can consult books written about this case (which was decided by the U.S. Supreme Court), published

court opinions, and the Pentagon Papers themselves, which have been published with an introduction. The Internet may also serve as a source for material about this case and the issues raised by it.

∞ The Declaration of Independence (1776)

THOMAS JEFFERSON

The author of the Declaration was thirty-two-year-old Thomas Jefferson (1743–1826) who could, in the words of a contemporary, "break a horse, play the violin, dance the minuet" and of whom the usually acerbic John Adams said, he had a "reputation for literature, science, and a happy talent of composition. His writings were remarkable for their felicity of expression." Jefferson was, in succession, a member of the Continental Congress, governor of Virginia, ambassador to France, the first secretary of state, vice-president, and then president for two terms, during which he authorized the Louisiana Purchase, doubling the size of the United States. He founded the University of Virginia; designed it and his home, Monticello; and collected the books that formed the basis for the Library of Congress.

In 1962, when President Kennedy invited a group of Nobel Prize winners to dinner, he said it was the greatest concentration of intellect in the White House since the evenings when Thomas Jefferson dined there alone. Jefferson died on July 4, 1826— fifty years to the day after the signing of the Declaration of Independence. In the text that follows, the underlined words and phrases were in the first draft but were removed in the final draft. The words and phrases in the margin are those that appeared in the final version.

A DECLARATION BY THE REPRESENTATIVES OF THE UNITED STATES OF AMERICA, IN GENERAL CONGRESS ASSEMBLED.

When in the course of human events, it becomes necessary for one people to dissolve the political bands which have connected them with another, and to assume among the powers of the earth the separate and equal station to which the laws of nature and of nature's God entitle them, a decent respect to the opinions of mankind requires that they should declare the causes which impel them to the separation.

We hold these truths to be self evident: that all men are created equal, that they are endowed by their Creator with <u>inherent and</u> un- certain
alienable rights; that among these are life, liberty, and the pursuit of happiness; that to secure these rights, governments are instituted among men, deriving their just powers from the consent of the governed; that whenever any form of government becomes destructive of these ends, it is the right of the people to alter or to abolish it, and to institute new government, laying its foundation on such principles, and organizing its powers in such form, as to them shall seem most likely to effect their safety and happiness. Prudence, indeed, will dictate that governments

long established should not be changed for light and transient causes; and accordingly all experience hath shown that mankind are more disposed to suffer while evils are sufferable, than to right themselves by abolishing the forms to which they are accustomed. But when a long train of abuses and usurpations, <u>begun at a distinguished period and</u> pursuing invariably the same object, evinces a design to reduce them under absolute despotism, it is their right, it is their duty to throw off such government, and to provide new guards for their future security. Such has been the patient sufferance of these colonies; and such is now the necessity which constrains them to <u>expunge</u> their former systems of [alter] government. The history of the present king of Great Britain is a history of <u>unremitting</u> injuries and usurpations, <u>among which appears no soli-</u> [repeated] <u>tary fact to contradict the uniform tenor of the rest, but all have</u> in direct [all having] object the establishment of an absolute tyranny over these states. To prove this, let facts be submitted to a candid world <u>for the truth of which</u> <u>we pledge a faith yet unsullied by falsehood.</u>

He has refused his assent to laws the most wholesome and necessary for the public good.

He has forbidden his governors to pass laws of immediate and [5] pressing importance, unless suspended in their operation till his assent should be obtained; and, when so suspended, he has utterly neglected to attend to them.

He has refused to pass other laws for the accommodation of large districts of people, unless those people would relinquish the right of representation in the legislature, a right inestimable to them, and formidable to tyrants only.

He has called together legislative bodies at places unusual, uncomfortable, and distant from the depository of their public records, for the sole purpose of fatiguing them into compliance with his measures.

He has dissolved representative houses repeatedly <u>and continu-</u> <u>ally</u> for opposing with manly firmness his invasions on the rights of the people.

He has refused for a long time after such dissolutions to cause others to be elected, whereby the legislative powers, incapable of annihilation, have returned to the people at large for their exercise, the state remaining, in the meantime, exposed to all the dangers of invasion from without and convulsions within.

He has endeavored to prevent the population of these states: for [10] that purpose obstructing the laws for naturalization of foreigners, refusing to pass others to encourage their migrations hither, and raising the conditions of new appropriations of lands.

He has <u>suffered</u> the administration of justice <u>totally to cease in</u> [obstructed] <u>some of these states</u> refusing his assent to laws for establishing judi- [by] ciary powers.

He has made <u>our</u> judges dependent on his will alone for the tenure of their offices, and the amount and payment of their salaries.

He has erected a multitude of new offices, <u>by a self-assumed power</u> and sent hither swarms of new officers to harass our people and eat out their substance.

He has kept among us in times of peace standing armies <u>and ships of war</u> without the consent of our legislatures.

He has affected to render the military independent of, and supe- 15 rior to, the civil power.

He has combined with others to subject us to a jurisdiction foreign to our constitutions and unacknowledged by our laws, giving his assent to their acts of pretended legislation for quartering large bodies of armed troops among us; for protecting them by a mock trial from punishment for any murders which they should commit on the inhabitants of these states; for cutting off our trade with all parts of the world; for imposing taxes on us without our consent; for depriving us [   ] of the benefits of trial by jury; for transporting us beyond seas `in many` to be tried for pretended offenses; for abolishing the free system of `cases` English laws in a neighboring province, establishing therein an arbi- `in many` trary government, and enlarging its boundaries, so as to render it at `cases` once an example and fit instrument for introducing the same absolute rule into these <u>states;</u> for taking away our charters, abolishing our `colonies` most valuable laws, and altering fundamentally the forms of our governments; for suspending our own legislatures, and declaring themselves invested with power to legislate for us in all cases whatsoever. `by declaring`

He has abdicated government here <u>withdrawing his governors,</u> `us out of his` <u>and declaring us out of his allegiance and protection.</u> `protection` `and waging`

He has plundered our seas, ravaged our coasts, burnt our towns, `war against` and destroyed the lives of our people. `us`

He is at this time transporting large armies of foreign mercenaries `scarcely par-` to complete the works of death, desolation and tyranny already begun `alleled in the` with circumstances of cruelty and perfidy [   ] unworthy the head `most bar-` of a civilized nation. `barous ages,` `and totally`

He has constrained our fellow citizens taken captive on the high 20 seas, to bear arms, against their country, to become the executioners of their friends and brethren, or to fall themselves by their hands.

He has [   ] endeavored to bring on the inhabitants of our `excited` frontiers, the merciless Indian savages, whose known rule of warfare `domestic` is an undistinguished destruction of all ages, sexes and conditions <u>of</u> `insurrection` <u>existence.</u> `among us,` `and has`

<u>He has incited treasonable insurrections of our fellow citizens,</u> <u>with the allurements of forfeiture and confiscation of our property.</u>

<u>He has waged cruel war against human nature itself, violating its</u> <u>most sacred rights of life and liberty in the persons of a distant people</u> <u>who never offended him, captivating and carrying them into slavery</u>

in another hemisphere, or to incur miserable death in their transportation thither. This piratical warfare, the opprobrium of INFIDEL powers, is the warfare of the CHRISTIAN king of Great Britain. Determined to keep open a market where MEN should be bought and sold, he has prostituted his negative for suppressing every legislative attempt to prohibit or to restrain this execrable commerce. And that this assemblage of horrors might want no fact of distinguished die, he is now exciting those very people to rise in arms among us, and to purchase that liberty of which he has deprived them, by murdering the people on whom he also obtruded them: thus paying off former crimes committed against the LIBERTIES of one people, with crimes which heurges them to commit against the LIVES of another.

In every stage of these oppressions we have petitioned for redress in the most humble terms: our repeated petitions have been answered only by repeated injuries.

A prince whose character is thus marked by every act which may define a tyrant is unfit to be the ruler of a [   ] people who mean to be free. Future ages will scarcely believe that the hardiness of one man adventured, within the short compass of twelve years only, to lay a foundation so broad and so undisguised for tyranny over a people fostered and fixed in principles of freedom.

Nor have we been wanting in attentions to our British brethren. We have warned them from time to time of attempts by their legislature to extend a jurisdiction over these our states. We have reminded them of the circumstances of our emigration and settlement here, no one of which would warrant so strange a pretension: that these were effected at the expense of our own blood and treasure, unassisted by the wealth or the strength of Great Britain: that in constituting indeed our several forms of government, we had adopted one common king, thereby laying a foundation for perpetual league and amity with them: but that submission to their parliament was no part of our constitution, nor ever in idea, if history may be credited: and, we [   ] appealed to their native justice and magnanimity as well as to the ties of our common kindred to disavow these usurpations which were likely to interrupt our connection and correspondence. They too have been deaf to the voice of justice and of consanguinity, and when occasions have been given them, by the regular course of their laws, of removing from their councils the disturbers of our harmony, they have, by their free election, reestablished them in power. At this very time too, they are permitting their chief magistrate to send over not only soldiers of our common blood, but Scotch and foreign mercenaries to invade and destroy us. These facts have given the last stab to agonizing affection, and manly spirit bids us to renounce forever these unfeeling brethren. We must endeavor to forget our former love for them, and hold them as we hold the rest of mankind, enemies in war,

25

free

an/unwarrantable/us

have
and we
have
conjured
them by/
would
inevitably

in peace friends. We might have been a free and a great people together; but a communication of grandeur and of freedom, it seems, is
below their dignity. Be it so, since they will have it. The road to hap-   We must
piness and to glory is open to us, too. We will tread it apart from   therefore
them, and acquiesce in the necessity which denounces our eternal
separation [   ]!   and hold

We therefore the representatives of the United States of America   them as we
in General Congress assembled, do in the name, and by the authority   hold the
of the good people of these states reject and renounce all allegiance   rest of
mankind
and subjection to the kings of Great Britain and all others who may   enemies in
hereafter claim by, through or under them; we utterly dissolve all po-   war, in
litical connection which may heretofore have subsisted between us   peace
and the people or parliament of Great Britain: and finally we do assert   friends
and declare these colonies to be free and independent states, and that
as free and independent states, they have full power to levy war, conclude peace, contract alliances, establish commerce, and to do all other
acts and things which independent states may of right do.

And for the support of this declaration, we mutually pledge to
each other our lives, our fortunes, and our sacred honor.

We, therefore, the representatives of the United States of America
in General Congress assembled, appealing to the supreme judge of the
world for the rectitude of our intentions, do in the name, and by the
authority of the good people of these colonies, solemnly publish and
declare, that these united colonies are, and of right ought to be free
and independent states; that they are absolved from all allegiance to
the British crown, and that all political connection between them and
the state of Great Britain is, and ought to be, totally dissolved; and that
as free and independent states, they have full power to levy war, conclude peace, contract alliances, establish commerce, and to do all other
acts and things which independent states may of right do.

And for the support of this declaration, with a firm reliance on the   30
protection of divine providence, we mutually pledge to each other our
lives, our fortunes, and our sacred honor.

For Journals

Is the content of the Declaration of Independence what you expected it
would be? What parts of it, if any, were familiar to you?

For Discussion

1.   Read the entire Declaration out loud, with each person in the class
reading part of it. Then do five minutes worth of freewriting. Using
your freewriting as a basis, compare your thoughts about the Declaration with those of your peers.

2. The Declaration was the justification for the idea of a democratic republic when no such republic had ever existed before. Working with someone else in your class, find three good examples of Jefferson's argument for the form of government he wants. What is the main point in each example? What is the supporting evidence? What is the conclusion?

3. The two most famous phrases in the Declaration of Independence declare that "all men are created equal" and that we are endowed by our Creator with the rights to "life, liberty, and the pursuit of happiness." What do you think those particular phrases mean? What does it mean to be created equal? Equal in what way? Equal spiritually? Equal legally? Equal intellectually? How do you think an American pursues happiness?

4. Jefferson, who was trained as a lawyer, was accustomed to framing arguments. Reread the Declaration as though you were a member of a jury listening to a trial lawyer's closing statement on behalf of his client. How does he refute the idea that George III is a just king and that Americans owe him their loyalty under any circumstances? What kind of evidence does he present about the injustices committed by the king and Great Britain to prove that Americans are entitled to decide on their own?

5. Many Americans did not support the Revolution and remained loyal to the English government. What arguments do you think they might have made to refute Jefferson's assertions? What holes would they have tried to find in his argument?

6. What do you think Jefferson wanted an American audience to take away from the Declaration? What do you think he wanted a British audience to learn?

For Writing

1. Look at the underlined phrases that were in the first version of the Declaration but were eliminated or changed in the final version; then examine the words in the margin that replaced them. For example, in the first draft, Jefferson included a long denunciation of slavery; in the final draft it is taken out because the southern slaveholders would not vote for a document that included it. Write an essay in which you respond to the following: What changes were the most surprising to you? Are there any cases in which you prefer the first version over the final one? Which ones do you think present a stronger argument against British injustice? Why?

2. There were many lawyers among the founding fathers; yet although they all opposed British rule, at least one of them was willing to defend British soldiers in court in the name of justice and civil liberties. Research and write a documented paper on the story of how John Adams defended British soldiers accused of murdering five colonials during the Boston Massacre. Include his reasons for taking on the case, what the colonial community thought of Adams's decision, and your own reaction.

∞ FROM *Civil Disobedience* (1850)

HENRY DAVID THOREAU

Henry David Thoreau (1817–1862) spent almost his entire life in and around Concord, Massachusetts, and found there all the subject matter he needed. An ardent abolitionist, diarist, nature writer, and natural scientist, he challenged American materialism and complacency as no other writer has before or since. Always an individualist, he wrote his most famous book, Walden *(1854), while living alone for two years at Walden Pond, where he said he could live a life of "simplicity, independence, magnanimity, trust." It was at Walden that he was arrested—willingly—and spent a night in jail for having refused to pay taxes supporting slavery and the Mexican-American War.* Civil Disobedience, *which explains Thoreau's theory of passive resistance, challenged his neighbors—and us—to examine our lives and our ethics, and to act.*

I heartily accept the motto—"That government is best which governs least"; and I should like to see it acted up to more rapidly and systematically. Carried out, it finally amounts to this, which also I believe,—"That government is best which governs not at all"; and when men are prepared for it, that will be the kind of government which they will have. Government is at best but an expedient; but most governments are usually, and all governments are sometimes, inexpedient. The objections which have been brought against a standing army, and they are many and weighty, and deserve to prevail, may also at last be brought against a standing government. The standing army is only an arm of the standing government. The government itself, which is only the mode which the people have chosen to execute their will, is equally liable to be abused and perverted before the people can act through it. Witness the present Mexican war, the work of comparatively a few individuals using the standing government as their tool; for, in the outset, the people would not have consented to this measure.

The American government,—what is it but a tradition, though a recent one, endeavoring to transmit itself unimpaired to posterity, but each instant losing some of its integrity? It has not the vitality and force of a single living man; for a single man can bend it to his will. It is a sort of wooden gun to the people themselves; and, if ever they should use it in earnest as a real one against each other, it will surely split. But it is not the less necessary for this; for the people must have some complicated machinery or other, and hear its din, to satisfy that idea of government which they have. Governments show thus how successfully men can be imposed on, even impose on themselves, for their own advantage. It is excellent, we must all allow; yet this government never of itself furthered any enterprise, but by the alacrity with which it got out of its way. *It* does not keep the country free. *It* does not settle the West. *It* does not educate. The character inherent in the American people has done all that has been accomplished; and it would have done somewhat more, if the government had not sometimes got in its way. For government is an expedient by which men would fain succeed in letting one another alone; and, as has been said, when it is most expedient, the governed are most let alone by it. Trade and commerce, if they were not made of india rubber, would never manage to bounce over the obstacles which legislators are continually putting in their way; and, if one were to judge these men wholly by the effects of their actions, and not partly by their intentions, they would deserve to be classed and punished with those mischievous persons who put obstructions on the railroads.

But, to speak practically and as a citizen, unlike those who call themselves no-government men, I ask for, not at once no government, but *at once* a better government. Let every man make known what kind of government would command his respect, and that will be one step toward obtaining it.

After all, the practical reason why, when the power is once in the hands of the people, a majority are permitted, and for a long period continue, to rule, is not because this seems fairest to the minority, but because they are physically the strongest. But a government in which the majority rule in all cases cannot be based on justice, even as far as men understand it. Can there not be a government in which majorities do not virtually decide right and wrong, but conscience?—in which majorities decide only those questions to which the rule of expediency is applicable? Must the citizen ever for a moment, or in the least degree, resign his conscience to the legislator? Why has every man a conscience, then? I think that we should be men first, and subjects afterward. It is not desirable to cultivate a respect for the law, so much as for the right. The only obligation which I have a right to assume, is to do at any time what I think right. . . .

How does it become a man to behave toward this American 5 government to-day? I answer that he cannot without disgrace be associated with it. I cannot for an instant recognize that political organization as *my* government which is the *slave's* government also.

All men recognize the right of revolution; that is, the right to refuse allegiance to and to resist the government, when its tyranny or its inefficiency are great and unendurable. But almost all say that such is not the case now. But such was the case, they think, in the Revolution of '75. If one were to tell me that this was a bad government because it taxed certain foreign commodities brought to its ports, it is most probable that I should not make an ado about it, for I can do without them; all machines have their friction; and possibly this does enough good to counterbalance the evil. At any rate, it is a great evil to make a stir about it. But when the friction comes to have its machine, and oppression and robbery are organized, I say, let us not have such a machine any longer. In other words, when a sixth of the population of a nation which has undertaken to be the refuge of liberty are slaves, and a whole country is unjustly overrun and conquered by a foreign army, and subject to military law, I think that it is not too soon for honest men to rebel and revolutionize. What makes this duty the more urgent is the fact, that the country so overrun is not our own, but ours is the invading army. . . .

Practically speaking, the opponents to a reform in Massachusetts are not a hundred thousand politicians at the South, but a hundred thousand merchants and farmers here, who are more interested in commerce and agriculture than they are in humanity, and are not prepared to do justice to the slave and to Mexico, *cost what it may.* I quarrel not with far-off foes, but with those who, near at home, co-operate with, and do the bidding of those far away, and without whom the latter would be harmless. We are accustomed to say, that the mass of men are unprepared; but improvement is slow, because the few are not materially wiser or better than the many. It is not so important that many should be as good as you, as that there be some absolute goodness somewhere; for that will leaven the whole lump. There are thousands who are *in opinion* opposed to slavery and to the war, who yet in effect do nothing to put an end to them; who, esteeming themselves children of Washington and Franklin, sit down with their hands in their pockets, and say that they know not what to do, and do nothing; who even postpone the question of freedom to the question of free-trade, and quietly read the prices-current along with the latest advices from Mexico, after dinner, and, it may be, fall asleep over them both. . . .

The American has dwindled into an Old Fellow,—one who may be known by the development of his organ of gregariousness, and a manifest lack of intellect and cheerful self-reliance; whose first and chief concern, on coming into the world, is to see that the alms-houses are in good repair; and, before yet he has lawfully donned the virile garb, to collect a fund for the support of the widows and orphans that may be; who, in short, ventures to live only by the aid of the mutual insurance company, which has promised to bury him decently. . . .

Unjust laws exist: shall we be content to obey them, or shall we endeavor to amend them, and obey them until we have succeeded, or shall we transgress them at once? Men generally, under such a government as this, think that they ought to wait until they have persuaded the majority to alter them. They think that, if they should resist, the remedy would be worse than the evil. But it is the fault of the government itself that the remedy *is* worse than the evil. *It* makes it worse. Why is it not more apt to anticipate and provide for reform? Why does it not cherish its wise minority? Why does it cry and resist before it is hurt? Why does it not encourage its citizens to be on the alert to point out its faults, and *do* better than it would have them? Why does it always crucify Christ, and excommunicate Copernicus and Luther, and pronounce Washington and Franklin rebels? . . .

If the injustice is part of the necessary friction of the machine of 10 government, let it go, let it go: perchance it will wear smooth,—certainly the machine will wear out. If the injustice has a spring, or a pulley, or a rope, or a crank, exclusively for itself, then perhaps you may consider whether the remedy will not be worse than the evil; but if it is of such a nature that it requires you to be the agent of injustice to another, then, I say, break the law. Let your life be a counter friction to stop the machine. What I have to do is to see, at any rate, that I do not lend myself to the wrong which I condemn.

As for adopting the ways which the State has provided for remedying the evil, I know not of such ways. They take too much time, and a man's life will be gone. I have other affairs to attend to. I came into this world, not chiefly to make this a good place to life [*sic*], but to live in it, be it good or bad. A man has not everything to do, but something; and because he cannot do *every thing*, it is not necessary that he should do *something* wrong. It is not my business to be petitioning the governor or the legislature any more than it is theirs to petition me; and if they should not hear my petition, what should I do then? But in this case the State has provided no way: its very Constitution is the evil. This may seem to be harsh and stubborn and unconciliatory; but it is to treat with the utmost kindness and consideration the only spirit that can appreciate or deserves it. So is all change for the better, like birth and death which convulse the body.

I do not hesitate to say, that those who call themselves abolitionists should at once effectually withdraw their support, both in person and property, from the government of Massachusetts, and not wait till they constitute a majority of one, before they suffer the right to prevail through them, I think that it is enough if they have God on their side, without waiting for that other one. Moreover, any man more right than his neighbors constitutes a majority of one already. . . .

Under a government which imprisons any unjustly, the true place for a just man is also in prison. The proper place to-day, the only place which Massachusetts has provided for her freer and less desponding spirits, is in her prisons, to be put out and locked out of the State by

her own act, as they have already put themselves out by their principles. It is there that the fugitive slave, and the Mexican prisoner on pa-
role, and the Indian come to plead the wrongs of his race, should find
them; on that separate, but more free and honorable ground, where
the State places those who are not *with* her, but *against* her,—the only
house in a slave-state in which a free man can abide with honor. If any
think that their influence would be lost there, and their voices no
longer afflict the ear of the State, that they would not be as an enemy
within its walls, they do not know by how much truth is stronger than
error, nor how much more eloquently and effectively he can combat
injustice who has experienced a little in his own person. Cast your
whole vote, not a strip of paper merely, but your whole influence. A
minority is powerless while it conforms to the majority; it is not even a
minority then; but it is irresistible when it clogs by its whole weight. If
the alternative is to keep all just men in prison, or give up war and
slavery, the State will not hesitate which to choose. If a thousand men
were not to pay their tax-bills this year, that would not be a violent
and bloody measure, as it would be to pay them, and enable the State
to commit violence and shed innocent blood. This is, in fact, the definition of a peaceable revolution, if any such is possible. If the taxgatherer, or any other public officer, asks me, as one has done, "But
what shall I do?" my answer is, "If you really wish to do anything, resign our office." When the subject has refused allegiance, and the officer has resigned his office, then the revolution is accomplished. But
even suppose blood should flow. Is there not a sort of blood shed
when the conscience is wounded? Through this wound a man's real
manhood and immortality flow out, and he bleeds to an everlasting
death. I see this blood flowing now. . . .

I have paid no poll-tax for six years. I was put into a jail once on
this account, for one night; and, as I stood considering the walls of
solid stone, two or three feet thick, the door of wood and iron, a foot
thick, and the iron grating which strained the light, I could not help
being struck with the foolishness of that institution which treated me
as if I were mere flesh and blood and bones, to be locked up. I wondered that it should have concluded at length that this was the best
use it could put me to, and had never thought to avail itself of my services in some way. I saw that, if there was a wall of stone between me
and my townsmen, there was a still more difficult one to climb or
break through, before they could get to be as free as I was. I did not for
a moment feel confined, and the walls seemed a great waste of stone
and mortar. I felt as if I alone of all my townsmen had paid my tax.
They plainly did not know how to treat me, but behaved like persons
who are underbred. In every threat and in every compliment there
was a blunder; for they thought that my chief desire was to stand the
other side of that stone wall. I could not but smile to see how industri-

ously they locked the door on my meditations, which followed them out again without let or hindrance, and *they* were really all that was dangerous. As they could not reach me, they had resolved to punish my body; just as boys, if they cannot come at some person against whom they have a spite, will abuse his dog. I saw that the State was half-witted, that it was timid as a lone woman with her silver spoons, and that it did not know its friends from its foes, and I lost all my remaining respect for it, and pitied it.

Thus the State never intentionally confronts a man's sense, intel- 15 lectual or moral, but only his body, his senses. It is not armed with superior wit or honesty, but with superior physical strength. I was not born to be forced. I will breathe after my own fashion. Let us see who is the strongest. What force has a multitude? They only can force me who obey a higher law than I. They force me to become like themselves. I do not hear of *men* being *forced* to live this way or that by masses of men. What sort of life were that to live? When I meet a government which says to me, "Your money or your life," why should I be in haste to give it my money? It may be in a great strait, and not know what to do: I cannot help that. It must help itself; do as I do. It is not worth the while to snivel about it. I am not responsible for the successful working of the machinery of society. I am not the son of the engineer. I perceive that, when an acorn and a chestnut fall side by side, the one does not remain inert to make way for the other, but both obey their own laws, and spring and grow and flourish as best they can, till one, perchance, overshadows and destroys the other. If a plant cannot live according to its nature, it dies; and so a man. . . .

I do not wish to quarrel with any man or nation. I do not wish to split hairs, to make fine distinctions, or set myself up as better than my neighbors. I seek rather, I may say, even an excuse for conforming to the laws of the land. I am but too ready to conform to them. Indeed I have reason to suspect myself on his head; and each year, as the taxgatherer comes round, I find myself disposed to review the acts and position of the general and state governments, and the spirit of the people, to discover a pretext for conformity. I believe that the State will soon be able to take all my work of this sort out of my hands, and then I shall be no better a patriot than my fellow-countrymen. Seen from a lower point of view, the Constitution, with all its faults, is very good; the law and the courts are very respectable; even this State and this American government are, in many respects, very admirable and rare things, to be thankful for, such as a great many have described them; but seen from a point of view a little higher, they are what I have described them; seen from a higher still, and the highest, who shall say that they are, or that they are worth looking at or thinking of at all?

However, the government does not concern me much, and I shall bestow the fewest possible thoughts on it. It is not many moments that

I live under a government, even in this world. If a man is thought-free, fancy-free, imagination-free, that which *is not* never for a long time appearing *to be* to him, unwise rulers or reformers cannot fatally interrupt him. . . .

The authority of government, even such as I am willing to submit to,—for I will cheerfully obey those who know and can do better than I, and in many things even those who neither know nor can do so well,—is still an impure one: to be strictly just, it must have the sanction and consent of the governed. It can have no pure right over my person and property but what I concede to it. The progress from an absolute to a limited monarchy, from a limited monarchy to a democracy, is a progress toward a true respect for the individual. Is a democracy, such as we know it, the last improvement possible in government? Is it not possible to take a step further towards recognizing and organizing the rights of man? There will never be a really free and enlightened State, until the State comes to recognize the individual as a higher and independent power, from which all its own power and authority are derived, and treats him accordingly. I please myself with imagining a State at last which can afford to be just to all men, and to treat the individual with respect as a neighbor, which even would not think it inconsistent with its own repose, if a few were to live aloof from it, not meddling with it, nor embraced by it, who fulfilled all the duties of neighbors and fellowmen. A State which bore this kind of fruit, and suffered it to drop off as fast as it ripened, would prepare the way for a still more perfect and glorious State, which also I have imagined, but not yet anywhere seen.

For Journals

Thoreau states that the government which governs best is the one which governs least. What functions does he seem to think government should stay out of? Which areas today would you want government to stay out of, and which do you think it should pursue more actively?

For Discussion

1. What is your response to Thoreau's ideas that an individual American following his or her conscience is a majority of one, and that fighting injustice by persuading the majority to change the law takes too long? What traditional ideas of good government and citizenship does he refute in these statements?

2. Thoreau says that the government does not keep the country free, that it does not settle the West, that it does not educate. In his opinion, then, what does it do?

3.   Democracy is supposed to be governed by the rule of the majority, but Thoreau says that his only obligation is "to do what I think is right." How do you respond to this assertion? Do you think that the two principles—majority rule and individual conscience—are compatible or mutually incompatible? Why?

4.   Thoreau refused to pay a poll tax as a protest against slavery and the war American was waging against Mexico. Do you find withholding taxes or going to jail reasonable ways of protesting injustice? If not, what would you say to refute Thoreau's belief in civil disobedience? Are there any principles for which you would be willing to break the law, go to jail, or otherwise practice civil disobedience yourself?

5.   What does Thoreau think constitute the responsibilities of a good citizen? Why does he think most Americans, even the ones opposed to slavery, are not truly good citizens?

6.   How would the government function if everyone followed his or her conscience the way Thoreau did? Did you see him as an extremist? A patriot? Both?

For Writing

1.   Write an essay in which you compose your own definition of patriotism. Be sure to identify the principles—political, personal, or ethical—on which your definition is based. You can refer to Thoreau, the Declaration, or any other readings, and either refute these arguments or draw on them to support your own views.

2.   Read one of Thoreau's other works—for example, *Walden,* the diary of his year-long adventure of living alone and being self-sufficient; or *A Week on the Concord and Merrimack Rivers,* an account of his canoeing trip in the American wilderness. Write a review critiquing Thoreau's skill as a naturalist and observer, and share the review with your peers; you should use secondary library sources (articles, biographies, and so on) if possible.

∞ *Independence Day Speech at Rochester* (1852)

FREDERICK DOUGLASS

At the time Frederick Douglass gave this speech, he had been living in Rochester, New York, for several years and editing his abolitionist newspaper, the Northern Star. *His autobiography had been published in 1845, after he escaped from slavery, and he subsequently spent two years in England lecturing and earning money to buy his freedom so that he could not be captured and returned to the South. He had a remarkable career as a diplomat, civil rights leader before and after the Civil War, marshal of the District of Columbia, organizer of black combat units, campaigner for women's rights, newspaper editor, and writer. He was asked to deliver the Fourth of July speech in Rochester in 1852. Fourth of July speeches were already an old American political tradition. Like parades and fireworks, the speeches on such occasions are usually celebratory, uncritical, and immediately forgettable. Douglass's speech, made nine years before the start of the Civil War, is the exception.*

Fellow citizens, pardon me, allow me to ask, why am I called upon to speak here today? What have I, or those I represent, to do with your national independence? Are the great principles of political freedom and of natural justice, embodied in that Declaration of Independence, extended to us? and am I, therefore, called upon to bring our humble offering to the national altar, and to confess the benefits and express devout gratitude for the blessings resulting from your independence to us?

Would to God, both for your sakes and ours, that an affirmative answer could be truthfully returned to these questions! Then would my task be light, and my burden easy and delightful. For who is there so cold that a nation's sympathy could not warm him? Who so obdurate and dead to the claims of gratitude that would not thankfully acknowledge such priceless benefits? Who so stolid and selfish that would not give his voice to swell the hallelujahs of a nation's jubilee, when the chains of servitude had been torn from his limbs? I am not that man. In a case like that the dumb might eloquently speak and the "lame man leap as an hart."[1]

But such is not the state of the case. I say it with a sad sense of the disparity between us. I am not included within the pale of this glorious anniversary! Your high independence only reveals the immeasurable distance between us. The blessings in which you, this day, rejoice are not enjoyed in common. The rich inheritance of justice, liberty, prosperity, and independence bequeathed by your fathers is shared by you, not by me. The sunlight that brought light and healing to you has brought stripes and death to me. This Fourth of July is yours, not mine. You may rejoice, I must mourn. To drag a man in fetters into the grand illuminated temple of liberty, and call upon him to join you in joyous anthems, were inhuman mockery and sacrilegious irony. Do you mean, citizens, to mock me by asking me to speak today? If so, there is a parallel to your conduct. And let me warn you that it is dangerous to copy the example of a nation whose crimes, towering up to heaven, were thrown down by the breath of the Almighty, burying that nation in irrevocable ruin! I can today take up the plaintive lament of a peeled and woe-smitten people![2]

---

[1]From the Bible, Isaiah 35:6.

[2]In 586 B.C.E., the near eastern kingdom of Babylon invaded Judea, burned the first temple in Jerusalem, and took the population into captivity.

"By the rivers of Babylon, there we sat down. Yea! we wept when we remembered Zion. We hanged our harps upon the willows in the midst thereof. For there, they that carried us away captive, required of us a song; and they who wasted us required of us mirth, saying, Sing us one of the songs of Zion. How can we sing the Lord's song in a strange land? If I forget thee, O Jerusalem, let my right hand forget her cunning. If I do not remember thee, let my tongue cleave to the roof of my mouth."[3]

Fellow citizens, above your national, tumultuous joy, I hear the mournful wail of millions! whose chains, heavy and grievous yesterday, are, today, rendered more intolerable by the jubilee shouts that reach them. If I do forget, if I do not faithfully remember those bleeding children of sorrow this day, "may my right hand forget her cunning, and may my tongue cleave to the roof of my mouth"! To forget them, to pass lightly over their wrongs, and to chime in with the popular theme would be treason most scandalous and shocking, and would make me a reproach before God and the world. My subject, then, fellow citizens, is *American slavery.* I shall see this day and its popular characteristics from the slave's point of view. Standing there identified with the American bondman, making his wrongs mine. I do not hesitate to declare with all my soul that the character and conduct of this nation never looked blacker to me than on this Fourth of July! Whether we turn to the declarations of the past or to the professions of the present, the conduct of the nation seems equally hideous and revolting. America is false to the past, false to the present, and solemnly binds herself to be false to the future. Standing with God and the crushed and bleeding slave on this occasion, I will, in the name of humanity which is outraged, in the name of liberty which is fettered, in the name of the Constitution and the Bible which are disregarded and trampled upon, dare to call in question and to denounce, with all the emphasis I can command, everything that serves to perpetuate slavery—the great sin and shame of America! "I will not equivocate, I will not excuse"; I will use the severest language I can command; and yet not one word shall escape me that any man, whose judgment is not blinded by prejudice, or who is not at heart a slaveholder, shall not confess to be right and just.

But I fancy I hear someone of my audience say, "It is just in this circumstance that you and your brother abolitionists fail to make a favorable impression on the public mind. Would you argue more and denounce less, would you persuade more and rebuke less, your cause would be much more likely to succeed." But, I submit, where all is plain, there is nothing to be argued. What point in the antislavery

---

[3]Psalm 137:1–6. This is the lament of the Judean exiles.

creed would you have me argue? On what branch of the subject do the people of this country need light? Must I undertake to prove that the slave is a man? That point is conceded already. Nobody doubts it. The slaveholders themselves acknowledge it in the enactment of laws for their government. They acknowledge it when they punish disobedience on the part of the slave. There are seventy-two crimes in the state of Virginia which, if committed by a black man (no matter how ignorant he be), subject him to the punishment of death; while only two of the same crimes will subject a white man to the like punishment. What is this but the acknowledgment that the slave is a moral, intellectual, and responsible being? The manhood of the slave is conceded. It is admitted in the fact that the Southern statute books are covered with enactments forbidding, under severe fines and penalties, the teaching of the slave to read or to write. When you can point to any such laws in reference to the beasts of the field, then I may consent to argue the manhood of the slave. When the dogs in your streets, when the fowls of the air, when the cattle on your hills, when the fish of the sea and the reptiles that crawl shall be unable to distinguish the slave from a brute, then will I argue with you that the slave is a man!

For the present, it is enough to affirm the equal manhood of the Negro race. Is it not astonishing that, while we are plowing, planting, and reaping, using all kinds of mechanical tools, erecting houses, constructing bridges, building ships, working in metals of brass, iron, copper, silver, and gold; that, while we are reading, writing, and ciphering, acting as clerks, merchants, and secretaries, having among us lawyers, doctors, ministers, poets, authors, editors, orators, and teachers; that, while we are engaged in all manner of enterprises common to other men, digging gold in California, capturing the whale in the Pacific, feeding sheep and cattle on the hillside, living, moving, acting, thinking, planning, living in families as husbands, wives, and children, and, above all, confession and worshiping the Christian's God, and looking hopefully for life and immortality beyond the grave, we are called upon to prove that we are men!

Would you have me argue that man is entitled to liberty? That he is the rightful owner of his own body? You have already declared it. Must I argue the wrongfulness of slavery? Is that a question for republicans? Is it to be settled by the rules of logic and argumentation, as a matter beset with great difficulty, involving a doubtful application of the principle of justice, hard to be understood? How should I look today, in the presence of Americans, dividing and subdividing a discourse, to show that men have a natural right to freedom? speaking of it relatively and positively, negatively and affirmatively? To do so would be to make myself ridiculous and to offer an insult to your understanding. There is not a man beneath the canopy of heaven that does not know that slavery is wrong for him.

What, am I to argue that it is wrong to make men brutes, to rob them of their liberty, to work them without wages, to keep them ignorant of their relations to their fellow men, to beat them with sticks, to flay their flesh with the lash, to load their limbs with irons, to hunt them with dogs, to sell them at auction, to sunder their families, to knock out their teeth, to burn their flesh, to starve them into obedience and submission to their masters? Must I argue that a system thus marked with blood, and stained with pollution, is wrong? No! I will not. I have better employment for my time and strength than such arguments would imply.

What, then, remains to be argued? Is it that slavery is not divine; 10 that God did not establish it; that our doctors of divinity are mistaken? There is blasphemy in the thought. That which is inhuman cannot be divine! Who can reason on such a proposition? They that can may; I cannot. The time for such argument is past.

At a time like this, scorching iron, not convincing argument, is needed. O! had I the ability, and could I reach the nation's ear, I would today pour out a fiery stream of biting ridicule, blasting reproach, withering sarcasm, and stern rebuke. For it is not light that is needed, but fire; it is not the gentle shower, but thunder. We need the storm, the whirlwind, and the earthquake. The feeling of the nation must be quickened; the conscience of the nation must be roused; the propriety of the nation must be startled; the hypocrisy of the nation must be exposed; and its crimes against God and man must be proclaimed and denounced.

What, to the American slave, is your Fourth of July? I answer: a day that reveals to him, more than all other days in the year, the gross injustice and cruelty to which he is the constant victim. To him, your celebration is a sham; your boasted liberty, an unholy license; your national greatness, swelling vanity; your sounds of rejoicing are empty and heartless; your denunciation of tyrants, brass-fronted impudence; your shouts of liberty and equality, hollow mockery; your prayers and hymns, your sermons and thanksgivings, with all your religious parade and solemnity, are, to Him, mere bombast, fraud, deception, impiety, and hypocrisy—a thin veil to cover up crimes which would disgrace a nation of savages. There is not a nation of savages. There is not a nation on the earth guilty of practices more shocking and bloody than are the people of the United States at this very hour.

Go where you may, search where you will, roam through all the monarchies and despotisms of the Old World, travel through South America, search out every abuse, and when you have found the last, lay your facts by the side of the everyday practices of this nation, and you will say with me that, for revolting barbarity and shameless hypocrisy, America reigns without a rival.

For Journals

Was Independence Day an appropriate time for Douglass to make his speech? Why or why not?

For Discussion

1. What do you think were the expectations of Douglass's audience when he began his speech? At what point in the speech do you think he begins to move toward his real topic?

2. Review Douglass's speech with one or two other people in your class, and identify the main points of his argument. (You might begin by identifying the crucial sentence in each paragraph.) What are his conclusions? What do you think he wants his audience to take away with them?

3. Refutation in Douglass's case is not only logically precise but full of emotion. Where in this speech do you find examples of Douglass's anger? Irony? Sarcasm? To what purpose does she express these? How do they help him make his point?

4. What evidence does Douglass accumulate to justify his conclusion that a slave is indeed a man? How would the argument be weaker without this proof? Are there any pieces of evidence that you would add?

5. Which phrases does Douglass quote or paraphrase from the language of the Declaration of Independence? How does he make use of those quotations to support his argument against slavery and to refute the idea that he should be celebrating the Fourth of July?

6. Douglass uses the technique of raising objections his audience might bring up and then refuting them himself. Find two or three examples of this strategy. Why do you think he employs it? In what ways is it effective in strengthening his argument?

For Writing

1. Douglass revised his autobiography, *The Life and Times of Frederick Douglass,* three times, adding information each time. For example, the first version, written before the Civil War, gives very few details about the people who helped him escape from slavery because Douglass didn't want to jeopardize anyone. The last version of the book, written many years later, is much more explicit. Write a research paper in which you compare elements of one version with another—for example, Douglass's childhood, his experiences as a slave, his education, his escape, or his relations with the Auld family. Consider these questions: What did Douglass add about a certain episode? Which version do you think is more effective? How was your initial response to the injustices Douglass fought against affected by reading the later version?

2.   Following the pattern of Douglass's speech, write a speech, for delivery at a formal occasion, about a political or social cause you believe in and which your audience may be hostile to or not enthusiastic about. Be sure to identify your audience—your parents, the people who came to your high school graduation, a historical figure (living or dead), a friend or acquaintance. Begin by making the conventional remarks expected on the occasion, and then focus on what you really want to speak about. Anticipate the objections of your audience, and then refute these objections.

∞ *Women's Right to Vote* (1873)

SUSAN B. ANTHONY

Susan B. Anthony (1820–1906) grew up in a Quaker family with strong abolitionist beliefs. A campaigner for women's rights even as a teenager, she was an early advocate of equal pay for women teachers and of coed education. At a time when women had almost no legal rights, she helped a bill through the New York legislature that gave women some control over their children and their earnings: both had previously been controlled by the husband. She supported the emancipation of slaves and was an active abolitionist, but devoted her life mainly to the fight for women's right to vote. In 1872, during a presidential election, she decided to test whether the Fourteenth Amendment to the Constitution—equal protection under the law—applied to women. She tried to register and was arrested and fined; the fine was never collected. This is the speech she gave to explain her views.

I stand before you under indictment for the alleged crime of having voted at the last presidential election, without having a lawful right to vote. It shall be my work this evening to prove to you that in thus doing, I not only committed no crime, but instead simply exercised my citizen's rights, guaranteed to me and all United States citizens by the National Constitution beyond the power of any State to deny.

Our democratic-republican government is based on the idea of the natural right of every individual member thereof to a voice and a vote in making and executing the laws. We assert the province of government to be to secure the people in the enjoyment of their inalienable rights. We throw to the winds the old dogma that government can give rights. No one denies that before governments were organized each individual possessed the right to protect his own life, liberty and property. When 100 to 1,000,000 people enter into a free government they do not barter away their natural rights; they simply pledge themselves to protect each other in the enjoyment of them through prescribed judicial and legislative tribunals. They agree to abandon the methods of brute force in the adjustment of their differences and adopt those of civilization. . . . The Declaration of Independence, the United States Constitution, the constitutions of the several States and the organic laws of the Territories, all alike propose to *protect* the people in the exercise of their God-given rights. Not one of them pretends to bestow rights.

> All men are created equal, and endowed by their Creator with certain inalienable rights. Among these are life, liberty and the pursuit of happiness. To secure these, governments are instituted among men, deriving their just powers from the consent of the governed.

Here is no shadow of government authority over rights, or exclusion of any class from their full and equal enjoyment. Here is pronounced the right of all men, and "consequently," as the Quaker preacher said, "of all women," to a voice in the government. And here, in this first paragraph of the Declaration, is the assertion of the natural right of all to the ballot; for how can "the consent of the governed" be given, if the right to vote be denied? . . . The women, dissatisfied as they are with this form of government, that enforces taxation without representation—that compels them to obey laws to which they never have given their consent—that imprisons and hangs them without a trial by a jury of their peers—that robs them, in marriage, of the custody of their own persons, wages, and children—are this half of the people who are left wholly at the mercy of the other half, in direct violation of the spirit and letter of the declarations of the framers of this government, every one of which was based on the immutable principle of equal rights to all. By these declarations, kings, popes, priests, aristocrats, all were alike dethroned and placed on a common level, politically, with the lowliest born subject or serf. By them, too, men, as such, were deprived of their divine right to rule and placed on a political level with women. By the practice of these declarations all class and caste distinctions would be abolished, and slave, serf, plebeian, wife, woman, all alike rise from their subject position to the broader platform of equality.

The preamble of the Federal Constitution says:

> We, the people of the United States, in order to form a more perfect union, establish justice, insure domestic tranquillity, provide for the common defence, promote the general welfare and secure the blessings of liberty to ourselves and our posterity, do ordain and establish this Constitution for the United States of America.

It was we, the people, not we, the white male citizens, nor we, the male citizens; but we, the whole people, who formed this Union. We 5 formed it not to give the blessings of liberty but to secure them; not to the half of ourselves and the half of our prosperity, but to the whole people—women as well as men. It is downright mockery to talk to women of their enjoyment of the blessings of liberty while they are denied the only means of securing them provided by this democratic-republican government—the ballot. . . .

When, in 1871, I asked [Senator Charles Sumner] to declare the power of the United States Constitution to protect women in their right to vote—as he had done for black men—he handed me a copy of all his speeches during that reconstruction period, and said:

> Put "sex" where I have "race" or "color," and you have here the best and strongest argument I can make for woman. There is not a doubt but women have the constitutional right to vote, and I will never vote for a Sixteenth Amendment to guarantee it to them. I voted for both the Fourteenth and Fifteenth under protest; would never have done it but for the pressing emergency of that hour; would have insisted that the power of the original Constitution to protect all citizens in the equal enjoyment of their rights should have been vindicated through the courts. But the newly-made freedmen had neither the intelligence, wealth nor time to await that slow process. Women do possess all these in an eminent degree, and I insist that they shall appeal to the courts and through them establish the powers of our American magna charta to protect every citizen of the republic.

But, friends, when in accordance with Senator Sumner's counsel I went to the ballot-box, last November, and exercised my citizen's right to vote, the courts did not wait for me to appeal to them—they appealed to me, and indicted me on the charge of having voted illegally. . . .

For any State to make sex a qualification, which must ever result in the disfranchisement of one entire half of the people, is to pass a bill of attainder, an ex post facto law, and is therefore a violation of the supreme law of the land. By it the blessings of liberty are forever withheld from women and their female posterity. For them, this government has no just powers derived from the consent of the governed. For them this government is not a democracy; it is not a republic. It is the most odious aristocracy ever established on the face of the globe. An oligarchy of wealth, where the rich govern the poor; an oligarchy of learning, where the educated govern the ignorant; or even an oligarchy of race, where the Saxon rules the African, might be endured; but this oligarchy of sex which makes father, brothers, husband, sons, the oligarchs over the mother and sisters, the wife and daughters of every household; which ordains all men sovereigns, all women subjects—carries discord and rebellion into every home of the nation. . . .

It is urged that the use of the masculine pronouns *he, his* and *him* in all the constitutions and laws, is proof that only men were meant to be included in their provisions. If you insist on this version of the letter of the law, we shall insist that you be consistent and accept the other horn of the dilemma, which would compel you to exempt women from taxation for the support of the government and from penalties for the violation of laws. There is no *she* or *her* or *hers* in the tax laws, and this is equally true of all the criminal laws.

Take for example, the civil rights law which I am charged with 10 having violated; not only are all the pronouns in it masculine, but everybody knows that it was intended expressly to hinder the rebel men from voting. It reads, "If any person shall knowingly vote without *his* having a lawful right." . . . I insist if government officials may thus manipulate the pronouns to tax, fine, imprison and hang women, it is their duty to thus change them in order to protect us in our right to vote. . . .

Though the words persons, people, inhabitants, electors, citizens, are all used indiscriminately in the national and State constitutions, there was always a conflict of opinion, prior to the war, as to whether they were synonymous terms, but whatever room there was for doubt, under the old regime, the adoption of the Fourteenth Amendment settled that question forever in its first sentence:

> All persons born or naturalized in the United States, and subject to the jurisdiction thereof, are citizens of the United States, and of the State wherein they reside.

The second settles the equal status of all citizens:

> No State shall make or enforce any law which shall abridge the privileges or immunities of citizens of the United States; nor shall any State deprive any person of life, liberty or property without due process of law, or deny to any person within its jurisdiction the equal protection of the laws.

The only question left to be settled now is: Are women persons? I scarcely believe any of our opponents will have the hardihood to say they are not. Being persons, then, women are citizens, and no State has a right to make any new law, or to enforce any old law, which shall abridge their privileges or immunities. Hence, every discrimination against women in the constitutions and laws of the several States is today null and void, precisely as is every one against negroes.

Is the right to vote one of the privileges or immunities of citizens? I think the disfranchised ex-rebels and ex-State prisoners all will agree that it is not only one of them, but the one without which all the others are nothing. Seek first the kingdom of the ballot and all things else shall be added, is the political injunction. . . .

However much the doctors of the law may disagree as to whether 15 people and citizens, in the original Constitution, were one and the same, or whether the privileges and immunities in the Fourteenth Amendment include the right of suffrage, the question of the citizen's right to vote is forever settled by the Fifteenth Amendment. "The right of citizens of the United States to vote shall not be denied or abridged by the United States, or by any State, on account of race, color or previous condition of servitude." How can the State deny or abridge the right of the citizen, if the citizen does not possess it? There is no escape from the conclusion that to vote is the citizen's right, and the specifications of race, color or previous condition of servitude can in no way impair the force of that emphatic assertion that the citizen's right to vote shall not be denied or abridged. . . .

If, however, you will insist that the Fifteenth Amendment's emphatic interdiction against robbing United States citizens of their suffrage "on account of race, color or previous condition of servitude," is a recognition of the right of either the United States or any State to deprive them of the ballot for any or all other reasons, I will prove to you that the class of citizens for whom I now plead are, by all the principles of our government and many of the laws of the States, included under the term "previous conditions of servitude."

Consider first married women and their legal status. What is servitude? "The condition of a slave." What is a slave? "A person who is robbed of the proceeds of his labor; a person who is subject to the will of another." By the laws of Georgia, South Carolina and all the States of the South, the negro had no right to the custody and control of his person. He belonged to his master. If he were disobedient, the master had the right to use correction. If the negro did not like the correction and ran away, the master had the right to use coercion to bring him back. By the laws of almost every State in this Union today, North as well as South, the married woman has no right to the custody and control of her person. The wife belongs to the husband; and if she refuse obedience he may use moderate correction, and if she do not like his moderate correction and leave his "bed and board," the husband may use moderate coercion to bring her back. The little word "moderate," you see, is the saving clause for the wife, and would doubtless be overstepped should her offended husband administer his correction with the "cat-o'-nine-tails," or accomplish his coercion with blood-hounds.

Again the slave had no right to the earnings of his hands, they belonged to his master; no right to the custody of his children, they belonged to his master; no right to sue or be sued, or to testify in the courts. If he committed a crime, it was the master who must sue or be sued. In many of the States there has been special legislation, giving married women the right to property inherited or received by bequest, or earned by the pursuit of any avocation outside the home; also giving them the right to sue and be sued in matters pertaining to such separate property; but not a single State of this Union has ever secured the wife in the enjoyment of her right to equal ownership of the joint earnings of the marriage copartnership. And since, in the nature of things, the vast majority of married women never earn a dollar by work outside their families, or inherit a dollar from their fathers, it follows that from the day of their marriage to the day of the death of their husbands not one of them ever has a dollar, except it shall please her husband to let her have it. . . .

Is anything further needed to prove woman's condition of servitude sufficient to entitle her to the guarantees of the Fifteenth Amendment? Is there a man who will not agree with me that to talk of freedom without the ballot is mockery to the women of this republic, precisely as New England's orator, Wendell Phillips, at the close of the late war declared it to be to the newly emancipated black man? I admit that, prior to the rebellion, by common consent, the right to enslave, as well as to disfranchise both native and foreign born persons, was conceded to the States. But the one grand principle settled by the war and the reconstruction legislation, is the supremacy of the national government to protect the citizens of the United States in their right to freedom and the elective franchise, against any and every interference on the part of the several States; and again and again have the American people asserted the triumph of this principle by their overwhelming majorities for Lincoln and Grant.

The one issue of the last two presidential elections was whether 20 the Fourteenth and Fifteenth Amendments should be considered the irrevocable will of the people; and the decision was that they should be, and that it is not only the right, but the duty of the national government to protect all United States citizens in the full enjoyment and free exercise of their privileges and immunities against the attempt of any State to deny or abridge. . . .

It is upon this just interpretation of the United States Constitution that our National Woman Suffrage Association, which celebrates the twenty-fifth anniversary of the woman's rights movement next May in New York City, has based all its arguments and action since the passage of these amendments. We no longer petition legislature or Congress to give us the right to vote, but appeal to women everywhere to exercise their too long neglected "citizen's right." We appeal to the inspectors of election to receive the votes of all United States citizens, as it is their duty to do. We appeal to United States commissioners and marshals to arrest, as is their duty, the inspectors who reject the votes of United States citizens, and leave alone those who perform their duties and accept these votes. We ask the juries to return verdicts of "not guilty" in the cases of law-abiding United States citizens who cast their votes, and inspectors of election who receive and count them.

We ask the judges to render unprejudiced opinions of the law, and wherever there is room for doubt to give the benefit to the side of liberty and equal rights for women, remembering that, as Sumner says,

"The true rule of interpretation under our National Constitution, especially since its amendments, is that anything *for* human rights is constitutional, everything *against* human rights unconstitutional." It is on this line that we propose to fight our battle for the ballot—peaceably but nevertheless persistently—until we achieve complete triumph and all United States citizens, men and women alike, are recognized as equals in the government.

For Journals

What was your reaction to the first sentence in Anthony's speech?

For Discussion

1. Almost all men in Victorian America, and many women, thought that women should not have the right to vote. What would you guess the arguments were against women's suffrage? What would the opponents of suffrage have been worried about if women did secure the right to vote?

2. How do Anthony's references to the language of the Declaration of Independence, the Constitution, and the Fourteenth and Fifteenth Amendments help her refute the belief that women should not be allowed to vote? Why do you think she chooses those particular quotations?

3. How does Anthony see the political condition of women in her own time as compared with the role of American men in the Revolution? As compared with the condition of former slaves? Considering your own knowledge, how valid do you find her comparisons?

4. Evaluate Anthony's argument that if laws refer only to "he" and "him," women shouldn't have to pay taxes to support the government or go to jail for breaking the law. What are the strengths and weaknesses of this argument? How would you make it stronger? What would Thoreau think of it?

5. Anthony argues that women are "persons" within the legal meaning stated by the Constitution. In an earlier selection in this chapter, Douglass argued that African Americans are men. Look back at Douglass's argument and compare it with Anthony's. Do they argue in similar ways or differently? Why do they feel compelled to argue these points at all?

6. Like Douglass, Anthony poses questions in her argument and then refutes them. What do you think are the advantages or disadvantages of this strategy? Which of her own questions do you think she answers best? In her place, what other questions would you ask? How would you answer them?

For Writing

1.   Write a paper in which you argue either for or against one of the following:

a. An American teenager today has as much right to emancipation from parental control as a married woman in Anthony's time had with respect to her husband's control.

b. Women should be allowed to serve in combat units in the armed forces.

c. The women's movement has become too aggressive and does more harm than good.

Whichever issue or side you take, follow Anthony's example in using the Constitution and the Declaration of Independence for your argument. Keep in mind what someone who disagrees with you would say, so that you can anticipate some of the serious objections and refute them.

2.   Using recent biographies of Anthony or *The Life and Works of Susan B. Anthony*, write a documented paper on one of the following topics:

a. The influence of her Quaker upbringing on her activism; her early fights for equal pay for women teachers.

b. Her support of emancipation during the Civil War.

c. Her refusal to support the vote for freed slaves because it did not include a vote for women.

d. The circumstances surrounding her attempt to register to vote and her subsequent arrest.

∞ *Plessy v. Ferguson* (1894)

U.S. SUPREME COURT

After the Civil War and Reconstruction, southern legislatures began passing Jim Crow laws, which instituted segregation against African Americans. In an earlier decision, the Court had repealed the Civil Rights Act of 1875, and the majority decision in Plessy *effectively made discrimination legal. Justice John Harlan, who had grown up as a slaveholder but who had become one of a long line of distinguished Supreme Court dissenters, was the only justice to vote against the decision.*

Majority Opinion (by Justice Henry Billings Brown)

Mr. Justice Brown, . . . delivered the opinion of the court.

This case turns upon the constitutionality of an Act of the general assembly of the state of Louisiana, passed in 1890, providing for separate railway carriages for the white and colored races.

The first section of the statute enacts "that all railway companies carrying passengers in their coaches in this state, shall provide equal but separate accommodations for the white, and colored races."

. . . [Plessy argued that he] was seven-eighths Caucasian and one-eighth African blood; that the mixture of colored blood was not discernible in him; and that he was entitled to every right, privilege, and immunity secured to citizens of the United States of the white race; and that, upon such theory, he took possession of a vacant seat in a coach where passengers of the white race were accommodated, and was ordered by the conductor to vacate said coach and take a seat in another, assigned to persons of the colored race, and, having refused to comply with such demand, he was forcibly ejected, with the aid of a police officer, and imprisoned in the parish jail to answer a charge of having violated the above act.

The constitutionality of this act is attacked upon the ground that it 5 conflicts both with the Thirteenth Amendment of the Constitution abolishing slavery, and the Fourteenth Amendment, which prohibits certain restrictive legislation on the part of the states.

1. That it does not conflict with the Thirteenth Amendment, which abolished slavery and involuntary servitude, except as a punishment for crime, is too clear for argument. Slavery implies involuntary servitude,—a state of bondage; the ownership of mankind as a chattel, or, at least, the control of the labor and services of one man for the benefit of another, and the absence of a legal right to the disposal of his own person, property, and services.

. . . "It would be running the slavery question into the ground," said Mr. Justice Bradley," to make it apply to every act of discrimination which a person may see fit to make as to the guests he will entertain, or as to the people he will take into his coach or cab or car, or admit to his concert or theater, or deal with in other matters of intercourse or business."

A statute which implies merely a legal distinction between the white and colored races—a distinction which is founded in the color of the two races, and which must always exist so long as white men are distinguished from the other race by color—has no tendency to destroy the legal equality of the two races, or re-establish a state of involuntary servitude. . . .

2. By the Fourteenth Amendment, all persons born or naturalized in the United States, and subject to the jurisdiction thereof, are made citizens of the United States and of the state wherein they reside; and the states are forbidden from making or enforcing any law which . . . shall deprive any person of life, liberty, or property without due process of law, or deny to any person . . . equal protection of the laws.

The object of the Amendment was undoubtedly to enforce the ab- 10 solute equality of the two races before the law, but in the nature of things, it could not have been intended to abolish distinctions based upon color, or to enforce social, as distinguished from political, equality, or a commingling of the two races upon terms unsatisfactory to either. Laws permitting, and even requiring, their separation, in places where they are liable to be brought into contact, do not necessarily imply the inferiority of either race to the other. . . . The most common instance of this is connected with the establishment of separate schools for white and colored children. . . .

So far, then, as a conflict with the Fourteenth Amendment is concerned, the case reduces itself to the question whether the statute of Louisiana is a reasonable regulation, and with respect to this there must necessarily be a large discretion on the part of the legislature. In determining the question of reasonableness, it is at liberty to act with reference to the established usages, customs, and traditions of the people, and with a view to the promotion of their comfort, and the preservation of the public peace and good order. Gauged by this standard, we cannot say that a law which authorizes or even requires the separation of the two races in public conveyances is unreasonable, or more obnoxious to the Fourteenth Amendment than the acts of Congress requiring separate schools for colored children in the District of Columbia, the constitutionality of which does not seem to have been questioned, or the corresponding acts of state legislatures.

We consider the underlying fallacy of the plaintiff's argument to consist in the assumption that the enforced separation of the two races stamps the colored race with a badge of inferiority. If this be so, it is not by reason of anything found in the act, but solely because the colored race chooses to put that construction upon it. The argument necessarily assumes that if, as has been more than once the case, and is not unlikely to be so again, the colored race should become the dominant power in the state legislature, and should enact a law in precisely similar terms, it would thereby relegate the white race to an inferior position. We imagine that the white race, at least, would not acquiesce in this assumption. The argument also assumes that social prejudices may be overcome by legislation, and that equal rights cannot be secured to the Negro except by an enforced commingling of the two races. We cannot accept this proposition. If the two races are to meet upon terms of social equality, it must be the result of natural affinities, a mutual appreciation of each other's merits, and a voluntary consent of individuals. . . . Legislation is powerless to eradicate racial instincts, or to abolish distinctions based upon physical differences, and the attempt to do so can only result in accentuating the difficulties of the present situation. If the civil and political rights of both races be equal, one cannot be inferior to the other civilly or politically. If one race be inferior to the other socially, the Constitution of the United States cannot put them upon the same plane.

Dissenting Opinion (by Justice John Harlan)

. . . In respect of civil rights common to all citizens, the Constitution of the United States does not, I think, permit any public authority to know the race of those entitled to be protected in the enjoyment of such rights. Every true man has pride of race, and under appropriate circumstances when the rights of others, his equals before the law, are not to be affected, it is his privilege to express such pride and to take such action based upon it as to him seems proper. But I deny that any legislative body or judicial tribunal may have regard to the race of citizens when the civil rights of those citizens are involved. Indeed, such legislation, as that here in question, is inconsistent not only with the equality of rights which pertains to citizenship, national and state, but with the personal liberty enjoyed by every one within the United States. . . .

The white race deems itself to be the dominant race in this country. And so it is, in prestige, in achievements, in education, in wealth and in power. So, I doubt not, it will continue to be for all time, if it remains true to its great heritage and holds fast to the principles of constitutional liberty. But in view of the Constitution, in the eye of the law, there is in this country no superior, dominant, ruling class of citizens. There is no caste here. Our Constitution is color-blind, and neither knows nor tolerates classes among citizens. In respect of civil rights, all citizens are equal before the law. The humblest is the peer of the most powerful. The law regards man as man, and takes no account of his surroundings or of his color when his civil rights as guaranteed by the supreme law of the land are involved. It is, therefore, to be regretted that this high tribunal, the final expositor of the fundamental law of the land, has reached the conclusion that it is competent for a State to regulate the enjoyment by citizens of their civil rights solely upon the basis of race. . . .

The arbitrary separation of citizens, on the basis of race, while they are on a public highway, is a badge of servitude wholly inconsistent with the civil freedom and the equality before the law established by the Constitution. It cannot be justified upon any legal grounds.

If evils will result from the commingling of the two races upon public highways established for the benefit of all, they will be infinitely less than those that will surely come from state legislation regulating the enjoyment of civil rights upon the basis of race. We boast of the freedom enjoyed by our people above all other peoples. But it is difficult to reconcile that boast with a state of the law which, practically, puts the brand of servitude and degradation upon a large class of our fellow-citizens, our equals before the law. The thin disguise of "equal" accommodations for passengers in railroad coaches will not mislead anyone, nor atone for the wrong this day done.

For Journals

In your own words, what did the Court decide in this case? Who won? Who lost?

For Discussion

1. Mr. Plessy argued that denying him the right to ride in the white railway carriage was a violation of the Thirteenth Amendment, which prohibits slavery, and the Fourteenth Amendment, which grants equal protection under the law. What reasons does Justice Brown give to refute Plessy's argument? Why does he think the two amendments do not apply to this case?

2. How does the Court define "separate but equal"?

3. In the majority opinion, Justice brown says that equality before the law doesn't have to mean social equality. Do you think it is possible to be equal before the law but not in any other way? What is your definition of equality?

4. How would you refute the Court's statement that if blacks felt inferior because they were forced to ride in a separate railway carriage, it was their fault because they chose to look at it that way?

5. In his minority opinion, what does Justice Harlan think is the real meaning of the separate-but-equal laws as far as the future of black–white relations is concerned? What kinds of injustices does he foresee in a segregated South?

6. Why do you think Harlan sees dangers to other minorities besides African Americans in the *Plessy* decision? What does he mean when he says that the decision would not mislead anyone and not atone for the wrong done? Do you agree with him?

For Writing

1. Research the term "Jim Crow." Write a documented paper in which you discuss the origins of the term and how Jim Crow laws affected the lives of southern blacks (give specific examples of segregation in everyday life). If you know someone who had firsthand experience with the Jim Crow laws, interview him or her for your paper.

2. Both Justice Harlan in *Plessy* and Thoreau in *Civil Disobedience* believed, with very different results, that legislation is not a good way to change people's behavior. Write an essay in which you argue for or against the proposition that injustice cannot be changed through legislation and that trying to eradicate differences through legislation can only make a situation worse. Focus your argument around an injustice you think needs changing. Use Thoreau, *Plessy*, or both to back up your assertions.

∾ *Dolls* (1935)

EUDORA WELTY

Eudora Welty (1909–) was born in Mississippi. She is most famous as a writer of novels and short stories, including Delta Wedding *(1946),* Golden Apples *(1949), and* Losing Battles *(1970); and she won the Pulitzer Prize for* The Optimist's Daughter *(1972). In her fiction, which is set in the South she knows so well, she often writes about familial conflicts and people who don't know themselves or those close to them as well as they should. In her photography, which also revolves mainly around Mississippi, she provides a compassionate and extraordinarily perceptive record of the lives of ordinary people, particularly the poor southern blacks whose dignity she portrays and respects. This photograph is one of a series she took in the 1930s, when she was hired by the Works Progress Administration to interview poor people and see how they coped with the additional burden of the Depression. Many of her greatest photographs, taken in the rural South, New York City, and Ireland, among other places, have been collected in a book called* Welty Photographs *(1989).*

For Journals

What is your most or least favorite childhood photograph of yourself? What does it remind you of?

For Discussion

1. Until recently, almost no dolls were manufactured with a skin color other than white. What do you think was the effect on the children in this picture of having only blond dolls to play with? Why would there be a connection between the toys and the way they see themselves?

2. This picture is usually called "Dolls." Based on your own first impressions of it, what new title would you give that would be more descriptive of its emotional impact? Why do you think Welty did not pick a more emotional title?

3. A photograph can establish a point of view, make an argument, or assert a moral viewpoint. Welty said that her photographs were facts. She took this photograph when life in the South was completely segregated and southern blacks lacked the most basic civil rights. Looking at the details of this picture—how the girls hold the dolls, the girls' facial expressions, the background, how the children and the dolls are dressed, and so on—explain in your own words what Welty was trying to communicate in this picture, and how well you think she succeeded.

For Writing

1. Bring to class a childhood photograph of yourself that brings back strong memories or a photograph of children from a magazine. Trade that photograph with someone else in class. Write an essay on the other person's photograph, analyzing it closely, as you did with Welty's photo. Make up a history for it: describe the mood it conveys, what happened just before and after the picture was taken, and so on. Use details from the photo as evidence for your interpretation. Then trade essays with your peer and compare the results; write follow-up notes on how accurate or inaccurate your interpretations were.

2.   Eudora Welty said her photographs were facts. Select another photograph from her book, and write an essay in which you evaluate and compare it with "Dolls," in the light of Welty's statement. Do you think she points a finger at injustice? Do you find her photos of black southern life under segregation objective? Sympathetic? Depressing? Refer directly to the photographs to support your argument.

∞ *Freedom of Speech* (1943)

NORMAN ROCKWELL

Norman Rockwell (1894–1978) was born in New York City. An artist and illustrator who specialized in portraying the archetypal American small town, he was best known for the covers he illustrated for the Saturday Evening Post. *He was famous for creating visual images that told stories and communicated detailed, if sometimes idealized, images of American life. This picture is from one of his best-known series,* The Four Freedoms, *which he painted in 1943, in the middle of World War II.*

For Journals

Have you ever made a speech at a public gathering? How comfortable are you with the idea of getting up to speak in a possibly hostile or indifferent setting?

For Discussion

1.   What would you think is the economic level or job status of the man who is speaking? How do you think it compares to that of the other people in the audience How can you tell that he's not accustomed to making speeches? Given the title of the painting, what purpose could Rockwell have had in making that particular person the central figure?

2.   Four words are visible on the papers held by the man in the forefront of the picture: *Annual Report, town,* and *Vermont.* Why do you think Rockwell chose a small-town setting? How might this painting be different if the setting were a poor city neighborhood? A middle-class suburb?

3. Rockwell wanted to make a patriotic statement about the freedoms that American soldiers in World War II were fighting to preserve. There are no American flags and we don't know what the subject matter is, so what makes this picture a persuasively patriotic statement in favor of freedom of speech?

4. What are the ages, postures, and expressions of the people listening to the speaker? How would you describe the clothing and expression of the older man to his right? In what ways do

For Writing

1. If your library or local bookstore has a book on Rockwell, look at the other three pictures he did in the series *The Four Freedoms*, portraying freedom from want, freedom from fear, and freedom of worship. Pick one or two of them, and write an analysis in which you examine the theme of the painting as it is expressed in individual figures, their clothing, body language, expressions, and so on; the relationship between them and the background, surrounding buildings and objects, and so on. Alternatively, choose a different painting by Rockwell that deals with a different aspect of American life, such as the World War II poster in Chapter 3, or such as family life, children playing, or adults doing their work.

∞ *Brown* v. *Board of Education* (1954)

U.S. SUPREME COURT

Brown v. Board of Education is the landmark decision of the Supreme Court, under Chief Justice Earl Warren, in the twentieth century. Its official result was to declare segregation in public schools unconstitutional and to overturn the Plessy doctrine of "separate but equal" facilities. It followed on the heels of other cases that had outlawed segregation in professional schools. Its effect was to take away the legal underpinnings of segregation in all areas, and it began a process of dismantling segregation that has had a profound effect on American life.

These cases come to us from the states of Kansas, South Carolina, Virginia, and Delaware. They are premised on different facts and different local conditions, but a common legal question justifies their consideration together in this consolidated opinion.

In each of the cases, minors of the Negro race, through their legal representatives, seek the aid of the courts in obtaining admission to the public schools of their community on a nonsegregated basis. In each instance, they have been denied admission to schools attended by white children under laws requiring or permitting segregation according to race. This segregation was alleged to deprive the plaintiffs of the equal protection of the laws under the Fourteenth Amendment. In each of the cases other than the Delaware case, a three-judge federal district court denied relief to the plaintiffs on the so-called "separate but equal" doctrine announced by this Court in *Plessy* v. *Ferguson*. . . . Under that doctrine, equality of treatment is accorded when the races are provided substantially equal facilities, even though these facilities be separate. . . .

The plaintiffs contend that segregated public schools are not "equal" and cannot be made "equal," and that hence they are deprived of the equal protection of the laws. Because of the obvious importance of the question presented, the Court took jurisdiction. . . .

There are findings below that the Negro and white schools involved have been equalized, or are being equalized, with respect to buildings, curricula, qualifications and salaries of teachers, and other "tangible" factors. Our decision, therefore, cannot turn on merely a comparison of these tangible factors in the Negro and white schools involved in each of the cases. We must look instead to the effect of segregation itself on public education.

In approaching this problem, we cannot turn the clock back to 5 1868 when the Amendment was adopted, or even to 1896 when *Plessy* v. *Ferguson* was written. We must consider public education in the light of its full development and its present place in American life throughout the nation. Only in this way can it be determined if segregation in public schools deprives these plaintiffs of the equal protection of the laws.

Today, education is perhaps the most important function of state and local governments. Compulsory school attendance laws and the great expenditures for education both demonstrate our recognition of the importance of education to our democratic society. It is required in the performance of our most basic public responsibilities, even service in the armed forces. It is the very foundation of good citizenship. Today it is a principal instrument in awakening the child to cultural values, in preparing him for later professional training, and in helping him to adjust normally to his environment. In these days, it is doubtful that any child may reasonably be expected to succeed in life if he is denied the opportunity of an education. Such an opportunity, where the state has undertaken to provide it, is a right which must be made available to all on equal terms.

We come then to the question presented: Does segregation of children in public schools solely on the basis of race, even though the physical facilities and other "tangible" factors may be equal, deprive the children of the minority group of equal educational opportunities? We believe that it does.

In *Sweatt* v. *Painter*, . . . in finding that a segregated law school for Negroes could not provide them equal educational opportunities, this Court relied in large part on "those qualities which are incapable of objective measurement but which make for greatness in a law school." In *McLaurin* v. *Oklahoma State Regents*, . . . the Court, in requiring that a Negro admitted to a white graduate school be treated like all other students, again resorted to intangible considerations: ". . . his ability to study, to engage in discussions and exchange views with other students, and, in general, to learn his profession." Such considerations apply with added force to children in grade and high schools. To separate them from others of similar age and qualifications solely because of their race generates a feeling of inferiority as to their status in the community that may affect their hearts and minds in a way unlikely ever to be undone. The effect of this separation on their educational opportunities was well stated by a finding in the Kansas case by a court which nevertheless felt compelled to rule against the Negro plaintiffs:

> Segregation of white and colored children in public schools has a detrimental effect upon the colored children. The impact is greater when it has the sanction of the law; for the policy of separating the races is usually interpreted as denoting the inferiority of the Negro group. A sense of inferiority affects the motivation of a child to learn. Segregation with the sanction of law, therefore, has a tendency to retard the educational and mental development of Negro children and to deprive them of some of the benefits they would receive in a racially integrated school system.

Whatever may have been the extent of psychological knowledge at the time of *Plessy* v. *Ferguson*, this finding is amply supported by modern authority. Any language in *Plessy* v. *Ferguson* contrary to this finding is rejected.

We conclude that in the field of public education the doctrine of "separate but equal" has no place. Separate educational facilities are inherently unequal. Therefore, we hold that the plaintiffs and others similarly situated for whom the actions have been brought are, by reason of the segregation complained of, deprived of the equal protection of the laws guaranteed by the Fourteenth Amendment. . . .

For Journals

Summarize the decision in the case. In your own words, write what you think the essence of the decision was.

For Discussion

1. In American law, precedent—what has been determined in previous legal decisions—is very important, so refuting the ruling of *Plessy* after almost fifty years required considerable justification. How does the Warren Court in *Brown* get around the fact that *Plessy* had stood since it was declared good law in 1896?

2. What are the Court's main points in its argument that education today and education right after the Civil War that a new interpretation of *Plessy* is appropriate?

3. Analyze what the Court says about the harmful effects of segregated schooling on black children. What injustice does the Court in *Brown* see in segregation that the Court in *Plessy* did not? Why wouldn't a school for black children do as good a job as an integrated school?

4. The decision of a court is called a ruling. In refuting *Plessy*, the Warren Court made a ruling that separate public schools could not also be equal. Why did the Court think that separate but equal was a contradiction?

5. If you had to pick the most crucial sentence from this ruling, what would it be? Why?

6. The Court says that if it only took into account "tangible" factors like buildings and curriculum for segregated schools, it would fail to see the situation in its entirety. What kinds of "intangibles" do you think the Warren Court considered in reaching its decision in *Brown*?

For Writing

1. Research one of the following and, in a documented essay, discuss its significance for civil liberties in the United States:

a. The life and career of Thurgood Marshall, who argued *Brown* and later became solicitor general of the United States and then the first African American justice of the Supreme Court.

b. Marshall's strategy, as leading attorney for the NAACP, in challenging segregation through the courts instead of in state legislatures, and in picking elementary school education as the point of attack.

c. The significance of the cases before *Brown* that are mentioned by Chief Justice Warren, especially *Sweatt* v. *Painter* and *McLaurin* v. *Oklahoma State Regents*.

2. Chief Justice Warren wrote that we must look at the intangibles to get a complete picture. Write an essay in which you compare the *Brown* decision and its use of intangible factors to either Douglass's Independence Day speech or Anthony's "Women's Right to Vote" speech. What tangible evidence and intangibles do the authors consider in arguing against injustice? Which category is more important to them? Which do you think is more important? Use examples from the selections as proof for your conclusions.

∞ *Letter from Birmingham Jail* (1963)

MARTIN LUTHER KING JR.

The strategy developed by the modern civil rights movement and its leader, the young Atlanta minister Martin Luther King Jr. (see Chapter 4), was the policy of non-violent resistance. Based on the teachings of the Bible, Mahatma Gandhi, and Thoreau, it revolved around peaceful marches, sit-ins at lunch counters, and economic boycotts of buses and businesses. In 1963, while leading demonstrations in Montgomery, Alabama, King was arrested. In jail he wrote a letter of justification and explanation addressed to eight southern clergymen who had issued a public statement objecting to the demonstrations King led and to demonstrations as a method for dealing with racial problems. Both letters are reprinted here.

Clergymen's Letter

We the undersigned clergymen are among those who, in January, issued "An Appeal for Law and Order and Common Sense," in dealing with racial problems in Alabama. We expressed understanding that honest convictions in racial matters could properly be pursued in the courts, but urged that decisions of those courts should in the meantime be peacefully obeyed.

Since that time there had been some evidence of increased forbearance and a willingness to face facts. Responsible citizens have undertaken to work on various problems which cause racial friction and unrest. In Birmingham, recent public events have given indication that we all have opportunity for a new constructive and realistic approach to racial problems.

However, we are now confronted by a series of demonstrations by some of our Negro citizens, directed and led in part by outsiders. We recognize the natural impatience of people who feel that their hopes are slow in being realized. But we are convinced that these demonstrations are unwise and untimely.

We agree rather with certain local Negro leadership which has called for honest and open negotiation of racial issues in our area. And we believe this kind of facing of issues can best be accomplished by citizens of our own metropolitan area, white and Negro, meeting with their knowledge and experience of the local situation. All of us need to face that responsibility and find proper channels for its accomplishment.

Just as we formerly pointed out that "hatred and violence have no 5 sanction in our religious and political traditions," we also point out that such actions as incite to hatred and violence, however technically peaceful those actions may be, have not contributed to the resolution of our local problems. We do not believe that these days of new hope are days when extreme measures are justified in Birmingham.

We commend the community as a whole, and the local news media and the law enforcement officials in particular, on the calm manner in which these demonstrations have been handled. We urge the public to continue to show restraint should the demonstrations continue, and the law enforcement officials to remain calm and continue to protect our city from violence.

We further strongly urge our own Negro community to withdraw support from these demonstrations, and to unite locally in working peacefully for a better Birmingham. When rights are consistently denied, a cause should be pressed in the courts and in negotiations among local leaders, and not in the streets. We appeal to both our white and Negro citizenry to observe the principles of law and order and common sense.

Signed by:

C. C. J. Carpenter, D.D., LL.D., Bishop of Alabama

Joseph A. Durick, D.D., Auxiliary Bishop, Diocese of Mobile, Birmingham

Milton L. Grafman, Rabbi, Temple Emanu-El, Birmingham, Alabama

Paul Hardin, Bishop of the Alabama-West Florida Conference of the Methodist Church

Nolan B. Harmon, Bishop of the North Alabama Conference of the Methodist Church

George M. Murray, D.D., LL.D., Bishop Coadjutor, Episcopal Diocese of Alabama

Edward V. Ramage, Moderator, Synod of the Alabama Presbyterian Church in the United States

Earl Stallings, Pastor, First Baptist Church, Birmingham, Alabama

King's Letter

April 16, 1963

My Dear Fellow Clergymen:

While confined here in the Birmingham city jail, I came across your recent statement calling my present activities "unwise and untimely." Seldom do I pause to answer criticism of my work and ideas. If I sought to answer all the criticisms that cross my desk, my secretaries would have little time for anything other than such correspondence in the course of the day, and I would have no time for constructive work. But since I feel that you are men of genuine good will and that your criticisms are sincerely set forth, I want to try to answer your statement in what I hope will be patient and reasonable terms.

I think I should indicate why I am here in Birmingham, since you have been influenced by the view which argues against "outsiders coming in." I have the honor of serving as president of the Southern Christian Leadership Conference, an organization operating in every southern state, with headquarters in Atlanta, Georgia. We have some eighty-five affiliated organizations across the South, and one of them is the Alabama Christian Movement for Human Rights. Frequently we share staff, educational and financial resources with our affiliates. Several months ago the affiliate here in Birmingham asked us to be on call to engage in a nonviolent direct-action program if such were deemed necessary. We readily consented, and when the hour came we lived up to our promise. So I, along with several members of my staff, am here because I was invited here. I am here because I have organizational ties here.

But more basically, I am in Birmingham because injustice is here. 10 Just as the prophets of the eighth century B.C. left their villages and carried their "thus saith the Lord" far beyond the boundaries of their home towns, and just as the Apostle Paul left his village of Tarsus and carried the gospel of Jesus Christ to the far corners of the Greco-Roman world, so am I compelled to carry the gospel of freedom beyond my own home town. Like Paul, I must constantly respond to the Macedonian call for aid.

Moreover, I am cognizant of the interrelatedness of all communities and states. I cannot sit idly by in Atlanta and not be concerned about what happens in Birmingham. Injustice anywhere is a threat to justice everywhere. We are caught in an inescapable network of mutuality, tied in a single garment of destiny. Whatever affects one directly, affects all indirectly. Never again can we afford to live with the narrow, provincial "outside agitator" idea. Anyone who lives inside the United States can never be considered an outsider anywhere within its bounds.

You deplore the demonstrations taking place in Birmingham. But your statement, I am sorry to say, fails to express a similar concern for the conditions that brought about the demonstrations. I am sure that none of you would want to rest content with the superficial kind of social analysis that deals merely with effects and does not grapple with underlying causes. It is unfortunate that demonstrations are taking place in Birmingham, but it is even more unfortunate that the city's white power structure left the Negro community with no alternative.

In any nonviolent campaign there are four basic steps: collection of the facts to determine whether injustices exist; negotiation; self-purification; and direct action. We have gone through all these steps in Birmingham. There can be no gainsaying the fact that racial injustice engulfs this community. Birmingham is probably the most thoroughly segregated city in the United States. Its ugly record of brutality is widely known. Negroes have experienced grossly unjust treatment in the courts. There have been more unsolved bombings of Negro homes and churches in Birmingham than in any other city in the nation. These are the hard, brutal facts of the case. On the basis of these conditions, Negro leaders sought to negotiate with the city fathers. But the latter consistently refused to engage in good-faith negotiation.

Then, last September, came the opportunity to talk with leaders of Birmingham's economic community. In the course of the negotiations, certain promises were made by the merchants—for example, to remove the stores' humiliating racial signs. On the basis of these promises, the Reverend Fred Shuttlesworth and the leaders of the Alabama Christian Movement for Human Rights agreed to a moratorium on all demonstrations. As the weeks and months went by, we realized that we were the victims of a broken promise. A few signs, briefly removed, returned; the others remained.

As in so many past experiences, our hopes had been blasted, and 15 the shadow of deep disappointment settled upon us. We had no alternative except to prepare for direct action, whereby we would present our very bodies as a means of laying our case before the conscience of the local and the national community. Mindful of the difficulties involved, we decided to undertake a process of self-purification. We began a series of workshops on nonviolence, and we repeatedly asked ourselves: "Are you able to accept blows without retaliating?" "Are you able to endure the ordeal of jail?" We decided to schedule our direct-action program for the Easter season, realizing that except for Christmas, this is the main shopping period of the year. Knowing that a strong economic-withdrawal program would be the by-product of direct action, we felt that this would be the best time to bring pressure to bear on the merchants for the needed change.

Then it occurred to us that Birmingham's mayoral election was coming up in March, and we speedily decided to postpone action until after election day. When we discovered that the Commissioner of Public Safety, Eugene "Bull" Connor, had piled up enough votes to be in the run-off, we decided again to postpone action until the day after the run-off so that the demonstrations could not be used to cloud the issues. Like many others, we waited to see Mr. Connor defeated, and to this end we endured postponement after postponement. Having aided in this community need, we felt that our direct-action program could be delayed no longer.

You may well ask: "Why direct action? Why sit-ins, marches and so forth? Isn't negotiation a better path?" You are quite right in calling for negotiation. Indeed, this is the very purpose of direct action. Nonviolent direct action seeks to create such a crisis and foster such a tension that a community which has constantly refused to negotiate is forced to confront the issue. It seeks so to dramatize the issue that it can no longer be ignored. My citing the creation of tension as part of the work of the nonviolent-resister may sound rather shocking. But I must confess that I am not afraid of the word "tension." I have earnestly opposed violent tension, but there is a type of constructive, nonviolent tension which is necessary for growth. Just as Socrates felt that it was necessary to create a tension in the mind so that individuals could rise from the bondage of myths and half-truths to the unfettered realm of creative analysis and objective appraisal, so must we see the need for nonviolent gadflies to create the kind of tension in society that will help men rise from the dark depths of prejudice and racism to the majestic heights of understanding and brotherhood.

The purpose of our direct-action program is to create a situation so crisis-packed that it will inevitably open the door to negotiation. I therefore concur with you in your call for negotiation. Too long has our beloved Southland been bogged down in a tragic effort to live in monologue rather than dialogue.

One of the basic points in your statement is that the action that I and my associates have taken in Birmingham is untimely. Some have asked: "Why didn't you give the new city administration time to act?" The only answer that I can give to this query is that the new Birmingham administration must be prodded about as much as the outgoing one, before it will act. We are sadly mistaken if we feel that the election of Albert Boutwell as mayor will bring the millennium to Birmingham. While Mr. Boutwell is a much more gentle person than Mr. Connor, they are both segregationists, dedicated to maintenance of the status quo. I have hope that Mr. Boutwell will be reasonable enough to see the futility of massive resistance to desegregation. But he will not see this without pressure from devotees of civil rights. My friends, I must say to you that we have not made a single gain in civil rights without determined legal and nonviolent pressure. Lamentably, it is an historical fact that privileged groups seldom give up their privileges voluntarily. Individuals may see the moral light and voluntarily give up their unjust posture; but, as Reinhold Niebuhr has reminded us, groups tend to be more immoral than individuals.

We know through painful experience that freedom is never volun- 20 tarily given by the oppressor; it must be demanded by the oppressed. Frankly, I have yet to engage in a direct-action campaign that was "well timed" in the view of those who have not suffered unduly from the disease of segregation. For years now I have heard the word "Wait!" It rings in the ear of every Negro with piercing familiarity. This "Wait" has almost always meant "Never." We must come to see, with one of our distinguished jurists, that "justice too long delayed is justice denied."

We have waited for more than three hundred forty years for our constitutional God-given rights. The nations of Asia and Africa are moving with jetlike speed toward gaining political independence, but we still creep at horse-and-buggy pace toward gaining a cup of coffee at a lunch counter. Perhaps it is easy for those who have never felt the stinging darts of segregation to say, "Wait." But when you have seen vicious mobs lynch your mothers and fathers at will and drown your sisters and brothers at whim; when you have seen hate-filled policemen curse, kick, and even kill your black brothers and sisters; when you see the vast majority of your twenty million Negro brothers smothering in an airtight cage of poverty in the midst of an affluent society; when you suddenly find your tongue twisted and your speech stammering as you seek to explain to your six-year-old daughter why she can't go to the public amusement park that has just been advertised on television, and see tears welling up in her eyes when she is told that Funtown is closed to colored children, and see ominous clouds of inferiority beginning to form in her little mental sky, and see her beginning to distort her personality by developing an unconscious bitterness toward white people; when you have to concoct an answer for a five-year-old son who is asking: "Daddy, why do white people treat colored people so mean?"; when you take a cross-country drive and find it necessary to sleep night after night in the uncomfortable corners of your automobile because no motel will accept you; when you are humiliated day in and day out by nagging signs reading "white" and "colored"; when your first name becomes "nigger," your middle name becomes "boy" (however old you are) and your last name becomes "John," and your wife and mother are never given the respected title "Mrs."; when you are harried by day and haunted by night by the fact that you are a Negro, living constantly at tiptoe stance, never quite knowing what to expect next, and are plagued with inner fears and outer resentments; when you are forever fighting a degenerating sense of "nobodiness"—then you will understand why we find it difficult to wait. There comes a time when the cup of endurance runs over, and men are no longer willing to be plunged into the abyss of despair. I hope, sirs, you can understand our legitimate and unavoidable impatience.

You express a great deal of anxiety over our willingness to break laws. This is certainly a legitimate concern. Since we so diligently urge people to obey the Supreme Court's decision of 1954 outlawing segregation in the public schools, at first glance it may seem rather paradoxical for us consciously to break laws. One may well ask: "How can you advocate breaking some laws and obeying others?" The answer lies in the fact that there are two types of laws: just and unjust. I would be the first to advocate obeying just laws. One has not only a legal but a moral responsibility to obey just laws. Conversely, one has a moral responsibility to disobey unjust laws. I would agree with St. Augustine that "an unjust law is no law at all."

Now, what is the difference between the two? How does one determine whether a law is just or unjust? A just law is a man-made code that squares with the moral law or the law of God. An unjust law is a code that is out of harmony with the moral law. To put it in the terms of St. Thomas Aquinas: An unjust law is a human law that is not rooted in eternal law and natural law. Any law that uplifts human personality is just. Any law that degrades human personality is unjust. All segregation statutes are unjust because segregation distorts the soul and damages the personality. It gives the segregator a false sense of superiority and the segregated a false sense of inferiority. Segregation, to use the terminology of the Jewish philosopher Martin Buber, substitutes an "I–it" relationship for an "I–thou" relationship and ends up relegating persons to the status of things. Hence, segregation is not only politically, economically and sociologically unsound, it is morally wrong and sinful. Paul Tillich has said that sin is separation. Is not segregation an existential expression of man's tragic separation, his awful estrangement, his terrible sinfulness? Thus it is that I can urge men to obey the 1954 decision of the Supreme Court, for it is morally right; and I can urge them to disobey segregation ordinances, for they are morally wrong.

Let us consider a more concrete example of just and unjust laws. An unjust law is a code that a numerical or power majority group compels a minority group to obey but does not make binding on itself. This is *difference* made legal. By the same token, a just law is a code that a majority compels a minority to follow and that it is willing to follow itself. This is *sameness* made legal.

Let me give another explanation. A law is unjust if it is inflicted on a 25
minority that, as a result of being denied the right to vote, had no part in enacting or devising the law. Who can say that the legislature of Alabama which set up that state's segregation laws was democratically elected? Throughout Alabama all sorts of devious methods are used to prevent Negroes from becoming registered voters, and there are some counties in which, even though Negroes constitute a majority of the population, not a single Negro is registered. Can any law enacted under such circumstances be considered democratically structured?

Sometimes a law is just on its face and unjust in its application. For instance, I have been arrested on a charge of parading without a permit. Now, there is nothing wrong in having an ordinance which requires a permit for a parade. But such an ordinance becomes unjust when it is used to maintain segregation and to deny citizens the First-Amendment privilege of peaceful assembly and protest.

I hope you are able to see the distinction I am trying to point out. In no sense do I advocate evading or defying the law, as would the rabid segregationist. That would lead to anarchy. One who breaks an unjust law must do so openly, lovingly, and with a willingness to accept the penalty. I submit that an individual who breaks a law that conscience tells him is unjust, and who willingly accepts the penalty of imprisonment in order to arouse the conscience of the community over its injustice, is in reality expressing the highest respect for law.

Of course, there is nothing new about this kind of civil disobedience. It was evidenced sublimely in the refusal of Shadrach, Meshach and Abednego to obey the laws of Nebuchadnezzar, on the ground that a higher moral law was at stake. It was practiced superbly by the early Christians, who were willing to face hungry lions and the excruciating pain of chopping blocks rather than submit to certain unjust laws of the Roman Empire. To a degree, academic freedom is a reality today because Socrates practiced civil disobedience. In our own nation, the Boston Tea Party represented a massive act of civil disobedience.

We should never forget that everything Adolf Hitler did in Germany was "legal" and everything the Hungarian freedom fighters did in Hungary was "illegal." It was "illegal" to aid and comfort a Jew in Hitler's Germany. Even so, I am sure that, had I lived in Germany at the time, I would have aided and comforted my Jewish brothers. If today I lived in a Communist country where certain principles dear to the Christian faith are suppressed I would openly advocate disobeying that country's antireligious laws.

I must make two honest confessions to you, my Christian and Jew- 30 ish brothers. First, I must confess that over the past few years I have been gravely disappointed with the white moderate. I have almost reached the regrettable conclusion that the Negro's great stumbling block in his stride toward freedom is not the White Citizen's Counciler or the Ku Klux Klanner, but the white moderate, who is more devoted to "order" than to justice; who prefers a negative peace which is the presence of tension to a positive peace which is the presence of justice; who constantly says: "I agree with you in the goal you seek, but I cannot agree with your methods of direct action"; who paternalistically believes he can set the timetable for another man's freedom; who lives by a mythical concept of time and who constantly advises the Negro to wait for a "more convenient season." Shallow understanding from people of good will is more frustrating than absolute misunderstanding from people of ill will. Lukewarm acceptance is much more bewildering than outright rejection.

I had hoped that the white moderate would understand that law and order exist for the purpose of establishing justice and that when they fail in this purpose they become the dangerously structured dams that block the flow of social progress. I had hoped that the white moderate would understand that the present tension in the South is a necessary phase of the transition from an obnoxious negative peace, in which the Negro passively accepted his unjust plight, to a substantive and positive peace, in which all men will respect the dignity and worth of human personality. Actually, we who engage in nonviolent direct action are not the creators of tension. We merely bring to the surface the hidden tension that is already alive. We bring it out in the open, where it can be seen and dealt with. Like a boil that can never be cured so long as it is covered up but must be opened with all its ugliness to the natural medicines of air and light, injustice must be exposed, with all the tension its exposure creates, to the light of human conscience and the air of national opinion before it can be cured.

In your statement you assert that our actions, even though peaceful, must be condemned because they precipitate violence. But is this a logical assertion? Isn't this like condemning a robbed man because his possession of money precipitated the evil act of robbery? Isn't this like condemning Socrates because his unswerving commitment to truth and his philosophical inquiries precipitated the act by the misguided populace in which they made him drink hemlock? Isn't this like condemning Jesus because his unique God-consciousness and never-ceasing devotion to God's will precipitated the evil act of crucifixion? We must come to see that, as the federal courts have consistently affirmed, it is wrong to urge an individual to cease his efforts to gain his basic constitutional rights because the quest may precipitate violence. Society must protect the robbed and punish the robber.

I had also hoped that the white moderate would reject the myth concerning time in relation to the struggle for freedom. I have just received a letter from a white brother in Texas. He writes: "All Christians know that the colored people will receive equal rights eventually, but it is possible that you are in too great a religious hurry. It has taken Christianity almost two thousand years to accomplish what it has. The teachings of Christ take time to come to earth." Such an attitude stems from a tragic misconception of time, from the strangely irrational notion that there is something in the very flow of time that will inevitably cure all ills. Actually, time itself is neutral; it can be used either destructively or constructively. More and more I feel that the people of ill will have used time much more effectively than have the people of good will. We will have to repent in this generation not merely for the hateful words and actions of the bad people but for the appalling silence of the good people. Human progress never rolls in on wheels of inevitability; it comes through the tireless efforts of men willing to be co-workers with God, and without this hard work, time itself becomes an ally of the forces of social stagnation. We must use time creatively, in the knowledge that the time is always ripe to do right. Now is the time to make real the promise of democracy and transform our pending national elegy into a creative psalm of brotherhood. Now is the time to lift our national policy from the quicksand of racial injustice to the solid rock of human dignity.

You speak of our activity in Birmingham as extreme. At first I was rather disappointed that fellow clergymen would see my nonviolent efforts as those of an extremist. I began thinking about the fact that I stand in the middle of two opposing forces in the Negro community. One is a force of complacency, made up in part of Negroes who, as a result of long years of oppression, are so drained of self-respect and a sense of "somebodiness" that they have adjusted to segregation; and in part of a few middle-class Negroes who, because of a degree of academic and economic security and because in some ways they profit by segregation, have become insensitive to the problems of the masses. The other force is one of bitterness and hatred, and it comes perilously close to advocating violence. It is expressed in the various black nationalists groups that are springing up across the nation, the largest and best-known being Elijah Muhammad's Muslim movement. Nourished by the Negro's frustration over the continued existence of racial discrimination, this movement is made up of people who have lost faith in America, who have absolutely repudiated Christianity, and who have concluded that the white man is an incorrigible "devil."

I have tried to stand between these two forces, saying that we 35 need emulate neither the "do-nothingism" of the complacent nor the hatred and despair of the black nationalist. For there is the more excellent way of love and nonviolent protest. I am grateful to God that, through the influence of the Negro church, the way of nonviolence became an integral part of our struggle.

If this philosophy had not emerged, by now many streets of the South would, I am convinced, be flowing with blood. And I am further convinced that if our white brothers dismiss as "rabble-rousers" and "outside agitators" those of us who employ nonviolent direct action, and if they refuse to support our nonviolent efforts, millions of the Negroes will, out of frustration and despair, seek solace and security in black-nationalist ideologies—a development that would inevitably lead to a frightening racial nightmare.

Oppressed people cannot remain oppressed forever. The yearning for freedom eventually manifests itself, and that is what has happened to the American Negro. Something within has reminded him of his birthright of freedom, and something without has reminded him that it can be gained. Consciously or unconsciously, he has been caught up by the *Zeitgeist*, and with his black brothers of Africa and his brown and yellow brothers of Asia, South America and the Caribbean, the United States Negro is moving with a sense of great urgency toward the promised land of racial justice. If one recognizes this vital urge that has engulfed the Negro community, one should readily understand why public demonstrations are taking place. The Negro has many pent-up resentments and latent frustrations, and he must release them. So let him march; let him make prayer pilgrimages to the city hall; let him go on freedom rides—and try to understand why he must do so. If his repressed emotions are not released in nonviolent ways, they will seek expression through violence; this is not a threat but a fact of history. So I have not said to my people: "Get rid of your discontent." Rather, I have tried to say that this normal and healthy discontent can be channeled into the creative outlet of nonviolent direct action. And now this approach is being termed extremist.

But though I was initially disappointed at being categorized as an extremist, as I continued to think about the matter I gradually gained a measure of satisfaction from the label. Was not Jesus an extremist for love: "Love your enemies, bless them that curse you, do good to them that hate you, and pray for them which despitefully use you, and persecute you." Was not Amos an extremist for justice: "Let justice roll down like waters and righteousness like an ever-flowing stream." Was not Paul an extremist for the Christian gospel: "I bear in my body the makers of the Lord Jesus." Was not Martin Luther an extremist: "Here I stand; I cannot do otherwise, so help me God." And John Bunyan: "I will stay in jail to the end of my days before I make a butchery of my conscience." And Abraham Lincoln: "This nation cannot survive half slave and half free." And Thomas Jefferson: "We hold these truths to be self-evident, that all men are created equal. . . ." So the question is not whether we will be extremists, but what kind of extremists we will be. Will we be extremists for hate or for love? Will we be extremists for the preservation of injustice or for the extension of justice? In that dramatic scene on Calvary's hill three men were crucified. We must never forget that all three were crucified for the same crime—the crime of extremism. Two were extremists for immorality, and thus fell below their environment. The other, Jesus Christ, was an extremist for love, truth and goodness, and thereby rose above his environment. Perhaps the South, the nation and the world are in dire need of creative extremists.

I had hoped that the white moderate would see this need. Perhaps I was too optimistic; perhaps I expected too much. I suppose I should have realized that few members of the oppressor race can understand the deep groans and passionate yearnings of the oppressed race, and still fewer have the vision to see that injustice must be rooted out by strong, persistent and determined action. I am thankful, however, that some of our white brothers in the South have grasped the meaning of this social revolution and committed themselves to it. They are still all too few in quantity, but they are big in quality. Some—such as Ralph McGill, Lillian Smith, Harry Golden, James McBride Dabbs, Ann Braden and Sarah Patton Boyle—have written about our struggle in eloquent and prophetic terms. Others have marched with us down nameless streets of the South. They have languished in filthy, roach-infested jails, suffering the abuse and brutality of policemen who view them as "dirty nigger-lovers." Unlike so many of their moderate brothers and sisters, they have recognized the urgency of the moment and sensed the need for powerful "action" antidotes to combat the disease of segregation.

Let me take note of my other major disappointment. I have been 40 so greatly disappointed with the white church and its leadership. Of course, there are some notable exceptions. I am not unmindful of the fact that each of you has taken some significant stands on this issue. I commend you, Reverend Stallings, for your Christian stand on this past Sunday, in welcoming Negroes to your worship service on a non-segregated basis. I commend the Catholic leaders of this state for integrating Spring Hill College several years ago.

But despite these notable exceptions, I must honestly reiterate that I have been disappointed with the church. I do not say this as one of those negative critics who can always find something wrong with the church. I say this as a minister of the gospel, who loves the church; who was nurtured in its bosom; who has been sustained by its spiritual blessings and who will remain true to it as long as the cord of life shall lengthen.

When I was suddenly catapulted into the leadership of the bus protest in Montgomery, Alabama, a few years ago, I felt we would be supported by the white church. I felt that the white ministers, priests and rabbis of the South would be among our strongest allies. Instead, some have been outright opponents, refusing to understand the freedom movement and misrepresenting its leaders; all too many others have been more cautious than courageous and have remained silent behind the anesthetizing security of stained-glass windows.

In spite of my shattered dreams, I came to Birmingham with the hope that the white religious leadership of this community would see the justice of our cause and, with deep moral concern, would serve as the channel through which our just grievances could reach the power structure. I had hoped that each of you would understand. But again I have been disappointed.

I have heard numerous southern religious leaders admonish their worshipers to comply with a desegregation decision because it is the law, but I have longed to hear white ministers declare: "Follow this decree because integration is morally right and because the Negro is your brother." In the midst of blatant injustices inflicted upon the Negro, I have watched white churchmen stand on the sideline and mouth pious irrelevancies and sanctimonious trivialities. In the midst of a mighty struggle to rid our nation of racial and economic injustice, I have heard many ministers say: "Those are social issues, with which the gospel has no real concern." And I have watched many churches commit themselves to a completely otherworldly religion which makes a strange, un-Biblical distinction between body and soul, between the sacred and the secular.

I have traveled the length and breadth of Alabama, Mississippi 45 and all the other southern states. On sweltering summer days and crisp autumn mornings I have looked at the South's beautiful churches with their lofty spires pointing heavenward. I have beheld the impressive outlines of her massive religious-education buildings. Over and over I have found myself asking: "What kind of people worship here? Who is their God? Where were their voices when the lips of Governor Barnett dripped with words of interposition and nullification? Where were they when Governor Wallace gave a clarion call for defiance and hatred? Where were their voices of support when bruised and weary Negro men and women decided to rise from the dark dungeons of complacency to the bright hills of creative protest?"

Yes, these questions are still in my mind. In deep disappointment I have wept over the laxity of the church. But be assured that my tears have been tears of love. There can be no deep disappointment where there is not deep love. Yes, I love the church. How could I do otherwise? I am in the rather unique position of being the son, the grandson, and the great-grandson of preachers. Yes, I see the church as the body of Christ. But, oh! How we have blemished and scarred that body through social neglect and through fear of being nonconformists.

There was a time when the church was very powerful—in the time when the early Christians rejoiced at being deemed worthy to suffer for what they believed. In those days the church was not merely a thermometer that recorded the ideas and principles of popular opinion; it was a thermostat that transformed the mores of society. Whenever the early Christians entered a town, the people in power became disturbed and immediately sought to convict the Christians for being "disturbers of the peace" and "outside agitators." But the Christians pressed on, in the conviction that they were "a colony of heaven," called to obey God rather than man. Small in number, they were big in commitment. They were too God-intoxicated to be "astronomically intimidated." By their effort and example they brought an end to such ancient evils as infanticide and gladiatorial contests.

Things are different now. So often the contemporary church is a weak, ineffectual voice with an uncertain sound. So often it is an archdefender of the status quo. Far from being disturbed by the presence of the church, the power structure of the average community is consoled by the church's silent—and often even vocal—sanction of things as they are.

But the judgment of God is upon the church as never before. If today's church does not recapture the sacrificial spirit of the early church, it will lose its authenticity, forfeit the loyalty of millions, and be dismissed as an irrelevant social club with no meaning for the twentieth century. Every day I meet young people whose disappointment with the church has turned into outright disgust.

Perhaps I have once again been too optimistic. Is organized religion too inextricably bound to the status quo to save our nation and the world? Perhaps I must turn my faith to the inner spiritual church, the church within the church, as the true *ekklesia* and the hope of the world. But again I am thankful to God that some noble souls from the ranks of organized religion have broken loose from the paralyzing chains of conformity and joined us as active partners in the struggle for freedom. They have left their secure congregations and walked the streets of Albany, Georgia, with us. They have gone down the high-ways of the South on tortuous rides for freedom. Yes, they have gone to jail with us. Some have been dismissed from their churches, have lost the support of their bishops and fellow ministers. But they have acted in the faith that right defeated is stronger than evil triumphant. Their witness has been the spiritual salt that has preserved the true meaning of the gospel in these troubled times. They have carved a tunnel of hope through the dark mountain of disappointment.

I hope the church as a whole will meet the challenge of this decisive hour. But even if the church does not come to the aid of justice, I have no despair about the future. I have no fear about the outcome of our struggle in Birmingham, even if our motives are at present misunderstood. We will reach the goal of freedom in Birmingham and all over the nation, because the goal of America is freedom. Abused and scorned though we may be, our destiny is tied up with America's destiny. Before the pilgrims landed at Plymouth, we were here. Before the pen of Jefferson etched the majestic words of the Declaration of Independence across the pages of history, we were here. For more than two centuries our forebears labored in this country without wages; they made cotton king; they built the homes of their masters while suffering gross injustice and shameful humiliation—and yet out of a bottomless vitality they continued to thrive and develop. If the inexpressible cruelties of slavery could not stop us, the opposition we now face will surely fail. We will win our freedom because the sacred heritage of our nation and the eternal will of God are embodied in our echoing demands.

Before closing I feel impelled to mention one other point in your statement that has troubled me profoundly. You warmly commended the Birmingham police force for keeping "order" and "preventing violence." I doubt that you would have so warmly commended the police force if you had seen its dogs sinking their teeth into unarmed, nonviolent Negroes. I doubt that you would so quickly commend the policemen if you were to observe their ugly and inhumane treatment of Negroes here in the city jail; if you were to watch them push and curse old Negro women and young Negro girls; if you were to see them slap and kick old Negro men and young boys; if you to observe them, as they did on two occasions, refuse to give us good because we wanted to sing our grace together. I cannot join you in your praise of the Birmingham police department.

It is true that police have exercised a degree of discipline in handling the demonstrators. In this sense they have conducted themselves rather "nonviolently" in public. But for what purpose? To preserve the evil system of segregation. Over the past few years I have consistently preached that nonviolence demands that the means we use must be as pure as the ends we seek. I have tried to make clear that it is wrong to use immoral means to attain moral ends. But now I must affirm that it is just as wrong, or perhaps even more so, to use moral means to preserve immoral ends. Perhaps Mr. Connor and his policemen have been rather nonviolent in public, as was Chief Pritchett in Albany, Georgia, but they have used the moral means of nonviolence to maintain the immoral end of racial injustice. As T. S. Eliot has said: "The last temptation is the greatest treason: to do the right deed for the wrong reason."

I wish you had commended the Negro sit-inners and demonstrators of Birmingham for their sublime courage, their willingness to suffer and their amazing discipline in the midst of great provocation. One day the South will recognize its real heroes. They will be the James Merediths, with the noble sense of purpose that enables them to face jeering and hostile mobs, and with the agonizing loneliness that characterizes the life of the pioneer. They will be old, oppressed, battered Negro women, symbolized in a seventy-two-year-old woman in Montgomery, Alabama, who rose up with a sense of dignity and with her people decided not to ride segregated buses, and who responded with ungrammatical profundity to one who inquired about her weariness: "My feets is tired, but my soul is at rest." They will be the young high school and college students, the young ministers of the gospel and a host of their elders, courageously and nonviolently sitting in at lunch counters and willingly going to jail for conscience' sake. One day the South will know that when these disinherited children of God sat down at lunch counters, they were in reality standing up for what is best in the American dream and for the most sacred values in our Judaeo-Christian heritage, thereby bringing our nation back to those great wells of democracy which were dug deep by the founding fathers in their formulation of the Constitution and the Declaration of Independence.

Never before have I written so long a letter. I'm afraid it is much 55 too long to take your precious time. I can assure you that it would have been much shorter if I had been writing from a comfortable desk, but what else can one do when he is alone in a narrow jail cell, other than write long letters, think long thoughts and pray long prayers?

If I have said anything in this letter that overstates the truth and indicates an unreasonable impatience, I beg you to forgive me. If I have said anything that understates the truth and indicates my having a patience that allows me to settle for anything less than brotherhood, I beg God to forgive me.

I hope this letter finds you strong in faith. I also hope that circumstances will soon make it possible for me to meet each of you, not as an integrationist or a civil-rights leader but as a fellow clergyman and a Christian brother. Let us all hope that the dark clouds of racial prejudice will soon pass away and the deep fog of misunderstanding will be lifted from our fear-drenched communities, and in some not too distant tomorrow the radiant stars of love and brotherhood will shine over our great nation with all their scintillating beauty.

Yours for the cause of Peace and Brotherhood

MARTIN LUTHER KING, JR.

For Journals

What does King mean, in response to accusations that the civil rights demonstrations have not come to Birmingham at the right time, that he has "yet to engage in a direct-nation movement that was 'well timed'" (paragraph 20)?

For Discussion

1. Why do you think the black clergymen opposed to King were so worried about the civil rights activists? Since they were subject to the same prejudice as King, why wouldn't they join in the demonstrations themselves?

2. How does King refute the accusations that he is an outsider in Birmingham?

3. What is your response to King's argument that there are legitimate reasons for breaking the law if it is unjust? What are his criteria for deciding if a law is unjust? What basis would you use to decide if a law is unjust?

4. King says that one reason injustice is so powerful is not the actions of bad people but the "appalling silence of the good people" (paragraph 33). Do you think he is right? What is the responsibility of ordinary people when faced with an evil in their society?

5. Why do you think it pleases King to be referred to by his religious opponents as an extremist?

6. What do King's criticisms of the contemporary church tell you about what he thinks the role an effective clergy should be in promoting justice in American society? How does King refute the idea that an uninvolved clergy is better than an active one? How does he make the transition from discussing unheroic clergy to heroic activists?

For Writing

1. Write an essay or a speech on a public topic that makes you angry. Use Douglass and King as models. Be very explicit about who your audience is; you can choose to address any audience you want. State the point of view that you disagree with; then refute it. If you want, write your essay as a letter to your editor of a local newspaper; mail it to the newspaper for possible publication.

2. Like Thoreau, King spent time in jail for his beliefs, although Thoreau was never in danger of being killed and King was. Review Thoreau's *Civil Disobedience,* and write an essay in which you discuss the way both men approach and implement political resistance. Include a consideration of the following questions: What is Thoreau's definition of nonviolent resistance, and how does it compare with King's? What does King owe Thoreau in the development of his own philosophy? How does each man argue for the need to sometimes go to jail?

❧ *What Is Hate Speech?* (1993)

ALAN M. DERSHOWITZ

Alan Dershowitz was the youngest person ever to become a professor of law at Harvard University. Professor Dershowitz has become famous for appeals on behalf of controversial clients, including Klaus von Bulow, accused of trying to murder his wealthy wife, and O. J. Simpson. The von Bulow case and Dershowitz's role in it were the basis of a movie called Reversal of Fortune, *and Dershowitz has written often and passionately, in such books as* The Advocate's Devil *(1994),* Reasonable Doubts: The O. J. Simpson Case and the Criminal Justice System *(1996), and* Just Revenge *(1999), about the importance of safeguarding civil liberties and constitutional freedoms. The following article appeared in the* San Francisco Chronicle *on July 22, 1993.*

A recent letter to the editor of the *Boston Herald* clearly illustrates why the Supreme Court was right on target in striking down hate speech laws as unconstitutional.

The writer argued that "abortion counseling" is a form of "hate speech," since it constitutes advocacy of "taking the life of a developing human child." This may sound like a bizarre application of the hate speech laws, but the writer has a point—if you believe that a fetus is "a developing human child."

An equally compelling point could be made by a feminist, who believes that a fetus is merely a temporary appendage to a woman's body, that Operation Rescue, by accusing young women who are seeking abortions of being murderers, is guilty of hate speech. Plainly, the concept of hate speech is in the mind and heart of the beholder. It is not capable of objective application, as evidenced by several other recent incidents.

A few years ago in Great Britain, a number of universities branded all Zionist speakers as hate mongers and racists, pointing to the now-repealed United Nations resolution equating Zionism with racism. In Israel, speakers from the Palestine Liberation Organization are branded as purveyors of hate and racism because of the PLO's unwillingness to recognize Israel. The late Rabbi Meir Kahane was also branded as hateful and racist because of his advocacy that Arabs be expelled from Israel.

To many women, pornography is hate speech; to many men, femi- 5 nist put-downs of men—as sexists and rapists—is hate speech. To religious fundamentalists, atheism and blasphemy are forms of hate speech; to many atheists, fundamentalist attacks on atheism as immoral is hate speech.

To some African Americans, opposition to race-specific affirmative action is racist and hateful; to some whites, advocacy of race-specific affirmative action is reverse discrimination and thus a form of racism and hate. The *Boston Globe* recently accused Harvard Law School of "bigotry" because it hired faculty on the basis of academic criteria rather than race or gender.

To policemen, rap songs that advocate "cop-killing" are hate speech; to rap singers, Bill Clinton's condemnation of Sister Souljah constituted bigotry.

To many gays, homophobic speech is hateful; to some literal readers of the Bible, advocacy of a gay life style is a hateful abomination. To most Jews, Holocaust denial is hate speech; to those who deny the Holocaust, any claim that Nazis engaged in genocide against the Jews is anti-German hate speech.

To some liberals, extreme reactionaries are hateful; to some reactionaries, extreme leftists are guilty of hate speech.

I could go on and on in demonstrating that there is no content- 10 neutral way of defining what constitutes hate speech.

Americans tend to feel very strongly about their opinions, especially if they involve race, religion, ethnicity, sexual preference and ideology. We often express our views with strong words, without concern for the sensibilities of others. We are an impolite people, when it comes to expressing our opinions on controversial issues. Ask the Europeans. They will tell you how "direct"—a euphemism for impolite or insensitive—Americans can be. It is part of our national character.

For that reason, among others, speech codes do not suit us as a people. We were brought up on the ditty that "sticks and stones may break our bones, but names will never harm us." Though names can hurt, it is part of our cultural mythology that we must all develop thick skins. The First Amendment is premised on a thick-skinned response to open debate, including name-calling, personal attacks and hate speech.

Asking an African American family to develop a thick skin when a cross is burned by a skinhead is asking an awful lot, and so is asking a Holocaust survivor to tolerate Nazi marchers in his neighborhood. But unless we make these demands, there will be no end to censorship. The speech-cops will have to be called any time anyone is deeply offended by what they see or hear.

And if a subjective feeling of being offended could trigger censorship, Americans would feel offended more easily.

We must encourage vibrant—yes, sometimes even impolite—debate about issues that matter deeply to Americans. We must not curtail the way people argue about race, sex, religion and ideology. 15

Nor can we—in a society founded on the equal protection of the law—be selective about what constitutes hate speech or who has the power to censor if offended. If we were to grant that power to one group, we would have tog rant it to all. There can be no affirmative action when it comes to censorship.

The only answer to offensive speech—if we are to preserve our traditional way of debate and discourse in this country—is a fully open marketplace of ideas in which hate speech is rejected on its own demerits, rather than censored by a benevolent big brother or sister.

For Journals

Which of the following Constitutional freedoms—freedom of speech, press, or religion—do you value the most? Why?

For Discussion

1. Do you think you or anyone close to you has engaged in what Dershowitz refers to as hate speech? Have you ever been the object of hate speech?

2. The "marketplace of ideas," in which Americans would have access to all varieties of political ideas, including those they find hateful, and pick the ones they want, goes back to Supreme Court opinions written early in the twentieth century by two of the most famous Justices, Oliver Wendell Holmes and Louis Brandeis. What is appealing about this notion of Americans "shopping" and choosing among all kinds of speech? Should it still apply today—to the Internet, for example?

3. Given that judging what constitutes hate speech is so subjective, what are Dershowitz's reasons for arguing against speech codes that would spell out what kinds of speech are not to be allowed?

4. Would you be in favor of or opposed to your school having a speech code to guard against various forms of hate speech? Why?

For Writing

1. Assume that you and one or two of your classmates have been assigned the job of coming up with a speech code for your school that would lay out what constitutes the boundaries of acceptable speech on campus, including e-mail between students. To help you with your research, you might check with other colleges in your area, or with the legal department in your school, to find out what regulations are in place, if any, about limits on student freedom of speech. Then come up with your own two to four pages on what rules should be applied at your school. Use some of the examples in Dershowitz's article as samples of what you would or wouldn't allow, or come up with your own examples. If your class is divided several groups doing this assignment, you can share your research and still come up with different speech codes. And it would be interesting to compare codes, to see what one group as opposed to another found really objectionable. In any case, along with your rules, write out your reasons for your choices, so that other people in the class can understand how you arrived at your conclusions.

2. Watch the movie about Dershowitz, *Reversal of Fortune,* and write a review of it. Consider the working relationship between Dershowitz and Klaus von Bulow and the portrayal of Dershowitz—heroic/publicity seeking/brilliant/etc.—and how he justifies helping such a generally disliked client. What rights does Dershowitz feel he is defending? If you were in serious trouble, would you want him to be your lawyer?

3. There are many legal decisions on freedom of speech in general and hate speech in particular. Look up the category of hate speech in newspaper microfiche, on the Internet, or in a law library, and find a ruling you disagree with, or a news story about hate speech that you had a strong reaction to. Write an argumentative essay in which you give your own definition of hate speech, or use Dershowitz's ideas, and explain, in three or four major points, why your definition would lead to a better resolution of the case, redress an injustice, or provide citizens with more useful guidelines for recognizing or dealing with hate speech when it occurs.

∽ Libraries, the Internet, and Freedom of Speech (2000)

VICKI CHIANG

Vicki Chiang is a first-year college student; she began writing about this topic when she was a senior in high school.

The turn of the century has brought perhaps one of the greatest technological resources this nation has ever seen. Just in the past few years the United States has experienced an Internet boom, and the number of homes and institutions that are connected to the "net" is growing at a rapid pace. With the growing popularity and accessibility of this technological tool comes a new dilemma: The Internet is an incredible forum for free speech, free thought, free expression, and free information. Yet it is precisely the accessible nature of the Internet that provides people with the opportunity to abuse it.

For example, while pornographic sites on the Internet are technically accessible only to persons over the age of eighteen, a minor may easily subvert this barrier by simply clicking "ok" when the dialogue box appears on the screen. Some parents and conservative groups are concerned about children having access to vulgar and obscene images, which would otherwise not be available to them, and thus they are calling for government-mandated censorship of the Internet. This policy would create a problem for government institutions, and, most specifically, public libraries. Libraries should provide freedom of information, but they are being pressured to install filtering programs onto their computers that would censor the Internet.

It is this writer's opinion that public libraries should not install filtering programs on their computers. This type of censorship is constitutionally unsound and would be more of a problem than a solution. For over two hundred years, we have respected the authority of the Constitution. Why tear it down now? The censorship of the Internet in public libraries would be an infringement of the First Amendment. Our right to freedom of speech has allowed us to generate a great intellectual community where information and opinions flow freely. Censorship of the Internet, the "information superhighway," would not only severely limit this public resource, but it would also be a step backward for democracy. A precedent has been established in this nation that intellectual freedom is more important than the need to protect our minds. Justice John Paul Stevens of the Supreme Court agrees: "The interest in encouraging freedom of expression in a democratic society outweighs any theoretical but unproven benefit of censorship."

It is true that the Internet differs from the current resources found in the library (i.e., books, newspapers, articles, paintings, etc.) in a few fundamental areas. Obviously, libraries do not carry everything that is published in society; there is usually a committee that screens texts and decides which texts to add to its collection. While libraries do follow a policy of intellectual freedom, the committee will usually screen out works that are extremely vulgar and inappropriate. This intermediate screening process does not exist for the Internet. A person may access virtually anything with a click of the mouse. Nevertheless, the Library Bill of Rights is the only guide we currently have to deal with the dilemma of the unrestricted freedom of the Internet. Until there is a new system established, which is declared to be constitutionally valid in all aspects, we must follow the precedent set by the American

Library Association. To censor the Internet now, simply because of a few worried parents, may jeopardize the right of free access to information for future generations. Clearly, the government cannot make a rash decision on this issue.

Even if censorship of the Internet were deemed constitutional, the process would be ineffective in public libraries. Software filters are the current technology used to prevent users from accessing certain Web sites on the Internet. While the filters are intended to block obscene images or texts, they often end up blocking a much broader spectrum of speech. For example, filters that block based on key words would exclude poetry by Anne Sexton simply because the word "sex" is in her last name. There was an instance of the White House Web site being blocked because it contained the word "couple" when referring to the "First Couple."

Aside from the technical pitfalls, Internet filters would be inhibiting because the software installers program them. Unlike the library process mentioned earlier, where an established committee is given the responsibility to screen texts, an arbitrary software installer would program which key words and which sites the filter would block. One person, uneducated in the needs of the patrons of the library, would be deciding what information people could and could not access. The government, let alone a software installer, cannot determine what is appropriate and what is indecent for each person or community.

Images that are offensive to one group of people may be appreciated expressions of art to another, and vice-versa. As Wini Allard, city librarian at Santa Monica Public Library, puts it, "One person's porn is another person's art, and it's not for any of us to decide for another person." It would be democratically irresponsible to install software filters that are programmed by one subjective source onto computers that are used by hundreds of different people. Therefore, as a whole, the currently available filtering system is inadequate. Too much important information is blocked from people who truly need it, so that the harm of filters outweighs the benefit of preventing Internet abuse.

Ultimately, it is the parents' responsibility to monitor their children's appropriate use of the Internet. While it is true that protecting the innocence of our youth should be one of the nation's top priorities, it is also true that the rights of freedom of expression and freedom of information for all people should not be compromised. Unfortunately, today's filtering systems only offer libraries two choices: either they continue to have an unrestricted Internet policy which runs the risk of Internet abuse; or they install extremely restrictive filters to censor the Internet and limit information available to their users.

At this point, the first option is the better of the two. While installing filters nearly guarantees that some important information will be blocked, having an unrestricted Internet does not necessarily leave the door wide open for abuse. There will be parents and teachers there to censor the actions of their children. If adults argue that they absolutely need Internet filters to censor what their children are exposed to, then perhaps they need to focus on their parental responsibilities first. The Internet is the information superhighway, and despite the fact that some may abuse it, the Internet should be a freely accessible road for everyone.

For Journals

What dangers did your family try to protect you from when you were a child? Was there anything you were not allowed to watch on television or to read, or any video games you were not allowed to play?

For Discussion

1. The coming of the new technology has been referred to as the New American Revolution. How persuasive is this analogy to you? Are there any specific ways in which you believe that the changes have been really revolutionary? How different would your life be without them?

2. Although the Constitution says that Congress shall make no laws abridging freedom of speech, in fact speech has never been entirely free, and obscenity is not protected on or off the Internet. The Supreme Court has defined obscenity as that which lacks any literary, artistic, political, or social value—a deliberately vague standard. Community value also have to be recognized. What standards do you think would be applied in your community or by you or your friends? As you need something by which to judge, pick an advertisement, cartoon, or photograph and use it as a test case for your discussion.

3. If you surf the Net, would you recommend any restrictions on what you could have access to in terms of subject matter or content? On what your little brother or sister could have access to? What rights do you think are involved here? How much access, if any, would you be willing to give up permanently so that children couldn't be exposed to pornography?

4. The author, however, says the best thing would be for parents to restrict how much time their kids could spend on the Internet. What do you think are the parameters of parental responsibility in this conflict?

For Writing

1. The Constitution says that Congress shall make no laws abridging freedom of speech, but that statement has always been interpreted so

that some kinds of speech are protected and some aren't. For example, Justice Oliver Wendell Holmes said that no one has the right to yell "Fire!" in a crowded theater when there is no fire, just to see what would happen. Write an essay in which you argue the limits of freedom of speech or freedom of the press; use the argumentative points in this article or in the Hamilton selection at the beginning of this chapter.

2.   Referring back to discussion question #1 above, write an essay in which you compare the revolutionary aspects of electric lights described in David Nasaw's "Going Out" (see the Work and Play chapter) with the Internet revolution now. You can do this as a persuasive paper or as a short research exercise, in which case you will need to look at computer articles and/or books about the development of the Internet for facts to support your analysis.

3.   If you have access to the Internet, look up the category of Internet and freedom of speech. Pick an entry which has a view different from your own, and write an essay in which you argue against it. Start with your strongest point, and give examples to illustrate any general statements you make about free speech. For an example of a good legal argument, look at the first selection in this chapter, Hamilton's defense of freedom of the press.

∞ *Film: The Long Walk Home* (1995)

In 1955, the American South was completely segregated. In one of the turning points of the civil rights movement, Rosa Parks, an African American woman who rode the bus to work every day in Montgomery, Alabama refused for once to give her seat to a white person and go sit in the back of the bus. She was arrested; in protest, a twenty-six-year-old minister from Atlanta, Martin Luther King, Jr., organized a bus boycott by African Americans in Montgomery. This film is about the effect of those events on two women: a black woman named Odessa Carter, who works as a housekeeper for a white family and decides to join the boycott, even though that means walking nine painful miles to and from work; and the middle-class white woman, Miriam Thompson, for whom she works and who begins to sympathize with what Odessa is doing. (98 minutes)

For Journals

Before you saw this film, what did you know about the Montgomery bus boycott?

For Discussion

1. This famous event is reported in movie newsreels, television news, and documentaries. Why do you think the writer and director told this story from the point of view of ordinary people on both sides, instead of looking at the larger political picture? What did they have to gain by sticking with the effects on just two families?

2. How differently does Odessa behave when she's working from the way she behaves at home? For specific examples, examine the humiliating scene in the park, the apology of the policeman to Miriam Thompson, and the Christmas dinner at which Mr. Thompson's mother makes racist remarks while Odessa is in the room.

3. Late in the film, the white husband who is opposed to his wife's driving Odessa to work says that Odessa is a wonderful maid but that's not who she is and they will never know what she's really like. How well does Mrs. Thompson in fact get to know her? What bonds are formed between the two women? What are those bonds based on?

4. In the climactic scene in the movie, the attack by white men on the carpoolers' parking lot, the behavior of both Odessa and Miriam—facing the crowd and joining hands—suggests a positive resolution, but also ends the movie rather abruptly. What do you think will be the personal consequences for each woman? What questions are left unanswered?

For Writing

1. Research the history of the Montgomery boycott and write about one aspect of it: the role of Martin Luther King Jr.; the economic and personal effect of the boycott on the black community; the decision by the city of Montgomery to capitulate; or any other aspect that you find particularly interesting. Two sources you might check are the documentary book *Eyes on the Prize* and the Pulitzer Prize–winning history *Parting the Waters* by Taylor Branch.

2. Write a comparison of this film and "Letter from Birmingham Jail" by Martin Luther King Jr., which you read earlier in this chapter. For example, the film does not deal with King's efforts in overcoming the resistance of more conservative black clergy and businessmen who were uneasy about rocking the boat, but King's letter specifically addresses that issue. Other possible contrasts include the film's attention to private unknown people and King's need to reach both immediate and distant audiences; and the fact that in his letter King describes discrimination and nonviolent resistance, whereas in the film Odessa and her family experience them.

Writing Assignments

1. Write an analytical essay comparing Frederick Douglass's Independence Day speech with Martin Luther King, Jr.'s "Letter from Birmingham Jail." Consider the audience each man was addressing; the way in which each criticizes his audience and why; the sources of their anger; and how successful each one is at refuting the argument of his opponents. Do Douglass and King have any persuasive or argumentative points in common? Do they evoke in you similar or different responses?

2. Investigate some of the Victorian stereotypes about women's behavior, weakness, and dependence that Susan B. Anthony had to refute in her efforts to secure the vote. Use periodicals and books, but, if they are available at your library, also look at nineteenth-century women's magazines, etiquette books, and so on. Write an essay on your findings.

3. Visit the nearest federal, state, or city courthouse, and sit in on a trial for a couple of hours. Call or write the court clerk in advance so that you will know what kinds of trials are scheduled for that week and can pick a case that interests you. Family court and juvenile court, for example, deal in emotional issues that are both immediate and comprehensible. Take notes on what you see and hear: the behavior of the judge and attorneys, the demeanor of the defendants, the issues being raised. Write a paper analyzing the experience: what you saw and learned, whether the trial was different from what you've learned to expect from television, and how effectively each attorney refuted the other's arguments.

4. Devise your own favorite example of American individualism coming up against either government regulations or majority opinion—anything from whether the government can make you fight a war to whether it can force you to wear a helmet when you're riding a motorcycle. Write an argumentative paper in favor of your opinion, and include quotations or ideas from *Civil Disobedience* as support for your refutation.

5. During the Civil War, Frederick Douglass petitioned President Lincoln for the formation of black army units. Eventually the Fifty-Fourth Regiment was formed, and two of Douglass's sons fought in it. Write a documented research paper on the history of this unit or on Douglass's role in getting it established. Alternatively, compare the results of your research with the way the unit is developed in the film *Glory*. Does the film support or refute the version you found during your research? Why or why not?

6. The U.S. armed forces remained officially segregated until President Truman integrated them by executive order in 1947. Research this decision, and write a paper on your findings. What were the arguments against integration? What ideas were advanced to refute them? What was the immediate reaction of the military? How was integration put into practice?

10

War and Violence

A s researcher and writer Arnold P. Goldstein points out, the Revolutionary War "began our two-century-long love affair with the gun," embedding in the national consciousness the importance of bearing arms and a sense of "frontier justice" romanticized for many years since through diverse media. Nowhere is American culture more preoccupied with guns and self-defense than in the cultural representations of war and of the enemy. As narrator Sam Keen notes in the introduction to the video *Faces of the Enemy*, "Before we make war, even before we make weapons, we make an idea of the enemy." As we make an image of the enemy, we clarify who we are and set ourselves in opposition to that enemy: we are good, they are evil; our cause is just, theirs is unjust; we are human, they are animals. There is a certain peace of mind accompanying that clarity: suicide rates go down in wartime, people feel they have a common purpose, citizens rally to the cause, gray tones disappear in an increasingly black and white world where there is a good side (us) and a bad side (them).

As we identify and characterize an enemy, we more clearly establish our own national identity. Our leaders then appeal to that identity and to the desire to belong in order to rally the nation to support the war effort. In encouraging the citizenry to identify with national goals and in vilifying the enemy, politicians and officials, and often private commercial interests, use primarily appeals to ethos and pathos. Appeals to *ethos* commonly establish a sense of values and ideals to which true Americans would subscribe; those wishing to be considered real Americans support the efforts identified as essential to the common good. Leaders can also appeal to ethos to establish their credibility and their sense of leadership and authority, to appear "presidential" and offer an image of stability and steadfastness in the face of potential chaos.

Appeals to *pathos* convince us to suffer for the common good. On the home front, such appeals urge us to support the war politically, to

435

work in factories, to conserve petroleum products, to do without luxuries, and sometimes necessities, to support the war effort in any way possible. Even more difficult can be the appeal to offer one's time and loss of independence and income through military service. Along with such service comes the risk of losing one's life, and appeals must be strong indeed to urge men and women to be prepared to give their lives for their country and the "American way of life."

War and Violence through History

Throughout recorded history on the American continent, conflicts between economic forces, between cultures and ways of life, and between competing claims on the land have created divergent views about whose rights to the land, to the resources, to political and economic power, should be superior. White settlements intruded on the indigenous peoples of America, and European settlers from various countries fought over land and resources.

Most notable in mainstream American history is the Revolutionary War against Britain. In the first selection, Thomas Paine writes persuasively about the kind of American who Americans would not want to be—the "summer soldier and sunshine patriot"—and the kind with whom they want to identify—"he whose heart is firm, and whose conscience approves his conduct, will pursue his principles unto death." Intertwined with his appeals to support American independence in its most desperate hour are his descriptions of the enemy, "A sottish, stupid, stubborn, worthless, brutish man." In setting up oppositions—of supporting America or not, of courage or fear—Paine relies on parallel phrasing and balanced sentences to outline and reinforce the choices Americans will need to make.

Speaking about the Civil War—a war that many argue was primarily economic yet pitted "brother against brother"—Abraham Lincoln sought, in "The Gettysburg Address," not to divide but to unite, by linking the themes of birth and death, the deaths of Gettysburg in exchange for "a new birth of freedom." Lincoln predicted in his address that "the world will little note nor long remember what we say here," but about that he was wrong: The world rightly sees "The Gettysburg Address" as a perhaps unparalleled statement of the poignance of war.

Just as each side in the Civil War saw itself as the rightful victor, so do we frequently need to see ourselves as good and the other side as bad; we need to avoid seeing the enemy as anything but dangerous and worthy of extinction. Mark Twain, a sharp if humorous critic of American society, lacerates the tendency to simplify the waging of war in "The War Prayer," a short satirical piece countering piety with the grim reminder that victory for one side brings with it defeat and blighted lives for the other.

An image from a twentieth-century war that sharply contrasts the two sides, an anti-Nazi poster entitled *"Deliver Us from Evil,"* appeals to emotion and to values in order to move its audience—not merely to buy bonds but to sacrifice for the innocent victims of war.

The act of asking Congress to declare war is probably the most solemn occasion at which a sitting president can speak, and President Franklin Delano Roosevelt's "Pearl Harbor Address" on December 8, 1941, after the bombings of Pearl Harbor and other bases on Oahu, Hawaii, is a prime example of a difficult rhetorical situation and the ways in which a nation's leader can use such an occasion to unite citizens against a common enemy. In asking for a formal declaration of war, Roosevelt's speech required appeals to patriotism and a strong characterization of a treacherous enemy.

Sometimes in creating an enemy, we see something of ourselves in the enemy and something of the enemy in ourselves. The two Vietnam War–era photographs included in this chapter illustrate contradictions of that war. In "Saigon Execution," Americans are brought painfully close to the actuality of the war and to the confusion about friends and enemies that characterized it. In "The Terror of War," war's most horrifying damage—to innocent children—challenged political arguments and domino theories of spreading communism and had a profound effect on Americans' perceptions of the war.

Simple, straightforward narratives of war hold their own compelling power as well and can teach us something memorable about suffering. Jacqueline Navarra Rhoads's narrative, "Nurses in Vietnam," is a story of healing in the midst of massive casualties and war waging. Rhoads's account of her tour of duty in Vietnam also reminds us of the power of the personal voice in bringing the pain and tragedy of massive warfare to an individual level.

Paul Fussell's essay, "Type-Casting," discusses the stereotypes endemic to war, providing some background for examining the ways in which we characterize both ourselves and our enemies. His essay, from the book *Wartime,* is a useful secondary source to use while analyzing many of the primary materials included in this chapter.

War is by no means the only manifestation of violent conflict that concerns Americans; from hate crimes to domestic violence to guns in schools, Americans find themselves in a culture that both endorses the right of all citizens to own firearms and recognizes that violence is endemic in the culture. Arnold P. Goldstein's *Violence in America* examines many diverse manifestations of violence in American cultures. The selections included here focus on both the principles that drive violent behavior and several manifestations of that behavior—in the media, on the playground, and in school, where sometimes students pack guns along with their lunches.

The Violence Policy Center tackles gun violence by treating gun control as a public health issue; one of their more persuasive visual images, "Teddy Bears," offers one example of the Center's strategy to shape public opinion and public policy.

Student Neil A. Van Os, examining the range of materials in this chapter, selected Roosevelt's Pearl Harbor Address as a way to explore the principles of persuasion and propaganda evident in those selections. Integrating secondary sources into his argument, he asserts that Roosevelt's speech is effective in utilizing strategies of propaganda, a label we usually reserve for "the enemy's" rhetoric. But Van Os does what we recommend that you do as you read these selections: think critically and carefully about assumptions, purpose, imagery, language—about the arts of persuasion.

We highly recommend the documentary film discussed in this chapter, *Faces of the Enemy*, as a context for understanding the processes of creating images and perceptions of the enemy. Viewing it as a class is particularly helpful and can provoke thoughtful discussion on the readings in this chapter.

Each of the selections in this chapter is an argument: to unite against a common threat; to renounce an enemy; to embrace a former enemy and "bind up the nation's wounds"; to unite as a people to defeat a treacherous foe; to challenge our assumptions about who our political friends and enemies are and about the role of violence in our culture. The arguments about the war, and about waging war, appeal to the ethics of Americans—to fair play, to leadership in the free world, to protecting the innocent—and to logic—to protecting American and allies' interests. They also appeal to pathos—to empathy for the weak and hurt, to manliness and virility, to hatred of the less-than-human enemy. These appeals are made through language: word choice, syntax or sentence structure, emphasis, and allusions or references that evoke images to which we respond. (See Chapter 2 for further explanation.)

The authors in this chapter are all highly attentive to the power of language to move people's emotions and to move them to action. The discussion after the reading selections will help you to analyze persuasive language in what you read, to develop persuasive strategies of language in your own writing, and to appreciate the power of language to unite and to divide.

As you read and reflect on the selections in this chapter, consider the changes, even over your own lifetime, that have created the context in which questions about war and violence must now be asked. In the last years of the twentieth century, given the changing world political order that has resulted from the breakup of the Soviet Union and the end of the Cold War, Americans increasingly look upon war—and this nation's role in establishing and maintaining world peace—with skepticism.

∞ These Are the Times That Try Men's Souls (1776)

THOMAS PAINE

Thomas Paine (1737–1809) came to America from England in 1774. A political radical and active writer and supporter of the American Revolution, Paine worked in a variety of occupations and held several official posts in the colonies, but it is for his crusades on behalf of democratic principles and rights, both in America and abroad, that he is best remembered. Paine's writings include Common Sense *(1776),* The American Crisis *(1776–1783),* Public Good *(1780),* The Rights of Man *(1791–1792), and* The Age of Reason *(1794–1796), a book for which he was denounced as an atheist.* The American Crisis, *a series of sixteen pamphlets supporting the American Revolution, was widely distributed in the American colonies. The selection that follows is from the famous first pamphlet in the series, which was read to American troops on the eve of the Battle of Trenton by order of General Washington.*

These are the times that try men's souls. The summer soldier and the sunshine patriot will, in this crisis, shrink from the service of his country; but he that stands it NOW, deserves the love and thanks of man and woman. Tyranny, like hell, is not easily conquered: yet we have this consolation with us, that the harder the conflict, the more glorious the triumph. What we obtain too cheap, we esteem too lightly: 'tis dearness only that gives every thing its value. Heaven knows how to put a proper price upon its goods: and it would be strange indeed, if so celestial an article as FREEDOM should not be highly rated. Britain, with an army to enforce her tyranny, has declared that she has a right (*not only to* TAX) but "to BIND *us in* ALL CASES WHATSOEVER," and if being *bound in that manner*, is not slavery, then is there no such a thing as slavery upon earth. Even the expression is impious, for so unlimited a power can belong only to God. . . .

I have as little superstition in me as any man living, but my secret opinion has ever been, and still is, that God Almighty will not give up a people to military destruction, or leave them unsupportedly to perish, who have so earnestly and so repeatedly sought to avoid the calamities of war, by every decent method which wisdom could invent. Neither have I so much of the infidel in me, as to suppose that He has relinquished the government of the world, and given us up to the care of devils, and as I do not, I cannot see on what grounds the king of Britain can look up to Heaven for help against us: a common murderer, a highwayman, or a housebreaker, has as good a pretence as he. . . .

I call not upon a few, but upon all: not on *this* state or *that* state, but on *every* state; up and help us; lay your shoulders to the wheel; better have too much force than too little, when so great an object is at stake. Let it be told to the future world, that in the depth of winter, when nothing but hope and virtue could survive, that the city and the country, alarmed at one common danger, came forth to meet and to repulse it. Say not that thousands are gone, turn out your tens of thousands: throw not the burden of the day upon Providence, but *"show your faith by your works,"* that God may bless you. It matters not where you live, or what rank of life you hold, the evil or the blessing will reach you all. The far and the near, the home counties and the back, the rich and the poor, will suffer or rejoice alike. The heart that feels not now, is dead: the blood of his children will curse his cowardice, who shrinks back at a time when a little might have saved the whole, and made *them* happy. I love the man that can smile in trouble, that can gather strength from distress, and grow brave by reflection. 'Tis the business of little minds to shrink; but he whose heart is firm, and whose conscience approves his conduct, will pursue his principles unto death. My own line of reasoning is to myself as straight and clear as a ray of light. Not all the treasures of the world, so far as I believe, could have induced me to support an offensive war, for I think it murder; but if a thief breaks into my house, burns and destroys my property, and kills or threatens to kill me, or those that are in it, and to *"bind me in all cases whatsoever,"* to his absolute will, am I to suffer it? What signifies it to me, whether he who does it is a king or a common man; my countryman or not my countryman: whether it be done by an individual villain, or an army of them? If we reason to the root of things we shall find no difference: neither can any just cause be assigned why we should punish in the one case and pardon in the other. Let them call me rebel, and welcome, I feel no concern from it; but I should suffer the misery of devils, were I to make a whore of my soul by swearing allegiance to one whose character is that of a sottish, stupid, stubborn, worthless, brutish man. I conceive likewise a horrid idea in receiving mercy from a being, who at the last day shall be shrieking to the rocks and mountains to cover him, and fleeing with terror from the orphan, the widow, and the slain of America.

There are cases which cannot be overdone by language, and this is one. There are persons too who see not the full extent of the evil which threatens them, they solace themselves with hopes that the enemy, if they succeed, will be merciful. It is the madness of folly, to expect mercy from those who have refused to do justice; and even mercy, where conquest is the object, is only a trick of war; the cunning of the fox is as murderous as the violence of the wolf; and we ought to guard equally against both. . . .

I thank God that I fear not. I see no real cause for fear. I know our 5 situation well, and can see the way out of it. . . . By perseverance and fortitude we have the prospect of a glorious issue: by cowardice and submission, the sad choice of a variety of evils—a ravaged country— a depopulated city—habitations without safety, and slavery without hope—our homes turned into barracks and bawdy-houses for Hessians, and a future race to provide for, whose fathers we shall doubt of. Look on this picture and weep over it! and if there yet remains one thoughtless wretch who believes it not, let him suffer it unlamented.

For Journals

Have you heard someone use the expression in the title of this selection? What did it mean to you? If you haven't heard it before, freewrite about your initial reactions to it.

For Discussion

1.   A number of the phrases in this essay became well-known expressions over time. Which ones have you heard before? Did you know they came from the Revolutionary War era? What did they mean to you when you first heard them? What emotions did they inspire in you?

2.   How does Paine characterize the kind of Americans who will answer the call? In what ways does he appeal to his audience so that they will want to support the cause of independence?

3.   How does Paine characterize the enemy? What evidence does he offer to support his characterization? Cite examples of vivid language and concrete images.

4.   Paine develops his argument with parallelism, or grammatically similar phrases; and antithesis, or the setting up of a statement that begins with what is *not* true and then states what *is* true: for example, "I call not upon a few, but upon all." Identify specific examples of these and other stylistic strategies that you believe are particularly effective, and analyze what they contribute to the argument.

5.   Compare this selection with the Franklin woodcut *Join, or Die* (Chapter 5). What common themes and appeals do you find?

For Writing

1. Using discussion question 2 as a starting point, develop an essay on Paine's ideal heroic American.

2. Look up some of Paine's other pamphlets from *The American Crisis.* Study several selections, and write an essay analyzing the most common strategies of language in his writings.

∽ *The Gettysburg Address* (1863)

ABRAHAM LINCOLN

The son of a pioneer, Abraham Lincoln was born in Hodgesville, Kentucky, in 1809 and moved to Illinois in 1831. After brief experiences as a clerk, postmaster, and county surveyor, he studied law and was elected to the state legislature in 1834. A prominent member of the newly organized Republican Party, Lincoln became president on the eve of the Civil War. In 1862, after the Union victory at Antietam, Lincoln issued the Emancipation Proclamation freeing the slaves—the crowning achievement of an illustrious presidency. He delivered "The Gettysburg Address," one of his greatest speeches, at the dedication of the Gettysburg National Cemetery in 1863. Lincoln was assassinated by John Wilkes Booth in 1865, shortly after Robert E. Lee's surrender and the end of the Civil War.

Four score and seven years ago our fathers brought forth on this continent, a new nation, conceived in Liberty, and dedicated to the proposition that all men are created equal.

Now we are engaged in a great civil war, testing whether that nation, or any nation so conceived and so dedicated, can long endure. We are met on a great battlefield of that war. We have come to dedicate a portion of that field as a final resting-place for those who here gave their lives that that nation might live. It is altogether fitting and proper that we should do this.

But, in a larger sense, we cannot dedicate—we cannot consecrate—we cannot hallow—this ground. The brave men, living and dead, who struggled here have consecrated it, far above our poor power to add or detract. The world will little note, nor long remember, what we say here, but it can never forget what they did here. It is for us the living, rather, to be dedicated here to the unfinished work which they who fought here have thus far so nobly advanced. It is rather for us to be here dedicated to the great task remaining before us—that from these honored dead we take increased devotion to that cause for which they gave the last full measure of devotion; that we here highly resolve that these dead shall not have died in vain; that this nation, under God, shall have a new birth of freedom; and that government of the people, by the people, for the people, shall not perish from the earth.

For Journals

What phrases from "The Gettysburg Address" have you heard before? What did they mean to you when you first heard them?

For Discussion

1.   After your first reading, do a slow, line-by-line reading out loud. Do you find that the address engages your intellect, or your emotions, or both? Discuss your answer.

2.   Analyze what Lincoln leaves out of the speech as well as what he includes; for example, the address does not mention slavery, or the animosity between North and South. What is the effect of his careful selection of themes and words?

3.   What key ideas does Lincoln evoke in the address? What images? How do they work together to support Lincoln's persuasive purpose?

4.   In what ways does Lincoln weave the themes of birth and death? How does the style—the sentence structure, or syntax; the diction, or word choice—convey those themes?

5.   The address is full of expressions we have heard in other contexts: for example, Martin Luther King, Jr.'s "I Have a Dream" (Chapter 6) echoes its opening, and countless military funerals have repeated the phrase "last full measure of devotion." Author Garry Wills wrote, "Hemingway claimed that all modern American novels are the offspring of *Huckleberry Finn*. It is no greater exaggeration to say that all modern political prose descends from 'The Gettysburg Address.'" Discuss this assertion in view of the examples and other prose you have heard or read that have sought to invoke "The Gettysburg Address."

For Writing

1.   Do a close textual analysis of the address, considering sentence-level strategies as they relate to the larger theme or paradox of the address and to Lincoln's persuasive purpose in speaking. Consider the rhythm of the language, parallelism, pauses, and diction in your analysis.

2.   Research the context of the Battle of Gettysburg or of the address itself, writing a documented essay that gives the reader an understanding of the significance of the battle and the context of the speech.

∞ *The War Prayer* (1904–1905)

MARK TWAIN

Mark Twain (1835–1910) is the pen name of Samuel Clemens. He was born in Florida, Missouri, and explored a variety of jobs—printer, riverboat pilot, gold prospector—before discovering success as a writer with the publication of The Celebrated Jumping Frog of Calaveras County and Other Sketches *(1867) and* The Innocents Abroad *(1869). Twain established his reputation as a humorist through his classic novels* The Adventures of Tom Sawyer *(1876) and* The Adventures of Huckleberry Finn *(1885). Twain was always a critic of American society—Huckleberry Finn attacks racism, for example—but in later years he grew especially somber, even pessimistic. "The War Prayer" exemplifies the darker side of his satire.*

It was a time of great and exalting excitement. The country was up in arms, the war was on, in every breast burned the holy fire of patriotism; the drums were beating, the bands playing, the toy pistols popping, the bunched firecrackers hissing and spluttering; on every hand and far down the receding and fading spread of roofs and balconies a fluttering wilderness of flags flashed in the sun; daily the young volunteers marched down the wide avenue gay and fine in their new uniforms, the proud fathers and mothers and sisters and sweethearts cheering them with voices choked with happy emotion as they swung by; nightly the packed mass meetings listened, panting, to patriot oratory which stirred the deepest deeps of their hearts, and which they interrupted at briefest intervals with cyclones of applause, the tears running down their cheeks the while; in the churches the pastors preached devotion to flag and country, and invoked the God of Battles, beseeching His aid in our good cause in outpouring of fervid eloquence which moved every listener. It was indeed a glad and gracious time, and the half dozen rash spirits that ventured to disapprove of the war and cast a doubt upon its righteousness straightway got such a stern and angry warning that for their personal safety's sake they quickly shrank out of sight and offended no more in that way.

Sunday morning came—next day the battalions would leave for the front; the church was filled; the volunteers were there, their young faces alight with martial dreams—visions of the stern advance, the gathering momentum, the rushing charge, the flashing sabers, the flight of the foe, the tumult, the enveloping smoke, the fierce pursuit, the surrender!—them home from the war, bronzed heroes, welcomed, adored, submerged in golden seas of glory! With the volunteers sat their dear ones, proud, happy, and envied by the neighbors and friends who had no sons and brothers to send forth to the field of honor, there to win for the flag, or, failing, die the noblest of noble deaths. The service proceeded; a war chapter from the Old Testament was read; the first prayer was said; it was followed by an organ burst that shook the building, and with one impulse the house rose, with glowing eyes and beating hearts, and poured out that tremendous invocation—

"God the all-terrible!   Thou who ordainest,
Thunder thy clarion and lightning thy sword!"

Then came the "long" prayer. None could remember the like of it for passionate pleading and moving and beautiful language. The burden of its supplication was, that an ever-merciful and benignant Father of us all would watch over our noble young soldiers, and aid, comfort, and encourage them in their patriotic work; bless them, shield them in the day of battle and the hour of peril, bear them in His mighty hand, make them strong and confident, invincible in the bloody onset; help them to crush the foe, grant to them and to their flag and country imperishable honor and glory—

An aged stranger entered and moved with slow and noiseless step up the main aisle, his eyes fixed upon the minister, his long body clothed in a robe that reached to his feet, his head bare, his white hair descending in frothy cataract to his shoulders, his seamy face unnaturally pale, pale even to ghastliness. With all eyes following him and wondering, he made his silent way; without pausing, he ascended to the preacher's side and stood there, waiting. With shut lids the preacher, unconscious of his presence, continued his moving prayer, and at last finished it with the words, uttered in fervent appeal, "Bless our arms, grant us the victory, O Lord our God, Father and Protector of our land and flag!"

The stranger touched his arm, motioned him to step aside—which the startled minister did—and took his place. During some moments he surveyed the spellbound audience with solemn eyes, in which burned an uncanny light; then in a deep voice he said:

"I come from the Throne—bearing a message from Almighty God!" 5
The words smote the house with a shock; if the stranger perceived it he gave no attention. "He has heard the prayer of His servant your shepherd, and will grant it if such shall be your desire after I, His messenger, shall have explained to you its import—that is to say, its full import. For it is like unto many of the prayers of men, in that it asks for more than he who utters it is aware of—except he pause and think.

"God's servant and yours has prayed his prayer. Has he paused and taken thought? Is it one prayer? No, it is two—one uttered, the other not. Both have reached the ear of Him Who heareth all supplications, the spoken and the unspoken. Ponder this—keep it in mind. If you would beseech a blessing upon yourself, beware! lest without intent you invoke a curse upon a neighbor at the same time. If you pray for the blessing of rain upon your crop which needs it, by that act you are possibly praying for a curse upon some neighbor's crop which may not need rain and can be injured by it.

"You have heard your servant's prayer—the uttered part of it. I am commissioned of God to put into words the other part of it—that part which the pastor—and also you in your hearts—fervently prayed silently. And ignorantly and unthinkingly? God grant that it was so! You heard these words: 'Grant us the victory, O Lord our God!' That is sufficient. The *whole* of the uttered prayer is compact into those pregnant words. Elaborations were not necessary. When you have prayed for victory you have prayed for many unmentioned results which follow victory—*must* follow it, cannot help but follow it. Upon the listening spirit of God the Father fell also the unspoken part of the prayer. He commandeth me to put it into words. Listen!

"O Lord our Father, our young patriots, idols of our hearts, go forth to battle—be Thou near them! With them—in spirit—we also go forth from the sweet peace of our beloved firesides to smite the foe. O Lord our God, help us to tear their soldiers to bloody shreds with our shells; help us to cover their smiling fields with the pale forms of their patriot dead; help us to drown the thunder of the guns with the shrieks of their wounded, writhing in pain; help us to lay waste their humble homes with a hurricane of fire; help us to wring the hearts of their unoffending widows with unavailing grief; help us to turn them out roofless with their little children to wander unfriended the wastes of their desolated land in rags and hunger and thirst, sports of the sun flames of summer and the icy winds of winter, broken in spirit, worn with travail, imploring Thee for the refuge of the grave and denied it—for our sakes who adore Thee, Lord, blast their hopes, blight their lives, protract their bitter pilgrimage, make heavy their steps, water their way with their tears, stain the white snow with the blood of their wounded feet! We ask it, in the spirit of love, of Him Who is the Source of Love, and Who is the ever-faithful refuge and friend of all that are sore beset and seek His aid with humble and contrite hearts. Amen."

(*After a pause*) "Ye have prayed it: if ye still desire it, speak! The messenger of the Most High waits."

It was believed afterward that the man was a lunatic, because 10 there was no sense in what he said.

For Journals

Do you think of Mark Twain as a humorous writer? As a writer of satire or social commentary? Write about your expectations of this selection based on the title.

For Discussion

1. Examine the diction in the first two paragraphs. What tone and stance are established? Through which particular words and expressions?

2. What is your understanding of what the worshippers are praying for? Do you envision people on the other side of the conflict doing the same?

3. What does the messenger want the people in church to understand? How does he help them to do so? How does Twain convey to us the people's response to the message?

4. How does Twain show the irony of their prayer and their "spirit of love"? Examine the language, and cite specific examples that support your point.

5. How do you interpret the ending of the selection, particularly the last two sentences? How do you think the people hearing the stranger would respond? Would the other side respond any differently?

6. What is Twain's persuasive purpose in writing this selection? Why do you think he selected this genre and format for his purpose?

For Writing

1. Using discussion question 4 as a starting point, develop an analytical essay examining the style of this selection and the strategies Twain uses to convey irony.

2. Write a contemporary war prayer that pertains to a geopolitical situation in the middle to late twentieth century. Irony is not an easy writing technique, so aim for a subtle effect; get feedback from peers, and revise your language carefully.

∞ *"Deliver Us from Evil"* (ca. 1940)

This poster reveals a number of typical strategies used by poster artists to invoke American desire to support the war effort in Europe during both world wars—in this case, World War II. As you examine this selection and other visual materials in the chapter, consider what types of appeals are being made and which audiences are being targeted.

For Journals

What could convince you to work toward a war effort, whether by joining the military or contributing money? What are the most compelling ways in which a writer or artist could appeal to you?

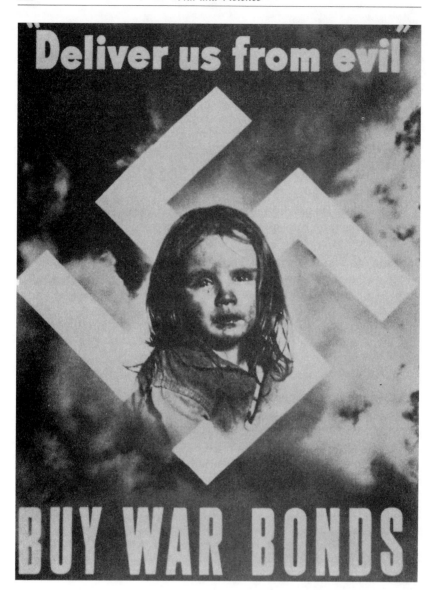

For Discussion

1. What is your immediate emotional response to the image?

2. What draws your eye? What do the shades and shapes emphasize?

3. Of what ethnicity does the child seem to be? How does that affect the viewer's reaction to the image?

4. The headline is from a Christian prayer. What is the significance of using this allusion?

For Writing

Using your journal entry as a starting point, if that would be helpful, write an essay on the different types of strategies that poster artists could use to elicit different kinds of support (monetary, military) from different segments of American society in a time of war. Pay special attention to the kinds of images you think would be most persuasive.

∾ *Pearl Harbor Address* (1941)

FRANKLIN DELANO ROOSEVELT

Franklin Delano Roosevelt (1882–1945) was the thirty-second president of the United States and the only president ever elected to four consecutive terms in office. His innovative New Deal economic recovery plan guided America through the difficult years of the Great Depression, and his cooperation with Winston Churchill helped secure an Allied victory in World War II. He died in Warm Springs, Georgia, in 1945, ironically, three weeks before the Nazi surrender. Roosevelt's address to the House of Representatives after the Japanese attack on Pearl Harbor in 1941, with such ringing phrases as "a date which will live in infamy," remains a classic call to action.

To the Congress of the United States: Yesterday, December 7, 1941—a date which will live in infamy—the United States of America was suddenly and deliberately attacked by naval and air forces of the Empire of Japan.

The United States was at peace with that nation and, at the solicitation of Japan, was still in conversation with its government and its emperor looking toward the maintenance of peace in the Pacific. Indeed, one hour after Japanese air squadrons had commenced bombing in Oahu, the Japanese ambassador to the United States and his colleague delivered to the secretary of state a formal reply to a recent American message. While this reply stated that it seemed useless to continue the existing diplomatic negotiations, it contained no threat or hint of war or armed attack.

It will be recorded that the distance of Hawaii from Japan makes it obvious that the attack was deliberately planned many days or even weeks ago. During the intervening time the Japanese government had deliberately sought to deceive the United States by false statements and expressions of hope for continued peace.

The attack yesterday on the Hawaiian Islands has caused severe damage to American naval and military forces. I regret to tell you that very many American lives have been lost. In addition American ships have been reported torpedoed on the high seas between San Francisco and Honolulu.

Yesterday the Japanese government also launched an attack 5 against Malaya.

Last night Japanese forces attacked Hong Kong.

Last night Japanese forces attacked Guam.

Last night Japanese forces attacked the Philippine Islands.

Last night the Japanese attacked Wake Island.

This morning the Japanese attacked Midway Island. 10

Japan has, therefore, undertaken a surprise offensive extending throughout the Pacific area. The facts of yesterday speak for themselves. The people of the United States have already formed their opinions and well understand the implications to the very life and safety of our nation.

As commander in chief of the army and navy I have directed that all measures be taken for our defense.

Always will we remember the character of the onslaught against us.

No matter how long it may take us to overcome this premeditated invasion, the American people in their righteous might will win through to absolute victory.

I believe I interpret the will of the Congress and of the people 15 when I assert that we will not only defend ourselves to the uttermost but will make very certain that this form of treachery shall never endanger us again.

Hostilities exist. There is no blinking at the fact that our people, our territory, and our interests are in grave danger.

With confidence in our armed forces—with the unbounded determination of our people—we will gain the inevitable triumph—so help us God.

I ask that the Congress declare that since the unprovoked and dastardly attack by Japan on Sunday, December 7, 1941, a state of war has existed between the United States and the Japanese Empire.

For Journals

Have your parents or grandparents ever talked about World War II or what they did in the war? Write for a few minutes on what you know about the war.

For Discussion

1.   Have you previously heard excerpts from this speech on television or radio? What was your reaction then? If you haven't heard the speech before, talk with people who heard the speech in 1941, and ask them about their reactions; share your findings with your peers, and compare accounts.

2.   How does Roosevelt seek to unite Americans? What sense of identity does he evoke? What themes does he dwell upon? What ethos appeals does he make? What pathos appeals?

3.   How does Roosevelt establish a sense of the enemy for his audience? What kinds of logos or other appeals does he use? How do syntax and diction reinforce the appeals? Look, for example, at his use of repetition in the series that opens "last night," at midspeech (paragraph 6).

4.   Examine the second-to-last sentence: "With confidence . . ." What effect does opening with a dependent phrase have on the emphasis in this sentence?

5.   Compare and contrast the rhetorical demands of a presidential address calling for war with an inaugural address or other presidential speech. Which type of speech do you believe would be the more difficult to write? Why?

For Writing

1.   Through library research or through taking oral histories, investigate reactions to this speech at the time it was given. You could examine newspaper commentaries and magazine articles and interview older people about their memories of the occasion. In what ways were they affected, practically and emotionally, by the address? How did the journalistic accounts of the times view the speech? Write an essay summarizing your findings.

2.   Write an essay discussing the ways in which Roosevelt seeks to write the American people and how he develops an image of the enemy in the speech. Pay special attention to Roosevelt's use of language, syntax, and repetition.

∞ *Saigon Execution* (1969)

EDWARD T. ADAMS

The following photograph became one of the most famous images of the Vietnam War. Colonel Nguyen Ngoc Loan, South Vietnam's police chief, executes a Vietcong suspect in Saigon. The filmed version of this execution was shown on television all over the world. Adams's photograph won the Pulitzer Prize for News Photography in 1969.

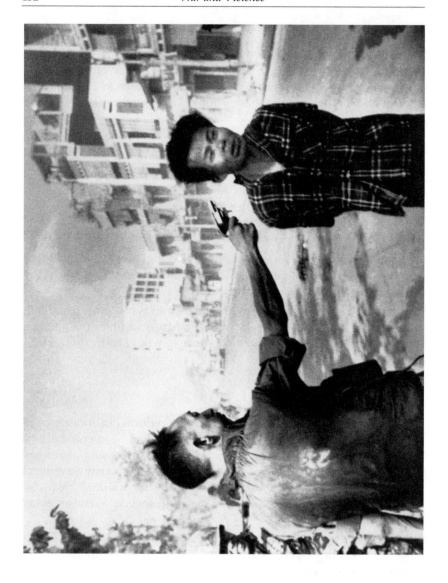

For Journals

Describe the visual images that come to mind when you think of the Vietnam War.

For Discussion

1. Analyze the photograph. What is emphasized? Whose face is more visible, and how does that visibility affect how you react to the photograph? How are the respective figures dressed? Where are their hands? What do these details tell you about the relative power of each man? How do such elements of the photograph contribute to your logical, ethical, and emotional reactions to the image.

2. In what ways is this sort of event expected in wartime? In what ways is it surprising?

3. What effects would this photograph have on Americans' perceptions of their "friends" and "enemies" during the war?

For Writing

1. What impact do you think that this photograph, and others like it, may have had on the American public and their perception of the Vietnam War?

2. Research the Vietnam War in pictures and photographs, and see if you can discern changes over time in the ways in which the war was covered in the popular print media.

∞ *The Terror of War* (1973)

HUYNH CONG "NICK" UT

> *The following photograph, taken by Associated Press photographer Huynh Cong "Nick" Ut, brought with it the horrifying realization of the many civilian participants in, and victims of, the war in Vietnam. Napalm, a gel developed in World War II, was used widely in Vietnam in flame throwers and incendiary bombs; it burns hotly and rather slowly and sticks to its target. The children pictured were apparently the victims of napalm bombs dropped by the South Vietnamese air force. This photograph won the Pulitzer Prize for News Photography in 1973.*

For Journals

Think about the truism that a picture is worth a thousand words. Do you agree?

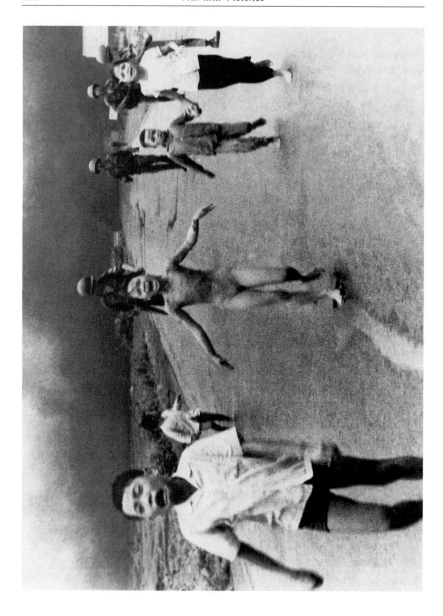

For Discussion

1. What are your immediate reactions to the photograph? Do you respond primarily on an emotional or intellectual level? What does your response tell you about the power of an image?

2. Examine the composition and content of the photograph. What is being conveyed? Do you find it more reportorial or persuasive? Of what might a viewer of this photograph be persuaded?

3. Who are the primary victims of war? To what extent do you think they are represented in war images? Do you think the image in the next photograph is more, or less, persuasive than images of young American men on the battlefield? Explain.

For Writing

1. Write a report describing the event portrayed in this photograph, using precise, concrete language. Then, in view of your journal entry, analyze the relative power of visual images and language.

2. Talk with people who remember the Vietnam War, and ask them about whom they perceived as America's friends and enemies during that war. Analyze the ways in which this photograph confirms or contradicts what you learned from your interviewees.

∞ *Nurses in Vietnam* (1987)

JACQUELINE NAVARRA RHOADS

Jacqueline Navarra Rhoads was born in 1948 in Albion, New York, resided for some time in San Antonio, and now lives in Albuquerque, New Mexico, where she is on the nursing faculty of the University of New Mexico. She served as an army nurse in Vietnam in 1970–1971 and spent most of her tour with the 18th Surgical Hospital in Quang Tri. Her personal account of her tour focuses the politically charged conflict on a personal level, dealing with both the pain and exhilaration of her work and the long-term effects it has had on her life.

We arrived in Vietnam on April 26, 1970, right in the middle of a rocket attack. We were ordered off the plane and everyone was supposed to lay down on the ground. So here I am with my dress uniform, stockings, shoes, and skirt, and suddenly I'm lying down on a cement pavement at Tan Son Nhut wondering, "My God, what did I get myself into?" The noise was so deafening. The heat—I remember how hot it was. We eventually got inside this terminal building where there were all these guys waiting to get on the plane to go home. They were whooping it up, running around with signs saying things like:

"Only one hour and thirty-five minutes left!" They saw us coming and one of them said, "Cheer up, the worst is yet to come." We stayed there sixteen hours before we could get out. When we got on the bus, all the windows were screened. I learned from the bus driver that this was to prevent the Vietnamese from throwing grenades in through the windows. I said, "But I thought the enemy was up north somewhere." He told me, "No, the enemy is all around you here. You never know who you're fighting."

My first assignment was in Phu Bai. I was there for thirty days because they needed some emergency room nurses there. Then I was transferred to the 18th Surgical Hospital in Quang Tri, just a few miles from the DMZ. They had just put a MUST (Medical Unit Self-Transportable) unit in there from Camp Evans and they needed operating and emergency room nurses right away. I was there the remainder of my tour.

I was a very young twenty-one. At St. Mary's School of Nursing in Rochester (New York), I kept these Army recruiting posters all over my room. There was a big push at that time for nurses, and we had recruiters coming to the school constantly from the time I started in 1966. I don't know what it was, I loved nursing as much. I always thought—I know it sounds crazy—but I wanted to do something for my country. I just had a feeling that being a nurse in the Army was what I wanted to do. And of course my uncles were all in the Army in World War II. There were nine brothers in my mother's family, and they all went into the Army within six months of each other.

Everyone thought I was crazy. I remember my mother saying, "Jacque, do you know what you're getting yourself into?" Of course, when you're young you have no fear.

I did basic training at Fort Sam Houston in San Antonio. My main 5 memory of that time is the parties, big parties. I never took basic training very seriously. It was only later I realized that I should have. What to do in case of a nuclear attack, what to do for chemical warfare, how to handle a weapon—these were things we laughed at. We went out to Camp Bullis and shot weapons, but as nurses we never thought that shooting a weapon was something we needed to know. True, we never had to fire weapons, but we had wounded who came in with weapons as splints, and they were loaded weapons. When that happened, I thought, "Why didn't I listen when they taught us how to take this weapon apart?" You know, an M-16 with a full magazine. We had a young guy come in, he had a grenade with the pin pulled wrapped in a handkerchief and stuffed into his fatigue pocket, a live grenade! I thought, "Gosh, if only I had listened."

I think the practice village out where we trained at Camp Bullis is still in existence. The bamboo sticks smeared with excrement, they were authentic. There was an instructor in black pajamas, camouflage makeup on his face. Well, we kind of laughed. We didn't take it seriously until we started seeing these kinds of injuries in Vietnam.

My first real exposure to the war came five days after I landed. It was at Phu Bai. We received twenty-five body bags in on this giant Chinook helicopter. You know, the Chinook is this great big helicopter, this two-blade deal that can carry one hundred to one hundred and fifty people. And this Chinook came in with twenty-five body bags aboard. One of the nurses' responsibilities was to look inside these body bags to determine cause of death. Of course, they couldn't release the doctors for such trivial work. What you had to do was open the bag, look inside and see what possibly could have killed this person, and then write down on the tag what you felt the cause of death was. It was so obvious most of the time. That's something I still have flashbacks about—unzipping those bags. It was my first exposure to maggots, something I had never seen before in my life.

One was a young guy who had had his face blown away, with hundreds of maggots eating away where his face used to be. Another one, he had his eyes wide open. He was staring up at me. I remember he had a large hole in his chest and I knew it was a gunshot wound or a grenade injury. It had blown his heart, his lungs, everything to shreds. He had nothing left but a rib cage. Evidently, they had lain out on the ground awhile before someone could get to them. The corpsmen were told to take care of the wounded first, instead of spending time getting the dead in the bags. There were GIs exposed to flame throwers or gas explosions. We used to call them "crispy critters" to keep from getting depressed. They'd come in and there would be nothing more than this shell of a person. That was a little easier to take, they didn't have a face. It could have been an animal's carcass for all you knew. But to have to go looking for the dog tags, to find the dog tags on a person, that bothered me. I remember the first time I looked in a body bag I shook so badly. One of the doctors was kind enough to help me through it, saying, "Come on, it's your duty and you're going to have to do this. It's just something that I'm going to help you through. It's just a dead person." It was such a close-knit group. We were considered the most beautiful women in the world. The guys treated us special. You could have been the ugliest woman in the world, but still you were treated special.

The mass-cal, that's mass-casualty situation, traditionally was anything more than ten or fifteen wounded. It was mass chaos, bordering on panic. There'd be a corpsman walking around saying, "Dust off just called and they're bringing in twenty-five wounded. Everybody get going." So we'd pull out all our supplies. The nurses would put extra tourniquets around their necks to get ready to clamp off blood vessels. The stretchers were all prepared, and we'd go down each row hanging IVs all plugged and ready to go. It was mass production. You'd start the IVs on those people where the doctor was able to say, "This one is saved, this one is saved." We put them in triage categories. The expectant ones were the ones who required too much care. We'd make them comfortable and allow them to die. I guess it was making us comfortable too.

I remember this guy named Cliff, a triple amputee we once had. 10 He came in with mast-trousers on. Mast-trousers is an apparatus you inflate that puts pressure on the lower half of your body to allow adequate blood flow to your heart and brain. When Cliff came in, he was conscious, which was amazing. He looked like a stage dummy who'd been thrown haphazardly in a pile. One of his legs was up underneath his chin so that he was able to look down at the underside of his foot. His left arm was twisted behind his head in a horrible way. We couldn't even locate his second leg. He had stepped on a land mine. With his legs that bad, we knew there probably wasn't much backbone left. He was alive because of these trousers. The corpsman must have been right there when he got wounded. He had put him in this bag and inflated it. Cliff should have been dead.

It was really funny because he looked at two of us nurses there and said, "God, I think I've died and gone to heaven . . . a round-eye, an American, you look so beautiful." He was so concerned about the way he looked because of us standing there, "Gee, I must look a mess." But he was alert, he knew where he was. "Doc, take good care of me. I know my leg is pretty bad because I can see it, but take good care of me, doc." The docs couldn't put him in the expectant category and give him morphine to make him comfortable, because he was too alert. The docs had trouble letting go. So one of them finally said, "Well, let's get him into the operating room, deflate the bag, and let's get in there and see if we can't do something."

Well, we knew just by looking at him in that condition that he wasn't going to last, that as soon as we deflated the bag he'd bleed to death in a matter of seconds. Somehow, he knew it too. I remember I was getting blood prepared for him. He called me from across the room, "Jacque, come here quick." I went over to him and said, "What's the matter Cliff, what's wrong?" He said, "Just hold my hand and don't leave me." I said, "Why, Cliff? Are you in pain?" We always worried about pain, alleviating pain. We'd do anything to alleviate pain. He said, "I think I'm going to die and I don't want to be alone." So I stood there crying, with him holding my hand. And when we deflated the trousers, we lost him in seconds. We found no backbone, no lower part of his body. Really, he had been cut in half.

The leg that was folded underneath his neck was completely severed from his body. It was just there. The corpsmen had evidently bundled him together into the bag hoping maybe something would be there that was salvageable. And he just died. I remember he had blond hair, blue eyes—cute as a button. I had to take his body myself to graves registration. I just couldn't let him go alone. I just couldn't do that. I had to pry my hand away from his hand, because he had held on to my hand so tightly. I had to follow him to graves registration and put him in the bag myself. I couldn't let go of him. It was something I had to do.

Usually the expectants had massive head injuries. They were practically gone, they couldn't communicate with you. You were supposed to clean them up, call the chaplain. You did all that stuff, I guess, to make you feel as though you were helping them. To preserve their lives, you would've had to put them on a respirator and evac them to a neuro facility, which in our case would have been all the way to Da Nang, which was hours, miles away. I was an operating room nurse, but when there was a mass-cal, since there were only twelve of us, we'd be called into triage to work there. After that, I'd follow them into the operating room and help do the surgery. A lot of the shrapnel extractions we'd do ourselves, and a lot of the closures too. The docs would say, "Why don't you close? I got this next case in the next room." You didn't have to worry about it too much, if you got into trouble he'd be right there next door.

We wanted to save everyone. We had a lot of ARVNs (Army of 15 the Republic of Vietnam), we called them "Marvin the ARVN." We tried to take care of the Americans first, but we also had to take care of whoever needed care—period, whether he was a Vietnamese, a POW, or whatever. In fact, when we tried to save Cliff, they brought in the Vietnamese who had laid the mine. He had an amputation. He was bleedingly badly and had to be treated right away. And we saved him. I guess in my heart I felt angry about what happened.

We were short on anesthesia and supplies. And we were giving anesthesia to this POW, which made me angry because I thought, "What if—what happens if someone comes in like Cliff and we don't—have any anesthesia left because we gave it all to this POW?" Again, because I was very strongly Catholic, as soon as I heard myself thinking this, I thought, "God, how can you think that? The tables could be turned, and what if it was Cliff in the POW's place, and how would I feel if he received no anesthesia simply because he was an enemy?" First of all, it shocked me and embarrassed me. It made me think, "Gosh, I'm losing my values, what's happened to me?" I had been taught in nursing school to save everybody regardless of race, creed, color, ethnic background, whatever. Life is life. But suddenly I wasn't thinking that anymore. I was thinking, "I'm American, and they're the enemy. Kill the enemy and save the American."

Before I went to Vietnam, I was kind of bubbly, excited about life. I haven't changed that much really, I'm still that way. But back then, suddenly, I began questioning things, wondering about what we were doing there. I remember talking with the chaplain, saying, "What are we doing? For what purpose are we here?" We were training Vietnamese helicopter pilots to go out and pick up their wounded and take them to their hospitals. And we treated plenty of them at our hospitals, too. Yet when we'd call up and say, "We got a wounded soldier in Timbuktu," they'd say, "It's five o'clock and we don't fly at night." We had soldiers in the hospital shot by ten-year-old boys and girls. We had women who'd invite GIs to dinner—nice women—and they'd have someone come out from behind a curtain and shoot them all down dead. I mean, what kind of war was this?

The chaplain told me, "Hey Jacque, you can't condemn the American government. We can't say the American government is wrong to put us in this position here. We can't say, because there is so much we don't know." It was good advice at the time, it really helped me. I was thinking, "Here I am judging, and I'm saying what the heck are we doing here, look at all these lives lost, all these young boys and for what? And who am I to judge that? There has to be a reason." I guess I'm still trying to hold on to that belief, even though people laugh at me when I say it. They think I'm living in a dream world because I'm hoping there was a good reason.

I didn't really have much time to worry about right and wrong back then, because during these mass-cals we'd be up for thirty-six hours at a stretch. Nobody wanted to quit until the last surgery case was stabilized. By that time, we were emotionally and physically numb. You couldn't see clearly, you couldn't react. Sounds were distant. We kind of policed each other. When we saw each other reacting strangely or slowly, we'd say, "Hey, Jacque, get some sleep, someone will cover, go get some sleep." That's how close we were. That's how we coped with stress.

You didn't have time to think about how unhappy you were. It was afterwards, when you couldn't go to sleep . . . here you were without sleep for thirty-six hours, lying in your bed expecting sleep to overwhelm you, but you couldn't fall asleep because you were so tensed and stressed from what you saw. I knew I had a problem the day I was with a nurse I was training who was going to replace someone else. I remember I had completed this amputation and I had the solider's leg under my arm. I was holding the leg because I had to dress it up and give it to graves registration. They'd handle all the severed limbs in a respectful manner. They wouldn't just throw them in the garbage pile and burn them. They were specially labeled and handled the good old government way.

I remember this nurse came in and she was scheduled to take the place of another nurse. When she saw me, I went to greet her and I had this leg under my arm. She collapsed on the ground in a dead faint. I thought, "What could possibly be wrong with her?" There I was trying to figure out what's wrong with her, not realizing that here I had this leg with a combat boot still on and half this man's combat fatigue still on, blood dripping over the exposed end. And I had no idea this might bother her.

We had a lot of big parties, too. The Army had all these rules about fraternization, how officers couldn't fraternize with enlisted. In Quang Tri, we were just one big family. You didn't worry about who had an E-2 stripe or who had the colonel's insignia. I'm not saying we didn't have problems with officers and enlisted people or things like insubordination. But everybody partied together.

I never had a sexual relationship over there. You have to remember how Catholic I was. Dating, well, you'd walk around bunkers and talk about home. Every hooch had a bunker, so you'd bring a bottle of wine and he'd bring glasses and—this sounds gross, I guess—you'd sit and watch the B-52s bomb across the DMZ. It produced this northern lights effect. The sky would light up in different colors and you'd sit and watch the fireworks. I know it sounds strange, watching somebody's village get blown up. We didn't want to think about the lives being lost.

The grunts always knew where the female nurses were. They all knew that at the hospital there was a good chance of seeing a "round-eye." Once, during monsoon season, we received a dust off call saying there'd been a truck convoy ambush involving forty or fifty guys. They were in bad shape but not far from the hospital, maybe seven or eight miles. We could stand on the tops of our bunkers and see flashes of light from where they were fighting the VC. One of these deuce-and-a-half trucks with a load of wounded came barreling up right into our triage area. Like I said, they all knew where the hospital was. The truck's canvas and wood back part were all on fire. Evidently they had just thrown the wounded in back and driven straight for us.

We were concerned about the truck, about getting it out of the 25 way, but we were also trying to get to the wounded. There were two guys in the back, standing up. There was a third guy we couldn't see, and the first two were carrying him and shrieking at the top of their lungs. One was holding the upper part of his torso, under the arms, and the other held the legs. Their eyes were wild and they were screaming. I couldn't see what was wrong with the guy they were carrying. Everyone else on the truck was jumping off. We were shouting to these guys to get off too, that the truck was about to explode. We were screaming, "You're OK, you're at the hospital."

Two of the corpsmen got up in the truck, grabbing them to let go and get moving. The corpsmen literally had to pick them up and throw them off the truck. Once they were off, they sat down in a heap, still shrieking. It wasn't until then that I got a look at the wounded one. He didn't have a head. He must have been a buddy of theirs. The buddy system was very strong, and these two evidently weren't going to leave without their friend. We brought them to the docs and had them sedated. We didn't have any psychiatric facilities, so we got them evac'd to Da Nang. We never heard what happened to them.

After awhile in Vietnam, I guess I wasn't so young anymore. I was seeing things, doing things that I never imagined could happen to anyone. I had to do a lot of things on my own, making snap decisions that could end up saving someone or costing him his life. Like once, when I'd been there about seven months, they brought in this guy who'd been shot square in the face. It was the middle of the night and I was on duty with a medical corpsman, no doctors around at all. They were sleeping, saving their strength. We got the call from dust off that this guy was coming in. Apparently he'd been shot by a sniper. Amazingly enough, he was conscious when they brought him in. As a matter of fact, he was sitting up on the stretcher. It was incredible.

His face was a huge hole, covered with blood. You couldn't see his eyes, his nose, or his mouth. There was no support for his jaw and his tongue was just hanging. You could hear the sound of blood gurgling as he took a breath, which meant he was taking blood into his lungs. We were afraid he'd aspirate. The corpsman was this older guy, over 40 anyway, an experienced sergeant. I took a look at this guy and knew we'd have to do a trach on him pretty fast. He couldn't hear us and we couldn't get him to lie down.

I told the sergeant, "We gotta call the doc in." He told me we didn't have time for that. We had to stabilize him with a trach and ship him out to Da Nang. I told the corpsman that the only time I'd ever done a trach was on a goat back in basic training at Fort Sam Houston. The corpsman said, "If you don't do it, he'll die." So he put my gloves on for me, and handed me the scalpel. I was shaking so badly I thought I'd cut his throat. I remember making the incision, and hearing him cough. The blood came out of the hole, he was coughing out everything he was breathing in. The drops flew into my eyes, spotting my contact lenses. After the blood finished spurting out, we slid the tube in. He laid back and I worried, "What's going on?"

But he was breathing. He didn't have to fight or struggle for breath anymore. I could see the air was escaping from the trach, just like it was supposed to. It was a beautiful feeling, believe me. We packed his face with four-by-fours and roller gauze to stop the bleeding. We told him what we were doing and he nodded his head. When they finally loaded him up for the trip to Da Nang, I was shaking pretty badly. The whole thing had taken less than forty-five minutes, from the time dust off landed to the time we packed him off. We never did get his name.

But three months later, I was sitting in the mess hall in Da Nang, waiting to take a C-130 to Hong Kong for R&R. I'd been in country ten months by then, and I was in the mess hall alone, drinking coffee and eating lunch, still in my fatigues. Somebody tapped me on the shoulder. I remember turning around. You have to remember, I was used to guys being friendly. I saw this guy standing there in hospital pajamas, the green-gray kind with the medical corps insignia on it. He had blond hair on the sides, bald on top. His face was a mass of scars, and you could see the outline of a jaw and chin. He had lips and a mouth, but no teeth. He looked like he had been badly burned, with a lot of scar tissue. You couldn't really tell where his lips began and the scar tissue ended.

The rest of his body was fine, and he could talk. "Do you remember me?" I was used to that, too, people coming up to me and saying, "Hey, I drove that tank by you the other day. . . ." Then he pointed to his trach scar and I said, "You can't be the same guy." He said something like, "I'll never forget you." I asked him how he knew who I was, because, I mean, there had been nothing left of his face. Apparently, the shot had flipped this skin flap up over his eyes so he could still see through the corners. I couldn't believe it. They called my flight right then, so I started saying a hasty goodbye. He mumbled something about how they had taken his ribs from his ribcage and artificially made a jawbone, and reconstructed portions of his face, taking skin from the lower legs, the buttocks.

Well, they began calling my name over the loud speaker. I remember giving him a big hug, saying I wished I had more time to talk to him. I wanted to learn his name, but I don't think he ever said it. I wanted to go back to the hospital and tell the others, "Hey, you remember what's-his-name? He's from Arkansas and he's doing fine." We always wanted to put names to faces, but we rarely got a chance to do it. You kept believing that everyone who left the hospital actually lived. When you found out someone actually had survived, it helped staff morale.

I came back home on a Friday, on a Pan American flight that landed in Seattle. I remember how we were told not to wear our uniforms, not to go out into the streets with our uniforms on. That made us feel worthless. There was no welcome home, not even from the Army people who processed your papers to terminate your time in the service. That was something. I felt like I had just lost my best friend. I decided to fly home to upstate New York in my uniform anyway. Nobody said anything. There were no dirty looks or comments. I was kind of excited. I wanted to say to people, "I just got back from Vietnam." Nobody cared. When I got home, my parents had a big banner strung up across the garage, "Welcome Home, Jacque." But that was about it. My parents were proud of me, of course. But other civilians? "Oh, you were in Vietnam? That's right, I remember reading something in the newspaper about you going there. That's nice." And then they'd go on talking about something else.

You were hungry to talk about it. You wanted so badly to say, 35
"Gee, don't you want to hear about what's going on there, and what
we did, and how proud you should be of your soldiers and your
nurses and your doctors?" I expected them to be waiting there, waving the flag. I remember all those films of World War II, with the tape
that flew from the buildings in New York City, the motorcades. Of
course, I had my mother. My mom was always willing to listen, but of
course she couldn't understand it when I started talking about "frag
wounds" or "claymore mines." There was no way she could.

The first six months at home, I just wanted to go back to Vietnam.
I wanted to go back to where I was needed, where I felt important.
The first job I took was in San Francisco. It was awful. Nobody cared
who I was. I remember the trouble I got into because I was doing
more than a nurse was supposed to do. I got in trouble because I was
a "mini-doctor." They kept saying, "You're acting like you're a doctor! You're doing all these things a doctor is supposed to do. What's
the big idea? You're a nurse, not a doctor." And I thought, how can I
forget all the stuff I learned—putting in chest tubes, doing trachs.
True, doctors only do that, but how do you prevent yourself from
doing things that came automatically to you for eighteen months?
How do you stop the wheels, and become the kind of nurse you were
before you left?

I was completely different. Even my parents didn't recognize me
as the immature little girl who left Albion, New York, just out of nursing school. San Francisco was a bomb, and there wasn't an Army post
for miles around Albion. So that's why I came back to San Antonio. All
my friends were back in and around Fort Sam Houston, so I just naturally gravitated back toward my network. I came to San Antonio in
1974 to get my B.S. in nursing from Incarnate Word College. The best
thing I did was to get into the reserve unit there. That's where I met
my husband. It gave me a chance to share my feelings with other Vietnam veterans. It kept me in touch with Army life, the good things and
the bad. It was like a family.

On weekends at North Fort Hood, we really do sit around the
campfire and talk about 'Nam, about what we as reservists can do to
be better prepared than we were back there. If there is another
Vietnam-type war, God forbid, I just know I'd want to be part of it. I
couldn't sit on the sidelines. We usually just talk about these things
among ourselves. I think the reason a lot of people are hesitant to talk
about it is that they don't know anyone who wants to listen. A lot of
people don't want to hear those kinds of stories. A lot of people just
want to forget that time altogether. I don't know why. I guess I'm just
not like that.

I'm not saying you don't pay a price for your memories. Last year,
I had an intense flashback while flying on a Huey (helicopter) around

North Fort Hood. It was the last day of this reserve unit exercise and I was invited on this tour of the area. We were flying a dust off, a medevac helicopter, just like the ones we had back then. It was my first time up in a helicopter since. I thought, "Gee, this is going to be great." One of the other nurses said to me, "Are you sure you want to do this? You're pretty tired." I brushed her aside, "No problem." We sat in back in seats strapped in next to where they held the litters. I was sitting in the seat, the helicopter was revving up . . . I don't know how to describe it. It was like a slide show, one of the old-fashioned kind where you go through this quick sequence . . . flick, flick, flick . . . now I know where they got the term flashback.

At first, it was as though I was daydreaming. What scared me to death was that I couldn't turn it off. I couldn't control my mind. The cow grazing in the field became a water buffalo. Fields marked off and cross-sectioned became cemeteries. We flew over this tent, it was the 114th (reserve hospital unit) and suddenly it became the 18th surg. I was scared. All I could do was grasp the hand of this friend of mine. We couldn't talk above the helicopter roar. I just started to cry, I couldn't control myself. I saw blood coming down onto the windshield and the wiper blades swishing over it. There was blood on the floor, all over the passenger area where we were sitting. The stretchers clicked into place had bodies on top of them. I was crying. The nurse next to me kept shouting about whether I was all right. My contacts were swimming around, I wanted the ride to end. I could see why GIs felt scared . . . I couldn't just turn around and open up to the nurse sitting next to me. How could you explain something like that?

I had had a flashback or two before, but the difference was I could control them. Even when the nurse started shaking me, I couldn't turn it off. I just looked past her toward the racks in the helicopter, with bodies on stretchers, body bags on the floor, blood everywhere. When we landed, everyone saw I was visibly upset. The pilot came over to see if I was OK. The only thing I could say was, "It brought back a lot of memories." How could I explain my feelings to these people at North Fort Hood. A lot of them were too young to remember Vietnam as anything more than some dim kind of image on the nightly news. I was scared to death, because all these feelings were brought back that I never knew I had.

I still try to think of the good memories from Vietnam, the people we were able to save. A flashback has certain negative connotations. It's a flashback when they can't think of another way of explaining it. I guess I'm lucky it took fourteen years for it to hit me like that. The one positive thing I can say about it is that it felt awfully good to come back and hover down to that red cross on the top of the tent. It felt good to come home.

For Journals

Do you know anyone who served in Vietnam? Do you know anyone who is a nurse or a nursing student? In what ways do they talk about their work?

For Discussion

1. What is your personal response to the story Rhoads tells and the ways in which she relates it? In what ways does her story confirm, or dispute, what you have heard about the Vietnam War?

2. Rhoads is a woman telling about an experience more often associated with men. In what ways do you think her perspective differs from or is similar to that of the men who served in Vietnam, leaving aside, for the moment, considerations of age and rank?

3. Doctors and nurses who serve in the military have in some ways a fundamentally different mission from the soldiers whose job, in the words of an army colonel, is to "kill people and break things." What kinds of personal conflicts do you imagine existed for the military health care workers in Vietnam? In what ways do you think they might have resolved this conflict?

4. The personal narrative can bring geopolitical conflict to a human scale. Examine the ways in which Rhoads clarifies your understanding of both the human cost of war and the painful homecoming of returning Vietnam veterans.

5. In what ways does Rhoads seem transformed by her experience? Do you sense a shift in her perspective, in her approach or attitudes, as she tells the story of her tour of duty?

For Writing

1. Interview someone who served in Vietnam or in some other war, using the oral history technique (see Studs Terkel's oral history in Chapter 8 as one possible model). Write up the oral history, and then compose a brief analysis that responds to the following questions: In what ways is the individual's story similar to, or different from Rhoads's story? In what ways does your interviewee's language compare with Rhoads's style?

2. Research newspaper and magazine articles from the late sixties and early seventies, selecting articles and opinion pieces that covered the Vietnam War. Examine the language in which stories about Vietnam are conveyed, and write an essay analyzing the attitudes about the war, and about the Vietnam service personnel, in the press coverage.

∞ Type-Casting (1989)

PAUL FUSSELL

A native of Pasadena, California, Paul Fussell (1924–) earned his Ph.D. in education from Harvard University in 1952. In 1976 he won the National Book Award and National Book Critics Circle Award for The Great War and Modern Memory. *In addition to being a Fulbright lecturer and Guggenheim fellow, Fussell was a member of the U.S. Army during World War II and the recipient of two Purple Hearts. More recently, he edited* The Norton Book of Modern War *(1991). His work reflects profoundly on the effect that war has on the individual and society. The selection that follows is from* Wartime *(1989).*

"The Chinese are fine fighting men," declares one of Horatio Stubbs's fellow soldiers. "Your Chink is brought up to fight on a handful of rice a day. A Chink'll go for days on just a handful of rice."[1] [Endnotes appear at the end of this selection—Ed.] That's an example, if a rather low one, of the kind of cliché classifications indispensable in wartime. If war is a political, social, and psychological disaster, it is also a perceptual and rhetorical scandal from which total recovery is unlikely. Looking out upon the wartime world, soldiers and civilians alike reduce it to a simplified sketch featuring a limited series of classifications into which people, in the process dehumanized and deprived of individuality or eccentricity, are fitted. In the Second World War many more things than conscripts underwent classifications from 1-A to 4-F. The British working girl Louie, in Elizabeth Bowen's *The Heat of the Day* (1948), receives the classifications determining her vision in 1942 from the newspapers she follows devotedly:

> Was she not a worker, a soldier's lonely wife, a war orphan, a pedestrian, a Londoner, a home and animal-lover, a thinking democrat, a movie-goer, a woman of Britain, a letter-writer, a fuel-saver and a housewife?[2]

Within the soldier's world, the classifications are clearly indicated by insignia of rank and branch of service. The result is that with people, you always know what to expect. A captain of artillery will be a certain type, and so will a major in the Judge Advocate General's department, a first lieutenant of Ordinance, and an infantry staff-sergeant. You can count on it. And gazing outward toward the civilian scene, the soldierly imagination rudely consigns people to four categories:

1. The female, consisting of mother, grandmother, and sister, on the one hand, and, on the other, agents of sexual solace.

2. Elderly men, who are running the draft boards, as well as the rationing, transportation, and propaganda apparatus.

3. The infantine, who will be in the war if it lasts long enough.

4. And the most despised of categories, the 4-F or physically unfit and thus defective, the more despicable the more invisible the defect, like a heart murmur, punctured ear-drum, or flat feet.

One might think the most vigorous soldierly contempt might be directed at conscientious objectors, but no: since most of them were set to hard labor in camps, they were regarded as virtually members, if a bit disgraced, of the armed services, and their circumstances were conceived to be little more degrading than those of the troops in, say, the non-combatant quartermaster corps. That the COs endured lots of chickenshit made them like brothers. Civilians were different, more like "foreigners," indeed rather like the enemy.

For the war to be prosecuted at all, the enemy of course had to be severely dehumanized and demeaned, and in different ways, depending on different presumed national characteristics. One way of classifying the Axis enemy was to arrange it by nationalities along a scale running from courage down to cowardice. The Japanese were at the brave end, the Italians at the pusillanimous, and the Germans were in the middle. This symmetrical arrangement also implied a scale of animalism, with the Japanese accorded the most feral qualities and the Italians the most human, including a love of music, ice-cream, and ostentatious dress.

Americans detested the Japanese the most, for only they had had the effrontery to attack the United States directly, sinking ships, killing sailors, and embarrassing American pretenses to alertness and combat adequacy. They must be animals to behave thus, and cruel ones at that. "Bestial apes"—that is what Admiral William F. Halsey termed them and added the good news that "we are drowning and burning [them] all over the Pacific, and it is just as much pleasure to burn them as to drown them."[3] A marine on Guadalcanal could perceive the Japanese only as beasts of various species. He told John Hersey, "They hide up in the trees like wildcats. Sometimes when they attack, they scream like a bunch of terrified cattle in a slaughter house." Another said, "I wish we were fighting against Germans. They are human beings, like us. . . . But the Japs are like animals. . . . They take to the jungle as if they had been bred there, and like some beasts you never see them until they are dead."[4] What harm, then, in cleaning, polishing, and sending home their animal skulls as souvenirs, so that a standard snapshot depicts a soldier or marine proudly exhibiting a cleansed Japanese skull, while a poem of the period, by Winfield Townley Scott, meditates without moral comment on "The U.S. Sailor with the Japanese Skull":

> our
> Bluejacket, I mean, aged 20, in August strolled
> Among the little bodies on the sand and hunted

Souvenirs: teeth, tags, diaries, boots; but bolder still
Hacked off this head and under a Ginkgo tree skinned it.[5]

Then dragged to behind his ship for many days and finally scrubbed it thoroughly with lye and had a perfect souvenir. Dealing that way with the skull of a German or Italian, that is, "a white man," would be clearly inappropriate, perhaps sacrilegious. This treatment of Japanese corpses as if they were animal became so flagrant as early as September, 1942, that the Commander in Chief of the Pacific Fleet ordered that "No part of the enemy's body may be used as a souvenir. Unit Commanders will take stern disciplinary action. . . ."[6]

The civil, unbloodthirsty American sailor James J. Fahey, a Roman 5
Catholic from Waltham, Massachusetts, and a respecter of all the decencies, after a *kamikaze* attack on his ship wrote home that "one of the men on our [gun] mount got a Jap rib and cleaned it up" because "his sister wants part of a Jap body."[7] No censorious reaction whatever from Fahey, for that rib is like one you can buy in a meat market. "Oh, the inhuman brutes!" exclaimed Mrs. John Milburn, as news of Japanese behavior reached the United Kingdom.[8] Among the Allies the Japanese were also known as "jackals" or "monkey-men" or "subhumans," the term of course used by the Germans for Russians, Poles, and assorted Slavs, amply justifying their vivisection. Personnel of the United States Marine Corps sought to popularize the term *Japes* (*Japs + apes*), but the word never caught on, and the Japanese remained *Japs*, or, slightly less contemptuously, *Nips.* Like the *Huns* of the Great War, *Japs*—"the yellow Huns of the East," Australian General Gordon Bennett called them[9]—was a brisk monosyllable handy for slogans like "Rap the Jap" or "Let's Blast the Jap Clean Off the Map," the last a virtual prophecy of Hiroshima. It is a truism of military propaganda that monosyllabic enemies are easier to despise than others. A *kraut* or *wop* is instantly disposable in a way a German or Italian isn't quite, just as in the Great War a *boche* or a *hun* betrayed by their very names their vileness and worthlessness. Like the later *gook.* In July, 1943, a large sign on the damaged bow of the U.S. Cruiser *Honolulu* quoted Admiral Halsey urging everyone to

> Kill Japs.   Kill Japs.
> Kill More Japs.[10]

Because they were animals, Japanese troops had certain advantages over Americans. They could see in the dark, it was believed, and survive on a diet of roots and grubs. The very tiny-ness of the Japanese was another reason for contempt. They were little the way insects and rodents are little—little but nasty. In 1942, in the pamphlet *Individual Battle Doctrine*, the United States Marine Corps assured its members of

Japanese combat inferiority by pointing out that "the Jap is much too short to enter the Marine Corps." One result of this puniness is that "he is really a poor bayonet fighter." Americans held in Japanese prison camps noticed the way their captors liked to get up onto something, a box, podium, platform, or stand, when haranguing the prisoners. "They loved to elevate themselves," one prisoner said.[11] Americans of standard height could understand the Japanese problem immediately as the "Runt's Complex," familiar from high school, the need of the short to "get back at" people of normal height and their customary use of guile or fraud to do so. The "sneak attack" on Pearl Harbor thus explains itself.

A rumor popular during the war told of a mother receiving a letter from her soldier son in a Japanese POW camp. He tells her that he is well and surviving OK and not to worry, and he adds that she might like to soak off the stamp on the envelope to give a friend who's a collector. When she does so, she finds written under the stamp, "THEY HAVE CUT OUT MY TONGUE." Given the notorious cruelty of the Japanese, in wartime that story could be received as entirely credible, making everyone forget that letters from captured soldiers bear no postage stamps. Typecasting assured that the Pacific War would be particularly cruel, and the cruelty was on both sides. The Japanese, as former marine E. B. Sledge says, "killed solely for the sake of killing, without hope and without higher purpose," and so did the Americans. The Japanese fired programmatically on stretcher-bearers and tortured to death Americans who fell into their hands. Sledge once encountered a group of dead marines whose bodies had been defiled, one man's penis having been sliced off and inserted in his mouth, another man's head and hands having been chopped off.[12] Similarly, the marines loved to use the few Japs who came forward to surrender as amusing rifle targets, just as they felt intense satisfaction watching them twist and writhe when set afire by the napalm of the flame-thrower. Japanese skulls were not the only desirable trophies: treasured also were Japanese gold teeth, knocked out, sometimes from the mouths of the still-living, by a USMC Ka-bar knife-hilt. During wartime it was impossible to complicate "the Japanese character" in any way, to recognize that the same auspices were behind the Bataan Death March and the Noh drama. It was not to be widely publicized that the same "types" who had bayoneted hospital patients in Hong Kong also flew out over the sea where they had sunk HMS *Repulse* and *Prince of Wales* and dropped a memorial wreath on the water. Once the war was over and the Americans were installed on the home islands as occupiers, the Japanese capacity for subtlety and delicacy could again be recognized. Then, Admiral Nimitz, doubtless with Halsey and such in mind, reminded his subordinates that "the use of insulting epithets in connection with the Japanese as a race or individuals does not now become the officers of the United States Navy."[13]

If the Japanese were type-cast as animals of an especially dwarfish but vicious species, the Germans were recognized to be human beings, but of a perverse type, cold, diagrammatic, pedantic, unimaginative, and thoroughly sinister. We had submarines, but they had U-boats. Their instinct for discipline made them especially dangerous, and their admitted distinction in technology made their cruelty uniquely effective. That it was the same people who were shooting hostages and hanging Poles and gassing Jews, on the one hand, and enjoying Beethoven and Schubert, on the other, was a complication too difficult to be faced during wartime. In March, 1942, John Steinbeck found that he had seriously misjudged the popular necessity of type-casting German troops as simply wicked. In his novella (later a play) *The Moon Is Down*, he depicted the Germans occupying a Norwegian town as human, subject like other people to emotions of love, pride, envy, and jealousy. None was characterized as an anti-Semitic monster. To his astonishment, a cascade of intellectual and moral abuse fell upon him. Artistically he may have deserved it: *The Moon Is Down* is a sort of narrative *Our Town* relocated to a wartime Continent. The story overflows with folksiness and jocosity, and the small-town scene is peopled with sentimental would-be lovable characters. But the badness of the book lies rather in its aesthetic clumsiness than in any ideological defect. As a writer dependent on popular suffrage, Steinbeck had simply not noticed that the days of light duty were past and henceforth Germans, all Germans— Wehrmacht, SS, sailors, housewives, hikers, the lot—had to be cast as confirmed enemies of human decency.

In normal times, the characteristic most often imputed to the Germans, thoroughness, would have constituted a compliment. But in wartime it was a moral defect, implying an inhuman mechanism, monotony, and rigidity. Heartless classification and analysis were considered a German specialty, and German soldiers were said to have a passion for straight lines and rigid postures. In one British theater showing a newsreel scene of German soldiers standing at exaggerated attention, someone was heard to shout, "Take t'coat hanger out then."[14] RAF bomber crews were not often deceived by decoy burning cities located five to ten miles from the actual ones because the fake fires were disposed in lines that were too straight. One photograph in Len Deighton's *Fighter* (1977) carries this legend:

> *Junkers JU 88 Bomber Crews Go to Work.* Most of the photographs . . . of the airmen, German and British . . . are strikingly alike—as the fliers pat their dogs, play chess, or relax near their aircraft—but it would be difficult to imagine RAF crews marching to their aircraft in the long rays of the early-morning sun singing as these men do.[15]

The German aircrewmen depicted there are marching in three precise files, an officer at their head, past a line-up of planes. And of course the group singing of such troops was more objectionably disciplined than that of the British or Americans could ever be. British General Sir John Hackett heard a lot of German army singing during his months as a prisoner of war, and he found himself offended by the communal abrupt "shortening of the final note of any line, as though according to a drill."[16] As a German characteristic, "thoroughness" was recognized even by the Germans. Visiting a Luftwaffe establishment in France in 1940, Josef Goebbels notes with satisfaction that it's operated with "German thoroughness," although it is "a very complex organizational machine."[17] Popular historiography especially preserves the German reputation for being foolishly "methodical." Thus Seymour Reit's *Masquerade: The Amazing Camouflage Deceptions of World War II* (1978) speaks critically of "the very methodical and systematic way" the Germans went about their visual deceptions. "Teutonic thoroughness" is the term for their technique,[18] and there is clearly something reprehensible about it.

While the Japanese were calumniated for being animals, the Germans were simply "sick," the very embodiment of disease. Hearing that the Germans have been manacling British prisoners of war (actually in retaliation for the British order to handcuff prisoners taken at Dieppe), Mrs. Milburn explodes: "One can't think of anything bad enough for these diseased Germans. Their minds are all wrong."[19] Indeed, "They are like a loathsome disease spreading and spreading over Europe."[20] And a disease is what they were held to resemble in a whimsical "receipt" by which General Troy Middleton took over the town of Bastogne from the 101st Airborne Division in January, 1945. The condition of the town was said to be "Used but Serviceable," and it was held to be "Kraut Disinfected."[21] Sick or not, the Germans were different in every way. Even their planes sounded different. Flying over England, their motors seemed to throb, sounding like "grunt-a-grunt-a-grunt-a-grunt-a." Some heard in the throbbing sound the message, "It's for you, It's for you, It's for you." One report printed in a newspaper ("ROUGED GERMAN AIRMEN") could never have been fastened on the bestial Japanese, namely, that some captured German fliers were found to have rouged cheeks, together with waved hair, lipstick, and painted finger- and toenails.[22]

Social envy and social snobbery, respectively, seem to lie behind Hitler's view of Churchill as "a superannuated drunkard supported by Jewish gold" and Churchill's view of Hitler as a "bloodthirsty guttersnipe."[23] Down below, where the troops were, the Germans had some respect for British soldiers but none for Americans. The Americans were spoiled, lazy, ignorant, unpolitical loud-mouths, and, as Goebbels put it, they seemed afflicted with "a spiritual emptiness that really makes you shake your head."[24] Few in Germany had any idea why the Americans had invaded Europe. One German officer could conclude only, as he told his interrogator, that they had attacked the Reich "in order to save Churchill and the Yews."[25] It was only their superiority in numbers, ordnance, and equipment that brought any victories to the Americans—and the British as well. High British officers privately admitted as much. Max Hastings observes of the state of Allied sensibility just before the invasion of Normandy:

> Four years of war against the Wehrmacht had convinced Britain's commanders that Allied troops should engage and could defeat their principal enemy only on the most absolutely favorable terms. Throughout the Second World War, whenever British or American troops met the Germans in anything like equal strength, the Germans prevailed.[26]

It was only wealth that tipped the scales in favor of the Allies.

A sensitive German woman, Christabel Bielenberg, accidentally came upon an American flier hidden in a room in her small town. She instantly perceived that the war was lost when she observed "the general air of health and well being, of affluence, about him." What struck her was

> the quality of the stuff his overalls were made of, his boots and the silk scarf which he had tied into his belt, and a soft leather wallet he held in one hand. Suddenly I felt shabby, old, dilapidated, and defeated. Everything he had on was so real: real wool, real leather, real silk—so real and he looked so young.[27]

German troops could often tell when the "Amis" were nearby. Their positions seemed to give off a sweet smell, probably because they smoked Virginia, rather than "Turkish" and ersatz, tobacco.

Those fighting on the same side type-cast each other just as enemies did. One reason the Italians were in such contempt by the Germans is that they seemed to resemble the Americans, with their unmilitary concern with comfort and their lack of the sacrificial impulse. But the Italians were patronized even by the Americans. One American officer in the North African desert was outraged to hear a German prisoner, asked what he thought of the American troops he'd encountered, assert: "The Americans are to us what the Italians are to you."[28] If the Germans were sadists and bullies, the Italians were dandies motivated by both vainglory and cowardice. Popular culture had them surrendering not just en masse but pomaded and scented, accompanied by framed pictures, birdcages, and similar domestic amenities, their elegant spare uniforms neatly folded in extra suitcases and trunks. One British prisoner of the Italians who was often moved from camp to camp was astonished at the Italian understanding of the comforts appropriate to commissioned rank, even when held by an enemy. He was allowed two suitcases, a pack, a blanket roll, and a case of books. "It never seemed to worry the Italians how much kit we took," he says, "since they regarded it as quite normal for officers. Their own took thirty large trunks, mostly full of different uniforms, wherever they moved, even on active service."[29]

Since it was not until late in the war that the Allies entered France, and since by that time there was little food there, Italy, even afflicted as it was by widespread starvation, became a place where the troops' food fantasies could sometimes be realized. In Taranto in June, 1944, one British soldier had an experience he set down in his diary this way: "Wonderful meal in T. Steak—eggs—cherries—white wine—macaroni—and Marsala." He added: "We should never have fought these people."[30] The Italian reputation as the surviving custodians of the cuisine depended in part on their fame in London as waiters and chefs and restaurant owners. Many were interned in the United Kingdom to be shipped to Canada out of harm's way. When a ship carrying them, the *Arandora Star*, was torpedoed and sunk, "a number of London's most famous *restaurateurs*," says Vera Brittain, "perished in the Atlantic."[31] Because the Italians were also associated with ice cream—making it, selling it, and eating it—British soldiers seldom let the idea of "Italians" pass through their understandings without some half-melancholy, half-contemptuous allusion to ice cream, a commodity rare in the British army. In one battalion magazine for February, 1941, a comic story, "Wops in Action," introduces its characters thus; "Alphonse and Toni were two soldiers in a crack Wop infantry regiment. On their right arms they wore three enamel ice cream cones, awarded by their C.O. for the smartest pair of heels."[32]

If the Germans were held to sing with conspicuous group disci- 15 pline, "shortening . . . the final note of any line, as though according to a drill," the Italians were likely to burst into song out of the sheer "Latin" joy of being alive, a feeling intensified beyond measure by the hazards of wartime. When Farley Mowat's unit invaded the Italian mainland near Messina, there were no Germans about, and "since the Italian troops manning the coast defenses already knew that Mussolini had fallen, they were in no mood to die heroically in a lost cause." Thus,

> As the Allied column labored upward like an attenuated khaki-colored snake, another descended parallel to it, this one bluish-green in hue. The Italian soldiers came down from the hills, not like members of a defeated army but in a mood of fiesta, marching raggedly along with their personal possessions slung about them, filling the air with laughter and song.[33]

"A lot of opera singers" was Roosevelt's characterization of resident Italian aliens as he decided not to intern them in 1942.[34] And speaking of the association between wartime and cliché, "*O Sole Mio*" was the song actually being sung when Edward Blishen saw a group of Italian prisoners in England for the first time,[35] while some of the British in North Africa maintained that it was "to the strains of *Aida*" that the Italians planned to march triumphantly into Egypt. Says Tanker H. L. Sykes, "We actually found the music, the instruments, and the ceremonial dress they intended to use."[36]

When in the earlier war Frederic Henry, in Hemingway's *A Farewell to Arms* (1929), feels some guilt about deserting, Catherine Barkley comforts him by reminding him that "It's only the Italian army."[37] This myth of Italian military haplessness served a useful psychological function in the Second World War, helping secretly to define what Allied soldiers wanted the "enemy" universally to be— pacifists, dandies, sensitive and civilized non-ideologues, even clowns. The antithesis of committed, fanatic National Socialists. At the same time the Italians could serve as the definition of incompetence, fraudulence, and cowardice: no one really wanted to be like them to be sure, but how everyone wished it were possible! The world was laughing at Italy, and yet the Italians were sensibly declining to be murdered. The Allied soldier couldn't help wondering that if contempt and ridicule are the price of staying alive, perhaps the price is worth paying. While constituting one of the war's most simple-minded clichés, the Italians thus posed a challenge to cliché, shaking up and complicating the standard uncomplex attitude toward "the enemy." It was their presence in the war that kept a degree of ambiguity and paradox alive in a wartime world of stark and easily dealt-with oppositions. Were the Italians properly sized up by ridicule, as in the popular London dance-step The Tuscana ("based on the Italians' way of fighting, . . . one step forward, two steps back")?[38] Was A. P. Herbert right to refer to Mussolini on the BBC as "the Top Wop"? Or were they a serious enemy, more correctly treated respectfully? One who fought them, Peter Cochrane, in his book *Charlie Company* (1977), praises their courage, flair, and discipline, and goes out of his way to celebrate Italian skill in road engineering and artillery ranging and to note Italian compassion toward wounded prisoners. Is that the correct view? Or did General Montgomery have the right attitude when he told the troops preparing to invade Sicily,

> "Someone said to me a few days ago that the Italians are really decent people and that if we treat them properly they will come over to us. I disagree with him. Our job is to kill them. That is what we have to do. Once we have killed them we can see if they are good fellows or not. But they must be killed first."[39]

Whatever the Italians actually were, the myth that they were the sweetest people in the war survives. The cover illustration of the

American magazine *Men Today* for July, 1963, depicts a scene from one of the sadoerotic narratives within. Two girls are busy torturing an American soldier of the Second World War. He is tied to a chair. One girl, dressed in tight blouse and short shorts, is playing a blowtorch over his chest. The other looks on, coiled whip at the ready. The first girl is shouting, "Scream for my kisses, Amerikaner Soldat!" She wears a swastika armband. The other girl wears a German officer's jacket and cap.[40] The Italian wartime image becomes doubly clear if one tries to imagine the insignia and trappings of Italian fascism used with significations like these. They would produce not a frisson or even an erection but a laugh.

The force and to a degree the validity of wartime type-casting can be appreciated by trying to imagine German troops crawling on their stomachs through the malarial jungles of the South Pacific. Just as hard to conceive as Japanese soldiers defending the Apennines from behind mountain barricades built up from stones of determined Italian youths resisting to the death the American assault on the Rhine or the Russian assault on Berlin. Each enemy has taken on the characteristics of primary geography, both literal and otherwise, and it is impossible to imagine them any other way. Similarly it is impossible to believe about one enemy what it is easy to believe about another. For example: according to Captain M. J. Brown, British troops once came up highly desirable billet abandoned by the Germans whose front was invitingly half-open. Entering cautiously through a window to avoid the likely booby-trap, they approached the front door from inside and found attached to it the expected explosive charge set to go off when the door was moved. They left the house carefully and tied a string to the outside knob of the front door, taking cover in a slit-trench across the road. When they were all in the slit-trench, they pulled the string and the slit-trench exploded, killing them all. "The layer of the trap had anticipated their process of reasoning," notes Captain Brown, "step by step."[41] The Japanese would probably not think such a caper funny enough to be worthwhile. The Italians would, but would be too "unmethodical" to set it up efficiently. The Americans and British would like the idea but would be too lazy to waste time on it. But assigned to the Germans, the story, apocryphal as it may be, rings true.

And although a whole book could be devoted to the sort of stereotyping necessary for Americans (and British) to see themselves as attractive, moral, and exemplary, some of the conventions can be noted briefly. A good way to get a feel for the subject would be to go through any number of *Life* magazine, or *Look*, or *Collier's*, or *The Saturday Evening Post* issued from 1942 to 1945. Attending to the display advertisements, mostly in color, one would immediately understand the wartime thrill Americans achieved by imagining themselves good-looking Aryans blond and tall, beloved by slim blonde women and surrounded by much-desired consumer goods. If the illustrations are to be believed, all young men are in the Air Corps, where they are officers almost by definition (or, in 1942, cadets destined soon to be officers). If by some misfortune they are in any other part of the army, they are almost never privates or NCOs but young officers beaming on their fiancée's assiduity in accumulating flatware of International Sterling. Notable is the absence of any features which might be interpreted as Jewish, or Central European, or in any remote way "Colored." The people on whose behalf the war is being fought are Anglo-Saxons, "nice people"—that is, upper-middle class. Readers of these advertisements could not help inferring that the war was designed primarily to defend and advance the interests of such tall, clean blondes, as well as the suppliers of the cars, tires, and refrigerators the blonds will own and exhibit once the war is won. If the Jews, like those in New York, liked to think the war was in some way about them, it's clear that most people didn't want to be like them in any way or even reminded of them. You could spend your life studying the magazine ads of wartime without once coming upon a yarmulkah or prayer shawl, or even features suggestive of Jewishness. Philip Roth's Alexander Portnoy, too young for the war but not too young to associate himself with the thrill of being on the winning and the righteous side, conceives of it as entirely an upper-middle-class Anglophile-American victory, less about the right to wear phylacteries than argyle socks and loafers.

The advertising artists sometimes had to face facts and recognize that many of those fighting the Axis were, regrettably, quite unromantic enlisted men, but such are generally depicted without women and usually alone, unwrapping a gift watch sent by the folks, celebrating the possession of a candy bar ("Boy! I'm strong for Milky Ways"), enjoying being included at a strange family's dinner table at Thanksgiving, waiting to board a train which, it is to be hoped, it not already full of idle civilians, or delighting in the Chelsea cigarettes included in a K-ration. The man shown in bed enjoying the luxury of Pacific Sheets is a Pfc., not an officer, because he is alone. Yawning and stretching in an ad in *Life* in February, 1945, he thinks, "'Hallelujah, what a day is coming! A day when a fellow can drop his gear in his tracks, climb into a real bed as soft as a marshmallow, and s-t-r-e-t-c-h every last muscle! A day when he can feel again the caress of sleek, soft, white Pacific Sheets against his tired body.'" But when women enter, the male models get promoted instantly to officer rank, and their looks improve, too. Thus the woman enjoying a Honeymoon in Mexico on behalf of DuBarry Beauty Preparations is attended by her young naval-officer husband in whites. A young woman fortunate enough to have found a lover who appreciates the benefits of an extremely smooth Barbasol Shave is doubly blessed, for he is also an officer (branch of service not revealed). One young woman appearing on behalf of a brand of woolen goods is being met at her front door at a snowy Christmastime by a young man in a sleigh bearing a Christmas tree. At first glance he seems to be wearing an enlisted soldier's rough overcoat, but the ad-man has saved the day by remembering to affix a gold bar to his shoulder. Another young woman, lonely, has been left behind as a result of Rough Hands, but in the background wiser women who have learned to use Campana Balm swarm past in crowds, each with her date: only two are servicemen, but one is a naval ensign, the other a commissioned Air Corps pilot. If an enlisted man must be depicted in close proximity to a desirable woman, as in one ad for Chesterfield cigarettes, the situation can be salvaged by displaying on his shoulder the insignia ("patch") not, surely, of the 3rd Armored Division but of the United States Army Air Corps. In fiction or film, the GI might be Jewish or Italian, Polish or Hispanic or "Colored," but never in advertising, a medium where only ideal imagery can be allowed to enter. In advertising, the Allied war is fought by white Anglo-Saxons, officers or aviators, with neat, short hair, clear eyes, gleaming teeth, and well-defined jawlines. That is the wartime "we," fighting against the beast-like yellow-skinned Japanese, the "sick" Germans, and the preposterous Italians. Naturally we won. As Admiral Halsey said in his victory message to his fleet when the Japanese surrendered, "The forces of righteousness and decency have triumphed."[42]

Endnotes

1. *A Soldier Erect, or Further Adventures of the Hand-Reared Boy* (London, 1971).
2. (New York, 1948 [1979]), 134.
3. Dwight Macdonald, *Memoirs of a Revolutionist: Essays in Political Criticism* (New York, 1957), 93.
4. *Into the Valley* (New York, 1943), 20, 56.
5. *Collected Poems: 1937–1962* (New York, 1962), 121.
6. Samuel Cosman Papers, U.S. Marine Corps Historical Center, Washington, D.C.
7. James Fahey, *Pacific War Diary* (New York, 1963), 231.
8. Peter Donnelly, ed., *Mrs. Milburn's Diaries: An Englishwoman's Day-to-Day Reflections, 1939–1945* (London, 1979 [1980]), 248.
9. *Why Singapore Fell* (Bombay, 1945), 58.
10. John W. Dower, *War Without Mercy: Race and Power in the Pacific War* (New York, 1986), 36.
11. Donald Knox, *Death March* (New York, 1981), 364.
12. *With the Old Breed* (Novato, Calif., 1981), 142, 148.
13. John Costello, *The Pacific War* (New York, 1981), 616.
14. Norman Longmate, *How We Lived Then* (London, 1971), 404.
15. No. 51, between pp. 248–49.
16. *I was a Stranger* (London, 1977 [1979]), 74–75.
17. Fred Taylor, ed., *The Goebbels Diaries, 1939–1941* (New York, 1983), 148.
18. (1980), 5, 148.
19. Donnelly, *Mrs. Milburn's Diaries*, 216.
20. *Ibid.*, 185.
21. Napier Crookenden, *The Battle of the Bulge* (New York, 1980), 124.
22. Arthur Marshall, "Odd Man In," *New Statesman*, Nov. 21, 1980, p. 15.

23. John Strawson, *Hitler's Battles for Europe* (New York, 1971), 113.

24. Louis Lochner, ed., *The Goebbels Diaries, 1942–1943* (Garden City, N.Y., 1948), 317.

25. Franklyn Johnson, *One More Hill* (New York, 1949), 157.

26. Hastings, *Overlord* (New York, 1984), 24.

27. *The Past Is Myself* (London, 1970), 148.

28. M. J. Brown, Diary, IWM.

29. Anthony Deane-Drummond, *Return Ticket* (London, 1953 [1967]), 82.

30. Oliver Carpenter, Diary, IWM.

31. *Testament of Experience,* 258.

32. C. C. Rand, *The Ordinary Fellow* (Magazine of the 1st Bn., London Irish Rifles), I, #5, 54–55.

33. *And No Birds Sang* (Boston, 1979), 143.

34. James MacGregor Burns, *Roosevelt: The Soldier of Freedom* (New York, 1970), 214.

35. Edward Blishen, *A Cackhanded War* (London, 1972), 119.

36. Memoir, IWM.

37. (New York, 1929), 260.

38. Longmate, *How We Lived Then,* 422.

39. Neil McCallum, *Journey with a Pistol* (London, 1959), 145.

40. Gillian Freeman, *The Undergrowth of Literature* (London, 1967), facing p. 86.

41. Diary, IWM.

42. E. B. Potter, *Bull Halsey* (Annapolis, Md., 1985), 348.

For Journals

Write about some common stereotypes that you are aware of and the ways in which they are depicted in film, paintings, advertisements, posters, or other media.

For Discussion

1. In view of Fussell's essay, discuss some kinds of typecasting or stereotyping that are familiar to you.

2. In what ways is constructing an "other," especially an enemy, similar to or different from the process of establishing a national identity? Review the readings in Chapter 5 as needed.

3. Fussell's preface to the book *Wartime,* from which this excerpt is taken, notes that the book is about "the rationalizations and euphemisms people needed to deal with an unacceptable actuality from 1939 to 1945." Does Fussell achieve his purpose of exposing such rationalizations and euphemisms?

4. In what ways, according to Fussell, are people "dehumanized and deprived of individuality" in wartime? Examine this claim, citing specific examples you find especially convincing.

5. Identify and analyze some of the metaphors used to stereotype different nationalities during World War II. From your own observation and experience, are any of these stereotypes still in popular use?

6. Contrast other nation's impressions of American soldiers in World War II with impressions you may have already gained from American popular culture—films, photographs, books and the like, or from family narratives.

For Writing

1. Follow Fussell's suggestion and research American popular magazines published during World War II—*Life* or *Time*, for example. You will find collections in your college library or in a public library, and you may need to work with microfilm or microfiche. A local historian may have information to share. Browse through a number of magazines, taking notes on what you see, particularly in the advertisements, but also reading editorials and letters to the editor as they seem relevant. Develop an essay based on your findings, focusing on some theme or aspect of your findings and supporting your core assertion with examples from your research.

2. Interview people who lived during World War II about their perceptions of the enemy during the war.

∞ *Violence in America* (1996)

ARNOLD P. GOLDSTEIN

Arnold P. Goldstein, PhD, professor of special education at Syracuse University, is an internationally recognized authority on prosocial skills training and interventions with aggressive youth. He founded and directs the Center for Research on Aggression at Syracuse University and codirected the New York State Task Force on Juvenile Gangs. His career interest, as both researcher and practitioner, has been difficult-to-reach youth. Since 1980, his main research and psychoeducational focus has been youth violence. The selections that follow are from his book, Violence in America: Lessons on Understanding the Aggression in Our Lives.

How Did We Get Here?

The United States was born in a spirit of freedom and democracy, yet also with a strong belief in the use of individual and group violence. The Revolutionary War lasted seven years and succeeded in its goal of a new and independent nation. It also began our two-century-long love affair with the gun, as four hundred thousand victorious citizen-soldiers helped proclaim the right to bear arms.

The new nation lay along the Eastern coast of a three-thousand-mile wide unexplored continent of buffalo and other game to kill, of Native Americans to displace, of a frontier to conquer. As our citizens began moving westward in the late 1700s, a frontier mentality went with them. Self-reliance, independence, and impatience with the poorly developed laws and law enforcement of the day were also part of this mentality. Justice often meant "frontier justice," in which groups of local citizenry took the law into their own hands: Hanging horse thieves or riding undesirables out of town were among the ways such early criminal sentencing was handled.

Though our mass media have long glamorized it, frontier living was rarely as easy and romantic as usually portrayed. Often, it was very difficult economically, which helped give rise to outlaw gangs, bank robbers, counterfeiters, and other criminal behavior. A tide of immigration to the United States commenced in earnest in the early 1800s, and grew to a flood of newcomers of diverse backgrounds to our shores as the twentieth century unfolded. The ingredients in this great, human melting pot often mixed poorly and often resulted in high levels of individual and group violence directed at these migrants, especially in the cities.

The Civil War, 1861 to 1865, pitted Northerner against Southerner and, at times, neighbor against neighbor, even cousin against cousin in bitter, lethal combat. Its price was high—well beyond the actual war casualties of 617,000 dead and 375,000 injured soldiers. Out of the war grew forces that yielded new and virulent forms of aggression throughout the country. Often stemming from war-related animosities, feuding, lynching, and high levels of vigilante activity erupted. The feud, primarily developing in Southern mountain states, was a kind of interfamily guerrilla warfare. Much more deadly in its effects was lynching, in which unorganized mobs captured and hung usually guiltless Black persons. It is the shame of America that 3,209 recorded lynchings occurred during the years 1889 to 1918.

Vigilante aggression also became more organized during this 5 post–Civil War period, with the Ku Klux Klan, the Bald Knobbers, the White Cappers, and many more such groups targeting not just Blacks but several other minority groups as well. Also at this time, the much-romanticized cowboy gang became prominent. Their specialities, stagecoach, train, and bank robberies, although to this day portrayed as exciting and heroic events, were plain and simple acts of criminal violence.

Much of the recorded violence in America in the late 1800s and early 1900s was group violence associated with the industrialization of our country. There were violent labor strikes in the mining, railroad, and auto industries as well as violent government response to the strikers. Though there are numerous accounts of violence by individuals during these years, actual numbers are largely unavailable because the F.B.I. did not begin compiling crime statistics for murder, assault, rape, and similar violent crimes until 1933. Nevertheless, it is clear that during the years in which Prohibition was the law of the land (1920 to 1933), murder and mayhem between and among bootleggers and liquor highjackers in their rivalry for market control was at a level of often lethal intensity. During the two world wars and the economic depression in the 1930s, there was less violence here for individuals and groups. The same was true in other countries. Perhaps when citizens feel joined together against a common enemy, there is less motivation to attack each other.

As the twentieth century moved along, feuding, vigilante groups, lynching, and labor violence all receded, but aggression in seemingly new and more serious individual forms appeared. Spouse and child abuse had been with us all along but was in a sense "discovered" as it became a matter for more public discussion and concern in the mid-1960s. It has since become recognized as widely practiced in our homes and severely damaging to many of our citizens. So too for the crime of rape, as the women's movement of this same period called our collective attention to its nature, its frequency, and its serious consequences. As is widely known, in this period, America's homicide rate far exceeded that of all other modern nations—and still does today.

Since the 1970s, the levels of murder, rape, abuse, and assault by adults are a continuing serious concern, but our main worry seems to be the flourishing of juvenile crime. Aided by the massive influx of drugs into our country, armed by our arsenal of weaponry, encouraged by its unremitting portrayal in the media, and in imitation of many of their heroes, our sons and daughters have reached new peaks of aggression in their lives, both as individuals and in growing numbers of gangs.

So America's history is contradictory. We are a free, democratic, progressive, creative country of protected citizen rights, rule by law, legal transfer of power, economic opportunity for at least most of our citizens, and much more that is good. We are also a country in which for more than two hundred years our people have insulted, injured, assaulted, abused, raped, and murdered one another at levels that are dismayingly high and seem to be growing. That is where we are and, briefly, how we got here.

Guns Go to School

The cartoon made the point with a punch: Titled "Back to School 10 Supplies," it shows a young adolescent on his way to school, knapsack slung over his shoulder, notebook and ruler sticking out of its top, pencil tucked behind his ear—and a .357 magnum revolver stuck in the waistband of his pants.

Is the situation really that bad, or are a small number of incidents causing far more concern than their numbers deserve? The facts, it seems, lie somewhere between.

More than 95 percent of our children go to school each day without a gun or any other sort of weapon, and most of them do so because their schools are safe, nonthreatening places.

Some children do bring weapons to school, mostly claiming they do so for protection. What weapons? Their variety is remarkable: weighted gloves, stun guns, steelies (in a bag), brass knuckles, auto batons, bayonets, bats, screwdrivers, box cutters (a metal detector-avoiding recent favorite), knives, and guns.

Guns have clearly caused the most concern, to the government, now seeking to declare legal gun-free zones around schools; to parents, fearing a goodbye on a school morning may be a goodbye forever; to school authorities, scrambling to find ever more effective ways to keep guns off the premises; and to students, the potential victims, fearful of attack in numbers well beyond actual frequency.

What are the facts surrounding gun use in school? About two- 15 thirds of the youths bringing guns to school got their arms from a friend or family member. Though in general there is more school violence in junior rather than senior high school (seventh grade is the most aggressive grade), approximately two-thirds of the gun-use incidents in American schools take place in senior high schools.

Although some guns are fired by accident in schools (13 percent of all incidents), 65 percent are intentional shootings. Why does one student intentionally shoot another? Where and when these shootings occur provides ample clues to their motivation.

Although students spend at least 90 percent of each school day in classrooms, three-quarters of the shootings in recent years took place elsewhere: the school yard, the parking lot, the cafeteria, athletic facilities, and, by far the favorite shooting ground, the hallways. While 22 percent of the shootings took place during classes, 32 percent occurred in the four-minute transition periods between classes.

Most classes are times of attention to lessons, restricted movement, and high levels of teacher supervision. Between class transitions are, for too many students keenly oversensitive to imagined insults, times of attention to "bad looks," "stare-downs," or "intentional" bumps from students passing the other way. These incidents occur in a context of lowered teacher supervision, to youngsters set to respond not with counter-insults or even their fists but instead with the metal equalizer weapon in their pockets or book bags.

In addition to such real or imagined insults, students have shot other students in schools over rights to drug-selling turf or romantic disagreements, as a culmination of racial disputes, and in fights over material possessions—jewelry, coats, and Walkmans.

What are schools doing in response? Increasingly, expulsion is 20 their answer, or at least suspension for long periods, perhaps with reassignment to special, alternative schools.

Many things are also being done to schools themselves in the effort to make them gun-free. Metal detectors are the most frequent change thus far. That they are of value is clear; that not a small number of weapons (including guns) still enter the building is also clear, as is the fact that such devices can indeed change the climate of a school, making it more prison-like.

Clear mesh book bags, locker searches and locker removal, weapons hot lines, and car searches are all also increasingly being used.

Our schools most definitely are not becoming armed camps. Yet the era of the school as neutral territory, a uniformly safe place for learning with no threat to its students beyond an occasional fistfight or wrestling match, is over. Bringing weapons to school, including guns, is still a rare event for the vast majority of students. Nonetheless, it does happen and is happening with increased frequency. Government, school authorities, parents, and students are wise to be concerned, and to continue their use of prudent responses.

Us versus Them

Groups may compete with each other, blame each other for this or that, grow angry with each other, and even fight and kill one another. Such aggression between groups has always been a main feature of human relations. Tribes; clans; gangs; ethnic, religious, or regional groups; or even whole nations are often in deadly conflict with one another.

The reasons are many, but one very important source is *us versus* 25 *them* thinking. A basic human quality is the desire to feel one is part of a group of people whom we see as being both like ourselves and special in some important way—such as better than other groups. One researcher described it as the need for allies and enemies.

Us versus them thinking is especially strong when groups compete. The competition may be among teens over the outcome of an athletic event, gangs over who owns a piece of turf, or nations struggling for resources or power. In all cases, the psychological outcome is the same—there is more attachment to one's own group (us) and more hostility toward the other group (them).

A group of British researchers, in their experiments on what they called the *minimal group,* showed the power of us versus them thinking even when the people involved were randomly put into one of two groups by a flip of a coin done in front of them. These were clearly not real groups to which the person had become attached. In fact, no one was even given the opportunity to meet the other members of his or her artificial group. Nevertheless, in a number of ways, people showed clear favoritism to their own group and regular discrimination toward the other group.

Our self-esteem, our sense of security, our own importance seems very much tied to the success of the groups to which we belong. We favor our own groups at the expense of other groups in order to build these positive qualities in ourselves. Unfortunately, "at the expense of" often means much more than friendly competition—and can mean deadly combat.

Is it inevitable that groups must fight? Are there ways of eliminating or at least reducing such aggression, and the suspicion, mistrust, tension, and stereotyping that seem to cause it?

One early view was that conflict between groups was a result of 30 ignorance. Bring us and them together, it was believed, and from such contact they would learn enough about each other that their misinterpreting would decrease and along with it their aggression toward each other. The brotherhood meetings, intergroup summer camps, interracial dinners, and educational campaigns of the 1940s and 1950s were among the several ways such us-them contact was carried out.

Research on these efforts, as well as on interracial housing and employment in the armed forces, showed that contact alone was not enough. For conflict between groups to decrease, there had to be certain types of contact. Contact between groups will decrease hostility if it is cooperative contact, such as when there is a challenging circumstance both wish to resolve but neither can resolve alone. Contact will also be successful when it is frequent, not rare; when it is personal, not casual; and when the meeting of us and them has the support of law, community climate, or another important source.

We fight partly because we are a "we" and they are somebody else. If the us-them gap can be narrowed, if they too can be seen as individuals and not as stereotypes, if they can be seen as like us in significant ways, such conflict between groups can diminish.

How to Hurt Someone and Not Feel Guilty

When a grievance, frustration, or anger makes me feel like punching you in the face, and yet I am held back by my civility, my upbringing, and my feelings of guilt as I imagine doing it, what may go on in my own head to tip the balance and permit me to punch away? More generally, how can people behave aggressively toward others, even cruelly, without condemning themselves for doing so? According to Professor Albert Bandura at Stanford University, several self-deceptive, rationalizing processes may take place.

- **Minimization of one's own aggression by comparing it with worse behavior by others.** "OK, I punched him and kicked him in the head, but at least I used my own fists and feet, not a knife or gun like some guys do."

- **Justification of one's own aggression in terms of higher moral principles.** Perhaps the best example of this type of self-vindication and denial of responsibility is the frequent recourse taken by nations at war to the claim that "God is on our side" and the companion notion that theirs is a righteous, holy battle.

- **Displacement of responsibility.** Here the individual avoids ownership of his or her own aggressive behavior by shifting responsibility for it to a higher authority, an authority willing to assume such responsibility. The commonly heard plea by those on trial for war crimes that they "were just following orders" is a prime illustration of such displacement to higher ranking others.

- **Diffusion of responsibility.** Aggression, especially on a large scale, may require for its enactment the services of many different people, each contributing their small part to the larger effort. It is often possible under such circumstances to make each contribution seem and feel relatively harmless, especially if the persons involved are kept (by others or themselves) relatively ignorant of the overall aggressive effort. The Nazi concentration camp death machine, a product composed of many individual contributions, well illustrates such diffusion of responsibility.

- **Dehumanization of victims.** It appears to be the case that the greater the empathy we feel for another person, the more we perceive his or her world and humanness, the less able we are to hurt him or her. The opposite also apparently is true. The more we are able to view someone as something less than human, or even as of another species, the more readily aggression toward that person is possible. Racial or religious stereotyping, the view of the enemy in wartime, or even our attitude toward fans of the other team at a heated sports contest are each good examples of our tendency to give such persons a demeaning label or name, see the others as "them" and unlike "us," and via such dehumanizing enable ourselves to hurt them.

- **Deindividuation.** This is a guilt-reducing, aggression-promoting phenomenon that often occurs in riots, mob or crowd violence, or other forms of group aggression. Each person, in a sense, temporarily loses his or her individual identity to become part of a larger collective. Rather than a spreading out, sharing, or diffusion of responsibility as we have described, deindividuation instead serves as a denial of responsibility. The highly emotional, aggressive collective violence by large groups of fans at soccer, football, or other athletic matches illustrates this quality well.

- **Attribution of blame to victims.** A related but different type of denial of responsibility for one's own aggressive behavior is to hold its target responsible. As Professor Bandura put it, here "aggressors see themselves as essentially persons of good will who are forced into punitive actions by villainous opponents." Victims, it is held, bring it on themselves. Not uncommonly, youths who are chronically delinquent or adults who are career criminals are adept at trying to explain away their antisocial behavior with detailed descriptions of how the victims' stupidity, resistance, hesitancy, or other qualities "made me do it."

- **Graduated desensitization.** Repeated performance of unpleasant behavior, especially when taken in small steps, can progressively decrease its unpleasantness and increase its perpetrator's tolerance for and acceptance of both the behavior itself and his or her own self-perception as an individual capable of doing such things. In this manner, the level of aggression can gradually increase, until eventually the perpetrator can carry out cruel and violent acts with little discomfort. A good illustration of such graduated desensitization is our description of the manner in which torturers are trained.

- **Hygienic positioning.** Here the aggressor positions himself or herself at sufficient distance from the impact or consequences of his or her own violent behavior in order to deny it. Sometimes this distancing is literally true, as when a soldier fires a missile or large artillery piece to a distant target or a bombardier drops bombs from an altitude of many miles. Other times, the distancing is figurative, such as when verbal deniers are used to describe one's own aggressive acts; for example, the victim was "offed" or "wasted," not "killed" or "murdered," or, as in concentration camp terminology, "units were processed" rather than "human beings were slaughtered."

When you stop and think about it, as we seldom do, our ability to avoid taking responsibility for our own aggression is both quite remarkable and quite dismaying.

Television as Tutor: Aggression 101

You have probably read the litany of numbers somewhere by 35 now: 99 percent of American homes have a television set, and two-thirds have two or more. The average American adolescent watches television approximately thirty-five hours per week. There are an average of six violent acts per hour on prime time evening programming and twenty-five such acts per hour on Saturday morning cartoons. By age sixteen, two hundred thousand violent acts have been seen, about thirty-three thousand of them murders or attempted murders.

Psychologists and other researchers studying human behavior almost always qualify their results when reporting them—"it seems to be," "it probably is true that," "it is likely the case that." No such hedging of bets is necessary here. Many dozens of studies have shown this heavy diet of violence viewing to have three serious and often long-lasting effects.

The first may be called the *copycat effect*. A substantial minority of the viewers will actually do what they have seen. Males copy more than do females, younger children more than older. There is more copying the more violence the youngster has seen, when the violence depicted is justified by the show's script (for example, when the "good guy" wins), when it "works," when it is shown in how-to detail, and when it has that odd quality of painlessness often depicted—no suffering, no injury, no bodily consequences. Violently erotic shows lead to the most copying; cartoons, sports, and soap operas next; followed by adventure, detective, and crime stories; with news and public affairs shows resulting in the least copying.

The second, well-demonstrated consequence has been called the *victim effect*. Increased fearfulness, mistrust, and self-protectiveness are its main features. We come to see the world differently, as more threatening, less safe. Millions of (especially elderly) American citizens sentence themselves to solitary confinement every night, fearful of becoming a crime victim to an extent that is out of proportion to its acturial likelihood. This fearfulness is, in part, an effect of television.

The final consequence, and perhaps the most serious, is the *desensitization effect*. As the violence levels depicted increase in intensity and graphic detail, we adapt, we adjust, we get used to it. Current fare includes spurting arteries, chainsaw dismemberment, violent rape scenes. We adapt, we adjust, we get used to it. Such desensitization and increased callousness present a major problem for the revenue-driven television industry, because, as we adapt to a level of violence, it becomes less stimulating, less interesting, and thus less desirable to watch. If we don't watch the program, we don't watch the commercial. Thus, to command our attention, producers must program ever-higher levels of violence. It is difficult to imagine what may be shown next: a type of "hemovision" in which blood spurts from the set onto your living room rug? Or the "snuff film," in which the actors are actually killed?

Thus far, corrective steps either contemplated or enacted at the in- 40 dustry or even at congressional levels have been ineffective, concentrating primarily on one or another type of rating system. Very little energy has been directed to encouraging or creating significant amounts of interesting nonviolent programming.

Our children go to two schools every day, often for five hours each. One is a building with teachers, classrooms, books, chalk, and erasers. The other is a box with a large picture tube, dials, cables, and the demonstrated ability to have a tremendous influence on the behavior of America's children. Thus far, most of the influence has been for the worse. The potential exists to make television an influence for the common good. As adults, as parents, as citizens, we owe our children no less.

Bullying: Schools' Not-So-Little Secret

Guns in school. Gangs in school. Drugs in school. Fights among students. We hear about these problems often. But what about the single most frequent expression of student aggression, bullying?

Bullying is the schools' secret, kept from others and even from themselves. Teachers and administrators often ignore it. After all, it doesn't usually disrupt the class, and besides, many adults mistakenly believe, it is a "natural" part of growing up. By enduring it, kids toughen up and are better prepared for life later on. Nothing could be further from the truth.

Bullies and their victims also keep it secret. The bully doesn't want to be punished; the victim fears reprisal. Victims also often feel pressure to deal with it on their own ("Be a big boy!") and believe no one will aid them if they do seek help.

More often than not, the victim's parents are unaware of the bully- 45 ing. They may wonder why she comes home during the school day to use the bathroom, or how his clothing got torn, or why she seems so hungry at supper (her lunch money was extorted earlier).

Just what are the facts, and what can be done to make this frequent and nasty behavior more public and less damaging?

Several experts estimate that between 15 to 20 percent of all schoolchildren are regularly bullied. The bullying may be verbal, such as threats, insults, teasing, starting rumors about the person, or trying to isolate or intimidate him or her. Often it is physical: pushing, tripping, kicking, hitting.

About two-thirds of the bullying is by boys and quite often is physical. Bullying by girls is usually more covert: such as gossiping, shunning, and the like.

Bullies tend to be hyperactive, domineering, impulsive, attention-seeking boys with little empathy for the feelings of others. Frequently, they bully not only fellow students but teachers, parents, and siblings also. They often come from homes in which the parents were (and frequently still are) bullies themselves. They commonly are parents who are strong believers, and users, of corporal punishment, yet are quite inconsistent in how they discipline, sometimes very strictly, sometimes very permissively.

Being a bully is bad for its victims but for the bully also. Research 50 shows, for example, that elementary school bullies are very likely to grow into antisocial adults with few friends, poor marriages, and trouble with the law. One study, on this last point, revealed that 60 percent of the bullies in grades six through nine had at least one criminal conviction by age twenty-four!

The victims, sometimes known as whipping boys or hostility sponges, are typically physically weaker children, socially insecure, frequently anxious, often lonely and abandoned by other children. As one school expert put it, they sit small in their seats. To the bully, such behaviors and demeanor signal that the person is an easy mark, unlikely to retaliate.

Since it so often is a hidden event, happening most commonly on a playground, or in a school corridor or other site with low adult supervision, the bullying may continue for a long time, even years. Its consequences are several and often severe. Its chronic target will often suffer in academic performance and increasingly avoid people, places, and even school itself (truancy and dropout are not unusual). As it becomes more extreme, the victim may begin bringing a weapon to school or seek to join a gang for protection. At its most severe, suicide or homicide may occur.

A good start in dealing effectively with this widespread form of aggression is any and all steps to bring it into the open. We have to first seek it out in order to root it out.

School administrators and teachers should plan and carry out a zero-tolerance policy for bullying. Announce what it is, why it is wrong, why it won't be tolerated, and what (nonviolent) punishments will be used with all who bully. Just as with good parenting, schools need to set a climate of positive adult involvement and firm limits on unacceptable behavior.

A few weeks into any school term, and usually before the teacher 55 knows it, most of the children in the class know who the class bullies and victims are. A bullying hot line, as used in Japan, or the creation of a "telling school" (where reporting serious aggression is urged as the school norm), as in England, both sound like workable ideas transportable to America.

Eighty-five percent of schoolchildren are neither bullies nor victims, but they can certainly help reduce it, not only by informing adults when they see it but also by being urged to welcome and include those students who are chronically left out of play and work activities.

Bullying is bad business: for the victim, for the bullies, for all of us. Let's get it out in the open, and start dealing with it. Every student has the right to learn in a safe environment.

For Journals

In what specific ways has violence touched you, your family, or your friends?

For Discussion

1. Goldstein's essays are discrete chapters in a collection. What themes or principles are common to all selections?

2. Because these essays appear in a book that is geared toward a mainstream audience rather than an academic one, the evidence is often attributed to specific sources but is not cited in scholarly footnotes or other citations. Are you willing to accept the author's authority and sources without citations? Why or why not?

3. Discuss Goldstein's description of an "us versus them" philosophy in view of "The War Prayer," "Type-Casting," or one of the propaganda posters included in this text.

4. Choose one of the selections—on bullying or on guns in school, for example—and discuss its assertions in view of your own experience in school.

For Writing

1. Articulate several key principles Goldstein discusses—rationalizing violence, for example—and assess one of this chapter's selections or propaganda images from another source in view of those principles.

2. Drawing from your discussion in 2 above, write an essay integrating assertions from this selection with an analysis of "The War Prayer." Include material from Fussell's "Type-Casting" as appropriate.

∞ *"Teddy Bears"* (1999)

VIOLENCE POLICY CENTER

The Violence Policy Center (VPC) is a national educational organization that works to reduce gun death and injury in America by approaching firearms violence as a public health issue and illustrating the need to hold firearms to the same health and safety standards we hold all other consumer products. The center conducts research on the gun industry, firearms violence, and federal regulatory approaches; develops public policy options and offers analyses of violence-reduction proposals; conducts public education; and builds working coalitions with organizations that have not traditionally been part of the gun control debate but that represent constituencies affected by firearms violence.

For Journals

In view of the Second Amendment and a national ethos of the "right to bear arms," how might you expect gun control advocates to appeal to Americans for stricter gun laws?

TEDDY BEARS
HAVE TO MEET CONSUMER
HEALTH & SAFETY STANDARDS

1 At least four types of federal safety standards cover teddy bears: sharp edges and points, small parts, hazardous materials, and flammability.

2 From 1994 and 1997, eight models of teddy bears were recalled by the United States Consumer Product Safety Commission due to possible choking hazards. The total number of teddy bears manufactured during this period was more than 750,000.

3 Teddy bears killed no one in the United States in 1997. From 1994 to 1997 there were 71 toy-related deaths in the United States.

BUT GUNS DON'T!

1 There are no federal safety standards for the domestic manufacture of firearms.

2 No federal health and safety agency has the authority to recall defective firearms or force changes in design.

3 Guns killed 32,436 people in the United States in 1997. From 1994 to 1997 there were 140,938 gun-related deaths in the United States. In 1997, for every time a firearm was used by a civilian to kill in self-defense, there were 4 unintentional deaths, 43 criminal homicides, and 75 suicides involving firearms.

981 unintentional
367 undetermined
13,522 homicides
17,566 suicides

THE SOLUTION

The Firearms Safety and Consumer Protection Act would end the gun industry's deadly exemption from health and safety regulation. Only then will America experience a meaningful reduction in firearms violence.

 Violence Policy Center · 1140 19th Street · NW · Washington · DC · 20036 · www.vpc.org

For Discussion

1.   Analyze the appeals to ethos, pathos, and logos in this image. Which do you find most persuasive and why?

2.   Analyze the image itself—placement of objects, graphics, and text within the overall argument. What does this assessment add to your sense of the appeals discussed above?

3.   Do you find the core analogy persuasive? Discuss why or why not. Do you notice any logical fallacies? Identify any and discuss.

For Writing

1.   Write an essay analyzing this image and the effectiveness of its appeals.

2.   Visit the website of the Violence Policy Center, *www.vpc.org*. Analyze the site and its presentation of research. Given its acknowledged advocacy position, how willing are you to accept the data and evidence its presents? Write an essay assessing the site itself or analyzing a specific piece of research it presents.

∞ Propaganda in Roosevelt's "Pearl Harbor Address" (2000)

NEIL A. VAN OS

Neil A. Van Os (1981–) is a college student attending a California university. He wrote this essay for an assignment in his writing class where he was asked to select one or more background texts and apply their principles to a primary text. He chose Roosevelt's Pearl Harbor Address, which his class had examined both in text and audio-recording.

On December 7, 1941, Japanese forces launched a surprise offensive against the United States of America at Pearl Harbor, Hawaii. The attack was recognized as a premeditated act of aggression against the United States, and thus a declaration of war against Japan became virtually inevitable. The attention of the American people was promptly directed toward President Roosevelt, but it is not the role of the president to declare war; the Constitution reserves this power for Congress. However, the president can address an emergency session of Congress and ask that such a declaration be made. In making this speech, Roosevelt knew that he would be addressing not only one room of Congressmen, but also millions of citizens listening to the radio as he spoke and reading newspapers the next day. In his address to Congress on December 8, 1941, President Roosevelt utilizes strategies of propaganda to portray the Japanese as inhuman aggressors while moving the American people to unite against them.

The notion that a president would intentionally manipulate the thoughts and emotions of U.S. citizens is disconcerting at first. Through propaganda, however, a government can add conviction to a cause and strength to a unified people. Propaganda exists to spread and promote a certain idea, cause, or policy through the populace. Effective propaganda is the greatest social weapon conceivable, for it is the force that reforms the minds of a people from individuals into elements of a unified whole, giving citizens beliefs and convictions that the government wants them to have, according to Jacques Ellul, author of *Propaganda: The Formation of Men's Attitudes.* To lead American forces to victory in the pending war, propaganda was the right tool at the right time.

President Roosevelt would deliver this speech to an enormous audience with anxious, attentive ears. The effectiveness of propaganda grows as the size and attention of the audience grows and, historically, propaganda is most useful in a state of war, a time when the unification of a nation is critical. Despite the undesirable circumstances, Roosevelt had an ideal opportunity to unite the Americans against their new foe, the Japanese.

Roosevelt begins by portraying the Japanese Empire as a heartless, faceless aggressor, a technique emphasized in the film, *Faces of the Enemy.* After setting a historical context with the words, "Yesterday, December 7, 1941,—a date which will live in infamy," he states that the "Empire of Japan" had "deliberately attacked" the United States of America. The president uses *empire* instead of *nation* or *people* because *empire* has a less appealing, imperialistic connotation. He does not want Americans to see the Japanese as individual people. A human being feels compassion and sympathizes with other human beings, and such feelings toward the Japanese, according to *Faces of the Enemy,* would only hinder this new American agenda to defeat them. Roosevelt's insinuation of an inhuman nature in the Japanese serves a further purpose. It suggests that the Japanese do not feel sympathy and compassion as Americans do. Therefore, the Japanese Empire seems even more evil and appears to pose a more aggressive threat to the United States. Stating that the empire had "deliberately attacked" American forces reminds the audience that this was not a random, accidental incident. The Japanese made a specific effort to strike against the United States.

Roosevelt now shifts his focus to accentuate the premeditated betrayal of trust committed by the Japanese. He explains that "the United States was at peace with that nation and, at the solicitation of Japan, was still in conversation with its government and its emperor 5 looking toward the maintenance of peace in the Pacific." He focuses on this point for a relatively long time, approximately one-third of his speech. The idea that the Japanese were hiding behind a mask of peaceful intention while actually planning aggressive action against the United States makes them more despicable in the eyes of an American citizen. Roosevelt reinforces his claims against Japan through appeals to logos when he says:

> It will be recorded that the distance of Hawaii from Japan makes it obvious that the attack was deliberately planned many days or even weeks ago. During the intervening time the Japanese government had deliberately sought to deceive the United States by false statements and expressions of hope for continued peace.

Roosevelt simultaneously makes appeals to pathos, provoking emotional response with charged words such as *deliberately* and *deceived* contrasting sharply with *hope* and *peace*. The Japanese Empire is again depicted as an aggressive and deceitful opponent with no sense of truce or negotiation. This causes citizens of the United States to feel even further removed from their new Japanese foes, an aspect of propaganda that *Faces of the Enemy* claims is essential.

President Roosevelt's next tactic is to remind his audience that the Japanese are not only attacking, but they are also killing as well. He says that the surprise attack "caused severe damage to American naval and military forces." More importantly, however, he makes the situation more real in saying, "I regret to tell you that very many American lives have been lost." Roosevelt's disclosure that "American lives have been lost" informs the people that this is not simply a fight between warships and airplanes, but a real attack with real consequences. To say that "very many American lives have been lost" adds still more to the seriousness of the situation. He wants America to know that the Japanese, like savages, have killed the sons, friends, and neighbors of many of the people listening to the address. This approach combines intellectual and emotional messages to the audience, an idea stressed by Ellul's *Propaganda*.

Roosevelt proceeds to broaden the scope of the Japanese aggression beyond one attack in Hawaii. He explains that the threat of the Japanese is not limited to one distant naval base. The President asserts that the Japanese threat is spreading like a plague of violence, and brings the threat closer to the common American by reporting that "American ships have been reported torpedoed on the high seas between San Francisco and Honolulu." The reference to San Francisco includes the continental United States as an area under threat by the Japanese, even though there had been no real fighting near San Francisco. Using anaphora to make a stronger impact, Roosevelt lists other recent victims of Japanese attack: "Last night Japanese forces attacked

Hong Kong. Last night Japanese forces attacked. . . ." These devices
add a sense of urgency to the situation. With the attitude Roosevelt encourages, an attitude explained in *Faces of the Enemy*, Americans
would feel compelled to stop the Japanese "monster" before it grew
too large.

Now that he has created this image of a demonic, bloodthirsty
Empire of Japan and ignited a fire of fear, anger, and hatred among
millions of Americans, Roosevelt's final task is to give direction to the
people and unite them under the cause of war. He leaves no room for
argument regarding interpretation of the Japanese action: "The facts of
yesterday speak for themselves." He tells the American people that
they "have already formed their opinions and well understand the
implications to the very life and safety of our nation." Not every
American has actually formed an opinion, but Roosevelt conveys the
mentality that no real citizen would have any convictions other than
those which he is expressing. He says "our nation" to tie the people to
the cause on a more personal level. Ellul addresses this aspect of social
manipulation on page 11 of *Propaganda:*

> Not only does propaganda seek to invade the whole man, to lead him
> to adopt a mystical attitude and reach him through all possible psy-
> chological channels, but, more, it speaks to all men. Propaganda can-
> not be satisfied with partial successes, for it does not tolerate
> discussion; by its very nature, it excludes contradiction and dis-
> cussion.

Roosevelt makes an appeal to ethos in the next sentence, reminding the audience that he is "commander in chief of the army and
navy" and therefore the utmost authority in matters of national defense. He then takes another jab at the Japanese while again reinforcing the historical significance of recent events. "Always will we
remember the character of the onslaught against us," he says. Roosevelt addresses the American people as a part of a whole, as propaganda is ineffective when applied toward an individual without direct
association with the nation. The intended mentality is that the individual is only valuable as a part of the cause or idea presented; one man
alone is not even worth mentioning. Roosevelt concludes by promoting the "righteous might" of the American people, implying that God
is with the Americans, and emphasizes that they will win this fight not
just to the point of victory, but to the point of "absolute victory." Both
Faces of the Enemy and *Propaganda: The Formation of Men's Attitudes* acknowledge the significance of this image: the nation as a whole, not individuals, fighting on the side of righteousness.

No small event has the power to reform the mind-set of a nation 10
from relative peace to ambitions of "absolute victory" over an adversary in two days' time. The December 7 bombing of Pearl Harbor was

among the most unsettling events in modern American history, and the shock of the attack evoked a range of emotions, from fear and confusion to anger and hatred, among millions of U.S. citizens. Public reaction could have amounted to chaos unless these emotions were channeled and the people united by common attitudes and goals. President Roosevelt recognized that America would prove triumphant in the war not as a random collection of individual ideals and intentions, but only as one collective whole: a nation. Roosevelt's use of propaganda brought the nation together to give Americans an advantage of unity and resolve that they would need in the years to follow.

Works Cited

Ellul, Jacques. *Propaganda: The Formation of Men's Attitudes.* Translated from the French by Konrad Kellen and Jean Lerner. With an introd. by Konrad Kellen. New York: Vintage Books, 1973, c1975.
Jersey, Bill. *Faces of the Enemy* [videorecording]. A Quest production for the Catticaus Corporation; produced and directed by Bill Jersey; edited and codirected by Jeffrey Friedman. Narrated by Sam Keen. 1987.

For Journals

Do you ever think of your country's political leaders as engaging in propaganda?

For Discussion

1. How would you define strategies of propaganda? Do you accept the author's use of the term? What is your reaction to Van Os's thesis that an American president has engaged in techniques of propaganda? Do you agree? Why or why not?

2. Van Os appeals to authority by citing his secondary sources. To what degree do these strengthen his argument?

3. Assess the structure, organization, and style of Van Os's essay. What suggestions would you make for him were he to revise his essay?

For Writing

1. Write a response to the author either agreeing or disagreeing with his argument. Support your view with examples from the text of the speech itself as well as from Van Os's essay.

2. Locate these secondary sources or other works that discuss strategies of propaganda. You could, for example, review Paul Fussell's essay, "Type-Casting," in this chapter. Apply the principles you have learned to a primary text, such as a piece of war rhetoric or a propaganda poster, and write an essay analyzing the persuasive text and incorporating secondary sources as appropriate.

∽ *Film: Faces of the Enemy* (1987)

Bill Jersey, Producer and Director; videorecording (58 minutes). Edited and codirected by Jeffrey Friedman, narrated by Sam Keen. Composer Mark Adler. Produced for Catticaus Corporation, Quest Productions, Berkeley, California.

This video may be available through your college library, and it is worth tracking down. The video examines the psychology of hatred and war and, by examining various sources, shows how those considered to be enemies must first be dehumanized in order to justify destroying them.

For Journals

Identify someone you consider an enemy. How did you formulate that belief?

For Discussion

1. Evaluate the narrator's process of evaluating evidence and drawing inferences in this video. How might it be similar to, and different from, your own research processes?

2. Which evidence do you find most persuasive in supporting Keen's assertion that we create dehumanizing images of enemies in order to destroy them?

For Writing

1. Drawing from the principles set forth in this video, apply several of Keen's core assertions to a text or image in this book or elsewhere. Core principles might include "us versus them" thinking; "we are victims/they are to blame," and "we are good, they are evil."

2. Compare and contrast Keen's assertions in this video to those implied in one of the war or antiwar films mentioned below.

Other films on war and violence:

Counterfeit Trader

The Guns of Navarone

Bridge on the River Kwai

Casablanca

Apocalypse Now

Platoon

Full Metal Jacket

There are any number of films you, your classmates, or your instructor may recommend for viewing. Whichever film you select, try to analyze the film in view of some principles discussed in this chapter, particularly in the Fussell and Goldstein readings.

Writing Assignments

1. Drawing from Fussell, Goldstein, or other secondary sources you research, write a documented essay analyzing several propaganda posters or one of the text selections in this chapter, integrating the secondary source as evidence to support your assessment of the propaganda. You may also find it helpful to find and review Jacques Ellul's book *Propaganda: The Formation of Men's Attitudes.*

2. Select a political event or issue of current interest, such as the 2000 presidential election and the vote-counting fracas that followed. Then select several magazines with divergent political viewpoints—*National Review, US News and World Report, Newsweek, New Republic,* or *The Nation.* Compare the coverage of events in the different sources. Do a close textual analysis of the sources, and write an essay presenting your findings.

3. Find and review Goldstein's entire book, *Violence in America,* and research one of the topics he discusses: domestic violence, gang violence, media representations of violence, and the like. Even though Goldstein is a psychologist and approaches the topic from his own disciplinary stance, you may want to take a different approach—examining the topic from more of a public health stance, for example, or analyzing representations of violence in literature or popular culture.

11

∞

Frontiers

A t the beginning of the nineteenth century, New York State was on
the frontier, and most people thought it would take a hundred
years to get to the Pacific, if in fact they ever thought in those terms at
all. They certainly would have been surprised to learn that by 1849
Americans had moved across the entire continent, all the way to California, thanks to the political and economic charms of expansion and
the incentive of the Gold Rush. What they would have found even
more unlikely is that a hundred years after the frontier had ceased to
exist as a geographic marker, Americans would still be so attached to
it, or to what it represents, that the search for new frontiers—even
technological ones—continues to occupy the American vocabulary
and the American psyche.

The American idea of frontier is of an invisible border between
settled and unsettled, civilized and uncivilized areas. It is recognized
more by what it is not than by what it is: it's not civilization as you
know it, it's not domesticated, it's not safe. Of course, the idea of the
frontier was a reality only to the European settlers who saw themselves as the bearers of culture and developers of empty country, not
to Native Americans who had their own indigenous cultures and
knew the country wasn't empty because they were already there.

Whether everyone accepted the idea of a frontier—receding before
the development of towns and farms but always out there somewhere,
leading to newer undiscovered places—it became so embedded in our
culture that it is what Americans think they know best about their
own country, and it is the way we are identified by the rest of the
world. In Germany, for example, there are vacation places complete
with wigwams so tourists can play cowboys and Indians. Blue jeans,
invented by young merchant Levi Strauss during the Gold Rush so
prospectors could put ore in their pockets without tearing them, are an
American national uniform and a status symbol in eastern Europe and
Russia. American theme parks have frontier towns; movie studios

have mock shoot-outs between good guys and bad guys; and Americans have been watching western movies as long as there have been movies to watch.

How much all of this re-creation has to do with what the frontier was actually like seems to matter much less than what most people prefer to think it was like. Wherever Americans live, they infuse some sense of the centrality of the frontier into their image of the United States. Whatever changes are wrought in that image are the cause of pitched emotional and intellectual battles between groups with an interest in preserving the idea of the frontier. In the last forty or fifty years, many scholars have explored the difference between the actual American frontier and the frontier of the American imagination, and many Native Americans have campaigned successfully for reevaluations of the image of Indians in American history.

Frontiers through History

Most Americans never saw the frontier, wherever it happened to be at the time. In the eighteenth and most of the nineteenth centuries, whether they lived in towns, on farms and in rural areas, or in the bigger eastern cities, they got their information about the frontier from newspaper reports, narratives—accurate or exaggerated—paintings by artists who had accompanied expeditions, and eventually from photographs.

The people who knew the frontier from firsthand experience were not only the settlers, trappers, hunters, and seekers for gold, and the frontier was not just the Far West. It existed as a permeable border between the white settlers and the Native Americans, or the Mexicans, or the English and the French, or wherever issues of control, power, and settlement arose, and it moved irregularly from the east coast to the west coast over a period of almost three hundred years; in the nineteenth century, as gold was discovered in California, the frontier receded with astonishing speed as far as it could go—to the Pacific Ocean and California.

For a lucky few, the idea of the frontier was an adventure of absolutely glorious proportions, and no one left a record of a better time than the young Samuel Clemens, otherwise known as Mark Twain. In 1861, accompanying his brother, who had been appointed secretary to the governor of the Nevada Territory, Clemens saw the continent as few other people but the Native Americans had ever been privileged to see it—stagecoaches, the Pony Express, the Southwest, clear lakes full of fish, early San Francisco, silver mining in Nevada, even Hawaii. His early book, *Roughing It,* is ironic from title to finish, but Twain's irrepressible humor communicates the reality of the frontier at the same time that it embroiders and sustains the mythology.

Twain could find amusement in almost anything, but the trip was extremely difficult, and relations between settlers and Indians deteriorated in proportion to the number of settlers who arrived and the realization that they were not going to stop coming. Some settlers both feared and pitied the Indians, but for Americans back East the picture was less complicated. People who went through their entire lives without ever seeing an Indian believed in the popular image of crazed savages bent on destroying civilization. A more respectful image, Albert Bierstadt's spectacular painting *Giant Redwood Trees of California*, gives us a sense of the symbiotic relationship between the Indians and the landscape.

There were real instances of brutality as competition for diminishing natural resources raised the stakes on both sides. But the tabloid newspapers such as the *Police Gazette* knew their audience and catered to its prejudices. In a typical example, the *Gazette* gives its version of a clash between U.S. Cavalry and Indians in South Dakota, complete with headline (*Indian Treachery and Bloodshed*) and violent illustration.

By 1893, the frontier was essentially closed; Oklahoma would not become a state until 1912, but the Indians were no longer a factor, the railroad had long since become transcontinental, industrialization had transformed American cities and multiplied their populations, and people who wanted to see Indians could buy a ticket to Buffalo Bill's show—the great Indian chief Sitting Bull was one of his acts.

Chicago, the youngest of America's great cities, celebrated its status by holding a World's Fair in 1893. A brilliant young professor, Frederick Jackson Turner, took the opportunity to speak about the impact the closing of the frontier had on the American consciousness. The result, his essay "The Significance of the Frontier in American History," is the first and still the most famous analysis of the frontier. Turner's address had profound effects on the development of economics as a discipline, as well as on the study of American history, and the argument he started about the significance of the frontier to the development of American character and democracy has continued ever since. Richard Hofstadter's response that follows is the most famous, but it is only one of many.

As the actual frontier disappeared, and with it the real conflict between whites and Indians, the need to preserve some portion of a pristine landscape grew, with the West and Far West as the primary beneficiaries. A conservationist movement led by naturalist and writer John Muir successfully campaigned for Yosemite and the Sequoias in California, which were declared national parks in 1890.

The size of the parks system has gradually increased over the years, but not without debate about the need for development versus the need for open space. One western writer who dedicated much of his work to the significance of the wilderness in an industrialized America was the novelist and conservationist Wallace Stegner. In his famous "Coda: Wilderness Letter," Stegner argues not just for the wilderness but for the *idea* of the wilderness, even for Americans who have never seen it and don't really want to, except in the movies.

Among the significant social changes which followed the closing of the frontier was the imaginative transformation of the west from a place of danger into one where a spectacular landscape and an exotic past—colonial Spanish and Mexican ranch life, cowboys and Indians, Gold Rush prospecting—became a subject for nostalgia and a tourist attraction. There are many examples of this kind of cultural reduction—posters inviting tourists to California to see a real Mexican fiesta, staged for their benefit; or paintings of Mexican grandees, aristocratic and gracious, on their enormous estates, even though those estates had been taken by Americans almost a half century ago in the wake of the Gold Rush.

The greatest degree of nostalgia, of course, was reserved for Native Americans. Because they had been perceived by whites as the greatest threat, they became, once they were powerless, the people who were the most thoroughly romanticized and fondly remembered. This change is not as strange as it sounds; it was, in a way, the strongest evidence of how completely they had been dismantled. The stereotypical image of the bloodthirsty savage was replaced by the equally stereotypical image of the noble savage. Indians maidens were now always pictured beautiful and demure, and Indian men as handsome and courageous.

One of the most interesting and aesthetically pleasing sources of romanticized Indian images were the ephemeral creations of the 1920s and 1930s known as crate labels. These packing labels, put on the sides of fruit and vegetable crates to make them recognizable and saleable at food auctions, are now collectors' items. The example in this chapter, called "Indian Belle," is a beautifully colored advertisement for navel oranges grown in central California for the consumption of easterners. It is not clear if the farmers and the largely anonymous artists they hired realized that they were selling not only the fruit inside the cartons, but the fantasy which decorated them.

For real Native Americans, movies provided one of their few chances to see themselves reflected in popular culture, but that reflection was, for many years, as much of a distortion as the overly idealized images on fruit crates. (In that sense their portrayals had much in common with that of African Americans, who were limited to movie roles as maids and servants, happy poor people and entertainers.) Actors playing the parts of Indians were invariably dressed in the clothing of Plains Indians no matter where the movie was set, and in the 1940s and 1950s, their chief function seemed to be that they got shot off their horses in battle scenes by members of the U.S. cavalry in general, and John Wayne in particular. In her poem, "Dear John Wayne," Native American writer Louise Erdrich captures the ironic experience of American Indian teenagers who go to a drive-in movie in the southwest to watch Hollywood versions of what happened to their ancestors.

Thanks to the Gold Rush, the creation of the movie industry, and its enormous economic and social influence, California is the place most Americans think of as the end of the frontier, the place, writer Joan Didion says, "we have to get it right because this is where we run out of room." And in fact writing about California, like everything else about California, is more abundant than writing about the rest of the west coast. But Oregon and Washington State, much more sparsely populated and less a part of the general imagination, have taken on the role of refuges from California's success, its crowds, its development, and what they perceive as its lost promise.

Irritated natives have bumper stickers on their cars asking that their states not be "Californiacated." Loggers fight with environmentalists about jobs versus old growth timber, livelihoods versus open space. Perhaps only someone who is not a westerner—like English writer Jonathan Raban—could explain these conflicts, as he does in his article about Washington State, Wyoming, and Montana, "The Next Last Frontier." Observant, curious, and a good listener, he is enough of an outsider to have the ear of both sides; coming from England, which would fit easily into one corner of Montana and which hasn't had a wilderness for a thousand years, he is visibly struck by the size and variety of the country, and his descriptions have the freshness of genuine surprise.

Ultimately, what may be most remarkable about the idea of the frontier is its incredible staying power. It has remained in our consciousness and our sense of ourselves, not only in the impassioned writing of Wallace Stegner or the elegiac and ironic poetry of Louise Erdrich, but also in every level of American culture, from high to low. Historian Patricia Nelson Limerick, in one of a series of essays on the frontier in American culture, writes in "Frontier Headlines" about the varied and sometimes ridiculous ways Americans contrive to identify every activity or product from the significant to the trivial with the frontier spirit.

Like any other powerful idea, though, the concept of the frontier must constantly be reexamined and reinterpreted in order to be meaningful. The Frontierland area at Disneyland or the fake shoot-outs staged for tourists in western ghost towns may be entertaining, but they are no more useful in that regard than the fake Mexican fiestas staged for tourists a century ago. A more intriguing approach comes from Clint Eastwood's revisionist western movie about the frontier,

Unforgiven. Eastwood became a movie star in a delightfully cynical series of Italian "spaghetti" westerns in which he played the ultimate silent gunfighter, inscrutable and alone, and a killer, but essentially heroic. In this film, he makes use of many of the elements of the traditional western, including the gunslinger, women in distress, good guys and bad guys, and the big gunfight at the end. But he turns many of those same elements on their heads: the good guy is a retired killer who is useless as a farmer, can barely get on a horse, and would rather stay home with his two children; the ladies in distress are prostitutes who hire him to kill a man who mutilated one of them; the most brutal character in the movie is the sheriff; and the epilogue to the film, which describes the gunslinger's change of career after all this is over, is a comic reversal of frontier clichés. The result is a movie that simultaneously revises, criticizes, and yet validates the frontier of myth. It may or may not be any more accurate than all the other versions of the frontier that have been with us for more than three hundred years, but it is another proof of our need for its continued presence, and for what we believe it tells us about who we are, or who we could be.

∞ FROM *Roughing It* (1872)

MARK TWAIN

Mark Twain (pseudonym of Samuel Clemens, 1835–1910), humorist, novelist, satirist, and lecturer, is one of the foremost writers in American literature, and probably the most beloved. He grew up in Missouri before the Civil War and worked as a printer and a Mississippi riverboat pilot before accompanying his brother Orion to Nevada in 1862. Roughing It, *with its adventures, tall tales, and absolutely American voice, came out in 1872.*

By eight o'clock everything was ready, and we were on the other side of the river. We jumped into the stage, the driver cracked his whip, and we bowled away and left "the States" behind us. It was a superb summer morning, and all the landscape was brilliant with sunshine. There was a freshness and breeziness, too, and an exhilarating sense of emancipation from all sorts of cares and responsibilities, that almost made us feel that the years we had spent in the close, hot city, toiling and slaving, had been wasted and thrown away. We were spinning along through Kansas, and in the course of an hour and a half we were fairly abroad on the great Plains. Just here the land was rolling— a grand sweep of regular elevations and depressions as far as the eye could reach—like the stately heave and swell of the ocean's bosom after a storm. And everywhere were cornfields, accenting with squares of deeper green, this limitless expanse of grassy land. But presently this sea upon dry ground was to lose its "rolling" character and stretch away for seven hundred miles as level as a floor!

Our coach was a great swinging and swaying stage, of the most sumptuous description—an imposing cradle on wheels. It was drawn by six handsome horses, and by the side of the driver sat the "conductor," the legitimate captain of the craft; for it was his business to take charge and care of the mails, baggage, express matter, and passengers. We three were the only passengers, this trip. We sat on the back seat, inside. About all the rest of the coach was full of mail-bags—for we had three days' delayed mails with us. Almost touching our knees, a perpendicular wall of mail matter rose up to the roof. There was a great pile of it strapped on top of the stage, and both the fore and hind boots were full. We had twenty-seven hundred pounds of it aboard, the driver said— "a little for Brigham, and Carson, and 'Frisco, but the heft of it for the Injuns, which is powerful troublesome 'thout they get plenty of truck to read." But as he just then got up a fearful convulsion of his countenance which was suggestive of a wink being swallowed by an earthquake, we guessed that his remark was intended to be facetious, and to mean that we would unload the most of our mail matter somewhere on the Plains and leave it to the Indians, or whosoever wanted it.

We changed horses every ten miles, all day long, and fairly flew over the hard, level road. We jumped out and stretched our legs every time the coach stopped, and so the night found us still vivacious and unfatigued.

It was now just dawn; and as we stretched our cramped legs full length on the mail-sacks, and gazed out through the windows across the wide wastes of greensward clad in cool, powdery mist, to where there was an expectant look in the eastern horizon, our perfect enjoyment took the form of a tranquil and contended ecstasy. The stage whirled along at a spanking gait, the breeze flapping curtains and suspended coats in a most exhilarating way; the cradle swayed and swung luxuriously, the pattering of the horses' hoofs, the cracking of the driver's whip, and his "Hi-yi! g'lang!" were music; the spinning ground and the waltzing trees appeared to give us a mute hurrah as we went by, and then slack up and look after us with interest, or envy, or something; and as we lay and smoked the pipe of peace and compared all this luxury with the years of tiresome city life that had gone before it, we felt that there was only one complete and satisfying happiness in the world, and we had found it. . . .

Really and truly, two thirds of the talk of drivers and conductors 5 had been about this man Slade, ever since the day before we reached Julesburg. In order that the Eastern reader may have a clear conception of what a Rocky Mountain desperado is, in his highest state of development, I will reduce all this mass of Overland gossip to one straight-forward narrative, and present it in the following shape:

Slade was born in Illinois, of good parentage. At about twenty-six years of age he killed a man in a quarrel and fled the country. At St. Joseph, Missouri, he joined one of the early California-bound emigrant trains, and was given the post of trainmaster. One day on the Plains he had an angry dispute with one of his wagon-drivers, and both drew their revolvers. But the driver was the quicker artist, and had his weapon cocked first. So Slade said it was a pity to waste life on so small a matter, and proposed that the pistols be thrown on the ground and the quarrel settled by a fist-fight. The unsuspecting driver agreed, and threw down his pistol—whereupon Slade laughed at his simplicity, and shot him dead!

He made his escape, and lived a wild life for a while, dividing his time between fighting Indians and avoiding an Illinois sheriff, who had been sent to arrest him for his first murder. It is said that in one Indian battle he killed three savages with his own hand, and afterward cut their ears off and sent them, with his compliments, to the chief of the tribe.

Slade soon gained a name for fearless resolution, and this was sufficient merit to procure for him the important post of Overland division-agent at Julesburg, in place of Mr. Jules, removed. For some time previously, the company's horses had been frequently stolen, and the coaches delayed, by gangs of outlaws, who were wont to laugh at the idea of any man's having the temerity to resent such outrages. Slade resented them promptly. The outlaws soon found that the new agent was a man who did not fear anything that breathed the breath of life. He made short work of all offenders. The result was that delays ceased, the company's property was let alone, and no matter what happened or who suffered, Slade's coaches went through, every time! True, in order to bring about this wholesome change, Slade had to kill several men— some say three, others say four, and others six—but the world was the richer for their loss. The first prominent difficulty he had was with the ex-agent Jules, who bore the reputation of being a reckless and desperate man himself. Jules hated Slade for supplanting him, and a good fair occasion for a fight was all he was waiting for. By and by Slade dared to employ a man whom Jules had once discharged. Next, Slade seized a team of stage-horses which he accused Jules of having driven off and hidden somewhere for his own use. War was declared, and for a day or two the two men walked warily about the streets, seeking each other, Jules armed with a double-barreled shotgun, and Slade with his history-creating revolver. Finally, as Slade stepped into a store, Jules poured the contents of his gun into him from behind the door. Slade was pluck, and Jules got several bad pistol wounds in return. Then both men fell, and were carried to their respective lodgings, both swearing that better aim should do deadlier work next time. Both were bedridden a long time, but Jules got on his feet first, and gathering his possessions together, packed them on a couple of mules, and fled to the Rocky Mountains to gather strength in safety against the day of reckoning. For many months he was not seen or heard of, and was gradually dropped out of the remembrance of all save Slade himself. But Slade was not the man to forget him. On the contrary, common report said that Slade kept a reward standing for his capture, dead or alive!

After a while, seeing that Slade's energetic administration had restored peace and order to one of the worst divisions of the road, the Overland Stage Company transferred him to the Rocky Ridge division in the Rocky Mountains, to see if he could perform a like miracle there. It was the very paradise of outlaws and desperadoes. There was absolutely no semblance of law there. Violence was the rule. Force was the only recognized authority. The commonest misunderstandings were settled on the spot with the revolver or the knife. Murders were done in open day, and with sparkling frequency, and nobody thought of inquiring into them. It was considered that the parties who did the killing had their private reasons for it; for other people to meddle would have been looked upon as indelicate. After a murder, all that Rocky Mountain etiquette required of a spectator was, that he should help the gentleman bury his game—otherwise his churlishness would surely be remembered against him the first time he killed a man himself and needed a neighborly turn in interring him.

Slade took up his residence sweetly and peacefully in the midst of this hive of horse-thieves and assassins, and the very first time one of them aired his insolent swaggerings in his presence he shot him dead! He began a raid on the outlaws, and in a singularly short space of time he had completely stopped their depredations on the stage stock, recovered a large number of stolen horses, killed several of the worst desperadoes of the district, and gained such a dread ascendancy over the rest that they respected him, admired him, feared him, obeyed him! He wrought the same marvelous change in the ways of the community that had marked his administration at Overland City. He captured two men who had stolen Overland stock, and with his own hands he hanged them. He was supreme judge in his district, and he was jury and executioner likewise—and not only in the case of offences against his employers, but against passing emigrants as well. On one occasion some emigrants had their stock lost or stolen, and told Slade, who chanced to visit their camp. With a single companion he rode to a ranch, the owners of which he suspected, and opening the door, commenced firing, killing three, and wounding the fourth.

From a bloodthirstily interesting little Montana book* I take this paragraph:

> While on the road, Slade held absolute sway. He would ride down to a station, get into a quarrel, turn the house out of windows, and maltreat the occupants most cruelly. The unfortunates had no means of

---

The Vigilantes of Montana, by Prof. Thos. J. Dimsdale. [Author's note] redress, and were compelled to recuperate as best they could. On one of these occasions, it is said, he killed the father of the fine little half-breed boy, Jemmy, whom he adopted, and who lived with his widow after his execution. Stories of Slade's hanging men, and of innumerable assaults, shootings, stabbings and beatings, in which he was a principal actor, form part of the legends of the stage line. As for minor quarrels and shootings, it is absolutely certain that a minute history of Slade's life would be one long record of such practices.

Slade was a matchless marksman with a navy revolver. The legends say that one morning at Rocky Ridge, when he was feeling comfortable, he saw a man approaching who had offended him some days before—observe the fine memory he had for matters like that—and, "Gentlemen," said Slade, drawing, "it is a good twenty-yard shot—I'll clip the third button on his coat!" Which he did. The bystanders all admired it. And they all attended the funeral, too.

On one occasion a man who kept a little whiskey-shelf at the station did something which angered Slade—and went and made his will. A day or two afterward Slade came in and called for some brandy. The man reached under the counter (ostensibly to get a bottle—possibly to get something else), but Slade smiled upon him that peculiarly bland and satisfied smile of his which the neighbors had long ago learned to recognize as a death-warrant in disguise, and told him to "none of that!—pass out the high-priced article." So the poor bar-keeper had to turn his back and get the high-priced brandy from the shelf; and when he faced around again he was looking into the muzzle of Slade's pistol. "And the next instant," added my informant, impressively, "he was one of the deadest men that ever lived."

The stage-drivers and conductors told us that sometimes Slade would leave a hated enemy wholly unmolested, unnoticed and unmentioned, for weeks together—had done it once or twice at any rate. And some said they believed he did it in order to lull the victims into unwatchfulness, so that he could get the advantage of them, and others said they believed he saved up an enemy that way, just as a schoolboy saves up a cake, and made the pleasure go as far as it would by gloating over the anticipation. One of these cases was that of a Frenchman who had offended Slade. To the surprise of everybody Slade did not kill him on the spot, but let him alone for a considerable time. Finally, however, he went to the Frenchman's house very late one night, knocked, and when his enemy opened the door, shot him dead—pushed the corpse inside the door with his foot, set the house on fire and burned up the dead man, his widow and three children! I heard this story from several different people, and they evidently believed what they were saying. It may be true, and it may not. "Give a dog a bad name," etc.

Slade was captured, once, by a party of men who intended to lynch him. They disarmed him, and shut him up in a strong log-house, 15 and placed a guard over him. He prevailed on his captors to send for his wife, so that he might have a last interview with her. She was a brave, loving, spirited woman. She jumped on a horse and rode for life and death. When she arrived they let her in without searching her, and before the door could be closed she whipped out a couple of revolvers, and she and her lord marched forth defying the party. And then, under a brisk fire, they mounted double and galloped away unharmed!

In the fulness of time Slade's myrmidons captured his ancient enemy Jules, whom they found in a well-chosen hiding-place in the remote fastnesses of the mountains, gaining a precarious livelihood with his rifle. They brought him to Rocky Ridge, bound hand and foot, and deposited him in the middle of the cattle-yard with his back against a post. It is said that the pleasure that lit Slade's face when he heard of it was something fearful to contemplate. He examined his enemy to see that he was securely tied, and then went to bed, content to wait till morning before enjoying the luxury of killing him. Jules spent the night in the cattle-yard, and it is a region where warm nights are never known. In the morning Slade practised on him with his revolver, nipping the flesh here and there, and occasionally clipping off a finger, while Jules begged him to kill him outright and put him out of his misery. Finally Slade reloaded, and walking up close to his victim, made some characteristic remarks and then dispatched him. The body lay there half a day, nobody venturing to touch it without orders, and then Slade detailed a party and assisted at the burial himself. But he first cut off the dead man's ears and put them in his vest pocket, where he carried them for some time with great satisfaction. That is the story as I have frequently heard it told and seen it in print in California newspapers. It is doubtless correct in all essential particulars.

In due time we rattled up to a stage station, and sat down to breakfast with a half-savage, half-civilized company of armed and bearded mountaineers, ranchmen and station employ[ees]. The most gentlemanly-appearing, quiet and affable officer we had yet found along the road in the Overland Company's service was the person who sat at the head of the table, at my elbow. Never youth stared and shivered as I did when I heard them call him SLADE!

Here was romance, and I sitting face to face with it!—looking upon it—touching it—hobnobbing with it, as it were! Here, right by my side, was the actual ogre who, in fights and brawls and various ways, *had taken the lives of twenty-six human beings,* or all men lied about him! I suppose I was the proudest stripling that ever traveled to see strange lands and wonderful people.

He was so friendly and so gentle-spoken that I warmed to him in spite of his awful history. It was hardly possible to realize that this pleasant person was the pitiless scourge of the outlaws, the raw-head-

and-bloody-bones the nursing mothers of the mountains terrified their children with. And to this day I can remember nothing remarkable about Slade except that his face was rather broad across the cheek bones, and that the cheek bones were low and the lips peculiarly thin and straight. But that was enough to leave something of an effect upon me, for since then I seldom see a face possessing those characteristics without fancying that the owner of it is a dangerous man.

The coffee ran out. At least it was reduced to one tin-cupful, and Slade was about to take it when he saw that my cup was empty. He politely offered to fill it, but although I wanted it, I politely declined. I was afraid he had not killed anybody that morning, and might be needing diversion. But still with firm politeness he insisted on filling my cup, and said I had traveled all night and better deserved it than he—and while he talked he placidly poured the fluid, to the last drop. I thanked him and drank it, but it gave me no comfort, for I could not feel sure that he would not be sorry, presently, that he had given it away, and proceed to kill me to distract his thoughts from the loss. But nothing of the kind occurred. We left him with only twenty-six dead people to account for, and I felt a tranquil satisfaction in the thought that in so judiciously taking care of No. 1 at that breakfast-table I had pleasantly escaped being No. 27. Slade came out to the coach and saw us off, first ordering certain rearrangements of the mail-bags for our comfort, and then we took leave of him.

For Journals

What had you previously read of Twain's works? What did you know about him or his work?

For Discussion

1. Tall tales are very characteristic of Twain and of western humor. Why do you think the frontier lent itself to such wildly exaggerated stories about people and places?

2. How do you respond to the idea that giving a biography to Slade or any other western character gives a history to a frontier that doesn't have any history of its own?

3. How does Twain's encounter with the real Slade make us revise our expectations of what he would be like?

4. What image of the frontier do you think Twain's eastern readers had? Does Twain's way of writing reinforce or revise that image?

5. How does Twain's humor contribute to his portrait of himself as a man who knows absolutely nothing about the frontier? Why do you think he chose that way of presenting himself?

For Writing

1.   Read a couple of other chapters from *Roughing It*—for example, on Mono Lake, on an earthquake in San Francisco, on Hawaii, on the desert, on striking it rich for ten days in a silver mine—and write a paper on how these episodes support or contradict your own expectations of what the frontier was like, what frontier heroes were like, and what American values these heroes lived by.

2.   Write an essay about a trip you took when you were younger to a place—a national park or a city, for example—that made a big impression on you at the time. Write a paragraph about it as you experienced it in childhood and a paragraph on the same experience as you recall it now. Analyze both paragraphs, and write an essay examining the ways you revised your understanding of your own experience.

∞ Giant Redwood Trees of California   (1874)

ALBERT BIERSTADT

Albert Bierstadt (1830–1902), was born in Germany but became famous in America as a painter of western scenery. After traveling and sketching the mountains of Europe, he went on a trail-making expedition to the West in 1859. He painted huge grand canvases, whose subjects included a Shoshone village, the last of the buffalo, the Rocky Mountains, and Yosemite, and his work was extremely popular.

For Journals

Who do you think was the original audience for this painting? What was your own first reaction to it?

For Discussion

1.   Why do you think Bierstadt includes human beings in the painting? How would the overall impression given by the sequoias be changed if there were no figures of people at all?

2.   How would the dramatic impact of the picture be changed if the figures in it were white rather than Native American? Why do you think Bierstadt made the choice he did?

3.   How would you describe the mood conveyed by this painting? How do its features—the angle from which you view it, the vertical placement of the trees, the subject matter—contribute to that mood?

4.   Today Americans take the sequoias for granted, but in the nineteenth century many easterners, faced with the spectacular western

Albert Bierstadt (1830–1902), "Giant Redwood Trees of California," 1874. Oil on canvas, 52 1/2 × 43 in. Gift of Zenas Crane. Courtesy of The Berkshire Museum 1903.15.

scenery of paintings like Bierstadt's, couldn't believe their eyes until they saw photographs of the same places. What would be the advantages and disadvantages of viewing a photograph of a scene like this versus a painting of the same scene?

For Writing

1. Compare this painting with the *California, the Cornucopia of the World* poster in Chapter 6, and write an analysis of their respective persuasive strategies: who their intended audiences might have been; what they told their audiences about California; what details conveyed that information; which one you find most effective, and why.

2. John Muir was the founder of the modern conservationist movement; his campaigns on behalf of Yosemite led to its establishment as a national park. Read John Muir's descriptions of Yosemite and the sequoias. Write an essay in which you include your analysis of his appreciation of the landscape, the relevance of his concerns as conservation issues today, and the attempt in his writing to revise the idea of land development as an unquestioned good.

✎ Indian Treachery and Bloodshed (1891)

POLICE GAZETTE

The Police Gazette *was a popular and lurid newspaper that was begun in 1846 but was at its height—or depth—in the 1880s and 1890s. It specialized in stories about crime, prostitution, and sports, was copiously illustrated, never had a story without a melodramatic title, and freely expressed the biases of its publisher, James Fox, who entertained lifelong prejudices against Chinese, African Americans, Jews, Native Americans, ministers, and college students, among others.*

The Indian war in South Dakota, so long anticipated, has at last become a reality, and with it has come the death of a number of brave troops of the United States Cavalry. The leader of the warriors was Big Foot and he and his braves tricked the troops into ambush. Then a wholesale slaughter began, the Indians being nearly annihilated, those who were not killed seeking refuge in the Bad Lands, where they will be frozen or starved out. As soon as the troops had cornered the Indians they fell upon them with Hotchkiss guns. The Indians fell in heaps but, determined to the last, they fought to the death even after being sorely wounded.

The saddest scene of the carnage was the killing of Captain George D. Wallace of the Seventh Cavalry, who was brutally tomahawked. Captain Wallace was appointed to the Military Academy from South Carolina in 1868 and upon being graduated in 1872 was commissioned a second lieutenant in the Seventh. He received his promotion to first lieutenant in 1876 and was commissioned captain in September 1885.

It is said that General Sheridan first remarked that "a dead Indian is the best Indian" and the action of the soldiers appears to coincide with Little Phil's views. The action teaches the lesson that if the Sioux are of any use at all they should be fairly dealt with, and if not, that they should at once be given free passes to the happy hunting grounds. As they speak highly of the happy hunting grounds, it might be as well to start them on the journey in any case, and then, if the decision be found unjust, to write them an apology.

For Journals

How does the news style of the *Police Gazette* compare with that of contemporary tabloid newspapers?

For Discussion

1. How would you describe the author's attitude toward the Indians? What values do you think the writer places on the lives of both Indians and soldiers?

2. How closely do you think the contents of the article and the illustration are related? What would you describe as the theme of the article? Of the illustration?

3. Look at the headline of the article and then at the first paragraph. How does the article support or revise the sentiments in the headline? Given the headline, what would you have expected?

4. Look at the illustration, starting at the top and working down to the bottom. How successfully does each grouping convey violent action? If there were no headline for the picture and text, what headline would you supply?

5. Who do you think read the *Police Gazette?* What would its audience have to do with the kinds of articles it published?

6. Suppose that Indians were writing the article and drawing the illustrations. In what specific ways do you think they would have revised the results?

For Writing

1. At the library, look at a book with copies of George Catlin's paintings of Native Americans—*North American Indians* or *Catlin's Indians*, for example—and write a paper in which you discuss and compare any two of the portraits. Among the points for you to consider: What is your impression of the character and personality of the Native Americans in the pictures? Exactly what in the paintings conveyed that impression to you—color, body posture, expression, background? What words would you use to describe the mood of the paintings? Your college library would be a good source of material on the history of the various tribes and on Catlin's artistry.

2. Research the development of the idea of the reservation: how it was developed, what treaties surrounded the setting up of reservations, or what conditions prevail on reservations today. If you write about reservations today, focus on one area of the country or one or two reservations.

∽ The Significance of the Frontier in American History (1893)

FREDERICK JACKSON TURNER

Frederick Jackson Turner (1862–1932) was born in Wisconsin and taught at the University of Wisconsin and Harvard. He presented this paper during the Chicago World's Fair of 1893 before the American Historical Association. Although Jackson did not publish a great deal, this essay alone made him one of the most famous historians in American studies.

In a recent bulletin of the Superintendent of the Census for 1890 appear these significant words: "Up to and including 1880 the country had a frontier of settlement, but at present the unsettled area has been so broken into by isolated bodies of settlement that there can hardly be said to be a frontier line. In the discussion of its extent, its westward movement, etc., it can not therefore, any longer have a place in the census reports." This brief official statement marks the closing of a great historic movement. Up to our own day American history has been in a large degree the history of the colonization of the Great West. The existence of an area of free land, its continuous recession, and the advance of American settlement westward, explain American development.

Behind institutions, behind constitutional forms and modifications, lie the vital forces that call these organs into life and shape them to meet changing conditions. The peculiarity of American institutions is, the fact that they have been compelled to adapt themselves to the changes of an expanding people—to the changes involved in crossing a continent, in winning a wilderness, and in developing at each area of this progress out of the primitive economic and political conditions of the frontier into the complexity of city life. Said Calhoun in 1817, "We are great, and rapidly—I was about to say fearfully—growing!" So saying, he touched the distinguishing feature of American life. All peoples show development; the germ theory of politics has been sufficiently emphasized. In the case of most nations, however, the development has occurred in a limited area; and if the nation has expanded, it has met other growing peoples whom it has conquered. But in the case of the United States we have a different phenomenon. Limiting our attention to the Atlantic coast, we have the familiar phenomenon of the evolution of institutions in a limited area, such as the rise of representative government; the differentiation of simple colonial governments into complex organs; the progress from primitive industrial society, without division of labor, up to manufacturing civilization. But we have in addition to this a recurrence of the process of evolution in each western area reached in the process of expansion. Thus American development has exhibited not merely advance along a single line, but a return to primitive conditions on a continually advancing frontier line, and a new development for that area. American social development has been continually beginning over again on the frontier. This perennial rebirth, this fluidity of American life, this expansion westward with its new opportunities, its continuous touch with the simplicity of primitive society, furnish the forces dominating American character. The true point of view in the history of this nation is not the Atlantic coast, it is the great West. Even the slavery struggle, which is made so exclusive an object of attention by writers like Professor von Holst, occupies its important place in American history because of its relation to westward expansion.

In this advance, the frontier is the outer edge of the wave—the meeting point between savagery and civilization. Much has been written about the frontier from the point of view of border warfare and the chase, but as a field for the serious study of the economist and the historian it has been neglected.

The American frontier is sharply distinguished from the European frontier—a fortified boundary line running through dense populations. The most significant thing about the American frontier is, that it lies at the hither edge of free land. In the census reports it is treated as the margin of that settlement which has a density of two or more to the square mile. The term is an elastic one, and for our purposes does not need sharp definition. We shall consider the whole frontier belt, including the Indian country and the outer margin of the "settled area" of the census reports. This paper will make no attempt to treat the subject exhaustively; its aim is simply to call attention to the frontier as a fertile field for investigation, and to suggest some of the problems which arise in connection with it.

In the settlement of America we have to observe how European life 5 entered the continent, and how America modified and developed that life and reacted on Europe. Our early history is the study of European germs developing in an American environment. Too exclusive attention has been paid by institutional students to the Germanic origins, too little to the American factors. The frontier is the line of most rapid and effective Americanization. The wilderness masters the colonist. It finds him a European in dress, industries, tools, modes of travel, and thought. It takes him from the railroad car and puts him in the birch canoe. It strips off the garments of civilization and arrays him in the hunting shirt and the moccasin. It puts him in the log cabin of the Cherokee and Iroquois and runs an Indian palisade around him. Before long he has gone to planting Indian corn and plowing with a sharp stick; he shouts the war cry and takes the scalp in orthodox Indian fashion. In short, at the frontier the environment is at first too strong for the man. He must accept the conditions which it furnishes, or perish, and so he fits himself into the Indian clearings and follows the Indian trails. Little by little he transforms the wilderness, but the outcome is not the old Europe, not simply the development of Germanic germs, any more than the first phenomenon was a case of reversion to the Germanic mark. The fact is, that here is a new product that is American. At first, the frontier was the Atlantic coast. It was the frontier of Europe in a very real sense. Moving westward, the frontier became more and more American. As successive terminal moraines result from successive glaciations, so each frontier leaves its traces behind it, and when it becomes a settled area the region still partakes of the frontier characteristics. Thus the advance of the frontier has meant a steady movement away from the influence of Europe, a steady growth of independence on American lines. And to study this advance, the men who grew up under these conditions, and the political, economic, and social results of it, is to study the really American part of our history. . . .

The Frontier Furnishes a Field for Comparative Study of Social Development

At the Atlantic frontier one can study the germs of processes repeated at each successive frontier. We have the complex European life sharply precipitated by the wilderness into the simplicity of primitive conditions. The first frontier had to meet its Indian question, its question of the disposition of the public domain, of the means of intercourse with older settlements, of the extension of political organization, of religious and educational activity. And the settlement of these and similar questions for one frontier served as a guide for the next. The American student needs not to go to the "prim little townships of Sleswick" for illustrations of the law of continuity and development. For example, he may study the origin of our land policies in the colonial land policy; he may see how the system grew by adapting the statutes to the customs of the successive frontiers. He may see how the mining experience in the lead regions of Wisconsin, Illinois, and Iowa was applied to the mining laws of the Rockies, and how our Indian policy has been a series of experimentations on successive frontiers. Each tier of new States has found in the older ones material for its constitutions. Each frontier has made similar contributions to American character, as will be discussed farther on.

But with all these similarities there are essential differences, due to the place element and the time element. It is evident that the farming frontier of the Mississippi Valley presents different conditions from the mining frontier of the Rocky Mountains. The frontier reached by the Pacific Railroad, surveyed into rectangles, guarded by the United States Army, and recruited by the daily immigrant ship, moves forward at a swifter pace and in a different way than the frontier reached by the birch canoe or the pack horse. The geologist traces patiently the shores of ancient seas, maps their areas, and compares the older and the newer. It would be a work worth the historian's labors to mark these various frontiers and in detail compare one with another. Not only would there result a more adequate conception of American development and characteristics, but invaluable additions would be made to the history of society.

Loria, the Italian economist, has urged the study of colonial life as an aid in understanding the stages of European development, affirming that colonial settlement is for economic science what the mountain is for geology, bringing to light primitive stratifications. "America," he says, "has the key to the historical enigma which Europe has sought for centuries in vain, and the land which has no history reveals luminously the course of universal history." There is much truth in this. The United States lies like a huge page in the history of society. Line by line as we read this continental page from west to east we find the record of social evolution. It begins with the Indian and the hunter; it goes on to tell of the disintegration of savagery by the entrance of the trader, the pathfinder of civilization; we read the annals of the pastoral stage in ranch life; the exploitation of the soil by the raising of unrotated crops of corn and wheat in sparsely settled farming communities; the intensive culture of the denser farm settlement; and finally the manufacturing organization with city and factory system. This page is familiar to the student of census statistics, but how little of it has been used by our historians. Particularly in eastern States this page is a palimpsest. What is now a manufacturing State was in an earlier decade an area of intensive farming. Earlier yet it had been a wheat area, and still earlier the "range" had attracted the cattle herder. Thus Wisconsin, now developing manufacture, is a State with varied agricultural interests. But earlier it was given over to almost exclusive grain-raising, like North Dakota at the present time.

Each of these areas has had an influence in our economic and political history; the evolution of each into a higher stage has worked political transformations. But what constitutional historian has made any adequate attempt to interpret political facts by the light of these social areas and changes?

The Atlantic frontier was compounded of fisherman, fur-trader, 10
miner, cattle-raiser, and farmer. Excepting the fisherman, each type of
industry was on the march toward the West, impelled by an irresistible attraction. Each passed in successive waves across the continent. Stand at Cumberland Gap and watch the procession of
civilization, marching single file—the buffalo following the trail to the
salt springs, the Indian, the fur-trader and hunter, the cattle-raiser, the
pioneer farmer—and the frontier has passed by. Stand at South Pass in
the Rockies a century later and see the same procession with wider intervals between. The unequal rate of advance compels us to distinguish the frontier into the trader's frontier, the rancher's frontier, or
the miner's frontier, and the farmer's frontier. When the mines and the
cow pens were still near the fall line the traders' pack trains were tin-
kling across the Alleghenies, and the French on the Great Lakes were
fortifying their posts, alarmed by the British trader's birch canoe.
When the trappers scaled the Rockies, the farmer was still near the
mouth of the Missouri. . . .

Land

The exploitation of the beasts took hunter and trader to the west,
the exploitation of the grasses took the rancher west, and the exploitation of the virgin soil of the river valleys and prairies attracted the
farmer. Good soils have been the most continuous attraction to the
farmer's frontier. The land hunger of the Virginians drew them down
the rivers into Carolina, in early colonial days; the search for soils took
the Massachusetts men to Pennsylvania and to New York. As the eastern lands were taken up migration flowed across them to the west.
Daniel Boone, the great backwoodsman, who combined the occupations of hunter, trader, cattle-raiser, farmer, and surveyor—learning,
probably from the traders, of the fertility of the lands on the upper
Yadkin, where the traders were wont to rest as they took their way to
the Indians, left his Pennsylvania home with his father, and passed
down the Great Valley road to that stream. Learning from a trader
whose posts were on the Red River in Kentucky of its game and rich
pastures, he pioneered the way for the farmers to that region. Thence
he passed to the frontier of Missouri, where his settlement was long a
landmark on the frontier. Here again he helped to open the way for
civilization, finding salt licks, and trails, and land. His son was among
the earliest trappers in the passes of the Rocky Mountains, and his
party are said to have been the first to camp on the present site of Den-
ver. His grandson, Col. A. J. Boone, of Colorado, was a power among
the Indians of the Rocky Mountains, and was appointed an agent by
the Government. Kit Carson's mother was a Boone. Thus this family
epitomizes the backwoodsman's advance across the continent. . . .

Composite Nationality

First, we note that the frontier promoted the formation of a composite nationality for the American people. The coast was preponderantly English, but the later tides of continental immigration flowed across to the free lands. This was the case from the early colonial days. The Scotch-Irish and the Palatine Germans, or "Pennsylvania Dutch," furnished the dominant element in the stock of the colonial frontier. With these peoples were also the freed indentured servants, or redemptioners, who at the expiration of their time of service passed to the frontier. Governor Spottswood of Virginia writes in 1717, "The inhabitants of our frontiers are composed generally of such as have been transported hither as servants, and, being out of their time, settle themselves where land is to be taken up and that will produce the necessarys of life with little labour." Very generally these redemptioners were of non-English stock. In the crucible of the frontier the immigrants were Americanized, liberated, and fused into a mixed race, English in neither nationality nor characteristics. The process has gone on from the early days to our own. Burke and other writers in the middle of the eighteenth century believed that Pennsylvania was "threatened with the danger of being wholly foreign in language, manners, and perhaps even inclinations." The German and Scotch-Irish elements in the frontier of the South were only less great. In the middle of the present century the German element in Wisconsin was already so considerable that leading publicists looked to the creation of a German state out of the commonwealth by concentrating their colonization. Such examples teach us to beware of misinterpreting the fact that there is a common English speech in America into a belief that the stock is also English.

Industrial Independence

In another way the advance of the frontier decreased our dependence on England. The coast, particularly of the South, lacked diversified industries, and was dependent on England for the bulk of its supplies. In the South there was even a dependence on the Northern colonies for articles of food. Governor Glenn, of South Carolina, writes in the middle of the eighteenth century: "Our trade with New York and Philadelphia was of this sort, draining us of all the little money and bills we could gather from other places for their bread, flour, beer, hams, bacon, and other things of their produce, all which, except beer, our new townships begin to supply us with, which are settled with very industrious and thriving Germans. This no doubt diminishes the number of shipping and the appearance of our trade, but it is far from being a detriment to us." Before long the frontier created a demand for merchants. As it retreated from the coast it became less and less possible for England to bring her supplies directly to the consumer's wharfs, and carry away staple crops, and staple crops began to give way to diversified agriculture for a time. The effect of this phase of the frontier action upon the northern section is perceived when we realize how the advance of the frontier aroused seaboard cities like Boston, New York, and Baltimore, to engage in rivalry for what Washington called "the extensive and valuable trade of a rising empire." . . .

Growth of Democracy

But the most important effect of the frontier has been in the promotion of democracy here and in Europe. As has been indicated, the frontier is productive of individualism. Complex society is precipitated by the wilderness into a kind of primitive organization based on the family. The tendency is anti-social. It produces antipathy to control, and particularly to any direct control. The tax gatherer is viewed as a representative of oppression. Professor Osgood, in an able article, has pointed out that the frontier conditions prevalent in the colonies are important factors in the explanation of the American Revolution, where individual liberty was sometimes confused with absence of all effective government. The same conditions aid in explaining the difficulty of instituting a strong government in the period of the confederacy. The frontier individualism has from the beginning promoted democracy.

The frontier States that came into the Union in the first quarter of a 15 century of its existence came in with democratic suffrage provisions, and had reactive effects of the highest importance upon the older States whose peoples were being attracted there. An extension of the franchise became essential. It was *western* New York that forced an extension of suffrage in the constitutional convention of that State in 1821; and it was *western* Virginia that compelled the tide-water region to put a more liberal suffrage provision in the constitution framed in 1830, and to give to the frontier region a more nearly proportionate representation with the tide-water aristocracy. The rise of democracy as an effective force in the nation came in with western preponderance under Jackson and William Henry Harrison, and it meant the triumph of the frontier—with all of its good and with all of its evil elements. . . .

So long as free land exists, the opportunity for a competency exists, and economic power secures political power. But the democracy born of free land, strong in selfishness and individualism, intolerant of administrative experience and education, and pressing individual liberty beyond its proper bounds, has its dangers as well as its benefits. Individualism in America has allowed a laxity in regard to governmental affairs which has rendered possible the spoils system and all the manifest evils that follow from the lack of a highly developed civic spirit. In this connection may be noted also the influence of frontier conditions in permitting lax business honor, inflated paper currency and wild-cat banking. The colonial and revolutionary frontier was the region whence emanated many of the worst forms of an evil currency. The West in the War of 1812 repeated the phenomenon on the frontier of that day, while the speculation and the wild-cat banking of the period of the crisis of 1837 occurred on the new frontier belt of the next tier of States. Thus each one of the periods of lax financial integrity coincides with periods when a new set of frontier communities had arisen, and coincides in area with these successive frontiers, for the most part. The recent Populist agitation is a case in point. Many a State that now declines any connection with the tenets of the Populists, itself adhered to such ideas in an earlier stage of the development of the State. A primitive society can hardly be expected to show the intelligent appreciation of the complexity of business interests in a developed society. The continual recurrence of these areas of paper-money agitation is another evidence that the frontier can be isolated and studied as a factor in American history of the highest importance. . . .

Intellectual Traits

From the conditions of frontier life came intellectual traits of profound importance. The works of travelers along each frontier from colonial days onward describe certain common traits, and these traits have, while softening down, still persisted as survivals in the place of their origin, even when a higher social organization succeeded. The result is that to the frontier the American intellect owes its striking characteristics. That coarseness and strength combined with acuteness and inquisitiveness; that practical, inventive turn of mind, quick to find expedients; that masterful grasp of material things, lacking in the artistic but powerful to effect great ends; that restless, nervous energy; that dominant individualism, working for good and for evil, and withal that buoyancy and exuberance which comes with freedom—these are traits of the frontier. Since the days when the fleet of Columbus sailed into the waters of the New World, America has been another name for opportunity, and the people of the United States have taken their tone from the incessant expansion which has not only been open but has even been forced upon them. He would be a rash prophet who should assert that the expansive character of American life has now entirely ceased. Movement has been its dominant fact, and, unless this training has no effect upon a people, the American energy will continually demand a wider field for its exercise. But never again will such gifts of free land offer themselves. For a moment, at the frontier, the bonds of custom are broken and unrestraint is triumphant. There is not *tabula rasa.* The stubborn American environment is there with its imperious summons to accept its conditions; the inherited ways of doing things are also there; and yet, in spite of environment, and in spite of custom, each frontier did indeed furnish a new field of opportunity, a gate of escape from the bondage of the past; and freshness, and confidence, and scorn of older society, impatience of its restraints and its ideas, and indifference to its lessons, have accompanied the frontier. What the Mediterranean Sea was to the Greeks, breaking the bond of custom, offering new experiences, calling out new institutions and activities, that, and more, the ever retreating frontier has been to the United States directly, and to the nations of Europe more remotely. And now, four centuries from the discovery of America, at the end of a hundred years of life under the Constitution, the frontier has gone, and with its going has closed the first period of American history.

For Journals

What is your own idea of what the American frontier represents? Cowboys and Indians? The Gold Rush? The space program? Movie westerns?

For Discussion

1. Turner saw the existence of a frontier as crucial to the formation of the American character and American democracy. What are his premises in this argument? What evidence does he provide to support them?

2. How do you respond to Turner's assertion that the frontier was the meeting point between civilization and savagery "the outer edge of the wave—" (paragraph 3)? How positively do you regard the idea of settlers moving through the frontier in order to create a different and distinctly American civilization?

3. Why does Turner see the life of Daniel Boone as a prototype of the frontiersman? What combination of elements makes Boone, in Turner's thesis, so suitable an example of the positive side of westward expansion?

4. How do you think Turner defines the idea of progress in American civilization? Progress from what to what? What do you think of as an example of progress in America?

5. One writer has said that Turner's essay is not *an* explanation of American history but rather *the* explanation of American history. Why would an analysis of the frontier be an analysis of American history altogether?

6. Turner said that the frontier had made the American character expansive, and that once the free land disappeared, Americans would have to find other ways of stretching their horizons. Where do you think Americans have turned to find psychological substitutions for the western frontier?

For Writing

1. Watch a video of one of the following movies: *High Noon; Shane; A Fistful of Dollars; Little Big Man; She Wore a Yellow Ribbon; Unforgiven.* Then write an essay in which you address the following issues: What picture does the movie give of life in the West? How closely does that picture coincide with your own idea of that life? What are the primary ethical and social values expressed in the movie, and who in the film embodies them?

2. Since it was written, there have been many revisions of Turner's thesis. Read one of them, such as David Potter's *People of Plenty*, and then write your own evaluation of whether the revision refutes all of Turner's claims effectively. Then write your own response to Turner's ideas.

∽ The Thesis Disputed (1949)

RICHARD HOFSTADTER

Richard Hofstadter (1916–1970) was a highly original American historian who spent his career at Columbia University. His amazingly diverse body of work paid particular attention to the importance of ideas in American history and to the development of political institutions. He won the Pulitzer Prize twice. When he wrote this essay, the most famous analysis of Frederick Jackson Turner's thesis on the role of the frontier in American history, the thesis had just undergone a period of attack by other historians. Hofstadter was able to appreciate the significance as well as the faults of Turner's theory.

American historical writing in the past century has produced two major theories or models of understanding, the economic interpretation of politics associated with Charles A. Beard, and the frontier interpretation of American development identified with Frederick Jackson Turner. Both views have had a pervasive influence upon American thinking, but Beard himself felt that Turner's original essay on the frontier had "a more profound influence on thought about American history than any other essay or volume ever written on the subject." It is the frontier thesis that has embodied the predominant American view of the American past. . . .

American evolution, Turner believed, had been a repeated return to primitive conditions on a continually receding frontier line, a constant repetition of development from simple conditions to a complex society. From this perennial rebirth and fluidity of American life, and from its continual re-exposure to the simplicity of primitive society, had come the forces dominant in the American character. And as the frontier advanced, society moved steadily away from European influences, grew steadily on distinctive American lines. To study this advance and the men who had been fashioned by it was "to study the really American part of our history."

Of all the effects of the frontier, the most important was that it promoted democracy and individualism. So long as free land existed, there was always opportunity for a man to acquire a competency, and economic power secured political power. Each succeeding frontier furnished "a new field of opportunity, a gate of escape from the bondage of the past." The lack of binding tradition and organized restraints promoted a distinctively American passion for individual freedom, antipathy to direct control from outside, aggressive self-interest, and intolerance of education and administrative experience. But by the year 1890, this process had come to an end; the frontier, the hither edge of unsettled land, no longer existed, and with its passing the first epoch of American history had closed. . . .

The initial plausibility of the Turner thesis lies in the patent fact that no nation could spend more than a century developing an immense continental empire without being deeply affected by it. Few critics question the great importance of the inland empire, or that Turner originally performed a service for historical writing by directing attention to it. Many accept Turner's emphasis on the frontier as one of several valid but limited perspectives on American history. But it has been forcefully denied that the frontier deserves any special preeminence among several major factors in "explaining" American development. The question has also been raised (and frequently answered in the negative) whether Turner analyzed the frontier process itself clearly or correctly.

It became plain, as new thought and research was brought to bear 5 upon the problem, that the frontier theory, as an analytic device, was a blunt instrument. The terms with which the Turnerians dealt— the frontier, the West, individualism, the American character—were vague at the outset, and as the Turnerian exposition developed, they did not receive increasingly sharp definition. Precisely because Turner defined the frontier so loosely ("the term," he said, "is an elastic one"), he could claim so much for it. At times he referred to the frontier literally as the edge of the settled territory having a population density of two to the square mile. But frequently he identified "the frontier" and "the West," so that areas actually long settled could be referred to as frontier. At times he spoke of both the "frontier" and the "West" not as places or areas, but as a social process: "The West, at bottom, is a form of society rather than an area." When this definition is followed to its logical conclusion, the development of American society is "explained" by "a form of society"—certainly a barren tautology. Again, at times Turner assimilated such natural resources as coal, oil, timber, to the idea of "the West"; in this way the truism that natural wealth has an important bearing upon a nation's development and characteristics was subtly absorbed into the mystique of the frontier and took on the guise of a major insight.

However, the central weakness of Turner's thesis was in its intellectual isolationism. Having committed himself to an initial overemphasis on the uniqueness of the historical development of the United States, Turner compounded the error by overemphasizing the frontier as a factor in this development. The obsession with uniqueness, the subtly demagogic stress on "the truly American part of our history," diverted the attention of historical scholarship from the possibilities of comparative social history; it offered no opportunity to explain why so many features of American development—for example, the rise of democracy in the nineteenth century—were parallel to changes in countries that did not have a contiguous frontier. Historians were encouraged to omit a host of basic influences common to both American and Western European development—the influence of Protestantism and the Protestant ethic, the inheritance from English republicanism, the growth of industrialism and urbanism. More than this, factors outside the frontier process that contributed to the singularity of American history were skipped over: the peculiar American federal structure, the slave system and the Southern caste complex, immigration and ethnic heterogeneity, the unusually capitalistic and speculative character of American agriculture, the American inheritance of *laissez faire.* The interpretation seems particularly weak for the corporate-industrial phase of American history that followed the Civil War. Indeed, if the historian's range of vision had to be limited to one explanatory idea, as it fortunately does not, one could easily argue that the business corporation was the dominant dynamic factor in American development during this period.

As a form of geographical determinism, the frontier interpretation is vulnerable on still another ground. If the frontier alone was a self-sufficient source of democracy and individualism, whatever the institutions and ideas the frontiersmen brought with them, frontiers elsewhere ought to have had a similar effect. The early frontier of seignorial French Canada, the South American frontier, and the Siberian frontier should have fostered democracy and individualism. The frontier should have forged the same kind of democracy when planters came to Mississippi as when yeomen farmers came to Illinois.

Turner's dictum, "American democracy came out of the American forest," proved to be a questionable improvement upon the notion of his predecessors that it came out of the German forest. Plainly the whole complex of institutions, habits and ideas that men brought to the frontier was left out of his formula, and it was these things, not bare geography, that had been decisive. Turner's analysis, as George Warren Pierson aptly put it, hung too much on real estate, not enough on a state of mind. . . .

One of the most criticized aspects of Turner's conception of American history, the so-called safety-valve thesis, maintains that the availability of free land as a refuge for the oppressed and discontented has alleviated American social conflicts, minimized industrial strife, and contributed to the backwardness of the American labor movement. As Turner expressed it, the American worker was never compelled to accept inferior wages because he could "with a slight effort" reach free country and set up in farming. "Whenever social conditions tended to crystallize in the East, whenever capital tended to impede the freedom of the mass, there was this gate of escape to the free conditions of the frontier," where "free lands promoted individualism, economic equality, freedom to rise, democracy."

The expression "free land" is itself misleading. Land was relatively cheap in the United States during the nineteenth century, but the difference between free land and cheap land was crucial. Up to 1820 the basic price of land was $2.00 an acre, and for years afterward it was $1.25. Slight as it may seem, this represented a large sum to the Eastern worker, whose wage was generally about $1.00 a day. Economic historians have estimated that during the 1850s, $1,000 represented a fairly typical cost for setting up a farm on virgin prairie land, or buying an established one; and the cost of transporting a worker's family from, say, Massachusetts or New York to Illinois or Iowa was a serious additional burden. Farming, moreover, is no enterprise for an amateur, nor one at which he has a good chance of success. The value of "free land" in alleviating distress has been challenged by several writers who have pointed out that periods of depression were the very periods when it was most difficult for the Eastern worker to move. Scattered instances of working-class migration to the West can be pointed to, but detailed studies of the origins of migrants have failed to substantiate the Turner thesis. . . .

Finally, Turner acknowledged but failed to see the full importance 10 for his thesis of the fact that the United States not only had a frontier but was a frontier—a major outlet for the countries of Western Europe during the nineteenth century. From 1820 to 1929, the total European emigration to the United States was more than 37,500,000—a number only a million short of the entire population of the United States in 1870. In one decade alone, 1901–1910, 8,795,000 people came from Europe. If Europe shared to such a major extent in this safety-valve economy, its uniqueness for American development must be considerably modified. The mingling of peoples that took place in the United States must be placed alongside the presence of "free land" in explaining American development; the closure of the American gates after the First World War becomes an historical event of broader significance than the disappearance of the frontier line in 1890. And the facts of immigration probably provide a better key to the character of the American labor movement than any speculation about the effects of "free land" upon workers who could not reach it.

It should be added, in justice to Turner, that his historical writing was better than his frontier thesis, and not least because he regularly made use in practice of historical factors which were not accounted for in his theory. Although he often stated his ideas with the vigor of a propagandist, his was not a doctrinaire mind, and he was willing, as time went on, to add new concepts to his analysis. In 1925 he went so far as to admit the need of "an urban reinterpretation of our history." "I hope," he frequently said, "to propagate inquiry, not to produce disciples." In fact he did both, but he propagated less inquiry among his disciples than among his critics.

For Journals

Hofstadter says he is revising Turner, but in effect he comes up with a thesis of his own. How would you state Hofstadter's central idea?

For Discussion

1.   What do you think Hofstadter means when he states that, as an analytic device, Turner's frontier theory is "a blunt instrument" (paragraph 5)? What kinds of problems in Turner's approach does that phrase suggest?

2.   Hofstadter accuses Turner of intellectual isolationism. In revising Turner's thesis, what kinds of evidence does he include that he says Turner failed to consider in developing his ideas?

3.   Hofstadter revises Turner but does not reject him. Where do you find points of agreement or overlap in their theories?

4.   Hofstadter thought that Turner overstated the significance of rural life in American history at the expense of the city. Which do you think—rural life or urban life—was more significant as a source of values? Of power?

5.   Based on your other readings in this book, what do you think of Hofstadter's assertion that emigration to America of millions of people from Europe is a better key to the American character than the idea of available free land in the West?

6. Look back over Turner's thesis and Hofstadter's revision. Which one is more satisfying to you? Intellectually, are they equally interesting? Which one coincides more with your own ideas about why America developed as it did?

For Writing

1. In your college library, look for primary and secondary materials, including books, periodicals, or photographs, as material for a research paper on one of the following topics: African American cowboys and the West; the great Mexican ranches of California; the Indian cultures of the Southwest; or any other group that is not a part of Turner's thesis. You could focus on an aspect of this group's life in frontier days (for example, influential individuals, significant events, or contributions to American culture). How does being aware of the group cause you to revise your image of the frontier?

2. Turner and Hofstadter are both interested in the idea of American progress. Write an essay about a change in American life that has come about in your own lifetime that you think represents real progress. Is it a result of technology, or of social and political change? Why do you think this change is important? For contrast, you might ask someone in your parents' generation what they think of as a major contribution to progress in America.

∞ *"Indian Belle" crate label* (ca. 1920)

Decorative labels for wooden fruit and vegetable crates were designed to attract attention to a grower's produce at food auctions and distinguish his product from other farmers' produce. The labels remained very popular before World War II, when wood was needed for the war effort and wooden crates were replaced by metal ones. The labels had as their subjects anything from ethnic stereotypes to famous presidents to animals, flowers, and scenery. Porterville, California, the source of the oranges being advertised, is in the Central Valley, which became the richest agricultural land in the United States in the twentieth century.

For Journals

What do you think an honest and/or attractive image of your state would be? Why?

For Discussion

1. Look up the term "belle" in the dictionary. How was it traditionally applied, and why is it being used here?

2. Look at the young Indian couple. How would you describe their clothing, their posture, and their expressions? How would they be dressed if they were a white courting couple?

3. Crate labels are now much prized by collectors. Why do you think people want to have them?

For Writing

1. Research and write a paper on crate labels from your state or your part of the country, or from another state such as Florida, New York, California, Pennsylvania, Georgia, and others. There are several books with color illustrations of crate label art from different parts of the country, including *Fruit Crate Art*, by Joe Davidson. You can also write to the American Antiques Graphic Society, P.O. Box 924, Medina,

Ohio 44256, for further information on crate labels or other ephemera (perishable older items such as games, dolls, plastics, etc.). Points to consider include exactly what the label or other ephemera looks like; what its intended use was; who was expected to either buy or use it; whether it's a beautiful or enjoyable creation; and what became of the category to which it belongs. For example, if you did a paper on yoyos, you'd want to see what the newest ones look like, and whether there was any improvement over the originals.

2.   Write an essay based on question 2 above.

∽ *Coda: Wilderness Letter* (1960)

WALLACE STEGNER

Wallace Stegner (1909–1993) grew up in Canada and the American West, and much of his writing, including his novels and essays, reflects his love for the wilderness. Stegner was active in the conservationist movement, often working with photographer Ansel Adams to promote national parks and a balance between development and the preservation of open space. The recipient of both the National Book Award and the Pulitzer Prize, Stegner founded the Creative writing Program at Stanford University.

Los Altos, Calif.
December 3, 1960

David E. Pesonen
Wildland Research Center
Agricultural Experiment Station
243 Mulford Hall
University of California
Berkeley 4, Calif.

Dear Mr. Pesonen:
I believe that you are working on the wilderness portion of the Outdoor Recreation Resources Review Commission's report. If I may, I should like to urge some arguments for wilderness preservation that involve recreation, as it is ordinarily conceived, hardly at all. Hunting, fishing, hiking, mountain-climbing, camping, photography, and the enjoyment of natural scenery will all, surely, figure in your report. So will the wilderness as a genetic reserve, a scientific yardstick by which we may measure the world in its natural balance against the world in its manmade imbalance. What I want to speak for is not so much the wilderness uses, valuable as those are, but the wilderness *idea*, which is a resource in itself. Being an intangible and spiritual resource, it will seem mystical to the practical-minded—but then anything that cannot be moved by a bulldozer is likely to seem mystical to them.

I want to speak for the wilderness idea as something that has helped form our character and that has certainly shaped our history as a people. It has no more to do with recreation than churches have to do with recreation, or than the strenuousness and optimism and expansiveness of what historians call the "American Dream" have to do with recreation. Nevertheless, since it is only in this recreation survey that the values of wilderness are being compiled, I hope you will permit me to insert this idea between the leaves, as it were, of the recreation report.

Something will have gone out of us as a people if we ever let the remaining wilderness be destroyed; if we permit the last virgin forests to be turned into comic books and plastic cigarette cases; if we drive the few remaining members of the wild species into zoos or to extinction; if we pollute the last clear air and dirty the last clean streams and push our paved roads through the last of the silence, so that never again will Americans be free in their own country from the noise, the exhausts, the stinks of human and automotive waste. And so that never again can we have the chance to see ourselves single, separate, vertical and individual in the world, part of the environment of trees and rocks and soil, brother to the other animals, part of the natural world and competent to belong in it. Without any remaining wilderness we are committed wholly, without chance for even momentary reflection and rest, to a headlong drive into our technological termite-life, the Brave New World of a completely man-controlled environment. We need wilderness preserved—as much of it as is still left, and as many kinds—because it was the challenge against which our character as a people was formed. The reminder and the reassurance that it is still there is good for our spiritual health even if we never once in ten years set foot in it. It is good for us when we are young, because of the incomparable sanity it can bring briefly, as vacation and rest, into our insane lives. It is important to us when we are old simply because it is there—important, that is, simply as idea.

We are a wild species, as Darwin pointed out. Nobody ever tamed or domesticated or scientifically bred us. But for at least three millennia we have been engaged in a cumulative and ambitious race to modify and gain control of our environment, and in the process we have come close to domesticating ourselves. Not many people are likely, any more, to look upon what we call "progress" as an unmixed blessing. Just as surely as it has brought us increased comfort and more material goods, it has brought us spiritual losses, and it threatens now to become the Frankenstein that will destroy us. One means of sanity is to retain a hold on the natural world, to remain, insofar as we can, good animals. Americans still have that chance, more than many peoples; for while we were demonstrating ourselves the most efficient and ruthless environment-busters in history, and slashing and burning and cutting our way through a wilderness continent, the wilderness was working on us. It remains in us as surely as Indian names remain on the land. If the abstract dream of human liberty and human dignity became, in America, something more than an abstract dream, mark it down at least partially to the fact that we were in subtle ways subdued by what we conquered.

The Connecticut Yankee, sending likely candidates from King 5 Arthur's unjust kingdom to his Man Factory for rehabilitation, was over-optimistic, as he later admitted. These things cannot be forced, they have to grow. To make such a man, such a democrat, such a believer in human individual dignity, as Mark Twain himself, the frontier was necessary, Hannibal and the Mississippi and Virginia City, and reaching out from those the wilderness; the wilderness as opportunity and as idea, the thing that has helped to make an American different from and, until we forget it in the roar of our industrial cities, more fortunate than other men. For an American, insofar as he is new and different at all, is a civilized man who has renewed himself in the wild. The American experience has been the confrontation by old peoples and cultures of a world as new as if it had just risen from the sea. That gave us our hope and our excitement, and the hope and excitement can be passed on to newer Americans, Americans who never saw any phase of the frontier. But only so long as we keep the remainder of our wild as a reserve and a promise—a sort of wilderness bank.

As a novelist, I may perhaps be forgiven for taking literature as a reflection, indirect but profoundly true, of our national consciousness. And our literature, as perhaps you are aware, is sick, embittered, losing its mind, losing its faith. Our novelists are the declared enemies of their society. There has hardly been a serious or important novel in this century that did not repudiate in part or in whole American technological culture for its commercialism, its vulgarity, and the way in which it has dirtied a clean continent and a clean dream. I do not expect that the preservation of our remaining wilderness is going to cure this condition. But the mere example that we can as a nation apply some other criteria than commercial and exploitative considerations would be heartening to many Americans, novelists or otherwise. We need to demonstrate our acceptance of the natural world, including ourselves; we need the spiritual refreshment that being natural can produce. And one of the best places for us to get that is in the wilderness where the fun houses, the bulldozers, and the pavements of our civilization are shut out.

Sherwood Anderson, in a letter to Waldo Frank in the 1920s, said it better than I can. "Is it not likely that when the country was new and men were often alone in the fields and the forest they got a sense of bigness outside themselves that has now in some way been lost. . . . Mystery whispered in the grass, played in the branches of trees overhead, was caught up and blown across the American line in clouds of dust at evening on the prairies. . . . I am old enough to remember tales that strengthen my belief in a deep semi-religious influence that was formerly at work among our people. The flavor of it hangs over the best work of Mark Twain. . . . I can remember old fellows in my home town speaking feelingly of an evening spent on the big empty plains. It had taken the shrillness out of them. They had learned the trick of quiet. . . ."

We could learn it too, even yet; even our children and grandchildren could learn it. But only if we save, for just such absolutely non-recreational, impractical, and mystical uses as this, all the wild that still remains to us.

It seems to me significant that the distinct downturn in our literature from hope to bitterness took place almost at the precise time when the frontier officially came to an end, in 1890, and when the American way of life had begun to turn strongly urban and industrial. The more urban it has become, and the more frantic with technological change, the sicker and more embittered our literature, and I believe our people, have become. For myself, I grew up on the empty plains of Saskatchewan and Montana and in the mountains of Utah, and I put a very high valuation on what those places gave me. And if I had not been able periodically to renew myself in the mountains and deserts of western America I would be very nearly bughouse. Even when I can't get to the back country, the thought of the colored deserts of southern Utah, or the reassurance that there are still stretches of prairie where the world can be instantaneously perceived as disk and bowl, and where the little but intensely important human being is exposed to the five directions and the thirty-six winds, is a positive consolation. The idea alone can sustain me. But as the wilderness areas are progressively exploited or "improved," as the jeeps and bulldozers of uranium prospectors scar up the deserts and the roads are cut into the alpine timberlands, and as the remnants of the unspoiled and natural world are progressively eroded, every such loss is a little death in me. In us.

I am not moved by the argument that those wilderness areas 10 which have already been exposed to grazing or mining are already deflowered, and so might as well be "harvested." For mining I cannot say much good except that its operations are generally short-lived. The extractable wealth is taken and the shafts, the tailings, and the ruins left, and in a dry country such as the American West the wounds men make in the earth do not quickly heal. Still, they are only wounds; they aren't absolutely mortal. Better a wounded wilderness than none at all. And as for grazing, if it is strictly controlled so that it does not destroy the ground cover, damage the ecology, or compete with the wildlife it is in itself nothing that need conflict with the wilderness feeling or the validity of the wilderness experience. I have known enough range cattle to recognize them as wild animals; and the people who herd them have, in the wilderness context, the dignity of rareness; they belong on the frontier, moreover, and have a look of rightness. The invasion they make on the virgin country is a sort of invasion that is as old as Neolithic man, and they can, in moderation, even emphasize a man's feeling of belonging to the natural world. Under surveillance, they can belong; under control, they need not deface or mar. I do not believe that in wilderness areas where grazing has never been permitted, it should be permitted; but I do not believe either that an otherwise untouched wilderness should be eliminated from the preservation plan because of limited existing uses such as grazing which are in consonance with the frontier condition and image.

Let me say something on the subject of the kinds of wilderness worth preserving. Most of those areas contemplated are in the national forests and in high mountain country. For all the usual recreational purposes, the alpine and forest wildernesses are obviously the most important, both as genetic banks and as beauty spots. But for the spiritual renewal, the recognition of identity, the birth of awe, other kinds will serve every bit as well. Perhaps, because they are less friendly to life, more abstractly nonhuman, they will serve even better. On our Saskatchewan prairie, the nearest neighbor was four miles away, and at night we saw only two lights on all the dark rounding earth. The earth was full of animals—field mice, ground squirrels, weasels, ferrets, badgers, coyotes, burrowing owls, snakes. I knew them as my little brothers, as fellow creatures, and I have never been able to look upon animals in any other way since. The sky in that country came clear down to the ground on every side, and it was full of great weathers, and clouds, and winds, and hawks. I hope I learned something from knowing intimately the creatures of the earth; I hope I learned something from looking a long way, from looking up, from being much alone. A prairie like that, one big enough to carry the eye clear to the sinking, rounding horizon, can be as lonely and grand and simple in its forms as the sea. It is as good a place as any for the wilderness experience to happen; the vanishing prairie is as worth preserving for the wilderness idea as the alpine forests.

So are great reaches of our western deserts, scarred somewhat by prospectors but otherwise open, beautiful, waiting, close to whatever God you want to see in them. Just as a sample, let me suggest the Robbers' Roost country in Wayne County, Utah, near the Capitol Reef National Monument. In that desert climate the dozer and jeep tracks will not soon melt back into the earth, but the country has a way of making the scars insignificant. It is a lovely and terrible wilderness, such a wilderness as Christ and the prophets went out into; harshly and beautifully colored, broken and worn until its bones are exposed, its great sky without a smudge or taint from Technocracy, and in hidden corners and pockets under its cliffs the sudden poetry of springs. Save a piece of country like that intact, and it does not matter in the slightest that only a few people every year will go into it. That is precisely its value. Roads would be a desecration, crowds would ruin it. But those who haven't the strength or youth to go into it and live can simply sit and look. They can look two hundred miles, clear into Colorado; and looking down over the cliffs and canyons of the San Rafael Swell and the Robbers' Roost they can also look as deeply into themselves as anywhere I know. And if they can't even get to the places on the Aquarius Plateau where the present roads will carry them, they can simply contemplate the *idea*, take pleasure in the fact that such a timeless and uncontrolled part of earth is still there.

These are some of the things wilderness can do for us. That is the reason we need to put into effect, for its preservation, some other principle than the principles of exploitation or "usefulness" or even recreation. We simply need that wild country available to us, even if we never do more than drive to its edge and look in. For it can be a means of reassuring ourselves of our sanity as creatures, a part of the geography of hope.

Very sincerely yours,
Wallace Stegner

For Journals

Do you go hiking or camping in national parks or other wilderness areas? If not, do you nevertheless support the idea of saving wilderness?

For Discussion

1. Stegner says that he wants to argue not for the wilderness but for the idea of the wilderness (paragraph 1). What do you think he means by the idea as opposed to the reality of the wilderness? Why should the idea be protected?

2. How did you respond to Stegner's assertion that Americans— even Americans who have never set foot in the wilderness—will lose the wilderness if it is destroyed?

3. How does Stegner think the development of technology and urban life have affected Americans? What advantage does he feel Americans who were exposed to the frontier gained?

4. Why does Stegner think that the relatively undramatic prairies and the deserts are as worthy of preservation as the more spectacular forest and alpine areas? How does emphasizing them help or harm his thesis?

5. Stegner was always interested in conflicting attitudes toward nature and development. Where do his sympathies lie? Yours?

For Writing

1. Write an essay about an urban place you know—an open space, a part of an old neighborhood, a small city park, a favorite store, a place that a parent used to take you to or that you shared with a childhood friend—and you want to see preserved. Explain its emotional and spiritual value to you and why you would like it to stay the way it is. Your research may include firsthand observation, interviews with other people familiar with the place, and library research. For example, if you are interested in an old movie theater, look for source materials on historic preservation and old movie palaces.

2. Write a paper in which you compare Stegner's and Turner's ideas of the wilderness. How does each man think the idea of the wilderness has shaped Americans? What represents progress to each author? In which instances does Stegner sound like Turner? Revise Turner? How did reading Stegner revise your reading of Turner?

∞ *Dear John Wayne* (1984)

LOUISE ERDRICH

Louise Erdrich (1954–) is a Native American novelist, poet, and essayist who teaches at Dartmouth College. She was born in Minnesota and grew up near a reservation in North Dakota, where her Native American mother and German father worked for the Bureau of Indian Affairs. She is the author of the novels Love Medicine *(1984),* The Beet Queen *(1986),* The Bingo Palace *(1994),* The Blue Jay's Dance *(1995), and* The Antelope Wife *(1998), as well as short stories and poems. She and her recently deceased husband, Michael Dorris, coauthored a novel,* The Crown of Columbus *(1991). "Dear John Wayne" is a wonderful example of Erdrich's ability to explore how differently white Americans and American Indians experience the mythology of the frontier.*

August and the drive-in picture is packed.
We lounge on the hood of the Pontiac
surrounded by the slow-burning spirals they sell

at the window, to vanquish the hordes of mosquitoes.
Nothing works. They break through the smoke-screen for blood.   5

Always the look-out spots the Indians first,
spread north to south, barring progress.
The Sioux, or Cheyenne, or some bunch
in spectacular columns, arranged like SAC missiles,
their feathers bristling in the meaningful sunset.   10

The drum breaks. There will be no parlance.
Only the arrows whining, a death-cloud of nerves
swarming down on the settlers
who die beautifully, tumbling like dust weeds
into the history that brought us all here   15
together: this wide screen beneath the sign of the bear.

The sky fills, acres of blue squint and eye
that the crowd cheers. His face moves over us,
a thick cloud of vengeance, pitted
like the land that was once flesh. Each rut,   20
each scar makes a promise: *It is*
not over, this fight, not as long as you resist.

Everything we see belongs to us.
A few laughing Indians fall over the hood
slipping in the hot spilled butter.   25
The eye sees a lot, John, but the heart is so blind.
How will you know what you own?
He smiles, a horizon of teeth
the credits reel over, and then the white fields
again blowing in the true-to-life dark.   30
The dark films over everything.
We get into the car
scratching our mosquito bites, speechless and small
as people are when the movie is done.
We are back in ourselves.   35

How can we help but keep hearing his voice,
the flip side of the sound-track, still playing:
Come on, boys, we've got them
where we want them, drunk, running.
They will give us what we want, what we need: 40
The heart is a strange wood inside of everything
we see, burning, doubling, splitting out of its skin.

For Journals

Where do your own ideas of the West come from? Movies? If so, which ones? What other sources? Where else could you find information about the West?

For Discussion

1. Read the poem out loud, all the way through. Then go back to the beginning, and in each stanza find three or four words that are either unexpected or particularly effective. What do they contribute to the theme of each stanza? How?

2. Compare this poem with the article and illustration from the *Police Gazette*. How does the view of Indians in the *Gazette* compare with the portrayal of them in the John Wayne movie? With the Indians watching the movie at the drive-in?

3. What values does the image of John Wayne usually represent? How does Erdrich's attitude toward him revise that image?

4. How do you think Erdrich would see the settling of the West compared with the way Turner sees it? Whose evidence do you find more persuasive? Why?

5. If the Indians had written the film script, how do you think they would write the battle scene? What kind of movie do you think they could make about whites and Indians on the frontier?

6. How does Erdrich use ironic details like the drive-in movie and the fact that the American Indians have a car named for an Indian chief to suggest Indians' ambivalence toward American culture and their place in it? What other examples of this irony can you find in the poem?

For Writing

Investigate books and scholarly articles for material on the Battle of Little Big Horn. Write a documented paper in which you compare an earlier version of the story—from newspaper stories at the time of the battle, or older books about it—with recent versions, such as Evan Connell's *Son of the Morning Star.* How have evaluations of Custer, his strategy, and the battle been revised?

∞ The Next Last Frontier (1993)

JONATHAN RABAN

Jonathan Raban (1942–) was born in Great Britain but lives in Seattle. He is the author of novels, literary criticism, and works of social commentary, travel, and explo-

ration. This selection is from an article he wrote for Harper's *magazine, after he had traveled through the Northwest from Washington State to Idaho to Montana.*

In the spring of 1990 I packed up as much of my life in London as would fit into four tea chests and flew to Seattle to set up house. It was a selfish and irregular move. I had "met someone" and liked what I'd seen of the Pacific Northwest during a two-month stay there in the autumn of 1989: the aquarium lighting, the sawtooth alps forested with black firs, the compact cities encrusted in Romanesque stucco. Most of all, I liked the place's wateriness. At forty-seven I felt cracked and dry. My new home territory was as rainy as Ireland, puddled with lakes and veined with big rivers. Seattle was built out on pilings over the sea, and at high tide the whole city seemed to come afloat like a ship lifting free from a mud berth and swaying in its chains.

We took a house on the wrong side of Queen Anne, the innermost of Seattle's hilltop suburbs. The tall wooden house, built like a boat from massive scantlings of Douglas fir, carvel-planked with cedar, had been put up in 1906, in the wake of the Yukon gold rush, when the hill was logged. It had warped and settled through a string of minor earthquakes: the floors sloped, doors hung askew in their frames. In the silence of the night, the house groaned and whiffled like a sleeping dog.

Barely a mile from the new banking and insurance skyscrapers of downtown, the house felt hidden away in the woods. Shaggy conifers, survivors of the original forest, darkened the views from every window. The study looked down over the Ship Canal, where trawlers stalked through an avenue of poplars on their way to the Alaskan fishing grounds, eight hundred miles to the north. From the deck on the top floor, one could see out over the pale suburbs, like shell middens, to the serrated line of the Cascade mountains, still snowcapped in May.

For someone fresh off the plane from London, it was a big prospect to take in, and a hard one in which to make oneself at home. It had been fine to be a tourist in this landscape, when I had been enjoyably awed by its far-western heights and distances; but now that I'd signed up as a permanent resident, the view from the window seemed only to reflect my own displacement here.

Even the very near-at-hand was strange. I kept Peterson's *Western Birds* and the Audubon Society's *Western Forests* by the typewriter. I made lists, and pinned them to the wall. *Redwood, cedar, cypress, dogwood, laurel, madrona, maple,* I wrote, trying to distinguish individual personalities in the jumble of damp and muddy greens framed by the window. I took the tree book down to the garden and matched the real-life barks with their pictures; the peeling, fish-scale skin of the lodgepole pine, the frayed hemp rope of the coast redwood. It took a month, at least, to be able to see the black-crested Steller's jay in the madrona

5

with something like the comfortable indifference with which I'd used to notice a song thrush in the sycamore in Battersea. It took a good deal longer to adjust to the way the rufous hummingbird, like a tiny thrashing autogiro, redisposed itself in space, zapping from point to point too fast for the eye to follow. Glancing up from the typewriter, stuck for a phrase, I'd sight a bald eagle, circling on a thermal over the Ship Canal on huge stiff ragged wings, and lose the logic of the sentence to another bout of ornithology.

The German word for "uncanny," as in Freud's famous essay on the Uncanny, is *unheimlich*—unhomely. The tourist thrives on the uncanny, moving happily through a phenomenal world of effects without causes. This world, in which he has no experience and no memory, is presented to him as a supernatural domain: the language of travel advertising hawks the uncanny as part of the deal. Experience the *magic* of Bali! the *wonders* of Hawaii! the *enchantment* of Bavaria!

But for the newly arrived immigrant, this magic stuff is like a curse. He's faced at every turn with the unhomelikeness of things, in an uncanny realm where the familiar house sparrows have all fled, to be replaced by hummingbirds and eagles. The immigrant needs to grow a memory, and grow it fast. Somehow or other, he must learn to convert the uncanny into the homely, in order to find a stable footing in his new land. . . .

November 1992 and the snow level, said Harry Wappler, our TV weatherman, was down to 3,500 feet and dropping fast. In a week the mountain passes would be tricky and the back roads closed for the winter. I dug out of storage my never-used box of tire chains and set off on a wide swing around the neighborhood.

It was high time to make the trip: though I had been living in Seattle for more than two years, I was still confused as to its whereabouts. I knew the city better than its cabdrivers (a very modest boast), but I'd barely begun to work out how Seattle fitted into the larger story. A long drive, on empty western roads where it's still possible to think with one's foot down, would, with luck, thread the oddly assorted bits of the Pacific Northwest onto one string and set them in narrative order.

The afternoon rush hour had started by the time I got away, and 10 on Interstate 90 heading east, the cars were locked bumper-to-bumper on the floating bridge over Lake Washington. The sky was lightless, and the windshield wipers scraped on the glass in the fall moisture, typical of these parts, that was something more than mist and less than rain. The traffic jam was typical of these parts, too: a ceremonious procession, like a funeral, of VWs with ski racks on their tops and I'D RATHER BE SAILING stickers on their rear ends. A lot of higher education was stuck on the bridge that afternoon. The names of the universities from which the drivers had graduated were posted in their back windows—faraway schools, mostly, like Syracuse, M.I.T., Columbia, Missouri, Michigan.

My own car, a low-slung, thirsty, black Dodge Daytona with a working ashtray, marked me out as a Yahoo among the Houyhnhnms—too old, dirty, and wasteful to pass as a member of Seattle's uniquely refined middle class. Stuffed into the book bag beside the work of the northwestern writers whom I had brought along for the ride (Richard Hugo, Ursula K. Le Guin, Raymond Carver, Katherine Dunn, William Stafford, Norman Maclean, James Welch, James Crumley) was a bottle of Teacher's, two-thirds full, which would have been okay by the northwestern writers but thought a very low touch by these northwestern drivers. In Seattle, a double shot of non-decaffeinated espresso was thought to be pushing the boat out farther than was wise.

In shifts and starts, we lurched into Eastside Seattle, Houyhnhnm country, where the VWs began to peel off to the Bellevue exits. Bellevue and its satellites were not suburbs so much as—in the rising term—an "edge city," with its own economy, sociology, and architecture. Things made on the Eastside were odorless, labor-intensive, and credit-card thin, like computer software and aerospace-related electronics gear. They were assembled in low, tree-shaded factories, whose grounds were known as "campuses"—for in Bellevue all work was graduate work, and the jargon of college leaked naturally into the workplace. Seen from an elevated-freeway distance, Bellevue looked like one of its own products: a giant circuit board of color-coded diodes and resistors, connected by a mazy grid of filaments.

During the presidential campaign, Bill Clinton had jetted around the country, calling for the advent of the "high-growth, high-wage, smart-work society"—a fair description of Bellevue, with its lightly rooted, highly trained workforce, its safe streets, its scented malls sprayed with composerless light orchestral music, its air of bland good conscience. Bellevue was the new and hopeful face of American capitalism, and it had a strongly Japanese cast to its features. The one- and two-story campuses with their radial walkways reflected a style of business management that was closer to the industrial collectives of Tokyo than to the moribund hierarchies of Detroit and the American Rust Belt.

The place looked like somebody's utopia, more a model city than an actual one, and it was inhabited by the kinds of people whom architects like to place as strolling figures in the foregrounds of watercolor sketches of their projects. Wherever the eye wandered in Bellevue, it lit on another 31¾-year-old, with a master's if not a doctorate, dressed for work in hiking shoes and chunky sweater. Thousands of these diagrammatic people were housed along I-90 in white-painted, shingled

faux–New England condo blocks called "villages." Lakefront Village
... Redwood Village ... Olde Towne Village ... communities in
which the villagers met in the evenings at neighboring Exercycles in
the village health club or at a pre-breakfast tee-off on the village
driving range.

Eastside Seattle was a new kind of American city, though it had a   15
lot in common with the long-established retirement paradises of
Florida and southern California. People in their twenties and thirties
were now moving (as their parents had done only toward the ends of
their lives) for the sake of the climate and the natural amenities of a
place rather than just for the jobs offered there. They were coming to
Seattle in much the same way as people had gone to Venice, California, and to Miami Beach; the difference was that they were coming at
the beginnings of their careers. So they arrived, as kayakers, hikers,
balloonists, bird-watchers, skiers, and mountain bikers who also happened to have degrees in math and marketing and computer science.
Their Pacific Northwest was really a civic park, roughly the same size
as France, equipped with golf courses, hiking trails, rock-climbing
routes, boat-launch ramps, ski lifts, campgrounds, and scenic overlooks. This great migration of open-air hobbyists (which dated from
about 1980—the early Reagan years) had won Seattle a curious niche
in urban history, as the first big city to which people had fled in order
to be closer to nature.

Sixteen miles out of Seattle the eastward march of the city was
stopped in its tracks by the foothills of the Cascades. Beyond Issaquah
the black cliffs of the forest began, and the social character of the road
abruptly changed, as the last of the VWs melted into the last of the
white condo blocks. Up till now I'd been in the fast lane; no longer.
Mud-slathered pickups with jumbo tires charged past the Dodge
wearing angry slogans on their tailgates: JOBS BEFORE OWLS. SUPPORT THE
TIMBER INDUSTRY. SAVE A LOGGER—SHOOT AN OWL. Behind the glass of a
cab window, a Zippo lighter flashed in the gloaming.

Small charcoal-colored clouds were snagged in the firs. We were
climbing steadily now, the road wet, the light failing fast. Each bend in
the road opened on another wall of Douglas fir, the trees as dense and
regularly spaced as the bristles on a broom.

This wasn't true forest; it was a "tree farm"—a second- or third-
growth plantation, now ready for "harvesting." The terms were those
of the industry, and after two years of seeing them in use, I still found
myself putting quotation marks around them in my head. To me, farm
and harvest meant a two-acre wheat field in Essex, with rabbits
scarpering from between the cornstalks, and the words refused to stick
when I tried to attach them to a mountain range with 150-foot trees,
where bears and cougars ran out in place of rabbits and twin-rotor
helicopters served as baling machines. ...

That night I put up at a motel in Forks, twelve miles inland, on the slope of the invisible Olympics. It was a timber town, and a minor classic in its genre. I had been driving through timber towns all day and seen them at every stage of their evolution. Forks was the most highly evolved version so far.

The lowest form of timber-industry social life was a camp of trail- 20 ers parked in line along the roadside. It became a town with a name when the trailers were joined by three or four prefabricated ranch-style bungalows and a 7-Eleven convenience store with a gas pump out front. The next stage up the ladder required the addition of a gas station with a "deli" (which in these parts meant not a delicatessen but a basic horseshoe-counter diner, serving steak-and-egg breakfasts and sandwiches). Serious civic ambitions set in with the arrival of the video store and the motel. After that came the sculpture.

The sculpture was as formalized in its way as the statue of the bronze infantryman atop the war memorial in small English market towns. I'd seen a dozen variants of it in Oregon, Washington, and British Columbia. It was carved from a section of old-growth Douglas fir of massive diameter, and it represented, in heavy relief, sometimes painted and sometimes in bare varnished wood, a logger with an ax cutting down an old-growth Douglas fir.

The example outside the motel was a beauty, for Forks was the metropolis of the logging camps—a mile-long strip of neon business signs, with three stoplights and a string of tenebrous beer joints. But the carved and painted logger, a figure of heroic pastoral, was way out of tune with his real-life counterparts, who gloomed disconsolately over their drinks in the bars. None were Paul Bunyan types. The loggers were journeyman employees of billion-dollar outfits like the Weyerhaeuser Corporation, and they gave off the sour smell of years of negative profits, evaporating cash flows, and hard bottom lines.

They were now the endangered species. They put up homemade signs on their lawns that said THIS FAMILY LIVES ON TIMBER DOLLARS—and I'd find myself peering in at the windows of these houses as if, indeed, I might catch a glimpse of some rare owlish birds pecking at a tray of timber dollars while *Wheel of Fortune* played in the background.

The sculptures (and all the ones I saw were recently carved) were part of the counter-preservationist movement. They owed a lot to the carved totemic ravens and thunderbirds with which the local Indian tribes announced their special status. They made the assertion that timber-industry workers, like the Indians, had, in one of the hardest-worked American phrases of the late twentieth century, a unique and historic *culture*. Deny me my job, and you deny me my culture, my past, my ethnic identity. So the logging communities were busy manufacturing craft objects that gave them a tribal history and the right to be regarded as yet another beleaguered minority threatened with extinction.

It took some imaginative effort to identify the Weyerhaeuser fork- 25
lift operators and helicopter crews with the carved figures of lone
brawny woodsmen swinging axes. The sculptures seemed to me to be
self-defeating: they came across as sentimental tributes to a past so
long gone that it was far beyond the reach of preservation.

I picked at a meal in an overlit, almost empty restaurant. The view
through the window was of pickups and logging trucks plowing
through the wet and dark. The chicken and French fries tasted of saw-
dust and wood pulp. The only other customer removed his teeth and
pocketed them after he'd finished dining. Forks in the rain was an
unlovely place.

An elderly blue VW Beetle was stopped at the light. Its back end
was pasted over with slogans that looked misplaced in Forks: anti-
nuke, Clinton/Gore, and the brightest piece of folk wisdom that I'd
yet seen on the tribulations of the timber industry, SAVE A LOGGER & A
WHALE—SINK A JAPANESE SHIP.

For Journals

What is your reaction to the idea of limiting logging as a livelihood in
order to preserve a natural setting? To save a species?

For Discussion

1.   The author is an Englishman who moved to Seattle from London.
How does his status as an outsider help him assess the beliefs and experiences of loggers and conservationists? Is he in any way at a disad-
vantage in trying to understand them?

2.   Explain the title of the essay; does it undercut or support the notion of the American frontier? How many frontiers do you think there
have been or will be in the future?

3.   Compare the arguments of Wallace Stegner versus those of the
loggers in Raban's article; what are the most persuasive points each
makes? Try to consider both arguments in their own terms—that is,
based on the different assumptions about environment and livelihood
that each side starts out with.

4.   Protest sculptures of loggers felling Douglas firs remind Raban of
Indian totems; in what way is this an ironic comparison, and how do
you think the loggers would respond to it?

For Writing

1.   Going back to discussion question 2, write an essay in which you
compare and contrast Wallace Stegner's passionate letter for preserva-

tion of the wilderness with the loggers' equally passionate stance against conservationists. Try to present each side in the best possible light before you evaluate them.

2.   Raban mentions that Paul Bunyan, a logger, used to be a folklore hero. Write an essay in which you address the following issues: Why did the logger go from being a larger-than-life hero to a larger-than-life villain? What ideas and myths about the frontier did his character represent to most Americans in the past? What does his image seem to represent now?

∞ *The Headline Frontier* (1994)

PATRICIA NELSON LIMERICK

Patricia Nelson Limerick (1951–) is one of the United States' foremost historians of the American frontier. She is the author or editor of nine books, including The Legacy of Conquest: The Unbroken Past of the American West *(1985);* Trails: Toward a New Western History *(1991); and* The Frontier in American Culture *(1994) from which the following essay is excerpted.*

The headlines in 1986 looked as if they had been co-authored by Frederick Jackson Turner and the director of the 1890 census:

Frontier's Fate Still Uncertain

Frontier Still Has a Chance for Survival

Frontier Verges on Collapse

Time Runs Out for Frontier

Frontier Shuts Down

Too Late for Frontier

Frontier Throws in the Towel

Frontier Files for Bankruptcy

Politics Killed Frontier

Frontier Legacy Lives

The entity in question was Frontier Airlines, struggling for financial survival. For readers in Colorado in 1986, the fate of the airline was a subject of some anxiety; the ironic historical resonance of these headlines offered little in the way of consolation or diversion.

Seldom recognized for its ironic implications, the word "frontier" appears frequently in headlines. To serve their function, headlines have to convey some trustworthy clue to the contents of the story they introduce. But headlines are very short; they are virtually a freeze-dried form of communication. Thus, their writers tap out their message in a kind of code. In the necessary economy of the headline, the writers go in search of words that will convey big meanings. They have, under those circumstances, little interest in treacherous words, words that stand a chance of betraying their users.

Headline writers are, predictably, heavy users of the words "frontier" and "pioneer." They trust those words, and the words repay that trust. They are words that carry the master key to the reader's mind; with that key, they can slip into the mind and deposit their meanings before anyone quite knows they are there.

To assemble a set of artifacts demonstrating the persistent and widespread power of these words, I looked at roughly four thousand headlines, from 1988 through the first half of 1993, that made use of "frontier" and "pioneer." The first time through, I made a strategic error, and simply looked to see how silly these references were. This was an easy exercise, because many of the usages are indeed goofy. But at the end of the exercise, I had to realize that simply chuckling over these phrases was not accomplishing much for the cause of understanding.

The next time, then, I tried to find the patterns in the usage of 5
these words. What seems to be going on in people's minds in the late twentieth century when they call someone a pioneer or refer to an activity or an enterprise as a frontier? Answering this question can illuminate even the sillier usages, showing just how far from historical reality this historical reference has strayed. This exercise works best if the reader picks a nineteenth-century pioneer and then imagines how that pioneer might respond to his or her twentieth-century descendants. Or one might think only of Frederick Jackson Turner and imagine his response to what the twentieth century has done to his favorite term and his favorite people.

Let us begin on the comparatively neutral frontier of food. "Eating to Heal: The New Frontiers," the *New York Times* announced in 1990. Apparently fighting on the wrong side of this frontier was the "Cookie Pioneer," "creator of the fortune cookie folding machine and a line of risqué fortune cookies." The Cookie Pioneer may have held only a superficial kinship to the Cinnamon Roll Pioneers, but all of these pioneers could have joined forces with the Fast Food Pioneer and the Pioneer of the Snack Food Industry to defend their turf against the insinuations of the Natural Foods Pioneer, the Vegetarian Pioneer, and the Pioneer of the Edible Landscape. Occupying less contested territory were the Pasta Pioneers, the Potato Pioneer, and the Microwave Popcorn Pioneer, and surely the most memorable of the food pioneers—the Pioneer of the South Philadelphia Hoagie.

As striking as the food pioneers are the "lifestyle pioneers": the Passionate Pioneer of Fitness Franchising (the woman who founded

Jazzercise Inc.); the Surfing Pioneer ("he pioneered a whole way of surfing for thousands"); the Psychedelic Pioneer; the New Age Pioneer; the Sex-Change Pioneer; the Porn Pioneer; the Pioneer in the Crack Business; and the Peekaboo Pioneer, the founder of Frederick's of Hollywood. Frederick's pioneering work did not exhaust the possibilities of the underwear frontier: "Underwear Pioneers Targeting Men," one headline reads, and the story opens with this promising line: "The two designing women who revolutionized the bra industry in the 1970s with the invention of the first jogging bra have turned their talents to men's underwear." On the subject of fabrics and new materials, there is the memorable Polyester Pioneer, as well as a Pioneer of Plastics and a Stainless Steel Cookware Pioneer.

Forced into the discomfort and disorientation of time travel, Frederick Jackson Turner, or any of his contemporaries, would have to experience astonishment at the applications of the word "pioneer" in the late twentieth century, at this implied kinship between overland travelers and marketers of underwear, stainless steel, and hoagies. Of all these contestants, the award for the most unsettling pioneer would have to go to Dr. Louis Irwin Grossman, Pioneer in Root Canal Dentistry. And if there were an award for the twentieth-century pioneer of the product that nineteenth-century pioneers would have had the most occasions to appreciate, then that prize would go to Bernard Castro, described as the Pioneer of the Sleeper-Sofa.

Beneath and beyond the silliness of these references lies a clear set of patterns. The pioneers and frontiers cluster in particular areas and enterprises. Art, music, sports, fashion, commerce, law, and labor activism get their full share of the analogy. Technology holds the biggest cluster: technology of transportation (bicycles, automobiles, helicopters, airplanes, rockets, and spacecraft); technology of communications and information (radio, television, talk shows, CD players, laser discs, computers, software, programming); technology of medicine (heart transplants, plastic surgery, headache treatment, weight reduction, gene therapy); technology of weaponry (rocketry, atomic bombs). Indeed, it is impossible to read all these references to the frontiers of technology without recognizing that the American public has genuinely and completely accepted, ratified, and bought the notion that the American frontiering spirit, sometime in the last century, picked itself up and made a definitive relocation—from territorial expansion to technological and commercial expansion.

In November 1944, as the end of World War II neared, President [10] Franklin Roosevelt asked Vannevar Bush, director of the Office of Scientific Research and Development, to report on the prospects for American science after the war. "New frontiers of the mind," Roosevelt said, "are before us, and if they are pioneered with the same vision, boldness, and drive with which we have waged this war we can create a fuller and more fruitful employment and a fuller and more fruitful life." Called *Science—The Endless Frontier,* Bush's response to Roosevelt's request set the agenda for federally funded science. "It is in keeping with basic United States policy," Bush wrote, "that the Government should foster the opening of new frontiers," and federal investment in science "is the modern way to do it." Casting science as the nation's new frontier, a frontier maintained by hearty federal funding, Vannevar Bush captured and promoted the popular understanding of the frontier's relocation after Turner.

Certainly the space program has provided the best example of this pattern. The promoters of space exploration and development may well qualify as the nation's most committed and persistent users of the frontier analogy. *Pioneering the Space Frontier,* the 1986 Paine commission report on the future of the space program, shows the analogy at its most fervent. The story of the American nation, as imagined by the Paine commissioners, was a triumphant and glorious story of success, with the complex stories of Indian conquest and African American slavery simply ignored and eliminated. "The promise of virgin lands and the opportunity to live in freedom," the commissioners declared, "brought our ancestor to the shores of North America." The frontiers have not closed, and Manifest Destiny has just taken a turn skyward: "Now space technology has freed humankind to move outward from Earth as a species destined to expand to other worlds." The best that the Paine commissioners could offer in recognizing that frontiers might not always be vacant was this memorable line: "As we move outward into the Solar System, we must remain true to our values as Americans: To go forward peacefully and to respect the integrity of planetary bodies and alien life forms, with equality of opportunity for all." If one thinks of the devastation of Indians by disease, alcohol, war, loss of territory, and coercive assimilation, and then places that reality next to the Paine commissioners' pious intentions, one feels some obligation to take up the mission of warning the "alien life forms," to suggest that they keep their many eyes on their wallets when they hear these intentions invoked, especially the line about "equality of opportunity for all."

However this frontier experience plays out for alien life forms, the mental act of equating the frontier of westward expansion with the development of space proved to be an enterprise that ran itself. In the selling of space as "the final frontier," the aerospace industry, the National Aeronautics and Space Administration, presidents, the news media, and the entertainment business collaborated with perfect harmony, with no need for centralize direction or planning, with a seamless match in their methods and goals. The split infinitive was regrettable, but the writers of *Star Trek* came up with the phrase to capture the essential idea brought to mind at the mention of the words "frontier" and "pioneer": "to boldly go where no man has gone before."

For Journals

Of all the examples Limerick gives of how the frontier idea gets used, which did you think was the most amusing? The most understandable?

For Discussion

1. What point do you think Limerick was trying to make in choosing the example she did to begin this essay?

2. Why do you think the concept of the frontier is still important to Americans? What meanings does it seem to have for us that no other word possesses?

3. Limerick gives many examples of how the word "frontier" is attached to all kinds of activities and businesses. What definition or definitions of "frontier" can you come up with that make sense to you?

For Writing

1. Look through some newspapers and magazines for the word "frontier"; write an essay in which you explain how it is used in one or two articles you find, and why you think the way it's used does or doesn't make sense. You may find yourself agreeing or disagreeing with Limerick. In any case, state what Limerick's assertions are about how the frontier concept is being manipulated in contemporary America, and then use your article(s) to either support or refute her argument. If you want, you can follow the same form in your essay that Limerick does, and start by quoting the best newspaper headlines you find.

2. Write an essay based on question 3 above, but once you've written about what you think frontier means, pick one or two other words or terms that are similarly important to Americans, for example, pursuit of happiness, all men are created equal, freedom of speech, and so on. Choose whatever term or word you want, but in order to keep this essay from becoming too abstract, give specific examples of what it means to you, your friends, or members of your family. You can interview people you know at school or elsewhere and ask them significant questions.

3. Assume that you are in charge of an advertising campaign for one of your favorite products—a food, a kind of clothing, a song or CD you really like, a movie, and so on—and the frontier, in whatever way you choose to use it, is going to be at the heart of your campaign.

Write a memorandum to your boss explaining why the frontier would be a good analogy for your ad campaign, who your audience is, and how you intend to incorporate the frontier into the slogan for your ad. Illustrate your memorandum by doing a version of the ad, including the slogan. You can look to Limerick's examples to give you ideas.

∞ Film: Unforgiven (1993)

Two retired, down-on-their luck outlaws pick up their guns one last time to collect a bounty offered by the vengeful prostitutes of the remote Wyoming town of Big Whiskey. (131 minutes)

For Journals

Why do you think this movie is called *Unforgiven?* How many people are unforgiven, and for what?

For Discussion

1. In older westerns the good guys wore white hats and the bad guys wore black hats, so the audience would always know who was who. In this movie, the hero is a killer; what does Eastwood, both as director and as actor, do with the character to make him heroic?

2. Two young people have significant parts in this movie: a near-sighted gunslinger who pretends he is an experienced killer, and a near-sighted writer who is enchanted with the idea of meeting a real killer. In a way, both become accomplices to what happens. Look closely at the scenes in which they appear: Who is the more innocent? Who is more corrupted by the West? What kind of harm does each of them do?

3. There are considerable comic touches in the film: Will Monny can't ride a horse well, and the Scofield Kid can't see what he's shooting at. How do these touches play against the usual stereotypes of western gunslingers? What parts of the movie reinforce those images?

4. The movie begins and ends with a peaceful scene of Will's farm, accompanied by words on the screen. Look at what the words say in the beginning and in the end; who do you think is supposed to be the author of those words? Why does it sound like part of a novel? What point do you think Eastwood is making about the fictionalization of the frontier?

For Writing

1. View one of Eastwood's earlier spaghetti westerns or one of his early American westerns, such as *A Fistful of Dollars* (1964), *For a Few*

Dollars More (1966), *Hang 'Em High* (1968), and *The Good, the Bad, and the Ugly* (1967). Take two or three scenes from one of those films and two or three scenes from *Unforgiven,* and write an essay in which you compare them for the presence or absence of the following themes: guilt, conscience, memory, or a frontier ethic. How has Eastwood's archetype of the western hero evolved since the earlier films?

2. The western is one of the primary American film traditions; that has made it a target for humor and satire. Look at Mel Brook's *Blazing Saddles* (1974), the single most parodic version of a western ever made. Write an essay in which you identify as many stereotypes as you can, and how Brooks treats them; for example—cowboys and Indians, whites and blacks, the gunslinger, the crooked politician.

Writing Assignments

1. Write an essay on an issue you feel strongly about, but take a stand absolutely against your usual position. Analyze a poem, take a side of a debate, or examine an advertisement from the perspective of someone with a background or gender different from yours. Your paper can be research oriented, expository, or narrative. Then write a reflective essay on how the change in perspective affected your writing process and your conclusions, and whether or how it caused you to revise your previous certainties on the topic.

2. Go through copies of old magazines—*Century* or *McClure's* from the early twentieth century, or *Colliers, Harper's, Saturday Evening Post* through the 1950s and 1960s—and look for images of Native Americans in advertisements. Write a paper in which you include your reflections on the following questions: What are the Native Americans being used to sell? If there are any whites in the ads, what is the relationship between them and the Native Americans? What stereotypes or clichés do you find in these ads? If you were writing any of these advertisements, how would you revise the pictures or the text, or both?

3. Try to locate any of the following: the old television series on Daniel Boone and Davy Crockett (starring, incidentally, the same actor, Fess Parker, as though these historical figures were interchangeable) or the musical based on the life of Annie Oakley, *Annie Get Your Gun.* How does the image of these figures put forth by articles and books revise or coincide with the image of them in television and theater? What do you think is lost or gained when the revised versions of their lives become more important than the reality?

4. Write an essay in which you discuss the negative stereotyping of any group to which you belong: your gender, your racial heritage, the region of the country you come from, your religious affiliation, your love of computers. Consider the following questions: How do you think your group is perceived by others? What stereotyping, negative and positive, do you have to contend with? How would you revise the stereotype to make it a more accurate reflection of reality?

5. Research any American hero or heroine in sports, movies, politics, or some other area who has become the subject of a mythology. Some of the most obvious are Elvis Presley, Marilyn Monroe, F. Scott Fitzgerald, and JFK, but anyone who can persistently fascinate the American public and is the subject of endless restructuring and remaking would be a good subject. Concentrate on separating some of the reality from the subsequent revision or on the way your subject's standing is revised positively or negatively in people's estimation. What, would you argue, is the cultural significance of your subject to America?